John S. Partington (ed.)

H. G. Wells in *Nature*, 1893–1946

A Reception Reader

PETER LANG
Internationaler Verlag der Wissenschaften

Bibliographic Information published by the Deutsche Nationalbibliothek
The Deutsche Nationalbibliothek lists this publication in the Deutsche Nationalbibliografie; detailed bibliographic data is available in the internet at <http://www.d-nb.de>.

Cover illustration:

© Mark Charlesworth 2008

ISSN 1864-323X
ISBN 978-3-631-57110-1

© for the English edition:
Nature Publishing Group, London & New York,
and Peter Lang GmbH
Internationaler Verlag der Wissenschaften
Frankfurt am Main 2008
© for all other languages:
Nature Publishing Group, London & Now York,
and John S. Partington
© A. P. Watt Ltd. on behalf of the Literary Executors
of the Estate of H. G. Wells

Printed in Germany 1 2 3 4 5   7

www.peterlang.de

To A. J.

And to Isis

Contents

Part 3: Other Mentions 389

Abbreviations

AM	Master of Arts
BBC	British Broadcasting Corporation
BC	Before Christ
BSc	Bachelor of Science
Bt	baronet
Cf.:	compare
D.:	pence (predecimal British currency)
DLit:	Doctor of Literature
DSc:	Doctor of Science
DSc (Econ.):	Doctor of Science (Economics)
DSc (Eng.):	Doctor of Science (Engineering)
Ed(s).	editor(s).
Etc.	et cetera
E. g.	for example
F	Fahrenheit
FLS	Fellow of the Linnean Society
FRS	Fellow of the Royal Society
FZS	Fellow of the Zoological Society
H₂O	the chemical formula of water
I. e.	that is to say
I. L. N.	*Illustrated London News*
Jr	junior
LLD	Doctor of Laws
LNU	League of Nations Union
M.	monsieur
MA	Master of Arts
MD	Doctor of Medicine
Mr	mister
N. B.	observe particularly

O	the chemical formula of oxygen
O. B. E.	Officer of the British Empire
PEN	Poets, Playwrights, Essayists and Novelists.
Phil. Trans.	*Philosophical Transactions*
PM	Post meridian
Prof.	professor
PS	post script
S.	shilling (predecimal British currency)
Sic.	thus written
SPR	Society for Psychical Research
St	saint
Trans.	translator
UNESCO	United Nations Educational, Scientific and Cultural Organisation
USA	United States of America
USSR	Union of Soviet Socialist Republics
Viz.	used to introduce an amplification or explanation of a previous statement or word
Vol.	volume

General Introduction and Acknowledgements

Uniquely in H. G. Wells's long writing career, *Nature*[1] remained an important vehicle for both the publication of his writings, and their critical reception. Between 1893 and 1944, he published twenty-five separate items in the journal, be they reviews, essays or letters to the editor, while his works received fifty-three reviews during the same period. In addition to these, Wells's activities as a public figure received substantial coverage in the pages of the journal.

The reasons for this close relationship between author and journal are several. Wells was educated in science to degree level, and spent several years teaching science in schools and to university correspondence students. He started his writing career publishing science essays in the popular and the educational press (in addition to *Nature*, the pre-eminent science journal, then as now). He wrote science textbooks, not only in the 1890s but also again in the 1930s. From his student days in the 1880s until his death, he was a close friend of Richard Gregory, editorial assistant and later editor of *Nature* from the 1897 to 1939. Perhaps most importantly, however, Wells was convinced of the central role of science, both discovery and invention but also scientific method, in the shaping of the human future, and its salvation (if salvation be had) in a world of war and international rivalry. This conviction led Wells to promote science and the role of scientists in society throughout his life, in his writings and lectures, but also as a representative of the British Association and as a member of many other scientific organisations such as the British Science Guild, the Committee on the Neglect of Science, the Diabetic Association, the National Union of Scientific Workers and the Neo-Malthusian League. The centrality of science to Wells's socio-political vision and the longevity of his relationship with *Nature* is the main justification for the publication of *H. G. Wells in Nature*.

Given that critics consistently acknowledge the importance of science on Wells's work and thought,[2] there has been surprisingly few reprints of his scientific writings. The major exception, of course, is Robert Philmus and David Hughes's splendid *H. G. Wells: Early Writings in Science and Science Fiction* (1975). While Philmus and Hughes deliberately collected 'a selection of H. G. Wells's hitherto unreprinted writings of the 1880s and 1890s relating to science and the sciences' (Philmus and Hughes 1975, ix), this volume, while aiming at comprehensiveness vis-à-vis *Nature*, secondarily acts as a continuation to

---

1   The pre-eminent British multidisciplinary scientific journal, founded in 1869.

2   See Roslynn D. Haynes's *H. G. Wells: Discoverer of the Future. The Influence of Science on His Thought* (1980) and John R. Reed's *The Natural History of H. G. Wells* (1982) for the two most detailed studies of the influence of science of Wells's work and thought.

Philmus and Hughes's volume, extending Wells's science journalism from the 1890s to the 1940s. And while Philmus and Hughes's volume allows 'the reader to follow the outline of Wells's intellectual development', demonstrating in the fin-de-siècle Wells that 'The view of nature's laws disposing of what man proposes gives way to the idea of "artificial" evolution, man's consciously taking charge of his future by shaping his sociocultural environment, over which he can exert control' (Philmus and Hughes 1975, ix-x), this volume demonstrates, rather, the consistency of Wells's thought from the 1890s to the end of his life. While Philmus and Hughes reveal that, from 1897, Wells 'ceased to speculate in biological terms of how man became man or will become any other entity, and turned instead to cultural evolution, which he labelled "The Acquired Factor"' (Philmus and Hughes 1975, 184) – in other words, show how Wells came to terms with the debates around evolution, supporting and then reluctantly rejecting the Lamarckian theory in favour of Weismannism and turning from the notion of biological inheritance in humanity to that of cultural inheritance – this volume reveals the increased urgency with which Wells propagated such cultural inheritance through his promotion of the scientific method in all aspects of life, of education as the key driver of behavioural change and of his encouragement for scientific freedom and the need for independent research, unencumbered by private patronage or state sponsorship.

If Wells's promotion of science and the scientific method led him to be published and reported in *Nature*, his association with *Nature* was also very useful to Wells's career. As John Hammond notes, '*Nature* was an influential journal, widely read in scientific and educational circles; a favourable notice within its pages was a significant bonus for Wells' (Hammond 2004, 119). Patrick Parrinder concurs with this opinion, noting that 'from the beginning his stories were recognized as appealing to the "scientific reader". They continued to be reviewed in *Nature*, and their scientific basis was sometimes the subject of expert discussion' (Parrinder 1972, 8-9). The attention Wells received in *Nature* did not go unappreciated; in a letter to Bruce Ingram, the editor of the *Illustrated London News*,[3] dated 31 March 1932, for instance, Wells declared, 'I think the *I. L. N.* the best newspaper in the world. Only *Nature* can compare with it' (Smith 1998, III: 414).

Curiously, given the long association between Wells and *Nature*, and Wells's close friendship with Richard Gregory, there has been very little published on the subject, even in the major biographies of Wells. David Smith, for instance, only gives one substantial mention to Wells's involvement with *Nature*:

---

3   A popular newspaper, published weekly (1842-1971), monthly (1971-89) and, after 1989, bi-monthly, quarterly and (currently) bi-annually.

2

Wells, of course, always thought of himself as a scientist. He continued throughout his life to describe himself in this way, and attempted to keep up with the general trends and changes in research findings. This, in fact, was made much easier because his old friend Gregory was editor of *Nature*. Wells read the journal regularly and contributed reviews and comments to it. And Gregory provided another service. He was always available, having the information himself or suggesting another source if he did not, to answer the scientific questions raised in increasing number by Wells's fiction. Gregory monitored Wells's writings, and kept him from making gross errors. This sort of aid has made the Wells science-fiction work of the period still extremely readable, while much of that from his competitors simply was not very good science, and is now not very good reading. (Smith 1986, 44)

The case is the same with Norman and Jeanne MacKenzie:

[Wells] had come to hope for some public recognition of his work, and what he wanted most of all was election as a Fellow of the Royal Society.[4] Late in 1926, his old friend Richard Gregory, whose position as editor of *Nature* ensured that he had influential contacts in the scientific world, wrote to H. G. saying that the only possibility was through a special rule which permitted the choice every two years of two persons who 'either have rendered conspicuous service to the cause of science, or are such that their election would be of signal benefit to the Society'. Gregory sadly noted that H. G. might have dished himself by a recent slighting to the Prince of Wales.[5] He could have added that the scandals which clung about the name of Wells[6] would have been a further problem. But he was not deterred from trying to help, and one thing he could do was to ensure that H. G. got significant notice in the columns of *Nature*. He had already commissioned a long and favourable review of *William Clissold*, and he now rallied *Nature* behind Wells in the row with Belloc.[7] (MacKenzie and MacKenzie 1987, 349)

These two long quotations suggest an important role for Gregory and *Nature* in promoting Wells within the scientific community, and, indeed, as a kind of col-

---

4   In full, the Royal Society of London for the Improvement of Natural Knowledge, a British learned society for science. Founded in 1660, it is the oldest such society in the world.

5   In 1926, the Prince of Wales (1910-36) was the future King Edward VIII.

6   A reference to Wells's notorious reputation as a philanderer.

7   Hilaire Belloc, the famous Roman Catholic apologist, attacked Wells's *The Outline of History* for its presentation of the theory of evolution as fact, amongst other reasons (see 2.11).

laborator in researching information to bolster the 'believability' of Wells's scientific romances. While *H. G. Wells in Nature* is not the forum for detailed research into the Wells-Gregory relationship (one which started professionally as early as 1893 when the two co-authored *Honours Physiography*), it is to be hoped that the material contained herein will provide a useful resource for the scholar who takes up that task.

H. G. Wells in Nature is divided into three parts. Part 1, 'The Essays, Reviews and Letters by H. G. Wells', contains 13 sections where Wells's writings were initiators of an issue (though, admittedly, not all received responses). In addition to Wells's pieces, therefore, I have included all the replies that he received (in the form of letters to the editor) as well as editorial comments related to his writing that appeared. By being thus inclusive, I hope to encourage readers to consider Wells's writings within the wider context of *Nature*'s publications, which in turn will hopefully also provoke further exploration beyond the pages of *Nature*, to the many area where these debates continued.

Part 2, 'Reviews of the Works of H. G. Wells', contains thirty-six sections reprinting fifty-three reviews of forty-four of Wells's works. As some reviews treat more than one book by Wells, as Wells occasionally revised and retitled his works and as some books received more than one review, some sections include reviews of more than one title or several reviews treating different editions of the same book. In addition to the reviews, I have again included responses, both by Wells and by others who had criticisms to offer, and for the same reasons as in Part 1. The debates aroused by these reviews are sometimes cordial and often heated, and occasionally result in the reviewer clarifying or defending his or her position. Not only do these reviews reveal a historical reception of Wells's work, but more significantly they reveal how a literary artist and a world figure was considered by the scientific community, and how seriously Wells's writings were taken as contributions to a scientific discourse, not simply in terms of the science Wells used in his scientific romances, but also in his scientific approach to questions of education and politics. Interestingly, the reviewers generally shied away from making literary-critical comments on the fiction, either declaring lack of qualification to do so, or arguing that *Nature* was not the forum for such comments, but nonetheless they went on to give often lengthy and penetrating readings of Wells's works. The necessarily distinctive angle taken by reviewers in *Nature* will hopefully inspire scholars of Wells's literature to make new insights into his critical reception, and offer new readings of his works.

Part 3, 'Other Mentions', contains all the remaining material between 1894 and 1946 in which Wells plays a part, albeit in a generally tangential (though not insignificant) manner. Thus the reader will find a review of the first biography of Wells, comments by Wells on debates concerning scientific freedom and the organisation of scientists, reports of his speeches and the obituary notice published on the occasion of his death, among other items. Many of the pieces in Part 3 are simply brief reports, though there are also detailed debates and follow-up comments.

As *H. G. Wells in Nature* makes reference to a tremendous range of information, I have attempted to provide detailed editorial support. Thus the text is extensively footnoted[8] and all persons mentioned throughout the book are included in the 'Short Biographies' section. Also, I have produced an exhaustive 'Bibliography', listing not only all the articles, reviews, editorials and letters to the editor which I have reprinted, but also all the books under review and all the books, articles, poems, short stories, etc., mentioned (or alluded to) throughout the text. In addition, I have also provided a list of 'Abbreviations' appearing throughout the text. While I hope that this volume in its entirety is a useful reader of Wells's reception in *Nature*, perhaps the footnotes, the 'Abbreviations', the 'Short Biographies' and the 'Bibliography', as independent components, will also serve as valuable resources in their own right.

In addition to this 'General Introduction', the reader will find each Part of the book introduced separately. Parts 1 and 2 are introduced by detailed summaries, though, due to space limitation, Part 3 receives only a cursory introduction, and the material in that Part is left to speak largely for itself.

*   *   *   *   *

In preparing this volume, and especially for assistance in compiling the many footnotes and identifying the many persons and organisations mentioned in the text, and for help with translating the several foreign phrases, sentences and paragraphs, I would like to thank the following persons and organisations: Prof. Richard Aldrich of the Institute of Education, London; Isabelle Aubé; Claire Batley of the Royal Society of Arts, London; Samuel Bausson of the Muséum Toulouse; BBC School Radio, London; Glenn Branch of the National Center for Science Education, Oakland, CA; Colin Bruce; Geraldine Buckley of the Society of Authors, London; Maggie Burns of Birmingham Public Library; Dr Roger Cockrell of the University of Exeter; Gillian Cooke of Cambridge Assessment; Dr Paul Corthorn of Queen's University, Belfast; Dr Linda Dryden of Napier University, Edinburgh; Prof. Richard Dury of the Università di Bergamo; Prof. David Edgerton of Imperial College, London; Prof. Annie Escuret of the Université Paul Valéry, Montpellier; Emily Ezust; Anna Fahey-Flynn of Boston Public Library, MA; Bob Fleck of Oak Knoll Books, New Castle, DE; Dr Peter

---

8   Footnotes marked by numerals (1, 2, 3, etc.) are my editorial interjections; those marked by symbols (* or †) are original to the text as published in *Nature*.

Forsaith of Oxford Brookes University; Thomas Gangale of OPS-Alaska, Petaluma, CA; Kay Grimstead of Midhurst Grammar School; Dr Jason Harding of Durham University; Dr Negley Harte of University College, London; P. Hatfield of Eton College; Lisa Hendry of the British Association, London; Steve Holland; Nick Hollis of the University of Reading Library; Dr Rob Jackson of the British Association, London; Dr Simon J. James of Durham University; Nathalie Julien; Eric Korn; Prof. Bernard Loing of the H. G. Wells Society; Prof. Jean-Pierre Lumaret of the Université Paul Valéry, Montpellier; Dr Randy L. Maddox of Duke University, Durham, NC; Dr Alan Marchbank of the National Library of Scotland; J. Murray of the North London Collegiate School; Prof. Patrick Parrinder of the University of Reading; Prof. Ted Porter of the University of California, Los Angeles; Bill Radcliffe; Dr Jane Read of Roehampton University; Gene K. Rinkel of the University of Illinois, Urbana-Champaign; Baudry Rocquin; Dr Tom Ruffles of the Society for Psychical Research, London; Prof. Elmar Schenkel of the Univesität Leipzig; Dr Michael Sherborne of Luton Sixth Form College; Dr Christopher Stray of the University of Wales, Swansea; John Stringer of Midhurst Grammar School; Dr Richard Toye of the University of Exeter; Dr Anna Vaninskaya of the University of Cambridge; Mike Weaver of the Working-Class Movement Library, Salford; and Dr Richard Willis of Roehampton University. For contributing the cover illustration for this volume, I would like to thank Mark Charlesworth. For permission to reprint material from *Nature* I would like to thank Macmillan Publishers Ltd, and for permission to reprint the work of H. G. Wells I wish to thank A. P. Watt Ltd on behalf of the Literary Executors of the Estate of H. G. Wells. For access to their volumes of *Nature*, I gratefully acknowledge the University of Reading Library. For her assistance in preparing this manuscript, I would like to thank Ute Winkelkoetter of Peter Lang GmbH. Finally, for his encouragement and good wishes, I offer my gratitude to Myk Davis.

Part 1: The Essays, Reviews and Letters by H. G. Wells

In this first part of *H. G. Wells in Nature*, the essays and reviews which Wells published in *Nature* appear, as well as a critical letter concerning the prehistoric caves at Mas d'Azil in France and a joint appeal by Wells and others for research resources for scientists in post-revolutionary Russia, along with the debates which these contributions aroused.

In 'Popularising Science' (1.1), Wells sets out to promote popular science as a literary field which should be taken seriously by professional scientists. He insists that decent popular science is essential to the scientific profession itself, as it does not simply educate the public for the public's own sake, but, as a result of an interested and intelligent public, scientific research attracts additional state funding. Wells does not think it likely, in the contemporary climate, that scientific endeavour will fall out of fashion with the public, but he fears that an insufficiently educated public will clamour for pseudo-scientific novelties, such as the endowment of the Zetetic Society or the funding of research into 'Dr Platt's polar and central suns' or Orville Owen's 'Bacon-cryptogram wheel' rather than for 'saner enquiries'.

Wells acknowledges that much popular science 'is the mere obvious tinctured by inaccurate compilation' and blames in part 'editorial incapacity' for the volume of such publications. However, he insists that the public clamour for such reading should not deter professional scientists from writing for a mass audience. After all, he observes, that earlier generation of scientists, such as Charles Darwin, 'addressed themselves in many cases to the general reader'. Wells recognises that some contemporary scientists are writing for the general reader, but he sees many of their efforts failing due to the overuse of technical language – 'a book should be written in the language of its readers', he asserts. Having said that, Wells also observes that another approach of the scientific writer is to avoid technicalities altogether in the belief that the reader will not understand them, and so he or she 'too often rests contented with vague, ambiguous, or misleading phrases', and 'talks down' to the reader, using jokes to entertain in place of scientific exposition to educate.

In place of both the 'over-technical' and the 'talking down' varieties of scientific publication, Wells demands the exposition of inductive reasoning as applied to scientific research. As demonstrated by such imaginative writers as Edgar Allen Poe and Arthur Conan Doyle, the public craves 'the ingenious unravelling of evidence' and, according to Wells, most scientific fields are appropriate for the presentation of 'the problem, then the gradual piecing together of the solution'. Only through such an approach to popular science writing can professional scientists wrest the public imagination away from novelty journalism and continue the tradition of intelligent popular science writing 'that the generation of writers who are now passing the zenith of their fame created'.

In his article 'Science, in School and After School' (1.2), Wells considers the contemporary practice of science teaching in schools, distinguishing between the teaching of scientific facts (mere instruction) and the teaching of scientific method (real education); or the imparting of information as against the training of the pupils' minds. To Wells, the teaching of scientific method starts too late in the curriculum, by-passing the elementary stage of education when young minds are being fashioned and taught how to think and learn. It is at just this stage of mental development, according to Wells, that pupils should be taught scientific method, in order that they might apply such method to their general outlook – 'the school is a training place, that there the vessel is moulded rather than filled, and that the only justification for the introduction of science is its educational value'. However, what Wells observes in schools is the transplantation of university-style lecturing and dictation of information to young minds incapable of understanding scientific cause and effect. In reality, information was imparted to students by rote, and the logic of science was entirely ignored. According to Wells, such teaching practice is not only lost upon the pupils, it also 'seriously discredits the claims of science upon the school time'. The practice of awarding financial rewards to teachers whose pupils gained first- or second-class passes in the Science and Art Department examinations simply incentivised rote learning, thus placing teachers interested in teaching scientific method at a financial disadvantage to their more conventional peers. While Wells seeks the abolition of rote learning and the mere imparting of facts from elementary education, he is concerned to see such methods preserved in adult education classes, where students' 'curiosity about nature is already aroused, and whose practical needs are also pressing for scientific information'. In short, Wells seeks a tailored science education for both elementary pupils and further education students, and condemns the existing one-size-fits-all approach.

In 'Scientific Method in Board Schools', Henry Armstrong endorses the principles Wells expressed, introducing a science teacher-training course with the express 'object of inculcating *scientific* habits of mind and *scientific* ways of working'. Armstrong's emphasis differs from Wells's somewhat in that he prioritises the teaching of scientific method in secondary schools as against Wells's insistence on its introduction at the primary level. Nonetheless, Armstrong amplifies Wells's call for an inductive approach to science learning, stressing that pupils 'must not only learn a good deal *about* things; they must also be taught how to *do* things, and to this end must learn how others before them have done things by actually repeating – not by merely reading about – what others have done'. Armstrong's emphasis on practical work leads him to endorse Wells on a further point: 'Abolish learning lessons by rote as far as possible', he writes.

As a chemistry professor, and one involved in propagating the teaching of scientific method since 1884, Armstrong's article adds prestige and professional authority to Wells's argument; a fact demonstrated by the correspondence which the two articles provoked. William Crump's letter defends traditional science instruction, but more powerfully attacks the imbalance between the science curriculum and the examinations set by the various examination boards. Indeed, his letter raises awareness of the varying standards existing between the examining bodies. Grace Heath, on the other hand, fully endorses Wells's and Armstrong's arguments for the teaching of scientific method, providing examples of its success, though again questioning the appropriateness of the examinations being set for the pupils. In his comment on the ongoing discussion, Olaus Henrici criticises the divide between the teaching of scientific method and scientific facts from the perspective of mathematics, complaining of the historical (and persisting) bias in favour of pure mathematics as against applied mathematics. In order to encourage pupils to learn algebra and trigonometry (particularly challenging areas of the subject), Henrici suggests teaching mathematics through experimental science, thereby allowing pupils to learn the meaning of formulae and equations 'in the concrete form' which 'in the abstract form of pure mathematics remained a mystery to them'.

Wells ends the discussing with a final letter restating his criticisms of the examination system, with its bias against scientific method, and answers Crump's support for examination boards made up of scientists with the declaration that 'I fail to see why eminent scientific men should be expected to be experts in elementary science teaching'.

In 'Peculiarities of Psychical Research' (1.3), Wells reviews Frank Podmore's *Apparitions and Thought Transference*. Podmore was a leading light in the Society for Psychical Research, and a believer in telepathic power. Wells's review avoids blind scepticism in favour of agnostic questioning, querying the scientific basis of the evidence presented in psychical research rather than condemning its investigation altogether. Podmore compares the ostracism of psychical researchers with that of geologists and biologists of earlier generations, but Wells objects to this simile on two grounds; firstly, at the time when geologists and biologists were being condemned, magic in various guises was thriving, only to diminish in influence as the power of scientific research grew, and secondly, the raw materials of science are real and present, and scientific experiments are repeatable given the existence of similar conditions, whereas psychic experiments rely on generally imperceptible evidence (or 'hearsay' as Wells terms it) and cannot be generally repeated under scientific conditions. As Wells complains, 'In no other field of inquiry is so much faith in personal character and intelligence demanded, or so little experimental verification possible'. Although Wells welcomes research into psychical phenomena, he insists on a note of scepticism, as 'Any general recognition of the evidence of "psychical" research will be taken by the outside public [...] as undeniable facts', and it would be irresponsible of the scientific community to so influence the general public without rock-solid evidence and repeatable verification.

Wells's review provoked a storm of debate, though initially not from defenders of psychical research, but from the statistician, Karl Pearson, who applauds Wells's disposal of Podmore's claims to scientific methodology but criticises Wells's treatment of card-drawing experiments. Wells explains that the law of probability only applies when the number of experiments is infinite, so the fact that a person can state the identity of a drawn card more times than the law of probability allows for does not suggest any special powers in a finite number of guesses. Pearson, however, criticises the card-drawing experiments on another ground; while the experimenters were quick to announce the excess of correct guesses above the probable, Pearson notes that they did not assess whether there was an 'abnormal distribution' in the cards drawn. This failure, according to Pearson, eradicates any claim to a scientific approach by the psychical researchers, and so, in fact, the question of probability need not be considered.

Both Wells's and Pearson's pieces provoked a response from Edward Dixon. Dixon attempts to turn Wells's criticism against him by stating that Wells's task should be not merely to rubbish the findings of psychical researchers but to demonstrate 'that there is not even a *prima facie* case worth investigating', while he answers Pearson's questioning regarding the distribution of the cards by stating that the deck was shuffled and cut between each draw, a method Pearson refuses to consider 'scientific' in a second letter responding to Dixon. Dixon then contributes a second letter calling on Pearson to apply his scientific methods to a criticism of the evidence of psychical research. This call is reiterated in a letter from Oliver Lodge, a respected scientist who was also a psychical researcher.

Lodge complains that scientists do not assess the evidence gathered by psychical researchers, 'but are content to ridicule what they conjecture to be our methods and results from so great an altitude of assured contempt, that we fail to recognise ourselves in their travesty'. Lodge bemoans the misrepresentation of psychical researchers, stating that Podmore does not, despite what Pearson writes, claim that the card-drawing experiments reveal evidence of psychical phenomena, but argues that 'the figures are sufficient to prove [...] that *some* cause must be sought for the results other than chance'. Lodge ends his letter by calling on Pearson to reveal the evidence of his own experiments into probability and allow others to criticise his results.

Pearson responds to the debate with a third letter, ignoring Lodge's challenge but calling on Dixon to present him with the evidence that the distribution of the cards in the card-drawing experiments were scientifically recorded and considered when assessing the question of probability of the guesses.

In a winding-up of the debate, Wells contributes a letter in response to Lodge, claiming that he did not refer to Podmore as a 'bigoted upholder of the certainty of telepathy' as Lodge accused him of doing but criticised Podmore's 'air of open-mindedness' in his preface, which might lead the general reader to treat the evidence presented in the book as more scientifically trustworthy than Wells believed it was. Wells ends by asserting that he 'made no objection to the individual prosecution of psychical research – only to its public recognition before it has produced more definite results than it has done so far'.

In 'The Sequence of Studies' (1.4) Wells reviews Michael Foster and Lewis Shore's *Physiology for Beginners*, Peter Chalmers Mitchell's *Outlines of Biology* and Charles Clark's *Practical Methods in Microscopy*. He uses the review to urge a greater interdisciplinary approach to the pure sciences and the teaching of more background information to science students. Thus, Wells regrets that Foster and Shore do not insist upon 'the necessity of a preliminary acquaintance with Chemistry and Physics' by physiology students, and he criticises Chalmers Mitchell for producing 'cut and dried' answers to an exam he himself administers in a biology primer which sets out broad generalisations without sufficient anatomical fact for the student to learn by. Indeed, Wells considers Chalmers Mitchell's assertion of biological truths so unsubstantiated that it borders on dogmatism rather than education. Wells finds similar fault with Clark's otherwise well received volume; rather than suggest preparatory study for students taking up his book, Clark attempts to state in a paragraph information students ought to discover in a full-length primer, and the result, according to Wells, 'is really [...] to place a grave impediment in their way to genuine knowledge', as students fail to understand such 'snap-shot chapters' but are not persuaded to take up more advanced study in order to receive an adequate background for the topics which Clark's book is actually designed to teach.

In 'Bio-optimism' (1.5), Wells's review of *The Evergreen*, edited by Patrick Geddes, he takes issue with biologists, and biology students, perverting the teachings of their subject in the name of art. *The Evergreen* was a semi-annual periodical produced by the biology department of St Andrews University in which staff and students used their scientific knowledge to produce an assortment of art. As art, Wells states, 'it is bad from cover to cover; and even the covers are bad'. However, 'Of greater concern to the readers of *Nature* [...] is the attempt on the part of two biologists – real responsible biologists – writing for the unscientific public, to represent Biology as having turned upon its own philosophical implications'. Thus John Arthur Thomson is condemned for telling 'his readers that "the conception of the Struggle for Existence as Nature's sole method of progress," "was to be sure a libel projected upon nature"', while

'Prof. Geddes writes tumultuously in the same vein – a kind of pulpit science – many hopeful things of "Renascence," and the "Elixir of Life"'. Wells counters these biologists' 'sweeping assertions' by illustrating the continued existence of struggle as a biological fact, and by concluding that 'The names of the sculptor who carve out the new forms of life are, and so far as human science goes at present they must ever be, Pain and Death'. With specific regard to humanity, biological competition and the elimination of the weak is all the more imperative, claims Wells, due to the contemporary debunking of the theory of the inheritance of acquired characteristics, dooming 'decadent families' to continued decadence regardless of the influence of education on any one particular generation.

In 'The Discovery of the Future' (1.6), Wells outlines his futurist philosophy. He begins by observing the existence of two types of mind: the 'legal', which judges the present and acts upon it with reference to the past, and the 'creative', which sees actions in the here and now as being contributory to an unfolding future. The legal-minded person sees the future as a 'black non-existence' and considers the purpose of life to 'reap the consequences of the past'. The creative-minded person, however, believes 'the future is just as fixed and determinate, just as settled and inevitable, just as possible a matter of knowledge as the past' but, paradoxically, sees life's purpose as 'to prepare the future'. 'Things have been, says the legal mind, and so we are here. And the creative mind says, we are here, because things have yet to be'. This distinction between the two types of mind would remain in Wells's thought throughout his career, appearing in *A Modern Utopia* (1905) and *Phoenix* (1942), for example, as the 'poietic' and the 'kinetic' temperaments.

Wells's purpose in the essay is not simply to point out these differing ways of looking at things, but to demonstrate that future knowledge may be determinable depending upon which point of view is in the ascendant, for 'along certain lines and with certain qualifications and limitations, a working knowledge of things in the future is a possible and practicable thing'. Wells based his argument for a knowable future on the discoveries of the 'pre-human past' consequent on the application of inductive reasoning to geological evidence. In the same way that 'We know to-day [...] the form and the habits of creatures that no living being has ever met, that no human eye has ever regarded, and the character of scenery that no man has ever seen or can ever possibly see', Wells argued we can know the future: through the application of inductive reasoning to operating causes existent in our own time. Just as meteorologists work to determine the coming weather, just as chemists forecast elements theoretically before actually discovering them, so scientists, attacking collectively the common problem, can, according to Wells, determine the nature of 'things to come' and, more importantly, social scientists can observe the nature of human society and determine the future course that it will take. Wells argues against the 'great man' theory of history, preferring to believe in the forces behind seemingly significant individuals; hence 'the more one inclines to this trust in forces, the more one will believe in the possibility of a reasoned inductive view of the future that will serve us in politics, in morals, in social contrivances, and in a thousand spacious ways'. The future Wells has in mind, however, is the general future, not the individual. It is future knowledge to aid legislators, planners and the like, rather than the individual; 'it will be no sort of knowledge that will either hamper us in the exercise of our individual free will or relieve us of our individual responsibility'. Although such research into the future had barely begun, Wells nonetheless states that 'It is not difficult to collect reasons for supposing […] that in the near future […] humanity will be definitely and consciously organising itself as a great world State', a vision he held for the duration of his life and, indeed, worked for in almost all of his subsequent writings.

Having made the case in this essay for an inductive research into the future, Wells makes an apparent *volte-face*, writing that 'All this paper is built finally upon certain negative beliefs that are incapable of scientific establishment. Our lives and powers are limited, our scope in space and time is limited, and it is not unreasonable that for fundamental beliefs we must go outside the sphere of reason and set our feet upon Faith'. This shift from evidence-based inductive enquiry to faith is puzzling and is not explicitly stated in Wells's work again until the Great War, when he expressed belief in a 'finite God' (1916-19), and then only briefly. The only explanation for this twist is that Wells's adherence to Darwinian theory forced him to recognise that evolution does not necessarily operate for humanity's benefit, but that the species could as easily devolve as evolve. Indeed, Wells was haunted by this awareness throughout his life, and struggled to come to terms with the possibility of ultimate human extinction while crusading for a peaceful cosmopolitan solution to the world's ills.

Wells's essay resulted in two letters, from T. B. S. and Osmond Fisher, regarding a metaphoric slip concerning the bed of Procrustes.

In 'Education and Research' (1.7) occurs an exchange which reflects 'the educational conflict of the present time' between the teaching of science versus that of the humanities (and especially the classics) in schools and universities.

Although the *Nature* editorial praises the 'newly developed liberalism of some of the classical leaders', Wells, in his reviews of *Science and the Nation*, edited by Albert Seward, and *A Defence of Classical Education*, by Richard Livingstone, bemoans the lack of resources being put into science teaching, attacks the patronising tone of classicists who consider science a subject suitable for students incapable of learning the humanities, and berates those science advocates who appear to be compromising their demands by according the humanities too much prestige, and their own subject too little, in the educational curriculum. Returning to the argument presented in 'Science, in School and After School'

13

(1.2), Wells observes that 'scientific men have still to develop a definite policy with regard to schools and colleges and higher education' while he turns his pen against 'the Greek shibboleth', stating with emphasis that *there is no time for Greek*. He denies that only through the humanities can a person become cultivated and that 'to be cultivated and to be scientific are antagonistic states', while he calls Viscount Bryce's 'determination *to secure the pick of the available boys and the pick of the administrative posts* for the classical training' the 'invincible conceit of the classical scholar'. In conclusion, Wells calls on men of science to present a collective argument against the classics, and promote science education for its intrinsic value and for the benefit it affords society at large.

In a letter to the editor, Livingstone responded to Wells's review, claiming that he simply sought classical education to be 'within the reach of all boys in secondary schools *who wished to learn it*', though Wells responded, with regard to Livingstone's book that 'the readers of *Nature* will see in its phrasing just that implicit claim to monopolise the best of the boys for the classical side of which I complain', while 'Mr Livingstone does, under existing conditions, wish to retain compulsory Greek'.

Matthew Hill closes the debate by pointing out the fallacy that students have an especial 'aptitude' for science or the classics. With rare exceptions, he claims, 'The boys who are best at classics are also best at science'.

In 1920 Wells visited Soviet Russia, met Vladimir Lenin and published *Russia in the Shadows*. During his trip he was appalled by the conditions under which Russia's literary and scientific elite was working. Especially disturbing was the poor quality of equipment Russia's scientists were using, and their lack of recent scientific publications. On his return to Britain, therefore, Wells attempted to rouse the British intelligentsia into a response to the Russian intellectual calamity. Following an article in the *Sunday Express* highlighting the conditions he witnessed, Wells assisted in the formation of 'The British Committee for Aiding Men of Letters and Science in Russia', which attempted, through the publication of 'Men of Letters and Science in Russia' (1.8), to garner donations of books, equipment and other provisions for Russian intellectuals from British scientists.

In the letter by Wells entitled 'Scientific Neglect of the Mas d'Azil' (1.9), and the response by Henri Breuil, attention is brought to the dilapidated state of the prehistoric caves at Mas d'Azil. The caves were most thoroughly excavated by Édouard Piette in the late-nineteenth century, when painted pebbles, wall paintings and carved antlers were discovered. Both correspondents point to the need for preservation rather than further excavation, with much scientific work already achieved over the previous forty years.

Although something like a World Encyclopaedia was represented in Wells's works from at least 1915 (in *The Research Magnificent*), and was referred to as the 'Bible of Civilization' in *The Salvaging of Civilization* (2.12), it was in 1931 with *The Work, Wealth and Happiness of Mankind* (2.20) that he first gave substantial shape to what he considered a World Encyclopaedia should be. Through the rest of the 1930s Wells elaborated the World Encyclopaedia idea, in works of fiction such as *The Camford Visitation* (1937) and especially in his collection of lectures and essays, *World Brain* (1938), in which was published 'The Idea of a World Encyclopaedia' (1.10), which was also printed as a pamphlet in 1936.

This lecture was Wells's second to the Royal Institution, his first being 'The Discovery of the Future' (1.6). Here he argues for the need of a unified knowledge system for the benefit of all, but especially to inform those persons in positions of power and to ensure the creation of a global intellectual culture based upon shared collective wisdom. Wells states that the motivation behind his crusade for a World Encyclopaedia was the disjointed efforts of the peacemakers at the conclusion of the Great War:

> Possibly all the knowledge and all the directive ideas needed to establish a wise and stable settlement of the world's affairs in 1919 existed in bits and fragments, here and there, but practically nothing had been assembled, practically nothing had been thought out, nothing practically had been done to draw that knowledge and these ideas together into a comprehensive conception of the world.

Even since the Great War, however, Wells felt no efforts had been made to correct this intellectual fragmentation. Thus in the USA during the Great Depression, Franklin Roosevelt 'showed himself extremely open and receptive for the organised information and guidance ... *that wasn't there*', Wells complains.

Wells desired a uniform approach to intellectual presentation and that approach he described as 'scientific'. He wanted to systematise the availability and distribution of knowledge. By taking a scientific approach to the organisation of knowledge, 'I am sketching what is really a scheme for the reorganisation and reorientation of education and information throughout the world'.

Wells's scheme was not targeted at intellectual and political elites alone, but at everyone, 'for in a completely modernised state every ordinary citizen will be an educated citizen'. The key to the success of the World Encyclopaedia would be the connectivity of resources, from the 'row of volumes in his own home or in some neighbouring house or in a convenient public library or in any school or college' to 'a trustworthy and complete system of reference to primary sources of knowledge'. Thus one would turn initially to a conventional-looking encyclopaedia (a 'row of volumes'), and trace relevant connections through them to further sources of information and ultimately to 'primary sources of knowledge'. But while the World Encyclopaedia would encapsulate all original source material, artefacts and other such evidence, its essence would 'consist of selections, extracts, quotations, very carefully assembled with the approval of outstanding authorities in each subject, carefully collated and edited and critically presented. It would be not a miscellany, but a concentration, a clarification and a synthesis'.

In the creation of the world encyclopaedia Wells saw a more systematic role for the academic and the intellectual specialist. By feeding an encyclopaedia of general use, the specialist would receive 'just that contact with the world at large which at present is merely caricatured by his more or less elementary class-teaching, amateurish examination work and college administration', while he or she would contribute to the organic development of the project itself as 'He will be able to criticise the presentation of his subject, to suggest amendments and restatements'.

Wells saw the world encyclopaedia as a global web of knowledge:

> It is something that must be taken up [...] by the universities, the learned societies, the responsible educational organisations if it is to be brought into effective being. It is a super university I am thinking of, a world brain; no less. It is nothing in the nature of a supplementary enterprise. It is a completion necessary to modernise the university idea.

Through his suggestion of a 'super university' or a 'world brain', Wells's World Encyclopaedia has been heralded by some as an intellectual precursor to the world wide web (Garfield 1983; Campbell-Kelly 2006). Certainly Wells saw the potential of his project in similar terms as those who see the internet as representing an 'information revolution' (see Shenk 1999): 'without a World Encyclopaedia to hold men's minds together in something like a common interpretation of reality, there is no hope whatever of anything but an accidental and transitory alleviation to any of our world troubles. As mankind is, so it will remain, until it pulls its mind together'.

In 'Biology for the Million' (1.11), Wells reviews *The Uniqueness of Man* by one of his co-authors of *The Science of Life* (1930), Julian Huxley. Wells admires Huxley, complimenting him as 'the natural successor to Edwin Ray Lankester', and identifying the volume as an able exposition of popular science for 'the man of intelligence, mainly preoccupied with other work'. He does, however, criticise Huxley for his carelessness of phrase and his ambiguous assertion that 'My final belief is in life'. 'What', asks Wells, 'does this belief in life mean?'

In 'The Man of Science as Aristocrat' (1.12), Wells considers the role of the scientist in society, and the potential methods for nurturing the best in discovery and invention. After having acknowledged the existence of a variety of motives which drive the scientific enquirer, from those researchers 'completely disinterested in their contribution to human achievement' and those 'deliberately directed to gainful research' to those 'whose end is [...] a definite practical end', and the Marxists who believe 'invention and discovery has been a response to a very present need', he nonetheless asserts that 'there are centres to this peripheral vagueness'. Agreeing with Richard Gregory, Wells states that 'Exploration, fundamental research, discovery, is the root from which the immense wealth of modern invention springs', and this realisation places a responsibility upon the shoulders of men and women of science, as well as upon policy-makers.

> [T]he preservation, multiplication and cultivation of the 'pure' discoverer is the primary solicitude of all of us progressives, and it becomes an inquiry of primary importance to the liberal thinker to reveal what are the political and social circumstances that will produce this type in maximum abundance and satisfactory activity.

Wells argues that it is incumbent upon modern society to ensure the continued independence of the scientist. In prior times private patronage funded research and 'The endowment paid its money for distinguished achievement and the man of science had a free hand'. Latterly, in the USA for example, 'the younger men of science in all departments [have] a lively disposition to get on with a new world and to find in an extension of federal activities in the way of research and educational activities a substitute for the spontaneous and rather incalculable generosity of the now deflated wealthy'. Although Wells does not explicitly endorse either option (private endowment or state funding), he makes the contrast in terms of old practice and new and states that the challenge is to settle 'how the scientific worker is to adjust his pride and honour to this new and dangerous change in his sustaining conditions'.

Wells concludes by arguing for the emergence of a new scientific aristocracy, driven not by financial reward but by a dedication to research:

> By resolving to become a primary research worker he decides that he is one of a necessary *élite*, an aristocrat in a democratic world. [...] If he feels that his research work is better worth while than anything else in the world, then

probably it is worth while, and if he does not feel that, he had better turn to something 'with money in it'.

In sum, Wells rejects all forms of endowment, whether private or public, and asserts that 'in the end the research worker, the philosopher, the author or the artist must fall back upon his innate conviction of the supreme value of his work. His ultimate resource is pride. With that he must be prepared to sustain himself against adverse conditions. He must do his best always. He must endure the bludgeonings of fate', and political progressives 'must fight for that unrestricted freedom of expression without which he is muffled and made ineffective' because 'He is the key man of the New World'.

Wells's article received several responses, with John Moore-Brabazon ridiculing Wells's suggestion that scientists should avoid the corruption of wealth and should work for the love of research and discovery. After all, writes Moore-Brabazon, Wells himself has prospered through literature without the '"arrogance and the detestableness of his nature"' coming out – because that nature 'was not there'. More importantly for Moore-Brabazon, Wells's article is misplaced in privileging scientists in society. As valuable as their contribution is, he asserts that the scientist pursues his career 'because that is his bent in life and where he can best satisfy himself' rather than from any noble calling. It is to the neglected science of politics that Moore-Brabazon calls Wells's attention, for only through political solutions will the world be improved and the independence of the scientist ensured.

Richard Paget also criticises Wells, stating that the patronage of science must be maintained. In lieu of private wealth, public endowment should occur.

Commenting upon Wells's retelling of a cinematic patent application from 1895, Robert Paul writes to flesh out the story and correct Wells's exaggerations.

Wells returns to the debate, commenting upon Moore-Brabazon's letter, and clarifying that his desire is to see scientists 'refuse absolutely to be directed, controlled or silenced by anybody' and so, by implication, he suggests any form of endowment must ultimately lead to control.

Robert Jones also offers a reply to Moore-Brabazon, pointing out certain problems of reward for scientists attempting to expand into government administration and bemoaning the lack of respect such scientists receive and the lack of incentive offered to them to apply their knowledge beyond their narrow research interests.

In June 1943 Wells was awarded a doctorate of science by the University of London, for which he had submitted a thesis, *The Quality of Illusion in the*

Continuity of the Individual Life in the Higher Metazoa, with particular reference to Home sapiens. The thesis was published in 1942 and appended to *'42 to '44* (1944), while 'The Illusion of Personality' (1.13) is an abridgement which also appeared as a pamphlet.

The essence of Wells's thesis is that human individuality is '"a biologically convenient delusion"' as humans do not possess 'a mental unity'. He argues that gregariousness is the basis for this delusion, as 'Self-consciousness and a conception of other individuals as consistent persons are necessary to gregariousness'. Nonetheless, within every human mind there exists innumerable personalities continually replacing each other and often vying for primacy with each other. Speaking of the average person, 'John Smith', Wells writes that

> All the Smiths, from No. 1 to No. 5000 or No. 5,000,000, have a common belief that John Smith is really one person, because they are not only all aboard the same body, but also built around a similar conception of himself, his *persona* as Jung has it. *In fact, they are a collection of mutually replaceable individual systems held together in a common habitation.*

According to Wells the 'illusion of personality' in individual humans is a biological imperative which permits the individual to coexist within a larger community. For while Wells argues against the existence of a continuity in the individual human life (the 'John Smith' of 5 is not the same personality as the 'John Smith' of 55), he shifts the notion of continuity to the human species, stating that 'The biological reality is that while [a person] can interbreed with every variety of human being, he goes on as a unity in the whole species, and, whatever frame of community he adopts, it can, from the ecological point of view, have no narrower boundary than the species'.

Because the human species continues on the basis of individuals' developments, variations are responsible for species change. However, this observation does not mean Wells credits the 'great man' theory of history; rather, 'Most variations have no survival value at all' while, in times of stress, 'The causes of a variation will almost certainly be acting not merely in one case but also upon groupings of similarly situated genes'. Referring to historical cultures he points out that 'Palaeontology shows repeated evidence of a sort of flurry of abnormalities before the collapse and obliteration of some dominant group which has outstayed its welcome' and, writing at the height of the Second World War, he asserts that 'This seems to be the case with man to-day'.

Wells saw twentieth-century conflict as qualitatively and quantitatively different from that of previous centuries. From a natural biological check in the past, war had become a menace to the very survival of the human species. In order to escape self-annihilation, Wells believed a new variation of *Homo sapiens* was required:

> A modern community must be held together by stronger forces than are derived from the purely gregarious instincts. It cannot be a mob of slaves, clinging together, incapable of self-government and begging to be led; because it will always be led to disaster. It must consist of vigorous, self-reliant men, knit to one another by a strong, tense and elastic community of will and understanding.

Two years later, in *Mind at the End of Its Tether* (1945), Wells reasserted the need for a new human variation to replace the martial variety then in existence, though by that time he was despondent about humanity's chances.

At present, Wells claims, human individuals and culture groups operate on the basis of dominance. "'This,'" in effect says life, emerging to a consciousness of others, "is not going to beat me'". It is just this insistence on gaining 'the upper hand' which must be overcome by the new variety of *Homo sapiens* Wells hoped would emerge. While Wells demurred about the notion of a wholesale evolution of the human species, he did see the possibility of an intellectual elite emerging which would offer selfless leadership and possibly avert species self-annihilation. Rather than evolve, however, Wells suggests that such an elite would come about through the channelling of already-present emotions and the overcoming of religion-driven moral self-suppression:

> The dominant phases of the unrestrained man, as distinguished from the suppressed individual in our now disintegrating modern communities, are those of an inquirer and maker. His unrestrained phases discover an innate desire for mastery; in invention (artistic or 'practical') and construction, according to his aptitude. The profounder disposition of mankind is to make, and to sublimate self in the discovery, each man, of his own idiosyncratic creative possibility.

Here Wells describes the selfless intellectual aiming to master not his or her fellow human, but his or her specialist field. Implicit in this description is the dispassionate scientific approach to life which Wells promoted in most of his articles in *Nature*; the forward-looking escape from tradition, anticipatory of 'things to come', as expressed, for example, in his 1902 lecture 'The Discovery of the Future' (1.6).

1.1: 'Popularising Science'

H. G. Wells, 'Popularising Science' (26 July 1894).[1]

'Popular Science,'[2] it is to be feared, is a phrase that conveys a certain flavour of contempt to many a scientific worker. It may be that this contempt is not altogether undeserved, and that a considerable proportion of the science of our magazines, school text-books, and books for the general reader, is the mere obvious tinctured by inaccurate compilation. But this in itself scarcely justifies a sweeping condemnation, though the editorial incapacity thus evinced must be a source of grave regret to all specialists with literary leanings and with the welfare of science at heart. The fact remains that in an age when the endowment of research is rapidly passing out of the hands of private or quasi-private organisations into those of the State, the maintenance of an intelligent exterior interest in current investigation becomes of almost vital importance to continual progress. Let that adjective 'intelligent' be insisted upon. Time was when inquiry could go on unaffected even by the scornful misrepresentations of such a powerful enemy as Swift, because it was mainly the occupation of men of considerable means. But now that our growing edifice of knowledge spreads more and more over a substructure of grants and votes, and the appliances needed for instruction and further research increase steadily in cost, even the affectation of a contempt for popular opinion becomes unwise. There is not only the danger of supplies being cut off, but of their being misapplied by a public whose scientific education is neglected, of their being deflected from investigations of certain, to those of doubtful value. For instance, the public endowment of the Zetetic Society,[3] the discovery of Dr Platt's polar and central suns,[4] or the rotation of Dr Owen's Bacon-cryptogram wheel,[5] at the expense of saner inquiries might conceivably and very appropriately result from the specialisation of science to the supercilious pitch.

It should also go far to reconcile even the youngest and most promising of specialists to the serious consideration of popular science, to reflect that the ack-

---

1   Reprinted by permission from Macmillan Publishers Ltd: *Nature* (50: 1291), copyright (1894). An extract from this essay has previously been reprinted in Ruddick 2001, 246-47.

2   The presentation of science for the general reader.

3   A pseudo-scientific society (1890-1956) which promoted belief in a flat earth and generally opposed the theory of evolution.

4   I have been unable to identify 'Dr Platt' or the meaning of this reference to his 'polar and central suns'.

5   Orville Owen was an exponent of the theory that Francis Bacon was the author of the plays of William Shakespeare. Owen devised a cryptogram-wheel based on Bacon's ciphers as presented in *De Augmentis Scientiarum*.

nowledged leaders of the great generation that is now passing away, Darwin[6] notably, addressed themselves in many cases to the general reader, rather than to their colleagues. But instead of the current of popular and yet philosophical books increasing, its volume appears if anything to dwindle, and many works ostensibly addressed to the public by distinguished investigators, succeed in no notable degree, or fail to meet with appreciation altogether. There is still a considerable demand for popular works, but it is met in many cases by a new class of publication from which philosophical quality is largely eliminated. At the risk of appearing impertinent, I may perhaps, as a mere general reader, say a little concerning the defects of very much of what is proffered to the public as scientific literature. As a reviewer for one or two publications,[7] I have necessarily given some special attention to the matter.

As a general principle, one should say that a book should be written in the language of its readers, but a very considerable number of scientific writers fail to realise this. A few write boldly in the dialect of their science, and there is certainly a considerable pleasure in a skilful and compact handling of technicalities; but such writers do not appreciate the fact that this is an acquired taste, and that the public has not acquired it. Worse sometimes results from the persistent avoidance of technicality. Except in the cases of the meteorologist, archaeologist, and astronomer, who are relatively free from a special terminology, a scientific man finds himself at a great disadvantage in writing literary English when compared with a man who is not a specialist. To express his thought precisely he gravitates towards the all too convenient technicality, and forbidden that, too often rests contented with vague, ambiguous, or misleading phrases. It does not follow that, because, what from a literary standpoint must be called 'slang,' is not to be used, that the writer is justified in 'writing down' as if to his intellectual inferiors. The evil often goes further than lack of precision. Out of a quite unwarrantable feeling of pity and condescension for the weak minds that have to wrestle with the elements of his thought, the scientific writer will go out of his way to jest jests of a carefully selected and most obvious description, forgetting that whatever status his special knowledge may give him in his subject, the subtlety of his humour is probably not greatly superior, and may even be inferior to that of the average man, and that what he assumes as inferiority in his hearers or readers is simply the absence of what is, after all, his own intellectual parochialism. The villager thought the tourist a fool because he did not know 'Owd Smith.' Occasionally scientific people are guilty of much the same fallacy.

In this matter of writing or lecturing 'down,' one may even go so far as to object altogether to the facetious adornment of popular scientific statements.

6   I. e., Charles Darwin.

7   At this time Wells was reviewing for the *Educational Times*, the *Journal of Education*, and regularly for the *Pall Mall Gazette*.

Writing as one of the reading public, I may testify that to the common man who opens a book or attends a lecture, this clowning is either very irritating or very depressing. We respect science and scientific men hugely, and we had far rather they took themselves seriously. The taste for formal jesting is sufficiently provided for in periodicals of a special class. Yet on three occasions recently very considerable distress has been occasioned the writer by such mistaken efforts after puerility of style. One was in a popular work on geology,[8] where the beautiful problems of the past of our island and the evolution of life were defaced by the disorderly offspring of a quite megathereal[9] wit – if one may coin such an antithesis to 'ethereal.'[10] One jest I am afraid I shall never forget. It was a Laocoön struggle[11] with the thought that the huge subsidiary brains in the lumbar region[12] of *Stegosaurus* suggested the animation of Dr Busby's arm by the suspicion of a similarly situated brain in the common boy. The second disappointment was a popular lecture professing to deal with the Lick Observatory,[13] and I was naturally anxious to learn a little of the unique appliances and special discoveries of this place. But we scarcely got to the Observatory at all. We were shown – I presume as being more adapted to our intelligence – numerous lantern-slides[14] of the road to the Lick Observatory, most of them with the 'great white dome' hidden, portraits of the 'gentlemen of the party on horseback,' walks round the Observatory, the head of an interesting old man who lived in a cottage near, the dome by moonlight, the dome in winter, and at last the telescope was 'too technical' for explanation, and we were told in a superior tone of foolish things our fellow common people had said about it. For my own part, I really saw nothing very foolish in a lady expecting to see houses on the moon. My third experience was ostensibly a lecture on astronomy,[15] but it really was an entertainment – and a very fair one – after the lines of Mr Grossmith's. 'Corney Grain in Infinite Space' might have served as a title. It was very amusing, it was full of humour, but as for science, the facts were mere magazine *clichés* that we have grown sick of long ago. And as a pretty example of its scientific value I find a newspaper reporter, whose account is chiefly '(laughter)' with jokes in

---

8   The branch of science that deals with the physical structure and substance of the earth.

9   Ponderous or unwieldy.

10   Of unearthly delicacy or refinement.

11   A death struggle like that experienced by Laocoön, a character from the *Aeneid* by Virgil, who, along with his two sons, was crushed to death by two sea-serpents.

12   The small of the back, between the diaphragm and the pelvis.

13   The astronomical observatory belonging to the University of California, Santa Cruz, constructed between 1876 and 1887.

14   Filmic slides which are displayed on a white screen by a projector.

15   The science of celestial objects, of space, and of the universe as a whole.

between, carried away the impression that Herschel discovered Saturn[16] in the reign of George the Third.

Now this kind of thing is not popularising science at all. It is merely making fun of it. It dishonours the goddess we serve. It is a far more difficult thing than is usually imagined, but it is an imperative one, that scientific exponents who wish to be taken seriously should not only be precise and explicit, but also absolutely serious in their style. If it were not a point of discretion it would still be a point of honour.

In another direction those to whom the exposition of science falls might reasonably consider their going more carefully, and that is in the way of construction. Very few books and scientific papers appear to be constructed at all. The author simply wanders about his subject. He selects, let us say, 'Badgers and Bats' as the title. It is alliterative, and an unhappy public is supposed to be singularly amenable to alliteration. He writes first of all about Badger A. 'We now come,' he says, 'to Badger B'; then 'another interesting species is Badger C'; paragraphs on Badger D follow, and so the pavement is completed. 'Let us now turn to the Bats,' he says. It would not matter a bit if you cut any section of his book or paper out, or shuffled the sections, or destroyed most or all of them. This is not simply bad art; it is the trick of boredom. A scientific paper for popular reading may and should have an orderly progression and development. Intelligent common people come to scientific books neither for humour, subtlety of style, nor for vulgar wonders of the 'millions and millions and millions' type, but for problems to exercise their minds upon. The taste for good inductive reading is very widely diffused; there is a keen pleasure in seeing a previously unexpected generalisation skilfully developed. The interest should begin at its opening words, and should rise steadily to its conclusion. The fundamental principles of construction that underlie such stories as Poe's *Murders in the Rue Morgue*, or Conan Doyle's 'Sherlock Holmes' series,[17] are precisely those that should guide a scientific writer. These stories show that the public delights in the ingenious unravelling of evidence, and Conan Doyle need never stoop to jesting. First the problem, then the gradual piecing together of the solution. They cannot get enough of such matter.

The nature of the problems, too, is worthy of a little attention. Very few scientific specialists differentiate clearly between philosophical and technical interest. To those engaged in research the means become at least almost as important, and even more important than the end, but apart from industrial applications, the final end of all science is to formulate the relationship of phenomena

---

16   In fact, Frederick Herschel discovered Uranus in 1781.

17   Arthur Conan Doyle's 'Sherlock Holmes' short stories and novels appeared between 1887 and 1927.

to the thinking man. The systematic reference of *Calceola*,[18] for instance, *Theca*,[19] the Lichens, the Polyzoa,[20] or the Termites, is an extremely fascinating question to the student who has just passed the elementary stage, and so too is the discussion of the manufacture and powers of telescopes and microscopes; morphological questions[21] again become at last as delightful as good chess, and so do mathematical problems. But it must be remembered that morphology, mathematics, and classification are from the wider point of view mere intellectual appliances, and that to the general reader they are only interesting in connection with their end. To the specialist even they would not be interesting if he had not first had their end in view. The fundamental interest of all biological science is the balance and interplay of life, yet for one paper of this type that comes to hand there are a dozen amplified catalogues of the 'Cats and Crocodiles' description. I find again, presented as a popular article, a long list of double stars[22] with their chief measurements. Now, to a common man one double star is as good as a feast. Again, the botanist, asked to write about leaves, will get himself voluminously entangled in the discussion whether an anther[23] is a lamina,[24] or in an exhaustive and even exuberant classification of simple and compound, pinnate[25] and palmate,[26] and the like, making great points of the orange leaf[27] and the barberry.[28] But the kind of thing we want to have pointed out to us is *why* leaves are of such different shapes and so variously arranged. It is a thing all people who are not botanists puzzle over, and a very pretty illustrated paper might be written, and remains still to be written, linking rainfall and other meteorological phenomena, the influence of soil upon root distribution and animal enemies, with this infinite variety of beautiful forms.

Enough has been said to show along what lines the genuine populariser of science goes. There are models still in plenty; but if there are models there are

---

18 Properly, calceolaria, a South American plant of the figwort family, bearing slipper-shaped flowers.

19 A cup-like or tubular structure containing a coral polyp.

20 Properly, bryozoa, tiny colonial animals that generally build stony skeletons of calcium carbonate, superficially similar to coral.

21 Morphology is the branch of biology which deals with the forms of living organisms, and with relationships between their structures.

22 Pairs of stars that appear as one until viewed through a telescope.

23 The part of the stamen in which pollen is contained and from which it is shed when mature.

24 A thin layer of membrane or other tissue.

25 Resembling a feather.

26 Shaped like the outspread palm of the hand.

27 The leaf of the orange tree, being shinny and leathery and up to ten centimetres long.

28 Any of numerous shrubs of the genus *Berberis*, usually thorny with yellow wood.

awful examples – if anything they seem to be increasing – who appear bent upon killing the interest that the generation of writers who are now passing the zenith of their fame created, wounding it with clumsy jests, paining it with patronage, and suffocating it under their voluminous and amorphous emissions. There is, I believe, no critical literature dealing generally with the literary merits of popular scientific books, and there are no canons for such criticism. It is, I am convinced, a matter that is worthy of more attention from scientific men, if only on the grounds mentioned in my opening paragraphs.

1.2: 'Science, in School and After School'

H. G. Wells, 'Science, in School and After School' (27 September 1894).[1]

It is an unfortunate accident of the conditions under which instruction in science has grown up, that in speaking of science teaching two essentially dissimilar things should be confused. This confusion has very seriously affected – and still affects – the development of method in this country. It arises from the fact that, twenty or thirty years ago at least, the ordinary schoolmaster was quite without the knowledge necessary to teach science, and that even when his scientific knowledge was a measurable quantity, that ignorance of psychology which was and which remains one of his most constant characteristics, rendered him incapable of innovations upon the tradition of mental training he cherished. Consequently what knowledge people obtained of the growing body of science came after the elementary stage of education was over, when their minds and senses had already received a considerable amount of cultivation and were, for good or evil, definitely developed in a prescribed way. The teaching given, therefore, did not aspire to be so much educational as *instructive*; it made the best of a bad job, and without any belated attempts to alter the fundamental intellectual mechanism, placed therein so much of the new facts and views as the circumstances permitted. It was addressed primarily to adolescence and to the adult, its methods were by lecture, diagram and text-book, and the written examination or a practical examination, turning chiefly on the identification of specimens or the interpretation of diagrams, was the adequate measure of its value. Such teaching can affect the taught only through their opinions and knowledge; it can discover scientific capacity, but it can neither develop nor very largely increase it, because it comes too late in the mental life. It is typically represented by the innumerable classes over which the Science and Art Department[2] presides.

On the other hand, we have the science teaching that is *educational*, that takes the pupil still undeveloped and trains hand, eye, and mind together, enlarges the scope of the observation, and stimulates the development of the reasoning power. Such science teaching occurs at present most abundantly in theoretical pedagogics.[3] It is, however, undoubtedly the proper science teaching for the school, if science is to have a place in the school. For it is universally conceded nowadays that the school is a training place, that there the vessel is moulded rather than filled, and that the only justification for the introduction of science is its educational value. Equally indubitable is it that it should be con-

---

1   Reprinted by permission from Macmillan Publishers Ltd: *Nature* (50: 1300), copyright (1894).

2   A British government body (1853-99) created to promote science, technology and design through education.

3   The theory of teaching.

fined to school limits. An attempt to make the adult science teaching educational in the same sense, would be – to complete the image – extremely like putting a well-baked – if imperfect – vessel back upon the potter's wheel.

Now, hitherto the chief influence of this confusion has been to hamper truly educational science teaching in schools. Those who had as adults studied science under the Science and Art Department, or in University lecture theatres, took their text-books and the methods under which they had acquired their knowledge into the school, where the conditions were altogether different. The course of science lessons began as a lecture in which the class listened to colourable imitations at second or third hand of this or that eminent exponent of scientific theory. The more discerning teachers after a time realised the futility of requiring genuine lecture notes from such immature minds, and supplied the deficiency *by dictating* a colourable imitation. They also provided copies on the blackboard for such original sketches as were required, and indeed went to very considerable pains to keep the outward appearance of the lecture system intact. Examiners of schools – being selected without the slightest reference to their capacity to examine – fell very readily into this view, that school science-teaching was adult science-teaching in miniature; as some parents hold that infant costume should be a simple and economical adaptation of the parental garments. And so an elaborate system of lecturing, note dictating, 'model answer' grinding, has been evolved, which is not only not educational and a grievous waste of the pupils' energies, but which seriously discredits the claims of science upon the school time, in the eyes of ordinary educated people.

This has been particularly the case in many middle class schools, though the recent abolition of the second class pass in the May examination has done much, as the Forty-first Report of the Department shows, towards mending the mischief. In connection with countless higher grade and small grammar schools, classes, containing as a rule only elementary pupils, and aiming really only at second class passes, have been organised from year to year. Not only was the science-teaching given in the evening classes, but a considerable portion of the daytime was devoted to model answer drill and to mechanical copying out from the text-book. The minimum of apparatus required by the Department formed a picturesque addition to the schoolroom. This discipline resulted in remunerative grants for second class passes, but it resulted in very little else, except perhaps a certain relaxation of the pupil's handwriting and a certain facility in the misuse of scientific phrases. The certificates were framed and glazed, the teacher added a few modest comforts to his home, and there the matter ended.

The examinations of the Science and Art Department were scarcely to blame in this matter, although the blame has been generously awarded them. The Science and Art Department is a large and convenient mark, it is perfectly safe to throw at, and to attack it has something of the romantic effect of David against Goliath.[4] But we must remember that its classes were primarily, as they are still in intention, continuation and adult classes, an outcome of the Mechanics' Institute movement,[5] and it was an unforeseen accident, and one the full bearing of which only became apparent in the course of years, that they should so seriously affect the teaching of middle-class, and even of the higher standards of elementary, schools. For their proper purpose as a test of lecture teaching, the departmental examinations are generally efficient. Far more blameworthy are examining bodies whose work is specially directed to school needs. The College of Preceptors,[6] for instance, while subsidising lecturers upon Educational Theory, has done nothing to promote practical work in schools, and many of its examinations set a premium upon the vicious lecture and text-book cramming which educational theory condemns. And in public schools over which the Department has no influence, young gentlemen from the older universities, beginning educators without of course the faintest knowledge of educational technique, set up precisely the same imitation of the professorial course. We have in consequence such a standing argument against science teaching as that naïve testimony of a prominent headmaster, that he found boys who had followed the classical course for some years, and who then took up 'science as beginners,' speedily outstripped those who, to the exclusion of literary work, had been engaged during the same time in what he regarded as scientific studies.

So far the confusion between the two forms of elementary instruction has hampered science-teaching. But there can be no doubt that the educational reformer is abroad. A large, if somewhat inchoate, body of criticism has grown up, and good resolutions in the matter are epidemic. A really educational scheme of instruction in physics[7] and chemistry[8] now exists, having its base upon the Kindergarten,[9] and developing side by side with elementary work in mathematics. Mr Earl's recently published book upon Physical Measurements[10] is an admirable exposition of what is here intended by educational science-teaching.

---

4   A reference to the Biblical story in 1 Samuel 17 in which David, a poor shepherd boy, slays Goliath, a giant Philistine warrior, single-handedly, here used as a metaphor for the struggle between an underdog and a more powerful foe.

5   A movement started in 1821 in Glasgow to provide technical education to working-class men, often funded by industrialists.

6   A professional association for teachers, founded in 1849 and renamed the College of Teachers in 1998, which 'professionalised' teaching and set school examinations. Wells was a member, licentiate and fellow of the College, and won several prizes from it.

7   The branch of science that deals with matter and its motion, as well as space and time.

8   The branch of science that deals with the investigation of the substances of which matter is composed, and of the phenomena of combination and change which they display.

9   A nursery school.

10   A reference to *Practical Lessons in Physical Measurement* by Alfred Earl.

In this, information is entirely subordinated to mental development. His course is devoted to the measurement of space, mass[11] and time, and to the observation and methods of recording various changes involving precise determinations. The first exercise requires the pupil to 'measure the size or dimensions in inches of the paper on which you are writing, using for your standard a strip of paper one inch in length, and which you have divided into halves, quarters, and eighths'; and the book concludes with experiments upon torsion[12] and the rotation of suspended bodies. The course must inevitably constitute a firm foundation of definite concepts, and develop a clear and interrogative habit of mind. It marks the line along which school science teaching must move in the future, if it is to attain that predominance which its advocates claim for it. Yet at the same time it may not be premature to notice that the new movement has its dangers.

These dangers arise from the confusion between the two distinct forms of science-teaching whose existence is necessitated by the present condition of things. In the past the error has been to treat children like adults; in the future it may be that adults will be treated like children. Such exercises as the one we have noticed, are excellent in developing concepts, but scarcely anything could be devised more irksome and exasperating to a mind already provided with a basis of definite ideas. Nothing, for instance, could be better calculated to discourage an intelligent student of eighteen or nineteen, curious about physics, than a day or so manufacturing an unreliable millimetre scale. The problems of the science are already more or less vaguely in his mind, and there is every reason why these should be made the starting-point. To produce an intellectual parallel to the spiritual re-birth, is as impossible as it would be to refer an unsatisfactory chicken back to the egg to reconsider its ontogeny.[13] We have now, and shall have for an indefinite number of years, to provide for the needs of a great number of people whose intellectual development is nearly or quite at an end, whose curiosity about nature is already aroused, and whose practical needs are also pressing for scientific information, and yet who are ignorant of any but the veriest commonplaces of science. For them the Science and Art Department classes were designed and are well adapted. It will be an unfortunate thing if the criticisms of the educational reformer should so far overshoot the mark as to affect their instruction. Yet one might suggest that a downward age limit, similar to that of the London University Matriculation,[14] might save many a schoolmaster from the temptations of the possibility of grant-earning – a temptation, however, from which the abolition of the second class in the elementary stage has already to some extent relieved him.

---

11 The amount of matter making up an object.

12 Twisting by turning an object in two opposite directions.

13 The origin and development of the individual organism.

14 The examination for admission into the University of London.

From Henry Armstrong, 'Scientific Method in Board Schools' (25 October 1894)*.[16]

At the request of my friend and former pupil, Mr W. M. Heller, I have undertaken to say a few words by way of introduction to the course which he is about to give here to assist a number of you who are teachers in the schools in the Tower Hamlets and Hackney district under the School Board for London[17] – a course of lessons expressly intended to direct your attention to the educational value of instruction given solely with the object of inculcating *scientific* habits of mind and *scientific* ways of working; and expressly and primarily intended to assist you in giving such teaching in your schools.

Nothing could afford me greater pleasure, as I regard the introduction of such teaching into schools generally – not Board Schools[18] merely, but all schools – as of the utmost importance; indeed, I may say, as of national importance: and I now confidently look forward to the time, at no distant date, when this will be everywhere acknowledged and acted on. Personally I regard the work that I have been able to do in this direction as of far greater value than any purely scientific work that I have accomplished. At the very outset of my career as a teacher, I was led to see how illogical, unsatisfactory and artificial were the prevailing methods of teaching, and became interested in their improvement. My appointment as one of the first professors at the Finsbury Technical College[19] forced me to pay particular attention to the subject and gave me abundant opportunity of practically working out a scheme of my own. I was the more anxious to do this, as I soon became convinced that if any real progress were to be made in our system of technical education, it was essential in the first place to introduce improved methods of teaching into schools generally, so that students of technical subjects might commence their studies properly prepared; and subsequent experience has only confirmed this view. Indeed it is beyond question, in the opinion of many, that what we at present most want in this country are proper systems of primary and secondary education: the latter especially. Now, most students at our technical colleges, in consequence of their defective school training, not only waste much of their time in learning elementary principles with which they should have been made familiar at school, and much of our time by

*   'A revised address delivered at the Berners Street Board School, Commercial Road, London, E., on October 9, 1894, by Prof. H. E. Armstrong, FRS.'

16   Reprinted by permission from Macmillan Publishers Ltd: *Nature* (50: 1304), copyright (1894).

17   The first directly elected body representing the whole of London, responsible for education policy in that city (1870-1904).

18   The first British state-schools, established in 1870 and administered by local boards of education.

19   The first City and Guilds of London Institute college (1878-1926), teaching craft trades.

obliging us to give elementary lessons, but what is far worse, they have acquired bad habits and convictions which are very difficult to eradicate; and their mental attitude towards their studies is usually a false one.

The first fruits of my experience were made public in 1884, at one of the Educational Conferences held at the Health Exhibition.[20] On that occasion, and again at the British Association[21] meeting at Aberdeen in 1885, in the course of my address as president of the Chemical Section,[22] after somewhat sharply criticising the methods of teaching in vogue, I pointed out what I conceived to be the directions in which improvements should be effected. Others meanwhile were working in the same spirit, and consequently, in 1887, a number of us willingly consented to act as a committee 'for the purpose of inquiring into and reporting upon the present methods of teaching chemistry.' This committee was appointed at the meeting of the British Association in York, and consisted of Prof. W. R. Dunstan (secretary), Dr J. H. Gladstone, Mr A. G. Vernon Harcourt, Prof. H. McLeod, Prof. Meldola, Mr Pattison Muir, Sir Henry E. Roscoe, Dr W. J. Russell (chairman), Mr W. A. Shenstone, Prof. Smithells, Mr Stallard and myself. A report was presented at the Bath meeting in 1888, giving an account of replies received to a letter addressed to the headmasters of schools in which elementary chemistry was taught. In 1889 and 1890 reports were presented in which were included suggestions drawn up by myself for a course of elementary instruction in physical science.[23]

Let me at once emphasise the fact that these schemes were for a course of instruction in physical science – not in chemistry alone. These objects to be accomplished by the introduction of such lessons into schools have since been more fully dwelt on in a paper which I read at the College of Preceptors early in 1891, printed in the *Educational Times* in May of that year.[24] After pointing out that literary and mathematical studies are not a sufficient preparation in the great majority of cases for the work of the world, as they develop introspective habits

---

20 An international display held in 1884 in South Kensington, London, demonstrating the advances made in public health over time and the insanitary conditions experienced by previous generations.

21 In full, the British Association for the Advancement of Science, a learned society founded in London in 1831 with the object of promoting science and facilitating interaction between scientific workers.

22 The Chemistry Section of the British Association was formally established in 1895, though a section dealing with 'Chemical Science and Mineralogy' (including its application to agriculture and the arts) had existed from 1832.

23 According to Philip Magnus, Hugh Gordan's *Elementary Course of Practical Science* 'is based on a scheme drawn up by Prof. Armstrong for a committee of the British Association' (Magnus 1893, 121), mentioned above.

24 This article has not been traced.

too exclusively, I then said, in future boys and girls generally must not be confined to desk studies; they must not only learn a good deal *about* things; they must also be taught how to *do* things, and to this end must learn how others before them have done things by actually repeating – not by merely reading about – what others have done. We ask, in fact, that the use of eyes and hands in unravelling the meaning of the wondrous changes which are going on around us in the world of nature shall be taught systematically in schools generally – that is to say, that the endeavour shall be made to inculcate the habits of observing accurately, of experimenting accurately, of observing and experimenting with a clearly defined and logical purpose, and of logical reasoning from observation and the results of experimental inquiry. Scientific habits and methods must be universally taught. We ask to be at once admitted to equal rights with the *three Rs*[25] – it is no question of an alternative subject. This cannot be too clearly stated, and the battle must be fought out on this issue within the next few years.

Well, gentleman and ladies, you have the honour of forming part of the advanced guard in the army which is fighting this battle – for the fight is begun in real earnest, although as yet on a small scale: nevertheless, in this case, the small beginning *must* have a great ending.

[…]

I have thought it desirable thus to sketch the history of the introduction of our British Association scheme into School Board circles. Let me now further emphasise the importance of teaching *scientific method*, which after all is recognised by very few as yet. Let me endeavour to make it clear what I mean by scientific method: that when I speak of scientific method, I do not mean a branch of science, but something much broader and more generally useful. We may teach scientific method without teaching any branch of science; and there are many ways in which we may teach it with materials always close to hand.

I have very little belief in the efficacy of lecturing, and it is always difficult to persuade those who are not always persuaded – I would therefore refer those of you who are not yet with me to a book from which they may derive much information and inspiration. I mean Herbert Spencer's essay on *Education*, the cheap edition of which, published by Williams and Norgate, costs only one shilling and elevenpence! It is a book which every parent of intelligence desiring to educate his children properly should read; certainly every teacher should have studied it thoroughly; and no one should be allowed to become a member of a School Board[26] who on examination was found not to have mastered its contents. But as Herbert Spencer says – and the times are not greatly

---

25 Reading, writing and arithmetic.

26 In Britain (1870-1902), a board elected by the rate-payers of a district responsible for the provision and maintenance of local elementary education.

changed since he wrote – although the great majority of the adult males throughout the kingdom are found to show some interest in the breeding, rearing, or training of animals of one kind or other, it rarely happens that one hears anything said about the rearing of children. I believe the subject is seldom mentioned in School Board debates. Hence it happens that Herbert Spencer's book has had a smaller circulation than many novels, and that the 1893 edition [sic.] is but the 34th instead of being the 340th thousand. After very fully discussing the question 'What knowledge is of most worth?' he arrives at the conclusion that science is, and eloquently advocates the claims of the order of knowledge termed scientific. The following are eminently instructive passages in his essay: – 'While every one is ready to endorse the abstract proposition that instruction fitting youths for the business of life is of high importance, or even to consider it of supreme importance; yet scarcely any inquire what instruction will so fit them. It is true that reading, writing, and arithmetic are taught with an intelligent appreciation of their uses. But when we have said this we have said nearly all. While the great bulk of what else is acquired has no bearing on the industrial activities, an immensity of information that has a direct bearing on the industrial activities is entirely passed over. For, leaving out only some very small classes, what are all men employed in? They are employed in the production, preparation and distribution of commodities. And on what does efficiency in the production, preparation, and distribution of commodities depend? It depends on the use of methods fitted to the respective natures of these commodities; it depends on an adequate acquaintance with their physical, chemical, and vital properties, as the case may be: that is, it depends on science. This order of knowledge, which is in great part ignored in our school courses, is the order of knowledge underlying the right performance of those processes by which civilised life is made possible. Undeniable as is this truth, there seems to be no living consciousness of it: its very familiarity makes it unregarded.... That which our school courses leave almost entirely out, we thus find to be that which most nearly concerns the business of life. Our industries would cease, were it not for the information which men begin to acquire, as they best may, after their education is said to be finished. And were it not for the information, from age to age accumulated and spread by unofficial means, these industries would never have existed. Had there been no teaching but such as goes on in our public schools England would now be what it was in feudal times.[27] That increasing acquaintance with the laws of phenomena, which has through successive ages enabled us to subjugate nature to our needs, and in these days gives the common labourer comforts which a few centuries ago kings could not purchase, is scarcely in any

---

27 The mediaeval social order characterised by the legal subjection of a large part of the peasantry to a hereditary landholding elite exercising legislative and judicial power on the basis of reciprocal private undertakings.

degree owed to the appointed means of instructing our youth. The vital knowledge – that by which we have grown as a nation to what we are, and which now underlies our whole existence, is a knowledge that has got itself taught in nooks and corners; while the ordained agencies for teaching have been mumbling little else than dead formulas.'

Some improvement there has been since Herbert Spencer wrote, but chiefly in technical teaching; and there is yet no national appreciation of what constitutes true education: fashion and vested interests still largely dominate educational policy.

Another advocate of the teaching of scientific method to whom I would refer you is Charles Kingsley, the celebrated divine,[28] but also a born naturalist possessed of the keenest powers of observation, a novelist of the first rank, and a poet. Read his life,[29] and you will find it full of inspiration and comfort. Study his scientific lectures and essays (vol. xix. of his 'Collected Works,' Macmillan and Co.[30]), and you will not only learn why 'science' is of use, but will have before you a valuable model of method and style. A friend – a member of the London County Council[31] – to whom I happened to send some of my papers, noting my frequent references to Kingsley, remarked, 'How very fond you are of his writings!' Indeed I am, for they seem to me to display a truer grasp of the importance of scientific method and of its essential character than do any other works with which I am acquainted. I recommend them because they are pleasant as well as profitable reading, and because our text-books generally are worthless for the purpose I have in view. Any ordinary person of intelligence can read Herbert Spencer's and Kingsley's essays and can appreciate them, especially Kingsley's insistent application of the scientific principle of always proceeding from the known to the unknown; but few can read a text-book of science – moreover, the probable effect of most of these would be to dissuade rather than persuade.

Kingsley's great point – and Herbert Spencer's also – is that what people want to learn is not so much what is, still less what has been, but how to *do*. And the object which you must set before yourselves will be to turn out boys and girls who, in proportion to their natural gifts – for, as everyone knows, you cannot make a silken purse from a sow's ear[32] – have become inquiring, observant,

---

28 A clergyman or other person with knowledge of divinity or theology.

29 A reference to Charles Kingsley's *The Life and Works of Charles Kingsley*.

30 A reference to Charles Kingsley's *The Works of Charles Kingsley, Volume XIX: Scientific Lectures and Essays*.

31 The local government body for the county of London (1889-1965).

32 You cannot produce a particular thing from just anything, but must have certain basic ingredients.

reasoning beings, ever thoughtful and exact and painstaking and therefore trustworthy workers. To turn out such is the whole object of our scheme, which chiefly aims at the development of intelligence and the formation of character. In your schools information must be *gained*, not imparted. After describing how the intelligent mother trains her young child, Herbert Spencer remarks: – 'To *tell* a child this and to *show* it the other, is not to teach it how to observe, but to make it a mere recipient of another's observations: a proceeding which weakens rather than strengthens its powers of self-instruction – which deprives it of the pleasures resulting from successful activity – which presents this all attractive knowledge under the aspect of formal tuition...' You must train the children under your care to help themselves in every possible way, and give up always feeding them with a spoon. Abolish learning lessons by rote[33] as far as possible. Devote every moment you possibly can to practical work, and having stated a problem leave it to the children if possible to find a solution. Encourage inquisitiveness, but suggest methods by which they may answer their own questions by experiment or trial or by appeal to dictionaries or simple works of reference, part of the furniture of the schoolroom, and lead them to make use of the public library even: in after life you will not be at their elbows, but books will always be available, and if they once grow accustomed to treat these as friends to whom they can appeal for help, you will have done them infinite service and will undoubtedly infuse many with the desire to continue their studies after leaving school. Under our present system school books are cast aside with infinite relief at the earliest possible moment, and the desire for amusement alone remains. Teach history, geography and much besides from the daily papers, and so prepare them to read the papers with intelligence and interest, and to prefer them to penny dreadfuls[34] and the miserable, often indecent, illustrated rubbish with which we are nowadays so terribly afflicted. At the same time, make it clear to them that the editorial 'we' is but an 'I,' and that assertion does not constitute proof. If such be your teaching, and it have constant reference to things natural, you will also – as Herbert Spencer points out in a very remarkable passage – without fail be giving much *religious* culture, using the word in its highest acceptance, for, as he says, 'it is the refusal to study the surrounding creation that is irreligious.' As I have already said, one great – indeed the great – object of our teaching is the formation of character: and if you teach your pupils to be careful, exact and observant, and they become trustworthy workers, you are giving much training of the highest excellence; and if they have enjoyed such training, what does it matter what facts they know when they leave school?

---

33   In a mechanical or repetitious manner.
34   Cheap sensational novels.

But I hear you say that the inspectors[35] will not allow all this. Gentlemen, do not fear the inspectors – they also are advancing; they also are learning that literary methods are insufficient, that desk studies must not absorb the entire attention of the scholars; that greater latitude must be permitted to the teachers, and especially in the direction of devising more suitable methods. And a new race of inspectors is coming into existence. Mr Gordon, I know, had difficulties with the inspectors; but when they realised that he understood his business and learnt to appreciate his work, they soon became his supporters.

And with appreciative ministers like Mr Acland[36] at the head of affairs, we shall move far more quickly than heretofore, and shall be able soon to entirely throw off the cast-iron bonds of control by examination and payment on results – a refined method of torture affecting both teachers and taught most disastrously. We know that a holiday spent under healthy conditions at the seaside or in the country is of the greatest service. We are becoming accustomed to take care that our houses are properly ventilated and drained, and to rest satisfied that when this is the case their inhabitants may safely be left to themselves. In like manner, in future, we shall take care that our schools are fully provided with all necessary proper appliances – in which I include teachers – and we shall see that the teachers are working in accordance with a proper system; but we shall trouble ourselves little about the taught, feeling that if they have been placed under healthy conditions they cannot fail to have benefited, however little this may be apparent on the surface. In the days to come the work of the teachers will be directly criticised; they, not their pupils, will be examined: but always by competent and sympathetic inspectors who have become acquainted with the work and its difficulties practically, and are not mere theorists, whose main function will be that of guide, philosopher and friend – not that of inquisitor.

In the course which you are about to attend under Mr Heller – the demonstrator[37] upon whom has fallen the mantle previously worn by Mr Gordon, and who is equally desirous of promoting and devising rational methods of teaching – you will in the first place devote your attention to exercises in measurement, including much that is ordinarily taught under mechanics[38] and physics, the prime object of which is to teach accuracy of observation. You will then study a series of problems, mainly chemical, which have been arranged chiefly in order to cultivate reasoning powers and to teach the research method. In fact, what we

---

35 State-appointed school inspectors.

36 I. e., Arthur Acland

37 A college teaching assistant who demonstrates an experiment or process before students attempt it themselves.

38 Now classical mechanics, the branch of applied mathematics that deals with the motion and equilibrium of bodies and the action of forces, and includes statics, dynamics and kinematics.

want to do is, as far as possible, to put every scholar in the position of the discoverer. The world always has and ever will advance through discovery; discoveries, however, are rarely made accidentally – indeed we all pass from ignorance to knowledge by discovery, and by discovering how to do things that we have not done before we ever increase our powers of usefulness: we all require therefore to be taught how to discover, although we may never be called on to make original discoveries or have the opportunity. But as you proceed I trust that you will realise that the method which you are learning to apply is one which can be made use of in all your work – that the course has a broad educational value far transcending its special value as an introduction to physical science.

Lastly, I should like to take this opportunity of calling attention to the very great value to girls, as well as to boys, of teaching such as you are about to give. I fear that much that girls are being taught under the guise of domestic economy[39] is of slight value educationally or otherwise, and that they are but having imparted to them little tit-bits of information which they are as likely as not to misapply. Nothing is done by way of increasing their intelligence and forming their characters. Lessons which would lead them to be observant, thoughtful and, above all, exact – lessons in method – would be of far higher and abiding value. They would then carry out their household functions with greater ease; there would be far less waste; less unhealthiness; far more comfort. I believe the need for such training to be indeed far greater in the case of girls than in that of boys. Boys are naturally apt in many ways, and even if neglected at school, perforce develop when they go out into the world; but girls are of a different disposition, and rarely seem to spontaneously acquire the mental habits which a training in scientific method can confer, the possession of which would be of inestimable value to them. Extraordinarily little has been done as yet on their behalf, and they have been cruelly sacrificed at examinations – for which, unfortunately, they appear themselves to have an insatiable natural appetite. It is to be hoped that the new Board will give the most serious attention to this matter, and that it will take steps to secure the teaching of scientific method in all the schools under its charge, whether boys' schools or girls' schools. Unhealthy buildings have attracted much attention; but the existence of a far more serious evil – the absence of healthy teaching suited to the times – has not even been noticed.

[...]

---

39   A school course teaching girls and young women the art of managing a household.

Comment on Wells and Armstrong: William Crump, letter to the editor, 'Science Teaching in Schools' (15 November 1894).[40]

Two articles have recently appeared in *Nature* which call for some comment, if the columns of your journal are to be opened once more to a discussion of this question. Educational reformers will agree heartily with the general position taken up by Mr H. G. Wells, in 'Science, in School and after School' (vol. 1, p. 525), and by Prof. Armstrong in 'Scientific Method in Board Schools' (p. 631). But they either ignore or give very little credit for the honest science teaching that is actually being done at the present time. I realise, only too personally, the great difference between training in scientific method and mere instruction in science; and how few are the attempts to make use of the former in all grades of schools. But I hold that the old-fashioned instruction in science has, under favourable conditions, a considerable *educational* value. To have enabled a boy to realise the composition of the air and water is to have introduced him to the world of nature, and has widened his ideas and conceptions to an extent which justifies the means. Was this not one of the original pleas for the introduction of science into the school course? But having entered my protest, I will pass on.

Mr Wells admirably distinguishes between the two styles of science teaching, and points out the original function of the Science and Art Department in encouraging and examining only the one of them. But he admits that the field of operation of the Department has been very much widened in recent years, and that its examinations 'seriously affect the teaching of middle-class, and even of the higher standards of elementary schools.' Yet his only suggestion is that the Department should withdraw from this work; for that would be the effect of an age limit, and is intended to be the effect of the recent alteration in the regulations in the elementary stage.

But circumstances are such that the Department cannot and ought not to withdraw from its present control of science teaching in *day-schools*, for its influence is greater than that of any other examining body; not simply financially, but from the magnitude of its operations. It is a historical quibble to say that the Department is concerned primarily with continuation and adult classes, when it specially encourages the formation of organised science day-schools, and yet rigidly confines the teaching in them to the schedules devised for adult instruction.

Last session there were 94 organised science day-schools, containing about 10,000 pupils taught on the lines laid down by the Department. As is well known, the majority of these are what are otherwise known as Higher Grade

---

40   Reprinted by permission from Macmillan Publishers Ltd: *Nature* (51: 1307), copyright (1894).

Board Schools,[41] which are absolutely dependent for their existence on the grants obtained from the Department. I take it as indisputable that this is the very class of schools where the science ought to have an educational basis; where its function is 'to develop and train the hand, eye and mind together, enlarge the scope of the observation, and stimulate the development of the reasoning power.' I also believe that many of the teachers are anxious to make it so, judging from their liberal denunciations of the present 'pernicious system.' Equally axiomatic is it that, under the Science and Art Department, it is impossible to indulge in such teaching. Time will not permit. The pressure is so great that oxygen and water are almost always spoken of as O and H_2O.

Mr Wells considers other examining bodies, whose work is exclusively directed to school needs, are far more blameworthy. This I absolutely deny. In the first place, the South Kensington examinations[42] are the only ones which are entirely controlled by scientific men. The sole cause for the existence of the Department is the encouragement of science and art, whereas the other bodies referred to provide for the examination of secondary education generally; and the examining board may not have a single representative of science upon it. But further, assuming that the South Kensington examinations are neither better nor worse than others, there are two causes which make them an educational abomination.

(1) In one year the pupils have to be rushed through such an excessive amount of work that the teaching degenerates into the merest cram.[43] The Department distinctly states that students in the first year are to be prepared for the first stage, and in the second year for the second stage. Putting aside entirely the consideration as to whether the scheme is any particular subject, as chemistry, will any practical teacher deny that the requirements for either the first or second stage are far beyond what it is possible to accomplish with satisfaction within the given time? It must be kept in mind that the time-table has to provide not only for the seven or eight subjects of which the Department takes cognisance, but 'for instruction in those literary subjects which are essential for a good general education.' Do not these latter often suffer in favour of the former, especially at the approach of May?[44]

(2) The consequence of this restriction is that boys scarcely in their teens enter by thousands for an examination beyond their normal capacities. It is in

---

41   Publicly funded post-elementary schools, established in law in 1900 (though existing earlier), admitting students between the ages of 10 and 15 years.

42   The science examinations set by the Royal College of Science (now the Imperial College of Science, Technology and Medicine), South Kensington.

43   The preparation for examinations by intensive coaching or study.

44   The month of examinations.

this that the South Kensington examinations differ so entirely from those of the Universities. The difference in standing between the Department's examination in chemistry and the Cambridge Junior Locals[45] or London Matriculation is not great; but in practice, the average age of candidates in the latter is higher by two or three years. Time is allowed for the awakening and development of the powers of observation and reasoning. A boy is then able to describe intelligently what he has become thoroughly familiar with, instead of reproducing mechanically his notes or text-book.

In still another particular have the University Boards[46] a decided advantage. Either they dispense altogether with an examination in practical chemistry, or they make something more of it than an analytical drill. Not much, it is true, but it must be remembered that practical chemistry is the most perverted subject in the whole range of knowledge at the hands of both teachers and examiners. But the greatest mockery is that which passes under the name at South Kensington. Of the written part of the examination it is needless to say anything; no boy would regard it as a test of what he has done in the laboratory, but what he has seen in the lecture-room. As to the analysis of salts, what bearing has it on the chemistry he is being taught elsewhere? Though at a certain stage it has a considerable educational value, the amount of time wasted upon it is appalling. It is useless to reiterate how easily it lends itself to being converted into a mechanical grind.

Mr Wells is of the opinion that the recent abolition of the second class pass in the May examinations has had a beneficial effect. So it may, in extinguishing what might be termed 'bogus' classes. But it has only intensified the evils in organised science schools, and put a higher premium on the cleverest cramming. The change did not deter such schools from sending in their pupils as before, but now they had to obtain 60 per cent of the possible marks, or fail – and most of them failed. This year there were fewer failures, because the teaching has answered to the whip. Financially the result is satisfactory to them, but educationally it is disastrous. At that age the average boy is not capable of obtaining more than forty or forty-five per cent of the marks in such a subject as chemistry. Very often he does not understand the full meaning of the question; and when he does, he is unable to write down more than a moiety of what he knows, or what could be drawn from him by a series of oral questions. There is no consideration shown for the immaturity of the candidates, but the standard is pitched higher than that of any other public examination in the country.

---

45   A British school examination for under-16s, established by the Cambridge Local Examinations Syndicate and running from 1858 to 1939 (and for overseas examinations until 1953). Rather than be subject-specific, the student was required to pass in a number of subjects.

46   School examination boards administered by universities.

So far from agreeing with Prof. Armstrong that science must be admitted to equal rights with the *three R's*, I hold that it is taught too extensively as long as the present system of examination prevails, and that the first battle to be fought ought to be against the South Kensington examinations, until they truly perform their double function.

Comment on Armstrong: Grace Heath, letter to the editor (15 November 1894).[47]

Will you allow me to take the opportunity afforded by the publication, in *Nature*, vol. 1. p. 631, of Prof. Armstrong's address at the Berners Street Board School, to offer my testimony to the value of teaching, based on the principles which he advocates so eloquently? The *practical* difficulty of teaching what Prof. Armstrong has called scientific method in an ordinary school, is often the ground of the objection made to it, so that it may interest your readers to hear of any experiments in this direction.

My work has been amongst girls, and the attempts made thus far in teaching scientific method in girls' schools show that such a method will inevitably lead to the development desired by Prof. Armstrong.

Doubtless one of the drawbacks is the difficulty of giving to each member of a large class the opportunity of individual work. I am not sorry, however, to have sometimes laboured under this difficulty myself, as it has brought about the discovery of how much could still be done on the right lines. When necessary I have replaced individual work by a demonstration class, in which the pupils, three or four at a time, have taken it in turns to work in front of the others, the work consisting in the solution of problems such as those suggested in the British Association's report on chemical teaching. The principal results are these: the children take a growing interest in the work, and those who are doubtful how far girls may desire to work with their hands, instead of always sitting still, may be glad to hear that no greater incentive to invention can be given in a demonstration class than the reward of becoming the experimenter for the time being. There is never any lack of suggestion for the next step in the work, and the rapidity with which such work trains the girls to consider the value or defects of any new proposal for the solution of their problem, is sometimes astonishing. In these classes the teacher plays a very small part – at least, apparently – only from time to time directing the suggestions, and giving permission for new work to be started; invention, experiment, meaning of results, and criticism are all undertaken by the children, and the final 'discovery' is their own triumph.

---

47   Reprinted by permission from Macmillan Publishers Ltd: *Nature* (51: 1307), copyright (1894).

I have often been asked by teachers about the discipline of such a class, since experimental work goes so slowly that they think it would be impossible to keep those who are not actually at work attentive. I can only say that the class consists of a group of people genuinely interested in a common object, and it behaves in a way such groups generally do. If at times a girl's enthusiasm so far carries her away that she rushes from her seat to the experimenting table, the class, with a laugh, excuses her, sympathises with her feelings, and is not disturbed thereby.

It seems unquestionable that the result of such work should have a wider-reaching effect than the mere knowledge of certain facts in nature, though such knowledge is certainly obtained. Where children, through their own work, have been led to observe and then to think, the result may fairly claim to be truly educative, and one is often at a loss to understand what support can be found for the still largely-existing method of teaching not science but 'useful information.'

Another objection often made to teaching scientific method instead of facts, that it takes too much time, I have already answered in this journal. I may perhaps be permitted to repeat that experiment shows the result of elementary training, of the kind described, to have a lasting influence on the rapidity and comprehension with which new subjects are grasped later on. Books, too, which are never put into the hands of beginners, are used with more than ordinary sense at this later stage. I may say that, even from the examination test (which, however, is not always going to be our standard), the results are very favourable. One thing, however, cannot be done by the teaching of scientific method, and that is to prepare for the London Matriculation examination in chemistry in three months – but then, is that altogether to be regretted?

Comment on discussion: Olaus Henrici, letter to the editor, 'Science Teaching in Schools' (29 November 1894).[48]

In the discussion on the teaching of science, and in the schemes put forward for reorganising this teaching, mathematics has so far been left out of consideration.

At present mathematics is taught for its own educational value, which has been traditional since the time of Plato; only in modern times has its great practical value been recognised. The teaching in schools takes little account, however, of the applications of mathematics, and whatever Prof. Greenhill may say (in his review of Prof. Mach's excellent book),[49] there is still wanting complete

---

48   Reprinted by permission from Macmillan Publishers Ltd: *Nature* (51: 1309), copyright (1894).

49   In 'Historical Exposition of Mechanics' (1894), Alfred Greenhill states that 'Although the double system of natural laws [...] is now exploded, we still have a double system

harmony between those two points of view; not perhaps in the higher branches of the subject and its applications, but certainly in school teaching.

Boys, and girls too, in public schools are taught the elements of mathematics as if all were expected to become mathematicians, and the practical side is kept out of view. In the modern, or science side, which has been introduced at many schools, one finds too often chiefly those boys who show no talent either for classics or mathematics. Many of these have made little or no progress in Euclid; they cannot grasp the altogether abstract notions and symbols of algebra, and they therefore never come near trigonometry. But they are expected to understand the elements of chemistry, mechanics and physics; and it is instructive to find that they very often do understand a good deal of what is taught under these headings.

Now none of these subjects can be accurately taught – and inaccurate teaching is worse than waste of time – without the introduction of mathematical reasoning. Here we are in a vicious circle: the boys are considered incapable of learning mathematics, and therefore mechanics and physics have to be taught without any more than the most elementary notions of geometry and algebra; hence not much progress can be made.

In my opinion the order of procedure might be reversed. Mathematics might be taught through experimental science. If the boys themselves make, as they should do, experiments where they perform actual measurements, they will learn there are certain laws connecting various quantities; they will see that such laws can be expressed in simple symbols, and they will thus grasp in the concrete form the meaning of a formula or an equation which in the abstract form of pure mathematics remained a mystery to them.

Mathematics could in this manner be made very much easier and more interesting to the majority of boys. Geometry[50] can be treated to a very great extent experimentally by aid of geometrical drawing and a development of the Kindergarten methods;[51] the abstract logic of Euclid can then follow, or it can be treated at the same time.

---

of instruction in mechanical text-books, one theoretical, geometrical, rational; the other practical, mechanical, empirical, discoverable by experience. It should be the object of modern science to break down the barriers between these two systems, and to treat the subject of mechanics from one point of view' (52). This would seem to agree with what Henrici is arguing, though Henrici implies that Greenhill holds the contrary view.

50 The branch of mathematics that deals with the properties and relations of magnitudes in space.

51 Methods devised by Friedrich Froebel for developing children's intelligence by means of interesting objects, exercises with toys, games, singing, etc.

Trigonometry need not be at once as fully gone into as is generally done, but the definitions of sine, cosine, etc., as names for certain ratios, can be easily and early introduced and made use of at once in mechanics or physics. Here also special experiments may easily be devised where measurements of angles or lines are made, and lines and angles calculated.

To explain fully what I mean I should require a great deal of space; in fact it would almost be necessary to draw up a distinct syllabus for a course on the above lines, or to give at least a great number of examples.

At present I wish only to urge that, while many attempts are being made to improve science teaching, and with it technical education, mathematics should be included, and to express my opinion that this science also allows of experimental treatment.

Reply to Crump and Heath: H. G. Wells, letter to the editor (29 November 1894).[52]

Mr Crump (*vide* p. 56) though adopting a critical form and tone, really endorses the grounds of my suggestion that the Science and Art Department should dissever itself by an age limit from school science. He is inclined to be especially severe upon the defects of the Government examinations because they are controlled by scientific men, and to excuse the proper school examining boards because they have – according to Mr Crump – attempted to examine in science without any qualification to do so. But I fail to see why eminent scientific men should be expected to be experts in elementary science teaching, any more than distinguished *littérateurs*,[53] in the art of teaching to read, and it seems to me – in spite of Mr Crump's 'absolute' denial – that examining boards, neither professedly literary or scientific but professedly educational, are more to blame in following and abetting the Department's premium upon text-book cramming. The fact remains that the London Matriculate ignores practical teaching of any kind, and that the 'practical chemistry' of the Locals and College of Preceptors is essentially the same test-tube analysis as the South Kensington examination. Anyone who knows the London Matriculation examination – witness Miss Heath's concluding remark – will appreciate the quiet humour of Mr Crump's allusion to it as 'awakening and developing the powers of observation and reasoning.'

---

52 Reprinted by permission from Macmillan Publishers Ltd: *Nature* (51: 1309), copyright (1894). This letter has previously been reprinted in Smith 1998, I: 223-24.

53 French, writers of literary or critical works.

1.3: 'Peculiarities of Psychical Research'

H. G. Wells, 'Peculiarities of Psychical Research' (6 December 1894).[1]

Apparitions and Thought Transference. By Frank Podmore, MA. (London: Walter Scott, 1894).

Mr Podmore, in the opening chapter of this popular exposition of telepathy,[2] pleads for the recognition of psychical research[3] by the general body of scientific workers. He reminds us of the opposition geological and biological discoveries have encountered, and ventures to compare the circumstances of the small group of investigators with which he is connected, and more particularly the prejudice and derision they encounter, with the experiences of Cuvier and Agassiz. Convincing as this comparison may appear to the general reader, in one respect at least it fails. Three hundred years ago, all these phenomena of crystal gazing,[4] thought transference,[5] and apparitions[6] had a broader basis of belief than they have to-day; even a hundred years ago, the ordinary scientific investigator was at little or no advantage over the exponent of magic arts.[7] But though, as Mr Podmore reminds us, the leading propositions of natural science once encountered popular prejudice, ridicule, contempt, hatred, far more abundantly than has ever been the lot of psychical interpretations, they have won through and triumphed, while the credit accorded such evidence as the SPR accumulates has, if anything, diminished. A thing Mr Podmore scarcely lays sufficient stress upon is the fundamental difference in the quality of the facts of 'psychical research,' as distinguished from those of scientific investigation – using scientific in its stricter sense. It is true he has, with an appearance of frankness, devoted a chapter to 'special grounds of caution,' in which he concedes the truth of various criticisms, and owns to several undeniable impostures; but even here he passes from admissions to a skilful argument in favour of telepathy, and avoids the cardinal reason for keeping aloof from this field of inquiry, that lies in the quality of the evidence.

---

1   Reprinted by permission from Macmillan Publishers Ltd: *Nature* (51: 1310), copyright (1894).

2   The communication or perception of thoughts, feelings, etc., by apparently extrasensory means.

3   The examination of allegedly paranormal phenomena using scientific principles.

4   Concentrating one's gaze on a crystal to see images forecasting the future or representing distant events.

5   The supposed communication of thought from one mind to another apart from the ordinary channels of sense.

6   Supernatural appearances.

7   The supposed art of influencing the course of events and of producing extraordinary physical phenomena by the occult control of nature or of spirits.

The scientific advances of Cuvier and Agassiz, like all true scientific discoveries, were based upon things that could be perceived directly by themselves, and which could be reproduced whenever required, and completely examined under this condition and that, by those who doubted the facts. That is the essential difference between natural science and such a subject as history; science produces its facts, history at best produces reputable witnesses to facts. Scientific men have never attached much importance to unverifiable statements, however eminent the source. If, to suppose an instance, the greatest living anatomist were to announce that he had dissected a dogfish and discovered lungs therein, adduce his wife, a local general practitioner, two servants, and a lady 'named Miss Z.' in evidence, and add that he had lost the specimen, there can be scarcely any doubt that, in spite of his position and his character, the science of anatomy would remain exactly where it was before his discovery was proclaimed. But in this 'psychical research' the deliberate reproduction of phenomena under conditions that admit of exhaustive sceptical examination appears to be generally impossible, and we are repeatedly asked to form opinions on the hearsay of Mr Podmore and his fellow-investigators.

This is not all. Few of the phenomena are directly observed. Dr Dee had his Kelly, Prof. Oliver J. Lodge his Mrs Piper. If Prof. Sidgwick would read the thoughts of Prof. Oliver J. Lodge, or – as a phantasm[8] of the living – take to haunting some sceptical person, we should have at least a statement at first hand, to doubt; but as it is, these investigators manifest, as a rule, no other mental phenomena than belief and repetition. Reading through Mr Podmore's book, the student will be struck by the fact that the persons who are in immediate contact with the alleged phenomena, the hireling eyes of the psychological inquirer, are persons usually youthful and coming from a social level below that of the investigators. Take, for instance, the Guthrie[9] cases, to which Mr Podmore attaches considerable importance. Mr Guthrie is a draper[10] in Liverpool, and by some means, not stated, he became aware of psychic powers[11] possessed by two of his employees – young ladies – whose identity is for some reason veiled under the initials 'E.' and 'R.' These young ladies were accordingly liberated at intervals from the toils of shop or workroom, and made the subjects of various experiments; Mr Guthrie, for instance, putting cayenne pepper[12] in his mouth, during a profound silence, and Miss E. experiencing a taste of 'mustard.' Now we must insist upon the fact, because it seriously affects this question of evidence,

---

8   An apparition.

9   I. e., Malcolm Guthrie.

10   A dealer in cloth.

11   The supposed faculty of perceiving, as if by seeing, what is happening or exists out of sight.

12   A pungent red powder prepared from ground dried chillies, used as a seasoning.

that to a young lady following the irksome and precarious calling of a draper's assistant, the manifestation of psychic gifts opens up eminently desirable possibilities and interests. Then, among other of these intermediaries, we find 'Jane' – a pitman's[13] wife – 'Bertha J.,' a peasant woman, hospital nurses and out-patients, two men 'who had been subjects of an itinerant lecturer upon hypnotism,'[14] most of the letters of the alphabet, several American MDs, lady medical students, a baker's assistant, Mr P., 'a clerk in a wholesale house, aged nineteen, who possesses a good deal of humour,' and so forth.

Scarcely ever is the medium a person really independent, in a financial sense, of the investigators who are craving for phenomena. It is necessary for us to believe in the general good faith of this extremely dubious material, or in the adequacy of the precautions against fraud taken by persons whose scientific reputations are now hopelessly bound up with the reality of the alleged facts, before one can even begin to accept the experimental basis upon which the theory of telepathy rests. And this is the character of the investigations that Mr Podmore has compared with the work of Cuvier and Agassiz! In no other field of inquiry is so much faith in personal character and intelligence demanded, or so little experimental verification possible. Indeed, the book is oddly suggestive in places, with its use of initials and second-hand guarantees of character, of the testimony one finds adduced in favour of patent medicines.[15]

Now, to the attentive reader of Mr Podmore, the persuasion is unavoidable that the ordinary psychical investigator is endowed with a considerable facility of belief, and is by no means instinct with the scientific method. And this, where we are to take very much on faith, is a material consideration. Anonymous statements are accepted, and not only anonymous but self-contradictory ones. Mrs Piper hypnotised, personated a French physician Dr Phinuit, who did not know French, and failed to give a satisfactory account of himself. Mrs Piper, during her trance as Dr Phinuit, gabbled, made chance shots, 'fished' for information, and was generally a transparent enough imposition. Yet she occasionally spoke of things she could not, according to the investigators, have obtained a knowledge of by ordinary means. For that they give her credit, and forgive all her failures. Prof. Lodge, apparently eager to believe, compares her utterances to the experience of anyone listening at a telephone: 'you hear the dim and meaningless fragments of a city's gossip till back again comes the voice obviously addressed to you, and speaking with firmness and decision.' Imagine in a real scientific inquiry an investigator pursuing a theory through a complicated series of

---

13 A man who works in a pit or a mine, especially a coal mine.

14 The action or process of placing a person in a state of consciousness in which he or she appears to lose all power of voluntary action or thought and to be highly responsive to suggestions and directions.

15 Trademarked products sold as medicines, though of dubious benefit to the user.

observations, arbitrarily selecting those that advance his views, and calling the others 'dim and meaningless until back comes the result obviously addressed to you!'

As one instance of the absence of scientific method from these discussions, take M. Richet's and Mr Gurney's experiments with cards. In these experiments an agent looked at the card, and a percipient guessed the suit. M. Richet conducted 2927 trials, and 789 correct guesses were made, the theory of probability[16] only granting 732. The SPR trials numbered 17,653 with 4760 successes – 347 in excess of the probable number. Now this is adduced by Mr Podmore as evidence for telepathy; we are asked to believe that about once in sixty times – that is the excess above the probable ratio of successes – the mental impression of the agent recorded itself upon the brain of the percipient. Whether during the interval of fifty-nine trials telepathy was in abeyance, Mr Podmore does not say, and the failure of the American SPR[17] to confirm these results he sets aside because the details of their experiments are not given – an excellent example to the sceptic. Are we to believe that only once in sixty times did the transferred thought surge up into consciousness, or that the transference occurs only at the sixtieth time, or what? A most obvious collateral test seems to have been altogether overlooked, namely, for someone to guess cards *before* the agent saw them, and so to ascertain how far pure haphazard guessing of this kind, of guessing on any particular gambler's 'system,'[18] may fall away from the theory of probability. The deductions of the theory of probability, be it remembered, become certainties only when the number of cases is infinite. We have no grounds for assuming that in seventeen thousand or seventy thousand, or in any finite number of cases, facts come into coincidence with this theory. In an infinite number of sets of 17,653 trials we might have every possible divergence from the average result up to 17,653 successive failures or 17,653 successive successes. Taking a number of sets, they may be expected to fluctuate round a mean result in agreement with the theory of probability – that is all. These three sets of experiments manifestly prove nothing. And this is how Mr Podmore prefaces his account of them: 'In the following cases, where the exact nature of the impression received was not apparently classified by the percipient, it may be presumed to have been either of a visual or an auditory nature.' He begs the question, and in a book addressed to the untrained mind of the general reader! Nothing could show more clearly the tendency of this psychical research to accept

---

16   The extent to which a particular event is likely to occur as expressed by a number between zero and one and commonly estimated by the ratio of the number of favourable cases to the total number of all possible cases.

17   The American Society for Psychical Research founded in 1885 in New York for the scientific study of allegedly paranormal phenomenon.

18   A betting systems aimed at making profits from casino gambling.

as evidence what is really not evidence at all, its lack of critical capacity and severe confirmatory inquiry, and the missionary spirit of its exposition.

Enough has been said to show the essential difference between 'psychical' and scientific investigations, and to justify the attitude of scepticism. After all, that scepticism does nothing to hamper Mr Podmore and his associates from collecting their evidence, clarifying their opinions, and building up such a defensible case as their peculiar circumstances permit. And be it remembered the scientific man of to-day occupies a responsible position, that he possesses even a disproportionate share of the public confidence, because of his reputation for sceptical caution. The public mind is incapable of the suspended judgement; it will not stop at telepathy. Any general recognition of the evidence of 'psychical' research will be taken by the outside public to mean the recognition of ghosts, witchcraft, miracles, and the pretensions of many a shabby-genteel[19] Cagliostro, now pining in a desert of incredulity, as undeniable facts. Were Mr Podmore's case strong – and it is singularly weak – the undeniable possibility of a recrudescence of superstition remains as a consideration against the unqualified recognition of his evidence.

Comment on Wells: Karl Pearson, letter to the editor, 'Peculiarities of Psychical Research' (13 December 1894).[20]

Mr H. G. Wells disposes very aptly of most of the claims set up by Mr Podmore and his colleagues to be real scientific investigators. But, I think, he rather disguises the significance of the card-drawing experiments to which he refers. The experiments of M. Richet and those of the SPR belong to two very different categories. In the former case, 789 correct guesses were made in 2927 trials, or a deviation from the most probable result of 57 or 58; this is about 2.4 times the standard deviation, or the odds against a deviation *in excess* of this amount are only about 100 to 1, or odds of only about 50 to 1 of a deviation of this magnitude either way.

On the other hand, in the SPR trials we have a deviation from the most probable of 347, about six times the standard deviation. That is to say, the odds against such a result are in round numbers about 2,000,000,000 to 3! Now, this is of a totally different order to that given by M. Richet's numbers. I have obtained odds as great a 100 to 1 against the results of very carefully conducted lottery experiments. There is in reality nothing significant about such odds. But the odds against the SPR experiments are almost equal to the odds against the

---

19   Attempting to look genteel and keep up appearances in spite of shabbiness.

20   Reprinted by permission from Macmillan Publishers Ltd: *Nature* (51: 1311), copyright (1894).

Monte Carlo roulette[21] returns! The experiments are significant, very significant – not to my mind, however, of telepathy, but of the want of scientific acumen in the psychical researchers. The interesting point as to whether an abnormal distribution was also in the cards turned up as well as in the percipient, does not appear to have been recorded. Mr Wells has, however, passed over the difference between the two cases, and given, I fear, the psychical researchers the chance of a little self-glorification on the due appreciation of the significant.

Comment on Wells and Pearson: Edward Dixon, letter to the editor, 'Peculiarities of Psychical Research' (27 December 1894).[22]

May I enter an emphatic protest against the notion insinuated both by Mr Wells and Prof. Karl Pearson, that 'Psychical researchers' are a sort of sect engaged in spiritualistic[23] or other propaganda? Most people, I am afraid, fight shy of psychical research, either because they are afraid that *if* there is anything in it it is the devil, or because they have a scientific reputation which they are afraid of losing. I do not know to which category Mr Wells belongs, but apparently he fails to understand that in order to make out a case against psychical research he has got to show, not that the existence of telepathy and clairvoyance[24] has not been proved, but that there is not even a *prima facie* case worth investigating. When we remember that ten years ago 'mesmerism'[25] was included along with telepathy and clairvoyance, we shall not attach much importance to such efforts to stifle inquiry. Even if the results should be to confirm Mr Wells's anticipation, and show that all the coincidences that have been reported can be explained away as mistakes or misstatements, the inquiry will yet have been worth the labour bestowed on it, if only as affording a measure of the value of testimony to the miraculous. And if this comes to pass, the bigots[26] of science will be ready enough to claim a share in the work, if only by saying, 'I told you so!'

I do not know what Prof. Karl Pearson means by his quite gratuitous attack on 'the scientific acumen of the psychical researchers.' Surely he cannot imagine that they overlooked the point which he has unearthed? The instructions

---

21 A seventeenth century French gambling game, popular in casinos.

22 Reprinted by permission from Macmillan Publishers Ltd: *Nature* (51: 1313), copyright (1894).

23 Pertaining to spiritualism, the belief that the spirits of the dead can communicate with the living, especially through a medium.

24 The supposed faculty of perceiving, as if by seeing, what is happening or exists out of sight.

25 The process or practice of inducing a hypnotic state by the influence of an operator over the will of a patient.

26 Obstinate and unreasonable adherents to an opinion; narrow-minded intolerant persons.

to the experimenters were, that 'the agent should draw a card at random, and cut the pack between each draw' (*Phantasms of the Living*, vol. i. p. 33, foot-note[27]). Could an abnormal distribution of the cards affect the result if those precautions were taken, or has the Professor any reason to suppose the instructions were not carried out?

Reply to Dixon: Karl Pearson, letter to the editor (27 December 1894).[28]

The following are a few of my grounds for questioning the scientific acumen of the psychical researchers: – (1) M. Richet's experiments are cited as if they were significant of telepathic action. On the contrary, they give odds of so little weight that they are significant of nothing but want of acumen. I have in card drawing,[29] tossing[30] and lottery experiments, all conducted with every precaution to secure a random distribution, obtained results against which the odds were more considerable. (2) Mr Dixon is unable to see the importance of ascertaining whether there was an abnormal distribution in the cards cut or the cards guessed. His inability is a strong confirmation of my standpoint. (3) I have heard lectures, and read papers written by psychical researchers. Both alike seem to me akin to those products of circle squarers[31] and paradoxers,[32] with which, as a reviewer, I am painfully familiar. As a concrete example, I take my friend Dr Oliver Lodge's psychical papers. They are typical, to my mind, of the manner in which the scientific acumen of even a professed and most highly competent man of science vanishes when he enters this field of 'research.'

I do not intend to take part in a controversy on the subject at the present time, but I do suggest that no better exercise could be found for a strictly logical mind with plenty of leisure than a criticism of the products of the chief psychical researchers. Such a criticism would be of much social value, in the light of recent attempts to popularise the 'results' reached by these investigators.

---

27 By Edmund Gurney, Frederick W. H. Myers and Frank Podmore.

28 Reprinted by permission from Macmillan Publishers Ltd: *Nature* (51: 1313), copyright (1894).

29 The random selection of a playing card from its pack.

30 Throwing at random for gambling purposes (e. g. a coin).

31 Those who attempt to achieve the impossible, from the expression 'to square a circle'.

32 One whose arguments are logically unacceptable or self-contradictory.

Reply to Pearson: Edward Dixon, letter to the editor, 'Peculiarities of Psychical Research' (3 January 1895).[33]

In reply to Prof. Pearson: (1) His remark about 'scientific acumen' was not made apropos of M. Richet's experiments, but of those of the SPR; and hardly any stress is laid on M. Richet's results, either by Mr Gurney or Mr Podmore. Mr Gurney, on the contrary, expressly says: 'Clearly no definite conclusion could be based on such figures.' But if Prof. Pearson has made experiments which are equally striking in the opposite sense, I wish he would publish them, or communicate them to the SPR. (2) There was nothing in my letter to indicate that I under-estimated the importance of 'abnormal distributions'; but I asked Prof. Pearson to say whether he had any reason to suppose such distributions might have occurred in the case in dispute. This he has failed to do – he has evaded the point. (3) Prof. Pearson descends to vague generalities except in regard to Dr Oliver Lodge, who may be left to defend himself.

With the last paragraph of the letter, however, I heartily concur. There is nothing the SPR would welcome more than intelligent and independent criticism. Only the critic would have to study the evidence first, and the Professor apparently has the 'scientific acumen' to see that by doing so he would cut his own throat; for he would, *ipso facto*, become a psychical researcher!

Reply to Pearson and Wells: Oliver Lodge, letter to the editor, 'Peculiarities of Psychical Research' (10 January 1895).[34]

On page 200 I see that Prof. Karl Pearson suggests that it would be a good exercise for someone with a strictly logical mind and plenty of leisure to criticise 'the products of the chief psychical researchers.' May I say, as a member of the SPR, speaking for myself and fellow-workers, that we ask nothing better than such a studious and searching criticism. One of our main difficulties is that our critics will not take the trouble to study or even read our evidence, but are content to ridicule what they conjecture to be our methods and results from so great an altitude of assured contempt, that we fail to recognise ourselves in their travesty, and are therefore unable to derive much benefit from their utterances.

Thus, for instance, Prof. Karl Pearson, before writing his recent letters, has evidently not taken the trouble to refer even to the abbreviated summary of certain card-drawing experiments contained in Mr Podmore's little book; other-

---

33 Reprinted by permission from Macmillan Publishers Ltd: *Nature* (51: 1314), copyright (1895).

34 Reprinted by permission from Macmillan Publishers Ltd: *Nature* (51: 1315), copyright (1895).

wise he could hardly make the statements he does concerning the SPR record of them.

He objects to M. Richet's results as giving insufficient odds in favour of telepathy, so that, as he says, it shows want of acumen to adduce them. Would he then regard it as more scientific to suppress them? On the other hand, the enormous odds against chance, shown in Mr Gurney's trials, he also says, on page 153, show a want of acumen (I don't know why, but I expect because nothing could possibly exhibit anything else on the part of an SPR worker), and that such odds might be otherwise accounted for. Does he then suppose that the odds of, as he reckons them, two thousand million to three are accepted by us as the odds in favour of telepathy? Probably he does, because there is at present no need to be fair to investigators in an unorthodox field; but Mr Podmore is careful to state the opposite, as follows (footnote to p. 27 of Mr Podmore's little summary, in the *Contemporary Science Series*, of the evidence for Thought-transference so far as it exists at the present time): 'Of course the statement in the text' [viz. that 'the probability for some cause other than chance deduced from this result is .99999998'] 'must not be taken as indicating the belief of Mr Edgeworth, or the writer, or anyone else, that the above figures demonstrate thought-transference as the cause of the results attained. The results may conceivably have been due to some error of observation or of reporting. But the figures are sufficient to prove, what is here claimed for them, that *some* cause must be sought for the results other than chance.' And another quotation may be permitted from Mr Podmore's preface, which ought to silence irresponsible detractors like Mr H. G. Wells, and others, who seek to lead the world to suppose that we have some cause at heart other than the simple ascertainment of the truth, whatever it is, and that Mr Podmore, in particular, is a bigoted upholder of the certainty of telepathy. This is the quotation: 'The evidence, of which samples are presented in the following pages, is as yet hardly adequate for the establishment of telepathy as a fact in nature, and leaves much to be desired for the elucidation of the laws under which it operates. Any contribution to the problem ... will be gladly received....'

Now, I observe that Prof. Karl Pearson has a contribution to the problem, for in *Nature* of December 27, 1894, p. 200, he refers to certain experiments of his own, wherein by pure chance he obtained results against which the theory of probability also gave large odds. Would he be good enough to let us have these results more precisely, as recorded at the time and signed by witnesses, so that they may furnish us with an example of the methods of a 'real scientific investigator'? It will be very unsatisfactory if we have nothing but his memory to rely on for the facts; and as he well knows, it is necessary to have the whole of a large number of trials before deductions from the theory of probability are legitimately applicable.

I observe, finally, that Prof. Pearson, with plenty of good-nature but some lack of originality, has refurbished Dr Carpenter's old joke about an 'ortho-Crookes' and a 'pseudo-Crookes,'[35] and has directed it against me. I shall be well content if he never manages to find a keener and more effective weapon.

Reply to Dixon: Karl Pearson, letter to the editor, 'Peculiarities of Psychical Research' (17 January 1895).[36]

Mr Dixon asks in his first letter: Could an abnormal distribution of the cards affect the result, if certain precautions were taken? In his second letter he says there was nothing in his first letter to indicate that he under-estimated the importance of 'abnormal distributions.' Well and good, if the SPR have not under-estimated the importance of examining the actual distribution of cards cut and of cards guessed, they will have kept a record of each card cut and each card guessed, card for card. If they have not done so, then their experiment is scientifically of no value; if they have done so, then the analysis of the distributions of the cards cut and the cards guessed ought to have accompanied any publication of these experiments. It is an obvious, but by *no means sufficient*, condition for a proper experiment. If the Secretary of the SPR[37] will place in my hands the actual analyses of the cards cut and the cards guessed made by a competent mathematician, *before* the publication in their *Proceedings*[38] of the card guesses, and proving that they did at that time fully consider the point, and take the obvious precaution against deception, my estimation of the 'scientific acumen' of the SPR will at any rate on this point be modified.

I, of course, do not refer to my friend Prof. Edgeworth's investigations, which do not touch the question of the distributions of cards cut and cards guessed.

---

35 On William Crooke's scientific and spiritualistic research, respectively, William Carpenter stated, 'I hold the one to have been as scientific as the other was unscientific', leading Crookes to muse, 'I have, it appears, two allo-tropic personalities, which I may designate, in chemical language, Ortho-Crookes and Pseudo-Crookes' (quoted in Luckhurst 2002, 35-36).

36 Reprinted by permission from Macmillan Publishers Ltd: *Nature* (51: 1316), copyright (1895).

37 During 1894 and 1895 the joint-secretaries of the SPR were Frederic Myers and Frank Podmore.

38 Occasional papers published by the Society for Psychical Research.

Reply to Lodge: H. G. Wells, letter to the editor (17 January 1895).[39]

May I call attention to Prof. Lodge's method of 'silencing' me in your issue of January 10. It bears very closely upon this question of the effect of psychical research upon the investigator's reasoning. He quotes the preface of Mr Podmore's book to show that the gentleman is not a 'bigoted upholder of the certainty of telepathy,' and the casual reader would scarcely guess that, in truth, I never asserted that he was. I complained of the very air of open-mindedness in that preface to which Prof. Lodge's quotation witnesses, and showed by an instance, that in the body of the book question-begging occurred which was all the more dangerous on account of the liberal tone of the opening portion. I made no objection to the individual prosecution of psychical research – only to its public recognition before it has produced more definite results than it has done so far. So much for the 'silencing.' It shows either that Prof. Lodge has not read my review, or that he has misunderstood it; and in either case it enforces my contention that these investigators are over-hasty. The phrase 'irresponsible detractor,' points in the same direction.

---

39   Reprinted by permission from Macmillan Publishers Ltd: *Nature* (51: 1316), copyright (1895). This letter has previously been reprinted in Smith 1998, I: 228-29.

1.4: 'The Sequence of Studies'

H. G. Wells, 'The Sequence of Studies' (27 December 1894).[1]

Physiology for Beginners. By Professor M. Foster, MA, MD, FRS, and Lewis E. Shore, MA, MD. (London: Macmillan and Co., 1894).

Outlines of Biology. By P. Chalmers Mitchell, MA, FZS. (London: Methuen and Co., 1894).

Practical Methods in Microscopy. By C. H. Clark, AM (Boston: Heath and Co., 1894).

The scientific precision and modernness of a book of elementary physiology, written by Dr Shore, under the supervision of Prof. Foster, is scarcely to be called in question. This little volume is amply illustrated, and written with clearness as well as exactness. The authors are especially to be commended for laying stress in their preface upon the necessity of a preliminary acquaintance with Chemistry and Physics, and it is to be regretted that they had not the courage to insist upon this point. But here they are gravely open to criticism. 'Knowing,' they say, 'how frequently a book on physiology is taken up without any such previous acquaintance, we have given a few chemical and physical facts as preliminaries in chapter 1.' A few, and quite too few, it is – six complete pages – expanding scarcely any of the principles which are involved in the simplest physiological explanation, giving, of course, no conceptions of the relations of chemical combination to energy, nor of osmose,[2] diffusion,[3] solution,[4] isomerism[5] nor the action of ferments,[6] all of which come to the front directly one approaches respiration or digestion. We cannot but think that this concession to a common educational error is greatly to be deplored. The authors occupy a position of authority, and it was their privilege – a privilege they have neglected – to demand here, by assuming a sound basis of chemical and physical knowledge, the proper sequence of studies. As it is they have produced a little primer that by virtue of its clearness and attractiveness and the prestige of their names, will serve to uphold for a few years longer a fundamentally faulty system of scientific education.

---

1   Reprinted by permission from Macmillan Publishers Ltd: *Nature* (51: 1313), copyright (1894).

2   Of gradual assimilation.

3   Wide and general distribution.

4   The action of dissolving or uniformly dispersing a solid, liquid or gas in a liquid, or a solid in a solid.

5   Identity of percentage composition in compounds differing in properties.

6   Fermenting agents or leavens.

The evil of a neglect of the rational sequence of studies becomes particularly apparent in the chapters upon the eye and ear. In the former of these an attempt is made to convey all the optical principles involved, in seven lines – 'convex lens'[7] is not even defined – and in the latter comes a series of dogmatic statements about sounds and noises, without a particle of that progressive reasoning process which is the very essence of genuine scientific study. Once the initial concession was made, however, this kind of thing was an inevitable consequence. In order to explain the science in hand, three or four others have to be compressed to the limits of a paragraph.

The same unfortunate disposition to begin the wrong way about is apparent in the little book by Mr Chalmers Mitchell. But in his case there is even less excuse. His book is designed to prepare students for the Conjoint Boards Examination,[8] and therein he is an examiner. Since he calls the tune he might have danced as he likes, and he has, we conclude, preferred of his own free will to contravene the common-places of educational science. We find such a proposition as the following, printed in spaced type; so that the medical student, preparing for examination by Mr Chalmers Mitchell, who fails to learn it by heart will have only himself to blame for his failure. The earthworm, we are told,

> has reached the second stage of coelomate[9] development in that it is very highly segmented, and there is little or no trace of the third stage, the stage of the condensation of segments. [...] Vertebrates[10] are highly segmented animals, in which condensation of segments has become an important factor, resulting notably in the formation of a complicated head, and of kidneys formed by the aggregation of many nephridia.[11]

Now these propositions are illustrated rather than supported by a brief description of the anatomy of the earthworm, dogfish, and frog, and we find that even in the case of these types the metameric segmentation[12] of the cranial

---

7   A lens having a surface curved like the exterior of a circle.

8   A medical examination organised conjointly by the Royal College of Surgeons, the Royal College of Physicians and the Society of Apothecaries in the early nineteenth century leading to the English Conjoint Diploma. By the late nineteenth century, the Diploma was generally an initial qualification before students went on to take a Bachelor of Medicine or a Bachelor of Surgery degree. It was abolished in 1999.

9   Of an animal's coelom, a secondary body cavity between the body wall and the gut.

10 Those animals possessing a bony skeleton, skull and spinal column, including fish, amphibia, reptiles, birds and mammals.

11 Excretory or osmoregulatory tubules open to the exterior and present in various invertebrate groups.

12 Having a body consisting of similar segments.

nerves[13] is scarcely alluded to, and the homology[14] of the mandibular arch[15] with the branchial bars[16] is not presented as a probability, but stated as a fact. And, in brief, Mr Chalmers Mitchell, who is not a crammer, but a teacher, gives the medical student the impression almost in so many words – 'cut and dried' and ready to be cast into the oven – that the vertebrate type is merely a concentrated derivative (concertina fashion) of the chaetopod[17] type, advancing this pure, and as he gives it, baseless, speculation, in the face of the absence of any chaetopod stage in the embryology or palaeontology of the vertebrates, in the face of the lesser metamerism in the vertebral column of more primitive fishes, and in the face of the declared opinion of many prominent anatomists. But whether the view he gives is right or wrong is, from our point of view, the smaller issue; the great and grave objection is the unscientific spirit of the presentation, the narrowness of the base of anatomical fact upon which this far-reaching generalisation is raised. We find this disposition to what is really the old theological trick of dogmatism, again and again in his book, and it is the evident and necessary consequence of an attempt to touch the far-reaching theories of comparative anatomy without a sufficient preliminary study of individual types.

It is odd that we should find another aspect of the same mistake cropping up in one chapter of Mr Clark's extremely useful and well-arranged handbook for the beginner in microscopy.[18] It is in almost every way a well-arranged and well-written work, and will be particularly a boon to the amateur to whom experienced advice is inaccessible. But before proceeding to the petrographical instrument,[19] Mr Clark has attempted a 'concise description' of polarised light,[20] which begins –

---

13   Each of twelve pairs of nerves arising directly from the brain and passing through separate apertures in the cranium.

14   Correspondence in fundamental structure of an organ, part, etc., or correspondence in evolutionary origin.

15   Commonly, the first branchial arch, the lower jaw during its foetal stage of development.

16   Supports within a fish's gill clefts.

17   An order of Annelida, or segmented worms.

18   The use of a microscope.

19   Any of a number of tools used for the description and understanding of the composition and classification of rocks.

20   Having vibrations restricted to a particular direction.

The elasticity of the ether[21] in space is believed to be equal in all directions. The same is true of the ether in non-crystalline substances[22] and in crystalline substances[23] of the cubical system.[24] The particles of ether are consequently free to vibrate equally in all directions. In other crystalline substances the elasticity of the ether is modified by the crystalline structure. In some crystals there is one axis or direction about which the molecules[25] are arranged in a uniform manner; such crystals are said to by uniaxial.[26] In other crystals there are two such axes.

Now we believe a student who will clearly understand this will be sufficiently advanced not to require it, and that to the raw beginner, this passage, and its context, will be incomprehensible. Were it not for the actual evidence of these books it would seem the most unnecessary thing in the world to assert that a clear working idea of the *theory* of polarised light, or the general ideas of chemistry and physics, or a cyclopaedia of the anatomy of the metazoa,[27] cannot be imparted in half a dozen pages or so of the text. If it could, our textbooks in these subjects would be unnecessary, for the ultimate aim of all intelligent research and teaching in pure science is broader and simpler general notions, and there can be no need for a volume if a handbill[28] will suffice. Cannot the scientific writer insist upon the proper sequence of studies in his preface, and proceed on the assumption that his counsel will be observed? To positively encourage students to proceed to subjects for which they have not the necessary grounding, to proffer them snap-shot chapters upon these neglected preliminaries, is really, we are persuaded, to place a grave impediment in their way to genuine knowledge, all the graver because it seems a help, and to place one also in the way of our advance towards more efficient science teaching in the future.

---

21 A very rarefied and highly elastic substance formerly believed to permeate all space, including the interstices between the particles of matter.

22 Entities in which the constituent atoms, molecules or ions are packed irregularly.

23 Having the form or structure of a crystal.

24 A register of minerals that crystallise in the form of a cube.

25 Sufficiently stable electrically neutral groups of at least two atoms in a definite arrangement held together by strong chemical bonds.

26 Characterised by one axis of alignment or action.

27 Animals which have bodies composed of more than one cell and display differentiation of tissue.

28 A printed notice delivered or circulated by hand.

1.5: 'Bio-optimism'

H. G. Wells, 'Bio-optimism' (29 August 1895).[1]

The Evergreen. A Northern Seasonal. Published in the Lawnmarket of Edinburgh by Patrick Geddes and Colleagues. (London: Fisher Unwin, 1895).

It is not often that a reviewer is called upon to write art criticism in the columns of *Nature*. But the circumstances of the 'Evergreen' are peculiar; it is published with a certain scientific sanction as the expression of a coming scientific Renascence of Art, and it is impossible to avoid glancing at its aesthetic merits. It is a semi-annual periodical emanating from the biological school of St Andrews University.[2] Mr J. Arthur Thomson assists with the proem[3] and the concluding article ('The Scots Renascence'), and other significant work in the volume is from the pen of Prof. Patrick Geddes. It may be assumed that a large section of the public will accept this volume as being representative of the younger generation of biological workers, and as indicating the aesthetic tendencies of a scientific training. What injustice may be done thereby a glance at the original Almanac will show. In this page of 'Scots Renascence' design the beautiful markings on the carapace[4] of a crab and the exquisite convolutions of a ram's horn are alike replaced by unmeaning and clumsy spirals, the delicate outlines of a butterfly body by a gross shape like a soda-water bottle; its wings are indicated by three sausage-shaped excrescences on either side, and the vegetable forms in the decorative border are deprived of all variety and sinuosity in favour of a system of cast-iron semi-circular curves. Now, as a matter of fact, provided there is no excess of diagram, his training should render the genuine biologist more acutely sensitive to these ugly and unmeaning distortions than the average educated man. Neither does a biological training blind the eye to the quite fortuitous arrangement of the black masses in Mr Duncan's studies in the art of Mr Beardsley, to the clumsy line of Mr Mackie's reminiscences of Mr Walter Crane, or to the amateurish quality of Mr Burn-Murdoch. And when Mr Riccardo Stephens honours Herrick on his intention rather than his execution, and Mr Laubach, rejoicing 'with tabret[5] and string' at the advent of spring, bleats

> Now hillock and highway
> > Are budding and glad,

---

1   Reprinted by permission from Macmillan Publishers Ltd: *Nature* (52: 1348), copyright (1895). This review has previously been reprinted in Philmus and Hughes 1975, 206-10.

2   Scotland's oldest university, established between 1410 and 1413.

3   A preface or preamble to a book or speech.

4   The upper shell of a crustacean.

5   A small drum.

> Thro' dingle[6] and byway
>
> Go lassie and lad.

it must not be supposed that the frequenters of the biological laboratory, outside the circle immediately about Prof. Patrick Geddes, are more profoundly stirred than they are when Mr Kipling, full of knowledge and power, sings of the wind and the sea and the heart of the natural man.

But enough has been said of the artistic merits of this volume. Regarded as anything more than the first efforts of amateurs in art and literature – and it makes that claim – it is bad from cover to cover; and even the covers are bad. No mitigated condemnation will meet the circumstances of the case. Imagine the New English Art Club[7] propounding a Scientific Renascence in its leisure moments! Of greater concern to the readers of *Nature* than the fact that a successful professor may be an indifferent art editor, is the attempt on the part of two biologists – real responsible biologists – writing for the unscientific public, to represent Biology[8] as having turned upon its own philosophical implications. Mr Thomson, for instance, tells his readers that 'the conception of the Struggle for Existence[9] as Nature's sole method of progress,' 'was to be sure a libel projected upon nature, but it had enough truth in it to be mischievous for a while.' So zoologists honour their greatest! 'Science,' he says, has perceived 'how false to natural fact the theory was.' 'It has shown how primordial, how organically imperative the social virtues are; how love, not egoism, is the motive which the final history of every species justifies.' And so on to some beautiful socialistic sentiment and anticipations of 'the dominance of a common civic ideal, which to naturalists is known as a Symbiosis.'[10] And Prof. Geddes writes tumultuously in the same vein – a kind of pulpit science – many hopeful things of 'Renascence,' and the 'Elixir of Life.'[11]

Now there is absolutely no justifications for these sweeping assertions, this frantic hopefulness, this attempt to belittle the giants of the Natural Selec-

---

6   A tree-shaded dell.

7   An organisation established in 1885 as an alternative to the Royal Academy, by British painters who had studied and worked in Paris.

8   The science of life.

9   The relation between coexisting species which must compete for restricted resources necessary for survival.

10 In biology, a beneficial interaction between two dissimilar organisms living in close physical association.

11 A supposed drug or essence capable of prolonging life indefinitely.

tion[12] period of biological history. There is nothing in Symbiosis or in any other group of phenomena to warrant the statement that the representation of all life as a Struggle for Existence is a libel on Nature. Because some species have abandoned fighting in open order, each family for itself, as some of the larger carnivora[13] do, for a fight in masses after the fashion of the ants, because the fungus fighting its brother fungus has armed itself with an auxiliary alga,[14] because man instead of killing his cattle at sight preserves them against his convenience, and fights with advertisements and legal process instead of with flint instruments, is life therefore any the less a battle-field? Has anything arisen to show that the seed of the unfit[15] need not perish, that a species may wheel into line with new conditions without the generous assistance of Death, that where the life and breeding of every individual in a species is about equally secure, a degenerative process must not inevitably supervene? As a matter of fact Natural Selection grips us more grimly than it ever did, because the doubts thrown upon the inheritance of acquired characteristics[16] have deprived us of our trust in education as a means of redemption for decadent families. In our hearts we all wish that the case was not so, we all hate Death and his handiwork; but the business of science is not to keep up the courage of men, but to tell the truth. And biological science in the study still faces this dilemma, that the individual in a non-combatant species, if such a thing as a non-combatant species ever exist, a species, that is to say, perfectly adapted to static conditions, is, by virtue of its perfect reactions, a mechanism, and that in a species not in a state of equilibrium, a species undergoing modification, a certain painful stress must weigh upon all its perfectly adapted individuals, and death be busy among the most imperfect. And where your animal is social, the stress is still upon the group of imperfect individuals constituting the imperfect herd[17] or anthill, or what not – they merely suffer by wholesale instead of by retail. In brief, a static species is mechanical, an evolving species suffering – no line of escape from that *impasse* has as yet presented itself. The names of the sculptor who carve out the new forms of life are, and so far as human science[18] goes at present they must ever be, Pain and Death. And

---

12 In Darwinian evolutionary theory, the survival and preferential propagation of organisms better adapted to their environment.

13 An order of animals which consists mainly of carnivorous mammals.

14 Commonly, seaweed, though properly, any of a large group of non-vascular mainly aquatic cryptograms capable of photosynthesis.

15 A person whose mental or physical health falls below a desired standard.

16 The discredited biological theory that claims that changes in physiology acquired over the life of the organism are transmitted to offspring.

17 A biological group being gregarious and mutually influenced.

18 The investigation of human life and activities by a rational, systematic and verifiable methodology that acknowledges the validity of both data derived through sensory experiences and that derived through psychological experience.

the phenomena of degeneration rob one of any confidence that the new forms will be in any case or a majority of cases 'higher' (by any standard except present adaptation[19] to circumstances) than the old.

Messrs. Geddes and Thomson have advanced nothing to weaken these convictions, and their attitude is altogether amazingly unscientific. Mr Thomson talks of the Gospel of the Resurrection[20] and 'that charming girl Proserpina,'[21] and Baldur the Beautiful[22] and Dornröschen,[23] and hammers away at the great god Pan,[24] inviting all and sundry to 'light the Beltane[25] fires' – apparently with the dry truths of science – 'and keep the Floralia,'[26] while Prof. Geddes relies chiefly on the Alchemy[27] of Life for his literary effects. Intercalated among these writings are amateurish short stories about spring, 'descriptive articles' of the High School[28] Essay type, poetry and illustrations such as we have already dealt with. In this manner is the banner of the 'Scots Renascence,' and 'Bio-optimism' unfurled by these industrious investigators in biology. It will not appeal to science students, but to that large and important class of the community which trims its convictions to its amiable sentiments, it may appear as a very desirable mitigation of the rigour of, what Mr Buchanan has very aptly called, the Calvinism of science.[29]

---

19   In evolution, the process of change in species when adjusting to their environment.

20   The Christian teaching that Jesus Christ was raised from the dead and ascended into Heaven.

21   The Roman goddess of springtime.

22   In Norse mythology, the god of innocence, beauty, joy, purity and peace.

23   German, Briar Rose, the name given by Jacob and Wilhelm Grimm to the title character in the German translation of the fairytale, 'La belle au bois dormant' ('Sleeping Beauty'), originally collected in Contes de ma Mère l'Oye by Charles Perrault in 1697.

24   The Greek god of shepherds and flocks, of mountain wilds, hunting and rustic music, half man, half goat and often highly sexualised in art and literature.

25   An ancient Scottish and Irish festival celebrated on 1 May at which great bonfires were lit.

26   An ancient Roman festival dedicated to the goddess Flora, held between 27 April and 3 May to symbolise the renewal of the cycle of life.

27   The pursuit of the transmutation of baser metals into gold, and the search for the elixir of life.

28   In Scotland, a secondary school.

29   Quoting Robert Buchanan's The Coming Terror (1891), this refers to the rule of nature, which human endeavour can palliate but not alter.

1.6: 'The Discovery of the Future'

H. G. Wells, 'The Discovery of the Future' (6 February 1902)*.[1]

It will lead into my subject most conveniently to contrast and separate two divergent types of mind, types which are to be distinguished chiefly by their attitude towards time and more particularly by the relative importance they attach and the relative amount of thought they give to the future of things.

The first of these two types of mind, and it is, I think, the predominant type, the type of the majority of living people, is that which seems scarcely to think of the future at all, which regards it as a sort of black non-existence upon which the advancing present will presently write events. The second type, which is, I think, a more modern and much less abundant type of mind, thinks constantly and by preference of things to come, and of present things mainly in relation to the results which must arise from them. The former type of mind, when one gets it in its purity, is retrospective in habit, and it interprets the things of the present, and gives value to this and denies it to that, entirely with relation to the past. The latter type of mind is constructive in habit, it interprets the things of the present and gives value to this or that, entirely in relation to things designed or foreseen. While from that former point of view our life is simply to reap the consequences of the past, from this our life is to prepare the future. The former type one might speak of as the legal or submissive type of mind, because the business, the practice and the training of a lawyer dispose him towards it; he of all men must constantly refer to the law made, the right established, the precedent set, and most consistently ignore or condemn the thing that is only seeking to establish itself. The latter type of mind I might for contrast call the legislative, creative, organising or masterful type, because it is perpetually attacking and altering the established order of things, perpetually falling away from respect for what the past has given us. It sees the world as one great workshop, and the present is no more than material for the future, for the thing that is yet destined to be. It is in the active mood of thought, while the former is in the passive; it is the mind of youth, it is the mind more manifest among the western nations while the former is the mind of age, the mind of the oriental.

---

*   'A discourse delivered at the Royal Institution on Friday, January 24, by Mr H. G. Wells.' [Editor's note: this lecture was originally scheduled for 1899 but was cancelled due to Wells's ill-health (see Partington 2007). As well as appearing in *Nature*, it was published as a pamphlet later the same year. Patrick Parrinder has said of the lecture, it 'marked Wells's emergence in the public view as a potential great man, a mind and a force to be reckoned with' (Parrinder 1989, 9).]

1   Reprinted by permission from Macmillan Publishers Ltd: *Nature* (65: 1684), copyright (1902).

Things have been, says the legal mind, and so we are here. And the creative mind says, we are here, because things have yet to be.

Now I do not wish to suggest that the great mass of people belong to either of these two types. Indeed, I speak of them as two distinct and distinguishable types mainly for convenience and in order to accentuate their distinction. There are probably very few people who brood constantly upon the past without any thought of the future at all, and there are probably scarcely any who live and think consistently in relation to the future. The great mass of people occupy an intermediate position between these extremes, they pass daily and hourly from the passive mood to the active, they see this thing in relation to its associations and that thing in relation to its consequences, and they do not even suspect that they are using two distinct methods in their minds.

But for all that they are distinct methods, the method of reference to the past and the method of reference to the future, and their mingling in many of our minds no more abolishes their difference than the existence of piebald[2] horses proves that white is black.

I believe that it is not sufficiently recognised just how different in their consequences these two methods are, and just where their difference and where the failure to appreciate their difference takes one. This present time is a period of quite extraordinary uncertainty and indecision upon endless questions – moral questions, aesthetic questions, religious and political questions – upon which we should all of us be happier to feel assured and settled, and a very large amount of this floating uncertainty about these important matters is due to the fact that with most of us these two insufficiently distinguished ways of looking at things are not only present together, but in actual conflict in our minds, in unsuspected conflict; we pass from one to the other heedlessly without any clear recognition of the fundamental difference in conclusions that exists between the two, and we do this with disastrous results to our confidence and our consistency in dealing with all sorts of things.

But before pointing out how divergent these two types or habits of mind really are, it is necessary to meet a possible objection to what has been said. I may put that objection in this form – Is not this distinction between a type of mind that thinks of the past and of a type of mind that thinks of the future a sort of hair-splitting almost like distinguishing between people who have left hands and people who have right? Everybody believes that the present is entirely determined by the past, you say; but, then, everybody believes *also* that the present determines the future. Are we simply separating and contrasting two sides of everybody's opinion? To which one replies that we are not discussing what we know and believe about the relations of past, present and future, or of the rela-

---

2   Having irregular patches of two different colours, especially black and white.

tion of cause and effect to each other in time. We all know the present depends for its causes on the past and that the future depends for its causes upon the present. But this discussion concerns *the way in which we approach things* upon this common ground of knowledge and belief. We may all know there is an east and a west, but if some of us always approach and look at things from the west, if some of us always approach and look at things from the east, and if others again wander about with a pretty disregard of direction, looking at things as chance determines, some of us will get to a westward conclusion of this journey, and some of us will get to an eastward conclusion, and some of us will get to no definite conclusion at all about all sorts of important matters. And yet those who are travelling east, and those who are travelling west, and those who are wandering haphazard, may be all upon the same ground of belief and statement and amidst the same assembly of proven facts. Precisely the same thing will happen if you always approach things from the point of view of their causes, or if you approach them always with a view to their probable effects. And in several very important groups of human affairs it is possible to show quite clearly just how widely apart the two methods, pursued each in its purity, take those who follow them.

I suppose that three hundred years ago all people who thought at all about moral questions, about questions of right and wrong, deduced their rules of conduct absolutely and unreservedly from the past, from some dogmatic injunction, some finally settled decree. The great mass of people do so to-day. It is written, they say. Thou shalt not steal,[3] for example – that is the sole, complete and sufficient reason why you should not steal, and even to-day there is a strong aversion to admit that there is any relation between the actual consequences of acts and the imperatives of right and wrong. Our lives are to reap the fruits[4] of determinate things, and it is still a fundamental presumption of the established morality that one must do right though the heavens fall.[5] But there are people coming into this world who would refuse to call it right if it brought the heavens about our heads, however authoritative its sources and sanctions, and this new disposition is, I believe, a growing one. I suppose in all ages people in a timid, hesitating, guilty way have tempered the austerity of a dogmatic moral code by small infractions to secure obviously kindly ends, but it was, I am told, the Jesuits[6]

---

3   The eighth of the Ten Commandments of the Bible, considered the fundamental law of Jews.

4   To obtain a reward or gain benefits.

5   From the Latin, '*fiat justitia, ruat caelum*', 'let justice be done though the heavens fall', signifying the belief that justice must be done even if the powerful are brought low and the foundations of the state are shaken.

6   Members of the Society of Jesus, a Roman Catholic order founded in 1534 to propagate the faith among unbelievers.

who first deliberately sought to qualify the moral interpretation of acts by a consideration of their results. To-day there are few people who have not more or less clearly discovered the future as a more or less important factor in moral considerations. To-day there is a certain small proportion of people who frankly regard morality as a means to an end, as an overriding of immediate and personal considerations out of regard to something to be attained in the future, and who break away altogether from the idea of a code dogmatically established for ever. Most of us are not so definite as that, but most of us are deeply tinged with the spirit of compromise between the past and the future; we profess an unbounded allegiance to the prescriptions of the past, and we practise a general observance of its injunctions, but we qualify to a vague, variable extent with considerations of expediency. We hold, for example, that we must respect our promises. But suppose we find unexpectedly that for one of us to keep a promise, which has been sealed and sworn in the most sacred fashion, must lead to the great suffering of some other human being, must lead, in fact, to practical evil? Would a man do right or wrong if he broke such a promise? The practical decision most modern people would make would be to break the promise. Most would say that they did evil to avoid a greater evil. But suppose it was not such *very* great suffering we were going to inflict, but only some suffering? And suppose it was a rather important promise? With most of us it would then come to be a matter of weighing the promise, the thing of the past, against this unexpected bad consequence, the thing of the future. And the smaller the overplus[7] of evil consequences, the more most of us would vacillate. But neither of the two types of mind we are contrasting would vacillate at all. The legal type of mind would obey the past unhesitatingly, the creative would unhesitatingly sacrifice it to the future. The legal mind would say, 'they who break the law at any point, break it altogether,' while the creative mind would say, 'let the dead past bury its dead.'[8] It is convenient to take my illustration from the sphere of promises, but it is in the realm of sexual morality that the two methods are most acutely in conflict.

And I would like to suggest that until you have definitely determined either to obey the real or imaginary imperatives of the past, or to set yourself towards the demands of some ideal of the future, until you have made up your mind to adhere to one or other of these two types of mental action in these matters, you are not even within hope of a sustained consistency in the thought that underlies your acts, that in every issue of principle that comes upon you, you will be entirely at the mercy of the intellectual mood that happens to be ascendant at that particular moment in your mind.

---

7   Excess or surplus.

8   A quotation from 'A Psalm of Life' (1838), a poem by Henry Longfellow.

In the sphere of public affairs also, these two ways of looking at things work out into equally divergent and incompatible consequences. The legal mind insists upon treaties, constitutions, legitimacies and charters; the legislative incessantly assails these. Whenever some period of stress sets in, some great conflict between institutions and the forces in things, there comes a sorting between these two types of mind. The legal mind becomes glorified and transfigured in the form of hopeless loyalty, the creative mind inspires revolutions and reconstructions. And particularly is this difference of attitude accentuated in the disputes that arise out of wars. In most modern wars there is no doubt quite traceable on one side or the other a distinct creative idea, a distinct regard for some future consequence. But the main dispute even in most modern wars and the sole dispute in most mediaeval wars will be found to be a reference, not to the future, but to the past; to turn upon a question of fact and right. The wars of Plantagenet[9] and Lancastrian[10] England with France, for example, were based entirely upon a dummy claim, supported by obscure legal arguments, upon the crown of France.[11] And the arguments that centre about the present war in South Africa[12] ignore any ideal of a great united South African State almost entirely, and quibble this way and that about who began the fighting and what was or was not written in some obscure revision of a treaty a score of years ago.[13] Yet beneath the legal issues, the broad creative idea has been very apparent in the public mind during this war. It will be found more or less definitely formulated beneath almost all the great wars of the past century, and a comparison of the wars of the nineteenth century with the wars of the middle ages will show, I think, that in this field also there has been a discovery of the future, an increasing disposition to shift the reference and values from things accomplished to things to come.

Yet though foresight creeps into our politics and a reference to consequences into our morality, it is still the past that dominates our lives. But why? Why are we so bound to it? It is into the future we go, to-morrow is the eventful thing for us. There lies all that remains to be felt by us and our children and all

---

9   An English royal house which ruled from 1154-1399.

10   Pertaining to the royal House of Lancaster which ruled England from 1399 to 1461 and 1470 to 1471.

11   A reference to the Hundred Years' War (1337-1453), a series of dynastic conflicts between England and France over claims by the English kings to the French throne.

12   A reference to the Second Boer War (1899-1902) fought between Britain and the southern African states of the Transvaal Republic and the Orange Free State, resulting in the incorporation of the latter two into the British Empire.

13   A reference to the 1884 London Convention which revised the Pretoria Convention of 1881 (which had ended the First Boer War), the revision ending British suzerainty over Transvaal Province and denying Britain's right to protect the native population of the Transvaal.

those that are dear to us. Yet we marshal and order men into classes entirely with regard to the past, we draw shame and honour out of the past; against the rights of property, the vested interests, the agreements and establishments of the past, the future has no rights. Literature is for the most part history or history at one remove, and what is culture but a mould of interpretation into which new things are thrust, a collection of standards, a sort of bed of King Og,[14] to which all new expressions must be lopped or stretched?[15] Our conveniences, like our thoughts, are all retrospective. We travel on roads so narrow that they suffocate our traffic; we live in uncomfortable, inconvenient, life-wasting houses out of a love of familiar shapes and familiar customs and a dread of strangeness, all our public affairs are cramped by local boundaries impossibly restricted and small. Our clothing, our habits of speech, our spelling, our weights and measures, our coinage, our religious and political theories, all witness to the binding power of the past upon our minds. Yet – we do not serve the past as the Chinese have done. There are degrees. We do not worship our ancestors or prescribe a rigid local costume; we venture to enlarge our stock of knowledge, and we qualify the classics[16] with occasional adventures into original thought. Compared with the Chinese we are distinctly aware of the future. But compared with what we might be, the past is all our world.

The reason why the retrospective habit, the legal habit, is so dominant and always has been so predominant, is of course a perfectly obvious one. We follow the fundamental human principle and take what we can get. All people believe the past is certain, defined and knowable, and only a few people believe it is possible to know anything about the future. Man has acquired the habit of going to the past because it was the line of least resistance for his mind. While a certain variable portion of the past is serviceable matter for knowledge in the case of everyone, the future is, to a mind without any imagination trained in scientific habits of thought, non-existent. All our minds are made of memories. In our memories each of us has something that without any special training whatever will go back into the past and grip firmly and convincingly all sorts of workable facts, sometimes more convincingly than firmly. But the imagination, unless it is strengthened by a very sound training in the laws of causation, wanders like a lost child in the blackness of things to come and returns – empty.

Many people believe, therefore, that there can be no sort of certainty about the future. You can know no more about the future, I was recently assured

---

14   According to the Old Testament Bible, an ancient Amorite king of Bashan who lived to be 3000 years old.

15   See the letters to the editor from T. B. S. and Osmond Fisher, below, for a discussion of this expression, and Wells's error in its use.

16   The standard ancient Greek and Latin authors and their works, or the culture, art, architecture, etc., of Greek and Roman antiquity generally.

by a friend, than you can know which way a kitten will jump next. And to all who hold that view, who regard the future as a perpetual source of convulsive surprises, as an impenetrable, incurable, perpetual blackness, it is right and reasonable to derive such values as it is necessary to attach such things from the events that have certainly happened with regard to them. It is our ignorance of the future and our persuasion that that ignorance is absolutely incurable that alone gives the past its enormous predominance in our thoughts. But through the ages, the long unbroken succession of fortune tellers[17] – and they flourish still – witness to the perpetually smouldering feeling that after all there *may* be a better sort of knowledge – a more serviceable sort of knowledge than that we now possess.

On the whole there is something sympathetic for the dupe of the fortune teller in the spirit of modern science; it is one of the persuasions that come into one's mind, as one assimilates the broad conceptions of science, that the adequacy of causation[18] is universal; that in absolute fact, which constitutes the individual life, in absolute fact the future is just as fixed and determinate, just as settled and inevitable, just as possible a matter of knowledge as the past. Our personal memory gives us an impression of the superior reality and trustworthiness of things in the past, as of things that have finally committed themselves and said their say, but the more clearly we master the leading conceptions of science the better we understand that this impression is one of the results of the peculiar conditions of our lives and not an absolute truth. The man of science comes to believe at last that the events of the year A. D. 4000 are as fixed, settled and unchangeable as the events of the year 1600. Only about the latter he has some material for belief and about the former practically none.

And the question arises how far this absolute ignorance of the future is a fixed and necessary condition of human life, and how far some application of intellectual methods may not attenuate even if it does not absolutely set aside the veil between ourselves and things to come. And I am venturing to suggest to you that, along certain lines and with certain qualifications and limitations, a working knowledge of things in the future is a possible and practicable thing.

And in order to support this suggestion I would call your attention to certain facts about our knowledge of the past, and more particularly I would insist upon this, that about the past our range of absolute certainty is very limited indeed. About the past I would suggest we are inclined to overestimate our certainty, just as I think we are inclined to underestimate the certainties of the fu-

---

17   Persons purportedly capable of telling people's futures by reading their palms.

18   In law, an argument put by a defendant which claims that the plaintiff did not take adequate care to prevent the alleged crime and therefore shares some liability for the crime occurring.

ture. And such a knowledge of the past as we have is not all of the same sort, or derived from the same sources.

Let us consider just what an educate man of to-day knows of the past. First of all he has the realest of all knowledge, the knowledge of his own personal experiences, his memory. Uneducated people believe there memories absolutely, and most educated people believe them with a few reservations. Some of us take up a critical attitude even towards our own memories; we know that they not only sometimes drop things out, but that sometimes a sort of dreaming or a strong suggestion will put things in. But for all that memory remains vivid and real as no other knowledge can be, and to have seen and heard and felt is to be nearest to absolute conviction. Yet our memory of direct impressions is only the smallest part of what we know. Outside that bright area comes knowledge of a different order, the knowledge brought to us by other people. Outside our immediate personal memory, there comes this wider area of facts, or quasi-facts, told us by more or less trustworthy people, told us by word of mouth or by the written word of living and of dead writers. This is the past of report, rumour, tradition and history, the second sort of knowledge of the past. The nearer knowledge of this sort is abundant and clear and detailed, remoter it becomes vaguer, still more remotely in time and space it dies down to brief, imperfect inscriptions and enigmatical traditions, and at last dies away, so far as the records and traditions of humanity go, into a doubt and darkness as black, just as black, as futurity. And now let me remind you that this second zone of knowledge outside the bright area of what we have felt and witnessed and handled for ourselves, this zone of hearsay and history and tradition completed the whole knowledge of the past that was accessible to Shakespeare, for example. To these limits man's knowledge of the past was absolutely confined save for some inklings and guesses, save for some small, almost negligible beginnings, until the seventeenth century began. Beside the correct knowledge in this scheme of hearsay and history a man had a certain amount of legend and error that rounded off the picture in a very satisfying and misleading way, according to Bishop Ussher, just exactly 4004 years BC.[19] And that was man's universal history – that was his all, until the scientific epoch[20] began. And beyond those limits–? Well, I suppose the educated man of the sixteenth century was as certain of the non-existence of anything before the creation of the world as he was, and as most of us are still, of the practical non-existence of the future, or at any rate he was as satisfied of the impossibility of knowledge in the one direction as in the other.

---

19   This is the date at which Archbishop Ussher dated the creation of the earth based upon Biblical and contemporary geological evidence.

20   The period from the seventeenth century onwards when major scientific discoveries began transforming the material world.

But modern science, that is to say, the relentless systematic criticism of phenomena, has in the past hundred years absolutely destroyed the conception of a finitely distant beginning of things; has abolished such limits to the past as a dated creation set, and added an enormous vista to that limited sixteenth century outlook. And what I would insist upon is that this further knowledge is a new kind of knowledge, obtained in a new kind of way. We know to-day, quite as confidently and in many respects more intimately than we know Sargon, or Zenobia, or Caractacus, the form and the habits of creatures that no living being has ever met, that no human eye has ever regarded, and the character of scenery that no man has ever seen or can ever possibly see; we picture to ourselves the labyrinthodon[21] raising its clumsy head above the waters of the Carboniferous swamps[22] in which he lived, and we figure the pterodactyls,[23] those great bird lizards, flapping their way athwart the forests of the Mesozoic age[24] with exactly the same certainty as that with which we picture the rhinoceros or the vulture. I doubt no more about the facts in this further picture than I do about those in the nearest. I believe in the Megatherium[25] which I have never seen as confidently as I believe in the hippopotamus that has engulfed buns from my hand. A vast amount of detail in that further picture is now fixed and finite for all time. And countless number of investigators are persistently and confidently enlarging, amplifying, correcting and pushing further and further back the boundaries of this greater past, this pre-human past[26] that the scientific criticism of existing phenomena has discovered and restored and brought for the first time into the world of human thought. We have become possessed of a new and once unsuspected history of the world – of which all the history that was known, for example, to Doctor Johnson, is only the brief concluding chapter. And even that concluding chapter has been greatly enlarged and corrected by the exploring archaeologist working strictly upon the lines of the new method, that is to say, the comparison and criticism of suggestive facts.

I want particularly to insist upon this, that all this outer past – this non-historical past – is the product of a new and keener habit of inquiry, and no sort of

---

21 Properly, labyrinthodont, any of various large fossil amphibians of the Palaeozoic and Triassic periods characterised by teeth of labyrinthine structure having the enamel deeply folded.

22 The swamps of the Palaeozoic period in which many coal deposits were formed.

23 Properly, pterosaurs, winged reptiles of the Triassic and Cretaceous periods.

24 The epoch, 245 million years ago to 65 million years ago, when the earth was dominated by dinosaurs.

25 Any of several large extinct mammals known as ground sloths of the upper tertiary of South America.

26 The time before humankind appeared on earth, about 130,000 years ago.

revelation.[27] It is simply due to a new and more critical way of looking at things. Our knowledge of the geological past, clear and definite as it has become, is of a different and lower order than the knowledge of our memory, and yet of a quite practicable and trustworthy order, a knowledge good enough to go upon. And if one were to speak of the private memory as the personal past, as the next wider area of knowledge as the traditional or historical past, then one might call all that great and inspiring background of remoter geological time, the inductive past.[28]

And this great discovery of the inductive past was got by the discussion and rediscussion and effective criticism of a number of existing facts, odd-shaped lumps of stone, streaks and bandings in quarries and cliffs, anatomical and developmental details that had always been about in the world, that had been lying at the feet of mankind so long as mankind had existed, but that no one had ever dreamt before could supply any information at all, much more could reveal such astounding and enlightening vistas. Looked at in a new way they became sources of dazzling and penetrating light; the remoter past lit up and became a picture. Considered as effects, compared and criticised, they yielded a clairvoyant vision of the history of interminable years.

And now – if it has been possible for men by picking out a number of suggestive and significant looking things in the present, by comparing them, criticising them, and discussing them, with a perpetual insistence upon *why?* without any guiding tradition, and indeed in the teeth of established beliefs, to construct this amazing searchlight of inference into the remoter past – is it really, after all, such an extravagant and hopeless thing to suggest that, by seeking for operating causes[29] instead of for fossils and by criticising them as persistently and thoroughly as the geological record has been criticised, it may be possible to throw a searchlight of inference forward instead of backward and to attain to a knowledge of coming things as clear, as universally convincing and infinitely more important to mankind than the clear vision of the past that geology has opened to us during the nineteenth century?

Let us grant that anything to correspond with the memory, anything having the same relation to future that memory has to the past, is out of the question. We cannot imagine, of course, that we can ever know any personal future to correspond with our personal past, or any traditional future to correspond with our traditional past. But the possibility of an inductive future to correspond with

---

27 A sudden disclosure of something previously unknown or not realised.

28 The past as understood primarily through reasoned hypothesis applied to scant material evidence.

29 Processes which occur in the scheme of things and from which future events can be determined.

the great inductive past of geology and archaeology[30] is an altogether different thing.

I must confess that I believe quite firmly that an inductive knowledge of a great number of things in the future is becoming a human possibility. I believe that the time is drawing near when it will be possible to suggest a systematic exploration of the future. And you must not judge the practicability of this enterprise by the failures of the past. So far nothing has been attempted, so far no first-class mind has ever focussed itself upon these issues. But suppose the laws of social and political development, for example, were given as many brains, were given as much attention, criticism and discussion as we have given to the laws of chemical combination[31] during the last fifty years – what might we not expect?

To the popular mind of to-day there is something very difficult in such a suggestion, soberly made. But here, in this Institution[32] which has watched for a whole century over the splendid adolescence of science, and where the spirit of science is surely understood, you will know that as a matter of fact prophecy[33] has always been inseparably associated with the idea of scientific research. The popular idea of scientific investigation is a vehement, aimless collection of little facts, collected as the bower bird[34] collects shells and pebbles, in methodical little rows, and out of this process, in some manner unknown to the popular mind, certain conjuring tricks – the celebrated wonders of science – in a sort of accidental way emerge. The popular conception of all discovery is accident. But you will know that the essential thing in the scientific process is not the collection of facts, but the analysis of facts; facts are the raw material and not the substance of science; it is analysis that has given us all ordered knowledge, and you know that the aim and the test and the justification of the scientific process is *not* a marketable conjuring trick, but prophecy. Until a scientific theory yields confident forecasts you know it is unsound and tentative; it is mere theorising, as evanescent as art talk[35] or the phantoms politicians talk about.[36] The splendid

---

30 The systematic description or study of human antiquities as revealed by excavation.

31 A law, more commonly known as the law of multiple proportions; discovered by John Dalton in 1803 which states that if two elements form more than one compound between them, then the ratios of the masses of the second element which combines with a fixed mass of the first element will be ratios of small whole numbers.

32 The Royal Institution of Great Britain, an organisation dedicated to science education and research, founded in London in 1799.

33 The foretelling or prediction of future events.

34 Any of various passerine birds of the family *Ptilonorhynchidae*, native to Australia and New Guinea, which construct elaborate runs adorned with feathers, shells, etc., during courtship.

35 Notions based on impressions or emotions.

body of gravitational astronomy,[37] for example, establishes itself upon the certain forecast of stellar movements,[38] and you would absolutely refuse to believe its amazing assertions if it were not for these same unerring forecasts. The whole body of medical science[39] aims, and claims the ability, to diagnose. Meteorology constantly and persistently aims at prophecy, and it will never stand in a place of honour until it can certainly foretell. The chemist forecasts elements[40] before he meets them – it is very properly his boast – and the splendid manner in which the mind of Clerk Maxwell reached in front of all experiment and foretold those things that Marconi has materialised[41] is familiar to us all.

And if I am right in saying that science aims at prophecy, and if the specialist in each science is in fact doing his best *now* to prophesy within the limits of his field, what is there to stand in the way of our building up this growing body of forecast into an ordered picture of the future that will be just as certain, just as strictly science, and perhaps just as detailed as the picture that has been built up within the last hundred years to make the geological past? Well, so far and until we bring the prophecy down to the affairs of man and his children, it is just as possible to carry induction forward as back; it is just as simple and sure to work out the changing orbit of the earth in the future until the tidal drag[42] hauls one unchanging face at last towards the sun as it is to work back to its blazing and molten past.[43] Until man comes in, the inductive future is as real and convincing as the inductive past. But inorganic forces are the smaller part and the minor interest in this concern. Directly man becomes a factor the nature of the problem changes, and our whole present interest centres on the question whether man is, indeed, individually and collectively incalculable, a new element which entirely

---

36 Political diagnoses of social ills, which are not necessarily grounded in fact but in popular appeal.

37 Properly, gravitational wave astronomy, a nascent branch of observational astronomy which aims to use gravitational waves to discern observational data about objects such as neutron stars and black holes, about such events as supernovae and about the early universe shortly after the big bang.

38 Properly, stellar dynamics, the scientific description in statistical terms of the collective motions of stars subject to their mutual gravity.

39 Research disciplines related to health, such as biochemistry, experimental psychology, pathology, pharmacology, physiology, anatomy and genetics.

40 Atoms as defined by the number of protons in their nuclei.

41 A reference to experiments by James Clerk Maxwell in which he described the theoretical basis of the propagation of electromagnetic waves essential for Guglielmo Marconi's later work on radio communication.

42 The action of gravity which ensures one side of a satellite remains constantly facing its parent planet.

43 The notion that planets began as molten infernos, and have gradually cooled and solidified over time.

alters the nature of our inquiry and stamps it at once as vain and hopeless, or whether his presence complicates, but does not alter, the essential nature of the induction. How far may we hope to get trustworthy inductions about the future of man?

Well, I think on the whole, we are inclined to underrate our chance of certainties in the future just as I think we are inclined to be too credulous about the historical past. The vividness of our personal memories, which are the very essence of reality to us, throws a glamour of conviction over tradition and past inductions. But the personal future must in the very nature of things be hidden from us so long as time endures, and this black ignorance at our very feet, this black shadow that corresponds to the brightness of our memories behind us, throws a glamour of uncertainty and unreality over all the future. We are continually surprising ourselves by our own will or want of will; the individualities about us are continually producing the unexpected, and it is very natural to reason that as we can never be precisely sure before the time comes what *we* are going to do and feel, and if we can never count with absolute certainty upon the acts and happenings even of our most intimate friends, how much the more impossible is it to anticipate the behaviour in any direction of states and communities?

In reply to which I would advance the suggestion that an increase in the number of human beings considered may positively simplify the case instead of complicating it, that as the individuals increase in number they begin to average out. Let me illustrate this point by a comparison. Angular pit sand[44] has grains of the most varied shapes. Examined microscopically you will find all sorts of angles and outlines and variations. Before you look, you can say of no particular grain what its outline will be. And if you shoot a load of such sand from a cart you cannot foretell with any certainty where any particular grain will be in the heap that you make. But you can tell, you can tell pretty definitely, the form of the heap as a whole. And further, if you pass that sand through a series of shoots, and finally drop it some distance to the ground, you will be able to foretell that grains of a certain sort of form and size will for the most part be found in one part of the heap, and grains of another sort of form and size will be found in another part of the heap. In such a case, you see, the thing as a whole may be simpler than its component parts, and this I submit is also the case in many human affairs. So that because the individual future eludes us completely, that is no reason why we should not aspire to, and discover and use, safe and serviceable generalisations upon countless important issues in the human destiny.

But there is a very grave and important-looking difference between a load of sand and a multitude of human beings, and this I must face and examine. Our

---

44   Sand containing grains of the most varied shapes.

thoughts and wills and emotions are contagious. An exceptional sort of sand grain, a sand grain that was exceptionally big and heavy, for example, exerts no influence worth considering upon any other of the sand grains in the load. They will fall and roll and heap themselves just the same, whether that exceptional grain is with them or not. But an exceptional man comes into the world, a Caesar[45] or a Napoleon or a Peter the Hermit, and he appears to persuade and convince and compel and take entire possession of the sand heap – I mean the community – and to twist and alter its destinies to an almost unlimited extent. And if this is indeed the case, it reduces our project of an inductive knowledge of the future to very small limits. To hope to foretell the birth and coming of men of exceptional force and genius is to hope incredibly, and if, indeed, such exceptional men do as much as they seem to do in warping the path of humanity, our utmost prophetic limit in human affairs is a conditional sort of prophecy. *If* people do so and so, we can say, then such and such results will follow, and we must admit that that is our limit.

But everybody does not believe in the importance of the leading man. There are those who will say that the whole world is different by reason of Napoleon. But there are also those who will say the whole world of to-day would be very much as it is now if Napoleon had never been born. There are those who believe entirely in the individual man and those who believe entirely in the forces behind the individual man, and for my own part I must confess myself a rather extreme case of the latter kind. I must confess that I believe that if by some juggling with space and time Julius Caesar, Napoleon, Edward IV, William the Conqueror, Lord Rosebery and Robert Burns had all been changed at birth, it would not have produced any serious dislocation of the course of destiny. I believe that these great men of ours are no more than images and symbols and instruments taken, as it were, haphazard by the incessant and consistent forces behind them; they are the pen-nibs[46] Fate[47] has used for her writing, the diamonds upon the drill that pierces through the rock. And the more one inclines to this trust in forces, the more one will believe in the possibility of a reasoned inductive view of the future that will serve us in politics, in morals, in social contrivances, and in a thousand spacious ways. And even those who take the most extreme and personal and melodramatic view of the ways of human destiny, who see life as a tissue of fairy godmother[48] births and accidental meetings and promises and jealousies, will, I suppose, admit there comes a limit to these things, that at last personality dies away and the greater forces come to there own. The great man, however great he be, cannot set back the whole scheme of things;

---

45   The title of the ancient Roman emperors, also used to refer to an autocratic ruler.

46   The tips of fountain pens or dip pens.

47   The goddess of destiny represented in Greek, Roman and Scandinavian mythology.

48   A benefactress.

what he does in right and reason will remain, and what he does against the greater creative forces will perish. We cannot foresee him, let us grant that. His personal difference, the splendour of his effect, his dramatic arrangement of events will be his own – in other words, we cannot estimate for accidents and accelerations and delays – but if only we throw our web of generalisation wide enough, if only we spin our rope of induction strong enough, the final result of the great man, his ultimate surviving consequences, will come within our net.

Such, then, is the sort of knowledge of the future that I believe is attainable, and worth attaining. I believe that the deliberate direction of historical study and of economic and social study towards the future, and an increasing reference, a deliberate and courageous reference, to the future in moral and religious discussion, would be enormously stimulating and enormously profitable to our intellectual life. I have done my best to suggest to you that such an enterprise is now a serious and practicable undertaking. But at the risk of repetition I would call your attention to the essential difference that must always hold between our attainable knowledge of the future and our existing knowledge of the past. The portion of the past that is brightest and most real to each of us is the individual past, the personal memory. The portion of the future which must remain darkest and least accessible is the individual future. Scientific prophecy will not be fortune telling, whatever else it may be. Those excellent people who cast horoscopes,[49] those illegal fashionable palm-reading[50] ladies who abound so much to-day, in whom nobody is so foolish as to believe, and to whom everybody is foolish enough to go, need fear no competition from the scientific prophets. The knowledge of the future we may hope to gain will be general and not individual; it will be no sort of knowledge that will either hamper us in the exercise of our individual free will[51] or relieve us of our individual responsibility.

And now, how far is it possible at the present time to speculate on the particular outline the future will assume when it is investigated in this way?

It is interesting, before we answer that question, to take into account the speculations of a certain sect and culture of people who already, before the middle of the last century, had set their faces towards the future as the justifying explanation of the present. These were the positivists,[52] whose position is still most eloquently maintained and displayed by Mr Frederic Harrison, in spite of the great expansion of the human outlook that has occurred since Comte. If you read

---

49 Predictions of people's futures based on observations of the sky and the configuration of the planets at a particular moment, especially at a person's birth.

50 Divination by examination of the lines and configurations of the palm of the hand.

51 The power of directing one's own actions unconstrained by necessity or fate.

52 Adherence of positivism, a philosophy which recognises only positive facts and observable phenomena and rejects metaphysics and theism.

Mr Harrison, and you are also, as I presume your presence here indicates, saturated with that new wine of more spacious knowledge that has been given the world during the last fifty years, you will have been greatly impressed by the peculiar limitations of the positivist conception of the future. So far as I can gather, Comte was, for all practical purposes, totally ignorant of that remoter past outside the past that is known to us by history, or if he was not totally ignorant of its existence, he was, and conscientiously remained, ignorant of its relevancy to the history of humanity. In the narrow and limited past he recognised, men had always been like the men of to-day; in the future he could not imagine that they would be anything more than men like the men of to-day. He perceived, as we all perceive, that the old social order was breaking up, and after a richly suggestive and incomplete analysis of the forces that were breaking it up, he set himself to plan a new static social order to replace it. If you will read Comte, or, what is much easier and pleasanter, if you will read Mr Frederic Harrison, you will find this conception constantly apparent – that there was once a stable condition of society with humanity, so to speak, sitting down in an orderly and respectable manner; that humanity has been stirred up and is on the move, and that finally it will sit down again on a higher plane, and for good and all, cultured and happy, in the re-organised positivist state. And since he could see nothing beyond man in the future, there, in that millennial[53] fashion, Comte had to end. Since he could imagine nothing higher than man, he had to assert that humanity, and particularly the future of humanity, was the highest of all conceivable things.

All that was perfectly comprehensible in a thinker of the first half of the nineteenth century. But we of the early twentieth, and particularly that growing majority of us who have been born since the *Origin of Species*[54] was written, have no excuse for any such limited vision. Our imaginations have been trained upon a past in which the past that Comte knew is scarcely more than the concluding moment; we perceive that man, and all the world of men, is no more than the present phase of a development so great and splendid that beside this vision epics[55] jingle like nursery rhymes,[56] and all the exploits of humanity shrivel to the proportion of castles in the sand. We look back through countless millions of years and see the great will to live struggling out of the intertidal slime,[57] struggling from shape to shape and from power to power, crawling and then walking confidently upon the land, struggling generation after generation to

---

53   Of the millennium, a period of peace, happiness, prosperity and ideal government.

54   By Charles Darwin (1859).

55   Grand and heroic narratives impressive in scope and grandeur.

56   A simple traditional song or story in rhyme for children.

57   The supposed compound on the first seashores in which water-based creatures evolved into primitive land-based creatures.

master the air, creeping down into the darkness of the deep; we see it turn upon itself in rage and hunger and reshape itself anew, we watch it draw nearer and more akin to us, expanding, elaborating itself, pursuing its relentless inconceivable purpose, until at last it reaches us and its being beats through our brains and arteries, throbs and thunders in our battleships, roars through our cities, sings in our music and flowers in our art. And when – from that retrospect – we turn again towards the future, surely any thought of finality, any millennial settlement of cultured persons, has vanished from our minds.

This fact that man is not final is the great unmanageable disturbing fact that rises upon us in the scientific discovery of the future, and to my mind at any rate the question what is to come *after* man is the most persistently fascinating and the most insoluble question in the whole world.

Of course we have no answer. Such imaginations as we have refuse to rise to the task.

But for the nearer future, while man is still man, there are a few general statements that seem to grow more certain. It seems to be pretty generally believed to-day that our dense populations are in the opening phase of a process of diffusion and aeration.[58] It seems pretty inevitable also that at least the mass of white population in the world will be forced some way up the scale of education and personal efficiency in the next two of three decades. It is not difficult to collect reasons for supposing, and such reasons have been collected, that in the near future, in a couple of hundred years as one rash optimist has written, or in a thousand or so, humanity will be definitely and consciously organising itself as a great world State,[59] a great world State that will purge from itself much that is mean, much that is bestial, and much that makes for individual dullness and dreariness, greyness and wretchedness in the world of to-day. And although we know that there is nothing final in the world State, although we see it only as something to be reached and passed, although we are sure there will be no such sitting down to restore and perfect a culture as the positivists foretell, yet few people can persuade themselves to see anything beyond that except in the vaguest and more general terms. That world State of more efficient, more vivid, beautiful and eventful people is, so to speak, on the brow of the hill, and we cannot see over – though some of us can imagine great uplands beyond and something, something that glitters elusively, taking first one form and then another, through the haze. We can see no detail, we can see nothing definable, and it is

---

58 Wells observed in 'Anticipations' (1901) that urban conglomerations will give way to suburban sprawls, and this was borne out by the 1901 census which showed a population shift in Britain from the cities to the suburbs.

59 A further reference to 'Anticipations' (1901), in which Wells, the 'rash optimist', predicts a world state emerging around the year 2100.

simply, I know, the sanguine necessity of our minds that makes us believe those uplands of the future are still more gracious and splendid than we can either hope or imagine. But of things that can be demonstrated we have none.

Yet I suppose most of us entertain certain necessary persuasions, without which a moral life in this world is neither a reasonable nor a possible thing. All this paper is built finally upon certain negative beliefs that are incapable of scientific establishment. Our lives and powers are limited, our scope in space and time is limited, and it is not unreasonable that for fundamental beliefs we must go outside the sphere of reason and set our feet upon Faith.[60] Implicit in all such speculations as this, is a very definite and quite arbitrary belief, and that belief is that neither humanity nor in truth any individual human being is living its life in vain. And it is entirely by an act of faith that we must rule out of our forecasts certain possibilities, certain things that one may consider improbable and against the chances, but that no one upon scientific grounds can call impossible. One must admit that it is impossible to show why certain things should not utterly destroy and end the entire human race and story, why night should not presently come down and make all our dreams and efforts vain. It is conceivable, for example, that some great unexpected mass of matter should presently rush upon us from out of space, whirl sun and planets aside like dead leaves before the breeze, and collide with and utterly destroy every spark of life upon this earth. So far as positive human knowledge goes, this is a conceivably possible thing. There is nothing in science to show why such a thing should not be. It is conceivable, too, that some pestilence may presently appear, some new disease, that will destroy, not 10 or 15 or 20 per cent of the earth's inhabitants as pestilences have done in the past, but 100 per cent, and so end our race. No one, speaking from scientific grounds alone, can say – that cannot be. And no one can dispute that some great disease of the atmosphere, some trailing cometary poison, some great emanation of vapour from the interior of the earth, such as Mr Shiel has made a brilliant use of in his *Purple Cloud*, is consistent with every demonstrated fact in the world. There may arise new animals to prey upon us by land and sea, and there may come some drug or a wrecking madness into the minds of men. And finally there is the reasonable certainty that this sun of ours must some day radiate itself towards extinction;[61] that at least *must* happen, it will grow cooler and cooler, and its planets will rotate ever more sluggishly until some day this earth of ours, tideless and slow moving, will be dead and frozen, and all that has lived upon it will be frozen out and done with. There surely man must end. That of all such nightmares is the most insistently convincing.

And yet one doesn't believe it.

---

60 Belief, not requiring evidence or proof.

61 A reference to the second law of thermodynamics which states that as the universe ages, the level of entropy increases.

At least I do not. And I do not believe in these things because I have come to believe in certain other things, – in the coherency and purpose in the world and in the greatness of human destiny. Worlds may freeze and suns may perish, but there stirs something within us now that can never die again.

Do not misunderstand me when I speak of the greatness of human destiny.

If I may speak quite openly to you, I will confess that, considered as a final product, I do not think very much of myself or (saving your presence) my fellow creatures. I do not think I could possibly join in the worship of humanity with any gravity or sincerity. Think of it. Think of the positive facts. There are surely moods for all of use when one can feel Swift's amazement that such a being should deal in pride.[62] There are moods when one can join in the laughter of Democritus;[63] and they would come oftener were not the spectacle of human littleness so abundantly shot with pain. But it is not only with pain that the world is shot – it is shot with promise. Small as our vanity and carnality makes us, there has been a day of still smaller things. It is the long ascent of the past that gives the lie to our despair. We now know that all the blood and passion of our life was represented in the Carboniferous time[64] by something – something, perhaps, cold-blooded and with a clammy skin, that lurked between air and water, and fled before the giant amphibia[65] of those days.

For all the folly, blindness and pain of our lives, we have come some way from that. And the distance we have travelled gives us some earnest of the way we have yet to go.

Why should things cease at man? Why should not this rising curve rise yet more steeply and swiftly? There are many things to suggest that we are now in a phase of rapid and unprecedented development. The conditions under which men live are changing with an ever-increasing rapidity, and, so far as our knowledge goes, no sort of creatures have ever lived under changing conditions without undergoing the profoundest changes themselves. In the past century there was more change in the conditions of human life than there had been in the previous thousand years. A hundred years ago inventors and investigators were rare scattered men, and now invention and inquiry is the work of an organised army. This century will see changes that will dwarf those of the nineteenth century as those of the nineteenth dwarf those of the eighteenth. One can see no sign any-

---

62 A reference to Jonathan Swift's *A Tale of a Tub* (1704), in which pride, amongst other things, is parodied.

63 The act of laughing at people for their folly or vanity, as Democritus is reputed to have done.

64 The fifth period of the Palaeozoic era, c. 354 to 290 million years ago, in which many coal deposits were formed.

65 Creatures that can live both in water and on land.

where that this rush of change will be over presently, that the positivist dream of a social reconstruction and of a new static culture phase will ever be realised. Human society never has been quite static, and it will presently cease to attempt to be static. Everything seems pointing to the belief that we are entering upon a progress that will go on, with an ever-widening and ever more confident stride, for ever. The reorganisation of society that is going on now beneath the traditional appearance of things is a kinetic reorganisation. We are getting into marching order. We have struck our camp for ever and we are out upon the roads.

We are in the beginning of the greatest change that humanity has ever undergone. There is no shock, no epoch-making incident – but then there is no shock at a cloudy daybreak. At no point can we say, here it commences, now, last minute was night and this is morning. But insensibly we are in the day. If we care to look we can foresee growing knowledge, growing order, and presently a deliberate improvement of the blood and character of the race.[66] And what we can see and imagine gives us a measure and gives us faith for what surpasses the imagination.

It is possible to believe that all the past is but the beginning of a beginning, and that all that is and has been is but the twilight of the dawn. It is possible to believe that all that the human mind has ever accomplished is but the dream before the awakening. We cannot see, there is no need for us to see, what this world will be like when the day has fully come. We are creatures of the twilight. But it is out of our race and lineage that minds will spring, that will reach back to us in our littleness to know us better than we know ourselves, and that will reach forward fearlessly to comprehend this future that defeats our eyes. All this world is heavy with the promise of greater things, a day will come, one day in the unending succession of days, when beings, beings who are now latent in our thoughts and hidden in our loins, shall stand upon this earth as one stands upon a footstool, and shall laugh and reach out their hands amidst the stars.

Comment on Wells: T. B. S., letter to the editor, 'King Og's Bed' (20 February 1902).[67]

I see that Mr Wells, in his interesting discourse on 'The Discovery of the Future,' mentions 'a sort of bed of King Og, to which all expressions must be lopped or stretched.' We are told in Numbers[68] that King Og had an iron bed-

---

66   A reference to eugenics, which Wells first considered in 'Anticipations' (1901).

67   Reprinted by permission from Macmillan Publishers Ltd: *Nature* (65: 1686), copyright (1902).

68   The fourth book of the Old Testament Bible. In fact, the reference to King Og's bed occurs in the fifth book of the Old Testament, Deuteronomy 3:11.

stead, which was 9 cubits[69] long and 4 cubits broad. But I cannot find that he put his bedstead to the use suggested by Mr Wells. Is it possible that this gentleman's memory is at fault, and that he is confusing King Og with the ancient Greek robber Procrustes,[70] who was accustomed to torture his captives by stretching them if they were too short for his bed, and by lopping of portions of their legs if they were too long to fit the bed?

Reply to T. B. S.: H. G. Wells, letter to the editor (20 February 1902).[71]

'T. B. S.' is quite right. I regret very much that I did not verify my quotation. A confusion of Og's bed and the lopping propensities of Adoni-Bezek[72] seems to have decayed to the likeness of Procrustes. I have lived in this error for years. I have often used the image of King Og's bed in conversation and, I think, in published matter. No one has ever detected my slip, and it is by no means impossible that I am the centre of propagation of a mistake that will turn up again.

Reply to T. B. S. and Wells: Osmond Fisher, letter to the editor, 'King Og's Bed' (27 February 1902).[73]

A Hebraist[74] once told me that he thought that Og's iron bed, mentioned in Deuteronomy 3:11, was a sarcophagus[75] of basalt.[76] The Hebrew word is 'barzel,' which is evidently the same as the Ethopic[77] 'basal,' iron, which Stormonth's dictionary gives as the derivation of 'basalt.'

---

69   Units of measure equivalent to the length of the forearm (i. e., one cubit equates to approximately 45 centimetres).

70   In Greek mythology, a bandit who invited every passer-by to lie in his bed, cutting off the head and feet of those too long for it, and stretching to size those too short for it.

71   Reprinted by permission from Macmillan Publishers Ltd: *Nature* (65: 1686), copyright (1902). This letter has previously been reprinted in Smith 1998, I: 394.

72   In Kings 1: 4-7, a Canaanite king who subdued seventy regional chiefs before being captured by the armies of Judea and Simeon and having his thumbs and toes cut off.

73   Reprinted by permission from Macmillan Publishers Ltd: *Nature* (65: 1687), copyright (1902).

74   A Hebrew scholar.

75   A stone coffin.

76   A dark, fine-grained igneous rock.

77   Correctly, Ethiopic, a Semitic language akin to Arabic spoken in Ethiopia and neighbouring areas.

1.7: 'Education and Research'

From 'University and Educational Intelligence' (12 April 1917).[1]

Those who desire to see the study of physical science[2] receive its due proportion of school time, of prizes and scholarships and other forms of encouragement, as well as social distinction equal to that traditionally allotted to scholars brought up on purely literary fare,[3] will rejoice to notice the newly developed liberalism of some of the classical leaders. Mr A. C. Benson's paper at the Royal Society of Arts[4] on December 20 last was noticed in *Nature* on February 1,[5] and now we find, in the *Fortnightly Review*[6] for April, an article by Lord Bryce entitled 'The Worth of Ancient Literature to the Modern World' (annual presidential address to the Classical Association[7]). This article concedes almost everything fundamental which has been demanded for many years past by the advocates of educational reform. It is no doubt true, as stated by Lord Bryce, that the present popular desire for more science has been created, not as a result of any appreciation of its educational value or of pride in the achievements of human intellect, but as a consequence of the association in the minds of the people between a knowledge of applied science and material prosperity. This is no ground for refusing to satisfy the demand, which, for other reasons, is fully justifiable. The time has come, we are told, when everyone should approach the subject, not as the advocate of a cause, but in an impartial spirit. Then Lord Bryce goes on to inquire, What is the chief aim of education? And the reply is: First, teaching the child how to observe, and from the beginning directing his attention to external Nature. Along with this he must be taught how to use language so as to be able to convey accurately what he wishes to say. An article by Mr H. G. Wells[8] follows that of Lord Bryce, and the subject is a review of Mr R. W. Livingstone's recent book entitled *A Defence of Classical Education*. It supplies interesting

---

1   Reprinted by permission from Macmillan Publishers Ltd: *Nature* (99: 2476), copyright (1917).

2   The sciences which deal with inanimate matter and energy, such as astronomy, physics, chemistry and geology.

3   An offering of literature.

4   Fully, the Royal Society for the Encouragement of Arts, Manufactures and Commerce, a British multi-disciplinary institution, founded in London in 1754.

5   The lecture was entitled 'Literature and Science in Education', and it was noticed anonymously in *Nature* under the same title (1917).

6   A British liberal journal (1865-1934), initially appearing fortnightly, then monthly from 1866.

7   An international body founded in 1903 for the promotion of the study of ancient Greece and Rome.

8   'The Case Against the Classical Languages' (1917).

and amusing reading, which will be relished probably by everyone except the author of the book.

H. G. Wells, 'Education and Research' (19 April 1917).[9]

Science and the Nation. Essays by Cambridge Graduates, with an Introduction by the Rt. Hon. Lord Moulton. Edited by Prof. A. C. Seward. (Cambridge: At the University Press, 1917.) Price 5s. net.

It is the fate of many symposia[10] to fail as a whole by the very excellence of the parts; relationship and proximity as well as stars are needed to form a constellation;[11] and this unsatisfactoriness of *ensemble*[12] is all too manifest in this well-intentioned volume that the Master of Downing[13] has gathered together rather than edited, to which Lord Moulton contributes an introduction. Individually the chapters are of the utmost interest to the general reader; they give him compactly and authoritatively a sound idea of the scope and value of contemporary work in chemistry, physics, botany, geology, medicine, mathematics, and anthropology by such eminent Cambridge[14] hands as Profs. Pope, Bragg, Hobson, Biffen, Wood, Nuttall, and Gowland Hopkins; and it is only when his heart, glowing responsively, demands, 'And in return for all these benefits, in a lively hope of more to come, what do you want the general public to do for you?' that the book becomes ineffective. This is not for want of a common intention. There are clear indications of a common intention to cry up 'pure' science[15] and to insist upon the importance of scientific studies and scientific research, but the cry never becomes more than a vague cry, and the need of the present time is for definite proposals. The present reviewer, who is a journalist very anxious for the advancement of science and very eager to serve it if he can, turns from this book with an uncomfortable sense that scientific men have still to develop a definite policy with regard to schools and colleges and higher education. They do not seem to realise how far science progress is bound up with these matters.

---

9   Reprinted by permission from Macmillan Publishers Ltd: *Nature* (99: 2477), copyright (1917).

10 Collections of essays or papers, written or spoken, on various aspects of a particular subject by a number of contributors.

11 A group or cluster of stars, but here a metaphor for a group of associated ideas.

12 French, the parts of something viewed as a whole.

13 Downing College, a college of the University of Cambridge, founded in 1800.

14 University of Cambridge, British university founded in 1209.

15 The basic knowledge of developing scientific theories considered independently of the application of science.

Here, for example, is a passage from Prof. Keeble's contribution. It shows an extraordinary blindness to the difficulties of the educational conflict at the present time.[16] To the keen parent of promising boys, or to the keen patriot in these urgent times,[17] its easy, ill-informed carelessness will be almost maddening.

> In our own sphere we might well make a beginning by calling a friendly truce between the big-endians and the little-endians[18] of Classics and Science. For if the protagonists were to confer instead of to contend, they would discover that in the ample years of leisure which our youth enjoy there is room in plenty for both classical and scientific education. In such a spirit of sweet reasonableness the scientific and the classico-clerical[19] might proceed together for a reform of our system of education – from top to bottom. There is room for it. It is essential that our statesmen and administrators, our teachers and our poets, know something of the work and method and beauty of science. It is no less essential that the men of science of the coming generation should be cultivated citizens as well as competent specialists.

The Master of Downing failed in his editorial duty when he let that passage stand. No parent, no schoolmaster of any intelligence will endorse Prof. Keeble's delusion that the swift years of youth are 'ample years of leisure.' From first to last through the whole curriculum the educationist[20] knows that he is up against an inexorable limitation of time. The contemporary dispute in education turns wholly upon the compulsory imposition of the Greek language on those who go on to a higher education[21] and upon its use as a medium of philosophical instruction.[22] The case of the moderns[23] is that *there is no time for*

---

16   A reference to the battle for educational resources then occurring between humanities subjects (especially classics) and the sciences.

17   A reference to the Great War or First World War (1914-1918), then in progress.

18   In Jonathan Swift's *Gulliver's Travels* (1726), the 'big-endians' is a name given to Catholics in the imaginary kingdom of Lilliput, who are considered heretics because they break their eggs at the big end, while 'little-endians' is a name given to Protestants because they break their eggs at the little end. The terms combine as an ironic expression of an unnecessary dichotomy.

19   In British education, the influence of and emphasis on the teaching of the Classics in school and university, and the role of the Anglican Church in maintaining the predominance of such education over the teaching of science.

20   Also educationalist, a scholar of the methods of education; an advocate of education.

21   A knowledge of Greek remained an entrance requirement for the universities of Oxford and Cambridge until 1919 and 1920, respectively.

22   In fact Greek was never used as a language of instruction in universities, though Wells could be referring to the prestige of 'Greats', the University of Oxford's classical hon-

Greek, and that the Greek shibboleth[24] cuts off philosophical studies from the general intelligence. No one anywhere is attempting to turn education into a manufacture of 'competent specialists,' and the idea Prof. Keeble favours, that to be cultivated and to be scientific are antagonistic states, is a suggestion of the enemy that has no real foundation in experience. A man may be a Greek scholar and a boor.[25] A man may be unable to construct half a dozen words in Greek and have a beautifully trained and subtly refined intelligence. The case for the defence of the Greek obstacle consists largely in ignoring these facts.

If scientific men who have not had the time to follow up this educational controversy closely wish to grasp its essential value, they cannot do better than weigh over the implications of this passage that follows, from an article by Lord Bryce in the current *Fortnightly Review*[26]:–

> I do not contend that the study of the ancients[27] is to be imposed on all, or even on the bulk, of those who remain at school till eighteen, or on most of those who enter a university. It is generally admitted that at the universities the present system cannot be maintained. Even of those who enter Oxford[28] or Cambridge, many have not the capacity or the taste to make it worth while for them to devote much time there to Greek and Latin.[29] The real practical problems for all our universities is this: How are we to find means by which the study, while dropped for those who will never make much of it, may be retained, and for ever securely maintained, for that percentage of our youth, be it 20 or 30 per cent or be it more, who will draw sufficient mental nourishment and stimulus from the study to make it an effective factor in their intellectual growth and an unceaing spring of enjoyment through the rest of life? This part of our youth has an importance for the nation not to be measured by its numbers. It is on the best minds that the strength of a nation depends, and more than half of these will find their proper province in letters[30] and history. It is by the best minds

---

ours course, in which ancient philosophers were read in the original Greek. Although not the most popular course, numerically, after the 1890s, 'Greats' continued to be considered the university's premier degree until after the Great War.

23   Educationalists who advocate the exclusion of compulsory Greek and Latin from the curriculum.

24   A long-standing idea held unreflectingly by or associated with a group.

25   An unrefined, rude, ill-mannered, inconsiderate person.

26   'The Worth of Ancient Literature to the Modern World' (1917).

27   A Greek or Roman of classical antiquity and the scholarship thereby.

28   The University of Oxford, the oldest British university, founded in the 11th century.

29   The language spoken in ancient Rome and its empire, which was used internationally in the Middle Ages as a medium of communication among educated people.

30   The humanities.

that nations win and retain leadership. No pains can be too great that are spent on developing such minds to the finest point of efficiency.

We shall effect a saving if we drop that study of the ancient languages in the case of those who, after a trial, show no aptitude for them.

Let the scientific man read that over carefully, and, if need be, re-read it. Let him note first the invincible conceit of the classical scholar in the superiority of his particular education to any other, and his firm determination *to secure the pick of the available boys and the pick of the administrative posts* for the classical training. Science and research are to have those rejected as unfit in this sublime progress of the elect. Instead of our boys – I mean the boys destined for real philosophy,[31] living literatures, science, and the study of actual social and political questions – having a straightforward, well-planned school course, they are to be *tried over* at Greek for just the most precious years educationally, and our modern world is to have the broken fragments. This claim is pressed even more impudently by Mr Livingstone in his recent *Defence of Classical Education*. He insists that all our sons are to be muddled about with by the teachers of Greek up to at least the opening of the university stage, entirely in the interests of Greek scholarship. Prof. Keeble's dream of 'sweet reasonableness' is a mere dream. These classical people are absolutely ignorant of their own limitations; they can imagine no compromise; they mean to ram compulsory Greek down the throat of every able English boy they can catch, and they mean to load the scales in favour of Greek at any cost to science, philosophy, and national well-being.

Against this strangle-grip of the classic-worshipping mandarins[32] on our higher English education such a book as *Science and the Nation* scarcely fights at all. Is it too much to suggest that scientific men should take a little more trouble collectively than they have hitherto done to master the essentials of this question, and to understand better what it is that really sustains the general contempt and mistrust of modern knowledge in Great Britain and blocks the way to a widespread national support of research?

31 A set or system of ideas, opinions, beliefs or principles of behaviour based on an overall understanding of existence and the universe.

32 Persons of official importance.

Comment on Wells: Richard Livingstone, letter to the editor, 'Classical Education and Modern Needs' (10 May 1917).[33]

A review by Mr H. G. Wells in *Nature* of April 19 contains the following words: 'This claim is pressed even more impudently by Mr Livingstone in his recent *Defence of Classical Education*. He insists that all our sons are to be muddled about with by the teachers of Greek up to at least the opening of the university stage.'

This is a complete misrepresentation of my views, the more gratuitous because in several passages I insist upon the importance of *not* teaching Greek and Latin to those boys who are unsuited for them – *e. g.* on p. 241: 'It ought to be a first aim ... to avoid diverting boys with mechanical or scientific tastes, who have no aptitude for linguistics, into studies that will be barren for them.' (The context shows that the studies referred to are Latin and Greek.)

With regard to the present system of 'compulsory Greek,' after pointing out that it was an undesirable system, maintained on the ground that without it Greek teaching would, in present circumstances, disappear in many important educational areas, I remarked that 'it would be possible, almost without opposition,' to abolish it, if such facilities were provided for the study of Greek as would put it within the reach of all boys in secondary schools *who wished to learn it.* This does not seem to me an impudent claim; it would be easy to satisfy; and I imagine that no one would take exception to it.

Reply to Livingstone: H. G. Wells, letter to the editor (10 May 1917).[34]

Mr Livingstone's letter is satisfactory, so far as it goes, in promising to spare such boys as are unworthy of classical blessings, but I think many of the readers of *Nature* will see in its phrasing just that implicit claim to monopolise the best of the boys for the classical side of which I complain. We do not want the imbeciles,[35] the calculating boys,[36] the creatures all hands and no head,[37] and so forth,

---

33 Reprinted by permission from Macmillan Publishers Ltd: *Nature* (99: 2480), copyright (1917).

34 Reprinted by permission from Macmillan Publishers Ltd: *Nature* (99: 2480), copyright (1917). This letter has previously been reprinted in Smith 1998, II: 506-07.

35 An archaic expression for persons of abnormally weak intellect, especially for adults with intelligence equal to that of a child of five.

36 Child prodigies who have extraordinary abilities to work out complex mathematical equations while not demonstrating exceptionality in other educational fields. It is often observed that this ability is lost as the children mature.

37 An expression, coined by Pierre-Edouard Lemontey in 'Influence morale de la division du travail' (1801), suggesting a critique of industrial society which was making mere machine operators out of working people.

for the modern side.[38] We want boys for scientific work who may be not 'unsuited,' but eminently suited for Greek and Latin, in order that they may do something better and more important. I write with some personal experience in this matter. I am very much concerned in the welfare of two boys[39] who have a great 'aptitude for linguistics,' and would make excellent classical scholars. I think I can do better with them than that, and that they can serve the world better with a different education. In each case I have had to interfere because they were being 'muddled about with' by the classical side masters, and have got Russian substituted for the futile beginnings of Greek. The fact remains that Mr Livingstone does, under existing conditions, wish to retain compulsory Greek.

Comment on Wells and Livingstone: Matthew Hill, letter to the editor, 'Classical Education and Modern Needs' (17 May 1917).[40]

In his reply to Mr Livingstone's letter in *Nature* of May 10 Mr Wells makes a point which classical apologists,[41] especially those who have not had experience in teaching boys, seem incapable of grasping. Mr Livingstone, on his own showing, would seem to have fallen into a like error. For more than twenty years it has been my lot to teach science to boys, most of whom are graded on their proficiency in linguistic studies, chiefly Latin and Greek. Experience has convinced me that it is a fundamental mistake to suppose that boys even of fifteen or sixteen show marked taste or ability for science or mechanics as opposed to linguistics, or *vice versa*. Those that do are the exceptions that prove the rule.[42]

The boys who are best at classics are also best at science. It is a question of general ability and nothing more. The fallacy that success in, or aptitude for, science denotes the possession of a special kind of intelligence, rarely forthcoming, but always clearly marked at an early age where it does exist, needs uprooting now and for ever; its prevalence is widespread, and the mischief it has done is great.

Every intelligent boy must be given equal opportunities in science and languages in the widest sense of the word, until he is old enough to show which line of study he can most profitably follow. Until this is done, and while only those boys who show a want of literary faculties are encouraged to 'take up sci-

---

38   The practical, scientific aspect of the educational curriculum.

39   A reference to Wells's oldest sons, George and Frank Wells, who were students at Oundle School at the time Wells was writing.

40   Reprinted by permission from Macmillan Publishers Ltd: *Nature* (99: 2481), copyright (1917).

41   Persons who defend a belief by argument.

42   An idiom often used to dismiss counter-examples that contradict stated examples.

ence,' so long will the best brains of our rising generation be imperfectly trained, and the potentialities of the nation towards achievement in science stunted and handicapped.

1.8: 'Men of Letters and Science in Russia'

From 'Notes' (11 November 1920).[1]

Mr H. G. Wells, who has recently been in Russia,[2] describes in the *Sunday Express*[3] of November 7[4] the position of some leading men of science whom he met at Petersburg, by which name, and not Petrograd, this city is now called.[5] He saw Pavlov, the physiologist, Karpinsky, the geologist, Belopolsky, the astronomer, Oldenburg, the Orientalist,[6] and Radlov,[7] the ethnologist, among others who have survived the complete social disruption which Russia has undergone since the catastrophe of 1917-18.[8] Such privileges as are possible in the country under existing conditions appear to be extended to scientific workers; for Mr Wells mentions that the ancient palace of the Archduchess Maria Pavlovna is now a House of Science,[9] where a special rationing system 'provides as well as it can for the needs of four thousand scientific workers and their dependants – in all, perhaps, for ten thousand people.' In spite of this, however, there are much privation and misery, and unless food and clothing are provided few are likely to survive the coming winter. What struck Mr Wells more than anything else was that even under the present disordered conditions, and with physical vitality reduced almost to its lowest limits, a certain amount of scientific work is still carried on, and there is a burning desire to know what has been done for the advancement of natural knowledge in other parts of the world since the Russian collapse. 'The House of Literature and Art,'[10] we are told, 'talked of want and miseries, but not the scientific men. What they were all keen about was the possibility of getting scientific publications; they value knowledge more than

---

1   Reprinted by permission from Macmillan Publishers Ltd: *Nature* (106: 2663), copyright (1920).

2   Wells visited Russia with his son, G. P. Wells, from 26 September to 10 October 1920.

3   British conservative newspaper, launched in 1918.

4   'Russia: The Effect in Europe' (1920).

5   St Petersburg was renamed Petrograd in 1914 before becoming Leningrad in 1924 and reverting to St Petersburg in 1991.

6   An expert in or student of Oriental languages or literature (i. e., those east of the Mediterranean).

7   As Wells's visit to Russia occurred two years after Vasily Radlov's death, the two men could not have met at this time.

8   This is a reference to the social upheaval experienced by Russia as a result of the February and October revolutions in 1917, the end of the Great War on the eastern front in March 1918 and the Russian civil war (1917-22).

9   A salvage establishment in Petrograd, headquarters of a special rationing system which provided for scientific workers and their dependents in the years following the Bolshevik Revolution.

10   A Russian club for artists and writers, established by Anatoly Lunacharsky c. 1920.

bread.' There would, we are sure, be no difficulty in obtaining the books and publications needed by, or funds for providing warm clothing for, the great survivors of the Russian scientific world, if their colleagues here were assured that the parcels would reach their destination. This specific aid is, however, a different matter from general provision for the physical and mental needs of the 'four thousand' scientific workers to whom Mr Wells refers. We should scarcely have placed so many men in that category even before the war,[11] and the ranks of scientific forces in Russia must have been greatly reduced by the revolution.

Resulting Appeal: Baron Montagu of Beaulieu, Ernest Barker, Edward Cathcart, Arthur Eddington, Israel Gollancz, Richard Gregory, Peter Chalmers Mitchell, Bernard Pares, Arthur Schuster, Charles Sherrington, Arthur Shipley, H. G. Wells, Arthur Smith Woodward and Charles Hagberg Wright, letter to the editor, 'The British Committee for Aiding Men of Letters and Science in Russia' (6 January 1921).[12]

We have recently been able to get some direct communication from men of science and men of letters in North Russia. There condition is one of great privation and limitation. They share in the consequences of the almost complete economic exhaustion of Russia;[13] like most people in that country, they are ill-clad, underfed, and short of such physical essentials as make life tolerable.

Nevertheless, a certain amount of scientific research and some literary work still go on. The Bolsheviks were at first regardless, and even in some cases hostile, to these intellectual workers, but the Bolshevik Government has apparently come to realise something of the importance of scientific and literary work to the community, and the remnant – for deaths among them have been very numerous – of these people, the flower of the mental life of Russia, has now been gathered together into special rationing organisations which ensure at least the bare necessities of life for them.

These organisations have their headquarters in two buildings known as the House of Science and the House of Literature and Art. Under the former we note such great names as those of Pavlov the physiologist and Nobel prizeman,[14] Karpinsky the geologist, Borodin the botanist, Belopolsky the astronomer, Tagantzev the criminologist, Oldenburg the Orientalist and permanent secretary of the

---

11   I. e., the Great War.

12   Reprinted by permission from Macmillan Publishers Ltd: *Nature* (106: 2671), copyright (1921).

13   Russia's economy and society were near collapse at this time due to the ongoing civil war, the Polish-Soviet War (1919-21) and the war of allied intervention waged against Russia by Britain, France, Japan and the USA (1918-20).

14   Ivan Pavlov won the Nobel Prize in Physiology or Medicine in 1904.

Petersburg Academy of Science,[15] Koni, Bechterev, Latishev, Morozov, and many others familiar to the scientific world.

Several of these scientific men have been interviewed and affairs been discussed with them, particularly as to whether anything could be done to help them. There were many matters in which it would be possible to assist them, but upon one in particular they laid stress. There thought and work are greatly impeded by the fact that they have seen practically no European books or publications since the Revolution.[16] This is an inconvenience amounting to real intellectual distress. In the hope that this condition may be relieved by an appeal to British scientific workers, Prof. Oldenburg formed a small committee and made a comprehensive list of books and publications needed by the intellectual community in Russia if it is to keep alive and abreast of the rest of the world.

It is, of course, necessary to be assured that any aid of this kind provided for literary and scientific men in Russia would reach its destination. The Bolshevik Government in Moscow, the Russian trade delegations in Reval and London, and our own authorities have therefore been consulted, and it would appear that there will be no obstacles to the transmission of this needed material to the House of Science and the House of Literature and Art. It can be got through by special facilities even under present conditions. Many of the publications named in Prof. Oldenburg's list will have to be bought, the cost of transmission will be considerable, and accordingly the undersigned have formed themselves into a small committee for the collection and administration of a fund for the supply of scientific and literary publications, and possibly, if the amount subscribed permits of it, of other necessities, to these Russian *savants*[17] and men of letters.[18]

We hope to work in close association with the Royal Society and other leading learned societies[19] in this matter. The British Science Guild[20] has kindly granted the committee permission to use its address.

We appeal for subscriptions, and ask that cheques should be made out to the Treasurer, C. Hagberg Wright, LLD, and sent to the British Committee for

---

15 Properly, the Russian Academy of Sciences, founded in 1724 and renamed the Academy of Sciences of the USSR in 1925 and relocated to Moscow in 1934 before reverting to its original name in 1991. It is Russia's pre-eminent national science institution.

16 I. e., the Bolshevik Revolution of October 1917 during which Russia became a Communist state.

17 Learned persons.

18 Scholars.

19 Intellectual societies, often academic, for the pursuit of one of many fields of knowledge.

20 An organisation for the promotion of science, founded in 1903 and merged with the British Association in 1936.

Aiding Men of Letters and Science in Russia,[21] British Science Guild Offices, 6 John Street, Adelphi, London, W. C. 2.

Follow-up Appeal: Leonard Schuster, letter to the editor, 'Literature for Men of Letters and Science in Russia' (3 February 1921).[22]

At the beginning of this year an appeal was issued for funds to enable a certain number of scientific and literary publications to be sent to the House of Science and the House of Literature in Petersburg, where the remnant of the intellectual life of Russia is mostly congregated. The British Committee for Aiding Men of Letters and Science in that country has assured itself that such publications will reach their destination, and has made arrangements for their transmission. There are probably many authors who would be willing to send copies of their works in the form of excerpts or otherwise to Russian workers who have been cut off from the outside world since the revolution. The British Committee will be glad to receive any such books or papers of a non-political type and to send them to Petersburg. It cannot guarantee delivery to individuals, but it can ensure that publications will reach the Houses of Literature and Science. Parcels for transmission should be addressed to the above Committee, care of Messrs Wm. Dawson and Sons, Ltd., Continental Department, Rolls Buildings, Fetter Lane, E. C. 4.

---

21 An organisation founded in 1921, following Wells's visit to Soviet Russia the previous year, to raise funds and purchase books and resources for shipment to Russian scholars.

22 Reprinted by permission from Macmillan Publishers Ltd: *Nature* (106: 2675), copyright (1921).

1.9: 'Scientific Neglect of the Mas d'Azil'

H. G. Wells, letter to the editor, 'Scientific Neglect of the Mas d'Azil' (14 August 1926).[1]

The other day in the course of an automobile tour I visited the Mas d'Azil.[2] I would like to direct the attention of the readers of *Nature*, and particularly of those with money and organising power, to the very unsatisfactory state of affairs in this beautiful and incomparable treasure-house of archaeological material. Practically there is no control, no protection and no organised excavation whatever at Mas d'Azil. There are masses of valuable material, but none of it is being worked at properly. Much of it, I fear, is being wasted and muddled up. There is a 'guide,' a pleasant untrained man, who pokes about in the caves, digs out bones which, as he remarks, fall to pieces, and presents the casual visitor with teeth or flint implements he has found in his own researches. He has no regular salary. He has to supplement his fees and tips by other work. Occasionally, isolated individuals obtain permission from the municipality[3] and prod in the rocks and extract this or that and publish their 'results' according to their lights. There is a small useless museum[4] without labels or arrangement at the *Mairie*.[5] The financial situation forbids the hope of Government direction. The essential trouble seems to be the want of funds. From Mas d'Azil came some of the most beautiful and interesting objects in the admirably arranged museum in Toulouse;[6] the carved horse head[7] and other carvings and the painted pebbles[8] from this site are well known. One would not need to go outside the scientific ability available in the region if money were forthcoming to mobilise it for the proper exploitation of these priceless deposits.

---

1   Reprinted by permission from Macmillan Publishers Ltd: *Nature* (118: 2963), copyright (1926). This letter has previously been reprinted in Smith 1998, III: 216-17.

2   A location in the French Pyrénées containing a rich heritage of Azilian artefacts, especially in the eponymous cave.

3   The governing body of a town, city or district, in this case the *Commune Le Mas d'Azil*.

4   A reference to the *Musée du Mas d'Azil* (now called the *Musée de la Préhistoire* and informally known as the *Musée Ladevèze* in former times) which is housed on the second floor of the town hall in Mas d'Azil.

5   French, town hall.

6   *Muséum de Toulouse*, France, founded in 1865.

7   This is a reference to a horse's head carved from reindeer antler and discovered in the Mas d'Azil by Édouard Piette in 1887, now housed in the *Musée des Antiquités Nationales* near Paris.

8   A distinctive Palaeolithic art form of southern France, the pebbles of the Mas d'Azil were first discovered by Piette in 1889.

Reply to Wells: Henri Breuil, letter to the editor, 'Scientific Neglect of the Mas d'Azil'[9] (21 August 1926).[10]

The derelict state of Mas d'Azil cave, which renowned writer Mr Wells has reported, is real and most unfortunate, although the consequences are probably not as serious as he may think. Mas d'Azil belongs to the State but the municipality has used it from time immemorial. The roadman in charge of the maintenance of the secondary road that runs across it, is also the official warden; he is the one who takes you to the dark galleries, more interesting indeed for their picturesque atmosphere than for prehistoric science, although some rare drawings can be seen on the walls, and here and there, a few tiny remnants of human activity. On the right bank, the main site was the *Salle du Foyer*[11] with its lower gallery. The *Salle du Foyer* was completely excavated a long time ago by Piette, Ladevèze, Maury etc., and lastly (1901-1902) by myself. I doubt that it currently contains anything but rubble from these excavations, except in its lower gallery which

---

9   This letter originally appeared in *Nature* in French thus:

L'état d'abandon que l'illustre écrivain M. Wells signale pour la caverne du Mas d'Azil est réel et fort regrettable, bien que les conséquences en soient probablement moins graves qu'il ne pense. Elle appartient à l'état, mais la commune en a l'usage de temps immémorial. Le cantonnier chargé de l'entretien de la route départementale qui la traverse en est le gardien officiel; c'est lui qui fait visiter les galeries obscures, plus intéressantes que pour la science préhistorique, bien que de rares dessins pariétaux s'y rencontrent, et, deci-delà, quelques menus vestiges de fréquentation humaine. Sur la rive droite, le point important était la salle du Foyer et sa galerie inférieur. La salle du Foyer a été fouillée depuis longtemps dans sa totalité par Piette, Ladevèze, Maury, etc., et en dernier lieu (1901-1902) par moi-même. Je doute qu'elle contienne actuellement autre chose que les déblais de ces fouilles, sauf son couloir inférieur, où existent quelques peintures étudiées par le Comte Bégouën et moi. Les couches archéologiques peu épaisses qui y subsistent vers le fond sont sans doute l'objet des grattages don't M. Wells nous entretient. Plus grave est le bouleversement réalisé l'année dernière dans cette région de la grotte par la municipalité pour y installer un théâtre. Mais je ne crois pas que les lieux de la caverne contenant encore du gisement, placés sur l'autre rive, aient été touchés récemment: une épaisse couche de pierrailles et de terre poudreuse les défend bien.

Reprinted by permission from Macmillan Publishers Ltd: *Nature* (118: 2964), copyright (1926).

10   Translated by permission from Macmillan Publishers Ltd: *Nature* (118: 2964), copyright (1926).

11   French, the main living space in the excavation.

contains some paintings studied by Count Bégouën and me. The sector of thin archaeological layers remaining at the bottom is probably the place subject to the scrapings Mr Wells tells us about. More serious is the disruption caused by the municipality last year in the area of the cave, to build a theatre. But I do not believe that the part of the cave located on the opposite bank and which still contains material, was recently tampered with – protected as it is by a thick layer of loose stones and powder earth.

1.10: 'The Idea of a World Encyclopaedia'

H. G. Wells, 'The Idea of a World Encyclopaedia' (28 November 1936)[*][1]

Most of the lectures that are given in this place to this audience are delivered by men of very special knowledge. They come here to tell you something you did not know before. But to-night I doubt if I shall tell you anything that is not already quite familiar to you. I am here not to impart facts but to make certain suggestions; and there is no other audience in the world to which I would make these suggestions more willingly and more hopefully than I do to you.

My particular line of country has always been generalisation and synthesis. I dislike isolated events and disconnected details. I really hate statements, views, prejudices and beliefs that jump at you suddenly out of mid-air. I like my world as coherent and consistent as possible. So far at any rate my temperament is that of a scientific man. That is why I have spent a few score thousand hours of my particular allotment of vitality in making outlines of history,[2] short histories of the world,[3] general accounts of the science of life,[4] attempts to bring economic, financial and social life into one conspectus[5] and even, still more desperate, struggles to estimate the possible consequences of this or that set of operating causes upon the future of mankind.[6]

All these attempts had profound and conspicuous faults and weaknesses; even my friends are apt to mention them with an apologetic smile. Presumptuous and preposterous they were, I admit, but I look back upon them, completely unabashed. Somebody had to break the ice. Somebody had to try out such summaries on the general mind. My reply to the superior critic has always been – forgive me – 'Damn you, do it better'.

The least satisfactory thing about these experiments of mine, so far as I am concerned, is that they did not at once provoke the learned and competent to produce superior substitutes. And in view of the number of able and disting-

---

*   'Friday Evening Discourse delivered at the Royal Institution on November 20.' [Editor's note: Richard Gregory, in a letter of 22 November 1936, told Wells, vis-à-vis the speech, 'the vast audience showed what a large number of people look to you for inspiration and guidance' (quoted in MacKenzie and MacKenzie 1987, 403).]

1   Reprinted by permission from Macmillan Publishers Ltd: *Nature* (138: 3500), copyright (1936).

2   A reference to Wells's *The Outline of History* (1920).

3   A reference to Wells's *A Short History of the World* (1922).

4   A reference to *The Science of Life* (1930) by H. G. Wells, Julian Huxley and G. P. Wells.

5   A reference to Wells's *The Work, Wealth and Happiness of Mankind* (1931).

6   This is probably a reference to Wells's *The Shape of Things to Come* (1933), a fictional account of the future to 2104.

uished people we have in the world professing and teaching economic, sociological, financial science, and the admittedly unsatisfactory nature of the world's financial, economic and political affairs, it is to me an immensely disconcerting fact that the *Work, Wealth and Happiness of Mankind* which was first published in 1932[7] remains – practically uncriticized, unstudied and largely unread – the only attempt to bring human ecology[8] into one correlated survey.

Well; I mention this experimental work now in order that you should not think I am throwing casually formed ideas before you to-night. I am bringing you my very best. The thoughts I am setting out here have troubled my mind, for years, and my ideas have been slowly gathering definition throughout these experiments and experiences. They have interwoven more and more intimately with other solicitudes of a more general nature in which I feel fairly certain of meeting your understanding and sympathy.

I doubt if there is anybody here to-night who has not given a certain amount of anxious thought to the conspicuous ineffectiveness of modern knowledge and – how shall I call it? – trained and studied thought in contemporary affairs. I think that it is mainly in the troubled years since 1914 that the world of cultivated, learned and scientific people, of which you are so representative, has become conscious of this ineffectiveness. Before that time, or to be more precise before 1909 or 1910,[9] the world, our world, our world as we older ones recall it, was living in a state of confidence, of established values, of assured security, which is already becoming now almost incredible. We had no suspicion then how much that apparent security had been undermined by science, invention and sceptical inquiry. Most of us carried on into the War[10] and even right through the War under the inertia of the accepted beliefs to which we had been born. We felt that the sort of history we were used to was still going on, and we did not realise at all that the War was a new sort of thing, not like the old wars, that the old traditions of strategy were disastrously out of date and that the old pattern of settling up after a war could only lead to such a thickening tangle of evil consequences as we contemplate to-day.

We know better now. Wiser after the events as we all are, few of us now fail to appreciate the stupendous ignorance, the almost total lack of grasp of so-

---

7   The British edition of the book was first published in 1932, though it appeared a year earlier in the USA.

8   The branch of knowledge that deals with the interaction of humans with their environment. The expression was coined by Wells in *The Shape of Things to Come*.

9   Wells's specific reference is unclear here, but such events as Austria-Hungary's annexation of Bosnia-Herzegovina, with its resulting antagonism of Serbia, and the first powered flight across the English Channel by Louis Blériot, both occurring in 1909, could be portents of the changed international situation which Wells had in mind.

10   I. e., the Great War.

cial and economic realities, the short views, the shallowness of mind, that characterised the treaty-making of 1919 and 1920.[11] I suppose Mr Maynard Keynes was one of the first to open our eyes to this world-wide intellectual insufficiency. What his book, *The Economic Consequences of the Peace*, practically said to the world was this: These people, these politicians, these statesmen, these directive people who are in authority over us, know scarcely anything about the business they have in hand. Nobody knows very much, but the important thing to realise is that they do not even know what is to be known. They arrange so and so, and so and so must ensue and they cannot or will not see that so and so will ensue. They are so unaccustomed to competent thought, so ignorant that there is knowledge and of what knowledge is, that they do not understand that it matters.

The same terrifying sense of insufficient mental equipment was dawning upon some of us who watched the birth of the League of Nations.[12] Reluctantly and with something like horror, we realised that these people who were, they imagined, turning over a new page and beginning a fresh chapter in human history, knew collectively scarcely anything about the formative forces of history. Collectively, I say. Altogether they had a very considerable amount of knowledge, uncoordinated bits of quite good knowledge, some about this period and some about that, but they had no common understanding whatever of the processes in which they were obliged to mingle and interfere. Possibly all the knowledge and all the directive ideas needed to establish a wise and stable settlement of the world's affairs in 1919 existed in bits and fragments, here and there, but practically nothing had been assembled, practically nothing had been thought out, nothing practically had been done to draw that knowledge and these ideas together into a comprehensive conception of the world. I put it to you that the Peace Conference at Versailles did not use anything but a very small fraction of the political and economic wisdom that already existed in human brains at that time; and I put it to you as rational creatures that if usage had not dulled our apprehension to this state of affairs, we should regard this as fantastically absurd.

If I might attempt a sweeping generalisation about the general course of human history in the eighteen years that have followed the War, I believe I should have you with me if I described it as a series of flounderings, violent ill-

---

11   A reference to the following peace treaties drawn up by Britain, France, the USA and their allies at the Conference of Paris which brought the Great War to an end: the Treaty of Versailles with Germany (28 June 1919), the Treaty of Saint-Germain with Austria (10 September 1919), the Treaty of Neuilly with Bulgaria (27 November 1919), the Treaty of Trianon with Hungary (4 June 1920) and the Treaty of Sèvres with Turkey (10 August 1920).

12   An international organisation (1920-46) established for the purpose of collective security and disarmament after the Great War.

directed mass-movements, slack drifting here and convulsive action there. We talk about the dignity of history.[13] It is a bookish phrase for which I have the extremest disrespect. There is no dignity yet in human history. It would be pure comedy, if it were not so often tragic, so frequently dismal, generally dishonourable and occasionally quite horrible; and it is so largely tragic because the human animal really is intelligent, can feel finely and acutely, expresses itself poignantly in art, music and literature, and – this is what I am driving at – impotently knows better.

Consider only the case of America during this recent period. America, when all is said and done, is one of the most intelligently *aware* communities in the world. Quite a number of people over there seem almost to know what is happening to them. Remember first the phase of fatuous self-sufficiency, the period of unprecedented prosperity, the boom, the crisis, the slump and the dismay.[14] And then appeared the new President, Franklin Roosevelt, and from the point of view of the present discussion he is one of the most interesting figures in all history. Because he really did make an appeal for such knowledge and understanding as existed to come to his aid.[15] America in an astounding state of meekness was ready to be told and shown. There were the universities, great schools, galaxies of authorities, learned men, experts, teachers, doctors, professors, gowned, adorned and splendid. Out of this knowledge mass there has since come many very trenchant criticisms of the President's mistakes. But at the time this – what shall I call it – this higher brain, these cerebrum,[16] this grey matter[17] of America was so entirely uncoordinated that it had nothing really comprehensive, searching, thought-out and trustworthy for him to go upon. The President had to experiment and attempt this and that, he turned from one promising adviser to another, because there was nothing ready for him. He did not pretend to be a divinity. He was a politician – of exceptional good-will. He was none of your dictator gods.[18] He showed himself extremely open and receptive for the organised information and guidance … *that wasn't there*. And it isn't there now.

---

13   The recitation of events with truth and accuracy; the consideration of history as the self-consciousness of humanity.

14   A reference to American history from the 1880s to the 1930s when that country's prosperity soared rapidly before plunging into extreme economic depression with the Wall Street Crash of 1929.

15   This is a reference to Roosevelt's 'Brain Trust', the diverse group of economists, academics and others who served as advisors during his early presidency.

16   The larger, anterior part of the brain, responsible for voluntary activity and mental processes.

17   Intelligence, brains.

18   A sarcastic reference to the contemporary dictators which were then in power nurturing cults of personality, such as Benito Mussolini, Adolf Hitler and Joseph Stalin.

Some years ago there was a considerable fuss in the world about preparedness and unpreparedness. Most of that clamour concerned the possibility of war. But here was a case of most fantastic unpreparedness on the part of hundreds of eminent men, who were supposed to have studied them, for the normal development of a community in times of peace. There had been no attempt to assemble that mechanism of knowledge of which America stood in need.

I repeat that if usage had not dulled us into a habit of acquiescence with this sort of thing we should think our species collectively insane to go about its business in this haphazard, planless, negligent fashion.

I think I have said enough to recall to anyone here who may have lapsed from the keen apprehension of his first realisation, of this wide gap between what I may call the at present unassembled and unexploited best thought and knowledge in the world and the ideas and acts not simply of the masses of common people, but of those who direct public affairs, the dictators,[19] the leaders, the politicians, the newspaper directors, and our spiritual guides and teachers. We live in a world of unused and misapplied knowledge and skill. That is my case. Knowledge and thought are ineffective. The human species regarded as a whole is extraordinarily like a man of the highest order of brain, who through some lesions[20] or defects or insufficiencies of his lower centres, suffers from the wildest uncoordinations, St Vitus's dance,[21] agraphia,[22] aphonia,[23] and suffers dreadfully (knowing better all the time) from the silly and disastrous gestures he makes and the foolish things he says and does.

I don't think this has ever been so evident as it is now. I doubt if in the past the gap was so wide as it is now between the occasions that confront us, and the knowledge we have assembled to meet them. But because of a certain run of luck in the late nineteenth century,[24] the existence of that widening gap and the menace of that widening gap were not thrust upon our attention as they have been since the War.

At first that realisation of the ineffectiveness of our best thought and knowledge struck only a few people, Mr Maynard Keynes for example, who were in what I may call salient positions, but gradually I have noted the realisa-

---

19   Rulers possessing absolute authority.

20   Injuries or harm.

21   Properly, Sydenham's chorea, a disease characterised by rapid uncoordinated jerking movements affecting primarily the face, feet and hands.

22   The inability to write as a symptom of cerebral disease or damage.

23   The loss or absence of voice through a defect in the vocal organs.

24   This is a reference to the period of European peace between 1877 and 1914 during which, Wells seems to suggest, the ruling classes forget the dislocating impact caused by wars between the great powers.

tion spreading and growing. It takes various forms. Prominent men of science speak more and more frequently of the responsibility of science for the disorder of the world. And if you are familiar with that most admirable of all newspapers, *Nature*, and if you care to turn over the files of that very representative weekly for the past quarter of a century or so and sample the articles, you will observe a very remarkable change of note and scope in what it has to say to its readers. Time was when *Nature* was almost pedantically[25] special and scientific. Its detachment from politics and general affairs was complete. But latterly the concussions of the social earthquake[26] and the vibration of the guns[27] have become increasingly perceptible in the laboratories. *Nature* from being specialist has become world-conscious, so that now it is almost haunted week by week by the question: 'What are we to do before it is too late, to make what we know and our way of thinking effective in world affairs?'

In that I think it is expressing a change which is happening in the minds of – if I may presume to class myself with you – nearly all people of the sort which fills this theatre to-night.

And consider again the topics that have been dealt with at the latest gathering of the British Association.[28] The very title of the presidential address: 'The Impact of Science upon Society'![29] Sir Josiah Stamp, as you will remember, stressed the need of extending endowment and multiplying workers in the social sciences. Professor Philip dealt with 'The Training of the Chemist for the Service of the Community'.[30] Professor Cramp talked of 'The Engineer and the Nation',[31] and there was an important discussion of 'The Cultural and Social Values of Science'[32] in which Sir Richard Gregory, Professor Hogben and Sir Daniel Hall[33] said some memorable things. There can be no doubt of the reality

---

25 In the manner of one concerned with trifling details or insisting on strict adherence to formal rules or literal meaning.

26 A reference to the social dislocation across Europe and the USA during the interwar period, especially with the onset of the World Depression.

27 A reference to the return of conflict in the world, with Japan's attack on China (1931), Italy's conquest of Abyssinia (1935) and the outbreak of civil war in Spain (1936-39).

28 In 1936, the British Association met in Blackpool.

29 On his presidential address, Stamp argued for 'The replacement of the present socially irresponsible financial control by socially responsible planning bodies'.

30 J. C. Philip gave the presidential address to the Chemistry Section of the British Association.

31 William Cramp's address to the British Association.

32 A panel discussion at the British Association featuring Richard Gregory, Lancelot Hogben and A. D. Hall.

33 I. e., A. D. Hall.

of this awakening of the scientific worker to the necessity of his becoming a definitely *organised* factor in the social scheme of the years before us.

Well, so far I have been merely opening up my subject and stating the problem for consideration. We want the intellectual worker to become a more definitely organised factor in the human scheme. How is that factor to be organised? Is there any way of implementing knowledge for ready and universal effect? I ask you to examine the question whether this great and growing gap between special knowledge and thought and the common ideas and motives of mankind can be bridged, and if so how it can be bridged.

Can scientific knowledge and specialised thought be brought into more effective relation to general affairs? Let us consider first what is actually going on. I find among my scientific and specialist friends a certain disposition – and I think it is a mistaken disposition – for direct political action and special political representation. The scientific and literary workers of the days when I was a young man were either indifferent or conservative in politics; nowadays quite a large proportion of them are inclined to active participation in extremist movements; many are leftish[34] and revolutionary, some accept the strange pseudo-scientific dogmas of the communist party[35] though that does no credit to their critical training, and even those who are not out on the left are restless for some way of intervening, definitely as a class, in the general happenings of the community. Their ideas of possible action vary from important-looking signed pronouncements and protests to a sort of strike[36] against war, the withholding of services and the refusal to assist in technical developments that may be misapplied. Some favour the idea of a gradual supersession of the political forms and methods of mass democracy by government through some sort of *élite* in which the man of science and the technician will play a dominating part.[37] There are very large vague patches upon this idea but the general projection is in the form of a modern priesthood, an oligarchy[38] of professors and exceptionally competent people.

---

34   Being sympathetic to radical, reforming or socialist views.

35   A political party established in most countries of the world between 1917 and the early 1920s following the success of the Bolshevik revolution in Russia which aimed to overthrow capitalism and create Marxist communist states. With the collapse of the Soviet Union in 1991, most parties were dissolved or liberalised.

36   An organised refusal to work by employees, or to cooperate in civil society generally by protesters.

37   This is a reference to the technocracy movement, founded in the USA in 1933 (though with antecedents in the nineteenth century), which advocates a form of society where human welfare is optimised by means of scientific analysis and the use of technology.

38   Government by a small group of people.

Like Plato they would make the philosopher king.[39] This project involves certain assumptions about the general quality and superiority of the intellectual worker that I am afraid will not stand scrutiny.

I submit that sort of thing – political activities, party intervention and dreams of an authoritative *élite* – is not the way in which specialists, artists and specialised thinkers and workers who constitute the vital feeling and understanding of the body politic can be brought into a conscious, effective, guiding and directive relationship to the control of human affairs. Because – I hope you will acquit me of any disrespect for science and philosophy when I say this – we have to face the fact that from the point of view of general living, men of science, artists, philosophers, specialised intelligences of any sort, do not constitute an *élite* that can be mobilised for collective action. They are an extraordinarily miscellaneous assembly, and their most remarkable common quality is the quality of concentration in comparative retirement – each along his own line. They have none of the solidarity, the customary *savoir faire*,[40] the habits arising out of practices, activities and interests in common, that lawyers, doctors or any of the really socially organised professions for example display. A professor-ridden world might prove as unsatisfactory under the stress of modern life and fluctuating conditions as a theologian-ridden world.

A distinguished specialist is precious because of his cultivated gift. It does not follow at all that by the standards of all-round necessity he is a superior person. Indeed by the very fact of his specialisation he may be less practised and competent than the average man. He probably does not read his newspaper so earnestly, he finds much of the common round a bother and a distraction and he puts it out of his mind. I think we should get the very gist of this problem if we could compare twelve very miscellaneous men of science and special skill, with twelve unspecialised men taken – let us say – from the head clerk's morning train to the city. We should probably find that for commonplace teamwork and the ordinary demands and sudden urgencies of life, the second dozen was individually quite as good as if not better than the first dozen. In a burning hotel or cast away on a desert island they would probably do quite as well. Yet collectively they would be ill-informed and limited men; the whole dozen of them would have nothing much more to tell you than any one of them. On the other hand, our dozen specialists would each have something distinctive to tell you. The former group would be almost as uniform in their knowledge and ability as tiles on a roof, the latter would be like pieces from a complicated jig-saw puzzle. The more you got them together the more they would signify. Twelve clerks or a hundred clerks; it wouldn't matter; you would get nothing but dull repetitions,

---

39   A member of an elite whose knowledge enables them to rule justly, as first portrayed in Plato's *Republic* (360 BC).

40   French, know-how.

and a flat acquiescent suggestible outlook upon life. But every specialised man we added would be adding something to the directive pattern of life. I think that consideration takes us a step further in defining our problem to-night.

It is *science* and not *men of science* that we want to enlighten and animate our politics and rule the world.

Now I will take rather a stride forward in my argument. I will introduce a phrase, *New Encyclopaedism*, which I shall spend most of the rest of my time defining. I want to suggest that something – a new social organ, a new institution, which for a time I shall call *World Encyclopaedia*[41] is the means whereby we can solve the problem of that jig-saw puzzle and bring all the scattered and ineffective mental wealth of our world into something like a common understanding and into effective reaction upon our vulgar everyday political, social and economic life. I warn you that I am flinging moderation to the winds in the suggestions I am about to put before you. They are immense suggestions. I am sketching what is really a scheme for the reorganisation and reorientation of education and information throughout the world. No less. We are so accustomed to the existing schools, colleges, universities, research organisations of the world; they have so moulded and made us and trained us from our earliest years to respect and believe in them; that it is with a real feeling of temerity, of alma-matricidal[42] impiety, so to speak, that I have allowed my mind to explore their merits and question whether they were not now altogether an extraordinarily loose, weak and out-of-date miscellany. Yet I do not see how we can admit, and I am disposed to think you have admitted with me, the existence of this terrifying gap between available knowledge and current social and political events, and not go on to something like an indictment of this whole great world of academic erudition, training and instruction from China to Peru – an indictment for, at least, inadequacy and uncoordination if not for actual negligence. It may be only a temporary inadequacy, a pause in development before renascence, but inadequate altogether they are. Universities have multiplied greatly, yes, but they have failed to participate in the general advance in power, scope and efficiency that has occurred in the past century. In transport we have progressed from coaches and horses by way of trains to electric traction, motor-cars and aeroplanes. In mental organisation we have, so to speak, simply multiplied our coaches and horses and livery stables.

---

41   A resource, first suggested by Wells in *The Work, Wealth and Happiness of Mankind* (1931), which would form the basis of his 'world brain', creating and spreading a world culture to maintain global peace and mutual understanding.

42   This is Wells's coin to mean murderous intent towards one's former university (Alma Mater), or academia in general.

Let me now try to picture for you this missing element in the modern human social mechanism, this needed connection between the percipient and informative parts and the power organisation for which I am using this phrase, World Encyclopaedia. And I will take it first from the point of view of the ordinary educated citizen – for in a completely modernised state every ordinary citizen will be an educated citizen. I will ask you to imagine how this World Encyclopaedic organisation would enter into his life and how it would affect him. From his point of view the World Encyclopaedia would be a row of volumes in his own home or in some neighbouring house or in a convenient public library or in any school or college, and in this row of volumes he would, without any great toil or difficulty, find in clear understandable language, and kept up to date, the ruling concepts of our social order, the outlines and main particulars in all fields of knowledge, an exact and reasonably detailed picture of our universe,[43] a general history of the world, and if by any chance he wanted to pursue a question into its ultimate detail, a trustworthy and complete system of reference to primary sources of knowledge. In fields where wide varieties of method and opinion existed, he would find, not casual summaries of opinions, but very carefully chosen and correlated statements and arguments. I do not imagine the major subjects being dealt with in special articles rather hastily written, such as has been the tradition of encyclopaedias since the days of Diderot's heroic effort. Our present circumstances are altogether different from his. Nowadays there is an immense literature of statement and explanation scattered through tens of thousands of books, pamphlets and papers, and it is not necessary, it is undesirable, to trust to such hurried summaries as the old tradition was obliged to make for its use. The day when an energetic journalist could gather together a few star contributors and a miscellany of compilers of very uneven quality to scribble special articles for him, articles often tainted with propaganda and advertisement, and call it an encyclopaedia, is past. The modern World Encyclopaedia should consist of selections, extracts, quotations, very carefully assembled with the approval of outstanding authorities in each subject, carefully collated and edited and critically presented. It would be not a miscellany, but a concentration, a clarification and a synthesis.

This World Encyclopaedia should be the mental background of every intelligent man in the world. It should be alive and growing and changing continually under revision, extension and replacement from the original thinkers in the world everywhere. Every university and research institution should be feeding it. Every fresh mind should be brought into contact with its standing editorial organisation. On the other hand its contents would be the standard source of material for the instructional side of school and college work, for the verification of facts and the testing of statements – everywhere in the world. Even journalists

---

43   All existing matter, space and other phenomena regarded collectively.

would deign to use it; even newspaper proprietors might be made to respect it. Such an encyclopaedia would play the role of an undogmatic Bible to a world culture.[44] It would do just what our scattered and disoriented intellectual organisations of to-day fall short of doing. It would hold the world together mentally.

It may be objected that this is a Utopian[45] dream. This is something too great to achieve, too good to be true. I won't deal with that for a few minutes. Flying was a Utopian dream, a third of a century ago. What I am putting before you is a perfectly sane, sound and practical proposal. But first I will notice briefly two objections – obstructions rather than objections – that one will certainly encounter at this point.

One of these is not likely to appear in any great force in this gathering. You have all heard and you have all probably been irritated or bored by the assertion that no two people think alike *'quot homines, tot sententiae'*,[46] that science is always contradicting itself, that economists like theologians can never agree. It is largely mental laziness on the defensive that makes people say this kind of thing. They don't want their intimate convictions turned over and examined, and it is unfortunate that the emphasis put upon minor differences by men of science, and belief in their strenuous search for the completest truth and the exactest expression sometimes give colour to this sort of misunderstanding. But I am inclined to think that most people overrate the apparent differences in the world of opinion to-day. Even in theology a psychological analysis reduces many flat contradictions to differences in terminology. My impression is that human brains are very much of a pattern, that under the same conditions they react in the same way, and that were it not for tradition, upbringing, accidents of circumstance and particularly of accidental individual obsessions, we should find ourselves – since we all face the same universe – much more in agreement than is superficially apparent. We speak different languages and dialects of thought and can even at times catch ourselves flatly contradicting each other in words while we are doing our utmost to express the same idea. And self love and personal vanity are not excluded from the intellectual life. How often do we see men misrepresenting each other in order to exaggerate a difference and secure the gratification of an argumentative victory! A World Encyclopaedia as I conceive it would bring together into close juxtaposition and under critical scrutiny many apparently conflicting systems of statement. It might act not merely as an assembly of fact and statement, but as an organ of adjustment and adjudication,

---

44   An artificial culture based on humanistic principles such as reason and education and developed through concerted effort, aimed at appealing to and embracing all the peoples of the world.

45   Ideal or visionary, but often considered impractical.

46   Latin, a quotation from *Phormio* by Terence, meaning 'there are as many opinions as there are men'.

a clearing house[47] of misunderstandings; it would be deliberately a synthesis, and so act as a flux and a filter for a very great quantity of human misapprehension. It would *compel* men to come to terms with one another. I think it would relegate '*quot homines, tot sententioe*' back to the Latin comedy from which it emerged.

The second type of obstruction that this idea of a World Encyclopaedia will encounter is even less likely to find many representatives in the present gathering and I will give it only the briefest of attention. (You know that kind of neuralgic[48] expression, the high protesting voice, the fluttering gesture of the hands.) 'But you want to *stereotype* people. What a dreadful, dreadful world it will be when everybody thinks alike' – and so they go on. Most of these elegant people who want the world picturesquely at sixes and sevens[49] are hopeless cases, but for the milder instances it may be worth while remarking that it really does not enhance the natural variety and beauty of life to have all the clocks in a town keeping individual times of their own, no charts of the sea, no time-tables, but trains starting secretly to unspecified destinations, infectious diseases without notification and postmen calling occasionally when they can get by the picturesque footpads[50] at the corner. I like order in the place of vermin, I prefer a garden to a swamp and the whole various world to a hole-and-corner[51] life in some obscure community, and to-night I like to imagine I am making my appeal to hearers of a kindred disposition to my own.

Next let us take this World Encyclopaedia from the point of view of the specialist and the super-intellectual.[52] To him even more than to the common intelligent man World Encyclopaedia is going to be of value because it is going to afford him an intelligible statement of what is being done by workers parallel with himself. Further, it will be giving him the general statement of his own subject that is being made to the world at large. He can watch that closely. On the assumption that the World Encyclopaedia is based on a world-wide organisation he will be – if he is a worker of any standing – a corresponding associate of the Encyclopaedia organisation. He will be able to criticise the presentation of his subject, to suggest amendments and restatements. For a World Encyclopaedia that was kept alive and up to date by the frequent re-issue of its volumes, could be made the basis of much fundamental discussion and controversy. It might

---

47   An agency for collecting and distributing information generally.

48   Of an intense burning or stabbing pain, typically along the line of a nerve, and especially in the face.

49   In a state of confusion or disarray.

50   Highway robbers operating on foot.

51   Secret, underhand.

52   A person of superior or supposedly superior intelligence.

116

breed swarms of pamphlets, and very wholesome swarms. It would give the specialist just that contact with the world at large which at present is merely caricatured by his more or less elementary class-teaching, amateurish examination work and college administration. In my dream of a World Encyclopaedia I have a feeling that part of the scheme would be the replacement of the latter group of professorial activities, the college business, tutoring, normal lecturing work and so on, by a new set of activities, the encyclopaedic work, the watching brief to prevent the corruption of the popular mind. In enlightening the general mind the specialist will broaden himself. He will be redeemed from oddity, from shy preciousness and practical futility.

Well, you begin to see the shape of this project; and you will realise that, except in so far as the nature of its reaction upon the world's affairs is concerned, it is far away from anything like the valiant enterprise of Denis Diderot and his associates a century and a half ago. That extraordinary adventure in intellectual synthesis makes this dream credible. That is our chief connection with it.

And here I have to make an incidental disavowal. I want to make it clear how little I have to do with what I am discussing. In order to get some talk going upon this idea of an Encyclopaedia, I have been circulating a short memorandum[53] upon the subject among a number of friends. I did not think to mark it *Private*, and unhappily one copy seems to have fallen into the hands of one of those minor pests of our time, a personal journalist, who at once rushed into print with the announcement that I was promising to *write* a brand new Encyclopaedia, all with my own little hand out of my own little head. At the age of seventy! Once a thing of this sort is started there is no stopping it – and I admit that announcement enables you to put me in my place in a pleasantly ridiculous light. But I think after what I have put before you now that you will acquit me of any such colossal ambition. I implore you not to let that touch of personal absurdity so difficult to avoid altogether belittle the greatness and urgency of the cause I am pleading. This Encyclopaedia I am thinking of is something in which manifestly I have neither the equipment nor the quality to play any but an infinitesimal part. I am asking for it in the role of a common intelligent man who needs it and understands the need for it, both for himself and his world. After that you can leave me out of it. It is just because in the past I *have* had some experience in the assembling of outlines of knowledge for popular use, that I realise, perhaps better than most people, the ineffectiveness of this sort of effort on the part of individuals or small groups. It is something that must be taken up – and taken up very widely and seriously – by the universities, the learned societies, the re-

---

53   This is a reference to Wells's 'Project for a Modern Encyclopaedia' (Smith 1998, IV: 52-56) which he circulated in late-1935 to over thirty close associates for their consideration.

sponsible educational organisations if it is to be brought into effective being. It is a super university I am thinking of, a world brain;[54] no less. It is nothing in the nature of a supplementary enterprise. It is a completion necessary to modernise the university idea.

That brings me to the last part of this speculation. Can such an Encyclopaedia as I have been suggesting to you, be a possible thing? How can it be set going? How can it be organised and paid for? I agree I have now to show it as a possible thing. For I am going to make the large assumption that you think that *if it is a possible thing* it is a desirable thing. How are we to set about it?

I think something in this way: To begin with we want a promotion organisation. We want, shall I call it, an Encyclopaedia Society to ask for an Encyclopaedia and to get as many people as possible asking for an Encyclopaedia. Directly that society asks for an Encyclopaedia it will probably have to resort to precautionary measures against any enterprising publisher who may see in that demand a chance for selling some sort of vamped-up[55] miscellany as the thing required, and who may even trust to the unworldliness of conspicuous learned men for some sort of countenance for his raid.

Next this society of promoters will have to survey the available material. For most of the material for a modern Encyclopaedia exists already – though in a state of impotent diffusion. In all the various departments with which an Encyclopaedia should deal, groups of authoritative men might be induced to prepare a comprehensive list of primary and leading books, articles, statements which taken together would give the best, clearest and most quintessential renderings of what is known and thought within their departments. This would make a sort of key bibliography to the thought and knowledge of the world. My friend Sir Richard Gregory has suggested that such a key bibliography for a World Encyclopaedia would in itself be a very worthwhile thing to evoke. I agree with him. I haven't an idea what we should get. I imagine something on the scale of ten or twenty thousand items. I don't know.

Possibly our Encyclopaedia Society would find that such a key bibliography was in itself a not unprofitable undertaking, but that is a comment by the way.

The next step on from this key bibliography would be the organisation of a general editorial board and of departmental boards dealing with separate fields of interest. These boards would be permanent bodies – for a World Encyclopaedia must have a perennial life. We should have to secure premises, engage a

---

54 An information system elaborated by Wells in *World Brain* (1938) through which all the people of the world would have practically instantaneous access to the world's knowledge.

55 Patched-up or refurbished.

118

literary staff and, with the constant co-operation of the departmental groups, set about the task of making our great synthesis and abstract. I must repeat that for the purposes of a World Encyclopaedia probably we would not want much original writing. If a thing has been stated clearly and compactly once for all, why paraphrase it or ask some inferior hand to restate it? Our job may be rather to secure the use of copyrights and induce leading exponents of this or that field of science or criticism to co-operate in the selection, condensation, expansion or simplification of what they have already said so well.

Now I will ask you to take another step forward and imagine our World Encyclopaedia has been assembled and digested and that the first edition is through the press. So far we shall have been spending money upon this great enterprise and receiving nothing; we shall have been spending capital, for which I have at present not accounted. I will merely say that I see no reason why the capital needed for these promotion activities should not be forthcoming. This is no gainful enterprise, but you have to remember that the values we should create would be far more stable than the ephemeral encyclopaedias representing sums round about a million pounds or so which have hitherto been the high-water mark of encyclopaedic enterprise. These were essentially book-selling enterprises made to exploit a demand. But this World Encyclopaedia as I conceive it, if only because it will have roped in the larger part of the original sources of exposition, discussion and information, will be in effect a world monopoly,[56] and it will be able to levy and distribute direct and indirect revenue, on the scale quite beyond the resources of any private publishing enterprise. I do not see that the financial aspects of this huge enterprise, big though the sums involved may be, present any insurmountable difficulties in the way of its realisation. The major difficulty will be to persuade the extremely various preoccupied, impatient and individualistic scholars, thinkers, scientific workers and merely distinguished but unavoidable men of whose participation its success depends, of its practicability, convenience and desirability.

So far as the promotion of it goes I am reasonably hopeful. Quite a few convinced, energetic and resourceful people could set this ball rolling[57] towards realisation. To begin with, it is not necessary to convert the whole world of learning, research and teaching. I see no reason why at any stage it should encounter much positive opposition. Negative opposition – the refusal to have anything to do with it and so forth – can be worn down by persistence and the gathering promise of success. A World Encyclopaedia has not to fight adversaries or win majorities before it gets going; and once this ball is fairly set rolling it will be fairly hard to stop. A great danger, as I have already suggested, will come

---

56   Exclusive possession, control or exercise of something.

57   Begin an activity.

from attempts at the private mercenary exploitation of this world-wide need – the raids of popular publishers and heavily financed salesmen, and in particular attempts to create copyright difficulties and so to corner the services and prestige of this or that unwary eminent person by anticipatory agreements. *Vis-à-vis*[58] with salesmanship the man of science, the man of the intellectual *élite*, is apt to show himself a very Simple Simon[59] indeed. And of course from the very start, various opinionated cults and propagandas will be doing their best to capture or buy the movement. Well, it mustn't be captured or bought, and in particular its silence must not be bought or captured. That danger may in the end prove to be a stimulus. It may be possible in some cases to digest and assimilate special cults to their own and the general advantage.

There will also be a constant danger that some of the early promoters may feel and attempt to realise a sort of proprietorship in the organisation, to make a group or a gang of it. But to recognise that danger is half way to averting it.

I have said nothing so far about the language in which the Encyclopaedia should appear. It is a question I have not worked out. But I think that the main text should be in one single language, from which translations in whole or part could be made. Catholic Christianity[60] during the years of its greatest influence[61] was held together by Latin, and I do not think that I am giving way to any patriotic bias when I suggest that unless we contemplate a polyglot[62] publication – and never yet have I heard of a successful polyglot publication – *English*, because it has a wider range than German, a greater abundance and greater subtlety of expression than French and more precision than Russian, is the language in which the original text of a World Encyclopaedia ought to stand. Moreover, it is in the English-speaking communities that such an enterprise as this is likely to find the broadest basis for operations, the frankest criticism and the greatest freedom from official interference and government propaganda. But that must not hinder us from drawing help and contributions from and contemplating a use in every community in the world.

So far I have laid no stress upon the immense advantage this enterprise would have in its detachment from immediate politics. Ultimately if our dream is realised it must exert a very great influence upon everyone who controls ad-

---

58   French, in relation to or with regards to.

59   A foolish person, from the nursery rhyme of the same name.

60   Wells is referring to the western Christian church before the Protestant Reformation of the sixteenth and seventeenth centuries.

61   This is a reference to the dominant Catholic influence in European politics during the medieval and early modern periods, until the Protestant Reformation challenged its authority.

62   Of several languages.

ministrations, makes wars, directs mass behaviour, feeds, moves, starves and kills populations. But it does not immediately challenge these active people. It is not the sort of thing to which they would be directly antagonist. It is not ostensibly anti-*them*. They would not easily realise its significance for all that they do and are. The prowling beast will fight savagely if it is pursued and challenged upon the jungle path in the darkness, but it goes home automatically as the day breaks.

You see how such and Encyclopaedic organisation could spread like a nervous network, a system of mental control about the globe, knitting all the intellectual workers of the world through a common interest and a common medium of expression into a more and more conscious co-operating unity with a growing sense of their own dignity and responsibility, informing without pressure or propaganda, directing without tyranny. It could be developed wherever conditions were favourable; it could make inessential concessions and bide its time in regions of exceptional violence, grow vigorously again with every return to liberalism and reason.

So I sketch my suggestion for a rehabilitation of thought and learning that ultimately may release a new form of power in the world, recalling indeed the power and influence of the Churches and religions of the past but with a progressive, adaptable and recuperative quality that none of these possessed. I believe that in some such way as I have sketched, the mental forces now largely and regrettably scattered and immobilised in the universities, the learned societies, research institutions and technical workers of the world, could be drawn together into a real directive world intelligence, and by the mere linking and implementing of what is known, human life as a whole could be made much surer, stronger, bolder and happier than it has ever been up to the present time. Until something of this sort is done, I do not see how the common life can ever be raised except occasionally, locally and by a conspiracy of happy chances, above its present level of impulsiveness, insincerity, insecurity, general under-vitality, under-nourishment and aimlessness. For that reason I think the promotion of an organisation for a World Encyclopaedia may prove in the long run to be a better investment for the time and energy of intelligent men and women than any definite revolutionary movement, Socialism,[63] Communism,[64] Fascism,[65] Imperial-

---

63 A political and economic theory or policy of social organisation which advocates that the community as a whole should own and control the means of production, distribution and exchange.

64 A movement, derived from the writings of Karl Marx, seeking the overthrow of capitalism by a proletarian revolution in favour of a system of society with property vested in the community and each member working for the common benefit according to his or her capacity and receiving according to his or her needs.

ism,[66] Pacificism[67] or any other of the current *isms* into which we pour ourselves and our resources so freely. None of these movements has anything like the intellectual comprehensiveness needed to construct the world anew.

Let me be very clear upon one point. I am not saying that a World Encyclopaedia will in itself solve any single one of the vast problems that must be solved if man is to escape from his present dangers and distresses and enter upon a more hopeful phase of history; what I am saying – and saying with the utmost conviction – is this, that without a World Encyclopaedia to hold men's minds together in something like a common interpretation of reality, there is no hope whatever of anything but an accidental and transitory alleviation to any of our world troubles. As mankind is, so it will remain, until it pulls its mind together. And if it does not pull its mind together then I do not see how it can help but decline. Never was a living species more perilously poised than ours at the present time. If it does not take thought to end its present mental indecisiveness catastrophe lies ahead. Our species may yet end its strange eventful history as just the last, the cleverest, of the great apes.[68] The great ape that was clever – but not clever enough. It could escape from most things but not from its own mental confusion and the destruction that is the inevitable consequence of incurable mental confusion.

---

65 A rightwing authoritarian ideology developed in Italy from 1919 and advocated by extreme nationalist groups in several other countries.

66 The belief in the desirability of, or practice of, the acquisition of colonies and dependencies, or the extension of a country's influence through trade, diplomacy, etc.

67 The advocacy of a peaceful policy in a particular instance.

68 Members of the biological family hominidae, including humans, chimpanzees, orangutans and gorillas.

1.11: 'Biology for the Million'

H. G. Wells, 'Biology for the Million' (1 March 1941).[1]

The Uniqueness of Man by Dr Julian Huxley. Pp. xiii + 300. (London: Chatto and Windus, 1941.) 10s. 6d. net.

The Uniqueness of Man is a book full of good reading, very diversified and occasionally very provocative, like the mind of its author. Julian Huxley is, among other things, the natural successor to Ray Lankester, the ripe and abundant author of *Science from an Easy Chair*. These papers vary in quality from the admirable essay which gives the book its title to a cheery little review of *Who's Who*, which lines up with its betters as 'The Analysis of Fame'. Such papers as 'Climate and Human History', 'The Origin of Species', 'The Concept of Race', and 'Mice and Men', are exactly what the man of intelligence, mainly preoccupied with other work, needs to keep him up to date with his biological ideas. The concluding three papers are 'religious' and very earnest in tone.

The title paper, written for the *Yale Review*,[2] is done with a carefulness and precision not always evident in Dr Huxley's fluent writing. It gives an extremely good survey of the profound gulf that has opened between *Homo sapiens*[3] and the rest of the animal kingdom out of which he has arisen in the brief space of at most a quarter of a million years,[4] a mere moment in geological time.[5] The gulf was cleft open by conceptual thought.[6] Already before then the anthropoid apes[7] were an odd outstanding group of animals descending gingerly from the trees; but although their hands were comparatively free, Dr Huxley tells us, they had no means of transmitting and handing on ideas. Then came words. With conceptual thought man established a mental and moral continuity and a power of assimilating social groups, additional to and far more effective

---

1   Reprinted by permission from Macmillan Publishers Ltd: *Nature* (147: 3722), copyright (1941).

2   Founded in 1819 as the *Christian Spectator* and renamed in 1911, the oldest literary quarterly in the USA, published by Yale University Press.

3   Modern humanity regarded as a species.

4   It has subsequently been observed that modern humans first appeared in the fossil record around 130,000 years ago.

5   The time which has elapsed since the earth's formation; time measured with reference to geological events.

6   A process of independent analysis in the creative search for new ideas or solutions which takes as its starting point the notion that none of the accepted constraints of contemporary reality need necessarily apply to or shape the future.

7   Those apes which are most human-like, gibbons, orang-utans, gorillas and chimpanzees, and their evolutionary ancestors.

than the links of consanguinity[8] and physical inheritance. He developed a novelty in the history of life, 'cumulative tradition',[9] and so by means of the word he escaped from the limitations of the small churlish family group hitherto characteristic of other anthropoids. That may not be wholly true. There may have been an intervening phase before the spoken word dominated us, when man had already achieved a certain power over general ideas by means of gesture. Many peoples can still converse by gestures with words as accessories. Man may have begun with gesture and mimicry, with grunts and sounds arising out of his movements. He may have been visual in his communications before he became vocal. He may have drawn and made tally marks[10] long before he used common nouns or numerals in counting.

It is perhaps an impertinence for a general reader to criticise the precision of a distinguished man of science; but occasionally there is a very perceptible laxity and tolerance in Dr Huxley's phrasing and mental attitude that is not in the best scientific tradition. He says that man has acquired the possibility of a unified mental life.[11] The work of Pavlov and the Behaviourists[12] goes all out to sustain the idea that he is only now acquiring it; and then, lapsing from a psycho-synthetic[13] to a psycho-analytic[14] phraseology, Dr Huxley speaks of 'the forces of disruption'. He cannot have it both ways.

Again he seems to me too ready to deal with telepathy and clairvoyance as something new and extraordinary in human experience. But has he really worried out the possibility that the mind may work at times with a swiftness that eludes observation? A friend of mine is a crossword puzzle addict. He tells me that occasionally he can take *The Times*[15] crossword puzzle and write down the solution with scarcely a hitch. At other times he sticks, and, sometimes, even after a considerable effort, he sticks hopelessly. Now *The Times* puzzles are very whimsical and various in their clues, and guessing them means that my friend must run over a very great store or memories, associations, possibilities and alternatives, and put this and that together. There can be no telepathy by means of

---

8   Relationship by descent from a common ancestor.

9   The ability to pass on through cultural inheritance (especially through speech and writing) knowledge from one generation to another.

10   Notches or scores representing a fixed quantity of items, used in accounting.

11   The supposed human ability to live a rational life in control of instinctual urges.

12   Psychologists who espouse the doctrine that objective investigation of stimuli and responses is the only valid investigative method.

13   Of or pertaining to psychosynthesis, the integration of separated elements of the personality through psychoanalysis.

14   Of or pertaining to the analysis of the unconscious forces believed to affect the mind.

15   British daily newspaper founded in 1788.

the printed page. His clairvoyance, I suggest, is just extremely swift clear-mindedness. He flashes to his end and the intermediate steps vanish. The rapid answers of a calculating boy probably fall into the same category of swift reactions with no record of the steps. There is no 'extra-sensory gift'[16] in such cases, but only indications of an enormous range in the pace of our mental processes. The same individual in different phases will vary between what we call intuition[17] and blank impenetrability. Observations on the reactions of a fly to stimuli[18] and of the quick decisions of a frightened cat escaping from some unfamiliar enclosure confirm the idea that ganglionic[19] and brain responses may be immensely accelerated in comparison with everyday humdrum human experience. I am still unconvinced that there is anything quasi-occult[20] in these apparent triumphs of the human mind over the theory of probability.

Let me now hurl a final reproach at the author for his curiously unscientific indisposition to pin himself down to unambiguous statements. His concluding papers on religion are rational and right-minded. I have no quarrel with their general trend. But this is how he winds up:

> I believe that we can never reduce our principles to any few simple terms. Existence is always too various and too complicated. We must supplement principles with faith. And the only faith that is both concrete and comprehensive is in life, its abundance and progress. My final belief is in life.

Here we are supposed to cheer and disperse in a mood of edification. I refuse to do so. What does this belief in life mean? We are alive. How can we avoid believing in life? What is the alternative? Is this an assertion that, to put it vulgarly, 'life is O. K. for me'? How can one accept that nowadays? I can understand the stoic's[21] stern pride in the life within himself. I can understand the scientific worker's devotion to truth – truth with the utmost possible precision at any cost – for how can one be a man of science without that? I can understand the man whose head is 'bloody but unbowed' under the bludgeonings of chance.

---

16 The supposed faculty for perceiving by means other than the known senses.

17 Immediate apprehension by the mind without the intervention of reasoning.

18 Things that provoke, increase or quicken bodily activity.

19 Relating to a structure within the central and automatic nervous system, forming a well-defined mass.

20 Seemingly magical.

21 A member of the ancient Greek school of philosophy founded by Zeno and characterised by its austere ethical doctrines; a person who practices repression of emotion, indifference to pleasure and pain, and patient endurance in adversity.

Maybe Dr Huxley will reply that he agrees with all that? Then why cannot he bring himself to say so quite distinctly?

1.12: 'The Man of Science as Aristocrat'

H. G. Wells, 'The Man of Science as Aristocrat' (19 April 1941).[1]

The other day I listened with great pleasure to Sir Richard Gregory's Aldred lecture,[*] and admired once again his instinct for bringing together into the most fruitful association, facts and consequences lying far apart, and extracting wide suggestions and new problems from the assemblage. But the readers of *Nature* do not need to be reminded that Sir Richard was a brilliant editor so that without any sacrifice of its world-wide scientific usefulness he also made this weekly journal a medium of interpretation and understanding between one type of specialist and another and between specialists in general and the man of general intelligence and broad curiosity outside the ranks of the specialist worker. The Royal Society began as an assembly of curious gentlemen, amateurs all, and how else could it have begun? It could include Pepys, for example, to his great benefit certainly and maybe to its own.

I find that very relevant to Sir Richard's discussion, and Prof. Hill's stimulating address on scientific co-operation[†] comes in at a different angle to the set of problems Sir Richard has set going in our minds. He gave us no solutions, and it may be there is no simple comprehensive final reply to the questions he had started. Is there a real hard-and-fast[2] difference between discovery and invention, between pure and applied science,[3] between philosophy and science, between the professional and the amateur, between gentlemen and players,[4] between the inventor and the patentee? One can imagine a sort of preposterous Royal Commission[5] sitting to define the boundaries and calling a fantastic crowd of witnesses. The discussion would slop over into the world of artists and writers and all who deal in thought and knowledge. Is it within the honour and

---

1 Reprinted by permission from Macmillan Publishers Ltd: *Nature* (147: 3729), copyright (1941). David Smith wrongly cites this essay as a review of Richard Gregory's 'new book [sic], *Discovery and Invention*' (Smith 1986, 438).

* 'The Royal Society of Arts Aldred Lecture, 1941: "Discovery and Invention", by Sir Richard Gregory, Bt, FRS.' [Editor's Note: the Aldred Lecture was an occasional lecture organised by the Royal Society of Arts between 1907 and 1948 on a scientific or literary theme, funded from a £100 bequest by George Aldred in 1868.]

† 'Address by Prof. A. V. Hill, "Science, National and International, and the Basis of Co-operation", *Nature*, 147, 250 (March 1, 1941).'

2 Strict, inflexible.

3 The exact science of applying knowledge from one or more natural scientific fields to practical problems.

4 A cricketing term to refer to matches between amateurs and professionals, used metaphorically for amateurs and professionals in any field.

5 A major government public enquiry into an issue.

dignity of a writer to write an advertisement? Or to write a book pandering to popular sentimentalities he despises?

But if we admit the boundaries are indefinable, it is still arguable that there are centres to this peripheral vagueness. There are types and groups and individuals, almost completely disinterested in their contribution to human achievement, and there are others whose activities are deliberately directed to gainful research. Again we have another group whose end is neither the good, the true or the beautiful, but a definite practical end. Thinkers unduly influenced perhaps by the materialist interpretation of history[6] have it that every step in invention and discovery has been a response to a very present need. Man had long wanted to practice agriculture in a methodical manner, and so he took up astronomy; he wanted to fix the boundaries of his fields in a wide flat plain and so he stretched out his hand into the unknown, and behold! geometry was there. He wanted to go places and so he leapt upon the hitherto merely edible horse and supplemented its insufficient sturdiness by breeding and the wheel. I put these things from one angle, but one can quite easily turn the point in the other direction. When man rumbled off in his first chariot,[7] was he looking for something practical he needed urgently, or was he just looking for trouble? No community would have kept and fed an astronomical and geometrical priesthood unless it had fulfilled a vital practical need. But how far the priest created the need he also satisfied is one of those head-spinning questions best dealt with by a gathering of convivial anthropologists after dinner. For the answer to almost all these conflicting questions seems to be: 'Well; to a certain extent – *yes*.'

But to push further into the luminous fog into which Sir Richard and Prof. Hill have lured me, and which I find so stimulating that it has kept me awake at nights, it is, I think, possible to define the practical problem to which their thoughts are directed. It is the protection of progress. They both think that human living should be and can be made more abundant and happier by the progress of discovery and invention, and they are agreed that that progress is only possible in an atmosphere of world-wide free expression, publication and exchanges. Free expression is the breath of human hope.

But neither of them stops at that. Sir Richard in particular upsets a whole beehive of notes of interrogation beyond that primary demand. The driving force responsible for the rapidity of human progress in the past century and a half has been, he evidently thinks, discovery. Exploration, fundamental research, discovery, is the root from which the immense wealth of modern invention springs.

---

6   Historical analysis based upon Karl Marx's assumption that 'it is not the consciousness of men that determines their existence, but, on the contrary, their social existence that determines their consciousness' (Marx 1981).

7   A wheeled conveyance, usually horse-drawn.

Lying abed at nights I have disputed that, but it is true. I thought of the bicycle as an invention that owed nothing to discovery, that might have happened any-when.[8] The idea of the hobby horse,[9] one might think, is as old as the wheel; a fair road was necessary, but there were good roads in the early empires, and I would not be surprised to find a hobby horse in a Sumerian[10] burial ground, just as one might find a prehistoric glider in Crete.[11] There would have been nothing fundamental in adding a treadle to the hobby horse. The penny-farthing[12] bone-shaker[13] was equally open to man, therefore, except – except that that big wheel was impossible, and it was impossible because of the backwardness of metallurgical practices. The 'safety'[14] was still more impossible because of the lack of skill and material for gearing. The invention of the practicable bicycle, like the glider, has had to wait throughout the ages therefore until the fruits of scores of remote explorations and discoveries had filtered down to practical exploitation. It could not have happened earlier than it did, and only as a consequence of that fundamental work.

So that the preservation, multiplication and cultivation of the 'pure' discoverer is the primary solicitude of all of us progressives,[15] and it becomes an inquiry of primary importance to the liberal thinker[16] to reveal what are the political and social circumstances that will produce this type in maximum abundance and satisfactory activity.

Last winter I flew over most of America.[17] I visited a number of universities and among others the great technological organisation at Pasadena.[18] I saw the great lens of the Lick Observatory being rubbed slowly to a perfect curva-

---

8   At any time ever.

9   Also known as a dandy horse, a two wheeled vehicle, precursor to the bicycle, propelled along by the stride of the rider, invented by Karl von Drais in 1818.

10   Relating to Sumer, the earliest known civilisation of the ancient Near East, located in the south-east of present day Iraq between the third and fourth millennia BC.

11   This is an allusion to the ancient Greek myth of Daedalus and Icarus who fashioned wings out of feathers and wax to escape imprisonment on Crete only for the latter to fly too close to the sun, resulting in the wax melting and his falling to his death.

12   An early form of bicycle having a large front wheel and a small rear one.

13   An early, jolting bicycle before the invention of rubber tyres.

14   The Safety bicycle, the modern bicycle characterised by a diamond-shaped frame, wheels of identical size and a chain driven rear wheel, invented in 1885 by John Starley.

15   Persons or groups advocating political or social reform.

16   One who favours free trade and gradual political and social reform and who advocates individual freedom and democracy.

17   Wells made a lecture tour of the USA between 3 October and 19 December 1940.

18   A reference to the California Institute of Technology, a private American research university founded in 1891.

ture, and I brought my knowledge of the chromosomes[19] of the fruit-fly up to date with my old friend Prof. T. H. Morgan. The atmosphere was charged with considerable political excitement because of the presidential election,[20] and I found a very curious divergence of opinion between the elder and the younger men of science. The older men had found their opportunity through the endowments provided by rich men, and they seemed to be unable and unwilling to contemplate any other way of sustaining research. Except in social and economic science, the yoke of the patron had been easy to bear, an almost imperceptible weight. The endowment paid its money for distinguished achievement and the man of science had a free hand, and the more he carried himself as a distinguished mental aristocrat, the more he gave satisfaction. But in our world of rapid revolution the very foundations of this conditional security are threatened, and these elder men of science are, so far as my knowledge goes, political Tories[21] to a man. They have a real and justifiable fear of the State politician, of journalistic denunciation, of a vast paralysing network of control. They do not want to change the rule of the wealthy patrician[22] for that of the political commissar.[23]

This, however, is not the case with the progressive recalcitrant sciences,[24] and among the younger men of science in all departments I found a lively disposition to get on with a new world and to find in an extension of federal activities in the way of research and educational activities a substitute for the spontaneous and rather incalculable generosity of the now deflated wealthy.[25] I will not take sides here and now. I report what is happening merely to raise the question of how the scientific worker is to adjust his pride and honour to this new and dangerous change in his sustaining conditions.

He may have to face not simply difficulty and poverty but bitter frustration. To do that he will have to set aside any pseudo-modesty that afflicts him. By resolving to become a primary research worker he decides that he is one of a necessary *élite*, an aristocrat in a democratic world. How can he decide that? If

---

19 Threadlike structures of nucleic acids and protein which carry a set of linked genes.

20 Democratic President Franklin Roosevelt won a third term of office in 1940, defeating the Republican candidate, Wendell Wilkie.

21 In American political discourse, rightwing antidemocratic supporters of social and political patronage.

22 A member of a noble class or order.

23 A political deputy or delegate.

24 This appears to be Wells's label for such social sciences as psychology, economics, sociology and anthropology.

25 This is a reference to the impact of the Great Depression on the rich American class of philanthropists, though Wells appears unaware of the relative security of that class during the economic collapse.

he feels that his research work is better worth while than anything else in the world, then probably it is worth while, and if he does not feel that, he had better turn to something 'with money in it'. He must not wait for a grant or anything, he must go ahead with it, whatever it is. Curie could do that. Think of the poverty of his life throughout, and how he died, and then think of all that the world owes to him. This world to-day is his.

My old friend, York Powell, told me years ago, 'Your first duty is to the gift within you. It does not matter whom you offend nor how you sacrifice your popularity. Do the thing that you are impelled to do. Everything else is secondary to that impulsion.' What holds good for the writer, holds good for the primary research worker. It is the same problem.

The philosophy for the essential research worker I submit is a stoical aristocracy. I note with interest and a certain cynicism the suggestions of our authors for gratuities and patents. Do any gratuities get to the original discoverers? I doubt it. Years ago I took up the idea of Diplock's pedrail[26] and applied it to the problem of trench warfare.[27] Diplock was the originating inventor. I described a tank and how it could be used to break an entrenched deadlock, in 1903, in a story called 'The Land Ironclads'. Years afterwards I discovered that some enterprising gentleman had secured a considerable gratuity as the 'inventor' of the tank.[28] His imagination stopped short just where my story stopped short. He had no idea of how to use the tank, and the British Higher Command[29] made an utter mess of the job. It might have decided the war[30] in 1916. I was kept in the dark as to what was going on or possibly I might have broken out with some saving suggestions. Later on, de Gaulle was quite unable to teach the elderly French generals the principles of mechanised warfare, and the Germans last year were the first people to make an intelligent use of the tanks.[31] But anyhow my gratuity (or Diplock's) was intercepted. That is likely to happen constantly. Interception will become an art if gratuities multiply, and I do not see

---

26   A vehicle that travels by means of wheels with spring-loaded pads or feet attached around the circumference, enabling it to pass over obstacles or rough ground.

27   Hostilities carried on from more or less permanent trenches.

28   The 1919 Royal Commission on Awards to Inventors rewarded Walter Wilson and William Tritton as co-inventors of the tank.

29   During the two world wars, a group of politicians and senior military personnel who determined British fighting strategy.

30   I. e., the Great War.

31   This is a reference to Germany's *Blitzkrieg* tactics in the Second World War (1939-45), where massed tanks advanced on the enemy at speed, supported by aircraft, and quickly overwhelmed the opposing army.

how one can circumvent the 'Smart Alecs'[32] without a tedious amount of litigation and worry that would distract one from one's proper work.

Much the same thing applies to patent rights. I doubt if many patents give any protection to original inventors. There also I have had some slight but edifying experience. I wrote a book about a 'time traveller',[33] and about that time the new 'instantaneous' photography[34] appeared. Mr Paul came along to me and we took out a provisional patent[35] that would have made us practically the ground landlords of the entire film industry. We nearly patented films! We did not go on with the patent. Happily. Otherwise we should have found ourselves corruptingly rich, and a heavy incubus on the development of the cinema. It would have been a mere fluke, a lucky anticipation of unsuspected possibilities, a hold-up.

I can't answer for Mr Paul, but I have no doubt that all that ill-gotten gain would have demoralised and wasted me completely. My egotism would have been inflated. It would have snatched me from honest work and brought out the latent arrogance and detestableness in my nature. I might have become a Press peer.[36] I might have endowed and dominated futile *ad hoc* research. I might have joined the privileged class which can treat men of science and civil servants and the like as though they are Greek slaves.[37] Happily, it did not dawn upon us until too late what a vast commercial opportunity we were missing. Our provisional patent[38] lapsed.

Those particular experiences make me equally sceptical of the effectiveness of the gratuity and the patent. It seems to me that in the end the research worker, the philosopher, the author or the artist must fall back upon his innate conviction of the supreme value of his work. His ultimate resource is pride. With that he must be prepared to sustain himself against adverse conditions. He must do his best always. He must endure the bludgeonings of fate. Those who detect his quality may be able to put laboratories, transport and material at his

---

32 Persons displaying ostentatious or smug cleverness.

33 A reference to Wells's novel, *The Time Machine* (1895).

34 Photography which captured an image on a negative instantly, rather than requiring lengthy exposure time.

35 On 24 October 1895 Paul and Wells filed a patent application for a moving picture journey through time in which the audience would experience the physical sensation of being transported through time and space using moving seats and film projections.

36 A holder of the British honour of Duke, Marquis, Earl, Viscount or Baron (or the female equivalents).

37 Chattel labour in ancient Greece, though who had liberty in most social functions except politics.

38 An initial patent application which only matures into a full patent once further developments of the idea have occurred.

service, but they must not insult him with offers of prizes and profits and honours, they must fight for that unrestricted freedom of expression without which he is muffled and made ineffective, and the rest lies with him. He has to hold to it and insist that so far as his work goes he is an aristocrat, an angular aristocrat it may be, but the only kind of aristocrat the new world has any use for. It matters very little if he is poor, gauche[39] or shabby. Without any pretence of false modesty he has to bear himself as an aristocrat not only within himself but among his peers, whether they like it or not. He is the key man of the New World.[40]

Comment on Wells: John Moore-Brabazon, letter to the editor, 'The Man of Science as Aristocrat' (3 May 1941).[41]

It is indeed a privilege that in *Nature* we can enjoy an article by Mr H. G. Wells. I, like him, would like to preface the remarks I have to make upon his contribution by paying my modest tribute to *Nature*. I know nothing more wholesome than a perusal of the 'Letters', at least 50 per cent of which must be pure gibberish to most people, but absorbing to the few interested in their particular subject raised. Humility of mind over such abysmal ignorance of so many subjects is a fine correction in these days of the 'cock-sure'.[42]

H. G. Wells obviously comes under the head of a man of 'general intelligence'. I make no such claim. I get included by virtue of 'a broad curiosity outside the ranks of the specialist worker'.

In a debate on Mr Wells's recent lectures in the United States[43] and why he was allowed to go and air such curious views, Mr Peake, speaking for the Government, put up an admirable defence of his conduct on the ground that we all knew Mr Wells and that we must look upon him as one of our 'invisible exports'.[44] I have never quite decided whether Mr Peake meant very subtly that we can all see through Mr Wells or not, for although he derides the patent laws and condemns them – 'we must all work for the common good' –, I see no urgent

---

39   Awkward.

40   The emerging time, according to Wells, in which talent will be free to blossom and the reliance upon patronage will have come to an end.

41   Reprinted by permission from Macmillan Publishers Ltd: *Nature* (147: 3731), copyright (1941).

42   To be convinced in one's own mind.

43   The title of Wells's lecture, delivered in various cities throughout the USA, was 'One World or Two Hemispheres'.

44   The export of non-tangible items, usually services.

advocacy of the abolition of copyright. The miserable capitalist[45] world that recognised Mr Wells's genius has by its machinery not only kept him from starvation and being 'bumped off',[46] but also made him incidentally one of the most privileged of the privileged classes.

Success in literature has been his, with its reward. If he had levied toll on the world for his invention of the cinematograph,[47] would the 'arrogance and the detestableness of his nature' have been brought out? Certainly not. It was not brought out by his success in literature for the reason it was not there. A more loveable, maddening man I have never met.

Mr Wells makes a plea for the man of science to look upon himself as an aristocrat. This, indeed, must make Robespierre turn in his grave, and surely in some States must put some of our friends in danger. To jump from the proletariat,[48] ignoring the *bourgeoisie*,[49] to be an aristocrat,[50] would certainly endanger, I should imagine, Prof. Kapitza's life. Dangerous advice from a socialist; but we get his meaning. I do not think his tongue was in his cheek[51] when he wrote that, but, when Mr Wells writes, the position of his tongue is important, which goes to show the superiority of the spoken over the written word.

My point is, why should the man of science look upon himself as an aristocrat? Granted, he may be doing work which will be of use to the world and not to himself; a soldier also does that. A man of science works at the subject he adorns because that is his bent in life and where he can best satisfy himself. It does not follow – brutal as it sounds, it must be made clear – that because a man of science is brilliant in his sphere he can take on any job and shine at it. A man can be a brilliant man of science but unable to make his way in life in any other direction. Even Sir Isaac Newton never shone as a member of Parliament.[52] A well-known fellow of the Royal Society complained to me the other day that working as he did in a particular Ministry he was valued for pay on the basis of a major,[53] and I am brutal enough to think that that is about right, once a specialist gets out of his groove.

---

45 Of a system in which private capital or wealth is used in the production or distribution of goods.

46 Murdered.

47 A film projector.

48 Wage earners collectively.

49 The middle class.

50 One born to hereditary wealth and social and political privilege.

51 Speaking with sly irony or humorous insincerity.

52 A British elected representative of the people in national elections.

53 An officer in the army.

I agree that the man of science and the specialist working in his groove have produced in our time the motor-car, the aeroplane and the radio, which by the 'wisdom' of man have been turned into the Panzer Division,[54] the night bomber[55] and lying propaganda. All this is indeed desperate, but it does show that technical minds outstrip political wisdom and that it is easier to discover X-rays[56] than to placate Europe.

The sort of article Mr Wells has given us tends to get all values wrong. Technical research may benefit the world or not, that depends on how it is ultimately used; but for the advancement of the general happiness of mankind concentration by the brains of the country is required on government and planning. That is the most difficult and important of all science. I suppose Mr Wells would class it as politics and fire squibs[57] at it; but because it is neglected and despised, because there are no chairs and no places for its students in the Royal Society, the most difficult of all subjects is being neglected as science.

Let us get our values right. The man who by his political efforts can get adequate milk to children deserves more of his fellow man than the inventor of the quantum theory;[58] but in the narrow world of science, who gets the most attention and encouragement?

Aristocracy means government by the best. If the man of science means to come out of his shell[59] and help us in the problems and perplexities of life, good luck to him. What we can do without, however, is the specialist, usually with the pen, divorced from all the responsibilities of public life but laying down high priestly[60] criticisms of all and sundry, as if knowledge, foresight and wisdom lay with him alone.

---

54   A German armoured unit.

55   An aircraft and its pilot that undertakes bombing raids at night.

56   Electromagnetic radiation of high energy and very short wavelength capable of passing through many substances opaque to light.

57   Small firecrackers; satirical or witty pieces of writing.

58   A theory of matter and energy based upon the notion of a discrete quantity of electromagnetic energy proportional in magnitude to the frequency of the radiation it represents.

59   To stop being shy and withdrawn and become more friendly and sociable.

60   Like a chief or the head of a cult.

Comment on Wells: Richard Paget, letter to the editor (3 May 1941).[61]

According to Mr H. G. Wells, it would appear that inventors and research workers must be stoically and aristocratically resigned to even worse conditions under democracy than they have hitherto endured under pluto-aristocracy.[62]

But, surely, if democracy abolishes the rich patron, it must be prepared to wear his mantle and do his job.

The precedent is already to hand, for example, in the Civil List,[63] from which State payments – pensions or gratuities – are already made to deserving individuals. It would, of course, be necessary to organise an extensive machinery for administering State patronage – as of right – to all deserving cases; but the advantage to the cause of national progress might be very great. Inventors, research workers, artists and the like would at least be protected from the 'Smart Alecs' – they would be rewarded by the State in proportion to the benefits they had rendered to the community.

As to the scale of payments – a progressive manufacturing firm may spend from 1 per cent up to 2 or 3 per cent of its annual turnover on research and development;[64] a wise and progressive democracy might well do the same, and spend as much on research and development as we have hitherto done on national defence.[65]

The same organisation might, with great advantage, have the duty of recommending the bestowal of national honours for public services rendered.

Reply to Moore-Brabazon: H. G. Wells, letter to the editor, 'The Man of Science as Aristocrat' (17 May 1941).[66]

If I may say a word more about 'The Man of Science as Aristocrat', I would like to point out to my friend Lieut.-Colonel Moore-Brabazon that my suggestion, as Sir Richard Paget realises, was of an inner aristocracy of the spirit in an entirely democratic world. I did not suggest that men of thought and knowledge should

---

61 Reprinted by permission from Macmillan Publishers Ltd: *Nature* (147: 3731), copyright (1941).

62 A conflation of plutocracy and aristocracy; rule by a class of hereditary wealthy people.

63 A register of the recipients of an annual allowance by parliament for the British monarch's official expenses, or the expenses of those voted an allowance by parliament.

64 In industry, work directed towards the innovation, introduction and improvement of products and processes.

65 Governmental effort to maintain the security of the nation-state through the use of economic, military and political power.

66 Reprinted by permission from Macmillan Publishers Ltd: *Nature* (147: 3733), copyright (1941). This letter has previously been reprinted in Smith 1998, IV: 296-97.

rule or control anybody or anything outside the range of their distinctive gifts. I suggested that within that range they should refuse absolutely to be directed, controlled or silenced by anybody, that they should bear themselves like brains with a backbone, and not like flexible slaves.

Comment on Wells: Robert Paul, letter to the editor (17 May 1941).[67]

Mr H. G. Wells states that he was once in danger of becoming corruptingly rich by patenting films, and that 'Mr Paul came along to me and we took out a provisional patent that would have made us practically the ground landlords of the entire film industry' (*Nature*, April 19, p. 465).

My provisional specification described means for presenting the main incidents in Mr Wells's story, *The Time Machine*. To create and illusion of travelling through time spectators were to be seated on a rocking and oscillating platform and subjected to wind and noise effects. Pausing at various epochs – past, present and future – they were to see appropriate events shown on a screen by means of animated photographs[68] and dissolving views.[69] It was to discuss details of such scenes that I invited Mr Wells to my office in Hatton Garden towards the end of 1895. He listened patiently to my proposals, gave his general approval to my attempting to carry them out, and proceeded to talk of subjects suitable for the primeval scenes. Having recommended for my perusal some books on extinct monsters he left without further discussion as to future action, and many years elapsed before I had the pleasure of meeting him again.

My scheme was promptly abandoned for reasons which can be guessed by those acquainted with animated photography in 1895. Then one-minute films could be watched by individuals who looked through the slot of an Edison kinetoscope[70] or one of its variants. In several countries inventors, including myself, were seeking means for showing films on a screen, and such projectors came into use early in 1896. The simplest scenes, coupled with the novelty of seeing photographs moving, sufficed to attract the public and to establish the new art of cinematography[71] in favour. A prolonged presentation, such as that of *The Time Machine*, was then unnecessary and indeed impracticable.

---

67   Reprinted by permission from Macmillan Publishers Ltd: *Nature* (147: 3733), copyright (1941). This letter has previously been reprinted in Stover 1996, 244-45.

68   Primitive cinema films.

69   In cinematography, to cause an image to fade away as another one appears.

70   An early motion-picture device in which the images were viewed through a peephole.

71   Film-making; the art of taking and reproducing moving pictures.

Reply to Moore-Brabazon: Robert Jones, letter to the editor, 'The Man of Science as Aristocrat' (31 May 1941).[72]

Lieut.-Colonel Moore-Brabazon has fallen into a common error of thought when he says that a politician who ensures a milk supply deserves more of his fellow men than does the inventor of the quantum theory. The boy who posts a lighted squib in a pillar box[73] commits the same offence whether the pillar box is empty or is filled with an unusually important mail. The fact that an action does not seem to the majority to be of immediate consequence is no guide to its importance. Colonel Moore-Brabazon's hypothetical politician will be deserving of the severest censure if he does not ensure the necessary milk supply, provided always that he is aware that our state of mechanical and scientific development is such as to make it possible; he deserves no credit for doing what is simply his job.

Our difficulties lie in the provision of such gifted public servants. Many of those we now have, by their lack of a scientific background, are unaware that the solutions of their problems exist, and in some instances there is even a suspicion that the existence of the problem itself goes unnoticed. The imperative need for men of science with a responsibility in public affairs, in a social system which has changed out of recognition in a period measured in months, is not at all appreciated.

It is true that, 'in the narrow world of science' the inventor of the quantum theory gets more attention than the average run of politicians do; but it must also be pointed out that the man of science who enters the public service is left in no doubt of the inferiority of his position compared with that of his lay colleagues. In consequence of this, cases are known of young men with the foundation stone of scientific knowledge laid at their universities who have seen the financial folly of building a superstructure of experience thereon, and have deliberately concealed their degrees in science in order to taste the fleshpots[74] of an 'administrative' post which could be filled by an intelligent clerk. Such a man is a waste of material, since it is only by the practice of science over a series of years that he gains a knowledge which is likely to be useful to his fellow men. By that time an attempt to 'come out of his shell' is usually out of the question on account of his age and lack of 'administrative' experience, for he will naturally prefer to remain in his shell rather than enter a new field as a junior.

---

72 Reprinted by permission from Macmillan Publishers Ltd: *Nature* (147: 3735), copyright (1941).

73 A public post-box shaped like a pillar.

74 A Biblical expression (Exodus 16: 3) meaning luxurious living.

1.13: 'The Illusion of Personality'

H. G. Wells, 'The Illusion of Personality' (1 April 1944)[*].[1]

The integrality of the individual in the higher Metazoa[2] is a 'biologically convenient delusion'. The expression 'psycho-analysis' implies a mental unity which can undergo analysis. This is the delusion. The reactions of the human machine are loosely linked behaviour systems, participating in a common delusion of being the self. Most lower animals react to stimuli without hesitation. As we ascend the scale *inhibition* appears. There is no longer a mere algebraic[3] summation of stimuli. There is reference back to a storage organ, a 'brain'. According to the record of that storage organ, the organism, not as a whole but as much of it as is affected by the recorded stimuli, reacts. Circumstances may have changed and it may act disastrously, or it may 'profit by experience'.

The *conception of self* appears most evidently in gregarious[4] animals, which have to conduct themselves with regard to the flock or pack. The sub-men[5] seem to have been gregarious running animals, less like the solitary great apes than the baboons. Self-consciousness and a conception of other individuals as consistent persons are necessary to gregariousness. The self-conscious social individual, *whatever it does and however much of it does it*, will ascribe its behaviour to its self, the same self, in continuous operation.

A man awakening from sleep imagines, when he has rubbed his eyes and yawned, etc., he is 'all there'. He is not. The evanescent impressions of dreamland give way to a more vivid reaction-memory-and-event-system which has established a by no means perfect control over what are called the voluntary muscles[6] of his body. Body holds mind together and not mind body. The body goes

---

*   'An abridgement of a thesis on "The Quality of Illusion in the Continuity of the Individual Life in the Higher Metazoa, with particular reference to *Home sapiens*", accepted for the doctorate of science of the University of London. Copies of the complete thesis are available to scientific institutions free of charge; otherwise it is two guineas unsigned, which will be devoted to the propaganda of the Natural Rights of Man, of which Mr Wells is acting secretary.'

1   Reprinted by permission from Macmillan Publishers Ltd: *Nature* (153: 3883), copyright (1944).

2   Multi-cellular animals which are bilaterally symmetrical and having three body layers.

3   Of, pertaining to or occurring in algebra.

4   Tending to live in flocks or loosely organised communities.

5   Prehistoric primates biologically closely related to human beings.

6   Skeletal muscles responsible for controlling the voluntary movements of the body.

as the dominant system in the neuro-sensitive apparatus[7] directs, but other reaction systems are either deflecting or ousting the dominant system.

There are endless variants of 'John Smith'.[8] He will admit in ordinary speech that he 'has his moods' and sometimes 'forgets himself'. It is John Smith No. 214, John Smith who had a dispute with his employer yesterday, who wakes up, the indignant employee. He rehearses a spirited conversation with his 'guv'nor'.[9] He sees his wife's portrait on the mantel and succumbs to resentment and jealousy. The recalcitrant employee is simply not present. John Smith, under control of No. 618, goes down to breakfast in a dark, unloving mood. All the Smiths, from No. 1 to No. 5000 or No. 5,000,000, have a common belief that John Smith is really one person, because they are not only all aboard the same body, but also built around a similar conception of himself, his *persona*[10] as Jung has it. *In fact, they are a collection of mutually replaceable individual systems held together in a common habitation.*

If the systems vary widely, John Smith is a moody man. If still more widely, you have at last a 'double personality'.[11] Whatever system dominates at the time owns John Smith and believes itself to be wholly and solely John Smith.

Conduct systems of reaction require a fable[12] to hold our *selves* together and put them over to others. The neuro-sensitive apparatus in social animals[13] cannot do a thing and forget, cat-fashion. Our conduct systems, whenever they invade simpler systems of reaction in us, set about attacking the independence of these other impulses and drawing them together. They go about like governesses,[14] drill-sergeants,[15] imposing an impossible uniformity of discipline upon the mute unconscious elbowing of our other drives and reactions.

---

7   A nerve cell in which the cell body is a receptor and has a single process by which impulses are transmitted.

8   A name often regarded as the archetype of a common personal name, representing the average man.

9   The cockney phonetic of 'governor', meaning employer.

10   An aspect of the personality as displayed to others.

11   Properly, dissociative identity disorder, a condition where a single individual evidences two or more distinct identities or personalities, each with its own pattern of perceiving and interacting with the environment.

12   A myth or legend, often conveying a moral.

13   Organisms that are highly interactive with other members of their species to the point of having a recognisable and distinct society.

14   Female teachers of children in a private household.

15   Non-commissioned officers who train soldiers in military exercises.

In order that the *persona* should be as consistent as possible in its autobiographical effort, these conduct systems, which concern themselves with the reputation of a human body, ignore aberrant impulses, push them away into what the analyst calls the unconscious,[16] that is, a multitude of reaction systems out of contact with the main directive system. The psycho-analyst says they are below in a dungeon; the behaviourist says they are at large outside. The contradiction is flat.

Jung called this excluded stir the *anima*.[17] It may contrast markedly with the material in the *persona*. It stirs, says the psycho-analyst, beneath the conscious life. It skulks, says the behaviourist, on the edge of the waking life.

That the integrality of the human individual is illusory does not sweep aside continuity from life. The individual belongs to his species, which existed before he appeared in the world, and will outlast him. Generally a man does not realise that. He may refer himself to a family, to a tribe, to a school, to a real or imaginary 'race', to a creed – indeed to a vast variety of larger aggregations. He may fluctuate in his terms of reference. So he thinks and feels. The biological reality is that while he can interbreed with every variety of human being, he goes on as a unity in the whole species, and, whatever frame of community he adopts, it can, from the ecological point of view, have no narrower boundary than the species. Every individual is in the nature of a unique experiment. There is no experimenter nor question behind it; it is an unpremeditated experiment.

It may be rejected at once; or it may have survival value in itself. By surviving it changes the totality of the species by its individual difference. In the generality of cases the difference is slight, and such individual cycles are called *normal*. Their collective effect is that of confirmatory experiments.

A marked and sudden difference is called a variation.[18] The causes of a variation will almost certainly be acting not merely in one case but also upon groupings of similarly situated genes.[19] So long as the individual variation has the qualities to enable it to survive and reproduce itself it will do so.

There is no benevolent bias in that survival. A species may go on varying and surviving through its individuals for a long time, although it is accumulating a variation that will disarm it against some conclusive danger. Most variations

---

16 Mental processes of which a person is not aware but which have a powerful effect on the person's behaviour.

17 In psychoanalysis, the inner self.

18 Heritable or genetic divergence in the structure, character or function of an organism from that considered typical in the species.

19 A unit of heredity which is transmitted from parent to offspring in gametes, usually as part of a chromosome, and which controls or determines a single characteristic in the offspring.

have no survival value at all; but when a species has drifted into disharmony with its surroundings – and that is the case with ours at the present time[20] – then abnormalities which would have been suppressed in the humdrum days of security may stand a chance of temporary establishment. Palaeontology[21] shows repeated evidence of a sort of flurry of abnormalities before the collapse and obliteration of some dominant group which has outstayed its welcome. This seems to be the case with man to-day.

From its first appearance, the human animal was too widespread and too thinly spread to produce a homogeneous *Home sapiens* throughout the earth. There has been more homoplasy[22] and less of diffusion in Homo[23] than is commonly believed.

Migrations began only in the past ten thousand years or so, when the social structure had developed means of conquest and exploitation. At a far remoter period exiguous[24] human races ranged seasonally over wide territories, incapable, for lack of transport or organisation, of sustained aggression or enslavement. The seasonal movement of gregarious food animals, horses, cattle and the like in response to pasture may have led to seasonal gatherings of these far-flung tribes from considerable distances, with little or no spirit of feud or aggression.

The leavings of Solutrean[25] men suggest a gregariousness in which the individuals were more self-reliant and socially tolerant than there descendants. These early nomads exchanged goods at these primordial[26] fairs, as the distances of many early artefacts far from their sources testify. With the dispersal of the food beasts this human gathering dispersed again, with quite possibly a woman or so and an artificer[27] going off with a new party. He or she would not need to learn a new language, when grunts and gestures remained the language of mankind.[28]

---

20 Wells came to believe during the Second World War that the human species was doomed, and that it could only survive through the appearance of a variation with greater survival value than *Homo Sapiens*. See his *Mind at the End of Its Tether* (1945) for a discussion of this.

21 The branch of science that deals with extinct and fossil plants and animals.

22 An instance of similarity of structure produced independently as by the operation of similar circumstances.

23 The genus to which human beings and certain of their fossil ancestors belong.

24 Extremely small.

25 Of or pertaining to an Upper Palaeolithic period of advanced flint-tool making dating to around 19,000 BC.

26 Existing at or from the beginning.

27 A craftsperson or skilled technician.

28 Modern anthropology dates the evolution of language in humans to c. 50,000 years ago.

Time estimates of these periods defeat even geologically trained imaginations. Our grip on big quantities is a feeble one. We have got beyond any other animal by checking with our digits,[29] but our sense of a hundred is foggy, and few will agree whether a crowd was a thousand or three thousand strong. Beyond these limits we *concertina*.[30] We have a 'gibus'[31] sense of time. A thousand years is a huge succession of yesterdays beyond our clear apprehension. If we reflect on the changes in social life since the Christian era,[32] we may achieve an intellectual if not a realistic comprehension of the remoteness of these wanderers from whom we spring. Many people believe that our ancestors were like the Australian aborigines.[33] These 'primitive peoples' are imagined as having been marking time for a hundred thousand years. But in that interval they have been subjected to climatic changes, changes of food, new environments. They have experienced dark ages[34] and phases of recovery. Anthropologists underestimate the intervals in which these systems have decayed and revived and changed and become something quite different. The 'primitive' Australian *talks*, and he has a complex grammar. He betrays traces of admixture, and, if we bring geographical shifting into consideration, we are forced to conclude that in the past there must have been trading, a 'pigeon' language,[35] and ideas and imitative stimuli from other drifting peoples. One may doubt if one can exaggerate the mental remoteness of these creatures whose lives are the basis of our thought and feeling. The makers of eoliths[36] and of Chellean[37] implements gave place to Acheuleans,[38] to Mousterians,[39] to Aurignacians,[40] Solutreans and Magdalen-

---

29 Fingers and toes.

30 Compress or collapse.

31 Collapsible.

32 The period, in Western culture, since the birth of Jesus Christ.

33 The indigenous population of Australia, believed to have arrived between 40,000 and 70,000 years ago.

34 Unenlightened or ignorant periods in a culture's history.

35 More commonly, pidgin, a form of language as spoken in a simplified or altered form by non-native speakers.

36 Roughly chipped stones found in Tertiary strata and originally thought to be the earliest human artefacts, but now regarded as naturally formed.

37 An archaic anthropological expression for a stone-tool tradition of the Lower Palaeolithic period now referred to as Olduwan (2.5 million to 1.5 million years ago).

38 Inhabitants of an early palaeolithic period in Europe, the Middle East, Africa and India (1.4 million years ago to 100,000 years ago) distinguished in particular by the manufacture of stone hand-axes.

39 Inhabitants of a middle palaeolithic Neanderthal culture of 300,000 to 30,000 years ago typified by flints worked on one side only.

40 Inhabitants of the upper palaeolithic period in Europe and south-west Asia between 34,000 and 23,000 years ago.

ians.[41] Meanwhile every species of large animal contemporary with the Acheulean had become extinct. Can we imagine, then, that the ascent of man has been simple and straightforward from Neanderthal[42] to Beckenham, Paris and the Riviera?

We make our way painstakingly to the fact that the mind of ancestral man was essentially unlike ours, and that the species was living under conditions still mostly unimaginable. He was not only different from anything human we can talk to, but, from the very beginning, he was also different *inter se*.[43]

A species is a species so long as it can interbreed and its kindred varieties, however divergent, can be recognised. There never was an original dog. Dogs are anything but select in their emotional phases. If an end came to dog fanciers,[44] Canis[45] would go back to a variety of mongrels,[46] reflecting the regional opportunities in which they found themselves.

Gregariousness is a subordination of the individual to the herd. The individual merges into a wider synthesis, a vast sentient web overspreading many acres; becomes shareholder in faculties always awake, eyes that see in all directions, ears and nostrils that explore a broad belt of air; a super-individual occupying every bit of ground where the approach of an enemy can be detected. Each individual receives a maximum of security at the cost of a minimum of individual animation. When an animal which has been accustomed to a gregarious life is isolated, it feels itself exposed to danger from every part of the circle around him, except the one point on which his attention is momentarily fixed. His glance is restless and anxious, and is turned in succession to different quarters; his movements are hurried and agitated, and he becomes a prey to the extremest terror. The blind instincts evolved under those conditions have been deeply ingrained into our breed, and they are a bar to that freedom the forms of modern civilisation could assure. A modern community must be held together by stronger forces than are derived from the purely gregarious instincts. It cannot be a mob of slaves, clinging together, incapable of self-government and begging to be led; because it will always be led to disaster. It must consist of vigorous, self-reliant men, knit to one another by a strong, tense and elastic community of will and understanding.

41　Inhabitants of the late upper palaeolithic period, between 18,000 and 10,000 years ago, in Europe characterised by fine bone and antler artefacts and a strong artistic tradition.

42　A palaeolithic fossil hominid with a retreating forehead and massive brow ridges which dwelt in Europe, Africa and Asia between 350,000 and 24,000 years ago.

43　Latin, meaning between or among themselves.

44　Those who have a particular interest in the breeding of dogs.

45　Latin, dog.

46　Dogs of no definable breed resulting from various crossings.

The personal life of the individual will still continue, held together by the individual body. Within its conditions that may be a very intense and passionate existence. Many of the bodily phases that constitute John Smith may be preoccupied with sex. The sexual stir of the contemporary Homo is renewed monthly, unlike so many of the larger Eutheria,[47] which have their annual rut. These phases are dependent upon the secretion of gonads,[48] which again seems to be determined by the fluctuations of innate rhythms under climatic and correlated physical influences.

There has been an enormous and biologically unserviceable over-development of those aspects of life in the handy and intelligent Primates.[49] The release of hand and brain by the adoption of the erect attitude during the human dawn, and the revival or continuation of some primitive monthly breeding cycle among the sub-human and human series, stimulated a recurrent or almost continuous interest in the orgasm that is only too manifest in a cageful of monkeys or any over-fed and idle social group – both confined and unemployed groups. But while the monkey's interest is unabashed, contemporary man is in a state either of defiant indulgence or passionate suppression that disorders all his social life. Christianity,[50] Islam[51] and Judaism[52] are all phallic religions,[53] and 'morality' over a large part of Christendom[54] means nothing more than values attached to sexual behaviour.

But we do not know how long this stress on sex as 'morality' has lasted. Dawning man, except under deprivation, may have been as shameless and casual as a monkey. Those primordial fairs were amiable corroborees,[55] free of competitive or possessive ideas. We may describe man, in those sparse days, as under-sexed. The male and the female of the species excited one another and achieved a mutual or substitutional relief; it was all over in no time, and that was all about it. The manner in which the sexual urge lies in wait, so to speak, and

---

47 The class of mammals which develop a placenta.

48 Organs in an animal, such as testes or ovaries, that produce gametes.

49 In zoology, a mammalian order which includes man, apes, monkeys and prosimians.

50 The religion developed out of the doctrines of Jesus Christ and his disciples.

51 The religious system established through the prophet Muhammad in 632.

52 The religion of Jews with a belief in one God and a basis in Mosaic and rabbinical teaching.

53 Religions in which phallic worship is an important component, often symbolising fertility.

54 Christians, or the nations professing Christianity, collectively.

55 Night-time dances, usually associated with Australian Aborigines, which may be either festive or warlike.

seizes upon and makes use of any unemployed mental energy in *Home sapiens* has still to be worked out in detail.

There have been and still are wide and rapid variations in the relationship-phases of men and women, and nowadays a woman will be either a subjugated meretrix[56] or a hard-minded and responsible equal, just in the measure that her sexual impulses and status dominate or are secondary in her *persona*. The decision rests upon womankind and the atmosphere they will create.

Every living thing, in obedience to its hormic[57] urge, seeks to assert itself over other things that move about – over other life or over inanimate things that are imagined as having life. 'This,' in effect says life, emerging to a consciousness of others, 'is not going to beat me.' This primitive uneasiness to reassure oneself that one has the upper hand of the not-me is still far more persistent than any other urge. We assert these selves through a huge miscellany of claims. The claims we make depend upon our upbringing and the ideas imposed on us. We pride ourselves on 'race', country, class, family, 'set' or dollars, intuitions, exceptional muscles or remarkable characters. We gravitate to the groupings in which these are key values.

Man in his dawn was certainly not so collectively maladjusted as the man of our own time. Contemporary man *en masse*[58] is definitely a degenerate creature, in the sense that he presents no collective resistance in the face of change. He experiments only feebly in adaptation; he persists in his follies.

But since we have some two thousand millions of him[59] varying about the average cases *of any particular quality*, whatever it may be, the exceptional instances are likely to have a wider range than in any previous period. These exceptional types will include, among others less biologically favourable, types of self-forgetfulness in some impersonal interest.

The factor in the individuals of this emergent *élite* is a development of the natural curiosity, the picking and searching hands and eyes of our ancestors. The dominant phases of the unrestrained man, as distinguished from the suppressed individual in our now disintegrating modern communities, are those of an inquirer and maker. His unrestrained phases discover an innate desire for mastery; in invention (artistic or 'practical') and construction, according to his aptitude. The profounder disposition of mankind is to make, and to sublimate self in the discovery, each man, of his own idiosyncratic creative possibility.

---

56   A prostitute.

57   Of vital or purposeful energy.

58   French, all together, as a group.

59   The estimated world population in 1944.

In the case of an intellectual *élite* there will be recurrent phases in their lives when an ecstasy of discovery will possess them. They will stand 'silent upon a peak in Darien'.[60] They will be looking upon something, hitherto hidden, which will now be the property of all mankind. They must descend again from that great moment into the shadow of their personal selves, but the achievement will remain as an enduring contribution to the human synthesis.

The spreading realisation that personality is illusory will not abolish the practical reality of individual living. This warp and woof[61] of hallucination provides the fabric upon which lives are lived, just as the cinema screen supplies the fabric on which personal dramas are played out. To realise that the drama is hallucinatory will be to escape from ultimate 'explanations' of life, from priest-crafts[62] and mental muddles that have embittered human relationships hitherto, but it will not release human beings from 'conduct'. It will, however, lift them into a new atmosphere, and mitigate profoundly the confused motivation of that long 'Martyrdom of Man'[63] which is now drawing to an end.

---

60 The last line from 'On First Looking into Chapman's Homer' (1816), a sonnet by British poet John Keats which tells of his astonishment at reading the works of Homer as translated by George Chapman.

61 Fabric.

62 Self-interested policies, practices and influences attributed to some priests.

63 A quotation from the title of the eponymous book (1872) by Winwood Reade.

Part 2: Reviews of the Works of H. G. Wells

In this second part of *H. G. Wells in Nature* all the reviews of Wells's works which appeared in *Nature* are reprinted, along with responses to them and subsequent replies. The range of coverage which Wells received in the journal is remarkable, for while notices of such works as *Text-book of Biology*, *Text-book of Zoology*, 'Human Evolution, an Artificial Process', *The Science of Life* and *Reshaping Man's Heritage* might be expected, and one might not be surprised at discovering coverage of his scientific romances (*The Time Machine*; *The War of the Worlds*; *The First Men in the Moon*; *The Food of the Gods*; *Star Begotten*), *Nature* also featured reviews of his speculative works (*Anticipations*; *Mankind in the Making*; *The Conquest of Time*), his utopias (*A Modern Utopia*; *Men Like Gods*; *The Shape of Things to Come*; *Things to Come*;), his fantasy literature (*In the Days of the Comet*; *Man Who Could Work Miracles*; *The Camford Visitation*), his historical works (*The Outline of History*; *Mr Belloc Objects to 'The Outline of History'*; *A Short History of the World*), his political tracts (*The Future in America*; *What is Coming?*; *The Salvaging of Civilisation*; *The Way the World is Going*; *The Open Conspiracy*; *What Are We To Do With Our Lives?*; *After Democracy*; *New America*; *World Brain*; *The Fate of Homo Sapiens*; *The New World Order*; *The Outlook for Homo Sapiens*; *Phoenix*; *'42 to '44*), his biographical works (*The Story of a Great Schoolmaster*; *Experiment in Autobiography*); his economics text (*The Work, Wealth and Happiness of Mankind*) and his novels and short stories (*The World of William Clissold*; *The Short Stories of H. G. Wells*; *Anatomy of Frustration*; *Babes in the Darkling Wood*). If *Nature* was aimed at a specialised, narrow readership, it can clearly be supposed that that readership's critical reception of Wells was shaped almost entirely by *Nature*, so wide was its coverage of his works.

The first review Wells received in *Nature*, 'Vertebrate Biology', was for Part I of his science primer, *Text-book of Biology* (2.1). William Parker praises it as 'far above the average as regards soundness of treatment and method', though is critical of the 'exceedingly rough' sketches and figures. In fact, for this first edition of the book, Wells produced the diagrams himself, though when the second edition appeared in 1894 they were replaced with fresh efforts by his future wife, Amy Catherine Robbins. Parker also identifies 'Numerous inaccuracies and awkward expressions' and states that 'Misprints are also fairly abundant throughout' but concludes by stating that 'the book will [...] serve the purpose for which it was written very satisfactorily'.

If Parker was generous in his review of Part I, he pulled no punches when he noticed Part II of *Text-book of Biology* in 'Our Book Shelf'. For, 'In dealing with a small number of vertebrate types in Part I of this book [...] the author showed distinct capability and promise; but we feel that he would have done well to wait and work for a few years before publishing this second volume, which covers a larger field'. Wells is accused of 'errors and misstatements' and criticised for the 'awkward terms and misprints' which abound while, again, the 'illustrations are exceedingly crude'.

In 1913 an anonymous notice of the sixth edition of the book, by now retitled *Text-book of Zoology*, appeared under the heading 'Our Book Shelf', though mention is only made to Joseph Cunningham's rearrangement and updating of material in the book. In fact, although Wells's name continued to appear on the title-page, he made no input into the volume, and he in fact unsuccessfully attempted to by back the copyright in the work (which he had sold outright when he produced the first edition for the University Tutorial College) as he wished to prevent its continued publication.

In the brief reviews of 'an eccentric story', *The Time Machine* (2.2), the anonymous reviewers in 'Science in the Magazines' and 'Our Book Shelf' consider it 'admirably-told' and assert that 'the story is well worth the attention of the scientific reader, for the reason that it is based so far as possible on scientific data, and while not taking it too seriously, it helps one to get a connected idea of the possible results of the ever-continuing processes of evolution'.

In the brief notice of Wells's 'Human Evolution, an Artificial Process' (2.3) which appeared in 'Science in the Magazines', the unnamed reviewer notes that, 'Starting from well-known biological facts, suggestive conclusions in ethics and educational science are reached'. As human development is uniquely affected by two factors, 'natural selection' and 'tradition, suggestion, and reasoned thought', Wells's essay argues that 'education should aim at the careful and systematic manufacture of the latter factor'.

In 1898 *The War of the Worlds* (2.4) became Wells's first book to receive detailed critical attention in *Nature*, appraised, significantly, by Wells's former classmate at the Normal School of Science, and the future editor of *Nature*, Richard Gregory in 'Science in Fiction'. Gregory credits Wells with using science in his fiction 'more successfully' than any of his predecessors and sees *The War of the Worlds* as 'more stimulating to thought than anything that the author has yet written'. Gregory praises Wells's portrayal of the Martians, stating that 'only a writer familiar with the lines of biological development could conceive them', and calls the Martians' death through contact with earthly microbes 'the best instance' of 'the ingenuity which the author displays in manipulating scientific material'. In addition to Wells's specific use of scientific knowledge in writing the story, however, Gregory offers more general praise for the value of his scientific romances, asserting that 'they attract attention to work that is being done in the realm of natural knowledge, and so create sympathy with the aims and observations of men of science'.

In the anonymous review of *The First Men in the Moon* (2.5), 'A Lunar Romance', Wells's story is described as 'a narrative which we will venture to say is not only as exciting to the average reader as Jules Verne's, but is full of interest to the scientific man'. It is this 'interest to the scientific man' for which Wells is singled out, as he was in Gregory's review of *The War of the Worlds*, as different from his literary predecessors. The reviewer finds few slips in Wells's science, except to suggest that his estimation of gravity and weightlessness in the moon-bound sphere might lack accuracy. Frank Constable writes to query the reviewers criticism, but the latter reinforces his case with an illustrated reply, demonstrating the effects of gravity upon the passengers in Wells's spacecraft.

From 1901 Wells's speculative writings began to receive attention in *Nature*, starting with *Anticipations, Mankind in the Making* and *The Food of the Gods* (2.6). In his review of *Anticipations* entitled 'The Present Judged by the Future', Edwin Ray Lankester summarises each chapter of the book in some detail before concluding that

> It is, truly enough, an unsparing indictment of existing government, society, education, religion and morality, but it contains also a confession of faith and is full of a spirit of hope and a belief in future development. It is a truthful statement of the outlook of a man who has grasped thoroughly the teachings of modern science and who still keeps hope alive in his breast.

Three years later, Frederick Headley, in 'The Future of the Human Race', reviewed a new edition of *Anticipations*, along with *Mankind in the Making* and *The Food of the Gods*. Headley takes a much more critical approach in his review, and clearly disagrees with Lankester's opinion that Wells is 'a man who has grasped thoroughly the teachings of modern science', for 'Though he expresses the greatest reverence for Darwin and his successors, he does not show a very thorough grip of the principles of evolution'. Headley argues that Wells 'seems unaware of the part in the national life that is played by the lower stratum of society' and he asserts that 'the upper strata do not keep up their numbers, and society has been truly described as an organism that is perpetually renewing itself from its base'. Furthermore, according to Wells, 'Reckless parentage must be in every way discouraged [but] he cannot devise any system of selection by which it would be possible to breed good citizens'. In response to this Headley observes that 'We are to introduce careful parentage, that is, put a stop to natural selection; but there is to be no scientific selection to take its place. The result would indeed be disastrous'. Finally, Headley concludes that both *Anticipations* and *The Food of the Gods* rest on a fallacy:

What is to make the world better? No doubt Mr Wells would say, 'The advance of science.' Science is his sheet anchor. It is to ennoble the national life so that even the idle holders of irresponsible wealth will be powerless to degrade it. But will this be so? [...] The striving after knowledge is the ennobling thing, and not the knowledge itself, the making of discoveries, not the enjoyment of them.

In *The Food of the Gods*, however, Wells presents the opposite reality; 'those who are fed on this food in their infancy and youth grow to a height of some forty feet. The inventors do not add to their inches'. Headley sees such a belief in science as generally liberating as intellectually unsound, and yet it runs through all three books under review.

Headley's review provoked an angry response from Wells, who felt his views were repeatedly misrepresented. Especially disturbing was Headley's criticism of Wells's views on the lower classes. In response to Headley's assertion that he 'seems unaware of the part in the national life that is played by the lower stratum of society', Wells retorted that 'no one does know what part is played by any stratum of society in national reproduction' and asserted that Headley's contention that the lower stratum of society 'is an absolutely necessity' is unsound; 'This is *not* a fact. It may or may not be true'. Headley responded to Wells's complaints point by point, citing Wells's works each time. Rather than being misrepresented by Headley, it seems more likely that Wells had altered his opinions since the publication of *Anticipations*, and his angry response was to his earlier self rather than to Headley (see Partington 2005).

In the review of *A Modern Utopia* (2.7) entitled 'Sociological Speculations', F. C. S. S. suggests that Wells has become 'more moderate and practicable and hopeful' than was revealed in *Anticipations* and *When the Sleeper Wakes*, though without compromising 'his ingenuity and originality'. Perhaps representing the interests of *Nature* readers, the reviewer hopes Wells 'will not, as he threatens, stick henceforth to his "art or trade of imaginative writing," but will continue from time to time to regale and stimulate us with sociological speculations'.

In *A Modern Utopia*, 'progress depends on individual initiative and variation, leading to successful experiments', though, while praising the protection of freedom in utopia, the reviewer suggests that the rule of the Samurai 'seems too rigid for the variety, and too cramping for the freedom of man'. Nonetheless, the book is highly praised, as

Mr Wells, on the whole, shows a wisdom far superior to that of former Utopists in not seeking to construct out of the imperfect materials which alone the actual can furnish a static order which shall be, and if possible remain eternally, perfect. He aims rather at laying down the principles of an order which shall be capable of progressively growing towards perfection.

The anonymous review of *In the Days of the Comet* (2.8), entitled 'Our Book Shelf', is a short, polite notice which simply comments on Wells's skilful use of the possible 'collision of the earth with the head of a comet' as 'the *deus ex machina* of the present romance'. Although the effects of the comet's vapours are fantastic, 'the theme is developed [...] with scientific knowledge, prophetic insight, lofty purpose, and human sympathy' and so the story 'cannot fail to excite interest and stimulate thought'.

John Perry's review of *The Future in America* (2.9), entitled 'Social Problems in America', is full of praise for Wells's analysis and lack of dogmatism and he predicts that 'during the next twenty years this book will be referred to and quoted from by every good writer on social problems'. Perry uses the opportunity of the review to air his own views on America's future, though he does offer one criticism of Wells: 'We are inclined to think that Mr Wells pays too much attention to America of the present, and that if he thought more of America of the past he would be altogether optimistic'.

Following Perry's review, William Thiselton-Dyer comments upon Wells's observations of racial interbreeding in *The Future in America*, calling Wells's reference to a black child being born to a white mother and a mixed-race father 'ultra-Mendelian', and doubting the accuracy of the description. Thiselton-Dyer, while keeping an open mind, favours the notion that in cases of racial interbreeding, the offspring would generally resemble the predominant racial strain of its ancestors.

This letter provoked a strong response from Wells, who disputed the story in his own book of 'The Pure White Mother and the Coal-black Babe'. Rather, Wells asserts that he 'told the anecdote simply to illustrate the nonsense people will talk under the influence of race mania' and he hopes the story will not be used to bolster the case for Mendelism.

In his review of *What is Coming?* (2.10) entitled 'Forecast by Mr Wells', Joseph Proudman mildly mocks Wells's assumptions concerning the outcome of the Great War. Due to the heavy loss of life, the financial burden of the war and the unlikelihood of any nation being completely defeated, 'Mr Wells thinks that the world peace is coming soon through universal self-sacrifice' and '"an ultimate confederation of the nations of the earth"', though Proudman calls this 'a guileless notion'. Instead, he suggests that peace will come to the world as a result of the 'loss of its wealth [...] by the exhaustion of its coal', and on this single assertion he ends his review.

Nature gave generous exposure to several editions of Wells's *The Outline of History* (2.11), and, through reviewing the debate on evolution between Wells and Hilaire Belloc (including Wells's *Mr Belloc Objects to 'The Outline of History'*), opened its pages to controversy.

The first review, 'The Dominion of Man', is of part one of the twenty-part publication of the first edition of the work, dealing with the formation of earth and the evolution of pre-mammalian creatures. While the anonymous reviewer merely abstracts this part one of the work, he or she does conclude that 'no other writer of the present day is so well equipped [...] to bring it to a successful completion'.

The second review of *The Outline of History*, 'A "Tour de Force"', also anonymous, is of the first book version (but second edition following its 20-part publication). The reviewer, while acknowledging the inevitable errors and omissions of a work of its nature, nonetheless asserts that 'Mr Wells has shown his day and generation the sort of history of the world that every educated man should have as a possession in his mind'. The book is called 'a *personal* document', reflecting 'the author's philosophy', though this is not condemned as 'Whether it makes for good history we do not know; it has made for a fascinating book which it does one good to read. Its influence will be far-reaching' and, in any event, 'it will be a still bigger gift when someone writes another like it from a different point of view. From out of the mouth of two or more witnesses there is some chance of the truth being stated'.

The third review of *The Outline of History*, 'Our Bookshelf', again anonymous, covers the first two parts of the 1925, 24-part fourth edition of the book. The reviewer praises Wells for virtually rewriting the work in light of new discoveries in the six years since it first appeared, and for greatly increasing the number of illustrations throughout.

The fourth review, also titled 'Our Bookshelf', assesses the same edition, though following the publication of all 24 parts, as well as *Mr Belloc Objects to 'The Outline of History'*, Wells's refutation of Hilaire Belloc's criticisms of the book as published in the *Tablet* and the *Catholic Herald*, a refutation which 'makes short work of Mr Belloc's criticisms'. Especially praiseworthy are the illustrations to *The Outline of History*, 'perhaps as remarkable a collection of photographs covering all sides of human evolution and history as has ever been gathered together within the covers of one book'. Wells's breadth of coverage, and the immediacy of his research, are credited: 'To have mastered so vast a body of material, and to have kept abreast of current opinion on so many technical subjects, is in itself no small intellectual feat'.

Belloc's sniping at Wells and Wells's return of fire provoked further criticisms from Belloc, and as the attacks centred on questions of evolution, Arthur

Keith, in 'Is Darwinism Dead?', was commissioned to review all the books in the debate: Wells's *Mr Belloc Objects to 'The Outline of History'* and Belloc's *A Companion to Mr Wells's 'Outline of History'* and *Mr Belloc Still Objects to Mr Wells's 'Outline of History*. Keith focuses his investigation on whether Belloc is an evolutionist and whether a fundamentalist, and he decides that Belloc must be both, for he agrees with St Thomas Aquinas that 'the creation of man was not mediate but direct' but also acknowledges kinship between the blood of humans and that of the anthropoid apes, and refers to 'the moment when a true man existed at all'. Belloc quibbles, however, with three aspects of Darwinism; he rejects humanity's gradual evolution (believing 'that man's emergence was of the nature of a leap'), he disbelieves that humanity continues to evolve (believing instead that 'he is now and will ever remain a "fixed type"') and he rejects natural selection as the medium of evolution. On this latter objection, Keith explodes Belloc's criticisms by revealing the dated source Belloc relies upon, and the subsequent arguments which have been made to discredit such critics of natural selection as St George Mivart.

Belloc responded to Keith's review, stating that the reviewer must not have read his books given the conclusions he draws, and both denies his reliance on Mivart as a source for his critique of natural selection and asserts that his books cite many noted biologists as evidence of the disregard with which natural selection has come to be held. Keith responded to Belloc, mentioning a further two other discredited sources which Belloc used (Louis Vialleton and Thomas Dwight), and standing by his review of Belloc's books.

James Garnett, in his review of *The Salvaging of Civilisation* (2.12) ('Education and World Citizenship'), calls Wells's works 'always important' and praises his 'remarkably clear and orderly thought'. The book under review emphasises the role of education in 'the political reconstruction of the world' as education will create the 'unity of purpose' required for world peace and harmony. 'Unity of outlook upon natural science, upon history, and upon literature, as well as upon the aim and purpose of human progress, he would secure by means of common text-books – "The Bible of Civilisation" – always being revised, but always and everywhere in use' – an early manifestation of what Wells would later call the 'World Encyclopaedia (see 1.10). To pay for the educational revolution Wells desired, he seeks a reduction in military expenditure, and so 'we need to come to an agreement with the other nations of the world [...] for a general limitation of armaments, that would enormously reduce the burden of taxation and set free far more than sufficient money to expand and improve our educational organisations as rapidly as is humanly possible'.

Garnett takes issue with Wells's globalist vision on two counts: first, he rejects as impossible Wells's desire that 'the world commonwealth [...] should be attained by the immediate absorption of the existing seventy or eighty independent sovereign States of the world into a single super-State', and second, 'Mr Wells is surely mistaken in supposing that we must get rid of patriotism if we are to have an adequate sense of world-citizenship'. Garnett believes loyalty to the nation can coexist alongside world citizenship in the way that county loyalties exist within Britain without detriment to counties or nation.

In his review of *A Short History of the World* (2.13), 'Unified Human History', Francis Marvin says the book covers 'the same ground as the *Outline of History* and in the same spirit, but re-written and better written, and correcting many of the faults of judgement and proportion which disfigured the earlier book' and he asserts that 'all who are interested either in history, in education or in the social progress of the world as a whole, are under a deep debt of gratitude to Mr Wells'. Writing of Wells's approach to 'teaching world-history to all nations on a common plan', Marvin states that he 'has provoked demands among working men to be taught history in that spirit; it has changed the outlook and the syllabuses of scores of teachers; it has helped to success other similar books'.

One fault Marvin does identify, there is 'a general tendency in the book to lay stress rather on the externals and the picturesque figures in history than on the deeper, spiritual, or intellectual factors. [...] Science appears as the transformer of industry, the generator of steam-engines and steam-ships, but not as the knitter-up of men's minds, the new universal doctrine which replaces theological dogma'. Supporting rather than rejecting Wells's ideological methodology in writing history, Marvin advises that,

> It would help his general cause, which is the salvation of mankind by education and unity, to lay more stress on the spiritual or intellectually constructive aspect of science and less on its mechanical applications. It is not the difficulties of posts and tariffs which will ultimately bring mankind together in harmonious progress: it will be a spiritual union of which knowledge and sympathy, science and law are co-operating factors, and may be traced growing, sometimes fitfully, and at various times and places, but never quite extinguished from the beginning of history till now.

In John Scott Haldane's review of *Men Like Gods* (2.14), 'Biology in Utopia', Wells's story is praised as good literature, but more relevantly, 'since Mr Wells is giving us not only a story, but his idea of what a properly-used human faculty might make of humanity in the space of a hundred generations, his romance has become a fit subject for biological dissection in these pages'. In his comprehensive estimation of Wells's book, Haldane notes a number of convincing prophecies within its pages: 'machinery has become so self-regulating that it does not make man captive [...] but is a real servant'; Wells's 'domestic-minded leopards and tigers [...] should not be lightly dismissed after recent experiments on the inheritance of tameness and wildness in rats – not to mention our knowledge of many breeds of dog'; Wells 'believes that, given real knowledge of the life-histories and inter-relations of organisms, man could proceed successfully to wholesale elimination of a multitude of noxious bacteria, parasitic worms, insects, and carnivores'. But the 'most radical and inevitably the most provocative of our author's imaginings' is Wells's thoughts on 'the alteration of [...] human nature itself'. Haldane calls this aspect of the novel 'extremely interesting', as Wells 'reduces the role of eugenics to a minimum, exalts that of education, or, if you prefer it, environment, to a maximum'. The 'change of heart' in humanity is achieved through 'the substitution of the ideal of creative service for that of competition'; through negative eugenics (the 'breeding out' of certain characteristics) and educational reform, 'a race has been produced of great beauty and physical strength, great intellectual and artistic capacities, interested primarily in two things – the understanding of Nature for its own sake, and its control for the sake of humanity'.

Haldane's review was responded to by Karl Pearson, who took exception to his recognition of eugenic change in animals (experiments on tameness and wildness in rats) while marginalising its potential in humans. Pearson concludes by stating that 'It is very strange how dominant is the wholly unwarranted belief that man is an animal for whom other laws hold than for his humbler mammalian kindred'.

Haldane replied to Pearson, stating that, in fact, 'other laws' of change do apply to humans due to humanity's ability to pass on tradition through successive generations, and also its ability to appreciate cultural achievement. Haldane summarises his views by concluding that human advance will not occur by eugenics alone, but 'alteration of environment, especially of social environment, must co-operate with eugenics if any human progress is to be achieved'.

In 'The Visioning of Science', V. B. uses a review of *The Story of a Great Schoolmaster* (2.15) to consider the possibility of a universal telling of life through a combination of history and biology. V. B. sees Frederick Sanderson, the 'great schoolmaster' in question, as a player in this new scientific telling of history or historical presentation of biology. Sanderson's efforts to create a scientific Hall of Vision to mirror the school chapel as dual foci within Oundle School is praised as an attempt to go beyond the historicisation of science to a merging of science and religion but 'The underlying problem of synthesis baffled him, for the sufficient reason that, as yet, official science is devoid of vision, and ecclesiastical vision is empty of science'.

Henry Armstrong, in 'Education, Science and Mr H. G. Wells', reviews *The World of William Clissold* (2.16), and begins by challenging its genre: 'The attempt is made, in a preface, to justify the contention that the book is a novel:

there is no novel in it: [...], we are dealing with autobiography [...]. It is a medical treatise – largely on social pathology'. Armstrong is quite critical of Wells's vision in the novel, seeing it as impracticable or deluded.

> He contemplates the organisation of a central police bureau to co-ordinate the protection of life, property and freedom throughout the world, without distinction of persons under a universally accepted code. [...] The coal strike was only begun when the book was issued. The history of Ireland, the love lost between the States of Europe, the growing development during many years past of local self-government in Great Britain – such items are left out of account.

Wells desires a new type of social commitment, which will bring with it an abundance of responsibility and power:

> The new social life will be aristocratic in the sense that it will have a decisive stratum of pre-eminent and leading individuals who will wield a relatively large part of the power and property of the community but it will be democratic in the sense that it will be open to every one with ability and energy to join that stratum and participate to the extent of his or her ability or energy.

This democratic elitism runs through Wells's works, such as with the Samurai of *A Modern Utopia* (2.7), and has been debated by critics ever since.

On Wells's indictment of modern education, Armstrong is in total agreement. In place of public schools and elite universities, 'The new system will be one of special schools, studios and laboratories for arts, sciences, language and every sort of technical work. The style of work will be new'.

In 'Science in Literature', Hyman Levy reviews Wells's *The Short Stories of H. G. Wells* (2.17). Of all the authors of fiction, old and new, Levy asserts that 'there is no novelist, with the exception of Mr H. G. Wells, in whom the dramatic element in scientific discovery evokes a sufficient response to urge him to action'. Levy relishes Wells's scientific approach to literature, noting that in 'The Land Ironclads' 'in 1903 trench warfare and tanks are described in unerring detail'. But more than just mechanical speculation, in Wells's short stories 'Mankind itself raises a problem of colossal magnitude – how to utilise the accumulating wealth of scientific knowledge in the design of a super-race – of a civilisation devoid of the stupidities and absurdities of social life as we know it'. Levy opposes the utopian Wells to the provocative Wells, and concludes that 'Wells on the constructive side is much less satisfying than at his favourite game of thought provoking'. Alas, Levy's interest in the early Wells of the short stories is countered by his disappointment in the later Wells: 'The kind of promise the imaginative Wells has held out in these early stories is not fulfilled by him in his later work. [T]he far-reaching and vital questions which Wells himself raised have really not been faced by him'.

In 'The Way the World might go' by Alexander Carr-Saunders, and 'The Politics of Science' by Louis Fenn, *Nature* prints reviews of *The Way the World is Going*, *The Open Conspiracy*, and the revised edition of the latter, *What are We to do with our Lives?* (2.18).

Carr-Saunders, in his review of the first two books, declares that 'Men of science owe a debt of gratitude to Mr H. G. Wells. He was born with a passion to make things better, and there is implicit in all his writings the view that the advancement of science and the application of scientific knowledge is the indispensable method whereby this end may be achieved'. In all the genres he has used, 'He wrote because he had lessons to teach', though, 'as he departs from the form of the novel, we become conscious of a certain thinness and a certain dryness'. Thus,

> The programme [of the 'Open Conspiracy'] as suggested in *William Clissold* is just definite enough to be real. It is not formalised or presented in an orderly fashion, but it comes through the incidental discussions and descriptions, and comes, moreover, with freshness. The book vibrates. It is exciting. It is concrete. Here [in *The Open Conspiracy*] Mr Wells attempts a fuller treatment, more logical and more abstract. It is not the same compelling force.

Fenn, in his review of *What are We to do with our Lives?*, observes that 'The book [...] is an attempt to impose the applications of science on the social and political world of to-day', stating that it is 'a highly concentrated essence, distilled from the author's sociological writings of the last twenty years' from *A Modern Utopia* onwards, though being 'mature and articulate beyond any other sociological book its author has produced'. Far from being a 'new movement', the 'open conspiracy' 'is a plan of world reconstruction made necessary by science and conceived in the scientific spirit [...] presented as a statement of a general tendency which its author perceives in the minds of intelligent contemporaries'. In sum, Wells believes that 'constructively-minded people should deliberately and progressively possess themselves of the nerve-centres of the world in order to establish a responsible world directorate in control of human affairs'. In the book Wells seeks an end to war, the replacement of the profit motive with 'organised production for use' with regards to 'credit, fuel, power, transport, and food' and scientific population control, especially through 'universal knowledge of contraceptive methods'.

From 1929 onwards, *Nature* published anonymous reviews of three versions of *The Science of Life* (2.19), which Wells co-authored with his eldest son, George Philip Wells, and with Julian Huxley. The first review, entitled 'Biology for All', deals with part one of the 30-part version of the book. The reviewer calls it a 'new educational venture of great attractiveness' in which 'Academic formalities have been thrown off without jettisoning accuracy, and everything is discussed in its bearing on everyday life'.

The second review, 'Biology and Human Life', treats the first deliberate book edition of *The Science of Life* (though the 30-part version had also been bound in book-form a year earlier). The reviewer sees the books as part of a movement to bring biology into everyday life for the planning of the destinies of the human race. Thus,

> while we appreciate *The Science of Life* for its wide reach, its educative lucidity, its fair-mindedness, its freshness of presentation, its arresting figures, and so on, we appreciate it most because the authors have had the courage of their convictions and have not hesitated to proclaim, as their particular gospel, that the utilisation of biological knowledge can do much to save man amid his sea of troubles.

Despite its part in such a movement, however, '*The Science of Life* rather disarms criticism by its frankness and sincerity and by its freedom from dogma'.

The final review, entitled 'The Living World', deals with the 9-book version of *The Science of Life*, revised and introduced anew by the three authors. In this positive review, the parent and teacher are urged to 'use these volumes so that their children or pupils may be educated, not merely crammed'.

'Social Economics' is an anonymous review of *The Work, Wealth and Happiness of Mankind* (2.20). The reviewer sees the book as succeeding *The Outline of History* and *The Science of Life*, the three of which present Wells's ideological case. 'He regards as essential for a modern ideology some understanding of world history (as against local, national, and period history), some assimilation of biological ideas, and – most urgently necessary of all – some conception of economic life, industrial processes, trade, and finance'; 'his third compendium, like its forerunners, is a remarkable, stimulating, valuable, and most readable book'. The book, while telling of work and the generation of wealth and material security, restates Wells's 'reiterated thesis that a civilised World State can only develop in correlation with the spread of the "educated" persona, with the replacement of the motives of profit and privilege by the motive of service in affairs of every kind'.

160

R. Brightman, in 'The Cost of a New World Order', reviews *After Democracy* (2.21) in which he calls Wells 'perhaps the most qualified of living writers to express either the implications of the scientific outlook in the life of society or the responsibilities which fall on the shoulders of scientific workers'. The work 'reiterates repeatedly the significant facts which our whole system of government and industry are still disposed to burke – the abolition of distance, the growth of human life into a world-wide community of interdependent human beings' and the need for a 'fusion of once separate economic systems'. Although Brightman is critical of Wells's attacks on internationalism, he acclaims the fact that the 'most significant note in the book is indeed to be found in the emphasis placed on education' and it is in this field that 'scientific workers everywhere might even yet contribute the decisive factor'.

Lancelot Hogben, in 'Mr Wells Comes Back', reviews *The Shape of Things to Come* (2.22) and writes of it, 'As literature, the dream book of Dr Raven surpasses anything which Mr Wells has written. [...] Few intelligent people will read the history without annoyance. No intelligent person will find it a dull book'. In his visions of the future, Wells 'sees the procession of human beings of diverse capacities and various endowments making their several contributions to the future and interacting with one another within the limits set by a social framework prescribed by the efforts of past generations and constantly being changed by human activities'. In his presentation of the evolving social organism and his advocacy of education as the motor of change, Hogben asserts that 'Wells justifies his claim to be regarded as the midwife of social biology', the chair of which Hogben held at the London School of Economics at the time of writing the review.

Wells's *Experiment in Autobiography* (2.23) received a review for each of its volumes, the second of which provoked an angry response from Wells about the nature of contemporary reviewing.

The first review is by T. LL. H. and is entitled 'Mr H. G. Wells Reveals Himself'. After giving a précis of the volume's content, the reviewer identifies a seeming contradiction in Wells:

> Mr Wells had two guiding principles in life: first, 'If you want something sufficiently, take it and damn the consequences'; and secondly, 'If life is not good enough for you, change it; never endure a way of life that is dull and dreary, because after all the worst thing that can happen to you, if you fight and go on fighting to get out, is defeat, and that is never certain to the end which is death and the end of everything'. Has not the first principle created the chaotic world which Mr Wells is obligingly going to set right?

However, rather than condemning Wells's philosophy on this score, we are told that 'Details are reserved for the second volume to be published in a few weeks'.

The review of the second volume, entitled 'The Autobiography of H. G. Wells', is penned by Hyman Levy. Reading Wells's life in the book, Levy observes that 'For two generations the author has striven with consummate journalistic skill and tireless energy, by educating his public, to get them to appreciate his theme and to desire its realisation. In particular he has succeeded: in general he has failed'. His success was that 'He jerked the youth of last generation out of their complacent acceptance of established tradition in politics, morals and religion'. His failure was that, in promoting his world state ideas, 'He is in fact addressing an intellectual and emotional argument to a group of individuals ['the people in key positions'] from whom he need not expect to receive an emotional response'. Levy is able to form this analysis due to the 'relentless objectivity' with which Wells has told his life story. In terms of the genre, 'he has smashed a staid and formal tradition and raised autobiography to a new level'.

Levy's review, and that of Charles Snow's *The Search* by J. N. and D. N. and a third (unidentified) review, provoked a response from Wells about the nature of reviewing, and especially the 'emotional doctrinaire mysticism' of Marxist critics. Wells felt the critics' emphasis on 'power' in achieving humanistic results was misguided and unscientific, and provoked by the authoritarianism of Nazi Germany and Soviet Russia. In contrast, Wells asserts that 'There is a limit to the concentration of power in human society, beyond which it becomes ineffective and undesirable', and critical analysis should be towards other factors than the usurpation and exercise of crude power.

Levy replied to Wells's letter, stating that 'Mr Wells seems to see [the lever for socio-political change] in the people in key positions, but paradoxically enough he complains that they have not the brains to see. What then?' Wells seeks a scientific solution to contemporary anarchism, but Levy claims that Wells's case for change is based on 'scientifically unverifiable assertions': Wells 'believes in man's ultimate sanity' and 'he *feels*' that 'Power will flow to the effective centres of direction'. Levy, however, does not 'share his sanguine feelings'.

The New America (2.24) receives a brief, anonymous review, in which Wells's observation of America's 'atmosphere of unbridled public discussion' and 'the relative unimportance of large mass antagonisms' in that country are highlighted.

Two anonymous reviews treat Wells's 'film story', *Things to Come* (2.25), and the actual film production, the latter review titled 'Mr H. G. Wells's Film *Things to Come*'. The first reviewer considers the film-script more vivid than the source novel, *The Shape of Things to Come*, in presenting the collapse and rebirth of civilisation and thinks that the 'scientific worker may well find as much interest in the technique with which Mr Wells develops his argument as in the picture he gives of an imaginary scientific age'. The film's reviewer waxes equally lyrical, stating that 'Science has put into the hands of civilised man the power to destroy himself or to make the world a celestial dwelling place; and the sooner this is widely realised the safer will the world be for humanity. There is no better way to-day of making this message universal than through the motion picture; and this is done in the marvellous film *Things to Come*'.

The anonymous, short review of *Man Who Could Work Miracles* (2.26), Wells's film treatment for the Alexander Korda production of the same name, simply makes the point that 'Mr Wells uses his new technique to expound his familiar theme of man's inability to use wisely the powers with which science has endowed him'.

In 'A Social Analysis', Alfred Hall reviews *The Anatomy of Frustration* (2.27). Hall asserts that, while Wells reveals 'the power of science to transform the material world' to the general public, to the scientific community, he 'has awakened them to a consciousness of social disorder, disorder remediable by the application to mankind of the methods by which science is learning to control the other departments of Nature'. Hall sees little construction in the novel, but acknowledges its stimulation, and writes that 'it is better to clear the mind than to trim it into a system'.

In John Burdon Sanderson Haldane's 'Messianic Radiation', a review of *Star Begotten* (2.28), it is noted that '*Star Begotten* [...] despairs of existing humanity, and demands beings of innate endowments superior to our own to deal with the present crisis of civilisation'. Haldane is sceptical of Wells's extra-terrestrial solution, stating that 'If this book encourages a single reader to think, even for one moment, that any natural or supernatural process will take the place of human effort and human thought, then it is a bad book'. However, he softens to conclude, writing that 'if it is read as a record of conversations between rather worried intellectuals, it is not only an excellent piece of writing, but also a valuable historical document'.

The short, anonymous review of *The Camford Visitation* (2.29) summarises the story and calls it 'stimulating, provocative and entertaining'.

In 'Knowledge and World Progress', Allan Ferguson reviews *World Brain* (2.30), observing that 'in most of these addresses Mr Wells seldom wonders far from his main theme – the gathering, indexing, digesting and clarifying of the sum total of present knowledge into an ever-changing, ever-growing World Encyclopaedia' and notes that Wells 'makes his appeal to youth'. Whilst pointing out the inertia of nationalism and the unteachableness of the middle aged, Ferguson is generally optimistic about Wells's educational scheme, concluding that 'If Mr Wells would continue the good work he has initiated in the volume under review, he would add very sensibly to the heavy debt which the civilised world already owes him'.

Three reviews and an editorial treat *The Fate of Homo Sapiens*, *The New World Order* and, the omnibus of these volumes, *The Outlook for Homo Sapiens* (2.31). Regarding the first-named volume, John Hardwick, in 'The Future of Mankind', summarises Wells's thoughts about the possibility of human survival by specifying that 'there will have to be something in the nature of a wholesale conversion of the species to more rational habits of thinking and behaving'. To escape extinction, humankind have to digest the following realities:

(1) the idea and tradition of war must be eliminated; (2) 'The vast and violent wastage of natural resources in the hunt for private profit [...] must be arrested and reversed by the establishment of a collective economy for the whole world'; (3) the resultant world organisation must be 'of an active, progressive, imaginatively exciting nature', so that the surplus energy of youth may be absorbed by it and not allowed to run to destructive waste in war.

Hardwick observes, however, that 'the educated [...] can be enlightened intellectually, without being in the least enlightened emotionally' and while he accepts that many educationalists are attempting the necessary change in emphasis, 'it is work that will not be done in a day'. In urging such change, Wells has produced 'a timely and sincere book and written without fear of giving offence'.

In 'Victorian Socialism', William Inge critically reviews *The New World Order*, writing of Wells's proposals,

We have only to make a clean sweep of emulation, ambition, love of private ownership, patriotism and pugnacity, and we shall be as happy, progressive and intelligent as a flock of sheep. That is always the way with Utopians. Abolish all the strongest passions and instincts of human nature, and a terminal state of blessedness, an earthly paradise, will be reached.

After critiquing liberalism, democracy, socialism and communism, all of which Wells draws on in his volume, Inge asserts that 'Although Mr Wells's Utopia seems to me utterly unrealisable, no one can read the book without admiration for his earnest longing for a new and better world'.

This review provoked an immediate response from Wells, who took exception to Inge's portrayal of the recently overthrown Republican government in

Spain and his support for the Nationalist attack upon it. Wells asks for evidence of Republican atrocities cited by Inge, and for Inge's assertion that the government butchered 300,000 civilians '"under orders from Moscow"'. In his reply, Inge cites Arthur Bryant and Walter Krivitsky for his anecdotes and statistics.

In an editorial entitled 'Civilisation and the Rights of Man', *Nature* commented upon the volumes reviewed by Ferguson and Inge, noting that in them Wells 'realises that the scientific method of inquiry can be profitably applied to political and social problems, as it is to other aspects of biological development'. The editorialist agrees with Wells's assessment that 'If the civilised world is to survive, the hour has come when measures will have to be devised to control the "gangster" element in human nature, whenever or wherever it manifests itself'. However,

> To strengthen one part by political balance of power or alliances makes other parts of the structure relatively weaker, with the result that the stability of the whole suffers. Mr Wells has, therefore, no sympathy with the movement for the federation of a number of European States, unless it is deliberately made the basis of a system designed ultimately to comprehend all the peoples of the world.

Rather than advocate a monolithic world state, 'It is towards such a world commonwealth, in which each nation can be free to follow its own course of cultural development, that Mr Wells would direct civilised thought'. Such cultural pluralism was to be protected by human rights law, and 'The intention is eventually to produce a Declaration which will represent world-wide opinion, and will crystallise the thoughts of men and women of all ranks and of all races who believe in the essential greatness of mankind'. The editorial urges men and women of science to partake in the 'Rights of Man' debate then being hosted by the *Daily Herald*, as, of its nature, 'The world of science is international in its constitution and aims, and citizenship can be claimed in it by men and women of any race or nationality who will respect the principles implied in the pursuit of scientific truth and endeavour to contribute to the advancement of natural knowledge by following them'.

With *The Fate of Homo Sapiens* and *The New World Order* published in amalgamated form as *The Outlook for Homo Sapiens*, John Hardwick reviewed it in 'Man's Present and Future'. In the revised volume 'Mr Wells speaks of "the triangle of collectivisation, law and knowledge"' upon which the 'new organisation of human life' must be constructed. Scientists are central to Wells's vision, though Hardwick wonders whether Wells too readily takes for granted 'how far the scientific outlook is *necessarily* bound up with humane and liberal ideals'.

In a short notice, James Crowther reviews *Babes in the Darkling Wood* (2.32) and commends Wells's preclusion of 'doctrinaire planning' through his suggestion 'that the problem of modern life should be approached in the spirit of the sculptor who contemplates a block of uncarved marble. The possibilities in it should be conceived by a flexible imagination, and all should hack away at it until they have carved out the figure of society that they desire'. In this late work of fiction, Crowther notes, Wells's 'belief in the future and continual wrestlings with the present are still a major inspiration'.

In 'The Triumph of Time', Herbert Dingle reviews at length *The Conquest of Time* (2.33), in which, rather like in 'The Illusion of Personality' (1.13), Wells argues that

> The individual is actually an element in a larger structure, the species, with which it interacts. The character of the species largely determines (through both physical inheritance and mental adaptation) the character of the individual, whose variations from the norm in turn react on and modify the character of the species.

In the crisis of the Second World War, 'The religion of the new man "demands the subordination of the self, of the aggressive personality, to the common creative task, which is the conquest and animation of the universe by life"'. Questioning the book's status as Wells's culminating philosophy, Dingle notes that it 'is as full of vigour and combativeness as anything that Mr Wells has written; it looks for strength in vitriolic protestation rather than in quietness and in confidence. It impresses one, in fact, as the product more of temporary excitement than of settled conviction'.

Turning to the substance of the book, the reviewer finds it 'unconvincing', as

> His 'conquest' of time is, in fact, a complete and whole-hearted surrender. He maps out the history of the individual and the species; shows where our various emotions and aspirations are located in the time sequence of the individual; is convinced that when he has so distributed all the experiences which come within range of his knowledge the individual ceases to be; and sums up our personality as merely 'serviceable synthetic illusions of continuity'.

Dingle argues that Wells's understanding of time is flawed due to his lack of grasp of Einsteinian relativity. Although Wells is not expected to understand such a complex philosophical concept, Dingle states that his attempted use of it in his philosophical discourse reveals that 'his magnificent castle is nothing but a mirage' and 'It is distressing to think that a life of such great achievement and penetrating vision should culminate in such an anticlimax'.

In 'World Reorganisation', Baron Horder appraises *Phoenix* (2.34), outlining Wells's vision for a socialised world based on universal rights, and developing out of wartime 'special commissions to deal with settlements needed for the winding up of the War'. Wells states that 'We must aim at a system of federally co-operative world authorities with powers delegated to them by the existing Governments'. Horder concludes that Wells has 'performed the prophet's major task – he has stabbed our spirit wide awake. He has shown us clearly the inescapability of our position and he has also shown us what is necessary for our successful emergence from it'.

In 'Science and Broadcasting', T. H. Hawkins reviews *Reshaping Man's Heritage* (2.35), a volume of radio broadcasts introduced, in 'Man's Heritage', by Wells, 'who spoke about man's accomplishments, opportunities and pitfalls'. Hawkins dwells not on the content of the talks, which he finds unimpeachable, but on their presentation. Thus, 'That a man or woman is an authority on a particular subject is not enough to make him a good broadcaster. He should have a microphone manner which will appeal to the largest body of listeners and make them want to listen again to the broadcast of a related subject'. To improve upon the presentation of such broadcast series as 'Reshaping Man's Heritage',

> The BBC should have on its directing staff a man of science of the standing of the co-ordinator of 'Reshaping Man's Heritage'. He should be instructed to develop the place of science in broadcasting and to use the necessary discrimination in the selection – and rejection – of speakers. He should be given a staff whose duty it would be to investigate the various methods of making scientific broadcasts attractive.

In 'The Supremacy of Reason', R. Brightman reviews *'42 to '44* (2.36), stating that, 'For the most part, it is journalism – inconsistent, sometimes irrelevant, even dogmatic or bullying, but always Mr Wells'. The book is full of vituperation, as 'It is obscurantism and prejudice, whether professional, political or religious, that arouse his wrath'. He maintains that 'Knowledge or extinction [...] is the only choice for man. He has no use or place for the emotions or for tradition: reason and the intellect must be the sole controlling factors'. Brightman argues that inconsistency lies at the heart of Wells's thesis, as, according to Wells,

Personality is an illusion; yet, he argues, it is compatible with an impersonal over-riding intelligence. But how in default of leadership and personality a new and broader education system throughout the world is to issue in a federated political and economic order and a common fundamental law of human rights, in which a great impersonal society with an unprecedented range of variability is to develop, is never explained.

While not recommending the volume as an introduction to Wells's oeuvre, Brightman commends the fact that, 'in a book that insists so strongly on the illusion of personality, it is Mr Wells's own personality that is dominant, sincere and forceful'.

2.1: *Text-book of Biology* and *Text-book of Zoology*

William Parker, 'Vertebrate Biology' (27 April 1893).[1]

Text-book of Biology. By H. G. Wells, BSc Lond., FZS. With an Introduction by G. B. Howes, FLS, FZS, Assistant Professor of Zoology, Royal College of Science, London. Part I. Vertebrata. (London: W. B. Clive and Co., University Correspondence College Press.)

Mr Wells's book is avowedly written mainly for the purpose of helping solitary workers to pass the Intermediate Science examination[2] of the University of London,[3] and it would therefore by unfair to criticise it from a wider point of view. The scope for originality in such a work is naturally somewhat limited, but it is a pleasant surprise to come across one that is far above the average as regards soundness of treatment and method. The author not only possesses a practical knowledge of the greater part of the subject he deals with, but also evidently takes pleasure in it for its own sake, and has a healthy dislike of 'that chaotic and breathless cramming of terms misunderstood, tabulated statements, formulated "tips," and lists of names, in which so many students, in spite of advice, waste their youth.' He states that 'the marked proclivity of the average schoolmaster[4] for mere book-work[5] has put such a stamp on study that, in nine cases out of ten, a student, unless he is expressly instructed to the contrary, will go to the tortuous, and possibly inexact, description of a book for a knowledge of things that lie at his very finger-tips' (p. 31); and again, on p. 125, that 'it is seeing and thinking much more than reading, which will enable' the student 'to clothe the bare terms and phrases of embryology[6] with coherent knowledge.' Throughout the book the importance of actual observation is insisted upon.

The present part deals with the Rabbit, Frog, Dog-fish and, Amphioxus,[7] and includes an account of the development of these animals and of the theory

---

1   Reprinted by permission from Macmillan Publishers Ltd: *Nature* (47: 1226), copyright (1893).

2   A former intermediate undergraduate examination at the University of London, between matriculation and the final degree examination, consisting of questions covering a variety of science topics, in use during the late-19th and early-20th centuries.

3   A federal university, made up of a number of semi-autonomous colleges and schools, founded in 1836.

4   A male school teacher.

5   The use of textbooks in science teaching as opposed to practical work.

6   The branch of science that deals with the development of an organism up to the time of birth or hatching.

7   A lancelet of the genus *Branchiostoma*.

of evolution,[8] as well as a number of questions, most of which have been set at the examinations of the London University. The morphological portions are, on the whole good and clearly written, and a fair amount of physiology[9] is also introduced. A syllabus of practical work is given at the end: this would in many respects bear amplifying. The student is not warned that his time will be wasted if he wanders off the direct path of the examination syllabus; and on the contrary, points of general biological interest are referred to here and there, and these go far to show what a good many of our elementary text-books do not – viz. that the London University syllabus, 'as at present constituted,' affords 'considerable scope for efficient biological study.' The student, moreover, is told that this 'little book is the merest beginning in zoology,'[10] and the last paragraph, on p. 131, indicates the aspect of mind with which the author regards his subject.

Twenty-four folding sheets of sketches are inserted in the text, but the figures are, on the whole, exceedingly rough; and though many of them may be found useful as guides, we feel that the student would do better to postpone drawing until his dissections[11] are made, or even copy some of the numerous good figures to be found elsewhere, than to 'copy and recopy' these sketches first, as advised by the author.

Numerous inaccuracies and awkward expressions occur, only a few of which can be here mentioned. The terms superior and inferior, as applied to the great veins,[12] are likely to confuse a beginner after reading the definitions of the regions of the body given on p. 3. 'Metabolism'[13] and 'metaboly'[14] occur even in consecutive sentences on p. 23. Peristaltic movement[15] is said to move the

---

8　The theory that present-day organisms have come into being by the differentiation and genetic mutation of earlier forms over successive generations.

9　The branch of science that deals with the normal functioning of living organisms and their parts.

10　The science of the structure, physiology, behaviour, classification and distribution of animals.

11　Procedures of methodically cutting up an animal or plant in order to show or examine its internal parts.

12　The *superior vena cava*, which carries deoxygenated blood from the upper part of the body to the heart, and the *inferior vena cava*, which carries deoxygenated blood from the lower part of the body to the heart.

13　The sum of the chemical processes in a cell or organism by which complex substances are synthesised and broken down, and growth and energy production sustained.

14　The change of shape characteristic of protists with a firm but flexible pellicle.

15　Properly, peristalsis, the involuntary muscular movement of the intestines and some other tubular organs by which their contents are propelled along, consisting of waves of alternate circular constrictions and relaxations.

food 'forward' (p. 41). It is stated that the thyroid[16] is similar in structure to the thymus[17] and to 'botryoidal tissue'[18] in general (p. 26), and that the epithelium[19] of the villi,[20] with its striated[21] border, 'is usually spoken of as leading towards "ciliated"[22] epithelium' (p. 22) [sic.]. It is misleading to say that 'a tarsus[23] (tarsalia) *equals* the carpus,'[24] and that the vomer[25] of the dog is paired (pp. 38 and 76). As the term 'Chordata'[26] is adopted on p. 96, it is unfortunate that the student is told on p. 60 that vertebrata occur in which cartilage is absent, and that Amphioxus possesses the 'essential vertebrate features,' 'is *twisted* as it were,' and that its 'vertebral column[27] is devoid of vertebrae:'[28] it is, moreover, inadvisable to use the term 'hyoidean'[29] with regard to this animal. On p. 61 'classes'[30] and 'orders'[31] are used in a correct and incorrect sense in the same sentence. The expression, 'carotid gland'[32] requires a better explanation on p. 67. The morphology of the cardinals,[33] azygos,[34] and post-caval[35] is incompletely explained

---

16 A gland located in the neck which secretes a hormone which regulates growth and development.

17 A glandular organ near the base of the neck.

18 Tissue resembling a cluster of grapes in shape.

19 Tissue of the kind that covers the surface of the body and lines some hollow structures in humans and animals, consisting of sheets of cells bound closely together without intervening connective tissue.

20 Slender hair-like processes or minute projections closely set on a surface, especially in the mucous membrane of the intestines.

21 Striped or streaked.

22 Adorned with delicate hairs along an edge.

23 A bone in the foot below the ankle.

24 The part of a tetrapod skeleton between the forearm and the metacarpus, consisting of eight small bones and forming the wrist.

25 A small thin bone forming the posterior part of the partition between the nostrils on most higher vetrebrates.

26 Animals which possess a notochord (for at least some part of their lives).

27 The spinal column.

28 The bony joints or segments composing the spinal column in vertebrates.

29 Of or pertaining to the hyoid, the bone or group of bones which supports the tongue, being situated at its base above the thyroid cartilage.

30 The principle taxonomic groupings ranking above orders and below phyla or divisions.

31 In biology, basic taxonomic groupings.

32 Properly, carotid body, a small mass of receptors in the carotid artery sensitive to chemical change in the blood.

33 Of or pertaining to the hinge of a bivalve mollusc.

34 A vein running up the right side of the thoracic vertebral column.

35 An alternative name for the *inferior vena cava*.

(pp. 87, 120, and 124). Several serious mistakes are made with regard to the homologies of the urinogenital apparatus[36] (*cf.*, *e. g.* pp. 92 and 114). Misprints are also fairly abundant throughout.

Most of these faults are, however, such as can be remedied in a future edition,[37] and the book will, we think, serve the purpose for which it was written very satisfactorily.

William Parker, 'Our Book Shelf' (14 December 1893).[38]

Text-book of Biology. By H. G. Wells, BSc Lond., FZS, Lecturer in Biology at University Tutorial College. With an Introduction by G. B. Howes, FLS, FZS, Assistant Professor of Zoology, Royal College of Science, London. Part II. Invertebrates and Plants. (London: W. B. Clive, University Correspondence College Press, 1893.)

In dealing with a small number of vertebrate types in Part I of this book (see *Nature*, vol. xlvii. 1893, p. 605), the author showed distinct capability and promise; but we feel that he would have done well to wait and work for a few years before publishing this second volume, which covers a larger field. As the types of plants and invertebrates[39] treated of have already been described in so many text-books, the writer had, at any rate, the opportunity of getting his facts and deductions second hand and fairly correctly stated, even without an extensive acquaintance with biological science. There is, therefore, all the less excuse for the many errors and misstatements that occur in this volume, the preface to which would lead one to expect better things in this respect, as well as in the selection and arrangement of facts. Prof. Howes's Introduction appeared in Part I; and before inserting his name on the title-page of Part II it would, we think, have been only just to have at least submitted the proofs[40] to him. The book would certainly have gained by so doing.

Apart from the more serious faults, which are so numerous that it is not easy to give a short selection of them, awkward terms and misprints abound.

---

36 Collectively, the components of the urinary and the genitals.

37 A second edition, revised by Wells, appeared in 1894.

38 Reprinted by permission from Macmillan Publishers Ltd: *Nature* (49: 1259), copyright (1893). On reading this review, Wells wrote, in a letter to his, mother Sarah Wells, dated 15 December 1893, 'Part II of my Biology has been slashed up most cruelly by this week's *Nature* in a review' (Smith 1998, I: 208).

39 The collective noun for animals without a backbone or a spinal column.

40 A trial impression of a text to be checked for errors and marked for correction before subsequent revision and final printing.

Prof. Goebel would probably be surprised to hear that he had written a text-book on botanical 'mythology'[41] (p. 94)!

The illustrations are exceedingly crude, and are mostly rough copies of well known figures. It is, however, only fair to state that the author has purposely made them 'as simple and diagrammatic as possible.'

'Our Bookshelf' (24 July 1913).[42]

Text-book of Zoology. By H. G. Wells and A. M. Davies. Sixth edition. Revised by J. T. Cunningham. Pp. viii + 487. (London: W. B. Clive, University Tutorial Press, Ltd., 1913.) Price 6*s.* 6*d.*

The supplement which Mr Cunningham added to the fifth edition of this popular text-book has now been incorporated in the body of the work, and the section dealing with the Invertebrata has been rearranged so that the types follow in general the descending order in classification. Important additions have been made explaining the facts and theories of most importance to modern biologists in relation to the problems of evolution.

---

41   Probably a reference to Karl von Goebel's book on plant morphology, *Grundzüge der systematik und speciellen pflanzenmorphologie* (1882).

42   Reprinted by permission from Macmillan Publishers Ltd: *Nature* (91: 2282), copyright (1913).

2.2: *The Time Machine*

From 'Science in the Magazines' (10 January 1895).[1]

[...]

In the *New Review*[2] are some verses having a singularly strange and appropriate rhythm, by the late R. L. Stevenson, in which he has expressed his keen sense of the struggle for existence;[3] and we find in the critical article upon this last among the many losses of 1894, by Mr Archer,[4] how profoundly modern scientific thought had affected his philosophy. There is also the first instalment of an eccentric story by Mr H. G. Wells, in which, after certain rather paradoxical dealings with the four dimensions, a 'Time Traveller' starts into futurity upon a *Time Machine*.[5] What he found there remains to be told in a subsequent number, but there certainly seems scope for the scientific imagination in such a story.

'Our Book Shelf' (18 July 1895).[6]

The Time Machine. By H. G. Wells. (London: Wm Heinemann, 1895.)

Ingeniously arguing that time may be regarded as the fourth dimension of which our faculties fail to give us any distinct impression, the author of this admirably-told story has conceived the idea of a machine which shall convey the traveller either backwards or forwards in time. Apart from its merits as a clever piece of imagination, the story is well worth the attention of the scientific reader, for the reason that it is based so far as possible on scientific data, and while not taking it too seriously, it helps one to get a connected idea of the possible results of the ever-continuing processes of evolution. Cosmical[7] evolution, it may be re-

---

1   Reprinted by permission from Macmillan Publishers Ltd: *Nature* (51: 1315), copyright (1895).

2   A British popular periodical, published from 1889 to 1897.

3   Probably a reference to Stevenson's poem, 'If This Were Faith' (1895).

4   'In Memoriam R. L. S.' (1895).

5   'The Time Machine' was serialised in the *New Review* from January to May 1895.

6   Reprinted by permission from Macmillan Publishers Ltd: *Nature* (52: 1342), copyright (1895). This review has previously been reprinted in Ruddick 2001, 268-69. John Hammond writes of it, 'This review is important since it highlights the fact that *The Time Machine*, though a work of fiction, is based on scientific data. The reviewer recognises that the novel is "admirably told" and that its author is acquainted with current ideas concerning evolution and the nature of time. By stressing that the novel "is well worth the attention of the scientific reader," the reviewer helped to ensure that *The Time Machine* received a wider readership than the normal fiction market' (Hammond 2004, 119).

7   Of or pertaining to the universe as a totality.

marked, is in some degree subject to mathematical investigations, and the author appears to be well acquainted with the results which have been obtained in this direction. It is naturally in the domain of social and organic evolution that the imagination finds its greatest scope.

Mounted on a 'time-machine' the 'time-traveller' does not come to a halt until the year eight hundred and two thousand,[8] and we are then favoured with his personal observations in that distant period. In that 'golden age,'[9] the constellations had put on new forms, and the sun's heat was greater, perhaps in consequence of the fall of a planet into the sun, in accordance with the theory of tidal evolution.[10] 'Horses, cattle, sheep, and dogs had followed the ichthyosaurus[11] into extinction'; but, most remarkable of all, 'man had not remained one species, but had differentiated into two distinct animals,' an upper-world people[12] of 'feeble prettiness,' and a most repulsive subterranean race[13] reduced to mere mechanical industry. It is with the time-traveller's adventures among these people, and their relations to each other, that the chief interest of the story, as such, belongs.

Continuing his journey to an age millions of years hence, nearly all traces of life had vanished, the sun glowed only with a dull red heat, tidal evolution had brought the earth to present a constant face to the sun, and the sun itself covered a tenth part of the heavens. These and other phenomena are very graphically described, and from first to last the narrative never lapses into dullness.

---

8   The year 802,701 to be precise.

9   An idyllic time of prosperity, happiness and innocence.

10   The theory, devised by George Darwin, that the planets of the solar system are slowing down, resulting in the moon drifting away from the earth, and planets eventually collapsing into the sun.

11   Any of a group of marine reptiles of Mesozoic times with paddle like limbs and a caudal fin.

12   The Eloi of the novel.

13   The Morlocks of the novel.

2.3: 'Human Evolution, an Artificial Process'

From 'Science in the Magazines' (15 October 1896).[1]

[...]

A third article in the *Fortnightly*[2] is by Mr H. G. Wells, and the title is 'Human Evolution, an Artificial Process.' Starting from well-known biological facts, suggestive conclusions in ethics and educational science are reached. 'Assuming the truth of Natural Selection,' says Mr Wells, 'and having regard to Prof. Weismann's destructive criticisms of the evidence for the inheritance of acquired [characteristics], there are satisfactory grounds for believing that man (allowing for racial blendings[3]) is still mentally, morally, and physically, what he was during the later Palaeolithic period,[4] that we are, and that the race is likely to remain, for (humanly speaking) a vast period of time, at the level of the Stone Age.[5] The only considerable evolution that has occurred since then, so far as man is concerned, has been, it is here asserted, a different sort of evolution altogether, an evolution of suggestions and ideas.' Taking the average rate at which rabbits breed, something like two hundred generations would descend from a single doe in a century, and would be subjected to the process of Natural Selection, whereas only four or five human generations would be amenable to the same process in the same time. 'Taking all these points together, and assuming four generations of men to the century – a generous allowance – and ten thousand years as the period of time that has elapsed since man entered upon the age of Polished Stone,[6] it can scarcely be an exaggeration to say that he has had time only to undergo as much specific modification as the rabbit could get through in a century.' The difference between civilised man and the Stone Age savage arises from the development of speech and writing,[7] so that, to follow the argument, civilised man represents (1) an inherited factor,[8] the natural man, who

---

1   Reprinted by permission from Macmillan Publishers Ltd: *Nature* (54: 1407), copyright (1896).

2   I. e., the *Fortnightly Review*.

3   Mixed race.

4   A prehistoric era distinguished by the development of stone tools, extending from 2.5 million years ago to 10,000 BC.

5   The prehistoric period characterised by the predominance of stone tools, divided into Palaeolithic, Mesolithic and Neolithic.

6   Properly, the Neolithic age, the last phase of the stone age, characterised by the rise of farming, occurring between 8500 BC and 4300 BC.

7   First developed in Mesopotamia in the 4th millennium BC.

8   The genetic characteristics acquired by an offspring from its parents.

is the product of natural selection, and (2) an acquired factor,[9] the artificial man, the highly plastic creature of tradition, suggestion, and reasoned thought. Obviously, then, education should aim at the careful and systematic manufacture of the latter factor.

---

9   The human ability to evolve through intellectual inheritance via such means as education, tradition, etc.

2.4: *The War of the Worlds*

Richard Gregory, 'Science in Fiction' (10 February 1898).[1]

The War of the Worlds. By H. G. Wells. Pp. 303. (London: William Heinemann, 1898.)

Many writers of fiction have gathered material from the fairy-land[2] of science, and have used it in the construction of literary fabrics, but none have done it more successfully than Mr H. G. Wells. It is often easy to understand the cause of failure. The material may be used in such a way that there appears no connection between it and the background upon which it is seen; it may be so prominent that the threads with which it ought to harmonise are thrown into obscurity; or (and this is the worst of all) it may be employed by a writer whose knowledge of natural phenomena is not sufficient to justify his working with scientific colour. Mr Wells makes none of these mistakes. Upon a groundwork of scientific fact, his vivid imagination and exceptional powers of description enable him to erect a structure which intellectual readers can find pleasure in contemplating.

The Time Machine – considered by the majority of scientific readers to be Mr Wells' best work – showed at once that a writer had arisen who was not only familiar with scientific facts, but who knew them intimately enough to present a view of the future. *The Island of Doctor Moreau*, though decried by some critics,[3] is a distinctly powerful work, and the worst that can be said of it is that the pabulum[4] it provides is too strong for the mental digestion of sentimental readers. But in several respects *The War of the Worlds* is even better than either of these contributions to scientific romance,[5] and there are parts of it which are more stimulating to thought than anything that the author has yet written.

The invasion of the earth by inhabitants of Mars[6] is the idea around which the present story is constructed. The planet is, as Mr Percival Lowell puts it, older in age if not in years than the earth; and it is not unreasonable to suppose that if sentient beings[7] exist upon it they would regard our world as a desirable

---

1 Reprinted by permission from Macmillan Publishers Ltd: *Nature* (57: 1476), copyright (1898). This review has previously been reprinted in Parrinder 1972, 74-76, and Danahay 2003, 229-31.

2 An enchanted region.

3 See Parrinder 1972, 43-56, for the outrage of several critics who considered *The Island of Doctor Moreau* either gory or blasphemous.

4 That which nourishes and sustains the mind or soul.

5 Fiction using science or pseudo-science as a plot device to engage readers and allow the author to explore fantastic themes and notions.

6 The fourth planet in order of distance from the sun.

7 Creatures capable of perception by the senses.

place for occupation after their own globe had gone so far in the secular cooling[8] as to be unable to support life. Mr Wells brings the Martians[9] to the earth in ten cylinders discharged from the planet and precipitated[10] in Surrey. The immigrants are as much unlike men as it is possible to imagine, and only a writer familiar with the lines of biological development[11] could conceive them. The greater part of their structure was brain, which sent enormous nerves to a pair of large eyes, an auditory organ,[12] and sixteen long tactile tentacles[13] arranged about the mouth; they had none of our complex apparatus of digestion, nor did they require it, for instead of eating they injected into their veins the fresh living blood of other creatures. Their organisms did not sleep any more than the heart of man sleeps; they multiplied by budding; and no bacteria entered into the scheme of their life. When they came to the earth they brought with them a means of producing a ray of intense heat[14] which was used in connection with a heavy vapour[15] to exterminate the inhabitants of London and the neighbourhood.

This bald outline does not, however, convey a good idea of the narrative, which must be read before the ingenuity which the author displays in manipulating scientific material can be appreciated. The manner in which the Martians are disposed of is undoubtedly the best instance of this skill. As the Martians had eliminated micro-organisms[16] from their planet, when they came to the earth their bodies were besieged by our microscopic allies, and they were destroyed by germs to which natural selection had rendered us immune. This is a distinctly clever idea, and it is introduced in a way which will allay the fears of those who may be led by the verisimilitude[17] of the narrative to expect an invasion from Mars. Of course, outside fiction such an event is hardly worth consideration; but that the possibility of it can be convincingly stated, will be conceded after reading Mr Wells' story. A remarkable case of the fulfilment of fiction is furnished by the history of the satellites of Mars. When Dean Swift wrote *Gulliver's Travels* (published in 1726), he made the astronomers on the island of Laputa[18] not

---

8   In astronomy, a planet's drop in temperature consequent on its gradual change in orbit.

9   The imagined inhabitants of Mars.

10   Thrown down headlong.

11   A reference to Wells's biological training at the Normal School of Science (1884-87) and his bachelor of science qualification from the University of London (1891).

12   An archaic equivalent of gustatory organ; the taste buds.

13   Slender flexible limbs or appendages in an animal.

14   The novel's heat-ray, an early example of a laser-beam weapon.

15   The novel's black smoke, an early example of the use of poison gas as a weapon.

16   Commonly, microbes, microscopic organisms.

17   The appearance of being true or real.

18   The flying island in Jonathan Swift's *Gulliver's Travels* (1726) whose inhabitants were addicted to visionary projects.

only observe two satellites, but caused one of these to move round the planet in less time than the planet itself takes to rotate on its axis. As every student of astronomy now knows, the satellites were not discovered until 1877, and one of them actually does revolve round Mars three times while the planet makes a rotation.[19] The coincidence is remarkable; but it is to be hoped, for the sake of the peace of mind of terrestrial inhabitants, that Mr Wells does not possess the prophetic insight vouchsafed[20] to Swift.

In conclusion, it is worth remark that scientific romances are not without a value in furthering scientific interests; they attract attention to work that is being done in the realm of natural knowledge, and so create sympathy with the aims and observations of men of science.

---

19   Mars's moons, Phobos and Deimos, were discovered by Asaph Hall in 1877, the former orbiting the planet three times during its rotation.

20   Granted to or assured.

2.5: *The First Men in the Moon*

'A Lunar Romance' (9 January 1902).[1]

The First Men in the Moon. By H. G. Wells. Pp. 312. (London: George Newnes, 1901.) Price 6*s*.[2]

It is many years now since Jules Verne wrote his imaginary account of a journey to the moon.[3] He supposed a party of three men enclosed in a projectile shot by a huge gun towards the moon, which they never reached; they fell back to earth and escaped in a marvellous manner to tell the tale. The work was imaginative enough to hold the attention, but full of scientific blunders and improbabilities of the most glaring character. Mr Wells has produced a book of a very different character; he has made himself master of the little we know about the moon, and thought out the possibilities with the greatest care, and the result is a narrative which we will venture to say is not only as exciting to the average reader as Jules Verne's, but is full of interest to the scientific man. We do not mean that the astronomer is likely to learn any new facts from this *résumé*,[4] for which he himself furnished the material; but he will be astonished to find how different the few scientific facts with which he is familiar look in the dress in which a skilful and imaginative writer can clothe them, and it is worth reading the book with minute care to see if one cannot catch Mr Wells in any little scientific slip. Some writers are so easy to catch that the game is not worth playing; but Mr Wells is a worthy opponent, and we are glad to see that his scientific rank has

---

1   Reprinted by permission from Macmillan Publishers Ltd: *Nature* (65: 1680), copyright (1902).

2   Norman and Jeanne MacKenzie have pointed out the role of Richard Gregory, an editorial assistant at *Nature* at this time, in assisting Wells in developing the scientific basis of *The First Men in the Moon*: Wells 'had some technical help from Gregory who, in June 1899, sent Wells a number of papers on lunar craters, and an article from *Nature* which was published in August 1900 in which a Professor Poynting gave an account of experiments made to determine whether any substance could screen off gravitation – the idea that Wells used under the name of "Cavorite" to carry Cavor's capsule between the earth and the moon' (MacKenzie and MacKenzie 1987, 151). Poynting's article, which was a printing of his Royal Institution lecture of 23 February 1900, concludes against the possibility of cutting off gravity in the way Wells suggests in his story: 'So while experiments to determine G are converging on the same value, the attempts to show that, under certain conditions, it may not be constant, have resulted so far in failure all along the line. No attack on gravitation has succeeded in showing that it is related to anything but the masses of the attracting and the attracted bodies. It appears to have no relation to physical or chemical condition of the acting masses or to the intervening medium' (Poynting 1900, 408).

3   A reference to Jules Verne's *De la terre à la lune* (1865) and *Autour de la lune* (1870).

4   French, a summary or epitome.

been recognised by the Royal Institution, who have invited him to lecture on January 24.[5]

The visit to the moon is made possible by the discovery of a substance (cavorite) impervious to gravitation. This interesting property only comes to cavorite at a critical temperature (60° F[6]), after 'the paste has been heated to a dull red glow in a stream of helium,'[7] and the suddenness with which the imperviousness arrives causes interesting events at first. When the new conditions are better realised, a glass sphere is built and covered with cavorite blinds which can be put up or down. When all are down the sphere is entirely free from attraction, and when any particular blind is up it is only attracted by the stars or planets seen in that direction. It is obvious that in these circumstances a comfortable voyage through space is manageable. The two occupants of the sphere journey to the moon and land upon it near the terminator,[8] on a snow drift of frozen air. With sunrise they find that the air melts and evaporates, and there is enough for them to breathe, so that they emerge from the sphere. They find their weight a trivial matter[9] and leap twenty or thirty yards at a step, and a wonderful fungus vegetation springs up before their eyes. In the exhilaration of exploring they lose their sphere and are thus thrown on their own resources. Presently they come across the Selenites, who emerge from the interior of the moon, where they have been spending the lunar[10] night. The first to emerge are those herding the moon calves – great beasts 200 feet long, that browse[11] in a vividly described and rather disgusting manner ('like stupendous slugs') on a speckled green mossy plant. The cowherd[12] was a 'mere ant' by comparison, and the intelligent Selenites generally turn out to be a sort of insect, varied physically in a grotesque manner at will. After various adventures in and on the moon, one of the voyagers recovers the sphere and gets back to earth; the other stays in the moon and sends messages by ethereal telegraphy[13] describing it more fully; and the interest never flags throughout. Following similar writings, Mr Wells sometimes allows himself a sly hint at terrestrial matters in describing lunar affairs. He describes a lunar artist thus (p. 302): –

---

5   A reference to Wells's lecture, 'The Discovery of the Future' (1902).

6   Equivalent to 15.6 degrees Celsius.

7   A colourless, odourless gaseous chemical element which is the lightest of the noble gases.

8   In astronomy, the line of separation between the illuminated and unilluminated parts of a planet or other heavenly body.

9   Wells accurately predicts the effects of reduced gravity on visitors to the moon.

10 Of or pertaining to the moon.

11 Feed on leaves or shoots of trees and bushes.

12 A person who tends grazing cattle.

13 Radio communication through the notional medium of ether.

Love draw. No other thing. Hate all who not draw like him. Angry. Hate all who draw like him better. Hate most people. Hate all who not think all world for to draw.

And two pages on there is a similar burlesque description of a mathematician. It is even easier to see the point than to find the pun in the following: –

> And since the density of the moon is only three-fifths that of the earth,[14] there can be nothing for it but that she is hollowed out by a great system of caverns. There was no necessity, said Sir Jabez Flap, FRS, that most entertaining exponent of the facetious side of the stars, that we should ever have gone to the moon to find out such easy inferences, and points the pun with an allusion to Gruyere[15]...

Of a book so full of unfamiliar things it is impossible to give a complete account. We will conclude this notice by heartily recommending the book to readers both scientific and unscientific, and by giving, with a triumph not free from trepidation, an instance where we think Mr Wells has been caught napping.[16] When the cavorite blinds are closed and the sphere starts on its journey, he describes the curious effects of the absence of external gravitational attraction – all the material occupants of the sphere slowly collect in the interior by their *mutual* attractions, and there is no 'up' or 'down.' Then a window is opened towards the moon and promptly everything gravitates towards the moon – the direction towards the moon is *down*wards, though the attraction is slight. Surely this is a slip? With bodies moving freely in space only the *differential* attraction would be felt, and this would be negligible compared with the mutual attraction of the occupants of the sphere. Even if it were not so small it could not act in the manner specified; its tendency would be to *separate* bodies (as in the case of the tides), not to bring them together, and thus a man near a 'floor' would not fall towards it but would rise from it.[17] But Mr Wells is so wonderfully careful in

---

14 The moon's mean density is 3,346.4 kg / m3 while that of the earth is 5,515.3 kg m3.

15 A firm, pale cow's-milk cheese from Switzerland with many cavities.

16 Found unaware of imminent danger or trouble.

17 According to an email on this subject sent to me by the aerospace technical expert, Thomas Gangale, when the Cavorite blinds are closed all objects inside the sphere would attract each other, so they would tend to cluster together. Additionally, the sphere would be a gravitational source, and the centre of attraction would be the centre of the sphere, so that is where the objects inside the sphere would cluster. When the blinds are opened towards the moon, all objects inside the sphere – and the sphere itself – would free fall toward the moon at the same rate of acceleration, thus objects inside the sphere would float freely. Objects would not fall toward the side of the sphere facing the moon. Any

general that we make this criticism with far less confidence than we should have felt in another case; we have an uneasy feeling that he may dextrously transfer the supposed slip from his account to ours.

Comment on Anonymous: Frank Constable, letter to the editor, 'A Lunar Romance' (6 February 1902).[18]

Is not Mr Wells right in the description of the effect referred to by the reviewer of his *First Men in the Moon* (p. 218)? The *sphere* itself, as a whole, is *not* attracted by gravity.[19] The action of gravity has effect only in the line through the open window, and, *quâ* [20] the sphere, would only affect that part which would be directly in a straight line from the moon through the window.

Reply to Constable: The Reviewer, letter to the editor (6 February 1902).[21]

In answer to Mr Constable, I think we cannot allow that the sphere is not attracted by gravity. I understand it to be a sphere of solid glass, PQ, inside a cavorite covering, RS (Fig. 1).

---

differential attraction would be negligible, since the objects in the sphere would have differential distances from the moon of only a few metres, whereas the objects would be hundreds of thousands of kilometres from the moon. The dominant forces that would be sensed inside the free-falling sphere would be the summed gravitation of the objects and the sphere.

18 Reprinted by permission from Macmillan Publishers Ltd: *Nature* (65: 1684), copyright (1902).

19 A force which all objects with mass are theorised to exert on each other.

20 Latin, in so far as, in the capacity of.

21 Reprinted by permission from Macmillan Publishers Ltd: *Nature* (65: 1684), copyright (1902). Referring to this letter, Arnold Bennett wrote in the *Cosmopolitan Magazine* in August 1902, 'Those who prefix "pseudo" to the scientific part of Mr Wells's novels are not the men of science. On the contrary, one may pleasantly observe the experts of *Nature*, a scientific organ of unrivalled authority, discussing the gravitational phenomena of *The First Men in the Moon*, with the aid of diagrams, and admitting that Mr Wells has the law on his side' (Wilson 1960, 264).

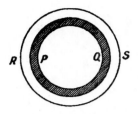

Fig. 1.

In the case considered, the covering is removed through a wide angle AB, thus described (p. 62): 'Four windows were open in order that the gravitation of the moon might act upon all the substances in our sphere.' Hence the gravitational beam reaches the whole of the glass sphere itself (Fig. 2); unless (Fig. 3) Mr Wells means to reserve little pieces, VW and MN, at the sides outside the beam. In this case the total mass of the sphere remains the same, but is not all acted on by gravity; so that the acceleration of the whole would be *less* than *g* (in the ratio of mass acted on to total mass), *i. e.* less than that of objects within, which would promptly settle on the 'floor.'

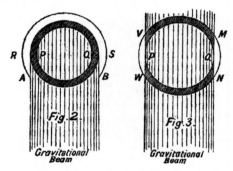

If Mr Wells was thinking in this subtle fashion I withdraw my criticism, and Mr Constable will see that I have left an open door for myself in the review for withdrawal. I may say it was left open expressly in view of this possibility. But the context does not suit this view at all well.

2.6: *Anticipations,* **Mankind in the Making and** *The Food of the Gods*

From 'Notes' (4 April 1901).[1]

Mr H. G. Wells commences, in the current number of the *Fortnightly Review,* a series of speculative papers[2] upon some changes of civilised life and conditions of living likely to occur in the new century. To construct a prehistoric animal from one or two fossil bones is a much easier task than the prediction of future developments from the point of view of the present; but Mr Wells attempts to do this, and even if his prophetic visions do not materialise they will convince the conservative mind that there is some virtue in dissatisfaction at many of the methods of to-day. The subject of the first article is land locomotion in the twentieth century, and it scarcely requires a prophetic afflatus[3] to know that the present systems will be largely superseded or modified. Horse traffic,[4] with its cruelty and filth, while the animals exhaust and pollute the air, must give place to motor carriages[5] in a few years. The railways will then develop in order to save themselves. There will be continuous trains, working perhaps upon a plan like that of the moving platform[6] of the Paris Exhibition,[7] or utilising the principle of the rotating platform outlined by Prof. Perry in these columns (vol. lxii. p. 412, 1900).[8] Nothing is said about the possibilities of aeronautics,[9] not because of any doubt as to its final practicability, but because 'I do not think it at all probable that aeronautics will ever come into play as a serious modification of transport and communication.' It is, of course, impossible to project ourselves into the future so as to say exactly what will or will not come to pass; for an estimate of future performances can only be made with the material now available, and it leaves out of account completely novel discoveries which often revolutionise the

---

1   Reprinted by permission from Macmillan Publishers Ltd: *Nature* (63: 1640), copyright (1901).

2   This refers to the serialisation of 'Anticipations', which ran in nine instalments in the *Fortnightly Review* between April and December 1901.

3   The communication of supernatural knowledge.

4   On public roads, vehicles drawn by horses, or horses themselves when used as transport.

5   Cars, automobiles.

6   Commonly, moving pavement, a footway arranged as a conveyor belt for the carrying of passengers.

7   A world's fair held in Paris, France, from 14 April to 10 November 1900 to celebrate the achievements of the past century and to accelerate development into the next.

8   A reference to John Perry's 'Railways and Moving Platforms' (1900). Perry's idea was for a rotating platform to spin at eight miles per hour, the rim of which would meet the continually moving train passing through the station, and passengers would simply step from the rotating platform onto the train without the train having to stop in the station.

9   The science, art or practice of controlled flight through the air.

whole conditions. Nevertheless, it is not unprofitable to meditate upon the promise of progress.

From 'Notes' (5 September 1901).[10]

'I returned, and saw under the sun, that the race is not to the swift, nor the battle to the strong,'[11] wrote the wise man. Writing in the same prophetic vein, M. J. de Bloch in the current *Contemporary Review*,[12] and Mr H. G. Wells in the *Fortnightly*[13] for September, depict in graphic colours the transformation which the immediate future will witness in the methods of warfare. Both writers are convinced that the military tactics of the past are irretrievably dead. The effective soldier of the future will be a man whose capacity for individual action has been cultivated and developed. The day for all the picturesque accompaniments of war is done, and exhibitions of mere brute courage will be of no avail. Mr Wells takes into account the resources which modern science has made available for the business of war, and proceeds to anticipate the most likely directions that future advances will take. Of one thing he leaves his reader in no doubt, victory is bound to be with the nation that most sedulously attends to the education of its people in the scientific method. The great war of the future will be fought by citizens familiar with destructive instruments of precision, who have learnt to utilise all the accessory helps which science is gradually perfecting. There will be few professional military men of the type of to-day in the ranks of the victorious nation. In Mr Wells's words, 'the warfare of the coming time will really be won in schools and colleges and universities, wherever men write and read and talk together. The nation that produces, in the near future, the largest proportional development of educated and intelligent engineers and agriculturists,[14] of doctors, schoolmasters, professional soldiers, and intellectually active people of all sorts; the nation that most resolutely picks over, educates, sterilises,[15] exports, or poisons its People of the Abyss;[16] ... the nation in a word, that turns the greatest

---

10 Reprinted by permission from Macmillan Publishers Ltd: *Nature* (64: 1662), copyright (1901).

11 A quotation from the Old Testament Bible, Ecclesiastics 9: 11.

12 A British monthly cultural journal founded in 1866 in Oxford. Bloch's article was entitled 'The Wars of the Future' (1901).

13 I. e., *The Fortnightly Review*.

14 Persons who study agriculture.

15 Renders unable to procreate through medical surgery.

16 H. G. Wells's expression, coined in 'Anticipations' (1901), to refer to the unteachable poor who could not adapt to modern life. Jack London popularised the phrase in his eponymous novel (1903).

proportion of its irresponsible adiposity[17] into social muscle, will certainly be the nation that will be the most powerful in warfare as in peace.'

Edwin Ray Lankester, 'The Present Judged by the Future' (13 March 1902).[18]

Anticipations of the Reaction of Mechanical and Scientific Progress upon Human Life and Thought. By H. G. Wells. Pp. 318. (London: Chapman and Hall. Ltd., 1902.) Price 7*s*. 6*d*.

This is a profoundly interesting and suggestive book by a very remarkable man. Mr Wells was educated at the Royal College of Science;[19] he has a thorough knowledge of, and considerable training in, the great branches of science – physics, chemistry, astronomy, geology and biology. This course of study operated, in the case of Mr Wells, upon a mind naturally gifted with an extraordinarily vivid imagination and the aptitude for true literary art. In one of his latest works, *Love and Mr Lewisham*, Mr Wells has told us the story of the struggle for life of a South Kensington student, and for the first time given the Royal College of Science the dignity of literary recognition. But it is by his audacious and fascinating 'imaginings' as to the arrival on our planet of the inhabitants of Mars,[20] the strange evolution and changes in the nature of men and the earth's surface as seen a million years hence,[21] the morphology and habits of the inhabitants of the moon, the nocturnal freezing and solidification of its atmosphere,[22] and as to other such topics that Mr H. G. Wells is best known. The really wonderful range of knowledge shown in these stories, the scientific accuracy of the abundant details, the absolute restraint of the weird histories recounted, within the limits of what scientific criticism must admit as possible – nay, even probable, given the one initial miracle of anyone having and recording experiences of such things – lend a special charm to Mr Wells' writings wanting in those of all other masters of this kind of literary craft from Swift to Jules Verne. One of his shorter stories, 'The Star' – calmly recording in the words of a survivor the approach and passage of a huge meteor which causes the ocean to sweep the land-surface of the earth in all parts to a depth of two hundred feet – is written with such faithful ad-

---

17   Obesity.

18   Reprinted by permission from Macmillan Publishers Ltd: *Nature* (65: 1689), copyright (1902).

19   A British higher education institution, founded in 1890 as the successor to the Normal School of Science, becoming a constituent part of Imperial College, London, in 1907 and being wholly absorbed into that College in 2002.

20   A reference to Wells's *The War of the Worlds* (1898).

21   A reference to Wells's *The Time Machine* (1895), set largely in 802,701.

22   A reference to Wells's *The First Men in the Moon* (1901).

herence to scientific possibility and such convincing art in narrative that I, for one, am haunted by the conviction that the thing has occurred in past epochs more than once, and may at any time occur again.

The character that Mr Wells has thus established for himself will necessarily tend to a misunderstanding of the nature of his work recently published under the title *Anticipations*. In this book the author is not seeking to amuse us by far-reaching speculation as to remote possibilities. Under the guise of prophecy as to the future, Mr Wells criticises the present. He imagines that before a hundred years are out (we must all wish this forecast to be realised) there will gradually come into existence

> a naturally and informally organised, educated class, an unprecedented sort of people, a New Republic[23] dominating the world.... A new social Hercules[24] that will strangle the serpents of war and national animosity in his cradle ... a conscious organisation of intelligent and, quite possibly in some cases, wealthy men.

Mr Wells hopes great things from the cosmopolitanism[25] and intelligence of this coming power. He tells us what the men of this new group will think on various subjects and do in regard to many things, and thus he makes them the vehicle for conveying his righteous indignation and just contempt for a large part of the present ways and beliefs of mankind. It is impossible to do justice in a brief review to a book which deals with nearly every subject under the sun[26] – from motor-cars to cooperative cookery to the struggle for dominion among the nations and the essence of religion. Mr Wells commences his far-reaching survey with a comparatively comfortable chapter on 'Locomotion in the Twentieth Century.' Special motor tracks and individual motor-cars will to a large extent replace railways. This leads on to the consideration of the 'Diffusion of Great Cities.' The country will cease to come into the town; the town will spread into the country in proportion as the facilities for locomotion enable a larger and larger area to be in easy touch with the great centres. Then follow chapters on the

---

23 Wells's imagined republican world state, based in part on Plato's *Republic* (360 BC).

24 In Roman mythology, the son of Jupiter, characterised by his great strength and courage. When an infant, his stepmother, Juno, sent serpents to his cot to kill him, but instead Hercules succeeded in strangling them.

25 The notion that the whole world is one's country; having no national attachments.

26 Any where on earth, from the Old Testament Bible, Ecclesiastics 1. 9, 'there is nothing new under the sun'.

domestic economy and the relations of class to class – the natural history[27] or bionomics[28] of the social organism in the past, the present and the immediate future of the twentieth century. 'War in the Twentieth Century,' 'The Conflict of Languages' and 'Faith, Morals and Public Policy in the Twentieth Century' are the titles of subsequent chapters.

I shall best enable the reader to judge of the manner in which these subjects are treated, and stimulate, I hope, his desire to read Mr Wells' book by a few quotations.

'The faeces[29] of the social fabric[30] has,' he says, 'changed and – as I hope to make clear – is still changing in a direction from which, without a total destruction and re-birth of that fabric, there can never be any return. The most striking of the new classes to emerge is certainly the share-holding class, the owners of a sort of property new in the world's history.... Share property is property that can be owned at any distance and that yields its revenue without thought or care on the part of its proprietor; it is, indeed, absolutely irresponsible property, a thing that no old world property ever was.... The shareholder owns the world *de jure*,[31] by common recognition of the rights of property; and the incumbency of knowledge, management and toil fall entirely to others. He toils not, neither does he spin;[32] he is mechanically released from the penalty of the Fall,[33] he reaps in a still sinful world all the practical benefits of the millennium – without any of its moral limitations.'

Among many other ways and habits which are pointed out for improvement in the nascent century, those of house-builders are criticised at some length. Here is a good sample:–

I find it incredible that there will not be a sweeping revolution in the methods of building during the next century. The erection of a house wall, come to think of it, is an astonishingly tedious and complex business, the final result exceedingly unsatisfactory.... I fail to see the necessity of (and, accordingly, I resent

---

27 Historically, the branch of science which dealt with all natural objects, animal, vegetable and mineral.

28 The branch of biology that deals with organisms' behaviour and modes of life in their natural environment.

29 The general aspect or appearance.

30 The common elements of society which keep it stable and functioning.

31 Latin, rightfully, according to law.

32 A quotation from the New Testament Bible, Luke 12: 27.

33 In the Old Testament Bible, Genesis 3: 1-24, Adam's lapse into a sinful state as a result of his eating from the Tree of Knowledge of Good and Evil.

bitterly) all these coral reef[34] methods. Better walls than this and less life-wasting ways of making them are surely possible.... I can dream at last of much more revolutionary affairs, of a thing running to and fro along a temporary rail, that will squeeze out wall as one squeezes paint from a tube, and form its surface with a pat or two as it sets. Moreover, I do not see at all why the walls of small dwelling-houses should be so solid as they are. There still hangs about us the monumental tradition of the pyramids.[35] It ought to be possible to build sound, portable and habitable houses of felted wire-netting and weather-proofed paper upon a light framework.

Mr Wells would improve the British workman.

'The average sanitary plumber[36] of to-day in England,' he says, 'insists upon his position as a mere labourer as though it were some precious thing; he guards himself from improvement as a virtuous woman guards her honour; he works for specifically limited hours and by the hour with specific limitations in the practice of his trade, on the fairly sound assumption that but for that restriction any fool might do plumbing as well as he; whatever he learns he learns from some other plumber during his apprenticeship[37] years – after which he devotes himself to doing the minimum of work in the maximum of time until his brief excursion into this mysterious universe is over.'

He has not much respect for the House of Commons.[38]

Even the physical conditions under which the House of Commons meets and plays at Government are ridiculously obsolete. Every disputable point is settled by a division; a bell rings, there is shouting and running, the members come blundering into the chamber and sort themselves with much loutish shuffling and shoving into the division lobbies.[39] They are counted, as illiterate farmers count sheep; amidst much fuss and confusion they return to their places and the

---

34 Aragonite structures produced gradually by living organisms, found in shallow, tropical marine waters with little or no nutrients in the water.

35 Monumental structures, often serving as tombs, built of stone, etc., with a usually square base and sloping sides meeting centrally at an apex.

36 A plumber specialising in sewerage systems.

37 A fixed period during which a learner of a craft is bound to serve, and receive instruction from, a fully qualified colleague.

38 The lower, representative house of the British parliament, established during the thirteenth century.

39 Corridors off the main chamber of the House of Commons where members of parliament go to vote on an act of parliament.

tellers vociferate the result. The waste of time over these antics is enormous, and they are often repeated many times in an evening.

Our author traces the origin of the modern democracy or democratic quasi-monarchy.[40] He has a wholesome contempt for the mode of Government it has produced and the conduct of affairs by party representative. Every such Government conducts its affairs, he says,

> as though there were no such thing as special knowledge or practical education. The utmost recognition it affords to the man who has taken the pains to know, and specifically to do, is occasionally to consult him upon specific points and override his councils in its ampler wisdom, or to entrust to him some otherwise impossible duty under circumstances of extreme limitation. The man of special equipment is treated always as if he were some sort of curious performing animal.

Of war, Mr Wells has much to say which is very important and, indeed, should be read, side by side, with the passionate appeal of a similar tendency recently made by Mr Rudyard Kipling in his 'Islanders.'

> 'War,' he tells us, 'in the past was a thing of days and heroisms; battles and campaigns rested in the hand of the great commander; he stood out against the sky, picturesquely on horseback, visibly controlling it all. War in the future will be a question of preparation, of long years of foresight and disciplined imagination.'

The picture given below is a fine sample of Mr Wells' style and matter:–

> There will be first of all the coming of the war, the wave of excitement, the belligerent shouting of the unemployed inefficients, the flag-waving, the secret doubts, the eagerness for hopeful news, the impatience of the warning voice. I seem to see, almost as if he were symbolic, the grey old general – the general who learnt his art of war away in the vanished nineteenth century, the altogether too elderly general with his epaulettes[41] and decorations,[42] his uniform that has still its historical value, his spurs and his sword – riding along on his

---

40   Wells's expression for a constitutional monarchy.

41   Decorative shoulder ornaments awarded as a military or other honour.

42   Ostentatious honours, such as ribbons or medals, worn by the recipient to demonstrate acclaim.

obsolete horse by the side of his doomed column. Above all things he is a gentleman – and the column looks at him lovingly with its countless boys' faces, and the boys' eyes are infinitely trustful, for he has won battles in the old time. They will believe in him to the end. They have been brought up in their schools to believe in him and his class, their mothers have mingled respect for the gentlefolk with the simple doctrines of their faith, their first lesson on entering the army was the salute. The 'smart' helmets His Majesty, or some such unqualified person, chose for them lie hotly on their young brows, and over their shoulders slope their obsolete carelessly-sighted guns. Tramp, tramp, they march, doing what they have been told to do; Religion and the Ratepayer[43] and the Rights of the Parent working through the instrumentality of the Best Club in the world have kept their souls and minds, if not untainted, at least only harmlessly veneered, with the thinnest sham of training or knowledge. Tramp, tramp, they go, boys who will never be men, rejoicing patriotically in the nation that has thus sent them forth, badly armed, badly clothed, badly led to be killed in some avoidable quarrel by men unseen. And beside them, an absolute stranger to them, a stranger even in habits of speech and thought, and at any rate to be shot with them fairly and squarely, marches the subaltern[44] – the son of the school-burking[45] share-holding class – a slightly taller sort of boy, as ill taught as they are in all that concerns the realities of life, ignorant of how to get food, how to get water, how to keep fever down and strength up, ignorant of his practical equality with the men beside him, carefully trained under a clerical headmaster to use a crib,[46] play cricket rather nicely, look alright whatever happens, believe in his gentility and avoid talking 'shop.'[47] ... So the gentlemanly old general – the polished drover[48] to the shambles[49] – rides, and his doomed column marches by, in this vision that haunts my mind. I cannot foresee what such a force will ever attempt to do, against modern weapons. Nothing can happen but the needless and most wasteful and pitiful killing of these poor lads, who make up the infantry battalions,[50] the main class of all European armies to-day, whenever they come against a sanely organised army. There is nowhere they can come in, there is nothing they can do. The scattered invisible marksmen[51] with their supporting guns will shatter their masses, pick them off individually, cover their line of retreat and force them into wholesale surrenders. It will be more like herding sheep than actual fighting. Yet the bitterest and cruellest things will have to happen, thousands and thousands of poor boys

---

43 A person liable to pay local taxes.

44 A military officer of junior rank.

45 The act of stifling or smothering, named after William Burke who suffocated victims before selling their corpses for medical research.

46 An illegitimate translated version of a text for use by students.

47 To speak inopportunely or tediously about one's occupation or business.

48 A person who drives cattle or other livestock to market.

49 A meat market.

50 Bodies of foot-soldiers.

51 Persons skilled or practised in shooting.

will be smashed in all sorts of dreadful ways and given over to every conceivable form of avoidable hardship and painful disease, before the obvious fact that war is no longer a business for half-trained lads in uniform, led by parson-bred sixth form[52] boys and men of pleasure and old men, but an exhaustive demand upon very carefully educated adults for the most strenuous best that is in them, will get its practical recognition.

Our author proceeds to emphasise

the inexorable tendency in things to make a soldier a skilled and educated man and to link him, in sympathy and organisation, with the engineer and the doctor, and all the continually developing mass of scientifically educated men that the advance of science and mechanism is producing.

He is led to think it not improbable that the present military hierarchy will be left in this country as a sort of ornamental court[53] attendants, and that an entirely new and independent army will be raised and organised on sound business principles.

'Already,' he says, 'recruiting is falling off.... Elementary education has at last raised the intelligence of the British lower classes to a point when the prospect of fighting in distant lands under unsuitably educated British officers of means and gentility with a defective War Office[54] equipment and inferior weapons has lost much of its romantic glamour.'

As to education, Mr Wells holds, and very many, like myself, will agree with him, that 'it is increasingly evident that to organise and control public education is beyond the power of a democratic Government.'

Schools alone are of no avail, universities are merely dens of the higher cramming.... At present, in Great Britain at least, the headmasters[55] entrusted with the education of the bulk of the influential men of the next decades are conspicuously second-rate men, forced and etiolated[56] creatures, scholarship boys

---

52   In British secondary school, classes for those over sixteen years of age.

53   In politics, the monarch with its ministers and councillors as the ruling power.

54   The former department of the British government in charge of the administration of the army from the seventeenth century to 1964.

55   Male headteachers of a school.

56   Pale and sickly due to a lack of light; figuratively, unenlightened.

manured with annotated editions,[57] and brought up under and protected from all current illumination by the Kale-pot[58] of the Thirty-nine Articles.[59] Many of them are less capable teachers and even less intelligent men than many Board School teachers.

There is need, Mr Wells declares, of a new type of school and also of a new type of university,

something other than a happy fastness for those precociously brilliant creatures – creatures whose brilliance is too often the hectic indication of a constitutional unsoundness of mind – who can 'get in' before the portcullis[60] of the nineteenth birthday falls.

The coming men, those whom Mr Wells calls the New Republic, will do away with

'the half-educated, unskilled pretenders, professing impossible creeds and propounding ridiculous curricula, to whom the unhappy parents of to-day must needs entrust the intelligences of their children.... The windy pretences of "forming character," supplying moral training and so forth, under which the educationalist of to-day conceals the fact that he is incapable of his proper task of training, developing and equipping the mind, will no longer be made by the teacher. Nor will the teacher be permitted to subordinate his duties to the entirely irrelevant business of his pupils' sports.' Hereafter 'the school and college will probably give only the keys and apparatus of thought, a necessary language or so, a sound mathematical training, drawing, a wide and reasoned view of philosophy, some good exercises in dialectics,[61] a training in the use of those stores of fact that science has made. So equipped the young man and young woman will go on to the technical school of their chosen profession and to the criticism of contemporary practice for their special efficiency and to the literature of contemporary thought for their general development.'

---

57 Scholarly editions of literary works, containing notes and other referential apparatus.

58 A large, semi-globular or full bottomed iron pot on three spiky legs.

59 The historic defining statements of Anglican doctrine, established by a Convocation of the Church of England in 1563.

60 A wooden or iron grating, usually suspended by chains above the gateway of a fortress and able to be quickly released to slide down vertical grooves in the sides of the gateway and secure the entrance.

61 The art of critically investigating the truth of opinions; logical disputation or argument.

198

The value of literature and the great question of the exclusive study of Greek and Latin writers[62] are alluded to thus:–

> After all, in spite of the pretentious impostors who trade upon the claim, literature, contemporary literature, is the breath of civilised life, and those who sincerely think and write the salt of the social body. To mumble over the past, to live on the classics, however splendid, is senility.

Many readers will find the final chapter the most interesting in this uncompromising book, where religion, morals and philosophy are briefly but frankly touched. The men of the New Republic will be, says Mr Wells, 'religious' men, and we gather that he is one, a forerunner so to speak, of those new men. They will find 'an effect of purpose in the totality of things.' That is the essence of being 'religious' and amounts to 'belief in God.' They will 'presume to no possibility of knowledge of the real being of God.' They will reject the conception of God[63] as an omniscient[64] mind as being as impossible as that which presents Him as an omnipresent[65] moving body.

> 'They will regard the whole of being, within themselves and without, as the sufficient revelation of God to their souls.' 'The same spacious faith that will render the idea of airing their egotisms in God's presence, through prayer, or of any such quite personal intimacy, absurd, will render the idea of an irascible and punitive Deity[66] ridiculous and incredible.' 'To believe completely in God' (as these men will believe) 'is to believe in the final rightness of all being.' 'If' (and this is said in comment on Huxley's Romanes lecture[67]) 'the universe is non-ethical by our present standards, we must reconsider these standards and reconstruct our ethics.'

---

62 A reference to the predominant position held by classics on the education curriculum from school to university.

63 A superhuman or supernatural being regarded as having power over nature and human fortunes; when capitalised, the deity of Christianity and Judaism believed to be the Creator of all things.

64 Having infinite knowledge.

65 Present in all places at the same time.

66 God.

67 A prestigious free public lecture delivered annually at the University of Oxford since 1892 and founded by George Romanes. T. H. Huxley's 'Evolution and Ethics' was the Romanes Lecture of 1893.

Mr Wells declares that no more 'shattering' book than the *Essay on Population* by Malthus has ever been or ever will be written. Darwinism,[68] as one outcome of it, has destroyed the basis of old-fashioned doctrines. An outline is given of the religion of the men of the New Republic. They will not seek to discover the final object of the struggle among existences; they will have abandoned the search for ultimates. They will seek God's purpose in the sphere of their activities and desire no more. They will find in themselves a desire, a passion almost, to create and organise, to put in order, to get the maximum result from certain possibilities. These men will hold life to be a privilege and a responsibility, 'not a sort of night refuge[69] for base spirits out of the void.' They will, accordingly, not punish criminals by inflicting pain, but will apply Nature's own method of improving her stock – the method of killing. And equally they will not encourage or applaud or support by charity (as many persons do at present)

> 'a mean-spirited, under-sized, diseased little man, quite incapable of earning a decent living even for himself, married to some underfed, ignorant, ill-shaped, plain and diseased little woman and guilty of the lives of ten or twelve ugly ailing children.' 'All Christian States of to-day are, as a matter of fact, engaged in slave-breeding. It is a result that endears religion and purity to the sweating employer, and leads unimaginative bishops, who have never missed a meal in their lives, and who know nothing of the indescribable bitterness of a handicapped entry into this world, to draw a complacent contrast with irreligious France.'[70]

It seems to me that this book should have – even for those whom it cannot fail to offend – more than the interest which attaches to clever fault-finding. It is, truly enough, an unsparing indictment of existing government, society, education, religion and morality, but it contains also a confession of faith[71] and is full of a spirit of hope and a belief in future development. It is a truthful statement of the outlook of a man who has grasped thoroughly the teachings of modern science and who still keeps hope alive in his breast.

---

68   The theory of evolution by natural selection as espoused by Charles Darwin.

69   A place where people may go at night who have no where else to stay.

70   A reference to the secular nature of the French Third Republic (1870-1940), the constitution (1875) of which pronounced France a secular republic.

71   A statement setting out ones essential religious doctrine or other personal principles.

Frederick Headley, 'The Future of the Human Race' (29 December 1904).[72]

(1) *Mankind in the Making.* Pp. viii + 429. Price 7*s*. 6*d*. (2) *Anticipations.* Pp. 122. Price 6*d*. (London: Chapman and Hall, Ltd., 1903.)[73] (3) *The Food of the Gods.* Pp. 317. (London: Macmillan and Co., Ltd., 1904.) Price 6*s*. By H. G. Wells.

Mr Wells is a man of imagination, and he has let his imaginative faculty play about the great problems that obtrude themselves when we contemplate the new conditions under which civilised man is now living, conditions which must inevitably undergo further change as science advances. Three books of his more especially claim to forecast the future of our race, and to lay down the lines on which education should proceed. These three are *Anticipations*, a very bold attempt to peer into the future; *The Food of the Gods*, a lively romance full of humour that does not pall from beginning to end of the book; and *Mankind in the Making*, a series of essays dealing mainly with education, and advocating radical changes in our methods.

As to style, Mr Wells is a hard hitter. He pounds at all classes or professions or trades which fall below his standard of efficiency, or who represent, as he thinks, mouldering[74] ideas and systems. He cannot talk patiently of bishops, schoolmasters, army men or plumbers. His philosophy has had its origin in the theory of evolution. He looks at the race of men in the past, the present, and the future, and he sees a long series of births. The individual is trustee for the race of the principle of life. The idea of this trusteeship is to Mr Wells a great and ennobling one. A man must not look upon his individual life as the all-important thing, but must find his true happiness in the propagation and education of offspring. Nevertheless, we find in *Anticipations* that this idea will be shared only by a limited number of people. In the world he pictures are many childless *ménages*,[75] and Mr Wells himself is prepared to tolerate relaxation of the marriage law and even 'sterile gratification.' But in this new world there will be also many men of strenuous earnestness and of religious purpose, though not professing a definitely Christian faith, who will be the leading spirits. As a rule they will be fathers of families, for the childless *ménages* will not fit in with their theory of things.

These men of energy – men of science, engineers, doctors, and so forth – will shape policy and administration. The result will be marvellous efficiency,

---

72 Reprinted by permission from Macmillan Publishers Ltd: *Nature* (71: 1835), copyright (1904).

73 Although *Mankind in the Making* was published in 1903, the edition of *Anticipations* here under review was actually published in 1904.

74 Decaying, rotting.

75 French, households, especially sexual relationships.

such as is rarely if ever seen now. There will be no king. Monarchy will have given place to the New Republic. Royalty is connected with all things out of date, with aristocratic privileges, ridiculous costumes and decorations. Therefore it must go. In the New Republic, though so efficiently managed, there will be many idlers. There will be an enormous development of irresponsible wealth, great numbers of people living on invested money, having no cares of management and no duties in connection with their property. It is among this class mainly that it will be found the childless *ménages*. The class that supplies unskilled labour, the old servile class, will tend to disappear. The invention of machines capable of performing more cheaply all the work that has hitherto fallen to the unskilled will make such men unnecessary. Peasant proprietors and all small land-holders must pass away. They represent stagnation, and there is room only for go-ahead,[76] adaptable people. Those who fail to adapt themselves will fall into the abyss, the great sink in which wallow all those who are unfitted for the new conditions. The people of the abyss are to be encouraged to extinguish themselves, to practice what would commonly be called vice without offspring resulting.

Mr Wells is quite alive to the need of an antiseptic in a wealthy society such as he foresees. To keep down excessive accumulations of wealth he proposes heavy death duties,[77] and heavy graduated duties[78] upon irresponsible incomes, 'with, perhaps, in addition, a system of terminable liability[79] for borrowers.' But besides this there will be at work for many years to come 'that most stern and educational of masters – war.' In its methods war will be very unlike anything of which we have as yet had experience. There will be marksmen few in number, but possessed of skill altogether beyond that of the marksmen of today. The army will no longer be officered by men too stupid and indifferent to use properly the inventions of science. No masses of raw, unskilled lads will be driven on to the slaughter.

Some greater synthesis will emerge. Mr Wells reviews the various large groups of peoples which make up the greater part of the population of the earth. There is the Russian group, the German, Latin, and English group, and there are the Yellow Races.[80] Mr Wells does not think the Russian or the German likely to predominate. In the French he has a great belief, though they do not 'breed like

---

76 Enterprising, having energy and initiative.

77 Taxes levied on a dead person's estate.

78 Differential taxes determined by the value of the commodity or the income being taxed.

79 A scheme for borrowers whereby interest charged is reduced over time.

80 A former designation for the oriental peoples of the far east, especially the Chinese and Japanese.

rabbits.'[81] The richness and power of their literature make him think their language will extend itself far. He laments the comparative poverty and meagreness of our literature. Still, he inclines to the belief that a great dominant synthesis of the English-speaking peoples may be formed. Germany will be cowed by the combined English and American Navies, and Anglo-Saxonism[82] will eventually triumph.

There remain the Yellow Races. Their star, too, will pale before that of the Anglo-Saxons. But all syntheses, however great, will eventually fuse into one. There will be a World State,[83] and rival nationalities will be a thing of the past. 'Against these old isolations, these obsolescent particularisms,[84] the forces of mechanical and scientific development fight and fight irresistibly.'

All these speculations are very interesting reading, but we cannot help regretting that Mr Wells did not study and reflect a little longer before writing. His imagination, unclogged by knowledge, is apt to run away with him. Though he expresses the greatest reverence for Darwin[85] and his successors, he does not show a very thorough grip of the principles of evolution. To begin with, he seems unaware of the part in the national life that is played by the lower stratum of society, the 'stagnant' masses as he would call them. From this stratum emerge the men of energy so dear to Mr Wells's heart. Occasionally the son of a poor man, say in Scotland or Yorkshire, rises to eminence. Far more often it takes more than one generation to climb the ladder. But this does not alter the fact that this substratum is an absolute necessity. For the upper strata do not keep up their numbers, and society has been truly described as an organism that is perpetually renewing itself from its base. But Mr Wells knows only of the abyss into which tumble all the failures of modern life. Such a valuable national asset as peasant land-holders he despises and wishes to abolish. Yet from such 'stagnant' classes spring the families that work upward and produce the men of energy that do the highest work of the nation. The downward movement of which Mr Wells talks so much is comparatively but a puny stream. No doubt there is an abyss, no doubt there are in our big towns not a few degraded families which are tending to die out. Yet even the most degraded produce here and there a man of grit, a man, for instance, who enlists and rises to be a non-commissioned officer.[86] The pick of the slum[87]-bred men make the finest fighters.

---

81   To breed rapidly, in an uncontrolled manner.

82   British-American power, collectively.

83   A theoretical world authority which would make, interpret and enforce global law.

84   Persons' exclusive attachments to their own party, sect, nation, etc.

85   I. e., Charles Darwin.

86   In the military, an officer not holding a commission.

Mr Wells wishes all citizens to be energetic and up to date. The inadaptable masses must be got rid of. They must be instructed so that the indulgence of their sexual instincts may not lead to their having offspring. Reckless parentage must be in every way discouraged. And yet Mr Wells declares that he cannot devise any system of selection by which it would be possible to breed good citizens; the qualities demanded are too diverse. So we are to get rid of the reckless classes and depend solely on the careful classes. We are to introduce careful parentage, that is, put a stop to natural selection; but there is to be no scientific selection[88] to take its place. The result would indeed be disastrous. As it is, our national physique may be poor, but what there is in the nation of physical vigour is due to the great amount of elimination, probably not far short of 50 per cent, that still goes on.

Here is another strange forecast. War is 'the most educational of all masters,' and yet after many years a great world state will arise and there will be a kind of millennium.[89] If war the great educator, the great antiseptic, is no more, surely the world is likely to be the worse for its absence. What is to make the world better? No doubt Mr Wells would say, 'The advance of science.' Science is his sheet anchor.[90] It is to ennoble the national life so that even the idle holders of irresponsible wealth will be powerless to degrade it. But will this be so? No doubt the inventor is ennobled by his brain labour, by his striving to make his dream a reality. And the men of energy who find practical applications of his discoveries are doing work of a kind that often, though not always, elevates the character. But what of the people who merely make use of the discoveries and inventions of others? The man who invents a locomotive engine is likely, at the lowest, to be above the pettiest meannesses. But the mere travelling in railway trains leaves men morally no better and no worse. The striving after knowledge is the ennobling thing, and not the knowledge itself, the making of discoveries, not the enjoyment of them.

This being so, there is a fallacy running all through that very humorous romance *The Food of the Gods*; in the story those who are fed on this food in their infancy and youth grow to a height of some forty feet. The inventors do not add to their inches. In its application this is not true. The mass of mankind remain small in brain and character – they grow, but do not grow much, when their youth is nurtured on the clearest and noblest ideas. The few thinkers, discoverers, inventors are the giants. As to education, Mr Wells has much to say

---

87 An overcrowded urban district having squalid housing conditions and inhabited by very poor people.

88 The use of scientific methodology to make choices, especially in relation to eugenics and human pairing.

89 An imagined period of peace, happiness, prosperity and ideal government.

90 Something on which one relies as a last resort; an ultimate source of security.

that is worth pondering. He wishes boys to make a real study of the English language and literature. On our success in teaching English and producing good literature depends the answer to the question: Will English retreat before the tongue of some rival synthesis, or will it become the language of the world? For educational purposes, the dead languages,[91] as we might expect, are tried and found wanting. Those who teach them are 'fumbling with the keys at the door of a room that was ransacked long ago.'

Comment on Headley: H. G. Wells, letter to the editor, 'Fact in Sociology' (2 February 1905).[92]

I addressed a letter to the editor of *Nature* replying to what I allege to be misrepresentations and misstatements in a review of three of my books by 'F. W. H.' (December 29, 1904, p. 193). After a delay of some weeks due to the absence of 'F. W. H.' abroad, the editor of *Nature* has written to ask me to modify and shorten my protest.

'F. W. H.' told the readers of *Nature* that my *Food of the Gods* 'claimed to forecast the future.' This was untrue, and I said so.

'F. W. H.' mixed up my discussion of probabilities in *Anticipations* with my general review of educational influences in *Mankind in the Mankind*, and presented this as my ideals. I pointed out that this was an unsound method of criticism.

'F. W. H.' presented the following as my opinions:– 'Germany will be cowed by the combined English and American Navies, and Anglo-Saxonism will eventually triumph. There remain the Yellow Races. Their star, too, will pale before that of the Anglo-Saxons.' I repudiated this balderdash[93] with some asperity. It is violently unlike my views.

He wrote of me, 'he seems unaware of the part in the national life that is played by the lower stratum of society, the "stagnant" masses as he would call them.' I denied that I should, and pointed out that no one does know what part is played by any stratum of society in national reproduction. It is a field of unrecorded facts. I commented on 'F. W. H.'s' assumption that he was in possession of special knowledge.

---

91   Languages which have stopped changing in grammar, vocabulary and the complete meaning of sentences, normally due to their being replaced by a different language.

92   Reprinted by permission from Macmillan Publishers Ltd: *Nature* (71: 1840), copyright (1905). This letter has previously been reprinted in Smith 1998, II: 63-64. Smith misidentifies the reviewer as F. W. Hirst, erroneously calling him a 'well-known scientist' (he was, in fact, a political economist).

93   A senseless jumble of words (spoken or written).

He wrote of 'the fact that this stratum is an absolute necessity.' This is *not* a fact. It may or may not be true. I commented on this use of the word 'fact' in view of 'F. W. H.'s' professorial sneer at my 'imagination unclogged by knowledge.'

He declared that I want to 'get rid of the reckless classes, and depend solely on the careful classes,' a statement which has not an atom[94] of justification. He not only 'guys'[95] my suggestions, but foists an absolutely uncongenial phraseology upon me.

Finally, he wrote, 'we are to introduce careful parentage, *that is*, put a stop to natural selection.' I quoted this in view of his statement that I had 'no very thorough grasp of the principles of evolution.' I discussed what appeared to be his ideas about evolution. They appeared to me to be crude and dull, and I regret I cannot condense my criticisms to my present limits.

I expressed some irritation at his method of misstatement followed by reply, and hinted a doubt whether my own style of inquiry – in spite of the fact that romances[96] blacken my reputation – was not really more scientific than his.

Reply to Wells: Frederick Headley, letter to the editor, 'Fact in Sociology' (16 February 1905).[97]

Mr Wells is a dangerous man to criticise. Such thunderbolts as 'crude,' 'dull,' 'balderdash,' come hurtling at one's head even from his modified letters (*Nature*, February 2). But I prefer to regard it all as meant only for sheet lightning.[98] Indeed, when I consider the courtesy that characterised my article (*Nature*, December 29), plain-spoken though it was on some points, I cannot take any other view.

Now to Mr Wells's points in order.

(1) '*The Food of the Gods* does not claim to forecast the future.' My mistake was natural. It only shows the risk Mr Wells runs in appearing before the world in two entirely different characters. Still, I hit upon a weak point. He pictures an ideal State, but cannot show us how it is to be realised. Archimedes had

---

94 A minuscule unit made up of a positively charged nucleus, containing most of the mass, surrounded by a number of electrons.

95 Mocks or trifles with.

96 Extraordinary works of fiction.

97 Reprinted by permission from Macmillan Publishers Ltd: *Nature* (71: 1842), copyright (1905).

98 Lightning which illuminates a wide area equally at once.

no fulcrum[99] for the lever with which he would have moved the world.[100] Mr Wells has no power to apply to his.

(2) '*I have mixed up Anticipations and Mankind in the Making.*' Why keep them separate? *Anticipations* also deals largely with ideals.

(3) *Re* the question – Which of the great national 'syntheses' will gain predominance, see *Anticipations*, chap. viii. *passim*,[101] and especially pp. 100, 101 (6*d*. ed., 1904). This chapter seemed to me an interesting speculation, but Mr Wells describes what I thought, and, on re-reading, think is to be found in it as 'balderdash.' True, through inadvertence I wrote 'Anglo-Saxon'[102] instead of 'English-speaking,' for which I am sorry.

(4) *Re* the recruiting of the upper strata of society from the lower, nothing, he says, is known about this. Still, those who have studied human evolution think they know something. Prof. Karl Pearson even says that there are 'class statistics' for the population of Copenhagen, and writes, 'the population would accordingly appear to be ultimately, and in the long run, reproducing itself from the artisan[103] classes' (*Natural Science*, May, 1896).[104] Dr Mercier (see the Sociological Society's papers, 1904, p. 55) regards 'a civilised community in the light of a lamp, which burns away at the top and is replenished at the bottom.'[105] As to 'stagnant' classes, I find in *Anticipations*, p. 121, 'It (the new Republic) will tolerate no dark corners where the people of the Abyss may fester, no vast diffused slums of peasant proprietors, no stagnant plague preserves.' See especially p. 117 for Mr Wells's plan for getting rid of undesirable types. As to careful parentage, see *Mankind in the Making*, p. 99:– 'The first step to ensuring them (the ends aimed at) is certainly to do all we can to discourage reckless parentage.'

In conclusion, let me described myself as a much-battered but not unfriendly critic of the New Republic.

---

99   The point against which a lever is placed to get purchase.

100   A reference to the quotation attributed to Archimedes, 'Give me a place to stand on, and I will move the Earth'.

101   Latin, of an allusion or reference in a published work, to be found at various places throughout the text.

102   A person of English descent wherever found (often used to refer jointly to British and Americans).

103   A craftsperson or skilled technician.

104   A reference to Pearson's 'Reproductive Selection' (1896).

105   An incorrectly dated reference to Mercier's 'Discussion' (1905).

2.7: *A Modern Utopia*

F. C. S. S., 'Sociological Speculations' (10 August 1905).[1]

A Modern Utopia. By H. G. Wells. Pp. xi + 393. (London: Chapman and Hall, Ltd., 1905.) Price 7s. 6d.

It is instructive to watch the growth, both in power and in hopefulness, of Mr Wells's criticism of life. In the *Time Machine* his forecast of the future of humanity was frankly appalling; in *When the Sleeper Wakes*, more lurid (albeit far more probable) than the worst imaginings of 'reforming' socialists. *Anticipations* was a most stimulating book, but so deliberately confined itself to exalting and exaggerating the prospects of a single aspect of life, so exclusively devoted itself to glorifying mechanical and material progress, that those sensitive to our spiritual and aesthetic possibilities might be pardoned for regarding the present order, with all its cruelty, waste, sordidness, and grotesqueness, as a golden age in comparison with Mr Wells's world. *Mankind in the Making* contained much vigorous criticism and many sensible and practical suggestions. In the present book Mr Wells has become still more moderate and practicable and hopeful, without in the least derogating from his ingenuity and originality. We sincerely hope, therefore, he will not, as he threatens, stick henceforth to his 'art or trade of imaginative writing,' but will continue from time to time to regale and stimulate us with sociological speculations.

Stripping off the romantic form – in which Mr Wells dreams himself and a companion, a botanist suffering from a chronic affair of the heart, into a distant planet which is an exact duplicate of our earth, save that it has realised all the good which is attainable with out present resources – his main argument may be condensed as follows.

As the philosophic foundation of his whole enterprise, Mr Wells assumes what he calls the 'metaphysical heresy' (though it is rapidly forcing itself upon the notice of even the most stagnantly 'orthodox' philosophers) that all classifications, though convenient, are crude, and that whatever is real and valuable in the world is individual, a thesis he had expounded in the brilliant contribution to *Mind*[2] entitled the 'Scepticism of the Instrument,' which he has now reprinted as an appendix to his book. From this philosophy he infers that progress depends on individual initiative and variation, leading to successful experiments. Hence the infinite preciousness of freedom, which the Utopian World-State must restrict only when and in so far as it would oppress the freedom of others. Hence, too, there will be extensive toleration of 'cranks,'[3] while even criminals would

---

1 Reprinted by permission from Macmillan Publishers Ltd: *Nature* (72: 1867), copyright (1905). This review has previously been reprinted in Scheick 1995, 65-67.

2 A British philosophic and analytic journal, founded in 1876.

3 Ill-tempered or nasty persons.

merely be segregated as failures and condemned to work out their ideas of a good life in a society of their likes, after a fashion charmingly described in the account of the arrival of involuntary immigrants at the 'Island of Incorrigible Cheats.' But though Utopia[4] is strangely kind to the cranky, the criminal and the inefficient, because it regards their occurrence as the measure of the State's failure, it does not allow them to reproduce their kind. Parentage is a privilege, and the production of superior offspring a service to the community for which a wise State will handsomely reward its women.[5]

But the efficiency and prosperity of the Utopian order ultimately depends on the ruling class, which Mr Wells seems to have taken bodily out of the Platonic Republic,[6] and, with a fine compliment to the unparalleled rise of Japan,[7] entitled the 'Samurai.'[8] The Samurai are conceived as a 'voluntary nobility' which (like the mediaeval Church) all may enter who are able and willing to lead the strenuous and somewhat ascetic life prescribed by the rules of the Order. Among these the obligations to buy and read every month at least one book published in the last five years, and every year to go out into the wilderness and to travel through it in silence and solitude for at least seven days, are perhaps the most noticeable, together with the prohibition of acting, singing and reciting, and the playing of games in public.

It is remarkable how Platonic is the general spirit of these institutions in all save the high appreciation of individual freedom, to the value of which Plato showed such singular blindness. Nor is their general aim hard to discover. At several points, however, a critic will be disposed to doubt whether Mr Wells's means are adequate to his ends. He has seen, indeed, what never seems to have occurred to Plato, that if wisdom is to control the State, elaborate precautions must be taken to keep learning progressive, and to prevent it from fossilising into pedantry.[9] The Platonic State, if it could have come into existence, would systematically have suppressed originality, and simply have stereotyped the condition of science and art prevailing at the date of its institution. If it could be conceived as surviving to the present day, it would still be sending its heroic hoplites[10] against quick-firing guns,[11] and still be punishing a belief in evolution or

4   An imaginary or hypothetical place or state of things considered to be perfect, coined by Thomas More in his eponymous novel (1516 / 1551).

5   Wells was a pioneering advocate of family allowances, which he called the 'Endowment of Motherhood' (1910).

6   Relating to *The Republic of Plato* (1904).

7   A reference to the modernisation of Japan from a mid-nineteenth century feudal society to a late-nineteenth century industrial one.

8   In feudal Japan, a member of a military caste.

9   Strict adherence to formal rules or literal meaning.

10   A heavily-armed foot-soldier of ancient Greece.

metageometry[12] as heresies worthy of death. Mr Wells seeks to guard against the universal human tendency to fix in rigid forms whatever man admires. But though he insists on the importance of preserving the 'poietic,'[13] *i. e.* originative, types of man and endowing their researches, it may be doubted that even under his laws they would not be overpowered by the 'kinetic,'[14] *i. e.* the efficient administrators, who everywhere conserve the established order. For these latter would control the Order of the Samurai.

Again, Mr Wells's distrust of eugenics,[15] justified as no doubt it is by the present state of our knowledge, seems unduly to disparage the prospects of scientific discovery in the future. It does not follow that because now we know too little to entrust the State with the function of controlling the reproduction of the race, this will continue to be unsafe, and it is easy to imagine circumstances in which such control would become almost inevitable. For example, if one of the many attempts to discover what determines the sex of an embryo should chance to be crowned with success, the numerical equality of the sexes would in all probability be gravely imperilled, and the State would almost certainly have to intervene. Again, while Mr Wells is doubtless within his rights in scoffing at the racial prejudices of the time, in his scorn of popular notions of 'superior' races, 'including such types as the Sussex farm labourer, the Bowery[16] tough, the London hooligan, and the Paris apache,'[17] and in his contention that 'no race is so superior as to be trusted with human charges,' his anticipation of wholesale racial fusions seems to involve a serious underestimate of the aesthetic instincts. Lastly, although Mr Wells has keenly perceived the spiritual value of a temporary retreat from society, it may be doubted whether he does not purchase its advantages at too high a cost. The solitary voyages of his Samurai would assuredly lead to a high death-rate among them, and though one type of mind was thereby strengthened, another would be unhinged. The rule, in short, seems too rigid for the variety, and too cramping for the freedom of man, both of which Mr Wells is elsewhere anxious to appreciate. But Mr Wells, on the whole, shows a wisdom far superior to that of former Utopists[18] in not seeking to construct out of the im-

---

11 Guns that can fire shots in rapid succession, such as automatic pistols or machine guns.

12 Non-Euclidean geometry.

13 Creative, formative, productive.

14 Active, dynamic, full of energy.

15 The science (or pseudo-science) dealing with factors that influence the hereditary qualities of a race and with ways of improving those qualities, especially by modifying the fertility of different categories of people.

16 Of, pertaining to, or characteristic of the Bowery in New York City; disreputable, rough, rowdy.

17 A violent street ruffian.

18 A writer or scholar of utopias.

perfect materials which alone the actual can furnish a static order which shall be, and if possible remain eternally, perfect. He aims rather at laying down the principles of an order which shall be capable of progressively growing towards perfection; and so it may well be that in his ideal society men will be less reluctant than now to learn from experience.

2.8: *In the Days of the Comet*

'Our Book Shelf' (6 December 1906).[1]

In the Days of the Comet. By H. G. Wells. Pp. 305. (London: Macmillan and Co., Ltd., 1906.) Price 6*s*.

Though the actual collision of the earth with the head of a comet is an extremely improbable event, it is not beyond the bounds of possibility. In 1861 the earth passed through the tail of a comet;[2] and the showers of meteors occasionally observed near the end of November[3] are probably due to encounters with fragmental remains of Biela's lost comet. The disc-like appearance of Holmes's comet in 1892 gave rise to the suggestion that the comet was approaching the earth head-on, and we believe Mr Wells then used the idea in one of his clever short stories.[4] In any case he would have no difficulty in finding justification for the supposed collision with a comet which forms the *deus ex machina*[5] of the present romance.

The comet which springs from Mr Wells's imaginative brain is seen in its early days by an enthusiastic amateur astronomer who forms one of the minor characters of the story as a 'quivering little smudge of light among the pinpoints,' while the spectroscope[6] showed 'an unprecedented band in the green.' The unknown element which this peculiar green radiation represented proves to be the Divine[7] afflatus that lifts the human race out of selfish individualism[8] into socialism understood in its finest sense. The struggle for existence and the survival of the fittest[9] no longer express operations of natural law,[10] and the world

---

1   Reprinted by permission from Macmillan Publishers Ltd: *Nature* (75: 1936), copyright (1906).

2   A reference to the Great Comet of 1861 (C/1861 J1) which passed the earth and was visible to the naked eye from May to August of that year.

3   A reference to the Andromedids meteor shower which was observed in late-November 1872 and several more times during the nineteenth century as a consequence of the destruction of the 3ED / Biela Comet in 1852.

4   A reference to Wells's 'The Star' (1897).

5   A providential (often rather contrived) interposition, especially in a novel or a play.

6   An instrument for the production and examination of spectra.

7   Heavenly.

8   The social theory which advocates the free and independent action of the individual; self-centred feeling or conduct as a principle.

9   In biology, the continued existence of organisms which are best adapted to their environment, and the extinction of others.

10 An observable law related to natural phenomenon.

becomes a place where the prevailing spirit is 'all for all and each for each.'[11] Love is transfigured, hate perishes, war and all other manifestations of our animal nature[12] are rendered unthinkable after the earth has passed through the comet. The change which evolution can scarcely anticipate in the distant future is brought about in a single night.

The idea is a noble one, and Mr Wells has dealt with the phenomenal and sociological aspects of the transformation in a masterly manner. What is the destiny of the human race cannot yet be foreseen, but what man might become when 'a new heaven and a new earth'[13] have been created is a worthy subject of speculation; and when the theme is developed, as it is in this book, with scientific knowledge, prophetic insight, lofty purpose, and human sympathy, it almost persuades us that the gospel it conveys points the way to the millennium. The message may not be understood, but the story in which it is presented cannot fail to excite interest and stimulate thought.

---

11   This is a rephrasing of the socialist or cooperative slogan 'all for each and each for all', which in turn probably has its origin in the phrase, 'from each according to his ability, to each according to his need', as published by Louis Blanc in *L'Organisation du travail* (1845).

12   The physical and instinctive side of human nature, as opposed to the spiritual and intellectual.

13   A quotation from the New Testament Bible, Revelation 21: 1.

2.9: *The Future in America*

John Perry, 'Social Problems in America' (17 January 1907).[1]

The Future in America – a Search After Realities. By H. G. Wells. Pp. 359. (London: Chapman and Hall, Ltd.) Price 10*s*. 6*d*. net.

We opened this book fearing that, like other books by the same author, it was an attempt to extrapolate[2] or foretell the future from a mere man's quite inadequate knowledge of the present and the past; but we have been delightfully disappointed. Mr Wells is acute in observation, he is well informed on English social problems, and he reasons carefully. His visit to America was very short, but it was preceded by much reading.[3] He nowhere speaks dogmatically; he evidently restrains his inclination to draw general conclusions from a sense that he may be neglecting important premises, and such conclusions as he comes to seem to us to be sound and of value.

Americans have never been tolerant of outside criticism, even when it was obviously honest and good; yet surely it is needed, and is found useful by other nations. Never was an outside critic more kindly and sympathetic than Mr Wells, and we have no doubt that during the next twenty years this book will be referred to and quoted from by every good writer on social problems, which, after all, are not peculiar to America. The American people are like the middle classes of England, France, and Germany; there is no feudal or aristocratic upper class, there is no earth-tied peasant.[4] The American idea is the middle-class idea everywhere, but in America it has been carried out without restrictions; it fosters that kind of individuality which thrives on open and undisciplined competition for wealth.

And the time is coming when the American formula will no longer suffice. Settled conditions and great possibilities of wealth given by nature to a large middle-class kind of population have produced their natural effects. The compound interest[5] law of increase of wealth is in action, and gigantic fortunes in the hands of quite common men have not only destroyed the idea of equality, but have become a danger to the community. Every energetic worker feels that there are limitations now being put to his chances of getting on. It is possible

---

1   Reprinted by permission from Macmillan Publishers Ltd: *Nature* (75: 1942), copyright (1907).

2   To predict on the basis of known facts or observed events.

3   Wells admits reading *American Notes* (1842) by Charles Dickens and *The American Scene* (1907) by Henry James in advance of his trip to the USA.

4   A member of an agricultural class dependent on subsistence farming.

5   Interest that is calculated not only on the original principal, but also on any unpaid interest that has been added to the principal.

quite legally for rich individuals to further their schemes by widespread corruption. Corruption everywhere, but especially in municipal governments, has assumed such large dimensions that it seems impossible to remedy the evil. The average man attends to his own personal affairs, and has no sense of his duties as a citizen. He resents all Government interference. Indeed, it is part of the American formula that the cultured and rich men, and one may say the best men, take no interest in Imperial or State or municipal affairs – to touch pitch is to be defiled[6] – and that the ordinary citizen thinks only of his own interests in this world and the next. Immigration is no longer British and Teutonic.[7] The German and Russian Jew, the lower classes from Austria and Italy and Turkey are – nearly one million of them a year – welcomed as necessary recruits in the serf[8] army of the capitalists. In this serf army the children and women are the chief sufferers. No story told of an old Lancashire factory can compete with some of the horrors of New Jersey at the present time.

There has always been in America a widespread contempt, not for the law, but for abstract justice,[9] so that even well-minded, influential people do not set themselves to remedy obvious wrong when by so doing they might hurt themselves or their party in the eyes of multitudes of base and busy, greedy and childish, malevolent and ignorant voters. The unfairness of the southerner to the Negro[10] is no longer confined to the south, and the crimes of a few Negroes exasperate white people so much that they forget the kindly ways of the average man of colour, and thus the Negro question is becoming more complex.

But thoughtful Americans are already feeling the inadequacy of their old formulas. New ideas are organising themselves out of the little limited efforts of innumerable men. Many universities are busy on the study of social problems. The younger generation is already raising an opposition to the tyranny of mere industrialism by cultivating religious, philosophic, literary, scientific, artistic, and political thought, and they are doing this, not as a mere matter of taste, but in their sacred duty as citizens.

One of the most interesting chapters in this book is entitled 'Culture.' If it were possible to get Boston to read anything of recent date, the perusal of this chapter would produce a much-needed revolution there. Between the Scylla, the

---

6   To associate with a criminal or a crime is to be as guilty as the perpetrator, from the Old
      Testament Bible, Leviticus 5, 'Neither can we touch pitch without being defiled'.

7   Of or pertaining to the Germans.

8   A slave.

9   The theory of justice which advocates the punishment of law-breakers in all instances,
      even where no person or persons have suffered wrongdoing.

10   Now derogatory, a black person.

fervid ignorance of the workers of Paterson, and that Charybdis,[11] the prestige and mere knowledge and genteel aloofness and culture which make Boston useless, the creative minds of the university reformers must steer their dangerous way. At futile Washington Mr Wells found a real man, the anxious, perplexed President, who is a microcosm of his hundred million subjects,[12] who sees all that is wrong and the difficulty of reform. Mr Roosevelt[13] assimilates all that makes for reform in contemporary thought, and causes it to reverberate over the land so that is becomes familiar to all people. At the root of all reform is political reform, creating a legislature[14] at Washington and an executive[15] which shall be in harmony with one another, and which under proper safeguards shall be able to put aside the present obstruction of the various States. Only a great educated and sustained agitation can bring about such a revolution.

Mr Wells would almost leave us still in doubt – may not America, after all, be a great futility? But just at the very end we find him optimistic. We are inclined to think that Mr Wells pays too much attention to America of the present, and that if he thought more of America of the past he would be altogether optimistic. Mrs Trollope and Cooper and Dickens differed but little in opinion, and can any candid student of their writings deny that America has surmounted social difficulties which looked almost insuperable sixty years ago? What Mr Wells says is all true, but there is also much more to be said. The average American neglects politics and selfishly thinks of his own interests; yes, but every now and again he shows himself capable of the highest kind of self-sacrifice. At the back of the futile Boston culture is the spirit of Charleston Neck[16] and Bunker's Hill;[17] and the cultured Bostonian had this great merit, he saw that Abraham Lincoln could save the country. We consider that the worst thing in America is Philistinism,[18] commonness or vulgarity of thought; the great merit of Boston is that she has always combated this. Then, as to immigration, we believe than an intermixture of all the European races (and, if we could

---

11   In Greek mythology, of two dangers such that to avoid one increases the risk from the other.

12   At the 1910 census, the American population was recorded as 92,228,496.

13   I. e., Theodore Roosevelt.

14   The body of people empowered to make or enact the laws of a country or state.

15   The group or body concerned with the administration or management of an organisation or a government.

16   The location of a battle of the American War of Independence, 11 May 1779, in South Carolina.

17   Properly, Bunker Hill, the location of a battle during the American War of Independence, 17 June 1775, in Massachusetts, during which the British won a Pyrrhic victory over the revolutionaries, suffering more than a thousand casualties.

18   The attitude of one who is indifferent or hostile to culture.

only get it, an assimilation of the Jews) would produce the very finest nation ever known. These lower races of which Mr Wells speaks are a danger only for a time; in the second and later generations their presence will be shown in a better appreciation of music and literature and painting.

The supreme danger to any State lies in the diminution of its middle class; this is the greatest lesson of history. We see no chance of such a diminution in America for a very long time to come. Furthermore, there is an evident growing determination in this middle class that social problems shall be solved at whatever cost. Lynching[19] is altogether evil, but it occurs only in certain parts of a country of enormous size still nearly empty of inhabitants; it certainly is altogether against the spirit of the American people, one of whose strongest characteristics has always been a respect for *law*. It was a product of the slave system,[20] and is diminishing.

The Europeanised American who scorns politics is truly a curse to himself and his own country and to Europe, but there is now a new revelation. Mr Roosevelt is not the only rich, educated American who has conquered his fear of touching pitch. We agree with Mr Wells as to the inferiority of American school education, the root of all evils; but the sole cause of this is poor payment for teachers, and, like many another great mischief in America, may be altered almost by the stroke of a pen.[21] Has not universal spitting, the habit most dreaded by Dickens, disappeared in one half-year?[22] Anything in the way of quick reform is possible in a country like America, where everybody reads, and where the cheapest monthly magazines, published by millions, contain serious articles about the great American problems and reforms; where in all States north of the Washington parallel[23] the people resemble the Scotch; that is, even the commonest labourers are accustomed to abstract reasoning[24] because of their early religious education. We cannot doubt that it will work out triumphantly its own and our salvation, for it is to be remembered that all the insoluble-looking problems of America are coming for solution more slowly upon England and France and Germany. We believe that Mr Wells has done something important towards solving such problems, and it is not merely America that ought to be grateful to him.

---

19 A hanging without a legal trial.

20 Plantation slavery as exploited in the USA between the 1640s and 1865.

21 In a quick, easy manner.

22 Dickens expressed disgust at the American habit of spitting in *American Notes* (1842), and in 1905, following the spread of tuberculosis assumedly through spitting tobacco, the habit became socially unacceptable within a year.

23 C. 38° north, the latitudinal line just south of Washington DC.

24 A field of deductive reasoning which uses symbols, logical operators and a set of rules which specify what processes may be followed to arrive at a conclusion.

Comment: William Thiselton-Dyer, letter to the editor, 'Mulattos' (12 December 1907).[25]

Mr H. G. Wells, in his interesting book *The Future in America* (1906), tells (pp. 269-270) a story at second-hand which apparently, however, he accepts as accurate in perfect good faith. I transcribe the facts as they were given to him:–

> A few years ago a young fellow came to Boston from New Orleans. Looked all right. Dark – but he explained that by an Italian grandmother. Touch of French in him too. Popular. Well, he made advances to a Boston girl – good family. Gave a fairly straight account of himself. Married.

The offspring of the marriage was a son:–

> Black as your hat. Absolutely Negroid.[26] Projecting jaw, thick lips, frizzy hair, flat nose – everything.

In this case Mr Wells observes:– 'The taint in the blood surges up so powerfully as to blacken the child at birth beyond even the habit of the pure-blooded Negro.'

This is, at any rate, ultra-Mendelian.[27] Such a story would hardly be told and repeated unless it corresponded to popular belief. What one would like to have is precise evidence that such cases actually occur. If verifiable, it would be of great importance both on scientific and political grounds. I find, however, nothing resembling it in such authorities as I am able to consult. No such case is mentioned in either Darwin[28] or Delage, though neither would have been likely to have passed over such a striking instance of reversion had it been known to him. Sir William Lawrence, in his *Lectures on Physiology, Zoology, and the Natural History of Man* (1822), a book still worth consulting, has industriously collected (pp. 472-484) all the facts available at the time about mulattos,[29] but has no instance of the kind.

---

25 Reprinted by permission from Macmillan Publishers Ltd: *Nature* (77: 1989), copyright (1907).

26 Resembling or having some of the characteristic physical features of black people.

27 Of the laws of heredity as espoused by Gregor Mendel in 1865 which state that offspring receive their genetic characterises from a combination of their parents genes.

28 I. e., Charles Darwin.

29 Persons having one white and one black parent.

The problem involved is thus stated by Galton (*Natural Inheritance*, p. 13):– 'A solitary peculiarity that blended freely with the characteristics of the parent stock, would disappear in hereditary transmission.'[30] He then discusses the case of a European mating in a black population:– 'If the whiteness refused to blend with the blackness, some of the offspring of the white man would be wholly white and rest wholly black. The same event would occur in the grand-children, mostly, but not exclusively, in the children of the white offspring, and so on in subsequent generations. Therefore, unless the white stock became wholly extinct, some undiluted specimens of it would make their appearance during an indefinite time, giving it repeated chances of holding its own in the struggle for existence.' *Mutatis mutandis*,[31] the same law would hold for a black mating in a white population.

Lawrence quotes a single case (p. 279) in which a refusal to blend certainly existed:– 'A Negress[32] had twins by an Englishman: one was perfectly black, with short, woolly curled hair; the other was light, with long hair.' He also points out that in 'mixed breeds' 'children may be seen like their grandsires,[33] and unlike the father and mother,' a fact observed by Lucretius.

Fit quoque, ut interdum similes existere avorum

Possint, et referant proavorum saepe figuras.[34]

On the other hand, according to Lawrence, there was a legal process in the Spanish colonies of South America by which a mulatto could claim a declaration that he was, at any rate politically, free from any taint of black blood. Of Quinterons,[35] who were one-sixteenth black, he says:– 'It is not credible that any trace of mixed origin can remain in this case,' and even of Tercerons,[36] who were one-quarter black, 'in colour and habit of body they cannot be distinguished from their European progenitors.' He says (p. 274) that Jamaica Quadroons[37] 'are not to be distinguished from whites.' But 'there is still a contamina-

---

30   The passing of biological characteristics to offspring through reproduction.

31   Latin, making the necessary changes.

32   A black woman.

33   Grandfathers.

34   A quotation from Lucretius's *De Rerum Natura*; the translation from the Latin reads: 'It may also happen at times that children resemble a grandfather and reproduce the features of a great-grandfather'.

35   Persons having one-sixteenth black blood.

36   More commonly terceroons, persons one-quarter black.

37   Persons having one quarter black blood.

tion of dark blood, although no longer visible. It is said to betray itself sometimes in a relic of the peculiar strong smell of the great-grandmother.' If these
statements can be relied upon, Galton's hypothetical law does not appear to apply to mulattos, and some doubt is thrown on the case cited by Wells. On the
other hand, Lawrence quotes from the *Philosophical Transactions*[38] ('v., 55') a
case of two Negroes who had a white child, the paternal grandfather being
white. This seems purely Mendelian.

Reply to Thiselton-Dyer: H. G. Wells, letter to the editor, 'Mulattos' (19 December 1907).[39]

May I have a line to correct Sir William Thiselton-Dyer's impression (p. 126)
that the tragic story of The Pure White Mother and the Coal-black Babe was accepted by me 'as accurate and in perfect good faith'? I suppose I ought to have
underlined the gentle sneer at a blackness transcending the natural blackness of a
Negro baby. At any rate, I told the anecdote simply to illustrate the nonsense
people will talk under the influence of race mania,[40] and I hope it will not be
added too hastily to the accumulation of evidence on the Mendelian side.

---

38   A journal of the Royal Society, founded in 1665.

39   Reprinted by permission from Macmillan Publishers Ltd: *Nature* (77: 1990), copyright
      (1907). This letter has previously been reprinted in Smith 1998, II: 202.

40   A xenophobic preoccupation with theories of race, and a consequent fear for one's own
      racial survival.

2.10: *What is Coming?*

Joseph Proudman, 'Forecast by Mr Wells' (10 August 1916).[1]

What is Coming? A Forecast of Things after the War. By H. G. Wells. Pp. 295. (London: Cassell and Co., Ltd., 1916.) Price 6*s*. net.

When Mr Wells writes upon social and political questions he is a prophet whom it is a pleasure to follow, even when we feel that time will prove his extrapolation careless. What mistakes he may have made in this book will declare themselves in a year of two, so that he has placed his reputation in more jeopardy than usual. He believes that Germany will be beaten, but not completely crushed by this war;[2] 'she is going to be left militarist and united with Austria and Hungary, and unchanged in her essential nature; and out of that state of affairs comes, I believe, the hope for an ultimate confederation of the nations of the earth.'[3] The Central Powers[4] remaining a menace, the Allies[5] and America will reform all their methods. It is in discussing these reforms that Mr Wells is at his best; he is on his own familiar ground, and he excites the admiration and sympathy of his most exacting critics. The chapter, 'Nations in Liquidation,' contains in one sentence his great idea: 'The landlord who squeezes, the workman who strikes and shirks, the lawyer who fogs and obstructs, will know, and will know that most people know, that what he does is done, not under an empty, regardless heaven, but in the face of an unsleeping enemy and in disregard of a continuous urgent necessity for unity.'

Thus we shall have a millennium induced by the German menace: we wish we could believe in it. In the chapter, 'The Outlook for the Germans,' we find that he relies upon the great middle class to save Germany from Junkerdom.[6] He does not take into account the fact that the German nation must get tired of being intense and perhaps may even get disgusted with 'Kultur.'[7] Read-

---

1   Reprinted by permission from Macmillan Publishers Ltd: *Nature* (97: 2441), copyright (1916).

2   I. e., the Great War.

3   Wells's preferred international accommodation from 1901 to 1916, though with *What is Coming?* (1916) he began a shift in emphasis towards cosmopolitan federalism and the need for nation-states to cede sovereignty to global authorities which would preoccupy his thinking for the rest of his life (see Wagar 1961 and Partington 2003).

4   The alliance of Germany, Austria-Hungary and the Ottoman Empire during the Great War.

5   During the Great War, the military combination of France, Russia, the British Empire and Italy.

6   An element of the Prussian aristocracy which aimed, between the eighteenth and the twentieth centuries, to maintain the exclusive privileges of their class.

7   A designation for German civilisation and culture by those who consider it racist, authoritarian and militaristic.

ers know his views on Socialism, and they can imagine how he mocks at our present want of organisation, our rottenness and dishonesty, and how in particular he makes war against the lawyers and schoolmasters. There is a good chapter on 'What the War is doing for Women.'

Mr Wells's whole scheme is based on his belief that the Central Powers will continue to menace the world, and this belief is itself based upon a certain hypothesis which might almost have been called an axiom five months ago, when Mr Wells wrote. This hypothesis is that in entrenched warfare the defensive has an advantage over the most brilliant strategy and over considerably superior numbers,[8] and that there must be a deadlock, followed by the complete exhaustion of both sides. If Mr Wells had waited only a few months he would have seen that the great wealth and patriotism of England and the enormous population of Russia and the intense feeling of France now enable the Allies to break through the long German fortifications at all points with advantages in power which get greater and greater every day, so that the deadlock is already at an end. Exhaustion in men is possible, and as there are more than twice as many available soldiers with the Allies as with the Central Powers, the speedier exhaustion of Germany in men is quite certain. As for exhaustion in wealth: in two years of the Napoleonic war[9] we spent one-third of a million pounds per day. In a week we spent as much as Charles II spent in a year. Now we have reached an expenditure of six millions per day, and yet unscientific persons refuse to recognise that the wealth of England is unimaginably great, and that the steam-engine[10] has given us the whole earth in fee.[*] Germany in 1871 thought, and everybody thought, that she had ruined France financially.[11] We know now that if she had enforced an indemnity ten times as great France would have paid it easily. We talk of the cost of the war to Germany spelling her financial ruin, whereas those scientific persons who have studied Germany know that at the end of this war, if we compel Germany to pay the total expenditure of the Allies (we do not recommend this), she will still be in a flourishing condition. Mr Wells thinks

---

8   This demonstrates Wells's debt to Jean de Bloch who claimed, in 'The Wars of the Future' (1901), that entrenched men would enjoy a fourfold advantage over infantry advancing across open ground.

9   A series of conflicts between France and her European neighbours between 1804 and 1815, extending into Asia, north Africa and the European colonies.

10   The mechanical invention at the centre of the industrial revolution which so increased production as to make Britain the preponderant global power of the nineteenth century.

*   'It has been proved that the steam-engine has multiplied the wealth of the world by some number between 200 and 1000.'

11   Following victory in the Franco-Prussian War (1870-71), Germany imposed an indemnity of five billion francs on France, to be paid within three years, which caused France surprisingly little economic hardship.

that the world peace is coming soon through universal self-sacrifice; it is a guileless notion. Peace will come to the world through such a loss of its wealth as people do not think about – by the exhaustion of its coal. The man in the street who reads scraps of scientific literature believes, like the spendthrift, in a miracle – namely, that unknown stores of wealth will be opened up when our coal fails. Before the war we recognised with sorrow that he was wrong, but we have less sorrow now when we know that our greatest blessing has become a curse.

2.11: *The Outline of History* and *Mr Belloc Objects to 'The Outline of History'*

'The Dominion of Man' (11 December 1919).[1]

The Outline of History: Being a Plain History of Life and Mankind. By H. G. Wells. With the editorial help of Mr Ernest Barker, Sir H. H. Johnston, Sir E. Ray Lankester, and Prof. Gilbert Murray. To be completed in about twenty fortnightly parts. Part I. Pp. 32. (London: George Newnes, Ltd.) Price 1*s*. 2*d*. net.

In the first part of his *Outline of History* Mr H. G. Wells has surpassed the old author who carried the Trojan war[2] back to Leda's eggs,[3] for he begins with our solar system[4] as a nebula[5] condensing into sun and planets, and our earth as a mass of glowing matter. He tells how, in the course of cooling, an ocean gathered on its surface, on the margin of which the first structureless organic matter at last appeared, from which, in the course of ages, the earth's living tenants were developed. He describes in graphic terms not a few characteristic members in their succession, some of which are well depicted by Mr J. F. Horrabin. Once or twice a phrase occurs to which we may demur: for instance, the nautilus[6] is not a genus of ammonite;[7] volcanic eruptions are more often a consequence than a cause of mountain upheaval; and we doubt whether the changes between the Mesozoic and the Kainozoic[8] were so 'catastrophic' as he implies. But these are trifles, and we find, after a discussion of the estimates of geological time, a good sketch of natural selection and the changes of species. As these changes in life depend not only on alteration's in the world's physical geography, but also on its climate, the causes of the latter are briefly explained.

---

1   Reprinted by permission from Macmillan Publishers Ltd: *Nature* (104: 2615), copyright (1919).

2   In Greek mythology, a war between Sparta and Troy, waged as a result of Paris of Troy stealing Helen from Menelaus, the King of Sparta. The Trojans were defeated following a ten-year siege, though the Spartans were punished by the gods for their behaviour.

3   In Greek mythology, the god Zeus, in the form of a swan, raped Leda who was then delivered of two eggs. From the eggs were born Castor and Pollux, and Helen and Clytemnestra.

4   The sun together with all the planets and other bodies connected with it.

5   A cloud of gas or dust in deep space, appearing lighter or darker due to the reflection or absorption of light.

6   A marine cephalopod mollusc.

7   Any of numerous fossil cephalopods of the order Ammonoidea which have a chambered cell, usually coiled into a plane spiral, and which are found mainly in Mesozoic rocks.

8   Properly, cenozoic, the most recent of the three classic geological eras covering the period from 65.5 million years ago to the present.

Next, Mr Wells, after sketching the strange living tenants of the earth in ages when no creature with a backbone existed in sea or on land, brings before his readers the strange aspects of the earlier vertebrates, such as Pareiosaurus,[9] which, low down as it is among the reptiles, seems as if striving to be a mammal.[10] This leads to the 'Age of Reptiles,'[11] which is illustrated by such huge forms as Brontosaurus[12] and Diplodocus,[13] Stegosaurus[14] and Triceratops,[15] which might be a first attempt at a Pachyderm,[16] together with Megalosaurus,[17] Tyrannosaurus,[18] and Iguanodon,[19] besides Plesiosaurus[20] and Ichthyosaurus in the sea, with flying creatures like Pterodactyls and Archaeopteryx,[21] half bird, half lizard; and then dentigerous[22] birds which pass on to the Kainozoic, and end the present part of the work, which when completed will be a broad survey of the world throughout time.

Mr Wells has undertaken a difficult task, and it is not too much to say that no other writer of the present day is so well equipped as he is to bring it to a successful completion. He possesses the rare combination of brilliant literary power with comprehensive and precise knowledge, and this distinctive quality makes his work one in which all intelligent readers will find profit and delight.

---

9   Properly, pareiasaurus, any of a group of herbivorous reptiles which roamed the earth between 280 million and 230 million years ago.

10 A warm-blooded animal characterised by the possession of mammary glands (in females), a four-chambered heart and a backbone (though with some exceptions).

11 The Mesozoic age.

12 A large herbivorous sauropod dinosaur of the genus *Apatosaurus* which lived during the Jurassic and Cretaceous periods.

13 A genus of gigantic herbivorous Jurassic sauropod dinosaur characterised by its long neck.

14 A large quadrupedal herbivorous dinosaur of the Jurassic period, having a double line of bony plates along its back.

15 A large herbivorous dinosaur having a horn on the snout, a horn over each eye and a bony frill over the neck.

16 A thick-skinned quadruped, especially an elephant, a hippopotamus or a rhinoceros.

17 A large bipedal carnivorous dinosaur of the Jurassic and Cretaceous periods.

18 A huge carnivorous dinosaur of the Upper Cretacious, having powerful hind legs and jaws, a large tail and small front legs.

19 Any of various large extinct ornithischian dinosaurs of late Jurassic and early Cretaceous times, with well-developed hind limbs and a long thick tail.

20 Any of a group of extinct marine reptiles of Mesozoic times having a small head, a short tail and four large paddle-like limbs.

21 The oldest known fossil bird, dating from the late Jurassic period and having several reptilian features.

22 Bearing teeth.

'A "Tour de Force"' (30 September 1920).[23]

There are three fundamental subjects in education – the history of our race,[24] the world around us, and the conditions of health, happiness, and effective work. They correspond to Le Play's 'famille, lieu, travail';[25] to the biologists 'Organism,[26] Environment, Function.' Fundamental they certainly are, but it is generally admitted that most men know little about any of them and understand less. We are perhaps deplorably slow to learn, but we are also very badly taught. Especially in regard to the history of mankind it is difficult to forgive our teachers, for we spent so long over it (the other fundamentals were for the 'modern' side) and we know that we were not unappetised. Yet for bread we got stones.[27] We find the same disappointment among most of our fellows, the disappointment of half-educated men who know their deficiencies. There are well-known ways of making the study of history grip – the use of graphs and charts, the biographical approach, with its calendar of great men, the emotional and dramatic methods so vividly illustrated by Dr Hayward,[28] and so on; but they seem rarely to be tested in schools or colleges, and widespread ignorance of a supreme subject prevails. We except, of course, those who are by birth historically minded, who learn in spite of bad methods or the absence of any; though even those who know many historical facts seem often like students who are familiar with fossils, but unaware of the aeonic[29] pulse and progress of life.

These bitter reflections are prompted, of course, by Mr Wells's *Outline of History,*[*] which convinces us of sin. For here we find what, in spite of its imperfections, is of the nature of a revelation – a sketch of the continuous movement from the nebula that became the earth to the League of Nations, a suggestion of the sweep and surge of civilisation, not in one corner, but all the world over, an attempt to focus attention on the things that have counted in the past and are living on, around us and in us, to-day. We use such words as 'sketch,' 'suggestion,' and 'attempt,' not in any disparaging way, but because no single man could offer anything else. The book is called 'The Outline.' There are probably big

---

23   Reprinted by permission from Macmillan Publishers Ltd: *Nature* (106: 2657), copyright (1920).

24   The human race; humankind.

25   French, 'family, place, work'.

26   An organised living body, especially an individual animal, plant, bacterium, etc.

27   From the New Testament Bible, Luke 11: 11, 'If a son shall ask bread of any of you that is a father, will he give him a stone?', meaning giving bad service to one in need.

28   This reference has proved untraceable.

29   Lasting an aeon, or an immeasurable period of time.

*   '*The Outline of History: Being a Plain History of Life and Mankind.* By H. G. Wells. Revised and corrected edition. Pp. xx + 652. (London: Cassell and Co., Ltd., 1920.) Price 21s. net.'

omissions, unconscious misinterpretations, mistaken accentuating, and so forth, but the point is that Mr Wells has shown his day and generation the sort of history of the world that every educated man should have as a possession in his mind. It is a fine thing to have achieved what has hitherto been called impossible. We recall two books of many years ago – Haeckel's *Natural History of Creation*[30] and Krause's *Werden und Vergehen* – which traced the cosmic genesis from nebula to consolidated earth, and the organic evolution from Protists[31] to Man, and did this in a vividly picturesque way. They may not have been quite so fine as we thought they were, but, errors and omissions excepted, they were fine books.

Mr Wells's *Outline* is another such big gift to education. Perhaps it will be a still bigger gift when someone writes another like it from a different point of view. From out of the mouth of two or more witnesses there is some chance of the truth being stated. But, as the author says, the book is an 'experimental contribution to a great and urgently necessary educational reformation, which must ultimately restore universal history, revised, corrected, and brought up to date, to its proper place and use as the backbone of a general education. We say "restore," because all the great cultures of the world hitherto, Judaism and Christianity in the Bible,[32] Islam in the Koran,[33] have used some sort of cosmogony[34] and world-history as a basis. It may indeed be argued that without such a basis any really binding culture of men is inconceivable. Without it we are a chaos.' We would also quote the striking sentence which expresses Mr Wells's appreciation of what a living conception of world-history may mean: 'A sense of history as the common adventure of all mankind is as necessary for peace within as it is for peace between the nations.' Yet we go on fumbling with educational methods, if such they may be called, which we know do not grip.

As is noted in the Introduction, it is usual to say that the time-table of instruction is full up, and that the idea of learning world-history is preposterous.

If an Englishman, for example, has found the history of England quite enough for his powers of assimilation, then it seems hopeless to expect his sons and daughters to master universal history, if that is to consist of the history of England, *plus* the history of France, *plus* the history of Russia, and so on. To which

---

30 Originally, *Natürliche Schöpfungsgeschichte* (1868).

31 Simple organisms regarded as intermediate between or distinct from animals and plants.

32 The canonical collection of religious writings or books of Judaism and Christianity.

33 The holy book of Islam, believed to be Allah's word as recorded by Muhammad in the 7th century.

34 A theory or account of, and the branch of science which deals with, the origin of the universe.

the only possible answer is that universal history is at once something more and something less than the aggregate of the national histories to which we are accustomed, that it must be approached in a different spirit and dealt with in a different manner. This book seeks to justify that answer. It has been written primarily to show that *history as one whole* is amenable to a more broad and comprehensive handling than is the history of special nations and periods, a broader handling that will bring it within the normal limitations of time and energy set to the reading and education of an ordinary citizen.... History is no exception amongst the sciences; as the gaps fill in, the outline simplifies; as the outlook broadens, the clustering multitude of details dissolves into general laws.

We are forced to add that there would be no difficulty about the time for instruction if the methods employed were psychologically sound, if the suggestions of 'historical associations' and clear-headed enthusiasts were put into practice. It is certain, for instance, that the purely intellectual presentation usually slips off the child's mind like water off a duck's back,[35] and that it ought to. Moreover, in higher classes what is wanted is not history *plus* history, but a discipline in the way of reading history of such a kind that it will be natural to continue learning. What we so often do not get are centres of crystallisation[36] – a less static metaphor than it used to seem.

There are nine books in *The Outline of History* – The Making of Our World; The Making of Man; The Dawn of History; Judea,[37] Greece, and India; The Rise and Collapse of the Roman Empire;[38] Christianity and Islam; The Great Mongol Empires[39] of the Land Ways and the New Empires of the Sea Ways; The Age of the Great Powers;[40] and then a prospect – The Next Stage in History. It was said of Buffon that he took all Nature for his province and was not embarrassed; but Mr Wells has an even wider reach. It seems almost superhuman – to be so well done; but the author tells us frankly: 'There is not a chapter that has not been examined by some more competent person than himself and very carefully revised. He has particularly to thank his friends Sir E. Ray Lan-

---

35 Not affected in the slightest.

36 The process of giving a definite or permanent shape to something vague or unformed.

37 The mountainous, southern part of the historic Land of Israel, now divided between Israel, the Palestinian Authority and Jordan.

38 The ancient empire of Rome, founded by Julius Caesar in 44 BC and ended through dismemberment in AD 305.

39 The largest contiguous land empire in history, lasting from 1206 to 1405, covering over 33 million square kilometres from east Asia to central Europe at its zenith and containing about 100 million people.

40 Nations or states that, through their economic, military, political and diplomatic strength, are able to exert power in the world.

kester, Sir H. H. Johnston, Prof. Gilbert Murray, and Mr Ernest Barker for much counsel.' There is a long list of authorities who have helped in various ways to keep the book true to the facts (their footnotes are illuminating); and he has been fortunate in securing in Mr J. F. Horrabin a skilful illustrator who has put brains into his drawings.

It need scarcely be said that *The Outline* is a *personal* document – materials had to be selected, much had to be left out; prominence has been given to some figures, others are in the background; the relative significance of various movements had to be judged, and all this has been obviously influenced by the author's philosophy. The difference here between Mr Wells and other historians is that he is so clearly aware of the relativity of his work. There is another way, of course, in which the book is personal: it is written in good style – clear, picturesque, and incisive – and it expresses throughout the serious purpose of improving things by understanding them. Another personal characteristic, familiar to readers of Mr Wells's books, is the courage of his convictions.

The First Book gives in very brief compass an account of the genesis of the earth and the evolution of organisms. There are a few points that puzzle us, such as an indication that the breastbone of Pterodactyls had no keel,[41] but the sketch is masterly. The Second Book deals with the ascent of man, his Primate ancestry, the extinct Neanderthal offshoot, the first true men[42] and their thoughts, the differentiation into races, with their various languages. The Third Book pictures the dawn of history, the primitive Aryan[43] life, the first civilisations, the early traders and travellers, the beginning of writing, the emergence of priests,[44] and the establishment of classes and castes. The treatment is a fine illustration of the art of leaving out what obscures the main issues and of the reward that comes to a man of science who has insisted on seeing things clearly. It is of great educational value to have this vivid and accurate picture of the rock whence we were hewn and the pit whence we were digged.[45]

What dominates the Fourth Book is the idea that by the beginning of the third century BC there had already arisen in the Western civilisation[46] of the Old

---

41 A central ridge along the back or convex surface of an animal or plant organ or structure.

42 The species Homo sapiens, which emerged around 130,000 years ago.

43 A native or inhabitant of Ariana, the eastern part of ancient Iran, or descendants thereof.

44 Clergymen, ministers of religion.

45 A paraphrase from the Old Testament Bible, Isaiah 51: 1, 'look to the rock whence ye are hewn, and to the hole of the pit whence ye are digged'.

46 A collective designation for the cultures which originated in Europe, and trace their origins back to Greek philosophy, Roman law and Catholic and Protestant Christianity.

World[47] the great structural ideas (1) of communicable and verifiable knowledge, as contrasted with priest-guarded mysteries; (2) of one universal God of Righteousness, whose temple is the whole world; and (3) of a world polity of which Alexander the Great became the symbol. 'The rest of the history of mankind is very largely the history of these three ideas of science, of a universal righteousness, and of a human commonweal.'[48] The Fifth Book gives an account of the rise and collapse of the Roman Empire – an account which seems to us to betray bias. It was a very unsound political system. 'The clue to all its failure lies in the absence of any free mental activity and any organisation for the increase, development, and application of knowledge.' It was 'a colossally ignorant and unimaginative Empire.' When the smash came 'there was one thing that did not perish, but grew, and that was the tradition of the world-empire of Rome and of the supremacy of the Caesars.' The Great War 'mowed down no fewer than four Caesars'[49] who insisted on keeping up the evil tradition. We do not hear much of Roman Law[50] from Mr Wells, but he frankly confesses that he 'contemplates the law and lawyers of to-day with a temperamental lack of appreciation.'

The Sixth Book is chiefly concerned with Christianity and its idea of the Kingdom of God,[51] and with Islam with its broad idea of human brotherhood under God. It is admitted that the founder of Islam 'had to tack on to his assertion of the supremacy of God an assertion that Muhammad was in especial his prophet, a queer little lapse into proprietorship, a touchingly baseless claim for the copyright of an idea which, as a matter of fact, he had picked up from the Jews and Christians about him.' Regarding Christianity, the author quotes with approval a sentence from Dean Inge's *Outspoken Essays*: 'St Paul understood what most Christians never realise, namely, that the Gospel of Christ[52] is not *a* religion, but religion itself in its most universal and deepest significance.' Thereafter follows a passage which will interest many, in which Mr Wells declares that there is no antagonism between science and religion. What he says seems to us to suggest rather that there is no antagonism between science and *morals*. 'The psychologist can now stand beside the preacher and assure us that there is no reasoned peace of heart, no balance and no safety in the soul, until a man in

---

47 The eastern hemisphere; Europe, Asia and Africa.

48 The body politic, a community in which everyone has an interest.

49 A reference to the fall of monarchism in Austria-Hungary, Germany, Russia and the Ottoman Empire as a result of the upheaval caused by the Great War.

50 The code of law developed by the ancient Romans and forming the basis of many modern codes.

51 The spiritual sovereignty of God or the sphere over which this extends, in heaven and / or on earth.

52 Jesus Christ's teachings as recorded in the Christian gospels.

losing his life has found it, and has schooled and disciplined his interests and will beyond greeds, rivalries, fears, instincts, and narrow affections.' And then he goes on to say, all too elliptically: 'The history of our race and personal religious experience run so closely parallel as to seem to a modern observer almost the same thing; both tell of a being at first scattered and blind and utterly confused, feeling its way slowly to the serenity and salvation of an ordered and coherent purpose. That in the simplest is the outline of history; whether one have a religious purpose or disavow a religious purpose altogether, the lines of the outline remain the same.'

In the Seventh Book the Age of the Land Ways is illustrated by the great empire of Jengis Khan and his successors, very sympathetically sketched ('the blood in our veins was brewed on the steppes[53] as well as on the ploughlands'). Land ways give place to sea ways and Western civilisation has its renascence ('Europe begins to Think for Itself,' 'Paper Liberated the Human Mind,' 'the expansion of human horizons,' 'intimations of a new and profounder social justice'). The Eighth Book is devoted to the Age of the Great Powers.

> Tremendously as these phantoms, the Powers, rule our minds and lives to-day, they are, as this history shows clearly, things only of the last few centuries, a mere hour, an incidental phase, in the vast, deliberate history of our kind. They mark a phase of relapse, a backwater, as the rise of Machiavellian[54] monarchy marks a backwater; they are part of the same eddy of faltering faith, in a process altogether greater and altogether different in general character, the process of the moral and intellectual reunion of mankind. For a time men have relapsed upon these national or imperial gods of theirs; it is but for a time. The idea of the world state, the universal kingdom of righteousness, of which every living soul shall be a citizen, was already in the world two thousand years ago, never more to leave it. Men know that it is present, even when they refuse to recognise it.

Glimpses of this same vision we find throughout the book; it is so dominant in Mr Wells's mind that he has seen all history in the light of it. Whether it makes for good history we do not know; it has made for a fascinating book which it does one good to read. Its influence will be far-reaching.

To what prospect does his study of universal history lead Mr Wells? The trend of human evolution points in the direction of internationalism[55] – but be-

---

53   The vast level grassy, usually treeless plains of south-east Europe and Siberia.

54   A person preferring expediency to morality, as suggested in *Il Principe* (1513 / 1532) by Niccolò Machiavelli.

55   The advocacy of a community of interests among nations.

yond. 'Our true nationality is mankind.' Religion and education, closely inter-woven influences, have been the chief synthetic forces throughout the great story of enlarging human co-operations: of the former we may look for a revival, of the latter a re-adjustment informed with science. As a necessary basis for world co-operation, for a preparation for a world league of men, there must be '*a new telling and interpretation, a common interpretation of history.*' And that this book will further. 'There can be little question that the attainment of a feder-ation[56] of all humanity, together with a sufficient measure of social justice, to ensure health, education, and a rough equality of opportunity to most of the children born into the world, would mean such a release and increase of human energy as to open a new phase in human history.' Mr Wells looks forward to 'the final achievement of world-wide political and social unity,' which will be reached by and based on righteousness as well as science, 'perhaps with long interludes of setback and disaster,' but 'it will mean no resting stage, nor even a breathing stage, before the development of a new struggle and of new and vaster efforts. Men will unify only to intensify the search for knowledge and power and live as ever for new occasions.' Almost the ending of what we cannot but regard as a great book is a key sentence: 'Life begins perpetually.'

'Our Bookshelf' (7 November 1925).[57]

The Outline of History: Being a Plain History of Life and Mankind. By H. G. Wells. New edition, fully revised. (Complete in 24 fortnightly parts.) Part 1. Pp. 32. Part 2. Pp. 33-64. (London: Cassell and Co., Ltd., 1925.) 1*s.* 3*d.* net each part.

Mr Wells's world history was first written in 1918-1919 and revised in 1920 and 1923. Even in the short period which has since elapsed, discoveries of new ma-terial have been made in almost every part of the world, and, whether by acci-dent of by design, new evidence is being brought to light daily which bears upon the early history of man upon this globe. It is, therefore, no matter for surprise that Mr Wells, in preparing the new edition of his *Outline of History*, should have found it necessary not merely to recast, but to rewrite a considerable part of it, especially in the earlier sections. It is inevitable that a work of this kind should be at the mercy of any new discovery which may at any moment throw doubt on a conclusion or necessitate a change in point of view. Mr Wells has done his utmost to protect his readers from this danger by bringing his informa-

---

56 A union of several states under a federal government, each retaining independence in internal affairs.

57 Reprinted by permission from Macmillan Publishers Ltd: *Nature* (116: 2923), copyright (1925).

tion fully up-to-date, and even so recent a discovery as that of the Galilean skull[58] receives due mention.

The first two parts which have now been issued afford an opportunity to test the quality of the work in its new form. They comprise from the beginnings of the earth down to Neolithic man in Europe, ending with an account of primitive trade. This, to many, will be the most interesting section of the whole work, as it deals with the earliest stages in the evolution of animal and human life and embraces so much that is new. It is inevitable that a writer of such strong individuality as Mr Wells should at times run counter to accepted views; but he is always prepared to argue his case on good grounds. His dates for the late stages of the Palaeolithic period on some views may appear too high, but this is of little moment beside the great advantage which his time charts and scales confer on the reader who is not an expert. To such a one they will be invaluable as an indication of perspective.

A special feature of this edition is the illustrations, which have been greatly increased in number and chosen with much discrimination and care.

'Our Bookshelf' (18 December 1926).[59]

The Outline of History: Being a Plain History of Life and Mankind. By H. G. Wells. New edition, fully revised. Parts 1-24. (London: Cassell and Co., Ltd., 1925-1926.) 1s. 3d. net each part.

Mr Belloc Objects to 'The Outline of History.' By H. G. Wells. (The Forum Series.) Pp. vii + 55. (London: Watts and Co., 1926.) 1s. net.

On the appearance of the first number we directed attention to the new edition of Mr H. G. Wells's *Outline of History*, the serial issue of which has recently been completed. The *Outline* has been almost entirely rewritten, brought up-to-date, and provided with a fresh set of illustrations – perhaps as remarkable a collection of photographs covering all sides of human evolution and history as has ever been gathered together within the covers of one book. Apart from matters of opinion, in which Mr Wells is characteristically individual – it is emphatically Mr Wells's outline of history – there is little even in matters of detail which requires criticism. To have mastered so vast a body of material, and to have kept abreast of current opinion on so many technical subjects, is in itself no small intellectual feat. To take an example only, he is prepared to assign the Taungs

---

58   The partial frontal cranial remains of a Neanderthal individual, discovered by Francis Turville-Petre in a cave in Wadi el-Amud near the Sea of Galilee in 1925.

59   Reprinted by permission from Macmillan Publishers Ltd: *Nature* (118: 2981), copyright (1926).

man[60] a place in his evolutionary scheme, although this skull was discovered only while the book was in process of writing. On certain points in dealing with the bronze[61] and iron ages,[62] and on ethnological[63] questions relating to the origin and migrations of races, the views adopted by Mr Wells are open to argument, just as his views of great personalities, such as Alexander, Julius Caesar, or Napoleon, invite or even provoke discussion. These, however, are little more than matters of detail in relation to the broad scheme of evolutionary history which Mr Wells has set himself to expound.

To those, be they men of science or historians, who grasp the broader issues of biological and anthropological science, Mr Wells may seem neither revolutionary nor iconoclast;[64] but it is evident that the *Outline* has been a stumbling block to a certain type of orthodoxy. Criticisms or Mr Wells and his views by Mr Hilaire Belloc have appeared in certain Roman Catholic newspapers[65] *pari passu*[66] with the fortnightly issue of the *Outline*. Mr Wells, having failed to secure adequate opportunity for reply in the periodicals in question, now replies in a little volume which he has issued himself. It is scarcely necessary to say that Mr Wells's humorous, if caustic, pen makes short work of Mr Belloc's criticisms as well as his views on the subjects of natural selection, evolution, and the ancestry of man.

Arthur Keith, 'Is Darwinism Dead?' (15 January 1927).[67]

(1) *A Companion to Mr Wells's 'Outline of History.'* By Hilaire Belloc. Pp. iv + 119. (London: Sheed and Ward, 1926.) 7*s*. 6*d*. net.

(2) *Mr Belloc Objects to 'The Outline of History.'* By H. G. Wells. (The Forum Series.) Pp. vii + 55 + 2 plates. (London: Watts and Co., 1926.) 1*s*. net.

---

60   More commonly Taung Child, a 2.5 million-year-old fossil of a skull discovered by a quarryman in Taung, South Africa, in 1924 and reported by Raymond Dart. It was unappreciated for several decades.

61   The age of human culture, c. 2500 BC to c. 1200 BC, when bronze was cast for making tools, weapons and jewellery.

62   The period, from the twelfth century BC to the early Middle Ages, when weapons and tools were first made from iron.

63   Pertaining to the branch of knowledge that deals with the characteristics of different peoples and the differences and relationships between them.

64   A person who attacks a cherished belief or respected institution.

65   Belloc published criticisms of *The Outline of History* in various newspapers, including *The Tablet* and the *Catholic Herald*.

66   Latin, simultaneously and equally.

67   Reprinted by permission from Macmillan Publishers Ltd: *Nature* (119: 2985), copyright (1927).

(3) *Mr Belloc Still Objects to Mr Wells's 'Outline of History.'* By Hilaire Belloc. Pp. x + 43. (London: Sheed and Ward, 1926.) Paper, 7d.; cloth, 1s.

Quite a dozen years ago statements began to appear in our public press announcing that 'Darwinism was dead,' and so often has this assertion been repeated in more recent days that there has arisen in the public mind a fear that some sort of fatality has overtaken the reputation of the great naturalist. If by Darwinism is implied the body of fact, inference, and doctrine contained between the covers of *The Origin of Species*, then assuredly Darwinism is not dead, for the revolution which that book began to work in the minds of thoughtful men sixty-seven years ago still continues its forward and unchecked progress.

The essence of Darwin's[68] teaching is to be found in the last paragraph of the introduction he wrote for the first edition of *The Origin*, and is repeated in all the later editions. There Darwin states that 'I can entertain no doubt, after the most deliberate study and dispassionate judgement of which I am capable, that the view which most naturalists[69] until recently entertained, and which I formerly entertained – namely, that each species has been independently created – is erroneous.' Through Darwin's influence 'special creationists'[70] in all the leading nations of the world were transformed into 'evolutionists.'[71] Thus in its widest sense Darwinism implies merely the acceptance of the belief that all living things have been evolved from other and older living things. There is no book which seems so certain of a place in the permanent literature of the world as Darwin's *Origin of Species*.

That Mr H. G. Wells, trained under Huxley,[72] should be a Darwinist in this wider sense occasions no surprise; but it was scarcely to be expected that Mr Belloc, a devoted son of the Roman Catholic Church,[73] should be of the number. Yet, like Darwin, Mr Belloc rejects special creation and accepts evolution; he even reproves Mr Wells for being ignorant of the fact that 'the conception of the Old Testament as an exact text-book of history and science, not a word of which must be taken as allegory[74] or generalisation, was mainly confined to England and her colonies. The Catholic Church never held it or could of its nature hold it' (*A Companion*, p. 32). Mr Belloc assures his readers that the theory of evolu-

---

68   I. e., Charles Darwin.

69   Experts in or students of natural history, concerned with observation rather than experiment.

70   Those who believe that humans, or even all creatures on earth, were created by supernatural means rather than through evolution over time.

71   Experts or students or believers in the theory of evolution.

72   I. e., T. H. Huxley.

73   A Christian denomination which acknowledges the pope as its head.

74   Symbolic representation.

238

tion is old, and that 'the ancients and fathers of the Church' were familiar with it.

Darwinism is confined by many people to cover merely the theory enunciated in the *Descent of Man*.[75] When used in this more limited sense Darwinism cannot be considered as dead, for I do not know of any living anthropologist[76] or student of the human body who believes that man arose by a special act of creation. Anthropologists may differ as to the kind of ape from which humanity has been evolved, and as to the geological date at which its face was turned manwards, but on the evidence now before them, which grows in volume and in trustworthiness every year, most of our authorities share Darwin's belief that the anthropoid apes and man have sprung from a common stem. In this narrow sense Mr Wells is a Darwinist, but so adroitly does Mr Belloc cover his verbal tracks with a smoke-screen that it is somewhat difficult for his readers to decide whether as regards man's origin he is a fundamentalist[77] or a Darwinist. He quotes with approbation the belief held by 'St Thomas, the great teacher of the Middle Ages,'[78] to the effect that 'the creation of man was not mediate but direct.' St Thomas must, on this evidence, be classed among the fundamentalists. Mr Belloc, however, gives his verbal assent to this narrower form of Darwinism which the fundamentalists find so objectionable; he believes in evolution; he regards the process by which man reached his present estate as open to debate; he speaks of 'the moment when a true man existed at all'; he directs Mr Wells's attention to the fact that certain tests show a close blood affinity between man and anthropoid. With such evidence before us we cannot say that Darwinism – even in this narrow sense – is dead.

Yet in justice to Mr Belloc it should be added here that he rejects two points in Darwin's theory of man's origin. Darwin believed that man's rise from apedom was a slow and gradual process, and he hoped that the evolutionary forces which had lifted him thus high might lift him still higher. Mr Belloc, on the other hand, prefers to believe that man's emergence was of the nature of a leap, and that he is now and will ever remain a 'fixed type.'[79] Our scanty knowledge of fossil[80] ape and man, and our much fuller information regarding their

---

75 By Charles Darwin (1871).

76 A student or researcher of the science of humankind in the widest sense.

77 One who strictly maintains orthodox religious beliefs or doctrines, especially belief in the inerrancy of Scripture and literal acceptance of the creeds.

78 Also, medieval times, the historical period roughly between the fall of the Western Roman Empire in 476 and the beginning of the Renaissance in the fourteenth century.

79 In creationism, the belief that humankind is unaffected by evolution, but is now biologically 'fixed' as God intended.

80 Anything preserved in the strata of the earth and recognisable as the remains or vestiges of a plant or animal of a former geological period.

embryological histories, are altogether against Mr Belloc's beliefs and in favour of Darwin's postulates, which have been rightly adopted by Mr Wells.

There is a third and more restricted sense in which the term Darwinism is used. As an intrinsic part of the machinery which he regarded as being concerned in the evolution of living forms, Darwin introduced the principle or form of 'Natural Selection,' which he defined thus: 'The *preservation* of favourable individual differences and variations, and the destruction of those which are injurious, I have called Natural Selection or the Survival of the Fittest' (*The Origin of Species*, sixth edition, p. 63). There can be no doubt that Darwin claimed the recognition of this law and its application to the problems of evolution as his particular discovery. 'Natural Selection,' writes Mr Belloc, 'is the only thing that properly can be called Darwinism,' and he reproves Mr Wells for being unaware that Darwinism in this sense has been 'riddled for a generation'; that it is 'done for'; that it is 'shaky'; that it is 'nonsense'; that it is 'old and exploded'; that it is 'moribund'; and also that it is 'quite dead.'

Mr Belloc devotes many pages to the exposition of Darwin's law of selection, and so little is the resemblance of the exposition to the original that one is forced to the conclusion that he has never read even the first chapter of *The Origin of Species*. Darwinism as expounded by Mr Belloc is certainly dead; indeed, it was never born. One does expect a historian, especially one who is ever accusing his antagonist – very unjustly – of being ignorant of recent events in the history of Darwinism, to be familiar with some of the chief happenings which followed the publication of *The Origin of Species*. Mr Belloc apparently does not know that Mr St George Mivart (*On the Genesis of Species*, 1871), a convert to the Catholic Church, and one of the ablest anatomists[81] of his time, formulated all the arguments which he now brings against Darwinism, and based them on an expert and first-hand knowledge of living things, such as Mr Belloc can lay no claim to. Nor is he aware that Darwin, patient with even unscrupulous and prejudiced opponents, devoted twenty-eight pages of the sixth edition of *The Origin of Species* (1872) (pp. 176-204) to answering Mivart's criticisms. From first page to last of this sixth edition, Darwin protests against those early critics who supposed that the variations utilised by natural selection occurred 'singly' and 'accidentally'; he admits time after time that although he does not know the 'efficient cause' which brings variations into existence, yet he is certain that their appearance is regulated by many laws, 'some few of which can be dimly seen,' one of these being the law of 'correlated growth'[82] whereby a whole series of structures may be modified together so as to serve more advantageously some functional purpose.

---

81   Researchers into the structure of the bodies of humans, animals and plants.

82   In evolutionary theory, the notion that a series of structures may modify together to the advantage of all structures concerned.

Mr Belloc resuscitates this ancient misrepresentation of 'accidental' and 'single' variations[83] and is thereby enabled, sitting in his armchair, unoppressed by any sense of modesty or burden of knowledge, to enumerate a dozen arguments, each ticked off after another with a triumphant emphasis, all of them demonstrating that the author of natural selection was an uncommonly stupid man and his modern critic a very clever fellow. One who presumes to criticise Darwin's *Origin of Species*, especially from a mathematical point of view, should have known that Prof. Fleeming Jenkin (*The Origin of Species*, sixth edition, 1872, p. 71), in 1867, had demonstrated the impossibility of a new breed or variety arising by natural selection if it had only 'accidental' variations[84] to work upon, and that Darwin had shown this erudite professor wherein his error lay. Mr Belloc knows nothing of this. Nor does he seem to be in touch with what is happening all around him. It is difficult to believe that any one who sees the unceasing struggle which goes on everywhere and every year for the possession of the continents of the world and has been waged since the dawn of history, a struggle which is attended by the spread and dominion of a few favoured races and the retrocession[85] and obliteration of many less favoured races, can doubt the potency of Darwin's law of selection as a factor in the process of evolution. We may not like the way in which evolution works out its effects, but I do not think man, devise as he may, can escape from them. Certainly animals and plants in a state of Nature cannot.

In the five and fifty years which have elapsed since the sixth and last edition of *The Origin of Species* was published, we have learned much concerning how evolutionary processes work in the world of living things, much that was unknown to Darwin. We now know something of the complex laws of heredity, and of the physiological means whereby the growth of the body is regulated, so that its several parts are modified together and made to serve a functional purpose. An example mentioned by Mr Belloc (*The Companion*, p. 22) will serve to illustrate the direction in which our knowledge has improved. After citing one of Darwin's early critics to prove that 'chance-made variations' could never have provided functionally useful structures, he proceeds thus: 'And another biologist has well said – What is the survival value of horns without the structure to support them and muscles to use them?' Having set down this question, Mr Belloc proceeds to answer it. 'The mathematical chances,' he informs his readers, 'are millions and millions to one' against 'the possibility of such a thing. Grant de-

---

83 Commonly, mutations, in genetics, changes in a species caused by exposure to ultraviolet or ionising radiation, or through copying errors in the genetic material during cell division.

84 In evolutionary theory, the notion that biological variations occur as a result of environmental circumstances rather than divine (or other) purpose.

85 The action or fact of moving backwards or receding.

sign moulding all nature – that is, God – and this process is explicable.' The impious biologist of to-day does not find it necessary to call in any divine or supernatural power to explain the multitude of changes which accompany the growth of horns in a young bull or antlers in a stag; the deity Mr Belloc appeals to lies in the testes[86] of these animals! The biologist knows that if a certain substance or hormone[87] formed in the testes is withheld, none of these changes take place; if they are permitted to enter the circulation, then as the horns grow the bones and muscles of the neck increase in size and strength, the lumina[88] of blood-vessels expand, and, what is still more wonderful, the temperament of the animal is transformed. The discovery of hormones, if it renders a direct appeal to the Almighty no longer necessary, does not in any way invalidate or lessen the efficiency of Darwin's law of natural selection; the hormone theory simply helps us to explain how variations of an adaptive nature can and do arise.

What is here written will suffice to show that Darwinism, in whatever sense we construe it, is neither an exploded creed nor a dead doctrine, and that those who assert the contrary not only sin against the light of truth, but also commit a crime by poisoning the springs from which a trusting public drinks its information.

It would be unfair to the memory of St George Mivart were I to conclude without indicating, however briefly, the remarkable manner in which he anticipated in 1871 (*The Genesis of Species*) the arguments which Mr Belloc has brought against Darwin in 1926. Mr Mivart began by asserting that a belief in evolution 'was perfectly consistent with the strictest and most orthodox Christian theology'; Mr Belloc echoes this statement but substitutes 'Catholic' for 'Christian.' Mr Mivart called the 'Fathers and Ancients' as witnesses for the orthodoxy of the theory of evolution, singling out St Thomas for special mention; so does Mr Belloc. Mr Mivart reproved Darwin for his total ignorance of the 'philosophy and teaching of the Catholic Church'; Mr Belloc scolds Mr Wells for the same offence. Mr Mivart believed that structural modifications of a really useful kind were wrought by a supernatural agency; so does Mr Belloc. Mr Mivart believed that by a miraculous intervention man became possessed of a soul only in the last stage of his evolutionary process; this apparently is also Mr Belloc's belief. Darwin, as I have already mentioned, took infinite pains to answer Mr Mivart's scientific objections, and I thought every one knew that Huxley[89] had answered his theological arguments in a famous essay ('Mr Dar-

---

86   The male reproductive organs.

87   Any of numerous organic compounds secreted into the body fluids of an animal by a specific group of cells, and regulating the activity of certain other cells.

88   The central space in blood vessels.

89   I. e., T. H. Huxley.

win's Critics,' 1871, Huxley's *Collected Essays*, vol. 2, p. 120), but it must have escaped Mr Belloc's attention, for he never alludes to it. Yet it is an essay which he might read with advantage, as should every one who honestly tries to reconcile Catholic beliefs with the truth of science. Even Mr Mivart, in the end, found a reconciliation impossible. His later books were placed on the *Index Librorum Prohibitorum*,[90] and in January 1900, when his last illness was upon him, he was excommunicated[91] by Cardinal Vaughan because he dared to assert what his investigations into science had taught him. Such was Mr Mivart's fate, and one wonders what would have happened to the author of *The Origin of Species* if his life had fallen in Catholic places and had his beliefs been in the keeping of Rome.

Comment on Keith: Hilaire Belloc, letter to the editor, 'Is Darwinism Dead?' (19 February 1927).[92]

The review in *Nature* of Jan. 15 of my criticism of Mr Wells's somewhat antiquated biology has only just been shown to me, hence the delay in my sending this letter. I will make it as brief as possible, for I am only concerned with showing that the distinguished reviewer, Sir Arthur Keith, though he has doubtless been given a few sentences from my book for the purposes of quotation, has not read the book itself.

(1) He says: 'So adroitly does Mr Belloc cover his verbal tracks with a smoke screen' that he cannot determine whether I am a 'fundamentalist' or a 'Darwinian.' As a fact, I cannot conceive myself being either, but the point is that no one who had read my book could have imagined that 'Fundamentalism' was the issue. The only issue was whether natural selection was the process whereby the differentiation of species came about.

(2) He says that I give 'with approbation' St Thomas's conclusion that the creation of man was (in scholastic language) 'immediate': that is, special and direct. Had the reviewer read my book he could never have sincerely written that. I quoted this *exceptional* conclusion on immediate human creation to show that St Thomas probably thought the creation of animate beings other than man to be 'mediate': that is, evolutionary.

---

90   Latin, the index of prohibited books, in the Roman Catholic Church an official list of heretical or otherwise undesirable books forbidden to the faithful or sanctioned only after the removal of objectionable passages, existing as a legal document from 1529 to 1966.

91   Expelled from a religious society or community.

92   Reprinted by permission from Macmillan Publishers Ltd: *Nature* (119: 2990), copyright (1927).

(3) The reviewer is 'forced to the conclusion' that I have never read *The Origin of Species*. If he had read my book he could not possibly have been 'forced' to so foolish a conclusion. All I say in it on this matter is written in direct relevance to that work – with its only original (and erroneous) thesis of natural selection as the machinery of differentiation.

(4) He says that 'Mr Belloc resuscitates this ancient misrepresentation of "accidental" and "single" variations,' and follows the sentence up with a good deal of irrelevant abuse. Had he read my book he would have found that I know all about Darwin's[93] retreat in this matter, *and* am careful to point out that it was a muddled retreat. For the mathematical argument against natural selection applies just as much to a thousand cases out of a million as to one out of a thousand.

(5) He so completely misunderstands the example I take from the growth of horns that he clearly has not read the original passage but is judging from a chance sentence put before him, and even that he fails to grasp. My point – clearly stated, emphasised, reiterated – was that multiple adaptation[94] is mathematically incompatible with the blind mechanical action of natural selection. Multiple adaptation presupposes design. The citation of the hormone as a disproof of God is wildly off my point. One might as well say that the presence of glue in a piece of woodwork disproved the presence of a carpenter.

(6) I have kept to the last the most damning count in this indictment. The reviewer sets me down as owing my remarks entirely to Mivart, as having merely copied Mivart's work of more than half a century ago: implying my ignorance of all since. Had he read my book he would have seen that I quoted from authority after authority among the highest names in modern biology from the beginning of the discussion to works which appeared so recently as three years ago. I give their actual words, which prove with what increasing force the old-fashioned Darwinian theory of natural selection has been beaten down. I end by a list of no less than forty such names – I might easily have made it a hundred. No one who had read my book could possibly have missed this continued and repeated citation of authority from every side, which is the principle feature of this section.

I conclude, therefore, that the reviewer has not read my book; for I hope that not even the most violent religious animosity could lead him to deliberate misrepresentation.

---

93 I. e., Charles Darwin.

94 In biological evolution, the theory that creatures have in the passed adapted through several simultaneous variations over a long period of time.

Reply to Belloc: Arthur Keith, letter to the editor (19 February 1927).[95]

Not only did I read Mr Belloc's book with great care, but I also took the trouble of turning up the works of some of the authorities he cites. On p. 12 he mentions, with bated breath as it were, 'the great work of Vialleton.' This 'great work' is a very good elementary treatise on embryology which Prof. L. Vialleton, of the University of Montpellier,[96] wrote for his students, and it stands in much the same relationship to the works of Charles Darwin as do those of Mr Belloc to Shakespeare's.

Mr Belloc cites Vialleton as his authority for denying the possibility of birds having been evolved from reptiles. On searching Prof. Vialleton's *Éléments de morphologie des vertébrés* – published in 1911 – I found on p. 611 that after citing what Huxley, Owen, Seeley, Mivart, and Gadow had to say about the matter, Prof. Vialleton concludes thus: 'L'origine des oiseaux reste donc dans le plus complet mystère,'[97] which is a very different thing from denying their origin from reptiles. I have collected many other errors of a like kind, enough to convince me that Mr Belloc's references are untrustworthy. Many of the authorities he cites, such as my friend the late Prof. Dwight, of Harvard,[98] belonged to the generation which never succeeded in assimilating the teachings of Darwin.

---

95 Reprinted by permission from Macmillan Publishers Ltd: *Nature* (119: 2990), copyright (1927).

96 French university, founded in 1289.

97 French, 'The origin of birds therefore remains a complete mystery'.

98 A private university in Cambridge, Massachusetts, founded in 1636.

2.12: *The Salvaging of Civilisation*

James Garnett, 'Education and World Citizenship' (4 August 1921).[1]

The Salvaging of Civilisation. By H. G. Wells. Pp. 202. (London: Cassell and Co., Ltd.) 7*s.* 6*d.* net.

A book by Mr Wells, and especially a book on education, is always important. *The Salvaging of Civilisation* is no exception. Part of the book has already been published as a separate essay,[2] part of it consists of lectures to an American audience,[3] and the third part was doubtless prepared for the present volume; but it all fits together, because it all belongs to Mr Wells's remarkably clear and orderly thought.

In his *Outline of History* Mr Wells has sketched, in amazingly firm lines, the uncertain origins of our race. In the present book he presents, with the same firm touch, our equally uncertain future. It would be tempting to compare Mr Wells as historian with Mr Wells as prophet, for this is a prophetic book. It is concerned with the purpose and future of mankind, but with the distant, rather than with the immediate, future. Mr Wells has gone scouting far ahead of those whose principal concern is with the next step towards international co-operation and world citizenship.[4] In this volume he tells us what he has seen of the distant goal, but he has little to say of the first practical steps towards it. One thing, however, he is sure about. If the goal is ever to be reached, it is education that will get us there. 'The task ... is not primarily one for the diplomatists[5] and lawyers and politicians at all. It is an educational one.'

It is true that thought tends always to end in action, and it follows that deeds are the ultimate (and ideas only the intermediate) product of a system of education. The universities, for example, because of their increasing concern with applied science, especially during the war,[6] are realising that their business is not only to discover and disseminate knowledge, but also to see that practical effect is given to it. The practical effect here in question is no less than the political reconstruction of the world, so that, as Mr Wells acknowledges, politicians, as well as educators, have a part to play; but 'world-wide educational develop-

---

1   Reprinted by permission from Macmillan Publishers Ltd: *Nature* (107: 2701), copyright (1921).

2   A reference to chapter one, 'The Probable Future of Mankind' (1920-21).

3   A reference to chapter two, 'The Project of a World State', written for a lecture tour in the USA in 1920 which was cancelled due to Wells's ill-health.

4   The status of a person who disapproves of traditional geopolitical divisions derived from national citizenship and advocates world government and democracy.

5   More commonly, diplomats, adroit negotiators engaged in diplomacy.

6   I. e., the Great War.

ment and reform are the necessary preparations for and the necessary accompaniments of a political reconstruction of the world. The two are the right and left hands of the same thing. Neither can effect much without the other.' But in the beginning, and for most of the way, it is the educator rather than the politician that plays the title-role in Mr Wells's outline of history yet to be.

If, then, the end of education, like the end of thought itself, is action, we are not to be educated passively to imagine, but actively to seek, the ideal future for mankind; and our immediate purpose must be 'to find release from the contentious loyalties and hostilities of the past which make collective world-wide action impossible at the present time, in a world-wide common vision of the history and destinies of the race.'[7] This purpose is to be central and dominant in the outlook that is to result from Mr Wells's scheme of education. (We remark parenthetically that Mr Wells's recognition of the supreme importance of purpose in the make-up of character might illustrate, if further examples were needed, how closely many of Mr Wells's views accord with much that is best in modern thought on education. But there are some of Mr Wells's opinions that would not obtain assent from those who are most competent to judge. Thus residence and tutorial superintendence were considered by Newman to be of the first importance in university education, but Mr Wells thinks that an undergraduate at Trinity College,[8] Cambridge, has 'no very marked advantage' over an evening student[9] in a northern industrial town.[10])

Mr Wells further recognises that, to get things done, there must be unity of purpose[11] among large numbers of men and women, as well as strong purposes dominating each of them individually. 'It is manifest that unless some unity of purpose can be achieved in the world ... the history of humanity must presently culminate in some sort of disaster.' But the unity which Mr Wells rightly demands for the central purposes of men and women the world over, he would also have for a large part of their outlook on the universe. Unity of outlook upon natural science, upon history, and upon literature, as well as upon the aim and purpose of human progress, he would secure by means of common textbooks – 'The Bible of Civilisation' – always being revised, but always and everywhere in use. Many of his readers will find this suggestion revolting; but they would be ill-advised to reject it without the most careful scrutiny. From

---

7   I. e., the human race, humankind.

8   A college of the University of Cambridge, founded in 1546.

9   One who attends classes held in the evening for adults who wish to learn about a particular subject or interest or to acquire a particular skill.

10   In Britain, the large towns of northern England and Scotland characterised by traditional heavy industries.

11   A unanimous aim of a disparate group of people.

many points of view it is far in advance of modern practice. Middle-aged students of mathematics will gratefully remember what Clerk Maxwell called

Hard truths made pleasant

By Routh and Besant

For one who hasn't

Got too much sense.[12]

The codification of elementary applied mathematics by these great Cambridge coaches enormously facilitated the progress of most students who would otherwise have had to depend upon comparatively incompetent teachers and 'overmuch tedious lecturing,' as Mr Wells has it. It created, among Cambridge mathematicians, a school of thought that was probably advantageous to their subject as well as to themselves.

But Mr Wells's scheme of world-wide education, like the national system of education foreshadowed for England in Mr Fisher's[13] great Act of 1918,[14] depends for its realisation upon the money being available. Mr Wells has no doubt where the money is to come from; and, in truth, there can be little doubt about the matter. According to a recent American book, the United States spent last year no less than 93 per cent of the national revenues upon wars old and new: that is, on war loan charges, on war pensions, and on maintaining military and naval forces. Great Britain, not being made up of forty-eight States[15] with separate incomes, naturally spent a smaller proportion of her national income on war charges; but last year, and again in the Estimates[16] for this year, the proportion of the national revenues that this country is spending on wars old and new is no less than 64 per cent – more than twelve shillings in every pound[17] of taxes. When we remember that a simple agreement between a few great naval Powers is all that is needed to abolish battleships, and that a battleship costs, in capital,

---

12   This is a misquotation from Maxwell's poem, 'To the Additional Examiner for 1875', the first two lines of which should read 'Dry proofs made pleasant / By Routh or Besant' (i. e., William Besant).

13   I. e., Herbert Fisher.

14   The British Education Act which raised the school-leaving age to 14 and made provision for medical inspection, nursery schools and centres for pupils with special needs.

15   The number of states making up the USA between 1912 and 1959.

16   In British politics, a series of legislative proposals to parliament outlining how the government will spend its money.

17   The equivalent of 60 pence in the pound in decimal currency.

some £8,000,000 sterling,[18] or, in income (for interest, depreciation, and repairs, but not including *personnel*), £1,000,000 a year – more than ten times the British contribution to the League of Nations – we wonder that this money is not diverted to remunerative expenditure. The whole contribution of the British Government to university education is only £2,000,000 (of which half a million pounds is a special grant for superannuation[19] purposes) this year, and used to be much less. It is thus equal to the cost of maintaining the structure and equipment of two battleships. Mr Wells says that we need to press 'for a ruthless subordination of naval, military, and Court expenditure to educational needs.' At all events, we need to come to an agreement with the other nations of the world, most of whose incomes are at present insufficient to meet their expenditure, for a general limitation of armaments, that would enormously reduce the burden of taxation and set free far more than sufficient money to expand and improve our educational organisations as rapidly as is humanly possible.

Mr Wells's book is marred by minor defects, which are only minor because of the greatness of the whole. Thus he would apparently have his readers believe that the world commonwealth,[20] which he regards as the ultimate goal, should be attained by the immediate absorption of the existing seventy or eighty independent sovereign States of the world into a single super-State.[21] Such a first step would certainly be a false step, even if it were in any way practicable. How would it, for example, be possible to persuade Japan to place the control of her destinies in the hands of a Parliament, Congress, or Assembly most of the members of which would be of European race? The first step towards increasing the political unity of the nations is surely their co-operation in multifarious works for the benefit of mankind,[22] and especially in the abolition of world-war. This is what is being done by the 'quite inadequate League of Nations at Geneva,' which consists, after all, of forty-eight sovereign States representing three-quarters of the population of the earth.

Moreover, Mr Wells is surely mistaken in supposing that we must get rid of patriotism[23] if we are to have an adequate sense of world-citizenship. Loyalty to a smaller group is not necessarily inconsistent with higher loyalty to a larger group that includes the smaller. An undergraduate[24] who is asked to play for his

---

18 The currency of the United Kingdom, divisible into pounds and pence (and shillings before 1971).

19 The paying of a retirement pension to an employee.

20 An alternative label for Wells's world state.

21 A dominant political community formed from an alliance or union of several nations.

22 This suggestion for a functional approach to world governance would, from 1923, become Wells's favoured formula (see Partington 2003, 101-25).

23 Devotion to one's country.

24 A university student who has not completed a first degree.

university and for his college on the same day will play for his university, and not for his college; but he is not on that account less loyal to his college. The Yorkshireman or the Cornishman who loves his county is not on that account an inferior Englishman; nor is one who loves England likely to be a less loyal member of the British Commonwealth of nations[25] than one who has no feeling for his own people; nor, again, has it ever been suggested that loyal members of the British Commonwealth are on that account feebler supporters of the League of Nations.

---

25 Now simply the Commonwealth of Nations, a voluntary association of sovereign states formally founded in 1931, made up of former members of the British Empire (plus Mozambique since 1995), though the expression predates formalisation.

2.13: *A Short History of the World*

Francis Marvin, 'Unified Human History' (30 December 1922).[1]

A Short History of the World. By H. G. Wells. Pp. xvi + 432. (London: Cassell and Co., Ltd., 1922.) 15s. net.

This is a new work covering the same ground as the *Outline of History* and in the same spirit, but re-written and better written, and correcting many of the faults of judgement and proportion which disfigured the earlier book. Mr Wells has digested his material in the interval and writes now with ease and mastery. The arrangement and general division of the space is quite satisfactory, and the production and illustrations[2] are excellent. It is a great feat, following so quickly on the labours of the *Outline*, and all who are interested either in history, in education or in the social progress of the world as a whole, are under a deep debt of gratitude to Mr Wells for carrying it out. Nothing has done so much to awaken the public to the social importance of history, and the readers of history to the unity of their subject. The books are a prodigy of industry and skill and in the realm of literature the best thing we owe to the war.[3] It was at a gathering of thinkers and social workers during the war that the idea of teaching world-history to all nations on a common plan was first mooted, and Mr Wells responded to the appeal. His *Outline* has sold in hundreds of thousands, especially in the United States. It has provoked demands among working men to be taught history in that spirit; it has changed the outlook and the syllabuses of scores of teachers; it has helped to success other similar books such as the fascinating *Story of Mankind* by Van Loon, which has come over to us from America this autumn.

In view of all this, it is paltry and unworthy to dwell on minor defects or on differences of judgements, and still worse to condemn Mr Wells because not being a 'historian,' he has done a work which 'historians' ought to have done over and over again before.

It was probably this fact, that he was not a historian in that sense, immersed in the details of some special period or aspect of history, which, added to his own incomparable powers of reception, production, and imagination, enabled Mr Wells to accomplish the feat. The freshness of his mind prompts him constantly to some interesting new view, some comparison especially of ancient and modern times, some wholesome challenge to accepted judgements; *e. g.* 'It

---

1   Reprinted by permission from Macmillan Publishers Ltd: *Nature* (110: 2774), copyright (1922).

2   The book includes 190 photographs and drawings, and 21 maps and diagrams by J. F. Horrabin.

3   I. e., the Great War.

was not so much the Jews that made the Bible, as the Bible that made the Jews.'
'How important a century this sixth BC was in the history of humanity. For not only were these Greek philosophers beginning the research for clear ideas about the universe and man's place in it, and Isaiah[4] carrying Jewish prophecy to its sublimest levels, but, as we shall tell later, Gautama Buddha was then teaching in India and Confucius and Lao Tse in China. From Athens to the Pacific the human mind was astir.'

Even in the case of Rome, to which Mr Wells still gives less than justice, it is enlightening to have the comparison with our modern empire.[5] 'The Roman empire was after all a very primitive organisation; it did not educate, did not explain itself to its increasing multitudes of citizens, did not invite their co-operation in its decisions. There was no network of schools to ensure a common understanding, no distribution of news to sustain collective activity.'

All such comparisons, whether of contemporary happenings or of earlier and later social states, are useful and inspiring and arise from the synoptic[6] frame of mind which qualifies a man for such work as this. It is an antidote to the excessive criticism and tendency to pessimism which mark so much of our literature at the present time. But it needs to be based on a sound knowledge and appreciation of the historical fact, and it is naturally on this latter side that Mr Wells is weaker. He does not estimate duly what Rome did for the world, the greatness of her legal work, its continued progress, its permanency in the modern world. Nor does he allow for the constructive value of the medieval Church and Catholic doctrine. No word of Dante (or of Descartes) with a whole chapter for Charles V! That is a blemish impossible to pass over. It goes with a general tendency in the book to lay stress rather on the externals and the picturesque figures in history than on the deeper, spiritual, or intellectual factors. Thus Archimedes and Hero appear but not Pythagoras. Stephenson and Watt but not Descartes and Leibniz, or even Newton. Science appears as the transformer of industry, the generator of steam-engines and steam-ships, but not as the knitter-up of men's minds, the new universal doctrine which replaces theological dogma. Even science as the healer and preventer of disease seems to find no place: there is no word of Hippocrates or Pasteur.

We know well how easy it is in reviewing such a book to draw up lists of inexcusable omissions. It would be ungrateful in this case, for Mr Wells has giv-

---

4   Jewish Biblical prophet, supposed author of the Book of Isaiah (c. 8th century BC).

5   The British Empire, at its height, the largest and most populous empire the world has ever known, was established in the fifteenth century and gradually dissolved over the course of the twentieth until, in 2008, it consists of fourteen British Oversees Territories.

6   Giving an overall view.

en us so useful and attractive a gift and has worked so valiantly for the cause both of history and of science, and especially of science coming into and modifying history. His answer, no doubt, to the last criticism would be that this was an introductory volume, and that therefore he avoided such matters as philosophy. But can one properly treat of religion without philosophy? And there are sympathetic chapters about Christ and Buddha. It would help his general cause, which is the salvation of mankind by education and unity, to lay more stress on the spiritual or intellectually constructive aspect of science and less on its mechanical applications. It is not the difficulties of posts[7] and tariffs[8] which will ultimately bring mankind together in harmonious progress: it will be a spiritual union of which knowledge and sympathy, science and law are co-operating factors, and may be traced growing, sometimes fitfully, and at various times and places, but never quite extinguished from the beginning of history till now. These should be the leading threads in any short sketch of human history as a whole, and it is because of their decisive contributions to those elements that Greece, Rome, Christianity, and modern times deserve a special place.

---

7   The system of distributing mail between persons and places.
8   Import duties levied on articles or group of articles.

2.14: *Men Like Gods*

John Scott Haldane, 'Biology in Utopia' (5 May 1923).[1]

Men Like Gods. By H. G. Wells. Pp. viii + 304. (London, New York, Toronto and Melbourne: Cassell and Co., Ltd., 1923.) 7*s*. 6*d*. net.

The columns of *Nature* are not the place to discuss the literary merits of Mr Wells's new book – although, for the matter of that, good style or artistic capacity and appreciation are qualities as natural as any other. Suffice it to say that he has achieved a Utopian tale which is not only interesting but also extremely readable. Most readable Utopias are in reality satires, such as *Gulliver's Travels*,[2] and the no less immortal *Erewhon*.[3] Mr Wells has attempted the genuine or idealistic Utopia, after the example of Plato, Sir Thomas More, and William Morris; and, by the ingenious idea of introducing not a solitary visitor from the present, but a whole party of visitors (including some entertaining and not-at-all-disguised portraits of various living personages[4]) has provided a good story to vivify his reflections.

However, since Mr Wells is giving us not only a story, but his idea of what a properly-used human faculty might make of humanity in the space of a hundred generations, his romance has become a fit subject for biological dissection in these pages.

Mr Wells pictures a world where, in the first place, the advance of physico-chemical science[5] and its application, to which we are already accustomed, has attained a far higher pitch of perfection. Further, machinery has become so self-regulating that it does not make man captive, as Samuel Butler prophesied, but is a real servant. Also, instead of machinery and mechanism occupying the foremost place in the life of the majority of men, as Bergson laments that they are tending to do to-day, they have apparently been rendered not only more efficient, but also more self-regulating, and are as subservient to the will of the community as a motor-car that never gets out of order is to its owner.

In the second place, life has been subjected to a similar control. This is a process which the biologist sees so obviously on its way that it should excite no

---

1   Reprinted by permission from Macmillan Publishers Ltd: *Nature* (111: 2792), copyright (1923).

2   By Jonathan Swift (1726).

3   By Samuel Butler (1872).

4   Among the thinly disguised portrayals in the novel are Cecil Burleigh, representing Arthur Balfour, Rupert Catskill, representing Winston Churchill, and Father Amerton, representing G. K. Chesterton.

5   Physical chemistry.

surprise. As our knowledge of genetics[6] increases, our application of it must outstrip the past achievements of empirical[7] breeding as much as the application of scientific knowledge of principle in chemistry, say, or electricity, has outstripped the achievements of empiricism in those fields. Mr Wells's wonderful flowers and trees are almost there already: we will not worry about them. Even his domestic-minded leopards and tigers, more 'kittenish and mild'[8] even than Mr Belloc's, should not be lightly dismissed after recent experiments on the inheritance of tameness and wildness in rats – not to mention our knowledge of many breeds of dog.

Meanwhile, Mr Wells also imagines a purging of the organic world. The triumphs of parasitology[9] and the rise of ecology[10] have set him thinking; and he believes that, given real knowledge of the life-histories and inter-relations of organisms, man could proceed successfully to wholesale elimination of a multitude of noxious[11] bacteria,[12] parasitic worms,[13] insects, and carnivores. Here again we have no right to quarrel. Mr Wells does not need to be reminded of the thistle in California[14] or the rabbits in Australia:[15] his Utopians proceed with exemplary precautions. All this is but an extension of what has already been begun.

In the third place, however, human as well as non-human life has been subjected to this control; and this in two ways. First, by an extension of the methods previously used. The accidents and circumstances of life have been altered – there has been a further control of external machinery. This has been, of course, chiefly in the fields of social and political institutions. A great part of

---

6   The branch of science that deals with heredity and the variation of inherited characteristics in living organisms.

7   Based on, guided by or employing observation and experiment rather than theory.

8   A quotation from Hilaire Belloc's 'The Tiger' (1896), the first line of which is 'The Tiger on the other hand, is kittenish and mild' (1939, 58).

9   The branch of biology and medicine that deals with parasites.

10 The branch of biology (and its study) that deals with organisms' relations to one another and to the physical environment in which they live.

11 Injurious, hurtful or harmful.

12 Microscopic, generally single-celled organisms, many of which are symbiotic or pathogenic, in animals and plants.

13 Worms that live in and nourish on the intestines of vertebrates, especially roundworms, tapeworms and flukes.

14 The Canada thistle (actually a native of Europe and Asia) was introduced to North America in the 17th century and is considered one of the most tenacious and economically important agricultural weed.

15 Twenty-four rabbits were deliberately taken to Australia for hunting in 1859 and within ten years, two million were being hunted per year.

258

such change is only intelligible as a corollary of the other supposed change. But we may here direct attention to one idea which is imagined as at the root of much of it – the idea that man is master in his own house[16] of Earth, as opposed to the idea which, with few exceptions, has until now dominated his history – the idea that he is the slave, sport, or servant of an arbitrary personal Power or Powers.

Finally, we come to the most radical and inevitably the most provocative of our author's imaginings – that which concerns not the alteration of things in relation to a constant human nature,[17] but the alteration of that human nature itself. Here Mr Wells is extremely interesting. He reduces the role of eugenics to a minimum, exalts that of education, or, if you prefer it, environment,[18] to a maximum. Eugenic change has been restricted to 'breeding out'[19] (Mr Wells does not initiate us into methods) certain temperamental qualities – habitual gloominess, petty inefficiency, excess of that 'sacrificial pity' Mr Wells dislikes so much, and so forth.

The rest has been accomplished by proper education, and, above all, by a 'change of heart' as regards the essential aims of life. Mr Wells sums this up in a phrase (in which one recognises his devotion to the late headmaster of Oundle[20]) as the substitution of the ideal of creative service for that of competition.

The realisation of this ideal is made possible in the first instance by a proper application of psychology[21] to early life, so that painful repression[22] and stupid suppression[23] shall not occur, and men and women shall grow up unridden by hags[24] of sex or fear, and yet without separation of any important fragment of their mental organism from the rest. Education *sensu restricto*[25] then steps in, and enlarges the capacities of the unhampered growing mind, while the substitution of a form of telepathy for speech reduces the time and energy needed for

---

16   In control.

17   The general characteristics and feelings attributed to human beings.

18   The set of circumstances or conditions in which a person or community lives, works, develops, etc.

19   The elimination of certain characteristics through controlled breeding.

20   A reference to F. W. Sanderson, headteacher of Oundle School from 1892 to 1922.

21   The science of the nature, functioning and development of the human mind.

22   The action, process or result of suppressing into the unconscious or of actively excluding from the conscious mind unacceptable memories, impulses or desires.

23   The action or result of conscious inhibition of unacceptable memories, impulses or desires.

24   Untroubled (from the expression 'hag-ridden' which means tormented by nightmares).

25   Latin, in a restricted sense.

communication. Meanwhile, a rational birth-control[26] provides a world not over-crowded or overstrained.

By these means, Mr Wells imagines, a race has been produced of great beauty and physical strength, great intellectual and artistic capacities, interested primarily in two things – the understanding of Nature for its own sake, and its control for the sake of humanity. By control Mr Wells means not only utilitarian[27] control, but that which, as in a garden, is to please and delight, and that highest control of material – artistic and scientific creation.

The Utopians, owing to their upbringing and social environment, come to think and act so that they need no central government, no law-courts, no police, no contracts. In this Mr Wells is only telling us what we all knew already, that in most men it seems theoretically possible to produce a 'change of heart' – *i. e.* substitute new dominant ideas for old – and that if this is effected, restrictive measures gradually become unnecessary. He is careful not to make his Utopia too ideal. It is as ideal compared with this world as would by Olympus:[28] but as short of perfection as Olympus seems to have been. The men and women there are often discontented and restless; criticism is abundant. Mr Wells knows that intellectual and aesthetic achievement opens the door to the highest known happiness of the present; he keeps them so, with all conditions and limitations of their being, in Utopia.

Let us go back and try to see how much of Mr Wells's speculations fall within the bounds of possibility. All Utopias must suffer from lack of familiar associations, for it is by familiar associations, especially with things of youth and childhood, that emotional appeal is made and real assent gained. Thus, whatever stores of loved memories a Utopian may have, whatever driving force he may draw from the sight of familiar places and objects, we can only see his emotional life from outside, as an Englishman on his first visit to the United States notices the differences from England rather than the resemblances. But if we remember that they must have each their private growth of life, and that this must be in many ways like ours, we get over the first stile.

We have already dealt with Mr Wells's applied physics and chemistry and his applied biology of lower organisms. That in a sense is commonplace – commonplace made surprising; none the less, it is good to have it so well done, to have people reminded that the rate of this sort of change not only need not slow down, but can continue, and continue to be accelerated, for a very long time. What of his applied biology of man? Minor criticisms are easy to make. The

---

26   Also contraception, methods for preventing unwanted pregnancy or limiting births.

27   Useful or for the benefit of a majority.

28   The traditional home of the twelve greater gods of Greek mythology, also used to mean an ideal.

Utopians, for example, go either almost naked, or else clothed in garb of the indeterminate simplicity that seems fashionable in all Utopias. Mr Wells is perhaps so revolted by the dullness of modern male attire that he underestimates the amount by which dress enlarges the human horizon, giving us a hundred extra variations of personality, raising the possibilities realised in the courtship[29]-decorations of lower animals to an infinitude of permutations.

With the rediscovery of Mendel's laws and their recent working out, we are introduced to the theoretical possibility of an analysis of the hereditary constitution[30] similar to the chemist's analysis of a compound; and so, presumably, in the long run to its control. There are great technical difficulties in higher organisms, and application to man presents yet further difficulties. Still, the fact remains that the theoretical possibility exists for us to-day, and did not exist twenty-five years ago. We must further remember that all discoveries concerning the history of man remind us that we must think, not in centuries as heretofore, but in ten-thousand-year periods when envisaging stages in human development.

We must further recall the lessons of evolutionary biology. These teach us that, however ignorant we may be regarding the details of the process, life is essentially plastic and has in the past been moulded into an extraordinary variety of forms. Further, that the attributes of living things have almost all been developed in relation to the environment – even their mental attributes. There is a causal relation between the absence of X-rays in the normal environment and the absence in organisms of sense-organs capable of detecting X-rays, between the habits of lions and their fierceness, of doves and their timidity. There is, thirdly, no reason whatever to suppose that the mind of man represents the highest development possible to mind, any more than there was to suppose it of the mind of monkeys when they were the highest organisms. We must squarely recognise that, in spite of proverbs[31] to the contrary, it is probable that 'human nature' could be considerably changed and improved.

Next, we have the recent rise of psychology. Much nonsense doubtless masquerades under the name of psycho-analysis or 'modern' psychology. None the less, as so shrewd a critic as the late W. H. R. Rivers at once saw, and as has been put to such practical uses in therapeutic treatment,[32] there is not only some-

---

29 Animal behaviour that precedes and leads up to mating.

30 In physiology, the character of the body as regards health, strength, vitality, etc.

31 Concise sentences, often metaphorical or alliterative in form, held to express some general truths.

32 The systematic treatment of mental or physical illness.

thing in it, but a great deal. Repression, suppression, sublimation,[33] and the rest are realities; and we are finding out how our minds do work, ought not to work, and might be made to work. It is clear that the average mind is as distorted and stunted as a much-below-average body; and that, by just so much as a great mind is more different from an average one than great from average bodily capacity, by so much would proper training be more efficient with mind than even with bodies. Here the extravagances of some eugenists[34] find their corrective; Mr Wells's imagination is pursuing to its logical end the line taken by such authorities as Mr Carr Saunders in his *Population Problem*.

Again, Mr Wells, being a major prophet, perceives without difficulty that the substitution of some new dominant idea for the current ideas of commercialism,[35] nationalism,[36] and sectarianism[37] (better not beg the question by saying *industry, patriotism*, and *religion*) is the most needed change of all. Here, again, he is in reality only adopting the method of Lyell and Darwin[38] – uniformitarianism[39] – and seeking the key of the future, as of the past, in the present. There is to-day a slowly growing minority of people who not only profoundly disbelieve in the current conceptions *and valuations* of the world and human life, but also, however gropingly,[40] are trying to put scientifically-grounded ideas in their place.

Belief is the parent of action; and so long as the majority of men refuse to believe that they need not remain the slave of the transcendental,[41] whether in the shape of an imaginary Being, of the Absolute,[42] or Transcendental Morality,[43] they cannot reap the fruits of reason.[44] If the minority became the majority, society and all its institutions and codes would be radically altered.

---

33   In psychoanalysis, the transformation of an instinctual drive so that it manifests in a socially acceptable way.

34   More commonly eugenicists, experts in, students of or advocates of eugenics.

35   The principles and practice of commerce; excessive adherence to financial return as a measure of worth.

36   Devotion to one's nation, often expressed in political action.

37   The bigoted or narrow-minded adhesion to a religious or other group.

38   I. e., Charles Darwin.

39   In geology, the theory that natural processes and phenomena have always been and still are due to causes or forces operating continuously and with uniformity.

40   Searching mentally with hesitation or uncertainty.

41   Of or pertaining to the divine as against the natural or moral world.

42   God.

43   The doctrine or branch of knowledge which deals with right and wrong conduct and with duty and responsibility.

44   The mental faculty which is used in adapting thought or action to a particular end.

Take but one example, and a current one – birth-control. When Mr Wells's 'Father Amerton' finds that it is the basis of Utopian civilisation he exclaims in horror: 'Refusing to create souls! The *wickedness* of it! Oh, my God!'

* * * * *

This is the great enemy of true progress – this belief that things have been already settled for us, and the consequent result of considering proposals not on their merits, but in reference to a system of principles which is for the most part a survival from primitive civilisations.

Mr Wells may often be disagreed with in detail: he is at least right in his premises. A perusal of his novel in conjunction with a commentary would be useful. *Men Like Gods* taken *en sandwich*[45] with, say, Punnett's *Mendelism*, Trotter's *Instincts of the Herd*, Thouless's *Psychology of Religion*, Carr-Saunders's *Population Problem*, Whetham on eugenics,[46] and a good compendium of recent psychology, would be a very wholesome employment of the scientific imagination.

Comment: Karl Pearson, letter to the editor, 'Biology of Man' (16 June 1923).[47]

In the review by J. S. H. of Mr Wells's *Men Like Gods* (*Nature*, May 5, p. 591) we are told that even domestic-minded leopards and tigers are not lightly to be dismissed after recent experiments on the *inheritance* of tameness and wildness in rats. Almost in the next paragraph we are further informed that the role of eugenics is to be reduced to a minimum, and its functions are to be replaced by education. Wildness in the lower animals is to be removed by selective breeding,[48] wildness and brutality in man is to be cured by education, by environment, and that mysterious process a 'change of heart.' It is very strange how dominant is the wholly unwarranted belief that man is an animal for whom other laws hold than for his humbler mammalian kindred.

Reply: John Scott Haldane, letter to the editor (16 June 1923).[49]

In referring to the reduction of eugenics to a minimum I was quoting Mr Wells, not putting forward my own views. Later on, in criticising Mr Wells, I expressly

---

45   French, sandwiched between.

46   A reference to *An Introduction to Eugenics* (1912).

47   Reprinted by permission from Macmillan Publishers Ltd: *Nature* (111: 2798), copyright (1923).

48   The scientific process of breeding animals for specific characteristics.

49   Reprinted by permission from Macmillan Publishers Ltd: *Nature* (111: 2798), copyright (1923).

referred to the possibility of the 'control of heredity' in man as well as in lower organisms.[50]

In the second part of his letter Prof. Pearson is ambiguous. He refers to 'the wholly unwarranted belief that man is an animal for whom other laws hold than for his humbler mammalian kindred.' In one sense of the word *other* this is of course wholly unwarranted – if, that is, we take it to mean 'wholly different.' If, however, we mean that, besides the laws applicable to lower organisms, there are 'other' *additional* laws at work in the sphere of human evolution, then I venture to say that we are enunciating a truism.[51] To take the simplest and most important example. No other organism can transmit tradition for more than one generation: man can. Or to take another example cognate to the 'change of heart' (which need be no less important for being 'mysterious'), you do not find cows or sheep or other of man's mammalian kindred stopping the business of their existence to look at the sunset or at a work of art; whereas man (or rather many men) do so.

One of the chief human characters of man is his greater modifiability (in the strict biological sense). This implies that alteration of environment, especially of social environment, must co-operate with eugenics if any human progress is to be achieved.

---

50 Plants and animals of slighter mental and physical complexity to humans; historical creatures from which humanity is believed to have evolved.

51 A self-evident or indisputable truth.

2.15: *The Story of a Great Schoolmaster*

V. B., 'The Visioning of Science' (19 April 1924).[1]

The Story of a Great Schoolmaster: Being a Plain Account of the Life and Ideas of Sanderson of Oundle. By H. G. Wells. Pp. vi + 151 + 3 plates. (London: Chatto and Windus, 1924.) 4s. 6d. net.

In his interpretative biography of Sanderson, the 'great schoolmaster' who made Oundle,[2] for his generation, what Rugby[3] was to that of Thomas Arnold, or Uppingham[4] to that of Thring, Mr H. G. Wells, with his customary penetration and lucidity, disentangles the main problem that emerges from this latest phase of progressive education. The last two or three years of Sanderson's life were increasingly directed towards conceiving and building a Hall of Scientific Vision.[5] He imagined it as the culminating edifice of all the secular buildings that house the everyday life and work of the school world. It was to pair with the School Chapel as crown and completion of those symbolic structures that link youth and age in the flowering generations. The scientific vision and the religious vision were to unite in the fullness of life perfected for boyhood and youth. How to fashion a new temple of science, true and worthy of its own tradition, yet harmonious with all that is ennobling in the vision of the old faith? To this issue Sanderson gave his last years, and his tragic death[6] in full career left it as a legacy to those concerned with the advancement of ideals through education.

The problem of integrating the facts of science with the 'values' of religion implies a prior solution of many puzzling enigmas; and above all, it implies the correlation of science with history, as Sanderson increasingly saw and stressed. But in his busy life at Oundle, he remained isolated from those newer schools of evolutionary doctrine, which are assiduously at work upon this and related problems. Let us try to sketch, in barest outline, their possible contribution to Sanderson's task of conceiving, planning, furnishing, a Hall of Vision, at once scientific, historic, futurist.[7]

---

1   Reprinted by permission from Macmillan Publishers Ltd: *Nature* (113: 2842), copyright (1924).

2   British public school founded in 1556 to which Wells sent his two eldest sons, George Philip and Frank Richard.

3   A reference to Rugby School, a British public school founded in 1567.

4   A reference to Uppingham School, a British public school founded in 1584.

5   An idea proposed by Sanderson to act as a temple to science as a counterpart to the school chapel. Sanderson's death prevented the hall being completed.

6   Sanderson died on a lecture platform at University College, London, on 15 June 1922 following his delivery of a speech on science education. Wells was in the chair, and was calling for questions from the floor when Sanderson collapsed.

7   Pertaining to human progress or the human future.

These newer evolutionists begin to glimpse, from their synthetic view-point of science and history, a whole Pageant of Vision, and, moreover, one sha-dowed forth in well-ordered sequence. For them there is, first, the ever-widening tale of evolution, and its procession of Nature's energies, as it were a word-play or cosmodrama.* Therewith unfolds a further tale of ever-opening secrets, those of the application of Nature's resources and energies to man's use; this is, as it were, the great play of labour, or technodrama.[8] With these two approaches to-wards unity, more commonly described as sciences physical and natural, pure and applied, not a few, even amongst men of science, remain satisfied, and so tend to stop short of real vision. There is, of course, also the story of life's strug-gles, in hunger and beyond, to sex and dawning love and care of offspring; hence man's rise from the brute, to higher groupings; first of family, gens,[9] and tribe, or cavern and hut-group to village; then to town and city, to nation and empire, in a word to ordered civilisations. Here is the life-play, or biodrama;[10] at least its first chapter, that of the play of selfdom, or autodrama,[11] and with much of psychodrama,[12] or soul-play, as well.

This psychodrama, or soul-play, does not end here: it begins anew; it takes lead and command, and henceforth no longer merely obeys natural condi-tions and simple natural impulses, but strives to control and direct them. Under this new imperative and guidance the autodrama, with its interests profoundly centred upon self and kin, however combined in an enlarging and more corpor-ate self, deepens its primal[13] impulses and motives, of nutrition and reproduc-tion, hunger and love, self-regarding and species-regarding, but transposes that order of them. Henceforth in the individual life and its pairings, through off-spring and race, the emphasis becomes transformed: love now overpowers hun-ger, to the subordination, and, if need be, even the sacrifice, of the individual life itself.

---

*   'The concept of science as presenting a dramatic interplay of three correlated unities –
        the World-process, the Life-process, the Social-process – has been vividly worked out
        by Prof. Patrick Geddes, as his many students know. It is as one of those students that
        the writer here sketches the visioning of science.'

8   A performance aimed to understand the essence of a sense-less but efficient mechanism.

9   A kinship group composed of people related through their male ancestors.

10   A transformational, healing dramatisation of life of the physical, mental and spiritual
        levels.

11   A dramatic exercise designed to bring the actor's biography on stage.

12   A form of dramatic therapy which explores, through action, the problems of people.

13   Of, pertaining to or designating the needs, fears, behaviour, etc., that are postulated to
        form the origins of emotional life.

It follows that ethics[14] is not, as it seemed to Huxley,[15] something external to life; and to be super-induced artificially so far as may be. The other-regarding instinct, the altruist impulse, is thus seen as the very secret of life, plain within the evolution of animal life, the mammals for conspicuous instance; and deep within the flower, the sex secret of which, though seemingly so obvious, yet remains unpopularised, and inadequately emphasised in most theories of organic evolution. To this more intimate understanding of flowers even Darwin[16] himself never really came, despite all his loving observation of the external aspects and relations in field and garden. Through such limitations his great theory, and with it most current biology, has remained but that of an autodrama of life, and has fallen short in discernment of that other-regarding factor, which is the profounder guiding secret of life's evolution, organic, human, and social. Out of this deep source, this transposition of the urge of life-impulses from the fundamental needs of simple nutrition to the supreme call of reproduction and sex, come the flower's beauty, the bird's song, the lover's lyric. From this elemental and organic process of real metamorphosis, or, as one might say, of true conversion, issues the universally human impulse of religion with its mystic and prophetic chants, of love, of faith, of hope, life triumphant over death. Autodrama is fundamentally but of the creeping and caterpillar phase of life, in hunger and struggle and danger, in growth and development, individual and alone; yet its chrysalis[17]-sleep and transformation, up to its emergence as winged Psyche[18] with the life of mating predominant over nectar-seeking, is also a natural process. Thus the evolutionary sciences, at once organic and psychic, meet the religions in mutual interpretations. Already, indeed, they are rising together, into what is at once science and religion. Their joint process, at once intellectual and emotional, we may call ethodrama.[19]

But the autodrama and the ethodrama, as we see (and share) them in the world, are so far at strife. Their views of the cosmodrama[20] differ, their grasps upon the technodrama also, indeed yet more. Hence, fresh struggles for existence, new tragedies in evolution. In the simpler world of life around us, we call this interplay (with Haeckel) 'ecology,' or (with Ray Lankester) 'bionomics,' each word but derived, though at opposite ends, from the 'economics' of man's

---

14 The branch of knowledge that deals with the principle of human duty or the logic of moral discourse.

15 I. e., T. H. Huxley.

16 I. e., Charles Darwin.

17 The pupa of a caterpillar from which a moth or butterfly emerges; figuratively, a quiescent, transitional form.

18 A butterfly or moth, from the ancient Greek.

19 A dramatic representation of the merging of science and religion.

20 The ever-widening tale of evolution.

own toil and effort, day by day. Given such evolutionary outlook, it naturally comes about that all active schools of social thought increasingly combine their economics with history; and see the social process not as a succession of catastrophes and escapes, but with a uniformitarianism as of the geologist, a product of everyday life and labour.

The chequered pages of history become but the material of a further and yet more difficult interpretative vision. They have thus once again suggested great yet imperfect philosophies of history; which now are seen more and more as the stuff of a needed science of history. Not merely as annals, nor as an empiric or encyclopaedic recording of events, nor even as psychologic readings of individual and incidental motives, a science of history interprets all these annals and stories as a mighty tree of becoming. Its modes of growth and branching are increasingly discerned; and even set forth, in their essential progressions, as the *arbor saeculorum*.[21]

A philosophy of history, yet of no mere philosophic abstractions, like those metaphysical[22] philosophies which have passed away, but of scientific character and verifiability, has indeed been in progress since the beginnings of sociology.[23] But, as yet, insufficiently do these initiatives of science and history move forward in unison. They need to grow together, alike in clearness and unity, yet in vivid presentment as well. Presentment how? As essential history. The pageants of civilisations and their religions, of their cities, nations, empires, for the halls and avenues of state; and the miracle plays[24] of religions and their cultures for temple-courts and cathedrals – all these renewals of evocative ritual are preparing. The newer evolutionists are labouring towards great issues. They foresee, and would get ready for, a time when the stately procession of philosophies, the varied masques[25] of learning, the quests of the sciences, the anthologies of muse[26]-inspired literatures, the joyous triumphs and mysteries of the arts, will be schemed not only in our universities and rehearsed in our cloisters,[27] but also replanned in our studios and enacted in our theatres. For staging of these

---

21 The 'tree of life', a biological diagram illustrating the historical progression of natural evolution devised by Charles Darwin and printed in *The Origin of Species* (1859).

22 Based on abstract general reasoning or *a priori* general principles.

23 The branch of knowledge that deals with the development, structure and collective behaviour and interaction of human society.

24 Medieval dramatic representations based on the life of Jesus Christ or the legends of the Christian saints.

25 Masked balls.

26 An inspirer of learning and the arts personified as a beautiful woman.

27 A covered place for walking, often round a quadrangle with a wall on the outer and a colonnade or windows on the inner side, especially of convent, college or cathedral buildings.

great spectacles and their due expression in song, and dance, and music, pioneers are emerging; and Sanderson was type and protagonist of this militant order. As they come into power, these evolutionary educationists will train up affirmative personalities eager and skilled to set forth, and before the people, in home, school, and street, in park, amphitheatre,[28] and temple, the pageant of man and his world, in their origins, being, and becoming. Yet all these histories and mysteries, these tragedies and comedies, are only partial visions; they are still but the material for that fuller ideal vision, which every man in measure may reach, yet none but the gods fully attain, that of the chronodrama,[29] the comedy divine yet human, of which the whole evolution of humanity, so far, is but the earnest and the beginning.

Here we touch the transcendences. For further advance in the visioning of fulfilments we need the collaboration of the orchestrated arts. For we have passed beyond the limits of history. We are no longer in the toil and effort of life, with its unrehearsed struggles, unpremeditated sacrifices, unorganised victories. We celebrate anew the explorations and adventures of the spirit creative, and now with skilled foresight and resolute hope. Our chronodrama, and with it all the preceding dramas of Nature and labour, of selfdoms and their transformation, have thus been uniting into the drama of creative art. For this climax of his vision the newer evolutionist needs a Greek term to round off the nomenclature of his sixfold synthesis. Terms like aesthetodrama, temenodrama, symbolodrama,[30] all suggest themselves, but without conclusive appeal.

Clearly at this point it is for poet and artist to take up the tale of unfolding vision, and with them, their quondam[31] ally the priest. Return then to our opening text. Towards solving that problem which, for Sanderson, was the supreme issue in education, men of science will contribute in measure that they sympathetically understand, and so make ready to co-operate with, not only poet and artist, but also priest and prophet. Yet a traditional barrier stands in the way. In his would-be role of seer, the man of science suffers a disabling handicap. He lacks as yet any adequate theory of evil, and its devastating part in arresting the evolution of man, and checking, even reversing, his ascent. This defect of science is more than merely negative. The failure of science, so far, to develop a social pathology[32] is accompanied by a great refusal. Pride and prejudice have

---

28 An oval or circular building with seats rising in tiers around a central open space, which hosts contests or other entertainments.

29 A dramatic presentation of the whole sweep of evolutionary history, including the human place within it.

30 Expressions to suggest the drama of creative art.

31 Latin, erstwhile, former.

32 Problems which afflict society such as war, crime, corruption and discrimination.

hitherto debarred the man of science from serious study of the central processes of religion. He has scornfully ignored the religious conception of sin as pollution of the inner life, and has explained away the purificatory rites[33] of the sacramental office,[34] with its consequent liberation of creative energies joyously militant. It was no romantic or sentimental attitude towards this central tradition of religion, but experience and grasp of its vital efficacy, that impelled Sanderson to labour for integration of his School Chapel and Hall of Vision. The underlying problem of synthesis baffled him, for the sufficient reason that, as yet, official science is devoid of vision, and ecclesiastical[35] vision is empty of science.

---

33 Ceremonies undertaken to purify one's mind, body or soul.

34 The priesthood in its role of administering Christian sacraments, such as penance or baptism.

35 Of or pertaining to the Christian church.

2.16: *The World of William Clissold*

Henry Armstrong, 'Education, Science and Mr H. G. Wells' (20 November 1926).[1]

The World of William Clissold: a Novel at a New Angle. By H. G. Wells. Vol. 1. Book the First: *The Frame of the Picture*; Book the Second: *The Story of the Clissolds – My Father and the Flow of Things.* Pp. 245. 7s. 6d. net. Vol. 2. Book the Third: *The Story of the Clissolds – Essence of Dickon*; Book the Fourth: *The Story of the Clissolds – Tangle of Desires.* Pp. 247-601. 7s. 6d. net. Vol. 3. Book the Fifth: *The Story of the Clissolds – The Next Phase*; Book the Sixth: *The Story of the Clissolds – Venus as Evening Star*; The Epilogue: Note by Sir Richard Clissold. Pp. 603-885. 7s. 6d. net. (London: Ernest Benn, Ltd., 1926.)

Although the critics have not been stirred by volumes 1 and 2 of William Clissold's achievements, there should be wigs on the green[2] over volume 3, if it be not above them. Book V is masterly in many ways – the less said of VI the better, perhaps. No writer, other than the author, could have preferred the indictment he does against our public-school system and the ancient universities.[3]

The attempt is made, in a preface, to justify the contention that the book is a novel: there is no novel in it: true it is, the story is told, ostensibly, by one William Clissold or through his brother Dickon but William is himself again, as he ever will be: from beginning to end, we are dealing with autobiography and early in the recital the writer gives himself away in saying – 'Autobiography, provided that it be not too severely disciplined may be an almost inexhaustible occupation. Nothing is altogether irrelevant. Whatever interests me or has ever interested me is material.' This, in a few clear words, is the book. It is a medical treatise – largely on social pathology.

The author is a photographer, working with a lens stopped down to a low aperture but of no great depth of focus, giving very clear pictures of superficial appearances. A photographer neither analyses nor constructs – he must record what is before him. However much he may fake his picture in development, out in the open he must take what is offered him by Nature and, at most, can await a favourable light and so play with the shadows.

At the moment there is what amounts to little short of a conspiracy to represent science and literature as moving along the same path. They never can,

---

1   Reprinted by permission from Macmillan Publishers Ltd: *Nature* (118: 2977), copyright (1926).

2   An Irish expression anticipating a conflict or disagreement, from the eighteenth century habit of discarding or losing one's wig before or during a fistfight.

3   The British and Irish universities of Oxford, Cambridge, St Andrews, Glasgow, Aberdeen, Edinburgh and Dublin which were founded before the seventeenth century.

unless and until we make a religion of our knowledge and recognise that, therefore, religion must be imperfect and ever correcting and shifting its boundaries. Science is ultimately the search after truth. Who can say what religion is? For every one the word has a different meaning. Our William, be it remarked, is a little fuzzy in his high lights. He can't be satisfied with what he has and may have and then leave it to the other fellow to have his turn, but hankers[4] for more. He is so spoilt by frequent reprinting, that he must contemplate a new edition of himself, no doubt with special binding:

> To me it is far easier to suppose that this present unfolding of consciousness and will is only a birth and a beginning and that I am not merely myself but a participator in a Being that has been born but need not die.

Surely, he is here but seconding a vote of thanks to 'that chap Oliver Lodge.' Still, 'belief in a living personal God – slight vestiges': we all have more or less as an ineradicable inheritance from primitive man.[5]

The lapse into such anthropomorphism[6] is proof how difficult it is for intelligence to prevail over convictions forced upon youth. The great problem before us soon in schools will be – how far we are entitled to go in retarding and repressing mental growth by forcing an 'established faith,' without explanation or qualification, upon children: whether parent and especially teacher be justified in misleading by baldly repeating assertions which have no authority other than tradition. The struggle is between knowledge and ignorance. Our William defines the position clearly and boldly:

> I do not know how Protestantism[7] will end. But I think it will end. I think it will come to perfectly plain speaking and if it comes to perfectly plain speaking it will cease to be Christianity. There is now little left of the Orthodox Church[8] except as a method of partisanship in the Balkans. The League of Nations may some day supersede that and then the only Christianity remaining upon earth will be the trained and safeguarded Roman Catholic Church. That is

---

4   Longs or craves for.

5   Prehistoric human culture characterised by isolation, low technology and simple social and economic organisation.

6   Ascription of human form, attributes or personality to a god, an animal or something impersonal.

7   The practices of the Christian churches or sects which repudiated papal authority at or since the Reformation.

8   The Christian churches which recognise the headship of the Patriarch of Constantinople and which split from the Roman Catholic Church in 1054.

less penetrable, a world within a world, it shields scores of millions securely throughout their lives from the least glimpse of our modern vision.

Teachers of science, and examiners, are equally concerned. Over and over again, when advocating *the teaching of scientific method*,[9] I have been told by my friends – 'You must teach something definite: students ask for assurance and will not countenance any philosophic doubt': examiners, too, ask for positive answers. Tennyson's lines are not yet accepted even of science:

> There lives more faith in honest doubt,
> Believe me, than in half the creeds.[10]

The attitude of all the schools is not merely unscientific but is one tending to systematise untruthfulness. Our William, at least, can think of better times:

> I can discover in all my world nothing enduring, neither in the hills nor in the sea, nor in laws and customs nor in the nature of man, nothing steadfast except for this – a certain growth of science, a certain increase of understanding, a certain accumulation of power. But there is that growth of science, there is that increase of understanding, there is that accumulation of power. I do not know why it should be so but so it is. It gathered its force slowly before man was. It goes on now with accumulating speed and widening scope and on it I build my working conception of the course of life. Man, unconscious at first, begins now, in an individual here and an individual there, to realise his possibilities and dream of the greatness of his destiny. A new phase of history is near its beginning. But it has not begun. Such science as we have brings us suggestions rather than direction.

William Clissold is not all religion, though considered under the conventional classification of *Wein, Weib* and *Gesang*,[11] it has a limited range of subject. Wine is only once referred to – a single bottle of Château Margaux 1917,[12]

---

9   A method of procedure consisting in systematic observation, measurement and experiment, and the formulation, testing and modification of hypotheses.

10   A quotation from Alfred Tennyson's poem *In Memoriam* (1850).

11   German, 'wine, women and song', attributed to Martin Luther by Johann Voss in 'Gesundheit' (1777).

12   The Château Margaux website notes for 1917 read: 'Quite a small crop, producing average quality wine' (http://www.chateau-margaux.com/en/Millesime.aspx); thus Armstrong's opinion of the wine is quite correct.

not a great vintage, produced at lunch by Sir Rupert Yorke. Still, this suffices to incite William's reflections upon Sir Rupert's sexual and religious outlook. It appears also to have led him to refrain from referring to certain questions he had intended to raise – the projected exchange of opinion would have been 'as possible as with a pensive lion in the zoo.' Pity it is perhaps that he has not met with more pensive lions in the course of his career and has not thereby been forced to concentrate upon some definite line of action.

After an over-full dose of *Weib*, we get music in the form of a study of futurism. Our William's swansong[13] foreshadows a metamorphosis of mankind – new ways of living – one terrestrial anthill: this he regards as the necessary, the only possible, continuation of human history. He contemplates the organisation of a central police bureau to co-ordinate the protection of life, property and freedom throughout the world, without distinction of persons under a universally accepted code. In fact, the lions and lambs are all to lie down comfortably together.[14] The coal strike[15] was only begun when the book was issued. The history of Ireland, the love lost between the States of Europe, the growing development during many years past of local self-government in Great Britain[16] – such items are left out of account.

The men of large material influence are to reconstruct the world upon broader, happier and finer lines. Their first struggle is to be with the Press. Civilisation must be by newspapers. Open, candid, full and generous, these are qualities the newspaper of the new life must possess. It must suppress nothing. It must bring to every mind capable of receiving it the new achievement of human and organising power, the victories of conscious change. The daily papers of educated people half a century ahead may be a tenth of the size and ten times the price of the present 'wildly flapping caricatures of contemporary happenings.' The Press apparently is to be the work of the men of affairs. Our William says, quite truly, the daily paper is a daily disappointment – but to how many? He has found but one newspaper that comforts his soul and that is *Nature*, to which flattering reference is made. 'Domestic bye-products,' such as sons, will have to

---

13 A final act or effort.

14 Referring to a situation where erstwhile enemies cooperate or compromise, a misquotation from the Old Testament Bible Isaiah 11: 6, 'The wolf shall lie with the lamb, / the leopard shall lie down with the kid, / the calf and the lion and the fatling together, / and a little child shall lead them'.

15 A reference to the General Strike of 3 to 12 May 1926, when trade unionists went on strike throughout Britain in opposition to the worsening conditions being enacted against coal miners.

16 A reference to the increased power of local authorities in Britain from 1900, with education, housing and welfare falling within the remit of local councils during the first third of the twentieth century.

justify their sonship – there is to be a diminution of inheritance in property. The new social life will be aristocratic in the sense that it will have a decisive stratum of pre-eminent and leading individuals who will wield a relatively large part of the power and property of the community but it will be democratic in the sense that it will be open to every one with ability and energy to join that stratum and participate to the extent of his or her ability or energy. In the formal picture presented to us of the world republic,[17] we shall be fully adult – a state to which few come now, doubtfully and each one alone:

> We shall put away childish things, childish extravagances of passion and nightmare fears. Our minds will live in a living world-literature and exercise in living art; our science will grow incessantly and our power increase. Our planet will become like a workshop in a pleasant garden and from it we shall look out with ever-diminishing fear upon our heritage of space and time amidst the stars. We shall be man in common and each one of us will develop his individuality to the utmost, no longer as a separated and conflicting being but as a part and contribution to one continuing whole.

Who shall say that our author is not an optimist and Holist?[18]

The contemplated metamorphosis of mankind, our William contends at an early stage of his dream, demands a life based on broader and sounder common ideas, expressed in new terms and new artistic forms, accompanied by nervous and other physiological changes. This necessity to change and expand extends from man's soul to man's chemistry.

It is strange that a reader of *Nature* and a pupil of the Royal College of Science should be so Lamarckian[19] as to proffer such doctrine or believe that it can be realised within any period that is worth our consideration. The lesson of Tutankhamen's tomb[20] seems to be lost upon him. Obviously, he has little knowledge of what is known in science. We have learnt sufficient of man's vital chemistry *to know* that it proceeds along lines which are little short of fixed. This must be so. If open to variation away from our type, we should be all over

---

17 An alternative label for Wells's world state.

18 One who believes that all the properties of a given system cannot be determined or explained by the by the sum of its component parts but rather the parts can only be understood through a knowledge of the system as a whole.

19 Of or pertaining to Jean-Baptiste Lamarck or his theory of organic evolution, which he ascribed to heritable modifications produced in the individual by habit, instinctive propensity and the direct action of the environment.

20 A reference to the discovery of the treasure-laden tomb in the Valley of the Kings, Egypt, by Howard Carter many years after most archaeologists had declared the Valley exhausted.

the shop,[21] to use a vulgarism.[22] Still, the human mind is strangely variable – subject at all times to the caprice of chemical change, every function apparently controlled by a chemical secretion. The woman, at regular intervals, we know, is heavily drugged. Male desire, of which our William has much to say in Book VI, is probably of chemical origin, due to chemical changes induced by mental processes.

Coming down to sense, human control of the world, as our William says, has been a control in detail; there has been no comprehensive control – because there has been no comprehensive understanding. Hence his indictment of our educational system in Book V. It is worth noting, he makes the point, that the mind of youth is the primitive, medieval mind – conservative and reactionary:[23]

> Few minds are mature enough and stout enough before thirty to achieve a genuine originality. The originality of the young is for the most part merely a childish reversal of established things. The independence of the young is commonly no more than a primitive resistance to instruction. The youthful revolutionary is merely insubordinate and his extremist radicalism an attempt to return to archaic conditions, to naturalism,[24] indiscipline, waste and dirt. The youthful anti-revolutionary turns back to mystical loyalties and romance.

It is necessary to educate the young for the new order. Sections 14 and 15 on supersession of schoolmasters and an inquest on universities must be studied to be appreciated – almost every word is telling. On an experience of sixty years, I am prepared to vouch for the substantial accuracy of the indictment. Much that is said, I have said over and over again.

Present-day education is nothing short of a pretentious farce – taking into account the changed and fast-changing state of the world. It promotes inaction, where action is needed above all things. It degrades and only accidentally promotes intelligence. It is in the hands of a class of men who are eyeless to the needs of the times, of men who never will respond to the call that is now made upon the teacher. Yet parents and guardians smugly accept what is and make no attempt to improve the conditions. Even our William, being a man of words, only half sees what is, what might and what should be. Education was begun in the monasteries,[25] to serve clerical ends. We have long since got rid of monasteries – Henry VIII did that for us. It were now time that we abolished the monastic in

---

21   An English idiom meaning completely disorganised or confused.

22   A common or ordinary expression.

23   Inclined or favourable to a reversion to a traditional mode of thinking or behaving.

24   Adherence or attachment to what is natural, and indifference to convention.

25   Places of residence for communities living under religious vows.

education. Only don't let us substitute co-education,[26] the emasculating invention of the Evil One.[27] The effect of the monasteries was of small account in comparison with that now being exercised by the survival of the system of training they instituted – it will yearly become a greater peril to us. Our William is explicit on this point:

> ... the last human beings in the world in whom you are likely to find a spark of creative energy or a touch of imaginative vigour are the masters and mistresses of upper middle-class schools ... these schoolmasters and schoolmistresses, ... to whom we entrust nearly all the sons and daughters of the owning and directing people of our world, are by necessity orthodox, conformist, genteel people of an infinite discretion and an invincible formality. Essentially they are a class of refugees from the novelties and strains of life. I do not see how, as a class, they can be anything else.... The whole crowd of upper-class youth has been picked over again and again before the schoolmasters come; the most vigorous and innovating men have gone in for diplomacy, the law, politics, the public services,[28] science, literature, art, business, the hard adventure of life; and at last comes the residue.... Its [the school's] mentality is the mentality of residue men.
>
> That is a neglected factor which has to be reckoned with in the history of the British Empire during the last hundred years. That is something the foreign observer has still to realise. A larger and larger proportion of its influential and directive men throughout this period have spent the most plastic years of their lives under the influence of the least lively, least enterprising, most restrictive, most conservative and intricately self-protective types it was possible to find. We have bred our governing class mentally, as the backward Essex farmer bred his pigs, from the individuals that were no good for the open market. The intelligent foreigner complains that the Englishman abroad has been growing duller and stiffer in every generation.
>
>   *   *   *   *   *
>
> The clue to the manifest change in character that Britain and its Empire have displayed during the last hundred years, the gradual lapses from a subtle and very real greatness and generosity to imitative imperialism and solemn puerility is to be found, if not precisely upon the playing fields of Eton,[29] in the mental and moral quality of the men who staff the public schools.

A true bill. Italy, the one country where there is government, has no public schools. No other explanation is possible of the way in which the courage has

---

26   The education of both sexes together.

27   The Devil.

28   Government employment; service provided for the community.

29   A British public school, founded in 1440.

gone out of us – of our loss of the art of government, the courage to govern, never more obvious than in the present coal strike – of the disappearance of the naturalist – of the decline of industry, *e. g.* the textile trade. The schools, to-day, it should be added, are greatly aided: golf and the motor-car serve to complete their insidious effect upon character.

Our William is nothing if not thorough – he would improve the public school and schoolmaster out of existence but recognises the need and desirability, under our present social condition, of schools of the preparatory class, largely staffed by women and not very big, where children up to fifteen could have a quasi-family life. (*N. B.* – The public school gone, these would be rid of the curse of the 'Common Entrance' examination.[30]) From fifteen onwards, the more directly a boy lives in contact with the real world, the better alike for the real world and himself. The reality of education for every one over fourteen, in a modern state, lies more and more outside any classroom; the fewer the school-made values a boy has, the juster will be his apprehension of reality. The new system will be one of special schools, studios and laboratories for arts, sciences, language and every sort of technical work. The style of work will be new.

All this is essentially sane. I saw the danger in early days and went so far as to express my opinion by saying that I would not send my sons to a public school to save their lives and kept my word but was lucky in having at my door what was long, probably, the best day-school in London, if not in the country. I have also always held, that seventeen was the *very latest age* up to which a boy should be kept under monastic school conditions. I took my four boys away at that age and sent them to places of higher instruction,[31] *where they were free to become men.* I have every cause to be satisfied: they may not be saints but neither are they serious sinners and the kick has not all been taken out of them.

The *Times*, on October 13,[32] contained a most feeling obituary notice of Dr E. A. Abbott, long well known as headmaster of the City of London School[33] and a noted scholar. He is brought into comparison with F. W. Walker, the famous headmaster of St Paul's School.[34] We are told that Abbott, who relished Walker's half-cynical frankness of speech, used to relate how the latter showed him over his grand new school buildings at Hammersmith and how, when he (Abbott) expressed his admiration of everything and especially of the magnificent chemical laboratories, Walker replied: 'Yes, they are very well in their way;

---

30 An examination established in 1904 which determines students' eligibility to join independent (i. e., private, non-state) schools.

31 Education in an institution of higher education such as a university.

32 'Dr E. A. Abbott' (1926).

33 An independent school for boys aged 10 to 18 in London, founded in 1834.

34 British public school, founded in London in 1509.

278

but, as we two are alone here, I may venture to say (lowering his voice to a confidential whisper) that you and I know that this sort of thing *is not education.*'

Surely such an episode is disgraceful to both men. If 'this sort of thing' were not education, why introduce it? If introduced, surely it was the headmaster's duty to see it made education. That two such men were able to scoff at a discipline that furnishes the key to the comprehension of life is but proof of the hopeless narrowness and impenetrability of the classical and literary mind. There attitude is that of most if not all our headmasters. 'Science,' we know, is a failure in schools – are the headmasters doing anything to improve the teaching, knowing as they must that to-day its dictates dominate the world?

Our William has something to say about science specifically but first let it be noted, that he extends his scepticism about schools to universities, particularly to 'the universities for juveniles like Oxford, Cambridge, Harvard and Yale.'[35] We are all alive to the fact that these are continuation boarding-schools,[36] not free institutions as are the German universities. He is justified in his indictment that there is a growing discontent with Oxford and Cambridge among those who have undergraduate sons – 'sending their boys trustfully and hopefully to these over-rated centres, they find themselves confronted with pleasant, easy-going evasive young men up to nothing in particular and schooled out of faith, passion or ambition.' I have said already, our William is an incomparable draughtsman. We must be prepared, he considers, to cut out this three or four-year holiday at Oxford or Cambridge and their American compeers from the lives of the young men we hope to see playing leading parts in the affairs of the world. So do I. We shall not get through with youths that are born tired, without method in their minds, such as we have to-day, who lapse into 're-search' but make it an armchair occupation and put neither heart nor guts into the work.

To pass to specific science, our William's presentation of the Royal Society is of a piece with his appreciation of the universities. Perhaps it is worth while occasionally to see ourselves as others see us. He reports a meeting with his brother Dickon, at which his brother fingers his first paper in the *Phil. Trans.* The comments he makes are amusing and delightful parody.

'Blastopore[37] of the snail,' he objected. 'Fancy poking about at the blastopore of the snail! It's – indelicate. And cryo-hydrates![38] This chap Oliver Lodge

---

35 A private American university, founded in 1701 and located in New Haven, Connecticut.

36 Schools, generally private, which offer accommodation to their pupils.

37 An opening formed by invagination of the surface of a blastula.

seems to be all over them. Wonder what they are. Well, this is your affair, Billy. It's up to you to display the name Clissold properly in these *Philosophical Transactions*. If that is the end of life. Not my pitch. Not in the least my pitch. I wouldn't try to see even a stethoscope[39] through these *Philosophical Transactions*. No.'

This is a confirmation, from outside, of the view I have often expressed, that the *Phil. Trans.* spell cremation, the *Proceedings*[40] 'decent burial' of scientific discovery.

The brother, who has made his fortune out of advertising, then suggests giving the 'dull old *Philosophical Transactions*' a real spirited Xmas[41] number, a genuine advertisement display, with which 'Temptation of St Antony'[42] won't be in the same field. The final opinion expressed by Dickon, to meet his brother's objection, that advertising would be vulgar, is again a noteworthy criticism:

'If there's anything vulgar about modern advertising it's because it's been so concerned about pills and soap and pickles. Just a passing phase. A man or a class or a religion or – anything that will not advertise isn't fit to exist in the world. It means it doesn't really believe in itself. To want to exist and not to dare to exist is something beneath vulgarity.... That's why I have such a contempt for your rotten, shy, sit-in-the-corner-and-ask-the-dear-Prince-of-Wales[43]-to-dinner-once-a-year-Royal Society. If the soap-boilers[44] did no more for soap than your old Royal Society does for science,' said Dickon, 'nobody would wash.'

Formerly, the opinion of the Society was often consulted in matters of importance to the State; now, the Department of Scientific and Industrial Re-

---

38   Substances such as salt or ammonium chloride which crystallise with water only at low temperatures.

39   A medical instrument for examining the chest and sounding the heart and lungs.

40   The *Proceedings of the Royal Society*, a journal of the Royal Society of London founded in 1800.

41   Properly, Christmas, the festival of Jesus Christ's birth, traditionally celebrated by Christians on 25 December or (in Orthodox Christianity) on 6 or 7 January.

42   The Christian account of Antony the Great who lived in isolation in the desert and, according to legend, was afflicted by the devil with boredom, laziness and the phantoms of women, but overcame these through prayer.

43   From 1910 to 1936 this title was held by Edward Windsor (later Edward VIII).

44   Manufacturers of soap.

search[45] is more and more usurping the office. The individual original scientific worker, like the naturalist, may easily soon be ruled out of existence and an unimaginative being put in his place. We confine our activity to publishing work which is either largely premature and unfinished or even better left unpublished. Few attend the meetings and, at these, soft nothings are said and no one dare criticise. 'We work submerged, we talk by no more than twos and threes,' says our mentor. This is the way of the Society. It cannot be brought, it makes no attempt, to realise, how essential it is to organise the forces of science into a living body – what it could do if it formed itself into a great consultative scientific House of Peers.[46] The only office it effectively serves is that of back-patting and bemedalling the supposed élite of the craft.

As our William truly remarks, 'No great creative development can go on in modern social life beyond a certain point without a literature of explanation and criticism.' We have no such literature: the result is that work is done and little use made of it. We keep no more than a casual profit-and-loss account and never seek systematically to balance our books. Our knowledge is never properly sifted and sorted and its values determined – no logical order is observed in filling in the blanks.

May it not be true that few would wash, if no more were done for soap than we do collectively for science? Is it policy to go on producing, paying insufficient attention to quality and demand, without taking proper steps to popularise and sell? Industry, to-day, we know is largely engaged in producing and forcing the sale of unnecessary goods: this is the manufacturers' conspiracy. If we are not coming very near to producing goods and leaving them to rot, we are doing little to secure the digestion of the food we provide. We finish nothing. To take an example. Cane sugar is now made, all but pure, in millions of tons and yet chemists cannot tell the manufacturer what it is – how its atomic bricks[47] are built together. Children are put to such work, not experts: to-day, these are engaged in the study of poison gases.[48]

Research work is fast being made an entirely selfish, narrow occupation, when not carried out for industrial purposes. A bureaucratic class of academic workers is fast growing up, fit for little more than drawing-room[49] service, with-

---

45 A British governmental department (1917-65) with responsibilities for enhancing research by means of government funding.

46 Colloquial name for the British House of Lords, the unelected legislative upper house created during the medieval period.

47 Atoms considered as the building blocks of all things.

48 Chemical weapons pioneered in the Great War to kill or injure large numbers of people on the battlefield.

49 A room where guests can be formally received and to which they can retire after dinner.

281

out practical outlook. We need a few Fords to introduce efficiency into the research machine – Mr Ford is said to have a greater annual turnover of work-people than any other employer, which means that he takes the efficiency of the worker into account: our up-growing civil service[50] research system does not: the threatened result is that 'research' will become a merely parasitic occupation. The term will disappear from the field of practice.

We work submerged, says our William. We hand on our impressions and vague intentions only by the most fragmentary hints. In education nothing is done to record, preserve and utilise successful trials of method. Sanderson left no record of method behind him and to-day, apart from his buildings, Oundle has nothing to show of his influence – it has reverted to the primitive school type. His Home of Vision[51] has no vision in it. One teacher succeeds another without ever considering his predecessor's methods. The Finsbury Technical College was proclaimed a success but its methods are on the dust heap.

Before attempting to form a world directorate,[52] we need to run our own little shanty:[53] to take notice of one another and be sympathetic and work together to make it really habitable for all. Not only leaders are needed but the apparatus also is not there. It is all very well to repeat Carlyle's saying, that the modern university is a university of books[54] – the books are not there. Even in leisure hours, you cannot live on the dull-as-ditch-water[55]-doings of a no-sight family, with or without spoons. Writers of the day have no knowledge within them to use, thanks to their schooling. Here is our William's future opportunity: he is only fifty-nine and has time to turn over many new leaves. Let him write up to his professions, to show, if possible, how the new and necessary knowledge may be brought home to youth and made of some general avail. He has recognised his and our limitations, in his preface, in a single line, which is probably the most significant in the book, in saying of the men of the type of 'the devout Mr Belloc, the aristocratic Duke of Northumberland, the political Mr Ramsay MacDonald,' that he can only comment on such types. *Their ultimate processes are inconceivable to him.*

We are all cryptic beings and no one of us is open to the complete inspection of his fellow-man. We differ vastly in mentality. This is why Oxford is ob-

---

50   All the non-military branches of state administration.

51   Properly, Hall of Scientific Vision.

52   An alternative label for Wells's world state.

53   A roughly-built dwelling.

54   A paraphrase of Thomas Carlyle in *On Heroes and Hero-Worship and the Heroic in History* (1840), where he writes, 'the true University in these days is a collection of books'.

55   Extremely uninteresting.

durate and will teach nothing that is needed by the world to-day. The word-slingers[56] it trains throw from empty slings – at times perhaps a few very beautiful stones from the past but not the bullets of to-day. By a strange process, by securing control of the schools by men of its own type, it has made itself a community of one type of mentality, with but few escapes from its rigidity: the mechanism for the appreciation of modern things is not built into the type. We shall never improve our system of education and make it fit the needs of the times until we take into account, in the most liberal manner possible, the strange variability of the human mind. Society being composed of all sorts and conditions of men,[57] to provide for all will always be very difficult, the less, however, the more we are alive to the differences and not too immodest in our individual opinions.

---

56 A derogatory expression for useless teachers.
57 An expression borrowed from the eponymous novel (1882) by Walter Besant.

2.17: *The Short Stories of H. G. Wells*

Hyman Levy, 'Science in Literature' (8 October 1927).[1]

The Short Stories of H. G. Wells. Pp. 1148. (London: Ernest Benn, Ltd., 1927.) 7*s.* 6*d.* net.

Nothing is so significant of the power of the old classical traditions as the extent to which the literature of fiction remains comparatively unmoved under the shock of scientific discovery. For the intellectual revolutions that have been effected during this past century by a mere handful of blandly inquiring scientists can be matched only by the social and industrial transformations to which they have unconsciously contributed in no small measure.

To a scientist a new field of human experience and expression is opened up. He sees life unfolding, not merely as the old interplay of human emotion and passion, but rather in response to the widening environment developed by man's increasing knowledge. In the field of science, for him who has eyes to see, dramatic material is not far to seek, but current fiction remains singularly aloof. Here and there a detective, a pathologist,[2] or a medical practitioner is created who plays his part against a suggestive background of mysterious knowledge, but there is no novelist, with the exception of Mr H. G. Wells, in whom the dramatic element in scientific discovery evokes a sufficient response to urge him to action.

The strong human impulses associated with love and sex which have formed the keynote of so much of modern fiction are not absent in the work of Wells – far from it – but the psychological behaviour of the scientist, his interests, his urges, the material he handles, and the stage he treads, constitute a region into which none other than Wells has dared to enter.

Coming to literary work from the field of technical knowledge, Wells has made the amazing discovery that a scientific training, far from being a handicap, is a positive blessing. A good novelist, if he is anything, is pre-eminently a psychologist. It is his function, by means of the technique of storytelling, to observe, to describe, and to analyse the thoughts and actions of mankind, and not merely that aspect of mankind constant throughout time, but mankind in the making.[3] He stands at the point of vantage who absorbs with understanding the newer knowledge. Being artistic, such an analysis – in the creation of a novel it is really a synthesis – is not scientifically systematic. It differs from a study of a

---

1   Reprinted by permission from Macmillan Publishers Ltd: *Nature* (120: 3023), copyright (1927).

2   A specialist in the laboratory examination of samples of body tissue, usually for diagnosis or forensic purposes.

3   An allusion to Wells's eponymous book of 1903.

scientific problem in this respect, that no two novelists in their treatment will produce the same result. The final product is dependent on the mentality of the solver. Thus the psychological study developed by the novelist is, as often as not, a reflected study of the author. Wells stands at this point of vantage; and in describing his vision opens up his mind.

Here, then, in the present group of short stories, we see Wells, a young imaginative artist, striding boldly into the field and with a few strokes creating a world which hums strangely in the ears of the old classical school. Tuned to the mentality of the scientist and alive to the trend of scientific thought, Wells enters the arena of fiction armed with weapons denied to his professional colleagues. He may manoeuvre in regions of the arena with assurance where others must hesitate to tread, and the earlier stories in this extraordinary collection show Wells deporting himself gaily and masterfully among the fantastic notions born of much of the speculative science of the late Victorian[4] era.

Early hesitant knowledge of time and space are handled with assurance and imagination in 'The Time Machine,' 'The Plattner Story,' 'The Remarkable Case of Davidson's Eyes.' Sometimes his boldness is preposterous, as when in 'My First Aeroplane' he makes a machine in 1912 stand up to treatment that no self-respecting aeroplane in 1927 would possibly tolerate without destruction. At other times it is almost prophetic, as in 'The Land Ironclads,' where in 1903 trench warfare and tanks are described in unerring detail. Again and again he traces the emergence of a world of wheels, and shafts, and furnaces.

It is easy to say that, in those early days of Wells's literary work, the young man is merely tickling the palate of the reader with a series of extravagant ideas. While it is probably true that a number of these stories are scarcely more than this, there recurs continually the suggestion that if mankind would only realise it, the potentialities for good and evil in modern scientific discovery on the mechanical side are enormous. There is, for example, 'A Dream of Armageddon,' 'A Story of the Days to Come,' and so on. There appears the implication to the scientific man that he must give himself pause to consider whither his newer knowledge may drive mankind, and to the layman the startling question as to whether he is indeed ready to receive this strange knowledge.

The theme changes slightly as Wells borrows from his biological experience.[5] The power of natural selection as a factor in evolution is violently forced to our notice here and there. In 'The Country of the Blind,' the capacity of the human organism to adapt itself to environment, and the extent to which refinement in the senses may proceed in response to needs, are brought out with the

---

4   Of, pertaining to or characteristic of the reign of Queen Victoria.

5   A reference to Wells's biological training at the Normal School of Science (1884-87) and his bachelor of science qualification from the University of London (1891).

skill of a master. 'The Empire of the Ants' teaches how the survival of the fittest is by no means identical with survival of the most desirable. In 'The Time Machine' we are projected forward into futurity and are horrified to discover that mankind has long passed the zenith of its highest development and a kind of retrogression[6] or involution[7] has set in, in place of the higher evolution.

These ideas may be fantastic; they may be mere examples of mental agility and imaginative strokes of a young man in a field yet unopened to assured knowledge. But we begin to perceive that in the background of Wells's mind there exists a dominating urge. Mankind itself raises a problem of colossal magnitude – how to utilise the accumulating wealth of scientific knowledge in the design of a super-race[8] – of a civilisation devoid of the stupidities and absurdities of social life as we know it.

These stories where they touch this issue scarcely do more than raise it. Some indication of Wells's own line of approach to this difficult issue is provided by glimmerings of Utopias of various kinds that sparkle out here and there. It is in his larger and more mature works that these ideas are worked out in greater detail, but, on the whole, Wells on the constructive side is much less satisfying than at his favourite game of thought provoking. Utopias are literally as old as Adam,[9] but it is permissible to doubt whether the mental exercise in their design ranks higher than that used in the solution of a crossword puzzle.

It is possible that in a sense they may serve the useful function of preparing the minds of some for the possibilities that might be achieved, for the ideals to which to strive. But imaginative gropings in a dim future, with roseate[10] pictures of the dawn of a new era when man will grasp the forces of Nature in the hollow of his hand, will not provide a solution of the immediately pressing problems of production, distribution, and exchange; for the question uppermost in every one's mind, both scientist and layman, is, 'What to do now?'

The kind of promise the imaginative Wells has held out in these early stories is not fulfilled by him in his later work. Doubtless, had his numerous love novels[11] been left unwritten, the world of literature would have been enormously the poorer, but the far-reaching and vital questions which Wells himself raised have really not been faced by him. Instead, he has left it to the politicians, con-

---

6   Movement in a backward or reverse direction.

7   Shrinkage, regression or atrophy due to inactivity.

8   A race of individuals with exceptional physical or intellectual qualities.

9   Ancient; (metaphorically) as old as the first man.

10   Happy, optimistic, promising.

11   A reference to such works as *Ann Veronica* (1909), *Marriage* (1912), *The Passionate Friends* (1913) and *The Wife of Sir Isaac Harman* (1914).

tent to be a mere finger-post[12] pointing towards an inaccessible region of the horizon.

---

12   A signpost at a crossroads or a junction.

2.18: *The Way the World is Going,* *The Open Conspiracy* **and** *What Are We To Do With Our Lives?*

Alexander Carr-Saunders, 'The Way the World might go' (7 July 1928).[1]

The Way the World is Going: Guesses and Forecasts of the Years Ahead. 26 Articles and a Lecture by H. G. Wells. Pp. xi + 301. (London: Ernest Benn, Ltd., 1928.) 7s. 6d. net.

The Open Conspiracy: Blue Prints for a World Revolution. By H. G. Wells. Pp. 156. (London: Victor Gollancz, Ltd., 1928.) 5s. net.

Men of science owe a debt of gratitude to Mr H. G. Wells. He was born with a passion to make things better, and there is implicit in all his writings the view that the advancement of science and the application of scientific knowledge is the indispensable method whereby this end may be achieved. The passion has lost none of its intensity as the years have passed. No trace of cynicism has crept in. He remains as eager, as impatient, as youthful as ever. He has not accumulated a series of tricks which he performs for the public amusement or 'pour épater les bourgeois.'[2] He argues, debates, and pleads like the young man just becoming aware of all the absurdities, complexities, and possibilities of life.

Not to have grown old, weary, formalised, or pontifical[3] is an achievement. Exuberance and vitality, a passion for the better ordering of society, a belief in science, are with Mr Wells as they have always been. Add to that a sixth sense[4] of understanding how ideas and experiences react upon different types of men and women brought up in different social strata, of sensing and expressing different social relationships with their economic background: remember that to religious and aesthetic experience Mr Wells is almost wholly insensitive, and we have some explanation of his positive achievements. His main achievement lies in his novels. In them is displayed an understanding of social as distinguished from individual relationships and experiences, which cannot be paralleled. The existence of Mr Wells's novels relating to the War[5] will make it possible in the future to understand how men and women were affected by that crisis in human affairs better than we can grasp how any crisis in the past affected those who lived through it.

This achievement, however, is incidental to Mr Wells's main purpose. He wrote because he had lessons to teach. Every now and then he has tried to con-

---

1   Reprinted by permission from Macmillan Publishers Ltd: *Nature* (122: 3062), copyright (1928).

2   French, 'to shock the middle classes'.

3   Pertaining to a bishop or a pope; preachy.

4   A supposed faculty giving intuitive or extrasensory knowledge.

5   I. e., the Great War.

vey his lessons in some other form. Thus he has given us utopias, histories, newspaper articles. No matter what form he selects, his vitality carries us along. Nevertheless, as he departs from the form of the novel, we become conscious of a certain thinness and a certain dryness. The further Mr Wells gets from men and women, though his powers may be limited to portraying types rather than personalities, some virtue seems to depart, some cunning to leave him. It appears that it is only contact with the flesh and the hot breath of struggling men and women that moves him to his best work. When he contemplates men in abstraction his temperature falls. When he visualised A, B, and C as types of social classes a, b, and c, and brings them together, his imagination is fully exerted, his humour is at work. He flashes out remarks which illuminate our social problems. But when he begins with classes a, b, and c, his powers are not stimulated in the same fashion, and the illumination is correspondingly reduced.

(1) It is a bold thing to collect and publish in book form articles from newspapers on topics of the day. But these articles stand the test. They have vitality and width of vision. The topics discussed are viewed in relation to a broad background, and thus stand in contrast to the common run of journalism in which the attitude of the day alone is represented. The thought common to all these discussions is expressed in the following sentence. 'While we are representing life in melodramatic colours as a struggle between the "Haves" and the "Have-nots,"[6] the less romantic and interesting reality of a struggle between scientific organisation on the one hand and the alliance of personal greed with chaotic stupidity on the other may be undermining all the grounds of our melodrama.'

It is on account of this emphasis on a scientific ordering of our affairs that we should be grateful to Mr Wells. Men of science are only too apt to content themselves with the application of scientific method to their particular sphere, and to watch without protest the unsystematic, short-sighted, and blundering attempts to mend our social and economic organisation. It may seldom fall to men of science to go themselves outside their spheres, but they are untrue to their guiding principles if they do not urge that those who move in the political arena should not attempt to plan and organise in what is essentially the spirit of science.

Mr Wells admirably fulfils this task of appearing as the prophet of the scientific method in the social field. He is at his best when he is in contact with a concrete problem. In this book is included a lecture given in Paris,[7] which is, as he tells us, 'much more closely written than the rest of the book.' It is not so

---

6   The advantaged and the disadvantaged, respectively.

7   A reference to 'Democracy Under Revision', a lecture delivered at the Sorbonne on 15 March 1927.

alive as the rest of the book. Mr Wells moves awkwardly in the world of abstractions. He seems to be wanting to get out of the study again and hear what people are saying and watch the expressions on their faces. His literary style, which is not unsuited to convey the jumble and flow of life and contact of man with man, is an uncouth weapon for dealing with academic niceties.

(2) What has just been said applies to *The Open Conspiracy*. Mr Wells has attempted to set down his programme. The book states 'the essential ideas of my life, the perspective of my world.... This is my religion. Here are my directive aims and the criteria of all I do.' Readers of *William Clissold*[8] will remember hearing of the 'open conspiracy.'[9] In that vivid work is conveyed the idea of the co-operation of men and women of good will and wide outlook in the task of producing world order and harmony. The programme as suggested in *William Clissold* is just definite enough to be real. It is not formalised or presented in an orderly fashion, but it comes through the incidental discussions and descriptions, and comes, moreover, with freshness. The book vibrates. It is exciting. It is concrete. Here Mr Wells attempts a fuller treatment, more logical and more abstract. It is not the same compelling force.

Interesting and conspicuously sincere as the book is, Mr Wells's genius is not well suited to this kind of presentation. In the novel form he can suggest the case for the control of population or the stabilisation of prices so as to make them overwhelming. He can show how absurdly some character fears the one and another character misunderstands the other. But when he tries to state the case in essay form, the result is somewhat commonplace and even jejune.[10] The nature of the programme must already be familiar to readers of the novels: the organisation of world peace, the world organisation of credit,[11] transport, and staple production, population control. He looks to its fulfilment coming through informal groups of people in substantial agreement with the main points in the programme who will work for it. It would appear that Mr Wells has been impressed by the success of Bolshevism[12] and Fascism in capturing the imagination and in focusing the energies of young people, and hopes that his very different programme may do as much.

---

8   A reference to Wells's *The World of William Clissold* (1926).

9   Wells's expression to describe the necessary public revolutionary movement for the replacement of capitalist nation-states with a cosmopolitan collectivist world state, first used in 'An Introduction to the 1914 Edition of *Anticipations*' (1924).

10   Intellectually unsatisfying, lacking substance, shallow, simplistic.

11   The sum at a persons disposal for use in purchase or exchange.

12   A form of revolutionary communism which was the ruling ideology in Russia from October 1917 to 1991.

Surely there is all the difference in the world between the ideals and dogmas of the Fascists and the Bolshevists, which demand from the mass of their adherents mere blind adherence, and Mr Wells's programme, which is that of following the light of science as an aid to social betterment and of accepting only that of which the informed intelligence approves. The 'open conspiracy' is not likely to achieve its peaceful revolution in that way. The best hope lies, perhaps, in the joint approach to these problems by teachers and students in our universities, of which Mr Wells speaks somewhat slightingly, and in the hope that some day the great body of men trained in science will refuse to remain content with the restriction of their methods to narrow fields, and will insist that they be applied to the wide and difficult problems of social organisation.

Louis Fenn, 'The Politics of Science' (19 March 1932).[13]

What are We to do with our Lives? By H. G. Wells. Pp. vi + 148. (London: William Heinemann, Ltd., 1931.) 3s. 6d. net.

There is nowadays scarcely an issue of *Nature* which does not call upon scientific men to unite for ends beyond the specialised discussion of their own work. That the appeal does not entirely fail of response is shown by the slowly growing professional and social organisation of the scientific world and by the formation of propagandist[14] societies which seek to impress upon the general public the importance of science in industry and government.

All this activity indicates a growing conviction among scientific men that science has something to contribute to the modern world beyond her technical applications: that its spirit and method carry with them implications of a rule of life, for human society as well as for the individual, and of a vision for the lack of which the people perish.

The practical working out of this increasing desire for a political movement based on science has proved, however, unexpectedly difficult. Scientific men are inevitably busy and preoccupied, and by the standard of their needs they are poor. Their calling has in the past made for a high degree of individualism; they have been able to combine for discussion and publication but for very little else. Moreover, the tradition of the pioneers who worked for knowledge and disdained its material prizes has prevented the development of the powerful 'trade union'[15] types of organisation which have elsewhere provided the economic

---

13　Reprinted by permission from Macmillan Publishers Ltd: *Nature* (129: 3255), copyright (1932).

14　Systematically advocating an idea or organisation.

15　The organised association of the workers in a trade for the protection and furtherance of their interests.

foundations of policy. A far more serious obstacle has been that the world of science has never made up its mind what it wants from politics. It has never got within sight of a political programme of its own, and it appears to accept conventional party divisions as real and important just when the general deliquescence of politics has revealed them as the superficial things they are.

The book at present under review, though addressed to intelligent people in general and not specifically to scientific workers, is an attempt to impose the applications of science on the social and political world of to-day. Its distinguished author, himself a scientific man turned publicist,[16] is perhaps more fitted than any other living writer to point the moral of our present discontents and to formulate political intentions for the world of science.

This book is really a highly concentrated essence, distilled from the author's sociological writings of the last twenty years. It looks back to the Samurai – the voluntary aristocracy of *A Modern Utopia* – and to the imagined State in *Men Like Gods* 'whose education was its government'. It considers and rejects the experimental anthropomorphism of *God the Invisible King*, and it carries on the scepticism about democratic institutions which has marked Mr Wells's writings ever since *The New Machiavelli*. It contains no new fundamental ideas, but it is mature and articulate beyond any other sociological book its author has produced; and it makes, very explicitly and with complete seriousness, a most daring proposal.

When, towards the close of the War,[17] Mr Wells sat down to consider what mankind must do to prevent the recurrence of that colossal tragedy, he discovered that, despite a respectable array of 'qualifications', he was very much at sea about a number of things which a properly educated citizen of the world ought to know. Fortunate in the possession of leisure and opportunity, he set to work, with the help of a number of distinguished specialists, to complete his education; and the result was three very important books the writing of which has left its mark on that at present under review. *The Outline of History* sought to tell the story of mankind from the primeval[18] lair to the Treaty of Versailles. *The Science of Life* recounts what is known of biology, especially in relation to human affairs; and *The Work, Wealth, and Happiness of Mankind* deals with the ways in which humanity earns its living at the present day. These three works form together a first draft of the necessary humanistic[19] education of the future,

---

16   A writer on contemporary public issues.

17   I. e., the Great War.

18   Of or pertaining to the first age of the world.

19   Of or pertaining to a belief or outlook emphasising common human needs and seeking solely rational ways of solving human problems, and concerned with humankind as responsible and progressive intellectual beings.

and in the writing of them the author's distinctive political ideas have gained clarity and precision.

The present work, which replaces an earlier sketch called *The Open Conspiracy*, contains the general conclusions of this mind-clearing process. It is a plan of world reconstruction made necessary by science and conceived in the scientific spirit. It does not claim to start a new movement. It is presented as a statement of a general tendency which its author perceives in the minds of intelligent contemporaries.

Mr Wells maintains that the changes in the scale of effective human association which have been brought about by scientific discovery necessitate certain wide innovations in social structure and policy if mankind is to survive, let alone to profit fully by the possibilities which modern knowledge holds out. The realisation of these innovations, he asserts, is likely to become an increasing preoccupation of intelligent people the world over; and in the service of these developing ideas we may hope to find expression and significance for our individual lives.

To this convergence of the creative intelligence of our race upon the political problems which science has set us to solve Mr Wells gives the name of 'The Open Conspiracy'; *conspiracy* because it is conceived as a revolutionary movement paying no superstitious respect to established constitutional usage, and *open* because its principal method is the frank discussion and publicly announced intention which have long been the practice of the scientific world. His proposal is that constructively-minded people should deliberately and progressively possess themselves of the nerve-centres of the world in order to establish a responsible world directorate in control of human affairs.

The first necessity for the Open Conspiracy arises from the technical evolution of modern warfare. What in pre-scientific ages was a relatively harmless bickering of governments has now become a danger which threatens the very life of civilised mankind; and the sixty or seventy sovereign States, with their arms and flags and their propaganda of specialist loyalties, have proved themselves an impossible method of government in a world which every day becomes more complete in its interdependence. The Open Conspirator, therefore, will work for the ending of war in the only way whereby war can be made finally impossible: by the ending of national governments the peculiar sovereignty of which consists in their right of ultimate resort to arms.

It is not only war, however, which science has rendered inadmissible in the modern world. The industrial and financial anarchy[20] which condemns that world to penury in the presence of plenty must also give place to comprehensive

---

20   A society in which formal government does not exist and individuals are absolute free.

and responsible direction. Our major economic concerns, such as credit, fuel, power, transport, and food, can no longer be left to chaotic competitive production on an alleged basis of profit-seeking. They must become the objects of organised production for use.

This, however, does not mean that these matters must be subject to popularly elected committees or councils or parliaments at the mercy of an ill-informed and only intermittently attentive electorate. Mr Wells maintains that real control should be in the hands of those who are sufficiently interested to exercise it seriously and competently. This control should be rendered responsible, not through elections made ridiculous by the arts of the politician, but through public criticism such as at present prevails in the scientific world. This rather startling proposal, which breaks sharply both with political and with industrial practice in Britain, merits a much more careful examination than is possible here. It recalls certain features of the social organisation of the Soviet Union[21] and the Italian Corporative State[22] – neither of which can be dismissed as a mere tyranny – and is curiously paralleled by a suggestion put forward some years ago over the signature of Mr Lloyd George, that industrial concerns should be made responsible simply by the statutory publication of very full information about their activities.

In the third place, the Open Conspirator must take account of population in a way which no previous statesmanship has dared to do. He must take steps to prevent any such uncontrolled increase in numbers as would cash in mere low-grade proliferation the material abundance which science offers to mankind. It is suggested that universal knowledge of contraceptive methods, combined with quite minor changes in our social and economic arrangements, would relieve us of the present fear of over-population even in India and the East, and would also rob the practice of birth control of its dysgenic[23] effects.

The Open Conspirator thus comes into necessary conflict with various religious and obscurantist[24] bodies, which at present seek to restrict the use of these important inventions in human biology. This, because of the value he attaches to free, abundant, and competent discussion and to the fullest diffusion of authenticated knowledge, he will in no wise regret. He will welcome also every opportunity to foster sound non-tendentious education. He will make no truce with

---

21 A federal Communist state of Eurasia from 1922 to 1991.
22 More commonly, corporate state, a state theoretically governed by representatives not of geographical areas but of vocational corporations of the employers and employees in each industry.
23 Exerting a detrimental effect on later generations; tending to racial degeneration.
24 Being opposed to reform and enlightenment.

those who seek to use the common schools[25] to inculcate nationalism or obstructive theological dogmas, or who set up barriers against the dissemination of modern knowledge. He will work for an education which will liberate minds instead of repressing them, and will answer the natural curiosities of questing youth by telling, as completely as contemporary knowledge makes possible, the place and task of the new generation in the world-wide drama of mankind.

There is nothing essentially new about all this. The dream of a world ordered and peaceful, of mankind deliberately grasping its opportunities and rising to the measure of its great occasions, has gleamed ever and again in literature and statecraft since the Hebrew[26] prophet spoke of nations which 'should learn war no more'.[27] What *is* new is the sense of urgency, of an imminent choice between world order and a disastrous retrogression from all the fine possibilities of the present day; and the conviction that a growing minority of intelligent people must add to there personal concerns an overriding solicitude about the unification of the world, must work for it and shape there careers towards it, and find in the promise of it there justification and significance.

---

25   State-supported schools.

26   Of an ancient people who lived in Canaan during the second millennium BC and who inhabited present-day Israel, both banks of the river Jordan, Sinai, Lebanon and coastal Syria.

27   This is a misquotation from the Old Testament Bible, Isaiah 2: 4, 'shall they learn war any more'.

2.19: *The Science of Life*

'Biology for All' (23 March 1929).[1]

The Science of Life. By H. G. Wells, Julian Huxley and G. P. Wells. To be completed in about 30 fortnightly Parts. Part 1. Pp. 32. (London: The Amalgamated Press, Ltd., 1929.) 1s. 3d. each Part.

A new educational venture of great attractiveness is *The Science of Life*, an exposition of biology, by Mr H. G. Wells, Prof. Julian Huxley, and Mr G. P. Wells, a young physiologist, son of the senior author. The work aims at doing for biological science what Mr H. G. Wells did for history in his famous *Outline*,[2] giving to the unlearned a vivid presentation of the essential data. It is to try to be 'clear, complete, and correct': and if the triumvirate[3] cannot do this, who can? There is wisdom in having three authors (tres faciunt collegium[4]); for there is always the possibility of a majority when opinions differ.

We cannot read Part 1 of this serial without envying those who are coming to biology in these days; for the presentation is so picturesque and gripping. Academic formalities have been thrown off without jettisoning accuracy, and everything is discussed in its bearing on everyday life. The increased availability of science promises well for the future, for it is one of the most hopeful lines of human progress that we should become more and more able to utilise our heritage of well-established knowledge.

If we were asked what every young student should know when beginning his voyage of life after schooldays, we should answer – (1) the most significant steps in the history of the human race: (2) how to find his way about in the world of Nature: and (3) the laws of health and happiness. We are not thinking at present of brain-stretching disciplines like mathematics, or of character-forming influences like poesy,[5] but of sheer knowledge. We can see that this *Science of Life* is going to help powerfully towards an understanding of animate Nature on one hand, and towards an understanding of the conditions of health and happiness on the other. We wish it the success it deserves.

The present part begins with the nature of life, a difficult problem to start with. But it is treated very concretely and with an interesting historical background. In any event the reader feels that if this is biology, he wishes some more. Then the story turns to the everyday life of the body – in mouse and in

---

1   Reprinted by permission from Macmillan Publishers Ltd: *Nature* (123: 3099), copyright (1929).

2   A reference to Wells's *The Outline of History* (1920).

3   A group of three people in a position of authority.

4   Latin, 'three makes company'.

5   Poetry.

man; and when this can be made vividly interesting, as here, we cannot have too much of it. It is tragic to think of the vast number of young people who leave school without any understanding of their bodily functions. Such ignorance may have been bliss, though we doubt it, long ago, when all the ways of living were more natural, but to-day it often means disaster. We do not wish to suggest that the new book is particularly designed for young people – though they will welcome it – for it appeals to all who wish more science for more life. In spite of all the expositors, it has to be confessed that a large proportion of the population remains in the Dark Ages[6] as regards the working of their bodies.

There are very effective and interesting illustrations, and the frontispiece shows a crowd of skeletons receding into the distance before the light of microscopy and biochemistry.[7] This we take to mean that necrology[8] will be recessive[9] and biology dominant throughout the book. We trust that this will be so, but it has been our sad experience that the skeleton shows great persistence in its efforts to sneak back to the feast. But all success to the triumvirate!

'Biology and Human Life' (28 March 1931).[10]

The Science of Life. By H. G. Wells, Julian Huxley and G. P. Wells. Pp. xvi + 896. (London, Toronto, Melbourne and Sydney: Cassell and Co., Ltd., 1931.) 21*s.* net.

This is in several ways a remarkable book, as its authorship would lead us to expect, for it gives us in one volume a competent comprehensive survey of the whole of biology – physiological, morphological, embryological, and evolutionary; it is written so that it can be 'understanded of the people'[11] and with a sparkle that engages the attention; and it is one of the few books, heralded by Sir Richard Gregory's *Discovery*, which make the reader feel that science is not only

---

6   The early mediaeval period between the fall of Rome and the appearance of vernacular documents (476 to c. 1000); a metaphor for any age of ignorance.

7   The branch of science that deals with the chemical and physico-chemical processes which occur in living organisms.

8   The history of the dead or extinct.

9   A characteristic, carried in both parents' genes (in a dormant form), which is passed on to their offspring but which remains dormant.

10   Reprinted by permission from Macmillan Publishers Ltd: *Nature* (127: 3204), copyright (1931).

11   A quotation from article 24 of the 'Thirty-Nine Articles of the Church of England' which decrees that church services should be spoken in the language of the congregation.

298

for illumination but also for 'the relief of man's estate',[12] as Bacon phrased it. If, as we believe, mankind is at the dawn of a new era, when an all-round appeal will be made to the biological sciences, as already to the physical, for guidance in the control of human life – then the big book of Wells, Huxley, and Wells will come to be regarded as an instalment of the relevant 'Law and Prophets'.[13] Along with biology, we are, of course, including psychology, for these two sciences are becoming almost as inseparable as chemistry and physics. No doubt the last scientific word will be with sociology; but that science, though born two millennia ago, has not yet come of age.

It may be said that the appeal to biology began very long ago when the early patients sought the aid of the early physicians; but this was an appeal to an art rather than to a science. For, while many of the physicians, from Hippocrates to Galen onwards, were biologically-minded in a high degree, biology is a modern science and a wide spread appeal to biology as a science is still incipient. The recent establishment of a professorship of social biology[14] in the University of London[15] is a natural supplement to a eugenics laboratory,[16] both expressing a movement of which Galton and Pasteur were pioneers. Thus, while we appreciate *The Science of Life* for its wide reach, its educative lucidity, its fair-mindedness, its freshness of presentation, its arresting figures, and so on, we appreciate it most because the authors have had the courage of their convictions and have not hesitated to proclaim, as their particular gospel, that the utilisation of biological knowledge can do much to save man amid his sea of troubles. We do not mean that this book stands alone in this respect; but it is perhaps the largest comprehensive treatise in which 'biology for life' is a dominant note. Cowdry's *Human Biology and Racial Welfare* (1930) is, to our thinking, a fine collection of specialised propagandist tracts; but the book before us is a treatise on biology, written primarily for the scientific instruction of the people, yet ever sounding the note of practical applicability. It would have pleased T. H. Huxley, who was so clearly convinced of the indispensableness of applying science to life, declaring 'that there is no alleviation for the sufferings of mankind except veracity of thought and of action, and the resolute facing of the world as it is'.[17] The same

---

12 A quotation from Francis Bacon's *Of the Proficience and Aduancement of Learning* (1605).

13 The whole of the Bible, including Old and New Testaments, or in this instance a secular equivalent in the making.

14 Commonly, socio-biology, the branch of science which deals with the biological, especially ecological and evolutionary, aspects of social behaviour.

15 Created in 1930 at the London School of Economics.

16 A reference to the Francis Galton Laboratory for National Eugenics, University College, London (1907-45).

17 A quotation from Huxley's 'Autobiography' (1893).

idea was finely expressed in a convincing address on Jan. 23 last by Sir Walter Morley Fletcher, which ended with the prophetic sentence 'that we can find safety and progress only in proportion as we bring into our methods of statecraft the guidance of biological truth'.[18]

It is time, however, to give some indication of the scope of this big book; and that is not difficult, for there is a progressive plan. It begins, physiologically, with the living body; it surveys, morphologically, the forms or patterns of life; it insists that the key to intelligibility is the concept of evolution; it discusses the factors in individual development and in racial history (ontogeny and phylogeny[19]); it sketches the ascent of life throughout the ages, the adventures and achievements of the ever-changing Proteus.[20] Then the book begins again, as it were, from the vantage-ground it has gained, and envisages the pageant and drama of life – a fine introduction to ecology. But the drama has its tragic side and this leads to a consideration of disease and the present very chequered health of *Homo sapiens*, who so often belies his specific name. But the activities, the ascent, the adventure, and the drama of life have all their subjective aspect, as real as the objective, though more elusive, and the eighth book of the treatise deals with behaviour, feeling, and thought, leading on to a tentative monistic theory[21] (not so far from the ancient hylozoism![22]) – the conception of 'a single universal world-stuff with both material and mental aspects, of which, so far as we know, life is the crowning elaboration, and human thought, feeling, and willing the highest expression yet attained'. The concluding 'Book' deals with the biology of man, and, with a bow to sociology, ends on a melioristic[23] note – 'Life under Control'.

The Science of Life rather disarms criticism by its frankness and sincerity and by its freedom from dogma. Thus, in discussing the trans-scientific question of purpose in or behind evolution, the authors state (1) the view 'of Bergson and Shaw' that organisms work out their own evolution purposively, if not even purposefully; and (2) 'the Creationism[24]-up-to-date' of some modernist[25] theolo-

---

18   Fletcher's address was entitled 'Biology and Statecraft' and was broadcast over the BBC, being noticed anonymously in *Nature* in 'News and Views' (1931, 172).

19   Properly, phylogenesis, the evolutionary development of a species or other group of organisms through a succession of forms.

20   In Greek mythology, a sea god capable of taking various forms at will.

21   A theory of thought which recognises a single ultimate principle.

22   The doctrine that all matter has life or that life is merely a property of matter.

23   Pertaining to the doctrine that the world may be made significantly better by rightly-directed human effort.

24   The theory which attributes the origin of matter, biological species, etc., to a special creation rather than to evolution.

gians,[26] that the world of life is the realisation of a divine purpose, which was dynamically embodied in the original institution of the order of Nature. When the reader has got these post-Paleyian[27] views before him as clearly as may be, he is told that *The Science of Life* must say 'No' to the first theory, and cannot say 'Yes' or 'No' to the second. Personally, we are not inclined to be bluffed by a too abstract science, as if it were the only pathway towards truth; but we must admit that the authors occupy a clear-headed and reasonable position – that biology, as biology, has no pronouncement to make on the reality of the philosophical or religious concept of a purpose behind evolution.

Though the book runs to nearly 900 pages, that is not much for an appreciation of the whole gamut of life. So we are not inclined to say that there should have been more about enzymes[28] and less about the humorous 'Margery' and the teleplasm[29] she produces from her mouth. We are sure that the authors must have thought out very carefully what seemed to them the best utilisation of the available space; and their restraint, relaxed just a little perhaps for 'Margery', is admirable.

In reading this remarkably successful presentation of the essentials of biology, our pleasure has been occasionally interrupted by finding a crumpled roseleaf; but it is in no carping mood that we give just a few illustrations. *The Science of Life* is certainly not an apsychic[30] biology, yet why does it insist that the body is a machine, and elaborate a comparison which eventually has to be withdrawn as inadequate? Similarly with the use of the word 'mechanism' for the nervous system and the like. The authors are all right, but will their readers be? If biologists say 'machine' often enough, people will begin to believe that they mean what they say. In this particular case, we think that would be a pity, for we believe with the authors that an organism is more than mechanism.

---

25 Pertaining to a usage, mode of expression, peculiarity of style, etc., characteristic of modern times.

26 Scholars of the organised body of knowledge dealing with the nature, attributes and governance of God.

27 A later advocate and interpreter of the ideas of William Paley or of his rationalist and utilitarian moral philosophy and his theology which styled God as the supreme craftsman in a mechanistic universe.

28 Proteins produced by living cells and functioning as catalysts in a specific biochemical reaction.

29 A mysterious vapour- or jelly-like substance apparently exuded from a medium's body for a distance during a seance, sometimes being moulded into recognisable shapes.

30 A coined expression used to mean mechanical, or without intelligence or consciousness.

A larger crumpled roseleaf is the picture of random variations[31] and blind selection.[32] No doubt there are saving clauses and corrective illustrations, but some readers will be apt to relapse to the old nightmare view of evolution as a chapter of accidents, which it certainly is not. For many variations are orthogenic;[33] and many are obviously congruent with the already established organic architecture and metabolic routine. Many express themselves in accordance with laws of growth and conditions of organic stability. How many plant variations in the present (and presumably in the irrecoverable past) are shortenings or elongations of the vegetative or floral axis! Similarly, many animal variations are shortenings-down or lengthenings-out of particular arcs on the general life-curve or trajectory. And so on at great length, for the authors know well that a very strong case can be made out for the frequency of definiteness in variation.

Then as to natural selection, it is inadequately summed up in such words as 'automatic' and 'blind'. How often the organism tries to play its hand of hereditary cards, endeavouring after well-being. It is often automatically selected, but it often deliberately selects. Many an able-minded bird or mammal is a factor in its own evolution, though it has no prevision of more than an immediate goal. Again, the general reader requires to be told that the everyday natural selection of nuance variations, though in a sense 'blind', is a sifting in relation to an already established *systema Naturae*[34] of intricate and stabilised inter-relations.

Then again, while we agree with a useful passage on the seamy side of evolution, which certainly includes, as Ray Lankester so well insisted,[35] its degenerations[36] and retrogressions as well as its advancements and achievements, we cannot agree with the statement that 'we find throughout the rest of life parallels to the diseases that haunt our own'. On the contrary, we are prepared to defend the thesis that wild Nature (that is, apart from man's interference) is characteristically marked by exuberant positive health, while in civilised society diseases are rife and sub-health is becoming almost normal!

---

31   Minor differences among the individual organisms in a population that are random and thus without foresight for the uses to which they may be put in the course of evolution.

32   In biological evolution, a term to express the survival of some species and extinction of others where no apparent adaptive advantage is detected.

33   Properly, orthogenetic, pertaining to evolutionary change in one direction, especially as supposedly caused internal tendency rather than external influence.

34   The hierarchical classification of species, as determined by the Carolus Linnaeus in his 1735 eponymous work.

35   A reference to Lankester's *Degeneration* (1880).

36   In biological evolution, changes towards a simpler structure or a less active form.

But enough of these minor criticisms, for we welcome the book with heartiness. It is an achievement of popular exposition in the best sense (and many professional biologists would do well to read it); it is written with learning and lucidity, and permeated with the idea of evolution, including a human evolution which will continue the more rapidly the more it is inspired by the science of life.

'The Living World' (18 September 1937).[37]

'Science of Life' Series by H. G. Wells, Julian Huxley and G. P. Wells. Vol. 1: *The Living Body*. Pp. xi + 223. Vol. 2: *Patterns of Life*. Pp. x + 239. Vol. 3: *Evolution – Fact and Theory*. Pp. x + 271. Vol. 4: *Reproduction, Heredity and the Development of Sex*. Pp. x + 222. Vol. 5: *The History and Adventure of Life*. Pp. x + 259. Vol. 6: *The Drama of Life*. Pp. x + 316. Vol. 7: *How Animals Behave*. Pp. x + 263. Vol. 8: *Man's Mind and Behaviour*. Pp. x + 271. Vol. 9: *Biology of the Human Race*. Pp. ix + 205. (London, New York, Toronto and Melbourne: Cassell and Co., Ltd., 1934-1937.) 4*s*. net each.

We confess that we commenced to read with a certain prejudice, for we thought of the many distinguished authors who combined to write the 'International Science Series'[38] and cheaper 'Primers'[39] of still earlier date. Each wrote on his own speciality, and we assumed a certain value in this. We were sceptical in respect to this combination of literary capacity, of imagination and of learning, perhaps expecting that the latter on account of its 'youthfulness' would not be allowed its full play. However, we found ourselves reading Volume 1 on a train journey, and a volume has been our inseparable companion on all such for the last three months. We admit 'second childhood'[40] with its consequent loss of memory – and thus our reading gave us pleasure, point following point as to life and the methods thereof, in such definite order that they produced in us a happy restfulness, not the boredom that induces sleep. We found a well-authenticated story and could read without the worry of hybrid names, too often coined to glorify an author rather than of necessity. 'We ought to have a name for it.' 'Why?' 'Well, someone else will give one, anyhow!' Far from valid reasoning.

Our authors are so merged that they might have been one. They start with *The Living Body* – and it is the human body – a machine reacting to its varied

---

37 Reprinted by permission from Macmillan Publishers Ltd: *Nature* (140: 3542), copyright (1937).

38 A popular science series, devised by Edward Youmans and published by Kegan Paul, Trench and Co. in London and D. Appleton and Co. in New York from 1871 to 1910. It was edited by T. H. Huxley, John Tyndall and Herbert Spencer.

39 Small introductory textbooks.

40 Childlike playfulness in an adult.

surroundings, its driver a nervous system, and efficient so long as it is properly fuelled and cleaned, until in course of time it wears out. This leads naturally to the various 'patterns' affected by animals and plants, and then our attention is directed to the way in which they may have been evolved. We are not allowed to assume without ample evidence the overwhelming positions of evolution and natural selection, which sometimes are rejected owing to man's pride or fear. 'Heredity' is all-important here, reproduction, sex and the body changes as the individual grows – a happily written and clear series of essays.

The History and Adventure of Life, weaving it into the conditions of each geological stratum, naturally appeals, but a map showing the proportional length of time of each period is not accessible where we want it, the table given devoting two-thirds of its length to man, its post-war[41] column especially in our opinion being out of place; this we disliked, but we found the rest of the volume corrective and admirable. The *Drama of Life* is scarcely a self-explanatory title for life in the sea and on the land and in its waters, and the swaying balance between the animals and plants in communities (ecology). To us this quite learned volume shows a curious lack of those personal and humorous touches which we had become accustomed to expect, and which recur in full measure in the consideration of 'behaviour' – a separate volume is devoted to man – and of the *Biology of the Human Race*.

Our suggestion to parents who have children going to a university for any science course, and to teachers, is to use these volumes so that their children or pupils may be educated, not merely crammed. There are nine of them, one for the summer vacation before the first term, and then one in each vacation until the student sits for final honours.[42] The examinational result – whether the student is biologist, physicist or chemist – a certain understanding, will be great, and the candidate will have something which will add permanently to his interest in life, and will help him in his relationship with his fellows and his community.

The series is a reproduction in convenient form of the volume entitled *Science of Life*, originally published in 1929 and reviewed in *Nature* of March 28, 1931; the separate and handy little volumes now before us have been appearing at intervals since 1934.

---

41 I. e., following the Great War.

42 The last examinations of an undergraduate course which determine whether the student is awarded an honours degree.

2.20: *The Work, Wealth and Happiness of Mankind*
'Social Economics' (16 April 1932).[1]

The Work, Wealth and Happiness of Mankind. By H. G. Wells. Pp. xiii + 850 + 32 plates. (London: William Heinemann, Ltd., 1932.) 10*s*. 6*d*. net.

Mr Wells writes of himself: 'He is attempting a book, a survey of the world, a scheme and map of *doing*, which will enable him to say to anyone whatever: "This is the whole world of work and wealth, of making and getting and spending, and here at this point is your place, and this is where you come in...."' Seeking Mr Wells's place in his own scheme, we find that he claims for his book the function of transmitting, correlating, and interpreting for the general mind the essential living thought of the world. In his *Outline of History* and *Science of Life* he attempted this task for history and for biology; now it is the turn of economics and sociology. Mr Wells holds that mankind's ideology,[2] or system of ideas about life in general, has become dangerously out of date, and out of correspondence with the realities of human affairs, since the 'change of scale', the 'abolition of distance',[3] of the last few decades. He regards as essential for a modern ideology some understanding of world history (as against local, national, and period history), some assimilation of biological ideas, and – most urgently necessary of all – some conception of economic life, industrial processes, trade, and finance. Valiantly he has attempted to supply all three sides of this ideological triangle, and his third compendium, like its forerunners, is a remarkable, stimulating, valuable, and most readable book.

In the development of a modern ideology, the first step, says Mr Wells, is to learn to think. 'Most of us do not think enough about thinking.' Children and primitive peoples do a large part of their thinking by imagination; their thinking is a spontaneous, uncontrolled flow of images, with which impulses to act are connected. There is no critical element, and scarcely any use of generalisations or abstract ideas. Things not themselves physically real are apprehended in a symbolical and often a personified form. The thinking of many adults is still of this kind, corresponding to what has been called the 'mythological'[4] phase of human development. This was followed by the gradual appearance of exacter

---

1   Reprinted by permission from Macmillan Publishers Ltd: *Nature* (129: 3259), copyright (1932).

2   A system of ideas or way of thinking regarded as justifying actions and especially to be maintained irrespective of events.

3   A phrase used frequently by Wells from October 1898 in 'Mr Ledbetter's Vacation' onwards to denote the geopolitical changes brought about by the industrial and technological revolutions of the nineteenth century which facilitated rapid movement and virtually instantaneous communication throughout the world.

4   Pertaining to mythology, a misinterpretation or fabulation of the truth.

discrimination; the mythological passed insensibly into the metaphorical;[5] abstraction became possible; classification and examination of ideas began, and 'logical' thinking[6] followed.

> This change from a mental life that was merely experience-checked imagining to an analytical mental life aiming at new and better knowledge and leading on to planned and directed effort, is still in progress.... Over a large range of his interests man has still to acquire the habits of thinking with self-control and precision.' 'The man who orders his knowledge and thinks things out is as far above the natural man of impulse and traditional usage as the latter is above an ape which has not even tradition but only instinct.[7]

Logical thinking, however, contains in itself a pitfall: Are words as true as material facts, or truer, or less true? If they are truer, then a logical conclusion is truer than an experience, and that, on the whole, was the 'Realist'[8] assumption of classical and medieval times, the view that classes or Platonic ideas[9] were the only reality, the view which nowadays is sometimes loosely called 'Idealism'.[10] Realism was opposed by the 'Nominalists',[11] for whom an experience is truer than a word. The defeat of philosophical Realism over large areas of human interest in the late Middle Ages and after was a necessary preliminary to the release of experimental science, and to the material triumphs following on the application of the scientific method of 'trying back to facts' all the time.

> The discovery of Evolution, the realisation, that is to say, that there are no strict limits set to animal and vegetable species, opened the whole world of life and its destiny to Nominalist thinking. The realisation by the world of mathematical physics that the universe can be represented as a four-dimensional universe of unique events has abolished the conception of a quantitative equivalence of cause and effect and made every atom unique.

---

5   Not literal, figurative.

6   Reasoning based on inference and scientific deduction.

7   An innate, usually fixed pattern of behaviour in most animals in response to certain stimuli.

8   In opposition to Nominalist, one who believes that universals have an objective or absolute existence.

9   The philosophy or doctrine of Plato or of his followers.

10   In philosophy, any of various systems of thought in which the object of external perception is held to consist of ideas not resulting from any unperceived material substance.

11   Believers in the notion that universals or abstract concepts are mere names without any corresponding reality.

The detachment of logical thinking from the Realist predispositions of the human mind remains, however, incomplete, and in the world of international politics the Realist way of thinking holds almost undisputed sway and lies at the root of the greatest dangers that threaten our race.[12]

Plainly the man who takes the Nominalist way and regards such a word as 'France' as merely covering a great area of country, climatic and social associations, and about forty million human beings of very diverse kinds (numbers of them not even speaking French) will regard international politics from an entirely different angle from a Realist who finds in the word France something more real and vital than any single individual or thing that contributes to the ensemble of that idea.... The Nominalist and Realist of contemporary life, all unaware of this difference in the very elements of their thought, find each the other stupefyingly obtuse.... The Realist 'patriot' calls his brother Nominalist 'traitor' or 'cosmopolitan scoundrel', and the like, and is amazed that he does not wince; the Nominalist humanitarian[13] calls the Realist, obdurate dogmatist[14] or romanticist,[15] and accuses him of a perverse taste for contention and blood.

Mr Wells, then, would have mankind abandon emotional for logical thinking, and in logical thinking beware of 'Realist' assumptions and remember the fruitfulness of the scientific appeal to fact. His early chapters recite some of the practical triumphs of science; the conquest of materials – iron and steel, rubber, petroleum, dyes, drugs, cellulose[16] – the conquest of power, the organisation of transport, the transmission of facts, the application of artificial fertilisers[17] and mechanical methods to agriculture, all the modern developments in the feeding and clothing and housing of mankind. He discusses the ways in which work is organised, and then turns aside to inquire why people work. He divides mankind into three classes, according to their guiding idea of themselves, or 'persona'; the 'peasant', characterised by the idea that toil is virtue, and by intense acquisitiveness; the 'aggressive nomad',[18] generous, reckless, and rapacious; and the

---

12   I. e., the human race.

13   A person advocating or practising humane action.

14   One who holds a narrow-minded assertion of a belief or opinion and who disregards alternative positions.

15   One tending towards romantic views.

16   A polymeric carbohydrate which forms the main constituent of the cell walls of plants, or a compound of this.

17   A natural or artificially prepared substance containing nitrogen, phosphorous or potassium added to soil in order to fertilise it.

18   One who leads a roaming or wandering life.

'educated' man, originally priestly in function, who works not for his own enrichment, or for his own honour and glory, but who is devoted to some end transcending personal considerations. With the peasant type and derived from it, Mr Wells places the peasant-minded townsman, giving rise on the one hand to a crop of 'petty' and 'big bourgeois', and on the other to a multitude of 'expropriated'[19] proletarians who have lost their grip upon property.

The peasant persona and its modifications will tend to cause the possessor to work for personal gain, the nomad persona for personal glory, the educated persona for some ideal of service. Mr Wells denies the Individualist creed that the peasant-craving for tangible property generally is a fundamental incentive to work: 'The human animal wants the feeling of security and it wants freedom and the feeling of power. These wants are truly fundamental.' The experience of the educated types shows, he thinks, that the satisfaction of these desires can be guaranteed in quite other ways than the actual possession of land, wife, children, goods, and chattels.[20] With the extension of literacy, the mentality of the learned clerk begins to penetrate everywhere, carrying its traditional disposition to find the satisfaction of good achievement greater than the satisfaction of possessions. The search for security, comfort, and liberty becomes the ruling motive in keeping mankind busy.

Mr Wells pauses to note a common confusion between independence and liberty: 'independence is no doubt being abolished ... in the case of individuals just as in the case of sovereign states, but independence is not freedom. An "independent" peasant or small tradesman is tied, with scarcely a day's holiday, to his cultivation or his shop.' But the worker under modern conditions has real personal freedom in the way of daily leisure, holidays, choice of activities and purchases. To provide such modern satisfactions, and to free himself from tangible burthensome ownership, man has made use of the abstraction of a monetary system. Mr Wells discusses currency, financial methods, banking, and investment, and gives an account of the world depression[21] with the monetary factors well emphasised. He describes recent proposals for monetary reform,[22] indicating here, as in many other parts of the book, the imperative need for international action.

---

19   Having suffered the loss of one's property for personal use by another.

20   Movable or transferable possessions.

21   A severe economic slump triggered by the American stock exchange crash of 29 October 1929 and which spread from the USA throughout the world. Its effects were felt throughout the 1930s, though its nadir occurred between 1929 and 1933.

22   Wells cites such monetary reformers as J. M. Keynes ('a barometric currency based on an index number'), J. F. Darling ('the remonetization of silver through an Imperial bimetallic standard of value') and Robert Eisler ('a world money of account').

The closing chapters bring him again to education, and to his reiterated thesis that a civilised World State can only develop in correlation with the spread of the 'educated' persona, with the replacement of the motives of profit and privilege by the motive of service in affairs of every kind. Such a co-operative outlook has become essential; nothing less than world planning for political and economic change can avert disaster. Mr Wells is optimistic enough to believe in the necessary educability of mankind, for is not educability the main distinguishing characteristic of *Homo sapiens*?

If *The Work, Wealth and Happiness of Mankind* is not on the whole as satisfactory as the *Outline of History* or the *Science of Life*, the defect is probably inherent in the less developed state of economic science as compared with history or biology, and perhaps also in our more primitive type of thought on economic subjects. One misses those diagrams and tables which were so useful a feature of the two earlier books, and which are replaced by a few casually selected photographs in the present volume. Yet Mr Wells has given us what is likely to remain for a long time the most comprehensive and lucid account available of the tangled complexity of economic processes in their human aspect, and the ways in which those processes are affected by the decisions we all have to make.

2.21: *After Democracy*

R. Brightman, 'The Cost of a New World Order' (11 February 1933).[1]

After Democracy: Addresses and Papers on the Present World Situation. By H. G. Wells. Pp. vii + 247. (London: Watts and Co., 1932.) 7*s.* 6*d.* net.

In this volume of essays, all the product of the last three years, we have the revelation of the thoughts on our present discontents of a student of science[2] turned publicist and perhaps the most qualified of living writers to express either the implications of the scientific outlook in the life of society or the responsibilities which fall on the shoulders of scientific workers.

There is little sequence or relation between the essays other than that conferred by the author's outlook. They range from parliamentary government, economics, planning and world peace to divorce and morals. Each subject is touched upon in the same open-mindedness and readiness to accept the consequences of change and development. Mr Wells reiterates repeatedly the significant facts which our whole system of government and industry are still disposed to burke – the abolition of distance, the growth of human life into a world-wide community of interdependent human beings – and he has no patience with the prejudices or the stupidity which refuse to accept the situation and to meet the consequences, above all with the neglect of the sovereign governments of the world to accommodate themselves to this fusion of once separate economic systems.

This impatience is apt at times to lead to excessive depreciation of factors which may have real value in the scientific order of society which he visualises as essential for the security of mankind. Thus Mr Wells's denunciation of the evils of nationalism, and his exposure of its persistent menace alike to world peace and to the economic structure of mankind, lead him to repudiate internationalism almost as forcefully. Is this either logical or wise? The international spirit as evidenced in certain forms of world co-operation, such as the health work of the League of Nations,[3] shows itself at least as practicable as the cosmopolitanism to which Mr Wells leans so strongly and is at least as likely to promote the development of the sense of world citizenship. A sense of civic and municipal responsibility or pride can be a national asset provided it does not displace or overshadow the larger and greater loyalty to the State as a whole. Nor need we assume that if we succeed in stripping our national governments of

---

1   Reprinted by permission from Macmillan Publishers Ltd: *Nature* (131: 3302), copyright (1933).

2   A reference to Wells's biological training at the Normal School of Science (1884-87) and his bachelor of science qualification from the University of London (1891).

3   A reference to the League of Nations' Health Organisation (1921-46) which worked on international health questions such as vaccination and inoculation programmes.

their militant manifestations, whether in military pageantry, armaments or tariffs, the national units may not learn to co-operate effectively and wisely for the good of mankind as a whole. The League at least offers a framework for constructive work, once the militancy of national governments has been replaced by a spirit of co-operation alike in the direction of a world police force[4] or a world economic policy.

So, too, Mr Wells's well-founded distrust of nationalism leads him to deny or ignore all its spiritual aspects and the rich contribution to civilisation made within the national framework. To the thinker, no doubt the vision of a world State and the allegiance of world citizenship may make a direct and a nobler appeal. But to lesser minds, the lesser loyalties may be more concrete, and rightly orientated may make the more effective appeal. We may yet see the day when the ordinary citizen is proud of his country according to her reputation for honourable dealing and co-operation in the world comity of nations in the same way that he is careful of his own reputation as a just and law-abiding citizen.

If Mr Wells has dealt with internationalism with rather unmerited severity, his strictures on the rising tide of nationalism and the many agencies that minister to it are well deserved and should indeed be supported and echoed fearlessly by all who wish to see a scientific order of society. The most significant note in the book is indeed to be found in the emphasis placed on education. It is only as man comes to an accurate knowledge of his environment and relates his knowledge to that action that Mr Wells sees any hope for the future.

Nowhere in the book is this more clearly stated than in the address on 'Liberalism and the Revolutionary Spirit' and on 'The Common-sense of World Peace'. In a footnote to the former address[5] Mr Wells outlines again the ideas recently formulated under the title *The Open Conspiracy*. The basis of his 'Z Society'[6] is declared to be 'the discussion, study, research and propaganda of the sciences of social biology' and 'the effective application of their principles to the reorganisation and enlargement of human life'. This is nothing else than a challenge to honest, lucid thought about the facts of the situation, and that is basic for the liberation of the world from sectionalism whether national or lesser units are involved. So, too, the basis for world peace lies in the elimination of nationalist teaching and teachers everywhere – the development of a history teaching which leads us on to the great possibilities of the collective human future. 'We need an education that will turn mankind from tradition to hope'.

---

4   A proposed international agency of law enforcement independent of nation states and with its own sovereign powers (or controlled by a global agency with sovereign powers).

5   A reference to chapter two, 'Project of a Liberal World Organisation'.

6   An alternative name for Wells's 'open conspiracy'.

Here indeed Mr Wells is on firm ground, and if his appeal succeeds in stimulating the wide circle of readers, into whose hands his reputation should carry the book, into thinking out some of these implications for themselves, and into refusing to tolerate the wrong kind of teaching or the perpetuation of obsolete jealousies, and sectionalisms, the first steps towards the new order will have been taken. There is no need to dwell on Mr Wells's obvious failure to show how the minority dictatorship he conceives in his 'Z Society' is to succeed while conceding full freedom of thought and expression. Once the vigour of mind, the willingness to accept new situations, to discard old prejudices, which characterise the distinguished author of this book have gained a firm hold of the minds of men generally, we should be in a fair way to realise his vision. But time presses and the danger that before any such widespread movement of thought can occur our civilisation may have tottered to its ruin, is even more acute than Mr Wells suggests in his somewhat pessimistic sketch 'Our World in Fifty Years Time'. It is in fact difficult to see how the vested interests[7] blocking the way to world security can be overcome except as governments are captured through the rapid orientation of some major political party to the outlook for which he pleads. To that orientation scientific workers everywhere might even yet contribute the decisive factor.

---

7   Persons or organisations with personal interests in a state of affairs, usually with the expectation of gain.

2.22: *The Shape of Things to Come*

Lancelot Hogben, 'Mr Wells Comes Back' (21 October 1933).[1]

The Shape of Things to Come: the Ultimate Revolution. By H. G. Wells. Pp. 432. (London: Hutchinson and Co. (Publishers), Ltd., 1933.) 10*s.* 6*d.* net.

Few realise that there is no longer any biological reason why a man should cease to be creative before he is eighty. Those of us who admired the earlier Wells could watch with resignation the steep descent from the wistful and sanctimonious penitence of Mr Britling[2] to the hearty and eupeptic[3] prosperity of William Clissold.[4] We were accustomed to the phenomena of senescence[5] and had not yet taken stock of the possibilities of rejuvenation. The cremation of Clissold was scarcely completed before the whimsicality of Dr Moreau[6] was reborn in the person of Mr Blettsworthy.[7] Then followed the incarnation of Mr Parham[8] with a polished irony lacking in the earlier romances. As literature, the dream book of Dr Raven[9] surpasses anything which Mr Wells has written. It engenders the impulse to read aloud and to go on reading. Its pages have been composed with a tragic distinction of language only to found among contemporary writings in some pages of Bertrand Russell's *Principles of Social Reconstruction*, in Briffault's *Making of Humanity* or in the final saga of men on Neptune in Olaf Stapledon's *Last and First Men*. It has the passionate and intoxicating earnestness of the *Dictionnaire*.[10] It is pervaded by a kindliness which was lacking in Voltaire, a kindliness which never degenerates into the obese complacency so repugnant in the middle period of the author's work. It is more than a history. It is an historic testament.

---

1 Reprinted by permission from Macmillan Publishers Ltd: *Nature* (132: 3338), copyright (1933).

2 The title character of *Mr Britling Sees it Through* (1916). Although this novel was never reviewed in *Nature*, Richard Gregory, in a letter to Wells dated 2 October 1916, wrote of it that 'The book is *the* masterpiece [...]. There is not a single writer of this generation who has ever produced or is likely to produce such a work of literary art and constructive thought. [...] I see more than ever before how distinctly you differ from other writers; it is in the free admission that you give to the workshop of your mind. We are not presented with puppets on a wooden stage but with the actual thoughts of a real man'.

3 Having good digestion.

4 The title character of *The World of William Clissold* (1926).

5 The process or condition of growing old or ageing.

6 The title character of *The Island of Doctor Moreau* (1896).

7 The title character of *Mr Blettsworthy on Rampole Island* (1928).

8 The title character of *The Autocracy of Mr Parham* (1930).

9 *The Shape of Things to Come* is the transcription of Dr Philip Raven's dreams.

10 A reference to the *Dictionnaire philosophique* (1764) by François-Marie de Voltaire.

The writer of the dream book is living in a communist Utopia. Those worthy and sententious scoutmasters[11] and storm troop[12] leaders, the Samurai of a younger Wells, have withered away. At a safe distance of two centuries from the conflicts of our own time, he can afford to criticise the shortcomings of Marx or the Soviet policies like a liberal historian of the early twentieth century pronouncing judgement on John Knox or the Kingdom of God in Münster. Naturally his strictures will irritate those who insist on adopting the historical approach to everything but their own actions. Still more will they infuriate the self-satisfied and socially indifferent. We see the Pompeian streets of contemporary civilisation spread beneath the shadow of a menacing Vesuvius.[13] In the cold corridors of the museum, our mummified[14] remains are caught in the act of gesticulation or in the affectation of negligence. Those of us who have an all too simple plan for precipitating the seismic[15] fury which is about to break upon us, and those of us who proudly boast a refined indifference to the properties of incandescent lava, seem a little ridiculous to the serene onlooker. Few intelligent people will read the history without annoyance. No intelligent person will find it a dull book.

Throughout the first half the reader is carried along by the circumstantial inevitability of the events. The great halt to social progress in 1933[16] has already become history. That the bulk of educated mankind in Western Europe will acquiesce or participate in the recrudescence of barbarism,[17] and march back towards the Neolithic behind the swastika[18] emblem, seems scarcely less certain than if the tale had already reached its disastrous climax in the epidemics[19] which follow in the trail of the European War of 1940.[20] There are oases of deliberate comic relief.[21] Such is the incident which precipitates the call to arms, the ill-fitting dental plate, the orange pip or, it may be, a small fragment of walnut. The prelude to the emergence of the World State is a monument of moving

---

11   Leaders of a band of boy scouts.

12   A member of the Nazi political militia, the *Sturmabteilung*.

13   A volcano located east of Naples in Italy which destroyed Pompeii in 79.

14   Preserved through embalming and drying.

15   Of, pertaining to or connected with earthquakes or other tectonic movements.

16   A reference to the rise to power of the Nazi Party in Germany in January of that year.

17   An uncivilised nature or condition; uncultured ignorance; the absence of culture.

18   Properly, *Hakenkreuz*, the bent-cross symbol of the National Socialist German Workers Party and other similar parties in other countries.

19   Temporarily widespread diseases.

20   In *The Shape of Things to Come*, Wells predicts the outbreak of a second world war in 1940.

21   A comic episode in a work of literature intended to offset more serious portions.

prose. For six pages (pp. 275-281) of sustained and pregnant rhetoric[22] which may be remembered with the *Areopagitica*,[23] Wells pleads the defence of that troublesome but vital part of the machinery of social change, the crank.

Thereafter the recital lacks the cogency of detail in the earlier part. Maybe this is the author's intention. Among the ruins of Europe there are few records for the historian to use. Communication comes to a standstill and mechanical production almost ceases. Locally a few aeroplanes and aeroplane factories are salvaged, and these form the only apparatus of trade exchange. The workers and technicians of the Transport Union are not hide-bound to the old loyalties. From their aerial Hanseatic League[24] a world government[25] takes shape in 1965. The dream book Russia, somewhat hampered in its further cultural development by a conservative adherence to rigid dogmas which had served well enough in the pioneer stage of the planned economy,[26] is readily assimilated in a wider and more cosmopolitan project. Elsewhere the competitiveness of the Acquisitive Society[27] is morally and materially bankrupt. There are local rebellions and obstructions. They are half-hearted and ill-equipped against a civilisation which controls all backward and forward movements of people and produce.

In spite of the inveterate dislike which Mr Wells displays towards Karl Marx, and the equally strong antipathy which such speculations will evoke from present-day disciples of Marx, his forecast has a plausibility which is eminently reminiscent of the author of the *Eighteenth Brumaire*.[28] Not until the introduction of steam power[29] did the struggling Protestant democracies[30] of the sixteenth and seventeenth centuries become the pattern of a well-nigh universal type of government and economy. The imaginative drive of the recital is such that one may well expect the political critics of Mr Wells to blame him for in-

---

22   The art of using language so as to persuade or influence others.

23   By John Milton (1644).

24   An alliance of trading guilds that established and maintained a trade monopoly over the Baltic Sea, to a certain extent the North Sea, and most of northern Europe between the thirteenth and seventeenth centuries.

25   An alternative label for Wells's world state.

26   An economy in which industrial production and development, etc., are determined by an overall national plan.

27   An expression coined by Richard Tawney in his eponymous book (1921), it refers to the culture of capitalism which promotes material acquisitiveness, which Tawney believed to be morally wrong and a corrupting social influence due to the distortions of economic policy resulting from concentrated wealth.

28   A reference to Marx's *Eighteenth Brumaire of Louis Napoleon* (1898).

29   The force of steam applied to machinery.

30   Governments in which power resides in the people and is exercised by them either directly or by means of elected representatives.

venting a future which need not happen, if they heed his warning. It is a memorable warning, the more memorable because, like the familiar warning of the elder Pitt, it may be destined to fall on deaf ears.[31]

In the final chapters Wells justifies his claim to be regarded as the midwife of social biology. He steers a rational course between the naïve environmentalism[32] of some Marxists[33] and the paralysing Calvinism[34] of most eugenists. He does not picture the historic environment moulding to its pattern a species from which all gene differences have been mysteriously obliterated. He does not conjure up a mosaic of gene combinations miraculously regulating the developmental process in a perfect vacuum. He sees the procession of human beings of diverse capacities and various endowments making their several contributions to the future and interacting with one another within the limits set by a social framework prescribed by the efforts of past generations and constantly being changed by human activities. Because the limits are constantly shifting, because man is at once a highly variable organism and the most teachable of animals, education is the supreme business which may fittingly engage the services of the most gifted men and women. It is a process which could be extended from birth until death. Mr Wells gives an object lesson of this more spacious conception of our capacity for continued growth. As an artist and as a leader of thought he has come back at sixty-seven to a world in which the Youth Movements[35] are clamouring for reaction while his contemporaries are committed to inaction.

---

31 The ignorance of a request or suggestion.

32 The view that the environment, especially as opposed to heredity, has a dominant influence on the development of an individual or society.

33 Followers of the political and economic theories of Karl Marx which argue that, as labour is basic to wealth, historical development must lead to the violent overthrow of the capitalist class and the taking over of the means of production by the proletariat.

34 A theological system and an approach to Christian life that emphasises the rule of God over all things; also a rigidly principled approach to a subject.

35 Those movements aimed at organising young people into a unified identity, often with a moral or political intent.

2.23: *Experiment in Autobiography*

T. LL. H., 'Mr H. G. Wells Reveals Himself' (13 October 1934).[1]

Experiment in Autobiography: Discoveries and Conclusions of a Very Ordinary Brain (since 1866). By H. G. Wells. Vol. 1. Pp. 414 + 8 plates. (London: Victor Gollancz, Ltd., and The Cresset Press, Ltd., 1934.) 10*s.* 6*d.* net.

A curious post-war[2] phenomenon is the spate of autobiographies and 'ought-not-to-biographies'[3] issuing from the publishers. The diapason[4] of the War resounds in these books. Silent and abashed, we stand before the cenotaph.[5] Some dream-child whispers: 'What did you do, daddy, in the Great War?'[6] The hand gropes for the fountain-pen.[7] Others, like Elihu,[8] the son of Barachel,[9] feel their bellies as wine which hath no vent, ready to burst. 'I will speak that I may be refreshed.'[10] Mr H. G. Wells's reason is akin to Elihu's – 'to clear and relieve my mind'. He explains that he has spent a large part of his life's energy 'in a drive to make a practically applicable science out of history and sociology' (p. 26). A jewel has formed in his head and 'through its crystalline clearness, a plainer vision of human possibilities, and the condition of their attainment appears' leading to 'an undreamt-of fullness, freedom and happiness within reach of our species'. Vast changes in the educational, economic and directive structure of society will be necessary. Details are reserved for the second volume to be published in a few weeks.

This first volume gives only hints of Mr Wells's design for the new world he wishes to create. His life as a shop assistant, here realistically described, suggests a dream. The draper's shop. Enter a shabby old lady. 'Our new model? Certainly, *Moddom.*[11] That counter! Mr Wells, forward.' A not very impressive

---

1   Reprinted by permission from Macmillan Publishers Ltd: *Nature* (134: 3389), copyright (1934).

2   I. e., after the Great War.

3   An expression coined by Catherine Spence in her autobiography (2006, 149).

4   Range, spectrum, scope.

5   A sepulchral monument commemorating the dead of war.

6   A reference to the 1915 British recruitment poster designed by Savile Lumley and entitled 'Daddy, what did <u>YOU</u> do in the Great War?'.

7   A writing instrument in which the nib is constantly replenished with ink from a reservoir contained within it.

8   In the Old Testament Bible, Book of Job, an antagonist of Job in debate.

9   According to Job 32: 2-6, father of Elihu.

10   A reference to the Old Testament Bible, Book of Job 32: 19-20, 'Behold, my belly is as wine which hath no vent; it is ready to burst like new bottles. I will speak, that I may be refreshed: I will open my lips and answer'.

11   A phonetic representation of an upper-class dialect pronunciation of 'madam'.

figure shuffles in, *our* Mr Wells, munching the last mouthful of his bread and butter breakfast, sniffs contemptuously at some dusty boxes labelled 'Karl Marx – *Das Kapital*', 'Abolish the retail distributor', 'Made in Russia', reaches down a box marked, let us suppose, 'World-State', and with voluble dialectic[12] succeeds in selling the new model for 1*s*. 11¾*d*.,[13] together with a packet of pins for the odd farthing.[14] Quite possibly the old lady will find that the pins alone serve some really useful purpose. Our post-war world is full of irony. 'To the saving of the universe,' says Conrad, a man of powerful judgement, 'I put my faith in the power of folly.'[15] If not folly, something simple, something unsophisticated – like the heart of a child. 'The perfectly efficient,' writes Gerald Heard in *These Hurrying Years*, 'is the perfectly finished.' A re-birth has to take place – 'foetalisation'[16] is the scientific word. If Mr Wells is going to tell us that the only way to save the world is to make it a macrocosm of Geneva[17] – but we will not indulge in anticipations, Mr Wells's own *cuvée reservée*.[18]

Mr H. G. Wells was born in 1866, 'blaspheming and protesting', and this first volume of his autobiography takes us to the year 1896, during which he earned £1,056 7*s*. 9*d*., and had definitely mounted the pedestal[19] of success. Students of the science of heredity will not find much raw material in his origin. His mother was 'a little blue-eyed, pink-cheeked woman with a large, serious, innocent face', and his father's chief claim to fame before the birth of Mr Wells – he was a professional cricketer – was having bowled four Sussex batsmen in four successive balls,[20] a super-hat trick[21] 'not hitherto recorded in county cricket'. In one of his reprinted letters (p. 400) Mr Wells asks his parents: 'If I haven't my mother to thank for my imagination and my father for skill, where did I get these qualities?' This may be a pleasing display of filial piety.[22] Even with the help of

---

12　Any formal system of reasoning that arrives at the truth by the exchange of logical arguments.

13　Twenty-three and three-quarters pence (or just under ten pence in decimal currency).

14　A coin representing a quarter of a penny (equal to a tenth of a penny in decimal currency) in use from c. 1222 to 1960.

15　A quote from a letter from Joseph Conrad to Robert Bontine Cunninghame Graham, 16 February 1905 (Conrad 1983, 218).

16　The retention into adult life of bodily characteristics which earlier in evolutionary history were only infantile.

17　A reference to the League of Nations, headquartered in Geneva.

18　French, a fine wine, used metaphorically here to refer to a person's special talent.

19　Achieved great success.

20　This feat, achieved by Joseph Wells on 26 June 1862, has been equalled 33 times but never bettered.

21　In cricket, the feat of taking three wickets with three successive balls.

22　A love and respect for one's parents and ancestors.

his autobiography, Mr Wells is not easy to explain, whether in terms of nature or of nurture.

His early education was spasmodic and was followed by apprenticeship to a draper. Emancipation came when Mr Wells became a student of Huxley's[23] at the Royal College of Science – then called the Normal School of Science[24] – his training as a science teacher being subsidised by the Government with a weekly grant of one guinea.[25] His unstinted praise of Huxley as 'the acutest observer, the ablest generaliser, the great teacher, the most lucid and valiant of controversialists' confirms current opinion. After a year's course of general biology and zoology, 'the most educational year of my life', the remaining two years of his course in the school were in the nature of an anti-climax. He writes with little enthusiasm of Guthrie,[26] the professor of physics, who 'maundered amidst unmarshalled facts', and with less of Judd, the professor of geology, to whom his antipathy was immediate; and he failed in his final examination in geology in 1887.

Tragedy? Not in the ordinary sense. The real tragedy was that Mr Wells should not have continued study and research in biology under Huxley. He might have discovered the cause of human cancer, leaving to others the investigation of the cause and cure of world cancer. Academically he may appear to have been butchered to make a Juddian holiday but, with feline[27] resuscitation, he soon took the BSc degree of the University of London with first class honours[28] in zoology and second class honours[29] in geology, a remarkable achievement, appreciated strangely enough by no one more important than William Briggs, principal of the University Correspondence College, and of the University Tutorial College. For these institutions, Mr Wells worked with diligence and success, until he abandoned teaching for literature, carrying away as booty one of his devoted women students, Amy Catherine Robbins, his second wife and mother of his children.[30]

---

23 I. e., T. H. Huxley.

24 A higher education institution founded in 1881, being renamed the Royal College of Science in 1890.

25 Twenty-one shillings (equal to £1.05 in decimal currency).

26 I. e., Frederick Guthrie.

27 Of or pertaining to cats.

28 In higher education, the highest division of an undergraduate examination list.

29 In higher education, the second highest and most common academic score, nowadays divided into upper and lower levels for bachelor's degrees.

30 I. e., of G. P. Wells and F. R. Wells.

This is an interesting book – especially for those who have trodden the same Calvary[31] without securing the same crown, undoubtedly golden in the case of Mr Wells – warm, human and ingenious, occasionally too ingenious. The young man emulating Mr Wells's colossal success who spends half a minted guinea to discover its secret will find (p. 157) that for some years Mr Wells had two guiding principles in life: first, 'If you want something sufficiently, take it and damn the consequences'; and secondly, 'If life is not good enough for you, change it; never endure a way of life that is dull and dreary, because after all the worst thing that can happen to you, if you fight and go on fighting to get out, is defeat, and that is never certain to the end which is death and the end of everything'. Has not the first principle created the chaotic world which Mr Wells is obligingly going to set right? It is the *stupid* people, as Sir Walter Raleigh remarked in one of his letters, who make the work and then do it. Mr Wells is not easy to explain....

There lurks in Mr Wells, on his own confession, 'the latent 'Arry in my composition' (p. 388), exhibited in his reference to religion, especially the unquotable account of his first communion[32] (p. 189), and in his exposition of his private benevolences, including the inevitable Christmas turkey. Some lapses from Mr Wells's high standard of scientific accuracy may be noted. The date of the great Education Act[33] was 1870, not 1871 (pp. 84, 93, 327) and the diamond jubilee[34] year was 1897, not 1896 (p. 403).

Hyman Levy, 'The Autobiography of H. G. Wells' (8 December 1934).[35]

Experiment in Autobiography: Discoveries and Conclusions of a Very Ordinary Brain (since 1866). By H. G. Wells. Vol. 2. Pp. viii + 417-840 + 11 plates. (London: Victor Gollancz, Ltd., and The Cresset Press, Ltd., 1934.) 10s. 6d. net.

This is an attempt on the part of the author to trace the development of his own mind, and, as he sees them now, the social forces and personal characteristics conditioning the changes that ensued. Thus we are presented with a slab of so-

---

31 Also knows as Golgotha, the place of crucifixion of Jesus Christ.

32 In the Roman Catholic and some Protestant churches, a believer's first reception of the sacrament of the Eucharist, or the body of Christ (literal in Roman Catholicism, figurative in Protestantism).

33 An enabling act passed in 1870 which empowered local authorities to levy rates to pay for elementary education for children between the ages of 5 and 13.

34 The sixtieth anniversary celebrations of the accession of Queen Victoria to the British throne in 1897.

35 Reprinted by permission from Macmillan Publishers Ltd: *Nature* (134: 3397), copyright (1934).

cial space-time,[36] and the world-line H. G. Wells has traced out in it. We see the ineffectual draper's assistant blossoming forth as a serious-minded science student, the student as a competent journalist, and the journalist, through external stress and struggle and internal strife, into a literary innovator and a social force. The drudgery and degradation of 'living in',[37] sow the seeds of rebellion and social discontent. A fleeting and not too academically successful passage through the Royal College of Science provides the quickening. The chrysalis unfolds and the grown Wells emerges, the literary and moral iconoclast, the pioneer of science for the common man,[38] the dreamer of a World State. The autobiography is like a swelling orchestra; as each new instrument adds its part it gradually assumes the appearance as a fugue[39] working up to its climax – the Modern Utopia,[40] the New Republic, the League of Free Nations,[41] the World State.

For two generations the author has striven with consummate journalistic skill and tireless energy, by educating his public, to get them to appreciate his theme and to desire its realisation. In particular he has succeeded: in general he has failed.

It began as a struggle against prudery, inhibitions, and falsehoods of the Victorian era, a fight to the success of which he contributed more than any living man. Few of us who read our modern novels and listen to our problem plays[42] realise how much we owe to the author of *Ann Veronica*. When the storm of abuse aroused by that novel had subsided, and the social ostracism meted out to the author had passed, it was evident that a long-awaited release had occurred; a new mood had entered into literature and with it into social life.

This, however, was one only of the fronts on which Wells waged his war. The inspiration of T. H. Huxley at the Royal College of Science had aroused him to the significance of the theory of evolution for mankind, and the possibilities for the future that lay in the fullest use of the findings of science. To him it

---

36 In physics, time and three-dimensional space regarded as fused in a four-dimensional continuum containing all events.

37 Residing in an employer's premises.

38 A reference to Wells's many popular science essays published in such journals as the *Pall Mall Gazette* in the 1890s.

39 In music, a contrapuntal composition in which a short melody or phrase is introduced by one part and successively taken up by others.

40 A reference to Wells's *A Modern Utopia* (1905).

41 The international organisation advocated by the League of Free Nations Association of which Wells was a member (1917-19) and which merged with the League of Nations Society to form the League of Nations Union in 1919.

42 A form of drama that emerged in the nineteenth century which deals with problematic social issues through debates between the characters, who typically represent conflicting points of view within a realistic social context.

meant a levelling of political frontiers and a new scale of life. The ideas can be seen germinating in his early scientific stories, and blossoming forth later in the scientific passages in his socially propagandist books. Finally it takes concrete shape in his *Modern Utopia*, that marvellous *tour de force*[43] the *Outline of History*, his *Work, Wealth and Happiness of Mankind*, his *Science of Life*, *The Shape of Things to Come*, *After Democracy* and numerous other volumes. It is an amazing performance, this steady and rapid output showing the gradual experimental groping towards precision in an idea at first faintly perceived and finally forcing itself more and more into definition with the logic of events.

In particular, Wells succeeded. He jerked the youth of last generation out of their complacent acceptance of established tradition in politics, morals and religion. In letters he smashed the classical tradition that science and literature are necessarily inimical. To the man in the street he brought an understanding of his history, and of the scientific make-up of himself and his environment.[44] In all this, and more, he succeeded, and he succeeded because he was supersensitive to the mood of his times.

For the 'seventies and 'eighties were a critical phase in the development of Great Britain. Industries had flourished steadily as England poured her manufactured goods into the Colonies[45] and Dependencies;[46] Free Trade[47] and Liberalism had provided the theoretical justification for our entry into all and every market of the world. They were principles that seemed to accord simultaneously with enlightenment and self-interest. Germany emerging now as a new united State from the Franco-Prussian war[48] consciously threw herself into the industrial struggle and turned to organise scientific knowledge and scientific research to assist her. In the face of this, Britain turned in the same direction, but not before a temporary stagnation had given warning of troubles ahead. Science was in the air, and the windows of schools and colleges were slowly being prised open to allow the new enlightenment and the new knowledge to penetrate. Trade schools[49] and evening classes,[50] colleges of science and scientific laboratories,

---

43   French, a feat of strength or skill.

44   A reference to Wells's trilogy of textbooks, *The Outline of History*, *The Science of Life* and *The Work, Wealth and Happiness of Mankind*.

45   Bodies of settlers in a new country forming a community fully or partly subject to the parent state.

46   Countries or provinces controlled by another.

47   An open and unrestricted trade, unhampered by tariffs and other forms of protection.

48   A war, ostensibly over the Spanish succession, between France and Prussia (in alliance with her south German allies), lasting from 19 July 1870 to 10 May 1871 and resulting in Prussian victory and the creation of the German Empire.

49   Schools in which manual skills are taught.

began to spring up, and for those who, like the young Wells, had noses to sniff, a new and stimulating atmosphere began to make itself felt. Huxley spread the gospel of Darwinism and fought the Bishops; the Trade Union movement strengthened, became militant and neo-Marxist, seeking its own special representation in Parliament as a special working class movement; and Wells and his associated intellectuals swept into the Fabian Society[51] to impregnate this movement on the political side with the policy of gradualness and planning for their social order. The names that stand out boldly in the period are Wells, the upstart scientific groper and visionary; Shaw, the sharp incisive critic and mental gymnast; and Sidney and Beatrice Webb, the embodiment of the British Museum.[52] These were the currents that swept Wells on his way, and through which he swam on his distinctive route.

What of the outcome of it all? What of the ideal to which Wells devoted so much of his life? In the last few pages of this extraordinary story he sums up his final conclusion:

'The truth remains that to-day nothing stands in the way to the attainment of universal freedom and abundance but mental tangles, egocentric preoccupations, obsessions, misconceived phrases and bad habits of thought, subconscious fears and dreads and plain dishonesty in people's minds – and especially in the minds of those in key positions.' And then apropos of the latter: 'I can talk to them and unsettle them but I cannot compel their brains to see.'

Now of one thing Wells can be quite certain: most of these individuals in key positions have brains. Then why, he must ask himself, do they not see? Perhaps after all it is not simply intellectual assent only that is needed, but also emotional harmony. To desire a new social order implies a valuation, and a valuation of a type that does not come into scientific or mathematical propositions. Why should he expect that the people in key positions would want the kind of world that Wells himself desires? They may see that in the long run it is inevitable, but why should he expect them to raise a finger to shorten the run? The answer is not to be found in the intellectual sphere. It must be expressed in terms of the physical circumstances that arouse the desire to which he is appealing. He is in fact addressing an intellectual and emotional argument to a group of individuals from whom he need not expect to receive an emotional response.

---

50   Classes aimed at working people interested in broadening their education held in the evenings.

51   A British socialist organisation founded in 1884, the purpose of which is to advance socialism by gradualist, reformist means.

52   Britain's national museum of history and culture, established in London in 1753.

The same weakness in the methodology of Wells's propaganda can be seen in another way. After almost half a century of energetic striving for his ideal, is his plaint not rather like the old statement that, if only everyone had goodwill, everything would be for the best? Surely the first question to ask is what are the material conditions requisite for goodwill? What are the material conditions for eliminating the egocentric preoccupations? Is it within the power of Mr Wells to produce these conditions, or is it the case that those who control the conditions are also those who possess the stubborn traits to which he objects? If this is so, is it not evident that Wells has not faced his problem squarely until he has faced the problem of how to acquire power?

The lack of a clear analysis of this issue shows itself over and over again, but particularly when he bitterly laments his failure to get Stalin to see that Russia and the United States are in fact treading the same path. The suggestion (apart from the trivial interpretation that we are everywhere treading the same path) is fantastic. The emotional motifs and the whole working structure of the two countries are poles asunder. The dislike of Roosevelt[53] for the Russian system is probably equalled only by the repugnance of Stalin for the American, and in any objective handling of propaganda for a World State these are facts to reckon with. In social science,[54] unlike physical science, the changing likes and dislikes of the human material play a significant role.

He who desires to forecast the future behaviour of social groups and to play his part in that development, as Wells does, must evolve a science of social dynamics.[55] He has to study society as a material phenomenon, and deduce its laws of change. He has at the same time to recognise that these laws are brought into existence by human beings in the teeth of opposition by others, each striving to carry out his desires. Only those desires that are consistent with material possibilities are therefore capable of reaching fruition. To bring them into being, either those who have the desires that can be realised must acquire power, or those who possess the power must acquire the realisable desires. Wells's complaint concerning the obtuseness of those in key positions is in effect an admission that those who have the power cannot acquire the desire. One can only conclude that either he must become a full-fledged active revolutionary or he is seeking to bring the wrong type of World State into being.

It is for these reasons, a false methodology in his propaganda or the pursuit of a false ideal, that the reviewer holds that while Wells has succeeded in particular he has failed in general. One of the particulars, however, in which he

---

53   I. e., Franklin Roosevelt.

54   Any academic discipline which studies the structure and functions of society and social relationships.

55   The study of forces that result in social changes.

has undoubtedly succeeded is in the creation of a new form to suit the content of autobiography. Throughout the whole of the work, in striking contrast to the babbling inconsequences and fatuous anecdotes of social nonentities invariably found in the compendious volumes that pass for autobiography, he has examined his own developing mind with relentless objectivity. With this and the preceding volume he has smashed a staid and formal tradition and raised autobiography to a new level.

J. N. and D. N., 'A Crystallographic *Arrowsmith*' (8 December 1934).[56]

The Search. By C. P. Snow. Pp. 429. (London: Victor Gollancz, Ltd., 1934.) 8*s.* 6*d.* net.

It is curious that in spite of the overwhelming influence exercised by science on our civilisation, there have been so few attempts to express its ethos in literature, especially in the field of imaginative romance. Many causes have probably contributed to this, not the least of which has been the fact that most writers are not in any sense within the boundaries of science, and have to take those essential structural details on which the whole complex of human relations must depend, at second or third hand. For this reason a book such as John Masefield's *Multitude and Solitude,* which deals with medical research in Africa, gives always a shadowy impression, failing to inspire confidence in the probability of its main theme. The *Martin Arrowsmith*[57] of Sinclair Lewis, in contrast, is a much more powerful book, and most of those who buy *The Search* will probably place the two novels side by side on their shelves.

It may be said at once that these purchasers will be many, and that *The Search* will rightly receive the general applause due to an almost unqualified success. It is to be noted, moreover, that the achievement is in more than meets the eye, for by the selection of crystal physics[58] as his protagonist's subject, Mr Snow abandons the popular appeal of the struggle against death and disease. The novel is in autobiographical form, and after a perhaps too Wellsian[59] introductory childhood, describes the life of a student at the University of London and his first researches both there and in Cambridge.[60] This is all excellent, becoming at times intensely exciting, with only traces of over-dramatisation. It leads to

---

56 Reprinted by permission from Macmillan Publishers Ltd: *Nature* (134: 3397), copyright (1934).

57 Properly, *Arrowsmith* (1925).

58 The phenomenon of crystals which behave like a liquid while having the molecular structure of a solid.

59 Of or pertaining to the ideas and writings of H. G. Wells.

60 I. e., the University of Cambridge.

an account of the proceedings of a committee appointed to set up a research institute, which is one of the most brilliant studies in character we have read for a long time. In the midst of this, the protagonist, who hopes for the post of director, becomes involved, somewhat to his detriment, in an unfortunate polemic,[61] which destroys his chances. After some years of further work he leaves science altogether and takes up social and political writing.

The parallels with *Martin Arrowsmith* are striking, though until we have finished the book, we are not at all conscious of them. Like Martin Arrowsmith, Arthur Miles struggles in the realms of methodological imperfection, and as the former failed to maintain his controls during the island plague, so the latter puts unjustifiable trust in some data obtained by his assistant, with depressing results. The women, too, arrange themselves similarly, for though Leora and Audrey are admirably and sympathetically drawn, Joyce and Ruth are but flat characters.

Of criticism, perhaps the most serious that might be made is that Mr Snow does not sufficiently make clear the nature of Arthur Miles's second enthusiasm. What is this for which an on the whole so successful scientific worker lays down his overall and slide-rule?[62] We are given to understand that the psychological and political education of mankind comes to seem more important to him than the search for detailed scientific truth. But the outlines of this need greater clarity. Had he turned to propagate a robuster political faith, this would not have been so necessary as it is when his aims seem so mild and moderate, so Lowes-Dickinsonian,[63] so LNU.[64]

In sum, we have in *The Search* a really important study of human life as it is lived in the world of science. If Mr Snow can push on along this line, we are not willing to suggest bounds for his possible achievement. But it will need a more definite socio-political outlook, and all the understanding that the closest and most sympathetic observation of human behaviour can give, whether it be of shop-assistant, railwayman, biologist, or parish priest. The results of such a life work are certainly no less valuable than a hundred papers in *Proceedings* and *Transactions*.

---

61   A controversial argument or discussion.

62   A ruler which has a sliding central strip and is graduated for making rapid calculations by appropriate movement of the sliding strip.

63   Of or relating to the thought of Goldsworthy Lowes Dickinson, especially his advocacy of the League of Nations as an institution for maintaining world peace.

64   The League of Nations Union (1918-46), a pressure group formed through the merger of the League of Nations Society and the League of Free Nations Association promoting the establishment of a League of Nations and later its democratic reform.

Comment on Levy, J. N. and D. N. and one other reviewer: H. G. Wells, letter to the editor, 'Power in Social Psychology' (22 December 1934).[65]

I do not know how far the columns of *Nature* are suitable for the discussion of 'power' (in the human community). But when I find no less than three of the nine chief reviews in the issue for December 8 dealing with this question, and Dr Snow and myself being scolded for 'false methodology' and the want of a 'robust' political faith, it is perhaps permissible to point out that the class-war[66] dogma which underlies this sort of criticism has no scientific standing.

Social psychology,[67] like every other branch of human ecology, is still in the squinting, vaguely exploratory stage of infancy; we have no adequate description of social 'power', no analysis of its miscellany of factors and no clear conception of its attainment or the scope of its operation. We have clear definitions of legal 'powers', but these definitions are independent of any qualifications by disregard, resistance or inaccurate or insufficient enforcement. The belatedness of social psychology is a misfortune for the world but it is a fact. That 'robust' political faith to which the reviewer urges Dr Snow, is really emotional doctrinaire[68] mysticism[69] born of impatience and trying to compensate for its poverty of assembled knowledge by a tawdry 'dialectic'.

The premeditated achievement of social resultants is a business for clearer heads and a stouter patience. Formal education, adult education, social stimulation, the mechanisms of production and distribution, a complex of diverse forces, all come into that process. Politicians and rulers of men have to 'get results', but as Dr Snow's recent novel demonstrates admirably, it is a primary crime against science for a man of science to produce 'results' unjustifiably.

So far as I am concerned, I am not a propagandist but an experimentalist in projection. This class-war stuff, this 'dialectic materialism'[70] is essentially unscientific talk, pseudo-scientific talk; it is literary, pretentious, rhetorical. As sincere, patient and steadfast scientific analysis spreads into human biology we shall begin to get the general concepts of human relationship and social process clear and plain – and then we shall not need to worry about 'power'; power will

---

65 Reprinted by permission from Macmillan Publishers Ltd: *Nature* (134: 3399), copyright (1934). This letter has previously been reprinted in Smith 1998, III: 560-61.

66 Conflict between social classes.

67 The branch of psychology which deals with social interactions, including their origins and effects on the individual.

68 The act of trying to apply principle without allowance for circumstance.

69 Belief characterised by self-delusion or dreamy confusion of thought.

70 Properly, dialectical materialism, the Marxist theory of political and historical events as due to the conflict of social forces caused by humanity's material needs and interpretable as a series of contradictions and their solutions.

flow to the effective centres of direction. Stalin in our recent conversation accused me of believing in the goodness of human nature. I do at any rate believe in man's ultimate sanity. The political and social imaginations of very many people nowadays seem to me to be obsessed by the transitory triumphs of violence in various countries, and a lot of this talk about the need to organise the illegal seizure of power for direct creative (revolutionary) ends by those masses of the population which presumably have the most unsatisfied desires, is due largely to a lack of perspective in the outlook of the intelligentsia[71] and a want of patience and lucidity in their minds. There is a limit to the concentration of power in human society, beyond which it becomes ineffective and undesirable. The limit has been passed in Germany and Russia to-day.

Reply to Wells: Hyman Levy, letter to the editor (22 December 1934).[72]

I cannot answer for the implications Mr Wells has drawn from the other reviewers. For myself, I am amazed that he does not see himself as a propagandist among his other roles. Others do; and that is good enough for scientific purposes. Talk of the *seizure* of power in present-day England is, of course, just rubbish. That question has not been raised. What was being discussed was, 'From which fulcrum would the lever for change to the Wellsian World State be finally applied?' Mr Wells seems to see it in the people in key positions, but paradoxically enough he complains that they have not the brains to see. What then? My contention was that it is not simply an intellectual 'seeing' that he must seek but an active desire, a liking for his world solution.

Mr Wells has left out the emotional content in assent to a social solution. His letter repeats it in simply demanding more scientific examination, as if objective science covered the whole of life, and yet he bases his case on two scientifically unverifiable assertions:

(1) He believes in man's ultimate sanity, meaning, I suppose, that he *feels* people in key positions will ultimately accept his solution.

(2) Power will flow to the effective centres of direction, meaning that he *feels* this will be so although he does not see it happening to-day in Russia and Germany.

I do not see why he should expect others to share his sanguine feelings.

---

71   A section of society regarded as possessing culture and political initiative.

72   Reprinted by permission from Macmillan Publishers Ltd: *Nature* (134: 3399), copyright (1934).

2.24: *The New America: The New World*

Review of *The New America: The New World* **(14 September 1935).**[1]

The New America: the New World by H. G. Wells. Pp. 96. (London: The Cresset Press, Ltd., 1935.) 2*s*. 6*d*. net.

Stressing the general problems rather than details, Mr Wells in a series of four short but brilliantly written chapters emphasises the necessity for the deliberate readjustment of the social mechanism, so as to recognise the possibilities of human expansion that are now running to waste and disaster. He holds that, if an effort is to be made at all to find a way out from catastrophe to a new lease of life for civilisation, the main part of it should come from America, as no other country has the necessary freedom of speech[2] and mind left and all other communities are confused by the war threat.[3]

During his recent visit to America, two aspects of that country's effort to adapt itself to the new conditions seemed to Mr Wells unique. The first is that the struggle to reconstruct in America goes on in an atmosphere of unbridled public discussion, whereas in Britain it is restrained by habit and custom and by the centralisation of the Press in London. The second is the relative unimportance of large mass antagonisms. There is no widespread conception of a class-war ruling the situation as in Russia,[4] or of racial incompatibility as in Germany[5] or any such exacerbation of xenophobia as in Italy or Japan.[6] There are conflicts of regional interests, indeed, but little regional bitterness.

---

1   Reprinted by permission from Macmillan Publishers Ltd: *Nature* (136: 3427), copyright (1935).

2   The right to express opinions of any kind without incurring a penalty.

3   A reference to the Abyssinian Crisis then in process, which saw an Italo-Abyssinian border clash at Walwal in December 1934 lead to the Italian conquest of Abyssinia by May 1936.

4   A reference to the ruling position of the Communist Party in the Soviet Union (1917-91).

5   A reference to the violently anti-Semitic nature of Nazi Germany (1933-45).

6   A reference to the extreme nationalism and racial bigotry of Fascist Italy (1919-43) and militarist Japan (1932-45).

2.25: *Things to Come*

Review of *Things to Come* (11 January 1936).[1]

Things to Come by H. G. Wells. A Film Story based on the Material contained in his History of the Future *The Shape of Things to Come*. Pp. 142. (London: The Cresset Press, 1935.) 3s. 6d. net.

Even more vividly than in the argument of *The Shape of Things to Come*, Mr H. G. Wells depicts the swift downfall of modern civilisation and the rise of a new and scientific order of society. His adaptation to the writing of a novel of something of the technique of a film story enables him to emphasise the more forcefully the inevitableness of some such order of society as an alternative to war. Equally without unduly stressing the horrors of warfare, his dramatic technique may perhaps stimulate many to realise the dangers of the present situation on whom the logical analysis of Sir Norman Angell, for example, would be lost. The scientific worker may well find as much interest in the technique with which Mr Wells develops his argument as in the picture he gives of an imaginary scientific age.

Even more pertinent, however, is the question which Mr Wells inevitably raises in the mind of all. Must mankind pass through such a period of disaster and collapse, or is there still time to regain control and so organise the resources and powers which science has put into man's hands that the surplus energies of the race spend themselves upon constructive and creative art and science?

The pictorial technique adopted by Mr Wells will prove more than justified if it can stimulate a forward look and a willingness to try new methods before catastrophe ensues in quarters which have hitherto been noted for mankind's direst peril – a belated mind.

'Mr H. G. Wells's Film *Things to Come*' (29 February 1936).[2]

Mr H. G. Wells is the only man of letters who understands the scientific spirit, and has consistently urged the use of it in the solution of social problems. In his imaginative romances, as well as in works on social, religious and political questions, he has always presented science as a progressive influence and has remonstrated against the unworthy ends for which it is often used. The hope expressed in his *Anticipations* and *A Modern Utopia* took different form in *The Shape of Things to Come* published two years ago and was accompanied by a warning of

---

1   Reprinted by permission from Macmillan Publishers Ltd: *Nature* (137: 3454), copyright (1936).

2   Reprinted by permission from Macmillan Publishers Ltd: *Nature* (137: 3461), copyright (1936).

disaster unless human purposes were determined by reconstructed principles. Science has put into the hands of civilised man the power to destroy himself or to make the world a celestial[3] dwelling place; and the sooner this is widely realised the safer will the world be for humanity. There is no better way to-day of making this message universal than through the motion picture;[4] and this is done in the marvellous film *Things to Come*,[5] the world première of which was given in London on Friday, February 21.[6] The film has been produced by Mr Alexander Korda; and Mr Wells, whose scenario of it was noticed in *Nature* of January 11 last, has taken an active part in the production of the picture.

The general story is that of the destruction of the civilised world by war-fever and pestilence, and after almost every material structure had been destroyed and intellectual culture had been lost, a new world government arises in which scientific leaders have control. Through the three generations represented in the film, some basic human attributes remain unchanged, and they are represented by Dr Harding's devotion to medical research even when the world is in ruins; Cabal, who never falters in his confidence in the power of science to promote human welfare; the military autocrat, who regards gladiatorial conflicts as the only means of securing peace; his mistress, Roxana, with the eternal 'sex appeal' diverting ethical aims; Theotocopulus, the sculptor who even in a beautiful and regenerate world, raises a revolt against mechanisation and looks with longing to the Golden Age of the past; and finally the two young people who, still with the spirit of adventure in them, start for a journey around the moon in spite of all efforts of reactionaries to restrain them. It is scarcely within our province to comment upon the technique of this remarkable production, but we have no hesitation in saying that every moment and movement of the picture has a meaning and that the film stands as high above the usual sentimental stock of the picture house[7] as a triumph of creative art does above a gaudy advertisement or a classical literary work is superior to a 'penny dreadful'.

---

3   Divine; heavenly.

4   A cinema film.

5   A film by produced by Alexander Korda and directed by William Cameron Menzies for which Wells produced a film treatment, 'Whither Mankind?' (Stover 1987, 121-79), and a published scenario, *Things to Come* (1935), though shooting was based on the postproduction script (Stover 1987, 181-297).

6   At Leicester Square Theatre.

7   Cinema.

2.26: *Man Who Could Work Miracles*

Review of *Man who could work Miracles* (6 June 1936).[1]

Man who could work Miracles by H. G. Wells. A Film Story based on the Material contained in his short story 'Man who could work Miracles'. Pp. 96. (London: The Cresset Press, 1936.) 3*s*. 6*d*. net.

In this film story Mr H. G. Wells applies again the treatment used in *Things to Come* to material drawn from the fantastic[2] vein of his earlier works. He describes how a draper's assistant in a small town suddenly becomes endowed with miraculous powers, how he uses his newly acquired gifts to further his own desires or those of friends, and how he loses his gift with dramatic suddenness just as he involves the world in disaster. Mr Wells uses his new technique to expound his familiar theme of man's inability to use wisely the powers with which science has endowed him, and to bring into high relief the moral as well as the material obstacles which beset the transformation of the present situation of unemployment and impoverishment in the midst of overproduction and sabotage[3] into an era of peace and plenitude for all.

---

1   Reprinted by permission from Macmillan Publishers Ltd: *Nature* (137: 3475), copyright (1936).

2   Existing only in the imagination, fabulous, unreal.

3   A reference to the economic depression in Britain during the 1930s, and the practice of destroying crops or scrapping manufactured commodities in order to raise prices while many people were in material need.

2.27: *Anatomy of Frustration*

Alfred Hall, 'A Social Analysis' (7 November 1936).[1]

The Anatomy of Frustration: A Modern Synthesis. By H. G. Wells. Pp. 274. (London: The Cresset Press, Ltd., 1936.) 7*s*. 6*d*. net.

To the generation of readers immediately preceding the Great War, H. G. Wells (as a member of a deputation remonstrated with the Minister of Fine Arts, 'On ne dit pas Monsieur Renoir, on dit Renoir'[2]) was the great illuminator, revealing the power of science to transform the material world, but on the men of science themselves his action has been different. He has awakened them to a consciousness of social disorder, disorder remediable by the application to mankind of the methods by which science is learning to control the other departments of Nature. In the laboratories either of the universities or the works, in the shops wherever the technicians congregate, the talk and thought are permeated by Wells, even though the participators have never read one of his books. Some of these men get labelled 'communists' because of their impatience with current government by slogans and the canons of good form; others incline to Fascism in the hope that a dictator would get things done. Even Wells has flirted with the Fascist idea of the need of a great man, though his leader would be the entrepreneur who had proved his quality in big business.[3] Whatever the particular manifestation may be, the young workers in science to-day no longer regard 'politics' as unworthy of their interest; they are looking for social reconstruction directed by science, and consciously or not, Wells has been the catalyst that has initiated the reaction.

In his latest book *The Anatomy of Frustration* Wells adopts an odd technique. He puts his opinions into the mouth of Mr Steele – inventor and business man, who after the War[4] had retired to the south of France in order to sort out his ideas about life. This gives Wells the opportunity of a running commentary and of anticipating in advance the scepticism which is part of the outfit of the man of science. He explains his title; Burton's *Anatomy of Melancholy* was an analysis of the despair with which the thinking man of his epoch must regard the world – a universe wholly and irremediably mad. Steele embarks on his examination of frustration in the modern world with the firm determination that a rem-

---

1   Reprinted by permission from Macmillan Publishers Ltd: *Nature* (138: 3497), copyright (1936).

2   French, 'You don't say Mister Renoir, you say Renoir'. I have been unable to trace the source of this reference.

3   A reference to *The World of William Clissold* (1926) in which the title character, a successful businessperson, suggests big-business and financial leaders could lead a world revolution.

4   I. e., the Great War.

edy can be found by the methods he has found valid in that section which he had experience. He starts with a brave assumption – that all men can and ultimately will think very much alike: 'Men have no right to a thousand contrasted faiths and creeds and … the multitudinousness of people in these matters is merely due to bad education, mental and moral indolence, slovenliness of statement and the failure to clinch issues'; and so we pass on to a discussion of religion and immortality, and of morality that needs re-expression in terms of daily life.

> Motives are things of deeper origin than intellectual convictions and the real will of *Homo sapiens* is still largely unaffected by his conscious and formulated wishes. His intentions are one thing; his behaviour quite another. The world's expressed desire, its conscious desire, is such and such; the total complex of human impulses is quite another system, darker, deeper and profoundly more real. These desires for world unity and sane economics are conscious and intellectual desires, and they scarcely penetrate at all into the more primitive and substantial mental mass which is the true reservoir of motives and impulses.

But for all that, Steele is not prepared to yield to the sub-conscious[5] – 'The essential purpose of all law, all discipline, all training, is the enthronement of a clear general purpose above a subjugated and directed subconsciousness'.

Steele would not be Wells if he did not knock a good many heads along his route; socialism is a case of 'habitual piecemeal thinking'; 'the Moscow frustration is a study in the deterioration of yet another blazing star of hope'; 'the League of Nations recognises, intensifies, and does its utmost to preserve the conventions of nationalism and the emotions of patriotism'; schools and colleges are to this day 'conducted to put back the new generation where its parents began'. Steele has no use for all sorts of things – The People, Zionism[6] and other separatist movements ('Why specialise in Erin[7] and Mother India and Palestine, when the whole world is our common inheritance. *Come out* of Israel'), Liberalism ('The stupid can co-operate loyally upon immediate objectives; the intelligentsia, it seems, cannot co-operate at all'), and the artistic temperament ('Indulgence of appetites to the detriment of fitness and the distraction of energy').

---

5   Of or pertaining to or existing in the part of the mind which influences actions without one's full awareness.

6   The movement for the creation and maintenance of a Jewish homeland in Palestine and present-day Israel.

7   The Anglicised version of the Irish Gaelic, *Éirinn*, meaning Ireland.

Is there nothing constructive about Steele? He attaches extraordinary importance to the production of that 'World Encyclopaedia'[8] of his. It seems to him that it is 'the most urgent need of our time. The main intellectual task of education is to put before the expanding mind everything that is clearly known about the nature of the world in which it finds itself'. Of such is to be the new education, and we may suppose that it was under the urge of Steele that Wells set about the *Outline of History*, and the *Science of Life*, as samples of that great and continuous synthesis the World Encyclopaedia is to be. And so Wells ends as he has begun and continued – a solvent and a loosener of mental inhibitions, for until freedom is obtained no orderly co-operation of men with men can proceed. 'Fine confused thinking' perhaps, but how stimulating; it is better to clear the mind than to trim it into a system.

---

8   A reference to Wells's 'The Idea of a World Encyclopaedia' (1936).

2.28: *Star Begotten*

John Burdon Sanderson Haldane, 'Messianic Radiation' (31 July 1937).[1]

Star Begotten: A Biological Fantasia. By H. G. Wells. Pp. vii + 199. (London: Chatto and Windus, 1937.) 6s. net.

It is always interesting to see what a scientific fact will look like after Mr Wells's imagination has been let loose on it. The facts on which this book is based are that particles[2] or photons[3] of high energy provoke mutation,[4] and that such particles and possibly photons are reaching our planet from outside. What if some intelligent extra-terrestrial[5] beings, perhaps on Mars, are treating us as we treat *Drosophila*?[6] If these beings are as benevolent as they are powerful, may we not expect that our mutations will be of a desirable character, and that the mutants will reform the world? So Mr Wells's characters argue. Two thousand years ago Virgil was writing 'Iam noua progenies coelo demittitur alto'[7]; and it is widely believed that his prophecy was fulfilled. Wells predicts not a single saviour, but millions of messianic[8] mutations.

It is worth while pointing out why such a theory, even if there were some evidence for it, would be unacceptable. First, as Wells himself remarks, the cosmic radiation[9] is undirected. As a theme for his next story, I offer him the radiation of about 15 metres wave-length[10] which Jansky found to be reaching our planet from the hub of the universe, or rather of our galaxy,[11] in Sagittarius.[12] Secondly, spontaneous mutation has a fairly high temperature coefficient,[13] and

---

1   Reprinted by permission from Macmillan Publishers Ltd: *Nature* (140: 3535), copyright (1937).

2   Subatomic constituents of the physical world that interact with each other.

3   Quanta of light, the energy of which is proportional to the frequency of the radiation.

4   A change in genetic material, especially one that gives rise to heritable variations in offspring; a distinct form produced by such change.

5   Existing or occurring beyond the earth's atmosphere.

6   A fruit fly much used as an experimental subject in genetics.

7   A quote from Virgil's Fourth Eclogue, line 7, meaning 'A new begetting now descends from heaven's height' (Virgil 1980).

8   Relating to a saviour.

9   The action or condition of sending out rays of light or other energy.

10   The distance between successive peaks of a wave.

11   Any of the numerous vast systems of stars, gas and dust that exist separately in the universe, the Milky Way being the galaxy which contains the earth's solar system.

12   Called Sagittarius A*, a bright, compact source of radio emission at the centre of the Milky Way Galaxy discovered by Karl Jansky in 1932.

13   The relative change of a physical property when its temperature is changed by one degree Celsius.

therefore cannot well be due to radiation. Müller discovered this fact before he showed that X-rays are more effective than heat in provoking mutation. But radiations are news, and temperature coefficients are not, so the discovery is generally ignored. Finally, cosmic radiation obeys (if one may use such a word) the uncertainty principle,[14] so even a superhuman marksman aiming at particular genes in human nuclei[15] could scarcely expect much success. It is interesting that temperature fluctuations are equally uncontrollable, so that at present we have no method which promises anything better than a random provocation of mutations, most of which are harmful.

Why, we may ask, has our author chosen this particular theme? Many of my younger contemporaries, in Flecker's words,

Take no solace from that palm-girt[16] Wells.[17]

I think they are wrong. He still represents an important tradition, he is a great stylist, and the workings of his mind are most instructive. *Star Begotten*, like Stapledon's *Last and First Men* and *Odd John*, but unlike his recent *Star-Maker*, despairs of existing humanity, and demands beings of innate endowments superior to our own to deal with the present crisis of civilisation, which it sketches in brilliant phrases. The author is obviously sceptical of the remedies which he and others have propounded. 'Haven't all civilised men nowadays the feeling of being dilettantes[18] on a sinking ship?' asks one of his characters. So with unconquered optimism he puts forward a panacea[19] which he knows to be fantastic.

Some of the undercurrents of Wells's thought are indicative. He is strongly anti-communistic, but he cannot help being influenced by communist ideas. Thus he uses the word ideology, and on p. 165 we find a phrase about mad dogs which perhaps owes something to a speech of Vishinsky's at the first trial of

---

14 In physics, the principle that certain pairs of observables (e. g., the momentum and position of a particle) cannot both be precisely determined at the same time.

15 In biology, the cores of living cells bounded by double membranes within which lie the chromosomes, and functioning as stores of genetic information and as directors of metabolic and synthetic activity in the cell.

16 Ringed by palm trees.

17 This is a misquotation from the James Flecker poem, 'The Golden Journey to Samarkand' (1913), in which is written, 'Take no more solace from the palm-girt wells'.

18 Persons who take an interest in a subject merely as a pastime and without serious study.

19 A remedy for all ailments.

Trotskyists in Moscow.[20] Many of his phrases remain apposite if the letter 'x' is substituted for 't' in Martian. Making this substitution, we read 'At the onset of a strange way of living we bristle like dogs at the sight of a strange animal. He hated these Marxians[21] as soon as he thought of them. He could not imagine that their interference with our nice world could be anything but devastating'. Another character is more tolerant. 'And now these new creatures from outside, these creatures called Marxians, are coming on board our drifting system. With their hard clear minds, and their penetrating unrelenting questions stinging our darknesses as the stars sting the sky. Are they going to salvage us? Shall we let them if they can?'

Whether or not the Marxians have correctly diagnosed the cause of our present distresses, it is clear that evolutionary processes, either natural, or directed by terrestrial or celestial eugenists, are most unlikely to end them. The timescale of evolution is altogether longer than that of history; and we probably have not many years, let alone generations, to save our civilisation from collapse. If this book encourages a single reader to think, even for one moment, that any natural or supernatural process will take the place of human effort and human thought, then it is a bad book. But if it is read as a record of conversations between rather worried intellectuals, it is not only an excellent piece of writing, but also a valuable historical document.

---

20 During the 1936 show trials of Soviet enemies, especially followers of Leon Trotsky, in Moscow, the prosecutor, Andrei Vishinsky, often ended his closing statements with the words 'Shoot these mad dogs'.

21 Marxists.

2.29: *The Camford Visitation*

Review of *The Camford Visitation* (12 February 1938).[1]

The Camford Visitation by H. G. Wells. Pp. 76. (London: Methuen and Co., Ltd., 1937.) 2*s*.

Mr Wells's address as president of the Educational Science Section of the British Association last year[2] dealt with certain aspects of education in the schools only. In his latest story, with its cover of dark and light blue, he deals with university education and its place in society. The story begins with an amusing sketch of a dyed-in-the-wool[3] scholar, the Master of Holy Innocents College, a preserver of culture, of true scholarship, born to appreciate without ever creating. His breakfast oration has got to the last stage of denouncing 'the dictatorship of the half-educated.... We are being endowed, Sir, and told what to know and teach, by the unholy wealth of ironmongers[4] and the overblown profits of syndicated[5] shop-keepers.' Then enters the visitant[6] as a voice, an unseen presence, asking: 'Half-educated? Now how can you measure education and divide it into halves and quarters? What do you *mean* by education?...' For the rest of the story the visitant subjects human life, and in particular its treatment by the University of Camford,[7] to a sympathetic but quite unsparing scrutiny. The general thesis is an appeal to the universities to play a part in 'so heroic an ordering of knowledge, so valiant a beating out of opinions, such a refreshment of teaching and such an organisation of brains as will constitute a real and living world university, head, eyes and purpose for Man.'

In the development of the thesis many topics are reviewed or touched, with Wellsian incisiveness and ironic humour – the claim that the humanities[8] are wisdom and that science is not, the pseudo-scientific[9] explanations of psycho-analysis, the fashionable philosophy-cum-politics-cum-religion called dialectical materialism. 'To see a novel proposition pass through a Marxist ga-

---

1 Reprinted by permission from Macmillan Publishers Ltd: *Nature* (141: 3563), copyright (1938).

2 A reference to 'The Informative Content of Education', a speech delivered on 12 September 1937.

3 Unchangeable, inveterate.

4 Hardware merchants or dealers in metal tools, utensils, etc.

5 Businesses which have been grouped for the purposes of co-operating in pursuing a scheme requiring large capital funds.

6 A spectre or ghost.

7 A portmanteau used to refer to the universities of Cambridge and Oxford coined by William Makepeace Thackeray in *The History of Pendennis* (1849-50).

8 Learning or literature concerned with human culture.

9 Related to a pretended or spurious science.

thering is like watching a breeze across a field of ripe corn. It passes, and the serried[10] minds return to their upstanding integrity.' Mr Wells is here as stimulating, provocative and entertaining as ever, but the visitant treats university science teaching more kindly than we should have expected.

---

10   Pressed close together; shoulder to shoulder.

2.30: *World Brain*

Allan Ferguson, 'Knowledge and World Progress' (23 April 1938).[1]

World Brain by H. G. Wells. Pp. xvi + 130. (London: Methuen and Co., Ltd., 1938.) 3*s.* 6*d.* net.

This, the latest of Mr Wells's books, may well be the latest-but-one before this review appears, so swift is the rush of his ideas, so urgent the message which he has for a civilisation clattering blindly towards chaos. Here, as in so much of his work, we have yet another contribution towards that orderly world-scheme so dear to the heart of the ever-young, wise and keenly interested recruit to the ranks of the septuagenarians.[2] The essays collected in the hundred and thirty pages of this slight and engrossing volume comprise a Friday evening discourse delivered at the Royal Institution,[3] a lecture given in America,[4] a contribution to the *Encyclopédie Française*,[5] the presidential address to Section L of the British Association on 'The Informative Content of Education'[6] and a series of appendices evoked by the comments of those sensitive souls ruffled by the more provocative parts of his addresses.

For provocative Mr Wells is – and long may he remain so! To some he may, now and then, seem to lay more stress on the material than the spiritual factors that have contributed to the making of history. As when he tells us that 'in the middle-nineteenth century all Europe thought the United States must break up into a lawless confusion. The railway, the printing press, saved that.' That is a literal truth. But the mind of Abraham Lincoln, a man as great as some of the strutting leaders of a later stage are small, was surely the determining factor in the preservation of the Union.[7]

These divagations,[8] however, are but incidental, and in most of these addresses Mr Wells seldom wonders far from his main theme – the gathering, indexing, digesting and clarifying of the sum total of present knowledge into an ever-changing, ever-growing World Encyclopaedia, which shall not only serve

---

1   Reprinted by permission from Macmillan Publishers Ltd: *Nature* (141: 3573), copyright (1938).

2   A person aged from 70 and 79 years.

3   Entitled 'World Encyclopaedia', Wells's lecture was delivered on 20 November 1936.

4   Entitled 'The Brain Organisation of the Modern World', Wells's lecture was delivered in October and November 1937 in various American cities.

5   Entitled 'The Idea of a Permanent World Encyclopaedia', the encyclopaedia appeared between 1935 and 1966.

6   Wells's address was delivered on 2 September 1937 in Nottingham.

7   The federal unity of the United States of America.

8   Wanderings from one subject to another.

the needs of the specialised student, but also shall give to the citizen of the nation of to-day something of the factual and critical knowledge necessary to make easy his progress towards citizenship of that world-federation to which he is, paradoxically enough, stumbling through a phase of intensified nationalism.

There never was a time in the history of mankind when it was more necessary that this ordered knowledge should be at the beck and call[9] of all of us – when the elements of success are in the hands of those who can combine an emotional drive towards the light with an intellectual appreciation of the difference between the true and the false dawn.

There's the rub. The two elements must be present and, whereas the emotions are easily, too easily, aroused, it is the hardest task in the world to persuade men to think objectively. In his so-called reasoning on matters directly concerning his relations with his fellows, man for the most part is content to allow a series of fleeting images to pass before his mind. He stamps down those he dislikes, seizes on those that appeal to him and terms the process 'coming to a reasoned judgement'. The result may be seen in a conversation overheard just after the Austrian coup[10] – a conversation which is, as near as may be, reported *literatim*:[11]

> *A*: Thank heaven we'd no League of Nations functioning this week-end – we'd have been in the middle of a first-class war now.
>
> *B*: Don't you think it would be more accurate to say that if we'd had a League of Nations this situation would never have arisen?
>
> *A*: Not a bit of it. Anything like the League means that England's left to hold the baby – as we were when Wilson founded the blessed League, and then cleared out[12] and let us down.'=
>
> *B*: Do you really feel that that's an accurate account of what Wilson did?
>
> *A*: Near enough. Anyway, we disarmed to the bone, to set a good example – and much notice anyone else took of us.
>
> *B*: Have you ever drawn curves of arms expenditure year by year to see if there was a dip in British expenditure that wasn't present in that of other countries?

---

9   Subservient to; at the absolute command of.

10   A reference to the seizure of power by the Austrian Nazi Party on 11 April 1938, followed by the German annexation of Austria the following day.

11   Latin, letter for letter, literally.

12   Woodrow Wilson negotiated the League of Nations into the Treaty of Versailles in 1919, but the American senate refused to ratify the treaty so the USA never joined the League.

A: No – and I don't intend to. And if there wasn't a dip then it was because money was spent in wages that should have been spent on ships.

There was more to the same tune.

And now remember that *A* is a well-to-do and competent man of business, multiply him by some millions, think of his like in other countries, and we see only too clearly that here is an immense mass of material not likely to be influenced in the slightest measure by the content of any World-Encyclopaedia.

Not that there is need for despair on this account. Mr Wells, himself perennially youthful, makes his appeal to youth and those whose minds have not acquired an incurable wry-neck[13] in the course of the process called education. Every year saved from war is a year gained to this end of education for world-citizenship. But what of the particulars of that education – how, in Rutherford's phrase, to 'get on with it'?[14] In these brilliant and discursive addresses, Mr Wells has sketched a general plan and has, very reasonably, not condescended to detail. Schemes may be over-elaborated and static on that account. In his own wise words, 'If a thing is really to live it should grow, rather than be made.' But a start must be made somewhere and somewhen.[15] Is it possible, *now*, to provide John Smith at least with pointers that will direct him to objective, critical and unbiased information concerning – well, concerning a thousand-and-one matters about which he should be conversant – the causes of the world war,[16] the reasons for the great depression,[17] the tragic story of these wasted twenty years, the meaning of money, credit, world-trade, Bolshevism, Communism, Fascism – how many of those whose votes may decide the fate of the world have the beginnings of knowledge of topics bandied about on all political platforms? If Mr Wells would continue the good work he has initiated in the volume under review, he would add very sensibly to the heavy debt which the civilised world already owes him.

---

13 Properly, torticollis, a medical condition in which a person's head is tilted towards one side while the chin is elevated and turned toward the opposite side.

14 In 1932, when American researchers developed a 1.5 million volt accelerator to emit particles at high speed in their endeavour to determine the structure and composition of the nucleus of an atom, Rutherford implored Ernest Walton and John Cockcroft to 'get on with it' – i.e., to better the Americans' invention.

15 At some time.

16 I. e., the Great War.

17 A period of global economic downturn which resulted from the Wall Street Crash of 24 October 1929, with recovery occurring unevenly throughout the 1930s.

2.31: *The Fate of Homo Sapiens*, *The New World Order* and *The Outlook for Homo Sapiens*

John Hardwick, 'The Future of Mankind' (2 September 1939).[1]

The Fate of Homo Sapiens: An Unemotional Statement of the Things that are Happening to him Now, and of the Immediate Possibilities Confronting Him. By H. G. Wells. Pp. vi + 330. (London: Martin Secker and Warburg, Ltd., 1939.) 7s. 6d. net.

No one having reached maturity in the reign of Queen Victoria and having survived into out present epoch can be expected to feel altogether at home. In those days, distant not so much in time as in atmosphere, although everyone believed in inevitable progress, 'there was a widespread feeling that nothing more of primary importance was ever likely to happen'. It was precisely because of this static condition of things that the public so eagerly took to Mr Wells's futuristic romances.

But all that has changed; the dominant question is: What is likely to happen? And the answers given to it are disturbing. Mr Wells's answer is no exception:

> There is no reason whatever to believe that the order of nature has any greater bias in favour of man than it had in favour of the ichthyosaur.... I perceive that now the universe is bored with him, is turning a hard face to him, and I see him being carried less and less intelligently and more and more rapidly ... along the stream of fate to degradation,[2] suffering and death.

Mr Wells does not consider that this fate is as yet absolutely inevitable, though to escape it there will have to be something in the nature of a wholesale conversion of the species[3] to more rational habits of thinking and behaving; and he does not appear to believe that this is very likely to happen.

The gravest menace to humanity at present springs, as everyone recognises, from war. The Marxists regard war as a necessary symptom of an economic system in decay; but Mr Wells repudiates Marxism. For him, war has been from primitive times a natural form of social blood-letting, caused by a surplus of young men. In the pre-scientific epoch only relatively puny means of destruc-

---

1   Reprinted by permission from Macmillan Publishers Ltd: *Nature* (144: 3644), copyright (1939).

2   Moral or intellectual debasement.

3   A biological grouping which contains organisms that are uniquely distinguished from others by certain shared characteristics and usually by an inability to interbreed with members of other such groupings.

tion were available. But the inventive urge of the species has altered the situation for the worse. Instead of being 'part of the accepted human rhythm', war has become 'a galloping consumption of the human species'.

Thus a situation has developed which threatens the human race with decline and ultimate extinction. The question is: Are human powers of self-adaptation[4] sufficient to enable the species to adjust itself to this new situation? The trouble is that speed seems to be called for; there is no time for the older and slower methods of adaptation. Of course, man's possession of a unique brain gives him an advantage; and the readjustment will have to be a *mental* one. This mental readjustment, says Mr Wells, must involve three main essentials: (1) the idea and tradition of war must be eliminated; (2) 'The vast and violent wastage of natural resources[5] in the hunt for private profit, that went on in the nineteenth century, must be arrested and reversed by the establishment of a collective economy for the whole world'; (3) the resultant world organisation[6] must be 'of an active, progressive, imaginatively exciting nature', so that the surplus energy of youth may be absorbed by it and not allowed to run to destructive waste in war.

These three principles, peace, collectivism, and incessant new enterprise, are interdependent and inseparable. In Mr Wells's view, the League Covenant[7] failed because it completely disregarded these principles. It overlooked the problem of the restless young men; and it gave not attention to 'the absolute necessity of reconstructing economic life upon a collectivist[8] basis throughout the world'.

In order to bring about the mental adjustment involving acceptance of his three principles, Mr Wells calls for 'such a *kultur-kampf*[9] as the world has never seen before'. Nothing less than the entire reconditioning of our mental life is required. What our generation needs is the kind of enlightenment that the French encyclopaedists[10] provided in the eighteenth century. It was the ideas of Diderot and his associates that 'materialised in the American[11] and French revolutions[12]

---

4   The ability to change one's own behaviour so as to better adapt to one's environment.

5   Commodities that are considered valuable in their relatively unmodified form.

6   An alternative label for Wells's world state.

7   The written constitution of the League of Nations.

8   Pertaining to the collective ownership of land and the means of production as a political principle.

9   German, a cultural struggle.

10   A group of intellectuals of the French Enlightenment, headed by Denis Diderot and Jean d'Alembert, who produced the *Encyclopédie* (1751-80).

11   During the American Revolution the American colonies revolted against the British Empire and gained their independence as the USA following a conflict lasting from 1775 to 1783.

and in a great heartening of the creative spirit of man'. Is it possible for this achievement to repeat itself on a larger scale to-day?

Mr Wells does not believe that our present educational institutions are likely to effect the change. The common schools 'are essentially conservative institutions, adapting the common man to the social order in which he finds himself', and they fail to provide 'the scientific vision of life in the universe'. Thus the existing educational organisation 'needs to be recast quite as much and even more than the political framework'.

It will be plain that what is here advocated is nothing less than a complete change of mentality, a redirection of public interest. The question is whether a new programme of intellectual education, even of the most enlightened kind, would suffice to achieve the change. The real trouble is that the educated, even those with an education in natural science,[13] can be enlightened intellectually, without being in the least enlightened emotionally. What is needed is a transvaluation of values,[14] and this is not to be achieved easily. Mr Herbert Read has suggested that we should 'try the experiment of educating the instincts instead of suppressing them'.[15] Many educationists (who as a class are very much more progressive and alive to realities than Mr Wells would seem to be aware) are trying to work along these lines, but it is work that will not be done in a day. Meanwhile, as Mr Wells says, the need is urgent.

This is a timely and sincere book and written without fear of giving offence.

William Inge, 'Victorian Socialism' (13 January 1940).[16]

The New World Order: Whether it is Attainable, How it can be Attained, and What Sort of World a World at Peace will have to be. By H. G. Wells. Pp. 192. (London: Martin Secker and Warburg, Ltd., 1940.) 6s. net.

---

12 A period (1789-99) of social and political upheaval during which time France passed from an absolute monarchy with feudal privileges for the aristocracy and the Catholic Church towards a more enlightened society based on democracy, citizenship and inalienable rights.

13 The branches of knowledge that deal with the natural or physical world, especially physics, chemistry, biology, geology, etc.

14 A central tenet of Friedrich Nietszsche's thought, which sought the rejection of Christian morality, such as pitying the weak and suppressing the sexual instinct, and its replacement by the promotion of strength and the celebration of sexual vitality.

15 This reference has proved untraceable.

16 Reprinted by permission from Macmillan Publishers Ltd: *Nature* (145: 3663), copyright (1940).

'Few human beings,' says Mr Wells in his new book, 'are able to change their primary ideas after the middle thirties. They get fixed in them and drive before them no more intelligently than animals before their innate impulses.' Here he does himself a great injustice. We used to wonder what panacea he would discover next. He was sure to advocate it in a brilliant and stimulating manner.

But the time comes to all of us – it came to me long ago – when our mind stiffens, and we become, as a Frenchman unkindly said, the comedians of our early convictions. The hardships of his early life[17] have permanently embittered Mr Wells against the class in which his genius has placed him. He sees Red[18] when he thinks of them, and exults in the destitution which he hopes awaits them.

So, since he is far too well-informed to be a Bolshevik, he has nailed his colours to[19] that waterlogged derelict, Fabian collectivism. We have only to make a clean sweep of emulation, ambition, love of private ownership, patriotism and pugnacity, and we shall be as happy, progressive and intelligent as a flock of sheep. That is always the way with Utopians. Abolish all the strongest passions and instincts of human nature, and a terminal state of blessedness, an earthly paradise,[20] will be reached.

It is pathetic to look at the row of deserted idols which we used to worship in the last century: Liberalism, Democracy, Human Perfectibility,[21] Socialism, Communism – there are few any more to do them reverence. Liberalism, which might sweep the suburbs with the Gladstonian[22] creed of peace and retrenchment, is content to limp feebly after Labour,[23] and has paid the penalty. Democracy is still a fetish in America, where it means anything, from an attribute of the Deity to a method of therapeutics, except what it really is, a not very successful experiment in government. 'Uric acid,'[24] I read in a New York medical

---

17 A reference to Wells's escape from retail trade and his self-education to become a successful author and world figure.

18 Gets extremely angry.

19 Commit oneself to a position.

20 The Garden of Eden or any other imagined perfect place on Earth.

21 A notion, originating during the Enlightenment, that humans (individually) or, more commonly, humankind could be perfected through cultural (especially educational), political (especially statist) or scientific (especially eugenic) means.

22 Of or pertaining to William Gladstone or his policies, especially in regard to limited government expenditure, low taxes, balanced budgets, free trade and equality of opportunity through institutional reform.

23 The Labour Party, a British social democratic political party, founded in 1900 as the Labour Representation Committee before being renamed in 1906.

24 An insoluble acid excreted in urine.

journal, 'is tottering on its throne. The triumphs of Democracy are not confined to politics.'[25] Elsewhere it is merely accepted from inertia, and from fear of something worse. No institution has lost in prestige so much as the House of Commons. Who now reads the dreary debates, which are not expected to turn a single vote? (Democracy as a form of society – equality of consideration – is a different matter; some other name ought to be found for it.) As for human perfectibility, nobody any longer believes in a law of progress. The fact of progress in the past – for example, in the eighteenth and nineteenth centuries – cannot be denied. But in the future? We began with faith, we went on with hope; now there is nothing left but charity.

Socialism has never recovered from giving birth to its misbegotten brat Communism. There was such a thing as Social Democracy,[26] though Socialism and Democracy are fundamentally incompatible. Nothing could be more ignominious than the total collapse of the Social Democrats in Italy and Germany at the first impact of Fascism.[27] The Bolsheviks found that the Social Democrats had not got the true milk of the word, and helped in their overthrow.[28] Mussolini and Hitler were quick to observe the signs of the times.

Communism is also practically dead. It exists in the USSR only for export; the Government of the Soviet Republic is pure Fascism or State capitalism.[29] It would be difficult to name any prediction of Marx that has not been falsified by history; but the most significant of all his miscalculations was that after the success of the social revolution the State would 'wither away'.[30] Instead of withering away, the State in Russia is omnipotent,[31] the most brutal and searching tyranny that the world has ever known. Communism at home is now the creed of a few *enragés*[32] and armchair doctrinaires,[33] and of callow[34] boys and girls at Oxford,[35] Cambridge[36] and the London School of Economics.[37]

---

25 This reference has proved untraceable.

26 A socialist system achieved by democratic means, or the advocates of such a system collectively.

27 A reference to the ineffectiveness of the social democratic opposition to the rise of fascism in Italy (1922) and Germany (1933).

28 A reference to the Bolsheviks overthrow of the Menshevik government in Russia in October 1917.

29 A socialist system whereby the state exerts exclusive control over production and the use of capital.

30 In Marxist theory, the natural disappearance of the state following a period of proletarian dictatorship.

31 Having unlimited power.

32 A radical group during the French Revolution of 1789 who argued that liberty for all meant more than mere constitutional rights; occasionally used as a label for later revolutionary practitioners.

The total failure of the prophecy that the State under Soviet Socialism would wither away is important because it affects other kinds of socialism. The inevitable result of collectivism is to deprive the citizen of all liberty, and to put him at the mercy of a horde of ignorant, indolent and insolent Jacks-in-office,[38] who take their orders from above. This is the crucial difference between State-socialism[39] and democracy. The bureaucracy under socialism must take their orders from above. Mr Wells wishes his citizens to be free to speak their minds; but your bureaucrat cannot stand criticism, and will know well enough how to gag it. Mr Wells's Gestapo[40] are to be 'sturdy and assertive'. There is no fear of their being anything else.

State-capitalism can make out a plausible case for itself. But apart from the difficulty of finding skilled administrators who are willing to give their best for a very small salary (in the USSR differential salaries are as steeply graded as in England) in the absence of competition it is most unlikely that the infinitely complicated affairs of a great industrial community would be competently handled by State officials. Such experience as is available is very discouraging to the advocates of that favourite Fabian slogan, 'a planned economy'.

I entirely agree with Mr Wells's detestation of the new idol which has dethroned the fetishes of the Victorians – frenzied nationalism. The deification[41] of the State is indeed a monstrous and Satanic form of idolatry. It is at present the strongest force in the world, though it must be said to the credit of the democratic countries that it has made few converts in England, France or the United States. It unfortunately commands the allegiance of some of the best as well as the worst elements in the totalitarian[42] countries, and is therefore the greatest danger that European civilisation has ever had to meet. Nevertheless, to speak of the possible 'extinction of mankind' (p. 18) is surely a violent exaggeration. The worst that can happened to Europe, if we persist in what are really civil wars,[43]

---

33   Ideologues who wear political labels but who take no constructive political action.

34   Inexperienced, raw, youthful.

35   The University of Oxford.

36   The University of Cambridge.

37   A constituent college of the University of London, established in 1895.

38   An insolent fellow in authority; a self-important minor official.

39   A political system whereby the state owns the public utilities and industries.

40   Abbreviated German, *Geheime Staatspolizei*, the state secret police of Nazi Germany (1933-45).

41   The process of rendering something godlike in character, spirit or quality.

42   Pertaining to a political regime in which only one party is tolerated and to which all other institutions are subordinated.

43   Military conflicts between citizens of the same country.

waged with greater fury than the old wars of religion,[44] is that we may be plunged into another 'dark age', which we may hope would not last six hundred years, like the welter of barbarism which followed the downfall of Graeco-Roman civilisation.[45] But America and the British Dominions[46] would survive and hand down the torch.[47] Count Keyserling, in his *Révolution Mondiale*, unaccountably forgot the not unimportant part of the human race who speak English. For I do not think that even Great Britain will either cease to exist or relapse into savagery.

I also agree with the author about the ruinous folly of the present war[48]; but perhaps at present the less said the better on that subject.

One protest I must make in conclusion. I am not supposed to be very fond of the Roman Catholic Church, but I deprecate Mr Wells's very harsh words about that institution. Catholicism is certainly anti-revolutionary. With its unequalled experience of human nature, that Church knows that revolutions always lead to reactions, and achieve very little at a terrible cost of human suffering. But it preserves some valuable traditions which are in some danger of being lost, including a philosophy which is far superior to modern systems. I am specially distressed to read what Mr Wells says about Spain.[49] I cannot understand how any decent person can deny that the Nationalists[50] were justified in taking arms against those devils in human shape, the Spanish Reds,[51] who, fighting under the 'hammer and sickle',[52] and under orders from Moscow, butchered three hundred thousand men and women, a hundred thousand in Madrid alone, in an attempt to extirpate whole classes of the population. It is difficult to forget what an American eye-witness saw in the town of Ronda, near Malaga. The Reds impaled on stakes all the male inhabitants who belonged to the middle class, and while they were dying in agony compelled them to watch their wives and daughters being

---

44 A series of conflicts in France between Catholics and Huguenots (1562-98) over dynastic control of the country.

45 The period, c. 476-1000, from the fall of Rome to the intellectual revival in Europe.

46 Self-governing territories within the British Empire, the first being Canada (from 1867).

47 Pass on a tradition or experience.

48 I. e., the Second World War.

49 A reference to the Spanish Civil War (1936-39), triggered by an attempted coup by Francisco Franco against the republican government in Spain, resulting in Franco's victory.

50 The forces in the Spanish Civil War supporting General Franco against the democratic government.

51 Communists or socialists.

52 The symbol of communism and of the Communist Party throughout the world, originally used in Soviet Russia after the 1917 Bolshevik revolution and forming an integral part of the Soviet flag from 1923 to 1991.

first violated[53] and then burnt alive.[54] There are scores of similar horrors equally well authenticated.

Although Mr Wells's Utopia seems to me utterly unrealisable, no one can read the book without admiration for his earnest longing for a new and better world. As Plato said of his *Republic*, the type of the perfect State is laid up in heaven,[55] and we need not inquire too curiously whether it is likely to be realised on earth. The obstacles are human sin and folly, and we shall soon have sharp enough lessons to cure all but the incurable.

Comment on Inge: H. G. Wells, letter to the editor, 'Victorian Socialism' (27 January 1940).[56]

In a very interesting essay entitled 'Victorian Socialism' which Dean Inge contributed to *Nature* of January 13 as if it were a review of my *New World Order*, he makes certain statements for which I think it is reasonable to demand documentation. He says that the Nationalists (that is, the Franco rebels) took arms 'against those devils in human shape, the Spanish Reds', etc. But is it not a matter of fact and common knowledge that Franco led his Moors[57] against a Liberal Republican[58] Government which had recently suppressed a very dangerous anarchist-socialist rising?[59] (see Sender's *Seven Red Sundays*, translated by Sir Peter Chalmers Mitchell, FRS). Further, he gives an explicit account of abominable atrocities committed at Ronda. But surely in *Nature* we want something more than an unnamed 'American eye-witness' for statements of that sort. Who was he? How can we check his testimony? Is he available for cross-examination? Then about that three hundred thousand men and women 'butchered under

---

53 Raped.

54 This evidence comes from *The Second and Third Reports on the Communist Atrocities Committed in Southern Spain from July to October, 1936, by the Communist Forces of the Madrid Government* (1937) by the Committee of Investigation Appointed by the National Government at Burgos.

55 In many religions, the abode of God, where the pious ascend after death.

56 Reprinted by permission from Macmillan Publishers Ltd: *Nature* (145: 3665), copyright (1940). This letter has previously been reprinted in Smith 1998, IV: 256-57.

57 A people of mixed Berber and Arab descent who inhabit Mauritania and parts of Morocco, Western Sahara, Algeria, Niger and Mali.

58 Of, belonging to or characteristic of a republic, a form of government which rejects hereditary rule.

59 A reference to the general strike of 1 October 1934 which turned into a leftwing rising on 6 October in Asurias, Spain, which was crushed by the army on the orders of the government. However, the government was a rightwing coalition under Alejandro Garcia and not the 'Liberal Republican Government' Wells refers to, which came to power in January 1936.

orders from Moscow'. Is there a single respectable scrap of evidence for any part of that statement which we may find quoted presently as a statement made in *Nature*.

Reply to Wells: William Inge, letter to the editor (27 January 1940).[60]

I have made a careful study of the Spanish horrors, and have accepted none but well-documented evidence. The Ronda story is from a book by Arthur Bryant.[61] I could have found several equally dreadful examples by Spanish eye-witnesses, but some of them I did not care to keep on my shelves. The estimate of 300,000 victims is official; some have put the number much higher. Krivitsky's *I Was Stalin's Agent* is most illuminating; for example, p. 120: 'The Ogpu[62] had done a brilliant piece of work. In Dec. 1936 the terror[63] was sweeping Madrid, Barcelona, and Valencia. The Ogpu ... carried out assassinations and kidnappings.... The Soviet Union had a grip on Loyalist Spain,[64] as if it were already a Soviet possession.' This book may be enough for my friend Mr Wells, who is a very honest man.

'Civilisation and the Rights of Man' (17 February 1940).[65]

Much has been said and written recently on the causes of the present conflict[66] between Germany and the Allies and the conditions of peace, but most of it has been from the point of view of national expediency and little from that of the history of civilisation or the future of mankind. In his two latest books – *The Fate of Homo Sapiens* and *The New World Order* – Mr H. G. Wells takes an eagle-eyed view of the world of man, as he did in his *Outline of History*, and brings his critical mind to bear upon what he sees. With a few other students of history he realises that the scientific method of inquiry can be profitably applied

---

60 Reprinted by permission from Macmillan Publishers Ltd: *Nature* (145: 3665), copyright (1940).

61 *The Second and Third Reports on the Communist Atrocities Committed in Southern Spain from July to October, 1936, by the Communist Forces of the Madrid Government* produced by the Committee of Investigation Appointed by the National Government at Burgos (1937), for which Bryant wrote a preface.

62 A secret police agency in the USSR (1923-34).

63 A period of brutal suppression or intimidation by those in power.

64 During the Spanish Civil War, those forces which supported the republican government against the nationalist opposition.

65 Reprinted by permission from Macmillan Publishers Ltd: *Nature* (145: 3668), copyright (1940).

66 I. e., the Second World War.

to political and social problems, as it is to other aspects of biological development. In the struggle for existence of all forms of life, many factors are involved; and the aim of scientific investigation is to discover their nature and influence. The history of civilisation shows that the chief causes of war have been migratory movements – represented in modern times by access to natural resources and the claim for *Lebensraum*[67] – aggressive nationalism, racial lust and religious hatred.

In the natural instincts which have led to struggles between groups of peoples, mankind is the same as it was at the beginning of civilisation six thousand years ago.[68] There has been great increase of knowledge but not a corresponding increase of wisdom in the use of it. If an individual or a nation has the will to avert a claim by force, he can acquire in an open market whatever power he is prepared to pay for and use. In a civilised community, citizens protect themselves from such dangerous disturbers of the peace by means of a police force; but there is no similar force to prevent breaches of the world's order by truculent nations, and no international court whose judgements upon disputes are accepted as final.

If the civilised world is to survive, the hour has come when measures will have to be devised to control the 'gangster' element in human nature, whenever or wherever it manifests itself. Authority to exercise such power will come only when nations believe that it is in their own interest to combine for the common good of the whole community of mankind. How this end will be attained, and the changes which will have to be made in social and political structures in order to achieve it, signify reconstruction of existing systems in a manner which may rightly be described as revolutionary. The aim of such a revolution is not, however, to readjust class relationships, but to create a world commonwealth of free peoples conscious of their responsibilities one to another, and accepting the principle of 'Live and let live'[69] rather than that of 'Lie and let lie', which is often an excuse for political diplomacy.

This is the type of revolution which Mr Wells foresees, if civilisation is to be saved from self-destruction. He urges that 'It is the system of nationalistic individualism and uncoordinated enterprise that is the world's disease'; and that the old foundations of the system have proved unable to support the ponderous structure which has been built upon them. To strengthen one part by political

---

67 German, space for living; territory which many German nationalists in the mid-twentieth century claimed was needed for the survival and healthy development of their nation.

68 The Sumer civilisation, beginning c. 4000 BC, is considered the first human civilisation by many anthropologists.

69 Be tolerant of others and be so tolerated.

balance of power[70] or alliances makes other parts of the structure relatively weaker, with the result that the stability of the whole suffers. Mr Wells has, therefore, no sympathy with the movement for the federation of a number of European States,[71] unless it is deliberately made the basis of a system designed ultimately to comprehend all the peoples of the world.

There is nothing new in the spirit of this intention. The philosophy of the Stoics included the principle of the brotherhood of man[72] and the merging of all nationalities in a cosmopolitan citizenship. Christianity adopted the same ethical doctrine, and still pursues it; yet neither in economic nor in political spheres are national policies or actions determined by it. After nearly two thousand years of teaching peace on earth, good will towards men,[73] this principle of all systems of ethics does not enter into the field of practical politics of Christian nations any more than it does in other communities. It may be that a world commonwealth of nations is just as far off as a world fellowship of religious faiths, but that does not make the ideal less worthy of effort to attain it. The mines and torpedoes which lie in the track of civilisation at the present time make it more necessary now than ever it was for navigators to be guided by a single light, instead of each ship of State,[74] or convoy, following a course which must cross the tracks of others and lead to collisions.

Though, in the past, war has played a part in the formation of certain groups, it represents only one phase in the development of civilisation. It is true that civilisation has developed through individual peoples, as, historically speaking, mankind has been organised on that basis, but we, as heirs of the ages[75] – to use a trite but expressive phase in this connection – are not interested in the survival of these peoples, except in so far as they have contributed to the general advancement of the human race. The trend of cultural achievement in the advancement of mankind has been to operate through larger and larger unities – tribe, people, nation, confederacy – eliminating war and the struggle for exist-

---

70 An objective in international relations whereby the dominant powers in world or regional affairs manipulate events and relationships, often through alliances, to prevent any one power predominating.

71 A reference to the Federal Union movement founded in 1939 for the immediate federation of all democratic states, to result in ultimate world federation after the war.

72 The first known philosophical concept of cosmopolitanism, espoused by the Stoics in the pre-Christian Greek and Roman worlds.

73 A quotation from the New Testament Bible, Luke 2: 14.

74 A reference to Plato's metaphor in *The Republic* which likens the governance of a city-state to the command of a ship, concluding that only benevolent men with absolute power are capable of captaining the ship.

75 Contemporary humanity as the inheritor of all the past's achievements.

ence as physical facts, and relying more and more on the struggle for existence between ideas.

It is towards such a world commonwealth, in which each nation can be free to follow its own course of cultural development, that Mr Wells would direct civilised thought. It may be held that this conception represents merely a reversion to primitive social structures; but the difference is in the extent of outlook. Whereas, in the primitive form, the sense of responsibility embraces the members of the same blood-kin[76] only, or those of the local group within which the members are more or less intimately acquainted, in a modern society it may reach out to embrace all members of a great nation, and possibly, when conflicting creeds and ideals agree to sink their differences, it may extend to all men of good will, to whom the dignity of man as an individual entity transcends racial and political boundaries.

When, if ever, this comes to pass, it will be possible to gauge how far mankind has advanced along the road of ethical as well as material progress. To many, the way seems long to go. The urge of nationalism and its ideals, combined with belief in might as the sole arbiter of right, has diverted the thoughts of peoples away from the main stream of human progress into narrower channels in which rocks and rapids threaten at every turn to shipwreck all that is best in civilisation.

In what is conceived to be the highest type of civilisation to-day, certain ethical and humane sentiments, such as those of truth and righteousness, justice and mercy, and sympathy with the weak and suffering, are possessed and practised by a greater number of the community than ever before. These high attributes of human nature have survived the ages of violence, cruelty and rapine[77] which have disgraced European history, and by which the recrudescence[78] in our own times will be remembered. In spite of the degrading influences, there has been an increase in the true, the humane and the just, and the standards of conduct towards others have become ethically higher, until now no people or nation which reverts to such methods can claim to be in the van[79] of modern civilisation. In so far as the present conflict is one of ideals, it may fairly be said that those of the Allies represent a far higher ethical standard than exists at present in Germany.

Freedom of thought and speech, belief and investigation, subject only to the recognition of the same liberty on the part of others, is threatened by the new

---

76   Persons related by blood as against marriage.

77   Plunder, pillage.

78   The state or fact of breaking out afresh.

79   Abbreviation of vanguard, the foremost part of a company of people moving or prepared to move forwards.

tyrannies[80] which through their aggressive militarism and economic national-ism[81] run mad, seek to reduce the citizen to a soulless unit and a condition of moral and intellectual servitude. The existence of economic antagonism and military rivalries among nations is as grave a danger to scientific thought and investigation, upon which so many material achievements are based, as it is to the general progress of civilised life. Science must, therefore, stand for high human values, as against slavery of the spirit of man, if civilisation is to be preserved from the dangers which now threaten it.

There are certain fundamental human rights[82] the recognition of which would do much to promote a sense of common interest among the peoples of the world. Mr Wells gives the first draft of such a Declaration of the Rights of Man[83] in his *New World Order*;[84] and the *Daily Herald*[85] is submitting it to free and wide discussion[86] with the view of constructing a new charter to represent man's just claims in a modern society. The intention is eventually to produce a Declaration which will represent world-wide opinion, and will crystallise the thoughts of men and women of all ranks and of all races who believe in the essential greatness of mankind. It is hoped that such a Declaration at the present epoch may have valuable consequences in shaping the structure of human society to the benefit of mankind.

Representatives of science are invited, with those interested in other fields of progressive life, to assist in making the final form of the Declaration a worthy and enduring statement of human needs. The time has come for an assertion of the rights of scientific and other intellectual workers in modern life, in view of the conditions of cruelty and suppression to which their work is now subject in some countries. Such a Declaration would insist that creative ideas are the essence of progressive thought and achievement in science, as in art and literature; and that to make them subversive to the principles of any social doctrine or political system is to restrain the expansion of the human mind and its means of

---

80   Cruel or oppressive governments or rule.

81   A term used to describe policies which are guided by the idea of protecting domestic consumption, labour and capital formation, even if this requires the imposition of tariffs and other restrictions on the movement of labour, goods and capital.

82   Rights held to be justifiably claimed by any person.

83   Fundamental rights of the individual which ought to be safeguarded in law. Wells led a campaign for the reassertion of these between 1939 and 1944.

84   In fact, the original draft was published as a letter to the *Times* on 25 October 1939 (Smith 1998, IV: 242-44).

85   British leftwing daily newspaper from 1912 to 1964.

86   Between 5 and 24 February 1940 Wells introduced each of the ten clauses of his 'Rights of Man' proposal in the *Daily Herald* and the paper published comments and suggestions regarding the clauses on its letters pages.

expression. Research can be organised and team-work be profitably applied to solve particular problems, but the true heart of science is in original independent thought; and this can neither be created nor regimented by political authority.

It has been suggested that a charter should be framed embodying these and other principles of liberty of thought, and freedom from the frustration by authority, which have long been assumed to be characteristic of scientific activity. Little encouragement has been given to this idea in scientific circles, otherwise the Society for the Protection of Science and Learning,[87] or the British Association's Division for Social and International Relations of Science,[88] would no doubt have produced such a charter. The world of science is international in its constitution and aims, and citizenship can be claimed in it by men and women of any race or nationality who will respect the principles implied in the pursuit of scientific truth and endeavour to contribute to the advancement of natural knowledge by following them. The Declaration of the Rights of Man which should emerge from the discussion organised by the *Daily Herald* will no doubt include these principles, among others which may be justly claimed by all the citizens of the modern world.

John Hardwick, 'Man's Present and Future' (21 March 1942).[89]

The Outlook for Homo Sapiens: An Unemotional Statement of the Things that are Happening to him Now, and of the Immediate Possibilities Confronting Him. By H. G. Wells. (An amalgamation and modernisation of two books – *The Fate of Homo Sapiens* and *The New World Order*, published severally in 1939 and 1940. Pp. 287. (London: Secker and Warburg, Ltd., 1942.) 8s. 6d. net.

The present volume is an amalgamation of two earlier books, *The Fate of Homo Sapiens* (1939) and *The New World Order* (1940). It will be remembered that in the earlier book Mr Wells stressed the need for some contemporary movement similar to that of the French Encyclopaedists of the eighteenth century, so that the human species, now dangerously out of harmony with its environment, might be enabled to make the necessary mental readjustments. He wants a campaign for a 'reinvigorated and modernised education', primarily scientific in character.

---

87 A British organisation which assists émigré scholars with research funding and assistance in finding employment, founded in 1933 (as the Academic Assistance Council, being renamed in 1936).

88 Founded in 1938 by the British Association as a mouthpiece for scientists to express opinions about the international impact of their research and discoveries. It was dissolved in the 1950s.

89 Reprinted by permission from Macmillan Publishers Ltd: *Nature* (149: 3777), copyright (1942).

The scientific vision of life in the universe and no other has to be his vision of the universe. Any other leads ultimately to disaster. And since the existing educational organisation of the world does not provide anything like that vision nor establish the necessary conceptions of right conduct that arise out of it, it needs to be recast quite as much and even more than the political framework. This will almost certainly involve such a kultur-kampf as the world has never seen before.

This new education will not stand by itself but will be a part of a new organisation of human life involving 'outright world-socialism scientifically planned and directed, *plus* a sustained insistence upon law, law based on a fuller, more jealously conceived restatement of the personal Rights of Man'. Summarising his programme, Mr Wells speaks of 'the triangle of collectivisation, law and knowledge'.

Mr Wells makes short work of current ideologies and religions. 'There is no creed, no way of living left in the world at all, that really meets the needs of the time.' He even seems somewhat dubious about the Division for the Social and International Relations of Science recently created by the British Association, and says that two divergent tendencies display themselves in it.

One is plainly to organise and implement the common creative impulse in the scientific mind so as to make it a vital factor in public opinion; the other is to restrain any such development of an authoritative and perhaps embarrassing criticism of the conduct of public affairs and to keep the man of science modestly to his present subordination.

Mr Wells is of the opinion that great possibilities await scientific research if his new and stirring education increased the numbers of workers available. 'I throw out the suggestion that in our present-day world, of all the brains capable of great and masterful contributions to "scientific" thought and achievement, not one in a thousand, not one in a score of thousands, ever gets born into such conditions as to realise its opportunities. And of the millions who would make good, useful, eager secondary research workers and explorers, not one in a million is utilised.'

Mr Wells writes with a strong sense of urgency. For the better part of his life this prolific and ingenious writer has been one of the foremost of our propagandists for an outlook which is at the same time scientific and humane. It has now become a question how far the scientific outlook is *necessarily* bound up with humane and liberal ideals, and perhaps Mr Wells is too ready to take such a connection for granted. For this reason it is perhaps a pity that Mr Wells is so impatient of the traditional religions, for though in the past they may have been, and may sometimes still be, obstacles to progress, yet they too are capable of leading men to make 'mental readjustments' of a desirable kind. To take one example. According to the Hindu[90] view of life, when a man has reached a certain age and fulfilled certain responsibilities, he should retire from active life and devote himself to the contemplation of the ultimate mysteries.[91] Mr Wells might consider this a waste of time; but by banishing all the men of sixty from active life it would ease the situation of those surplus and frustrated young men whose existence Mr Wells regards as the chief cause of wars.

---

90 Pertaining to Hinduism, a religion characterised by a belief in reincarnation, the worship of several gods and an ordained caste system as the basis of society.

91 The nature and origin of life, and the after-life.

2.32: *Babes in the Darkling Wood*

James Crowther, review of *Babes in the Darkling Wood* (28 December 1940).[1]

Babes in the Darkling Wood by H. G. Wells. Pp. 399. (London: Martin Secker and Warburg, Ltd., 1940.) 9*s*. 6*d*. net.

Mr H. G. Wells has done much to raise the prestige of science among the people. Here, at the age of seventy-four, he is still trying, with the intensest energy, to communicate to the generality of mankind the implications of science. In his latest book he has used the technique of the novel of ideas[2] to represent the attitude of young people to current events, and suggest what line they should pursue in the light of modern psychology. The ideas of Pavlov and Freud are discussed at length through the dialogues of the characters, but though an impression of their importance is conveyed successfully, they are not very clearly explained.

Mr Wells recommends that the problem of modern life should be approached in the spirit of the sculptor who contemplates a block of uncarved marble. The possibilities in it should be conceived by a flexible imagination, and all should hack away at it until they have carved out the figure of society that they desire. The advantage of this approach is that it precludes doctrinaire planning. The sculptor is unable to make a finished preliminary draft of the three-dimensional end at which he aims, and must trust to the guidance of intelligent imagination in the course of his work. But this does not prevent him from having some drafts, and a model in his imagination which undergoes continual adaptation and is therefore living. Though Mr Wells tends to become ever more discursive, his belief in the future and continual wrestlings with the present are still a major inspiration.

---

1   Reprinted by permission from Macmillan Publishers Ltd: *Nature* (146: 3713), copyright (1940).

2   A fictional work of literature used to exercise the author's socio-political ideas.

2.33: *The Conquest of Time*

Herbert Dingle, 'The Triumph of Time' (17 October 1942).[1]

The Conquest of Time by H. G. Wells. (The Thinker's Library, No. 92.) Pp. x + 86. (London: Watts and Co., Ltd., 1942.) 2*s*. net.

This little book has been written by Mr Wells to supersede *First and Last Things*, which was his attempt in 1908 'to get my ideas about the world and myself into some sort of order'. The new volume is stated on the cover to be the author's presentation of 'the final fruits of his philosophic thought', and he himself presents it as 'a fairly lucid and consistent summary of modern ideas concerning the fundamentals and ultimates of existence'. The change of title is at least appropriate, for one who has conquered time becomes as God, with whom there is no last or first, and the brevity of the book is as commendable as it is rare in a treatment of so large a theme.

Mr Wells's philosophy is as follows. The individual human life is a synthesis of isolated experiences, often mistakenly regarded as continuous. This illusion of temporal continuity creates a dread of its cessation, death, and of pain, and gives rise to an idea of persistence after death which imposes the tyranny of the dead past on the living present. The individual is actually an element in a larger structure, the species, with which it interacts. The character of the species largely determines (through both physical inheritance and mental adaptation) the character of the individual, whose variations from the norm in turn react on and modify the character of the species. The individual life is thus not 'a tale told by an idiot'; it is a factor in the progress towards 'the awakening of consciousness in the universe'. As the universe through the species advances to this goal, the successive generations of individuals gradually become freed from the tyranny of time. They cease to fear death, they acquire more knowledge of the forgotten past and more insight into the future, thus acquiring 'an ever-expanding Now'. The religion of the new man 'demands the subordination of the self, of the aggressive personality, to the common creative task, which is the conquest and animation of the universe by life'. The full course of the individual human life will be 'from action to an ultimate serene and impersonal contemplation. The body and the personality will die at length like and old garment laid aside'.

All this drama of evolution, however, is simply an appearance to our conscious life of what is actually a rigid, determined system in four-dimensional space-time. The latter is the reality; 'it is simply from the subjective and illusory point of view that there seems to be free movement' – that is, movement along the time axis. 'Our consciousness is a series of delusively unified conditioned

1   Reprinted by permission from Macmillan Publishers Ltd: *Nature* (150: 3807), copyright (1942).

reflexes'[2] – an 'illusion of a unified personality' which 'joins up a series of traces which constitute our conscious life'. The passage of time is an illusion; all that is actual in personal life is a discrete set of static points in the rigid four-dimensional system, and somewhere in that frame, at places having higher values of the t-co-ordinate[3] than ours, a very much larger number of points – 'the universe' – possesses consciousness (which presumably means that it also has illusions, though Mr Wells does not state specifically what the life of the universe is). This is the conquest of time.

As a summary of a lifetime's study of the fundamentals and ultimates of existence, the book is surprising in two respects. In the first place, it is written more carelessly than one would have thought fitting for the occasion. True, we sometimes meet the perfect phrase – for example, the reference to 'a God-shaped void' in the mind of the infant – but more often passages occur which seem meaningless, such as 'this present period of world warfare,[4] in which ... people die far more significantly than they have ever died before', or 'Natural Philosophy[5] ... went along the line of science, in the expectation that a great free correlation of individual effort would ensure without further effort as the collective truth'. Secondly, there is little of the 'serene and impersonal contemplation' which is to mark the maturity of the new man and which, we are told, one may 'share to a very considerable extent even now'. The book is as full of vigour and combativeness as anything that Mr Wells has written; it looks for strength in vitriolic protestation rather than in quietness and in confidence. It impresses one, in fact, as the product more of temporary excitement than of settled conviction.

It is, however, the substance of the book, and not its form, that calls for chief attention, and it may be said at once that it is unconvincing. To explain why, it is necessary to consider briefly what we mean by time, and how we have come to mean it.

It is not generally realised by modern scientific thinkers what little prominence time had in pre-Galilean[6] philosophies. It was taken for granted as being practically identical with consciousness itself, thus calling for no special thought on its own account. The great achievement of Galileo was to create conceptions in terms of which motion could be treated mathematically, and to this end he presented time as *a space-like dimension which could be measured* – divided up

---

2   Properly, classical conditioning, reflex responses to a non-natural stimulus established by training in a person or animal.

3   The plotting of time on a graph.

4   I. e., the Second World War.

5   The branch of knowledge that deals with the principles governing the material universe and perception of physical phenomena.

6   Pertaining to Galileo Galilei and his ideas.

into equal parts as a length is. But this dimension, or spacified extension, of time was so conceived for the one purpose of making motion amenable to mathematical treatment. The world describable in terms of it was specifically limited by Galileo to the world of mechanical phenomena. All else – even physical experiences like heat, sounds, smells, colours and the rest – he excluded from this world and located in the perceiving being.

It is difficult to over-estimate the value of this colossal achievement, for it has made possible the whole of modern physical science. It is difficult also to over-estimate the illusions it has created, for, having seen the value of the concept of 'spacified' time in mechanics, subsequent thinkers, less perspicacious than Galileo, have taken it to be a universal receptacle for the whole of human experience, and therefore as representing in a more precise form everything that human consciousness has ever meant by time. Consequently, the whole of experience has been distorted to fit a concept to which most of it is non-conformable. Our experiences have been ranged out in the mathematical continuum, and hopes and fears and passions (which are obviously non-spatial) have been placed cheek by jowl[7] with the spatial positions of mass particles[8] as occurring at such and such instants of spacified time, and the incongruous 'history' thus built up has been regarded as something objectively 'true' and infinitely more 'realistic' than the direct experiences which have been so regimented.

How different our modern conception of time is from that of pre-Galilean thinkers may be illustrated in several ways, of which perhaps the simplest is to ask what we mean by the 'reversal' of time.[9] We take this now to mean simply a reversal of the order of events in the time sequence, made visible by running a cinema film backwards, because we have lost the habit of thinking of time except as a space-like dimension. To a pre-Galilean, however, the phrase would have seemed rather silly, but it would have suggested a state of mind in which one knew the future but not the past, and as fast as the future became realised it would be forgotten except in so far as we might calculate it as we now calculate future eclipses.[10] The reversal of time would have been a passage from actuality into impotentiality, instead of that from potentiality into actuality of which we are, in fact, conscious. The loss of ready awareness of this aspect of time, and the imposition of another, admirably suited for its purpose, on the whole of experience, for most of which it is not at all suited, is the true tyranny, and the first

---

7   Side by side; close together; intimately.

8   Particles containing mass.

9   The reversal of the order of events.

10 The interception of the light of celestial objects by the intervention of other objects between the objects in question and the observer, or between the objects in question and what illuminates them.

step towards any conquest of time must be the release of our thought from this incubus.[11]

Towards this end Mr Wells contributes nothing. He accepts unquestioned the Galilean conception, in its Einstein-Minkowski rather than its Newtonian[12] development, and is blind to all that it ignores. He tries to mould experience to fit it, and thinks that he has thereby released experience from it. His 'conquest' of time is, in fact, a complete and whole-hearted surrender. He maps out the history of the individual and the species; shows where our various emotions and aspirations are located in the time sequence of the individual; is convinced that when he has so distributed all the experiences which come within range of his knowledge the individual ceases to be; and sums up our personality as merely 'serviceable synthetic illusions of continuity'.

Mr Wells's view of the space-time continuum of relativity[13] is fundamentally erroneous. That continuum is a conception, a development of the original Galilean terms more flexible than the Newtonian development, and so better fitted for the purposes of mechanical physics. It is not, as Mr Wells imagines, something independently existing to which experience must be adapted, but precisely the reverse. We do not explore the universe and count its dimensions; we try to rationalise out experience of movements, and choose as a means of doing so the concept of a continuum of 1, 2, 3, ... or n dimensions,[14] whichever makes our task simplest. In science experience is sacred. We may describe it as we like in order to establish rational relations between one experience and another, but what we cannot do is to deny it; hence whatever we do with motion cannot legitimately contain a denial of it. Now let us hear Mr Wells: 'From the standpoint of the space-time continuum there is no movement; the whole system is rigid. It is simply from the subjective and illusory point of view that there seems to be free movement.' He takes the Frankenstein monster[15] and puts the experience for which it was created under its control.

This inversion of the ordering of scientific reasoning, by which experience is subjected to the creations of reason instead of being the origin and end of their creation, is so vital to the whole subject that another example will not be out of place. 'In our universe', writes Mr Wells, 'the extreme limit of motion is

---

11   A thing which oppresses or troubles like a nightmare.

12   Designating the classical mechanics of Isaac Newton which is concerned with the set of physical laws governing and mathematically describing the motion of bodies and aggregates of bodies.

13   The theory that space and time are relative concepts.

14   'N' meaning number, this refers to any dimension.

15   A terrible creation, something that becomes terrible to its creator, from *Frankenstein* (1818) by Mary Shelley.

299,796 kilometres a second. Nothing has ever been know to go faster than that. You can imagine yourself doing so, you can imagine yourself on a rocket going at 299,796 kilometres a second, and you can imagine yourself standing up and leaping forward so as to go faster than that alleged maximum. But in reality you cannot do that. You are imagining the impossible.'

This is quite wrong. Whether the rocket is moving with any speed at all or is at rest, you can leap forward just the same; it is, in fact, the first principle of relativity that what happens in a system is independent of the uniform motion of that system as a whole. The finite maximum of material velocities is a characteristic not of motion but of *the terms in which we choose to measure motion*. What is true is that, when we leap forward from the rocket, an observer to whom the rocket is moving at Mr Wells's speed and who adopts our customary method of measuring velocities, will find our speed represented by the same number as that of the rocket. But we can with equal justification choose a different scale of velocity units such that any velocity up to infinity is possible. Bridgman has described a simple process which will serve our purpose. Imagine a framework carrying a string along which a transverse vibration[16] may be sent at a definite speed relatively to the framework. Call this unit speed. Now let the framework of an exactly similar system travel side by side with this vibration. The vibration of *its* string will then move forward (relatively to the first framework, which is the standard of rest throughout) at two of our units of speed. By continuing the process we can build up a scale of velocities extending upwards to infinity.

Now let us measure some naturally occurring speed – that of an α-particle,[17] say – by such a scale. Then there is no limit to the speed which may be reached. We may imagine a particle, when it is near the speed of light, emitting an electron[18] in the same direction which travels twice as fast by this scale as the particle itself. By our ordinary system of measurement the electron would be reckoned as moving only slightly faster than the α-particle. That is because the limitation is inherent in the method of measurement; it is not something imposed on the behaviour of the moving body.

We may take a third system of measurement. A moving body can exhibit a Doppler effect,[19] and we can measure its speed by the displacement of a spec-

---

16 A wave that causes vibration in the medium in a perpendicular direction to its own motion.

17 In physics, a positively-charged particle (a helium nucleus) which is one of the three main types of decay product emitted by radioactive substances.

18 A stable subatomic particle which has a constant charge of negative electricity, is a constituent of all atoms and is the primary carrier of electric current in solids.

19 The change in frequency and wavelength of (light, sound, etc.) waves as perceived by an observer moving relative to the source of the waves.

trum[20] line. Choose a scale of velocities such that velocity is proportional to the change of wave-length, $\delta\lambda$;[21] for any speed small compared with that of light this will be very close to our present scale. But now with this scale a speed of recession may be infinite, but the speed of approach cannot be greater than a certain finite value, simply because a wave-length can be *increased* without limit, but cannot be *decreased* below zero. The same moving body, measured from in front, moves with the finite speed of light, and, measured from behind, moves infinitely fast. The fact is we can impose a finite limit on speeds, or let them become infinite, by suitably choosing our arbitrary procedure for measuring them. This is literally true, because 'finite' and 'infinite' pertain to *measures*, and not to what is measured. They are characteristics of *numbers*; they have nothing to do with experiences – or with Nature, if one prefers that term.

The deeper insight into the character of scientific reasoning which relativity has made possible is not to be fully appreciated in a generation, and no reasonable person would expect Mr Wells, whose synoptic view takes the whole field of human endeavour as its field, to be familiar with all that many specialists still find strange and paradoxical. But when he takes this very point of the maximum attainable velocity as the text for a sermon on the 'great irritation of commonplace people' faced with the necessity of shedding cherished ideas; and, further, builds on his own misconceptions a system of philosophy which he presents with such blind dogmatism that he can declare that one who sees its worth 'is bound to regard a bishop or a contemporary statesman as somewhat of a barbarian and morally and mentally his inferior.... It is difficult to talk to them as equals' – even those who must admire Mr Wells's great gifts and are most conscious of the sincerity and disinterestedness of his efforts towards a better and happier state of existence, must feel the necessity of pointing out that his magnificent castle is nothing but a mirage, and that he has little chance of seeing anything more substantial until he is prepared to grant some measure of intelligence to those who announce a different prospect, even though to him it may seem only a sandy waste.

So much for the error which lies at the root of Mr Wells's philosophy. It remains to indicate the illusory character of the most prominent feature of the philosophy itself. He is clearly justified in regarding the individual, the self, as a conception ('illusion' is not the right word) of continuity binding together a discontinuous set of memories. I can remember some incidents in my life, between which gaps exist in the time-scale, and to rationalise my experience I therefore form a conception of a continuously existing individual, my 'self', of whose

---

20   The coloured band into which a beam of light is split by means of a prism.

21   A Greek expression used in physics and chemistry to mean a small change in wave-length.

career I have forgotten some portions. In the same way, if I observe a sunspot[22] on Monday, miss the cloudy Tuesday, see it nearer the centre of the sun's disk on Wednesday and later near one limb of the sun,[23] lose it for a fortnight of so, and then pick it up near the opposite limb, I form a conception of a continuously existing spot which has rotated uninterruptedly with the sun. There comes a time, however, when I no longer see it where the postulated continuity of existence would lead me to expect, and I say that it has ceased to be – I do not doubt it – but I see no reason to suppose that therefore I, who conceived it, will thereupon cease to be conscious, any more than I ceased to be conscious when the sunspot ceased to be. Anyone who thinks I will must give some reason for his belief; there is none in the mere ending of what Mr Wells goes so far as to call an 'illusion'.

The fallacy in Mr Wells's argument is that he confuses the subjective, conscious individual, which is never in the time dimension or time stream[24] or whatever it may be called, with the postulated object of consciousness – the continuously existing self which is conceived so that it does lie along the time axis.[25] The one fundamental and inescapable characteristic of the conscious individual is that it is always and only at the present; I cannot be conscious at any time but *now*, and this is not an accident, it is obviously of the very essence of consciousness. The conquest of time consists simply in realising that we already know that. All the interactions of the postulated individual and the postulated species which Mr Wells describes so succinctly are actual and important, but they do not touch the question of the destiny of the conscious individual; they refer to a few among the many things of which he is conscious.

Despite the length of Mr Wells's extension along the t-axis,[26] he is still mentally as young as ever. We may therefore hope that in after-years, when these wild ecstasies shall be matured into a sober pleasure, and he has reached the serenity of contemplation into which the individual life shall widen out, he will give us another version of the final fruits of his philosophic thought. It is distressing to think that a life of such great achievement and penetrating vision should culminate in such an anticlimax.

---

22 A spot or patch on the surface of the sun consisting of a relatively cool region.

23 The edge of the sun.

24 Time as the fourth dimension.

25 The directional projection of time on a graph, generally in relation to space.

26 Time axis.

2.34: *Phoenix*

Baron Horder, 'World Reorganisation' (3 April 1943).[1]

Phoenix: A Summary of the Inescapable Conditions of World Reorganisation.
By H. G. Wells. Pp. 192. (London: Martin Secker and Warburg, Ltd., 1942.) 8*s.*
net.

Whether it be only an expression of the lust of the human race to live, or whether it be a rationalisation of the mass of actual happenings of our times, the notion of the persistence of society is taken for granted by the great majority of us. The threat to civilisation which the present upheaval[2] is so often supposed to represent leaves most of us rather 'cold'. All the same, if we succeed in shaking ourselves out of that state of mental inertia to which, as a nation, we are specially prone, we see clearly enough that, when we emerge from this hurly-burly,[3] we have but two alternatives before us; either we drift once more into a state of *laisser-faire*,[4] 'lose the peace'[5] and await the next cataclysm, or we organise on a world basis so as to make war impossible.

Phoenix presents us with 'a summary of the inescapable conditions of world reorganisation'. We judge from the manner in which the conditions are presented that the author, despite his careful distinction between his hope and his faith, believes in the practicability of such re-organisation and therefore in an escape from a further, and even more terrible, disaster. 'There is good reason,' he says, 'for concluding that a rational reconstruction of the world ... can still be attempted.' Does the reader ask how? The author reiterates the imperatives which a world revolution[6] must obey: the establishment of an overriding federal world control of transport and inter-State communications, the federal conservation[7] of world resources of all the federated States in accordance with a common fundamental law.

Having thus enunciated his imperatives clearly, the author, in true Wellsian fashion, takes the reader round his project 'to view it from this point of view

---

1   Reprinted by permission from Macmillan Publishers Ltd: *Nature* (151: 3831), copyright (1943).

2   I. e., the Second World War.

3   Commotion, uproar, confusion.

4   French, 'allow to do'; government abstention from interference in the actions of individuals, especially in commerce.

5   The phenomenon of a victorious military power dictating peace terms to the defeated which results in another war in the near future.

6   The complete overthrow of a government or social order by those previously subject to it.

7   The preservation of the environment, especially of natural resources.

and that' in a series of interpolations which deal with the history of war, human temperaments and the place of money in the economic life. In the second part of the book the author returns to his aspects of the world revolution. He makes it clear that he is not thinking in terms of 'bloody revolution' and an initial reign of terror. The Wells revolution is 'the transformation of a going concern and not a fresh start'. Revolution in the 'bloody' sense is the antithesis of economy. 'The institutions of to-morrow cannot be anything else than a clarified and emancipated adaptation of the institutions of to-day.' The world revolution is a transformation by release. And again: 'The ... revolutionary movement can develop ... at the higher level of the Open Conspiracy and the Candid Life.' And there are things to be done *now*; we must not wait until armistice[8] is declared, or, if armistice be not the order of the day, until the moment of unconditional surrender.[9] We must make the most strenuous efforts to reappropriate[10] the material that has been socialised for greater collective efficiency during the War.[11]

But as to the foundation of this reconstruction there is no attempt to escape the issue. 'The fundamental issue of the world conflict is the banishment of mastery and ownership from the whole world.' The citizen (in Great Britain at all events) must be a Party politician rather than a mere patriot and must throw his weight to the left. As for 'federal super-government', we must sweep the idea to the winds; quite effective machinery would be provided by special commissions to deal with settlements needed for the winding up of the War. These may be stretched out to become the effective administrative organisations of the world's affairs. We must aim at a system of federally co-operative world authorities with powers delegated to them by the existing Governments. And the ultimate pattern of society to be aimed at? It cannot be, and it need not be, clearly predicted, but it may well be something larger and more satisfactory than hitherto achieved, even by equalitarian Soviet Russia, from the economic life of which ownership has been lifted. Soviet Russia is still crudely experimental, exhibiting an extreme ideological intolerance; that draft no one should wish to stereotype. As for the Communist party in the West, it is 'a yelping intervention and not an intermediary for the expansion of a common understanding'.

So much for the imperatives of the world revolution, and so much for the machinery by which this revolution is to be effected. What of the personnel necessary for organising its unity and its convergent activities? What of the individuals upon whose selfless and determined efforts the attainment of the desidera-

---

8   A cessation of hostilities.

9   Surrender without any negotiation.

10   To take back possession of, or take possession of something again in a more systematic
     manner.

11   I. e., the Second World War.

tum[12] depends? The author's answer lies in the Sankey Declaration of the Rights of Man, the universal acceptance of which is the paramount *sine qua non*[13] for success. These 'Rights' are the propaganda for the educational organisation of the new world.

Mackenzie King recently expressed the view that if the new world order[14] is not already on its way before the War is over, we may look for it in vain. This belief finds acceptance with the author of *Phoenix*, as it does with many of us. To the question, 'Can science save civilisation?' the answer surely is, No. The salvation of society can only come through a change of heart in society itself. 'The Kingdom of Heaven[15] is within you.' But as to whether there are enough men of good will to go round and to stand as a bulwark against the efforts that will certainly be made to force the world back into the slough[16] of pre-war apathy, our seer gives no answer. How can he? He has, in this book, performed the prophet's major task – he has stabbed our spirit wide awake. He has shown us clearly the inescapability of our position and he has also shown us what is necessary for our successful emergence from it.

In the presence of so weighty (to many of us) and so convincing an argument it is perhaps trivial to complain about the interruptions that tend to weaken its cogency. The reader surely knows his Wells sufficiently by now not to have his attention distracted unduly by digressions upon 'why Generals deteriorate', 'temperamental types' and 'love in a new world'. An edited Wells is unthinkable, and the reader can deal with these chapters separately. If he cannot, then he should forgive them to the man who writes such illuminating chapters as those on 're-education', 'the protection of the consumer' and 'the lay-out of the reorganised world'. Both people and the individuals get the rough side of the author's tongue now and again. Indeed, there are few, or no, soft words for anyone. To that also the reader is not unaccustomed. But the subject is a stark one and frills are, anyway, inappropriate. *Phoenix* lays bare for us our categorical imperative.[17]

---

12   A thing lacked and wanted, a requirement.
13   Latin, an essential thing or element.
14   A vision of the world ordered differently from the way it is at present.
15   The Kingdom of God.
16   A swamp or mire.
17   In ethics, an unconditional moral obligation derived from pure reason.

2.35: *Reshaping Man's Heritage*

T. H. Hawkins, 'Science and Broadcasting' (8 July 1944).[1]

Reshaping Man's Heritage: Biology in the Service of Man. By J. S. Huxley, H. G. Wells, J. B. S. Haldane, W. G. Ogg, J. C. Drummond and W. F. Crick, J. W. Munro and J. Fisher, W. H. Kauntze, L. J. Witts, Major P. G. Edge, J. M. Mackintosh, Sir E. V. Appleton. Pp. 96 + 7 plates. (London: George Allen and Unwin, Ltd., 1944.) 5*s.* net.

Reshaping Man's Heritage comprises a series of talks which were broadcast round the theme that, by the use of science, man is achieving greater freedom as well as surer control of his heritage. The series was introduced by H. G. Wells, who spoke about man's accomplishments, opportunities and pit-falls. The other contributors are specified under the title-heading above and their talks included such subjects as man's food, the good earth, reshaping plants and animals, the conquest of the germ, the banishment of pain, and preventive medicine.[2]

Of the talks themselves little need be said. The subjects were chosen carefully, the whole group was well co-ordinated, and the names of the distinguished persons who gave the talks lent sufficient appeal to attract the mass of listeners for whom they were intended. Further, the language used by the speakers was sufficiently clear and non-technical to make the presentation one that should not have taxed any listener unversed in science

Yet this group of broadcasts raises a problem which will need close attention by men of science. The present writer was privileged to arrange the series as material for an army listening group.[3] The men and women who attended were mostly of a fair standard of education and intelligence, and, although their knowledge of science was limited, attended the broadcasts voluntarily. What were their reactions? It cannot be said that the interest of the Service men and women[4] was aroused to any extent or that they were highly stimulated. In the main the talks were borne patiently, and little animation developed. It was difficult to find out why the majority of talks did not attract, but experience with other army groups may help to throw some light on the matter.

---

1   Reprinted by permission from Macmillan Publishers Ltd: *Nature* (154: 3897), copyright (1944).

2   The branch of medicine that deals with the prevention of disease.

3   A voluntary group of radio listeners from the British Army during the Second World War whose reaction to radio programmes was measured in order to gauge the success or failure of the broadcasts.

4   Persons serving in the armed forces.

Since the War-Time Army Education Scheme[5] was introduced in 1940, many thousands of talks and lectures have been given to troops on all kinds of 'educational' topics. Those which have been outstandingly successful have been derived from personal experiences of the speaker – travel, exploration, particular employment, etc. (The talk in this series on the control of rats reminds one of the broadcast some months ago by a Cockney[6] rat-catcher on how to trap rats. His methods may not necessarily have been the most successful ones, but troops are still discussing the talk.) Talks which have met with least response have been those which the audiences consider to be academic and detached from their lives. Here lies the crux of the problem.

If we wish to interest the masses[7] in the impact of science on society – we assume that the person who arranged this series of elementary talks[8] wished to interests as many listeners as possible – we must first recognise that the ordinary man and woman only too often regard science as academic and aloof, and are not infrequently a little afraid of it. It is essential, therefore, when planning a programme of popular science talks, to ensure that the subjects chosen fall within the daily interest of the listener. On this score alone, the series under discussion could have been little improved upon. The fault, if fault there be, lay with the presentation.

The time is long overdue when men of science, among others, began to learn of the effect which their discoveries have made, and are making, on the masses of the people. One shilling will produce a comfortable seat 'at the pictures'[9] where education can be absorbed pleasantly and without physical and mental exertion. A third of a shilling will produce a weekly journal where the many photographs are seductively displayed and unencumbered by much wearisome reading matter. These – and others – are the educative rods which inventive man has made for his own back.[10]

How can these opiate[11] effects be combated? It is not enough merely to say that we must raise the standard of films or give John Citizen[12] more information on how or what to read. We must also use the weapons available now and

---

5   A scheme introduced in 1940 to offer courses to military personnel to alleviate boredom during quiet times and to prepare servicepersons for employment in peacetime.

6   A native of London, especially of the East End or speaking its dialect.

7   The general public.

8   This was most likely Julian Huxley, though the editor has been unable to ascertain this for certain.

9   The cinema.

10 Things done which cause problems in the future.

11 Something that soothes or dulls the senses or causes drowsiness or inaction.

12 An ordinary man, especially as a member of the community.

help John Citizen to want to raise the standards himself. Broadcasting is one of the tools. But we must attend to presentation. In this connection we must take a hint from the Schools Broadcasting Department.[13] When a particular broadcast is being prepared, as much time is being given to the way in which a topic is to be 'put over'[14] as to the subject-matter itself. Straight talks, even of fifteen minutes duration, are seldom given. The appeal of different voices has been recognised and the question-answer or discussion method between two or more people is frequently used. (Of the twelve broadcasts under the heading of 'Reshaping Man's Heritage', ten were straight talks; two consisted of dialogue conversation.[15]) Again, when a straight talk is given, much more attention is paid to the speaker's degree of 'mike-worthiness'[16] than is the case with the Adults Talks Department[17] of the BBC. That a man or woman is an authority on a particular subject is not enough to make him a good broadcaster. He should have a microphone manner which will appeal to the largest body of listeners and make them want to listen again to the broadcast of a related subject. With the exception of two, and possibly three, of the speakers in 'Reshaping Man's Heritage', how many succeeded in making the listeners anxious to obtain further information about these all-important issues?

It may rightly be argued that there are few men – and less women – who are expert in a particular field and yet naturally have a microphone personality which is acceptable to the majority of listeners. It is a remarkable fact that the number of first-rate broadcasters on any special subject number less than half a dozen. How, then, can science topics be presented to make the appeal which they inherently possess for the bulk of the population?

One of the answers lies in the greater us of feature programmes.[18] Scriptwriters of the calibre of Louis MacNiece would have made any of the topics of 'Reshaping Man's Heritage' so attractive that many more listeners would have been attracted. It is not suggested that straight talks be eliminated from broadcasting. Great names are themselves an attraction and many people listen at first not for the subject-matter but because Dr So-and-So is broadcasting. But when Dr So-and-So is the authority on a particular subject which lends itself to broadcasting and he is not suitable either in manner or personality to make the subject

---

13   Founded in 1926 to provide educational programming for classroom use, it was absorbed into BBC Learning in the 1990s.

14   Presented.

15   These were 'Man's Food' by J. C. Drummond and W. F. Crick, and 'The Battle of Food' by James Fisher and J. W. Munro.

16   The ability to speak well over a microphone for the purpose of radio broadcasting.

17   Founded in 1927, the department of the BBC which commissioned educational and topical radio talks aimed at an adult audience.

18   Broadcasts based on specific subjects.

attractive over the microphone – this was even more evident in the recent series 'Science at Your Service'[19] than in 'Reshaping Man's Heritage' – he might well be asked to prepare a script which could be presented in 'feature' form by skilled broadcasters. To soften criticism on this point, perhaps it is worth mentioning that the BBC has a maxim, developed from experience, that to make a broadcast sound natural it must be 'staged'.[20] Examples of this are constantly being referred to by W. E. Williams in his sagacious column called 'The Spoken Word' which appears each week in *The Listener.*[21]

This brings the discussion to its focus. The BBC should have on its directing staff a man of science of the standing of the co-ordinator of 'Reshaping Man's Heritage'. He should be instructed to develop the place of science in broadcasting and to use the necessary discrimination in the selection – and rejection – of speakers. He should be given a staff whose duty it would be to investigate the various methods of making scientific broadcasts attractive.

In conclusion, it should be said that *Reshaping Man's Heritage* makes good reading for the elementary student wishing to extend his knowledge of the application of biological research to human welfare.

---

19   A BBC Home Service radio series of twelve broadcasts aired during the winter of 1943 and 1944.

20   Made into a performance, as on a stage.

21   The weekly magazine of the BBC (1929-91).

2.36: '42 to '44

R. Brightman, 'The Supremacy of Reason' (29 July 1944).[1]

'42 to '44: A Contemporary Memoir upon Human Behaviour during the Crisis of the World Revolution. By H. G. Wells. Pp. 212. (London: Martin Secker and Warburg, Ltd., 1944.) 42s. net.

Mr Wells is indefatigable, and advancing years seem in no way to diminish the output or readiness of his pen. This 'Contemporary Memoir' consists of two parts with three appendixes, the sequence and relation of which are by no means so apparent as they might be. Even the sedulity which Mr Wells demands of his reader at the point of his preface might well fail to reveal a common theme or dominant *motif*. Moreover, only part of the book is new – how much even one with the full range of Mr Wells's more recent writings in front of him might not be able to say with any certainty – and the high price will scarcely dispose a reader to excuse the compilation of so much material from previous writings without at least some biographical reference. Evasiveness or indefiniteness on this point is not confined to his own writings, for in this matter Mr Wells is thoroughly inconsistent. Sometimes he provides a complete reference to a book that has interested him, but he quotes several pages from what is presumably General Smuts's address to the South African Institute of Race Relations[2] in January 1942 without bothering to insert the line that would help a reader who wished to confirm his quotation or consult the full text to the New African Pamphlet No. 2, *The Basis of Trusteeship*, in which that speech has been printed.

What might be overlooked in the journalist can scarcely be condoned in a more serious study that claims to be an autobiography of ideas, in some ways continuing, supplementing and expanding Mr Wells's earlier *Experiment in Autobiography*. Moreover, as giving the mature views of Mr Wells as philosopher summing up his position after a life-time of work and study, the book might be placed in the philosophical class. That claim may indeed be contested, for if Mr Wells is a true philosopher, can his irrepressible vitality and imagination ever allow him to be mature? There are serious passages in the book and flashes of the brilliant and imaginative writing we expect from him. For the most part, it is journalism – inconsistent, sometimes irrelevant, even dogmatic or bullying, but always Mr Wells, as when the kindly *aria*[3] in praise of Beatrice Webb breaks

---

1   Reprinted by permission from Macmillan Publishers Ltd: *Nature* (154: 3900), copyright (1944).

2   An organisation for the promotion of constitutional and economic liberalism, founded in Johannesburg in 1929.

3   A long song for one voice, usually with accompaniment.

the thundering notes of the grand *oratorio*[4] of the private – or is it public? – hates of Mr Wells's which occupy so much of the second part of the book. Mr Wells tries hard at times; but his comments are seldom as detached as they purport to be. They are usually lively, often intemperate – as he readily admits – and sometimes stimulating and suggestive, which after all is one reason why this author is read.

In the first part of the book, Mr Wells discusses the reasons for the recrudescence of cruelty in this modern world, and ends on the optimistic note that the idea of a new world based on a universally valid declaration of equal human rights is now making headway against every device of its antagonists. In this part Mr Wells is happily irrelevant, and in view of the warning to the reader in his preface, one may well wonder whether he has not started off by deliberately making his argument obscure, or whether in some Puckish[5] mood Mr Wells has not written the whole book as a test for reader or reviewer to see what they would make of it. Certainly this first part completely falsifies the claim on the wrapper that it is detached from immediate contemporary political and social developments. Did Mr Wells make that claim himself with his tongue in his cheek, or does he also need deliverance from the writer of 'blurbs'?[6]

The idea of a declaration of the universal rights of man is the most substantial feature of the second part of the book. Entitled 'How We face the Future', and promising to study the drama of John Ball and Richard II in modern dress, its exposition of the idea of the universal rights of man proves but the overture to the oratorio of hate. Beginning with the Communist Party the tempo quickens and the stops are pulled out[7] as Mr Wells indulges in his dislikes of the War Office, Mr Alexander, President Roosevelt,[8] General de Gaulle, Sir Samuel Hoare and Lord Vansittart, culminating with Sir Richard Acland and the Roman Catholic Church as a grand finale.

There is nothing scientific in all this, but the objects of Mr Wells's dislikes appear to him to have a common feature in being obstacles to the penetration of a scientific spirit and outlook into public affairs. It is obscurantism and prejudice, whether professional, political or religious, that arouse his wrath. His

---

4   A semi-dramatic extended musical composition, usually based on a Scriptural theme, performed by a choir with soloists and a full orchestra.

5   Mischievous.

6   Publishers' brief, usually eulogistic, descriptions of books printed on their jacket or in advertisements.

7   Commonly, 'pull out all the stops', make every effort to achieve the desired end.

8   I. e., Franklin Roosevelt.

tirade against the Admiralty[9] in the section 'Invention and Professionalism apropos the U-boat War' is inspired by the Admiralty's apparent reluctance to examine thoroughly an idea for the use of the helicopter; but Mr Wells prejudices what appears to be a *prima facie*[10] case for searching official inquiry by his loose reference to 'hundreds' of battleships.

The three appendixes to the book are, first, a thesis accepted by the University of London for the doctorate of science[11] 'On the Quality of Illusion in the Continuity of the Individual Life in the Higher Metazoa, with Particular Reference to the Species *Homo sapiens*'; second, a memorandum on the relation of mathematics, music, moral and aesthetic values, chess and similar intellectual elaborations to the reality underlying phenomena; and, third, a memorandum on survival. The last is a reiteration of Mr Wells's conviction, so long and consistently and sincerely expounded, that the survival of man and of civilisation depend on our overcoming the stupid and uncritical resistance to thought and inquiry. Knowledge or extinction, he maintains, is the only choice for man. He has no use or place for the emotions or for tradition: reason and the intellect must be the sole controlling factors. Exactly how science alone is to reorganise human affairs for a new and happier adaptation of our interests and emotions to the state of affairs which the brighter factors of our life have brought about is not clear.

Mr Wells, though intensely individualistic himself, and with the faculty for looking at things at unusual angles, does not believe in individualism, and the main theme of his present thesis is that the integrality of the individual is a biologically convenient delusion. Personality is an illusion; yet, he argues, it is compatible with an impersonal over-riding intelligence. But how in default of leadership and personality a new and broader education system throughout the world is to issue in a federated political and economic order and a common fundamental law of human rights, in which a great impersonal society with an unprecedented range of variability is to develop, is never explained. The nearest approach to an explanation is the comment, in a chapter on 'The Propaganda of World Unity', that such bodies as the Combined Raw Materials Board,[12] the Production and Reserves Board,[13] the Food Board,[14] the Middle East Supply

---

9   The authority in the United Kingdom responsible for the command of the Royal Navy from the fifteenth century to 1964.

10 Latin, at first sight.

11 Wells was awarded this in 1943.

12 A joint USA-UK committee for the co-ordination of the development, expansion and use of raw materials during the Second World War (1942-45).

13 This is probably a reference to the Combined Production and Resources Board, created by the USA, UK and Canada for the joint production and utilisation of resources for the more efficient execution of the Second World War (1942-45).

Centre,[15] which we have already been obliged to set up for war purposes, must be developed for the establishment of world order when hostilities cease, and that from them world control of the new order must spring. Beneath the shelter of these world-wide settlement commissions and their over-riding powers, and so long as the universal rights of man are respected, national governments, great and small, can continue to develop the idiosyncrasies of their various nations and peoples, freely and securely.

Mr Wells's chief hope is this functional line of advance, and his underlying confidence in the supremacy of reason is as conspicuous as the sincerity of his passion for reform.

This is not one of Mr Wells's great books, and no one should read it as an introduction to his work. But in a book that insists so strongly on the illusion of personality, it is Mr Wells's own personality that is dominant, sincere and forceful. If his cosmic imagination is only evident here and there, and his philosophy uncertain, there is enough of the real Wells in this testament of impatience to redeem its shortcomings for those who measure it against earlier and finer books which have set the standard of judgement.

---

14 Properly, the Combined Food Board (1942-45), a joint USA-UK-Canada agency established during the Second World War to better utilise food resources during the conflict.

15 A British Second World War expedient for managing transport and supplies in the North African and Middle Eastern theatres of war (1942-45).

Part 3: Other Mentions

In this third part of *H. G. Wells in Nature*, material is reprinted in which Wells either features marginally in debates or receives a significant mention within a wider context, such as the report of a conference or other event. While significant enough for inclusion in the volume, space does not permit a detailed summary of the material.

3.1: 'Science Teaching – an Ideal, and some Realities' (1894)

From 'Notes' (20 December 1894).[1]

Under the title, 'Science Teaching – an Ideal, and some Realities,' Mr H. G. Wells delivered a lecture at the College of Preceptors last week.[2] Much attention is now being given to the methods of science teaching in our elementary schools and colleges, and Mr Wells' views on the subject are sound enough to be taken into consideration. In the course of his lecture, he pointed out that a rational course of science should grow naturally out of kindergarten. This should lead to object-lessons[3] proper, and demonstrations in physics and chemistry may be made to grow insensibly, without any formal beginning, out of such lessons. The best, about the only permanently valuable, preparation for a scientific calling that can be given to a boy in a secondary school, is the broad basis of physics and chemistry led up to in this way.

---

1   Reprinted by permission from Macmillan Publishers Ltd: *Nature* (51: 1312), copyright (1894).

2   The lecture took place on 12 December 1894 and was published the following year.

3   Striking practical illustrations of principles.

3.2: Richard Gregory, from 'National Aspects of Education' (17 April 1913).[1]

The raising of the leaving age of elementary schools,[2] the abolition of the 'half-time' system,[3] the establishment of compulsory continuation schools, and the co-ordination of elementary and secondary schools are reforms for which England ought no longer to wait, but of greater importance from the point of view of national progress is the development of higher technological instruction and research in our technical colleges and universities. The importance of this was emphasised by Mr H. G. Wells in three articles contributed to *The Daily Mail*[4] on April 7, 8, and 9.[5] Mr Wells's theme was the nature of our naval and military armaments and the national expenditure upon these preparations for war; and he urged that too much confidence is placed in obsolescent instruments of destruction and far too little encouragement given to organised technical research, military and naval experiment, and other means by which a secure position can be obtained by the aid of science. 'I will suggest,' he said, 'that we have the courage to restrain and even to curtail our monstrous outlay upon war material, and that we begin to spend lavishly upon military and naval education and training, upon laboratories and experiment stations, upon chemical and physical research, and all that makes for knowledge and leading, and that we increase our expenditure upon these things as fast as we can up to ten or twelve millions a year.' The arts of peace, no less than those of war, require the production of as many highly educated, inventive, investigating men as the nation can obtain from all classes of the community. The future of every modern State depends upon the work of its men of science and engineers. Let us hope that this will not be forgotten when the Government gives attention to the organisation of education, and that consideration will be given not only to the acquisition of knowledge by students of various grades, but also to its increase.

---

1   Reprinted by permission from Macmillan Publishers Ltd: *Nature* (91: 2268), copyright (1913).

2   The Education Act of 1918 raised the school-leaving age in Britain to 14.

3   An employment system, in operation from 1844 to 1918, in which factory owners were permitted to employ two children, working consecutively for six-and-a-half hours each, to do a full day's work, thus allowing the children to attend school for part of the day.

4   British conservative daily newspaper, established in 1896.

5   This refers to a three-part article entitled 'War and Common Sense' (1913).

3.3: The Eleventh Annual Meeting of the British Science Guild (1917)

From 'The British Science Guild' (3 May 1917).[1]

The eleventh annual meeting of the British Science Guild was held at the Mansion House[2] on Monday, April 30, when the Lord Mayor[3] presided. After the meeting had been welcomed by the Lord Mayor, Sir William Mather, president of the Guild, opened the proceedings, alluding briefly to the part taken by the British Science Guild in the encouragement of applied science during his tenure of office. He explained also the proposal of the committee of the Ramsay Memorial Fund[4] to raise £100,000 with the view of founding a chemical laboratory and a series of fellowships in memory of Sir William Ramsay at University College,[5] London. In conclusion, Sir William Mather announced his retirement and the nomination of Lord Sydenham to succeed him as president of the Guild.

[…]

Mr H. G. Wells, who followed Mr Fisher,[6] said that he had long been an enthusiast for education, on which any attempt at reconstruction must ultimately be based. If the education was right everything else would follow. He had followed the course of education in England for thirty years, and he was satisfied that all was *not* well with education in England. To defective education was due the general neglect of science and the habit of 'muddling through.'[7] The radical defect, both in the schools and in the universities, was the undue predominance of classical studies. In the school the classical side had received almost all the encouragement, obtained the best masters, and was allotted the best boys. There was no room for science, modern languages, or knowledge of potential industrial value when so many hours were allotted to Latin and Greek. The effect was constantly perpetuated by the encouragement given to classical studies in the form of scholarships, and the greater opportunities given in the public service to men trained in classics. As a result those responsible for the country's destinies were mainly without knowledge or appreciation of science. When one considered that during an average youth's period of education he could not get in more

---

1   Reprinted by permission from Macmillan Publishers Ltd: *Nature* (99: 2479), copyright (1917).

2   Completed in 1752, the official residence of the Lord Mayor of London, used for official functions of the City of London.

3   The head, generally ceremonial, of several municipal corporations in the United Kingdom and Ireland, that for London in 1917 being Charles Hanson.

4   Founded in 1923, a fund created in memory of Sir William Ramsay to improve the training of chemists for industrial work.

5   A constituent college of the University of London, founded in 1836.

6   Herbert Fisher, President of the Board of Education.

7   Progressing in a muddled or confused or unplanned manner.

than 5000 hours of real solid educational work, the importance of utilising these hours judiciously was evident.

Mr Wells did not underrate what was wise and beautiful in Latin and Greek and ancient philosophy,[8] and he regarded it as unfortunate that such knowledge was needlessly barred from the ordinary man by the insistence of pedants that it could be obtained only through the vehicle of the Latin and Greek languages. It was this insistence upon the rigid study of ancient languages which had raised a barrier between scientific and literary studies so that men of science and literary scholars tended to be separated into two camps, neither able to sympathise with or appreciate the aims of the other.[9]

A vote of thanks to the Lord Mayor and the speakers closed the proceedings.

---

8   In the Western world, pre-Christian philosophy.

9   Wells is here anticipating the 'Two Cultures' debate initiated by C. P. Snow in his 1956 article of that name.

3.4: The Sixteenth Annual Meeting of the British Science Guild (1922)

From 'British Science Guild' (3 June 1922).[1]

Much success attended the annual dinner of the British Science Guild, which was held at the Prince's Restaurant, Piccadilly, on May 23, with the president of the Guild, Lord Montagu of Beaulieu, in the chair.

[...]

The president gave the toast of 'The Guests,' and referred to the way in which science was solving modern problems. In one direction with which he was associated, the making of roads, we had only just begun to apply the teachings of science. The chemist is just as necessary to-day for making roads, for example, in deciding the proper mixture of bitumen[2] and sand to make the surface or carpet of the road, as he is for making dies, explosives, or medicines. The toast was acknowledged by Principal Ernest Barker, Mr H. G. Wells, and Mr F. W. Sanderson.

Mr H. G. Wells, who was called upon unexpectedly, said that science was to him a thing so great, so all-important, so entirely such salvation as man had before him, that it was with a feeling of irreverence that he found himself talking about it in an unprepared fashion. By science is meant a process of human intellectual energy which is exhaustively and reverently criticised, leading, it is hoped, to action exhaustively criticised before it is exhaustively planned. In that he expressed the whole of his faith, the whole of his belief in human life. An uncharitable person might entertain the view that the Guild had some idea of monopolising science or claiming science for the purposes of the British Empire, but there was something bigger in their minds than that. Science is a great thing that is going to carry human affairs above those levels, and when we think of science and of the Guild, it means that we of the British community hope to contribute our share to the bigger human process, and to play our part to the best of our ability, with no national and imperial aggressiveness, in the huge task of humanity which is involved in the scientific process.

---

1   Reprinted by permission from Macmillan Publishers Ltd: *Nature* (109: 2744), copyright (1922).

2   Any natural or artificial black or brown solid or viscous liquid consisting largely of hydrocarbons.

3.5: 'The Duty and Service of Science in the New Era' (1922)

From 'Current Topics and Events' (10 June 1922).[1]

A public meeting of the National Union of Scientific Workers[2] will be held in the Botanical Theatre, University College, Gower Street, London, on Thursday, June 15, at 5.30, when an address will be given by Mr F. W. Sanderson, Headmaster of Oundle, on 'The Duty and Service of Science in the New Era.' The chair will be taken by Mr H. G. Wells. Admission will be free.

---

1   Reprinted by permission from Macmillan Publishers Ltd: *Nature* (109: 2745), copyright (1922).

2   Founded in 1918 and renamed the Association of Scientific Workers in 1927, a trade union for laboratory and technical workers in universities, the National Health Service and chemical and metal manufacturing. In 1969 it was merged with other like organisations.

3.6: Wells as Labour Party Candidate (1922-23)

i) 'University and Educational Intelligence' (29 July 1922).[1]

Mr H. G. Wells has accepted the invitation of the Labour Party of the University of London to offer himself as the candidate of the Party at the election for a representative of the University in the House of Commons to be held after the retirement of Sir Philip Magnus at the end of the present session of Parliament. Mr Wells occupies such a distinguished position in the world of literature and among leaders of thought to-day that his early work in science and education is often overlooked. He was a student at the Royal College of Science, South Kensington, 1884-87, and was the first president of the Old Students' Association[2] of the College. He took his BSc with honours in zoology in 1890, and his first book was a *Text-book of Biology*, written particularly for London University students while he was a teacher of the subject. He is a fellow of the College of Preceptors, and for a short time edited the *Educational Times*.[3] Throughout his career he has been a steadfast supporter of scientific methods in schools and government, and in his books has pleaded the cause of scientific education and research with eloquence and conviction. It is not too much to say that no graduate of the University of London possesses such a rare combination of brilliant literary power and scientific thought or has used these gifts with greater effect than has Mr Wells in his many and various works.

ii) 'University and Educational Intelligence' (14 October 1922).[4]

London. – It was announced in *Nature* of July 29, p. 166, that Mr H. G. Wells had consented to offer himself as Parliamentary candidate for the University, at the invitation of the executive of the University Labour Party, upon the retirement of Sir Philip Magnus at the end of the present session of Parliament. At a general meeting of the party held on Friday, October 6, Mr Wells was adopted as Parliamentary candidate as recommended by the executive.[5]

---

1   Reprinted by permission from Macmillan Publishers Ltd: *Nature* (110: 2752), copyright (1922).

2   Alumni association of Imperial College, London, founded in 1907.

3   The journal of the College of Preceptors, published from 1847 to 1923.

4   Reprinted by permission from Macmillan Publishers Ltd: *Nature* (110: 2763), copyright (1922).

5   The result of the general election contest for the University of London seat on 15 November 1922 was: Sydney Russell-Wells (Conservative): 4,037 votes; Albert Pollard (Liberal): 2,593 votes; and H. G. Wells (Labour): 1,420 votes. The Conservative Party went on to form the government.

iii) 'University and Educational Intelligence' (24 November 1923).[6]

Party politics have no place in the columns of *Nature*, but we are concerned with what is promised or performed by our statesmen or politicians on behalf of scientific progress. We are, therefore, interested in the election address which Mr H. G. Wells, as Labour candidate for the University of London constituency, has issued, together with a report of a speech on 'Socialism and the Scientific Motive.'[7] The Labour Party believes, he says, in science and in the scientific motive as a motive altogether superior to profit-seeking. He appeals to university people as people who know something of the work of scientific investigators, artists, men of letters, teachers, and medical men; who know that none of these work for profit or on the profiteering system, but for service, and that the work they do is infinitely better and more devoted than the work that men do for the profit-making motive. This knowledge should enable them to see that if, in accordance with the doctrines of Labour Party Socialism, collective ownership[8] were to replace private ownership in nearly all the common interests and services of the community, these things would be better managed, especially as the Labour Party recognises 'the supreme need of scientific knowledge and the necessary leadership of professionally trained men ... and teachers.' The argument is not altogether convincing, but Mr Wells is at any rate capable of the philosophic point of view, and if he controlled the policy of the Labour Party, universities would not need to fear inconsiderate treatment at the hands of a Labour Government. One wonders, however, how far his attitude would be likely to be adopted by the people who would determine the policy of such a government. Some of the remarks by Labour members in the House of Commons debate on the Oxford and Cambridge Universities Bill[9] were the reverse of reassuring on this point.[10]

---

6   Reprinted by permission from Macmillan Publishers Ltd: *Nature* (112: 2821), copyright (1923).

7   This speech was delivered on 21 March 1923 at the University of London Club and published as a pamphlet shortly afterwards.

8   The public ownership of staple industries, generally through nationalisation.

9   When the Oxford and Cambridge Universities Bill was debated on 20 July 1923, the Labour Party supported compelling Cambridge to accept the admittance of women on equal status to men but MPs considered compulsion inappropriate government interference in university independence and the Labour Party was criticised for this reason.

10   The result of the general election contest for the University of London seat on 5 December 1923 was: Sydney Russell-Wells (Conservative): 3,833 votes; Albert Pollard (Liberal): 2,180 votes; and H. G. Wells (Labour): 1,427 votes. The Labour Party went on to form the government.

3.7: 'Evolution and Intellectual Freedom' (1925)

First editorial: 'Evolution and Intellectual Freedom' (11 July 1925).[1]

The agitation in the United States over the teaching of evolution is attracting such widespread interest that it has been proposed to build a stadium to accommodate twenty thousand people for the trial of J. T. Scopes,[2] a Tennessee High School science teacher, for having taught the truth of evolution in defiance of the State law. The trial is to open on July 10. The charge of the judge to the grand jury[3] began by reading the first chapter of Genesis[4] as the account of creation which Tennessee teachers must adopt. He pointed out that part of the value of education is mental discipline, and that flagrant defiance of the law by the school authorities would not be a wholesome influence in the State. He insisted that the integrity of the law must be upheld. The main issue, however, will be decided by the Federal Court in its decision as to the right of a State to prohibit the teaching of fundamental philosophical principles.

The defence of evolution has been undertaken by the American Association for the Advancement of Science,[5] which has appointed a committee of three distinguished biologists, Prof. E. G. Conklin, professor of biology at Princeton,[6] Dr C. B. Davenport, director of the Station for Experimental Evolution, Carnegie Institute of Washington,[7] and Dr H. F. Osborn, president of the trustees of the American Museum of Natural History,[8] New York, to prepare a resolution upon the subject. The resolution, which has been adopted by the Council of the Association, is as follows:

---

1   Reprinted by permission from Macmillan Publishers Ltd: *Nature* (116: 2906), copyright (1925).

2   The trial of John Scopes from 10 to 21 July 1925 who was convicted of breaching the State of Tennessee's Butler Act by teaching aspects of Darwinian evolution in a state-funded school. The appeal hearing in 1927 declared the Act constitutional but overturned Scopes's conviction on a technicality.

3   In the USA, a jury selected to examine the validity of an accusation prior to trial.

4   The first book of the Jewish Torah and the Christian Old Testament Bible, traditionally believed to have been written by Moses.

5   Founded in 1848, an organisation that promotes cooperation between scientists and the expansion of science education.

6   American university founded in 1746 as the College of New Jersey and renamed in 1896.

7   A foundation established by Andrew Carnegie in 1902 to support scientific research.

8   Founded in 1869 in New York, the pre-eminent institution for natural history research and education in the USA.

(1) The council of the association affirms that, so far as the scientific evidences of the evolution of plants and animals and man are concerned, there is no ground whatever for the assertion that these evidences constitute a 'mere guess.' No scientific generalisation is more strongly supported by thoroughly tested evidence than is that of organic evolution.

(2) The council of the association affirms that the evidences in favour of the evolution of man are sufficient to convince every scientist of note in the world, and that these evidences are increasing in number and importance every year.

(3) The council of the association also affirms that the theory of evolution is one of the most potent of the great influences for good that have thus far entered into human experience; it has promoted the progress of knowledge, it has fostered unprejudiced inquiry, and it has served as an invaluable aid in humanity's search for truth in many fields.

(4) The council of the association is convinced that any legislation attempting to limit the teaching of any scientific doctrine so well established and so widely accepted by specialists as is the doctrine of evolution would be a profound mistake, which could not fail to injure and retard the advancement of knowledge and of human welfare by denying the freedom of teaching and inquiry which is essential to all progress.

The American Medical Association[9] has expressed itself similarly in a resolution, passed by its House of Delegates, on the question of the teaching of evolution, 'that any restrictions of the proper study of scientific fact in regularly established scientific institutions be considered inimical to the progress of science and to the public welfare.'

The American Association is being helped in preparing a defence by the Science League,[10] which was founded last year in San Francisco in order to secure liberty of teaching in American education.

These organisations have to meet a widespread and well-organised attack. The teaching of evolution has already been prohibited by law in Oklahoma and Tennessee.[11] Bills for the same purpose were submitted to the State legislatures in Kentucky and in Texas and were rejected by the Upper House, in Kentucky by a majority of one vote.[12] In Florida the legislature passed a resolution advis-

---

9   Founded in Philadelphia 1847 to promote medical research and improved public health.

10   A defunct organisation, founded in 1924 to protect freedom in science teaching and to resist attempts to unite church and state in the USA.

11   In Oklahoma a law was passed in 1923 preventing State-funded institutions from purchasing textbooks that presented 'the Darwin theory of evolution', while in Tennessee the Butler Act, banning the teaching of Darwinian evolution, was passed in 1925.

12   In January 1922, three anti-evolution bills were introduced to the Kentucky legislature, one of which was defeated by one vote by the House of Representatives (not the upper

404

ing the educational authorities not to employ those who teach Darwinism, and the agitation for direct prohibition is still maintained. In North and South Carolina legislative action against the teaching of evolution was defeated, but textbooks and teachers who favour evolution are debarred from the State schools. Georgia has as yet no absolute legislation on the subject, but the State Education Committee last July advised the legislature to refuse grants to any school, college, or university that favoured the doctrine of evolution, and it has recently withheld a grant from a State library because it contains books on evolution. Bills against the teaching of evolution are being introduced or have been introduced into the legislatures of the States of Arizona, Arkansas, Georgia, Illinois, Indiana, Iowa, Minnesota, Mississippi, North Dakota, Oregon, and West Virginia.

In California the effort was made, as mentioned in *Nature* of May 9, p. 683,[13] to avert a struggle by reference of the question to a committee of the nine presidents of the State universities and leading colleges. Six of these colleges are under denominational[14] control, and the unsatisfactory compromise previously referred to in *Nature* has not satisfied either side.[15] A requisition is being signed for a reference of the question to a ballot at the next election; and the Fundamentalists are said to be confident that they will carry the State, unless books which give even a moderate approval of evolution are excluded from the schools.

The anti-evolution party is being supported to some extent by the publishers. Thus, one distinguished New York biologist has been requested by his publisher to omit any reference to evolution in any new editions of his text-book, owing to the objections of the Southern and Western States. The intellectual ter-

---

house), while in Texas three bills were introduced for the same purpose between January 1923 and February 1925, though none went to a vote.

13   In the anonymous article, 'Current Topics and Events' (1925).

14   Religious sectarianism, often in relation to education.

15   'The committee has issued a list of twelve text-books in which [...] evolution is presented as a theory – not as an established fact [...]. The committee quotes with approval from one of the text-books under judgement as among "Things that Evolution does *Not* Teach.... 'That man is descended from a monkey.'" Darwin's statement on this question is emphatic. He declared [...]: The Simiadae divided into "the New World and Old World monkeys; and from the latter, at a remote period, Man, the wonder and glory of the Universe, proceeded." It is significant of the strength of the anti-evolutionary movement in the United States that this committee [...] should endeavour to appease public opinion by its approval of such a misleading assertion, which suggests that the members of the committee are themselves in favour of teaching only a diluted Darwinism' ('Current Topics and Events' 1925, 683).

rorism[16] in some of the States may be judged by the fact that according to the *Boston Evening Transcript*[17] of May 23,[18] although, while the anti-evolution Bill was before the legislature in Tennessee, many clergy protested against the proposed infringement of freedom of opinion, 'there was never a word of protest from the State University.'[19] The North-eastern States show by the comments of the Press their deep regret at this outbreak of intellectual obscurantism, and it is to be hoped that an authoritative expression of opinion there may help the Southern and Western States to realise the heavy handicap they would be laying upon themselves, as well as upon their universities and schools, by the legal prohibition of well-established scientific principles.

In Great Britain, State interference with university teaching would not be tolerated. The proper body to decide what may or may not be taught in a university is the Senate[20] or Council,[21] and not a popularly elected civic chamber of any kind. It must not be forgotten, however, that education authorities in England exercise the right of control over the teaching of religious doctrine in schools, and that they could apply the same powers to the teaching of evolution if they wished. It is not for us, therefore, to attempt to justify what seems to have been a breach of law in the State of Tennessee, however much we may deplore that a State should pass a measure that is contrary to all modern ideas of progressive thought and intellectual freedom. What we are concerned with is the principle by which a political party or organisation should be able to put obstacles in the way of human enlightenment and independent thought, and should have the power of approving, or preventing, the teaching of scientific facts or conclusions of any kind. We have long passed the stage at which this was possible in England, and cannot help being astonished, therefore, that there should be States in the United States of America which deliberately adopt a policy of scientific stagnation.

In order to ascertain the views of leading authorities in the fields of university work, science and religious teaching, upon this attitude, advance proofs of this article have been sent to a number of representative men, whose com-

---

16 The systematic employment of violence or intimidation to coerce a government or community into acceding to specific demands.

17 A popular local newspaper in Boston, Massachusetts, USA, published from 1830 to 1941.

18 'War Against Evolution' (1925).

19 A reference to the University of Tennessee, headquartered in Knoxville and founded in 1794.

20 In British universities, the body which governs academic affairs.

21 In British universities, the body responsible for financial matters, buildings and the appointment of the vice-chancellor.

ments, here subjoined, will, we believe, be read with interest on both sides of the Atlantic.[22]

Second editorial: 'Truth and Doctrine in Science and Religion' (11 July 1925).[23]

The vagaries of those near to us in kin are proverbially harder to understand than those of strangers, and it is equally true that it is less easy to appreciate the shibboleths of the generations immediately preceding our own than those of a remoter date. It is undoubtedly a fact that the common element in British culture and that of the United States has often served to obscure certain fundamental differences of which the occasional manifestation sometimes amazes and more often bewilders us. The tendency shown by certain State legislatures in America in their attitude towards the doctrine of evolution, which has culminated in the prosecution of a teacher in the State of Tennessee for the use of a text-book in which a reference to that doctrine was included, is indicative of a public opinion of a force and character which it is difficult for us in Great Britain and in these days to appreciate.

Scientific workers on this side of the water are accustomed to meet their American colleagues on an equal footing. They expect to find among them a readiness equal to their own to accept the facts which scientific investigation may bring to light and an equal openness of mind in the discussion of the bearing of such facts upon accepted theory. It has, therefore, come as something of a shock to them to find that a movement upon which they may have looked with some feeling of amusement, and as such may not have regarded more seriously than as a passing phase, is likely to prove an obstinate barrier to intellectual progress and freedom of discussion. Those who have followed the trend of thought among the intellectual section of the general public in the United States for any length of time may not be equally surprised. They have been aware that sooner or later some such question as this was bound to arise. It is not so long ago that a well-known American novelist put before his public, as a living question of to-

---

22 This editorial was followed by a large number of comments from scientists, religious leaders and others and while space does not permit the inclusion of these comments, they can be found listed in the bibliography thus: Adami 1925, Ballard 1925, Barker 1925, Barnes 1925, Bateson 1925, Bather 1925, Berry 1925, Brown 1925, Cattell 1925, Clodd 1925, D'Arcy 1925, Day 1925, Dixey 1925, Ewart 1925, Fallaize 1925, Friend 1925, Gardiner 1925, Harmer 1925, Henson 1925, Hickson 1925, Keith 1925, Kerr 1925, Lankester 1925, Lidgett 1925, Lodge 1925, MacBride 1925, McIntosh 1925, Murray 1925, Nuttall 1925, Punnett 1925, Scott 1925, Shipley 1925, Smith 1925, Smithells 1925, Sollas 1925, Thompson 1925, Waterhouse 1925 and Workman 1925.

23 Reprinted by permission from Macmillan Publishers Ltd: *Nature* (116: 2906), copyright (1925).

day, in the church of an American city, the problems which exercised the readers of *Robert Elsmere*[24] when first that book was published in Great Britain nearly forty years ago.

The problem with which the more advanced section of intellectual America is now confronted is as old as the hills,[25] or at any rate as old as man himself. Every age and every country produces its Socrates and its Galileo. Everywhere the prophets are stoned when speculation or scientific discovery comes into conflict with the emotions of the majority.

In Great Britain, it is perhaps safe to say that the cause of intellectual freedom has been won. It is not likely that we shall witness again a struggle over a purely scientific doctrine, such as that which raged around the controversies of the middle and latter half of the last century. It is difficult for a generation brought up in the freer atmosphere which is a result of those fierce encounters, to enter fully into the intensity of feeling which was aroused by the theological disputes of the earlier Victorian era. The famous Gorham case[26] and the heated discussion of questions of church government which it aroused, and the Tractarian movement,[27] were only a prelude to the storm raised by the publication of F. D. Maurice's *Theological Essays* in 1853, repudiating the doctrine of eternal punishment, which forced his resignation of his professorial chair at King's College,[28] London; while the heated arguments over the archaeological discoveries of Boucher de Perthes in the Somme Valley, which relegate man to a vast antiquity,[29] merely paved the way for the tempest which followed the application of the Darwinian hypothesis to the problem of man's origin.

The recent celebrations of the centenary of Thomas Henry Huxley[30] have served to recall the many controversial questions in the discussion of which he

---

24 A novel by Mrs Humphrey Ward (1888).

25 Ancient; (metaphorically) referring to geological time when the mountains were created.

26 The case of George Gorham, an Anglican clergyman who was refused the living of Brampford Speke by Henry Phillpotts, the Bishop of Exeter, on the grounds that he was a Calvinist. Gorham appealed the decision to the Court of Arches, which upheld the bishop's decision, then appealed to the Privy Council, which reversed the decision and granted Gorham his living. The case was significant in that a secular court (the Privy Council) decided the doctrine of the Church of England.

27 More commonly, the Oxford Movement, an affiliation within the Church of England which sought to demonstrate the Church's direct descent from the Christian church as established by Jesus Christ's apostles.

28 A constituent college of the University of London, founded in 1829.

29 The ancient times, especially the period before the Middle Ages.

30 Papers to mark the centenary of T. H. Huxley's birth were published as 'The Centenary of Huxley' (1925) in *Nature*.

was a protagonist; of these, perhaps the encounters with Wilberforce at Oxford, and with Gladstone,[31] have remained most firmly fixed in public memory. To his fearless championship of the doctrine of evolution in the stormy years of the 'sixties of the last century, following on the publication of *The Origin of Species*, is due as much as to any the victory of freedom for scientific inquiry into, and speculation on, the great problems of the origin and development of the forms of life. His conception of the sanctity of truth, and his fearless acceptance of facts whatever might be their bearing upon dogma in any field of inquiry, remain the creed of the scientific investigator of to-day. But that it is generally recognised as right to hold that creed is due to those who bore the heat and burden of that day – Darwin,[32] Huxley, Tyndall and others of their time. Much must be attributed to the force of personality of those who participated in these controversies, and perhaps as much to the writings of one who took no active part in them himself, namely, Herbert Spencer. Spencer's writings, and particularly his sociological writings, by their application of the biological conception and the evolutionary point of view to the study of man as a social being, did much to secure acceptance for the doctrine of evolution among the intellectual public.

Further, in anthropology the work of Tylor in the comparative study of the beliefs of man demonstrated that behind the great religions of the world there lay a long process of growth which could be traced back stage by stage to the primitive animism[33] of the savage,[34] a work which has been extended and confirmed by the labours of Sir James Frazer. At the same time, the studies of the archaeologists, in conjunction with the geologists, were extending to more and more remote periods of time, and to an increasingly primitive stage, the evidence for man's existence, in the shape of the primitive stone implements which marked his early efforts to control and shape his environment to his needs. Concurrently, the critical study of the Bible – the Higher Criticism[35] – was demonstrating the composite character of its parts, while its sources – notably the story of the Creation deciphered by Smith from the cuneiform[36] inscriptions – were being derived from other than Jewish sources.

It would scarcely be worth while to recapitulate these familiar facts if it were not to recall that, immediately following upon the formulation of Darwin's theories and their discussion, there was a convergence of evidence bearing upon

---

31   I. e., William Ewart Gladstone.

32   I. e., Charles Darwin.

33   The attribution of a living soul to plants, inanimate objects and natural phenomena.

34   Formerly, a primitive or uncivilised person.

35   Literary analysis that investigates the origins of a text, especially the books of the Bible.

36   Designating or pertaining to writing in wedge-shaped impressed strokes, usually in clay, in the ancient inscriptions of Assyria, Persia, etc., from 3000 BC to AD 75.

the origin and history of man and on his beliefs, some of it derived from an extended application of the evolutionary method of study, which by superseding the traditional static view, tended to facilitate if not the acceptance at any rate the preservation of an open mind towards the central problem.

To the scientific mind, perhaps it is a temptation to over-estimate the extent to which the cogency of an argument has appealed to the general public. The freedom in discussion of matters of intellect which has been won in Great Britain must perhaps in part be attributed to the national temperament. The key may perhaps be found in the writings of Herbert Spencer, the apostle of the individualism which is the most marked characteristic of the Englishman. The appeal to authority which is the negation of the intellectual freedom postulated by scientific inquiry is by tradition and training alien to the British temperament. The nineteenth century in Great Britain was a time of intellectual ferment in the political as well as the scientific world, but in both cases it was the culmination of a movement which had been in being for centuries. The demand for 'Civil and Religious Liberty,' which was the war-cry[37] of one of the great political parties of the day, was merely the traditional spirit which gave rise to the Reformation,[38] to nonconformity[39] and to the reforms of the Philosophical Radicals[40] at the beginning of the nineteenth century.

It may be that it was by good fortune that the battle of the Darwinian hypothesis and its extension to the evolutionary theory was fought on favourable ground. That for us of to-day is a matter of history. But it lays upon those who hold the torch to hand it on undimmed and to watch jealously that, in changing conditions, no change can effect the unity of free and unfettered discussion in all matters that appertain to the pursuit of knowledge. In these days, when science is universal and co-operation in scientific research transcends national boundaries, it is impossible that what effects a part should not affect the whole. The whole scientific world will therefore watch with no little interest and anxiety the result of a trial which may by its results affect the intellectual progress of one of the great nations of the world. Not only may it stunt the intellectual growth of generations: it may also debar her from all participation in the advancement of one of the most important of the branches of knowledge.

---

37 A slogan of a political party.

38 The sixteenth century European religious movement for the reform of the doctrines and practices of the Church of Rome.

39 The act of not conforming to a particular practice or course of action; in Christianity, a person not conforming to the doctrine or discipline of the Established Church.

40 Advocates of thorough or far-reaching change.

Third editorial: 'Evolution and Intellectual Freedom' (18 July 1925).[41]

Since going to press last week, we have been favoured with several further messages on the subject of the campaign in the United States against the teaching of the principle of biological evolution. We are glad to be able to publish these expressions of opinion upon the attempt thus being made to restrain intellectual freedom and progressive thought. As to the trial now being held at Dayton to test the validity of the anti-evolution law of the State of Tennessee, there can be no question that leaders in all departments of intellectual activity in Great Britain regard it with amazement. It is not for us to suggest that a teacher was justified in breaking the law of a State of which he was the paid servant, but what does astonish us is that the citizens of the State should tolerate a law which makes references to evolution and the descent of man[42] illegal. So far as actual teaching of these subjects in schools is concerned, most men of science would not insist upon attention being devoted to them; but when the ban extends to colleges and universities, the matter becomes of prime importance.

There can be no research for truth in Nature if natural truth, including that of the creation of the universe, the earth, and man, has to be regarded as revealed, once for all, in the Biblical[43] record. It would be impossible for any teacher of science to be true to his intelligence and yet give instruction under such conditions. There is, fortunately, no probability of limitations of the kind advocated by Mr W. J. Bryan and the Fundamentalists being placed upon biological teaching in Great Britain; and for the sake of human progress, we trust that the reactionary movement which they represent will fail of its object. The attack has come from the advocates of traditional doctrine and not from workers in scientific fields, who ask only to be free to extend natural knowledge by research and instruction, without being bound by the words of any master. No one supposes that the problem of organic evolution has been solved, but of the fact of evolution there is not the slightest doubt, and only by further inquiry can we understand fully its course and significance. Whatever Mr Bryan and his followers may insist upon as regards belief, science declines to accept finality in the position of natural knowledge at any epoch, or to construct a standard which all discoverers must follow. As Huxley said, when unveiling Darwin's[44] statue in

---

41   Reprinted by permission from Macmillan Publishers Ltd: *Nature* (116: 2907), copyright (1925).

42   In Darwinian theory, the notion that humankind is descended through evolution from lower forms over a vast period of time.

43   Of, pertaining to or contained in the (Jewish or Christian) Bible.

44   I. e., Charles Darwin.

the Natural History Museum,[45] South Kensington, in 1885, science 'commits suicide when it adopts a creed.'[46]

We need scarcely say that it is not our wish to have a discussion in *Nature* upon Genesis and modern science, or religious belief and scientific evidence. Our sole object in taking up the subject of the prohibition of the teaching of evolution in certain States of the United States, and in inviting opinions upon this action from a number of leading authorities, has been to afford support to our colleagues fighting for scientific truth and progress against dogma and stagnation. We trust that the additional messages subjoined will give them the strength and courage they need to secure for them the position of intellectual freedom established in Great Britain many years ago, and existing unchallenged to-day.[47]

Comment on the debate: H. G. Wells, letter to the editor, 'Science and Intellectual Freedom' (25 July 1925).[48]

It is with considerable amusement that I have read the collection of opinions published in *Nature* upon the recent action of the State of Tennessee in forbidding the teaching of what we believe to be the established facts of human evolution in schools supported by public funds. There is an admirable undertone of contempt and condemnation in most of these contributions and a scorn that spreads at moments from Tennessee and Oklahoma to things American in general. Yet the British Government is at the present time in an almost parallel position to the Government of the benighted State of Tennessee in regard to a closely similar body of knowledge. At present if a medical officer of health[49] or a health visitor[50] in public employment gives information about contraceptives to a patient publicly paid for, he or she is liable to dismissal, and several cases of dismissal have occurred. The Minister of Health in both the previous and the

---

45   Opened in 1881 in South Kensington, London, Britain's premier natural history collection.

46   A quotation from T. H. Huxley's 'The Darwin Memorial' (1885).

47   This editorial was followed by a number of comments from scientists, religious leaders and others and while space does not permit the inclusion of these comments, they can be found listed in the bibliography thus: R. J. Campbell 1925, Gregory 1925, Marett 1925 and Morgan 1925.

48   Reprinted by permission from Macmillan Publishers Ltd: *Nature* (116: 2908), copyright (1925). This letter has previously been reprinted in Smith 1998, III: 195-96.

49   A doctor appointed by a public authority to attend to matters relating to health.

50   A trained person who visits people, especially expectant mothers and the elderly, in their homes to give them advice on their health.

present governments[51] has refused to allow these officials the freedom, at their discretion and with all circumstances of privacy, to give this sort of information to adults asking for it from them. There is no question of propaganda here or of forcing this kind of knowledge upon those unwilling to receive it. But British adults of the poorer classes wishing to know this much about their own bodies and to have this much of control over them, cannot get it in a private, seemly and proper manner from their publicly supplied and duly qualified medical advisers, but must resort to the one or two overworked privately supported clinics that exist, or to furtive expedients, to quacks and underhand and dubious sources of information. This is mainly a concession made by these successive Ministers of Health to the Roman Catholic vote. They plead that taxpayers of that persuasion might object to their money going to supply such knowledge to people with different views. But that is precisely the argument of the Tennessee legislators. They plead that a respectable body of old-fashioned Christians regard the doctrine of human evolution as a dangerous and sinful heresy[52] and that therefore they may object quite reasonably to their money being spent upon its diffusion.

In all these matters I am for open and accessible knowledge and free and frank discussion everywhere, in Britain as in Tennessee, but I submit that the *élite* of British science have no case against the State of Tennessee until they have done something to put our own house in order.[53] Perhaps later you will give us another Supplement of a rather wider scope and raise the whole problem of intellectual freedom in relation to these modern publicly endowed systems of education in which the teacher is at any time liable to the interruptions and direction of the government and the politician. The bulk of our educational organisation at every stage and much of current research could not exist without State support and subsidies, and the riddle of receiving maintenance without sacrificing freedom is a very fine and subtle one, which is not disposed of by damning Tennessee.

Reply to Wells: Norman Campbell, letter to the editor, 'Science and Intellectual Freedom' (8 August 1925).[54]

Mr Wells's letter in *Nature* of July 25, p. 134, fails to notice a most important distinction. Knowledge concerning the origin of species may be, and usually is, honestly and honourably desired for its own sake without any view of practical

---

51   These were John Wheatley, Labour Party minister from January to November 1924, and Neville Chamberlain, Conservative Party minister from November 1924 to June 1929.

52   Opinion or doctrine contrary to the orthodox doctrine of the Christian Church.

53   Solve one's own problems before criticising others.

54   Reprinted by permission from Macmillan Publishers Ltd: *Nature* (116: 2910), copyright (1925).

application. Knowledge concerning contraception is sought, either from mere prurience, or from intention to practise it or to teach others to do so. Many who hold that the State has no right to control its members' thoughts hold that it has the right to control their actions; and such persons, if they hold (as I do not) that the prevention of conception is wrong, may oppose the propagation of knowledge which has no value except in so far as it leads to such prevention, without being insincere in their desire for intellectual freedom.

There are, of course, doctrines, especially in ethical, political and economic theory, the intellectual and practical values of which are so closely associated that it is difficult to decide into which class they fall. But the solution of the problems raised by these border-line cases – which are those that cause real difficulty – is not aided by a refusal to recognise that they are border-line cases, and that the classes which they separate are generally distinct and present no difficulty whatever to a judicial mind.

Reply to Campbell: H. G. Wells, letter to the editor (22 August 1925).[55]

Dr Norman R. Campbell (*Nature*, August 8, p. 208) writes with a certain lack of charity about the numerous men of science, medical men, publicists, and so forth, who have ventured to inform themselves about birth control. To seek knowledge about the origin of species, he informs us, may be honest and honourable, but 'knowledge concerning contraception is sought, either from mere prurience, or from intention to practice it or to teach others to do so.' But that is just what a Tennessee Fundamentalist would say about curiosity about evolution. He would say men wanted to know they were beasts in order to make beasts of themselves. It is impossible to let Dr Campbell's sweeping indictment pass unchallenged. People in general want to know about this matter in order to judge it; they want to know the nature, the naturalness, the physical good or evil of these practices and what the mental and social reactions of this or that line of action may be. It is no more 'prurient' to be intelligently interested in the question than in dietary.[56] No one wants the publicly paid medical man to 'propagate' this knowledge where it is not desired. But we do want to see him free to give it, cleanly and discreetly, to people who know already that it exists and who will, failing him, probably seek it in shameful and dangerous ways. We object to any sect or section of the community coming with threats of dismissal or injury between him and those who want to know. And while this is the case in Britain I decline to line up to sneer at the Fundamentalists of Tennessee.

---

55 Reprinted by permission from Macmillan Publishers Ltd: *Nature* (116: 2912), copyright (1925). This letter has previously been reprinted in Smith 1998, III: 197-98.

56 Food intake, especially as prescribed for healthy living.

3.8: Chair of Social Biology (1930)

From 'News and Views' (1 November 1930).[1]

No one more appropriate than Mr H. G. Wells could have been found to introduce Prof. L. T. Hogben to his audience on Thursday, Oct. 23, when he read himself in as professor of social biology at the London School of Economics. Mr Wells hailed the new experiment in bringing biology and economics together as the portent of a complete change of direction and method for the social and economic sciences, and spoke of it as a most exciting event. He did not spare the traditional treatment of the dismal science,[2] which, dealing with human things, was, he said, entirely inhuman. While pretending to be a science, it began with hypotheses and definitions in the mediaeval manner, and maintained to the present time the flavour of scholasticism.[3] It would not have been Mr Wells if he had not clearly been rejoicing in the belief that the new chair would be revolutionary: with the rapid advances in the knowledge of the biology of man made in the last quarter of a century, the new body of knowledge which can be brought to bear on sociology and economics will bring them within the region of pure scientific treatment. He defined the scope of Prof. Hogben's work as the treatment of one special case of the science of ecology, the science of the balance and welfare of species – the study of the fluctuations of the human species under the fluctuating pressure of circumstances. Mr Wells paid the London School of Economics the compliment of finding the establishment of research into this new byway of science only what one would expect of it, and he described the new professor as a most hopeful and desirable adventurer.

Prof. Hogben's address, a synopsis of which appears elsewhere in this issue,[4] did nothing to damp the liveliness of Mr Wells's hopes and anticipations. It was a brilliant example of the exposition of a difficult scientific thesis in terms of smooth prose enriched by a wealth of humour and literary allusion. Prof. Hogben is not overwhelmed by the scope or the difficulty of the adventure on which he has embarked. Although Mr Wells suggested that he was about to cut the first furrow in an almost virgin soil, it is plain enough that the territory has already been surveyed, and that it will not be a random direction that this furrow will take. Nevertheless, Prof. Hogben sounded warning notes. He pointed out that the outlook which evolutionary biology brings to the study of human society is neither a philosophy of social reform nor a philosophy of social reaction but a

---

1   Reprinted by permission from Macmillan Publishers Ltd: *Nature* (126: 3183), copyright (1930).

2   The derogatory alternative name for economics, coined by Thomas Carlyle in 'Occasional Discourse on the Negro Question' (1849, 672-73).

3   Narrow-minded insistence on traditional doctrines and forms of exposition.

4   'Social Biology' (1930).

philosophy of social discovery. Above all, he drove home the need for discipline, restraint, and detachment in the discussion of the genetical foundations of racial and occupational stratifications in human society. To force the issues into the political arena at the present stage of inquiry would be to render these virtues impossible to exercise. In conclusion, Prof. Hogben, changing the metaphor, begged that an astronomical estimate should be taken of the time required for the seed now being sown to germinate. Accepting the conclusions of Sir James Jeans, the School of Economics has five million million years of life[5] in which to cherish and tend it. Prof. Hogben indicated that he confidently relied upon the School, with its tradition of free inquiry, to extend the necessary care and sympathy in its early, tender stages.

---

5   James Jeans's calculation of the time during which life will be able to survive on earth.

3.9: Hyman Levy, 'Science in Literature' (11 April 1931)[1]

H. G. Wells: A Sketch for a Portrait. By Geoffrey West. Pp. 316. (London: Gerald Howe, Ltd., 1930.) 10*s.* 6*d.* net.

If the function of a biographer is to produce a living picture of his subject for his own and future generations, he will not have succeeded in his task unless he himself fades completely in word and in spirit from the pages of his biography. In providing us with this story of the struggles of a great man, Mr Geoffrey West has done his work well, for as we turn over the pages of this volume and live through the intimate history of Mr H. G. Wells, the authorship of the work itself drops completely from our ken.[2] This is as it should be, and thus an excellent portrait has been produced.

Those of us who are now struggling through the lean and hungry forties and can look back on their early youth, twenty or more years ago, inspired as it then was by the glamour of the scientific romances and of the social philosophy of Mr H. G. Wells, are not likely to forget the debt which they owe him. The rising generation of the 1900s, caught between a decaying Victorianism and a rebellious modernism, threw itself with energy into the fight for what it, in its early enthusiasm, called Progress. Manhood may mature the judgement, or temper the impatience of youth, but if the altered values of this post-war[3] age in matters of convention and social outlook are at all to be associated with the activities of any group of men, eminent among that band must be the early Wells.

The story of the man is no tale of a silver spoon.[4] Born and bred in respectable poverty and Victorian gentility, dogged by persistent ill-health, he staggered through many vicissitudes, from inefficient drapery assistant through overworked private school teacher, to the feet of Huxley[5] at South Kensington. There early he saw a vision of science in the service of man, and he pursued it relentlessly. Material success came to him, but the vision remained a vision.

In a sense, one need not produce a biography to reveal the history of a writer. A craftsman proceeds straight from experience, and the writings of Wells reflect the structure of the man. A pioneer in scientific fiction, he quickly sensed the dramatic element in a field that had not so far been exploited at all, and so he insinuated into the minds of his readers the amazing possibilities of science. Throughout thirty years of strenuous writing, there runs this extraordinary thread

---

1   Reprinted by permission from Macmillan Publishers Ltd: *Nature* (127: 3206), copyright (1931).

2   Understanding.

3   I. e., after the Great War.

4   A sign of future prosperity.

5   I. e., T. H. Huxley.

of continuity in his work – the same theme – that the universal solvent of ignorance is scientific knowledge, scientifically applied: this, whether the problem be moral or pedagogic, social or industrial, national or international. To the young men who grew up in this hectic period of problem play and problem novel,[6] he was at once a strength and a goad. As boys, we passed easily from the schoolboy *Dormitory Flag*[7] stage, to Wells and the *Time Machine, War of the Worlds*, and *When the Sleeper Wakes*. A new universe stood revealed before us, a universe of science and imagination, a world of dizzy possibilities. It remained only to give direction to this awakened fervour, to set this torch to the ready sense of social and industrial injustice, in order to fire the reformist[8] and inflame the revolutionary spirits of the younger generation. *Anticipations, Mankind in the Making, A Modern Utopia, This Misery of Boots, New Worlds for Old, First and Last Things*, came in hammering succession, and the younger men became violent propagandists, a nuisance to friends and foes alike.

As we look back on these easily impressionable years, it is amazing to recognise the uncanny gift of the man. He said the things we ached to say. His work may date, but it was ripe, just ripe, for its time. Wells has never claimed to be more than a journalist, but if so, his journalism was unique.

The middle period of Wells is a tale of adolescent struggles, of the scientific exposure of sex, and of a determination to accustom the mind of the reading public to think boldly and openly of the matter, as one would of any scientific problem. In this he fought not merely a narrow Victorian convention, but also a taboo[9] with its roots deep in man's early history. In the eyes of those who still have faith in the open discussion and scientific analysis of secret matters, to H. G. Wells must be given a great measure of credit for a great achievement.

Times have changed and things have moved fast since these days, but the indefatigable Wells has effected some amazing revolutions. He has multiplied the reading public many-fold; he has forced it to read history in fat volumes[10] and to study biology[11] in the nude. Beginning his career as an underling in a small private school, he has become the greatest public teacher now living.

---

6   A form of fiction that emerged in the nineteenth century which deals with problematic social issues through debates between the characters, who typically represent conflicting points of view within a realistic social context.

7   A children's novel by Harold Avery (1899).

8   One who advocates gradual change as against sudden revolution.

9   Customary prohibitions.

10 A reference to Wells's *The Outline of History* (1920).

11 A reference to *The Science of Life* (1930) by H. G. Wells, Julian Huxley and G. P. Wells.

418

It is not easy to judge his later activity. In an atmosphere of sullen suspicion and industrial chaos, an aftermath of five years of slaughter, he is still idealist enough to pin his faith to international co-operation, and yet realist enough to disavow political parties and the League of Nations. And now at this stage, still yet in his prime, he projects a work on scientific economics.[12] The thread is still unbroken; the vision still beckons him on, but his young men are now mentally middle-aged and disillusioned. He has outlived them all; but the rising generation is equally disillusioned.

---

12   A reference to Wells's *The Work, Wealth and Happiness of Mankind* (1931).

3.10: 'British-American Understanding' (1 May 1937).[1]

Sir Frederick Whyte presided over a discussion, held on March 4 under the auspices of the English-Speaking Union,[2] on 'The Contribution of British Schools, Universities and other Educational Bodies to British-American Understanding'. The discussion was opened by Mr J. Wickham Murray, who outlined some of the work of the Union in developing contacts between Britain and America. He specially stressed schemes such as the Page Scholarships[3] scheme for men and women teachers, reciprocal scholarships under American direction, exchange of school boys and school masters and mistresses, and assistance given to visitors in both countries. He indicated, however, that the Union desires now to widen its work and to face the greater responsibilities which the present state of the world suggests it should undertake. To that end it has formed a Research and Discussion Committee, which is seeking the advice and guidance of experts in such fields as foreign affairs, economics, the Press of both countries, and general relationships such as would arise as a result of neutrality[4] legislation and American grievances against British policy. Already meetings of experts in these matters have been held, and, at every meeting, the importance of closer attention to matters of education has been stressed.

Mr Wickham Murray added that, in thinking it important for British students at school and university to get an accurate picture of English-speaking countries, the Union believes that because of similarities in our joint democratic institutions, experiments in those countries might be of greater relevance to Britain than experiments in such very different countries as Soviet Russia, Italy or Germany. In asking the meeting to consider what might be done to improve the contribution of British educational bodies so far as an understanding of problems in English-speaking countries is concerned, he raised the question of possible changes in examination syllabuses, special facilities for providing books on American and Dominion[5] history and affairs, the increase of scholarships and fellowships, and the introduction of special courses on the subject into curricula.

---

1   Reprinted by permission from Macmillan Publishers Ltd: *Nature* (139: 3522), copyright (1937).

2   An international educational charity founded in 1918 to promote global understanding through the shared use of English.

3   Created through a legacy from Walter Page, an annual study grant offered by the English-Speaking Union for British teachers to travel to the USA to study a specific aspect of American education.

4   An intermediate state or condition, especially in relation to conflict.

5   Any of the larger self-governing nations that belong or once belonged to the Commonwealth of Nations (or formerly the British Empire).

Mr H. G. Wells, president-elect of Section L (Education) of the British Association, who contributed to the discussion, thought there will be no peace in the world until education has been recast into a common basis of understanding throughout the world. He had little confidence in what has been called 'scientific' American, British, or other history. There is but one history – the history of mankind. The world is involved in great issues of human ecology and of economics, but little of these things is taught. He said that we shall have to realise – and it will be a wrench – that much of the history at present taught is stale, unprofitable and out of date. British people are curious about America. They devour American publications; they patronise American films; they are learning to think and speak American; but they are not interested in the history of the Constitution[6] or local points of pre-Civil War[7] days. The public is willing to react against limited histories and get into general understandings, but the schools hold up this natural development towards the human understanding of the world.

---

6   The supreme law of the USA, drawn up in 1787 and amended twenty-seven times since.

7   In the USA, the conflict (1861-65) between the southern confederate states and the northern unionist states over the southern states' attempt to secede from the American Union.

3.11: 'The Informative Content of Education' (4 September 1937).[1]

Mr H. G. Wells, in his presidential address to Section L (Education),[2] directs attention to an aspect of educational science that has received perhaps a disproportionately small amount of attention in educational literature, the question of information. He leaves the physical and mental training of our modern populations aside, he contributes nothing to the discussion of language teaching, mathematics, the cultivation of literary appreciation, music, drawing and aesthetic training generally, and he concentrates upon the question of what a modern human being should know in order to play the part of a citizen, happily and adequately. What sort of *fact system* should be and can be established in a normal human mind under the conditions existing in a contemporary civilised community?

Few people realise the restrictions set to the accumulation of knowledge by the exigencies of the time-table and the school-leaving age. When due allowance has been made for the other elements in educational work it is questionable whether we can allot more than six hours a week to imparting real knowledge (real, that is, as distinguished from methods of expression, etc.), or, assuming ten 40-week years, rather less than two thousand four hundred hours altogether in the school period of life. A vast amount of miscellaneous knowledge is, of course, picked up by talking, reading, observation and so forth outside the formal school scheme and we learn facts in vast variety to our dying days, but this is uncorrelated stuff, and it is within the limits of these two thousand four hundred precious hours that a sound framework of general knowledge must be established, if ever it is to be established in the growing mind.

At present we waste a considerable amount of this meagre allowance in imparting useless and unedifying information or information of secondary importance. We need a much more stringent economy in this respect and a more rigorous examination of what is included. The desire for knowledge, unless it is perverted and discouraged, is a natural impulse in the developing human being, and the informative side of educational work should be based on the natural curiosity of the child and should stimulate, develop and gratify it. The curiosity of the child turns mainly upon inanimate things and what can be done with them, upon animals and (secondarily) plants and upon personal and then social reactions. Upon the systematic exploitation of these primitive divisions of curiosity our teaching of the facts of physics, biology and historical and social sciences

---

1   Reprinted by permission from Macmillan Publishers Ltd: *Nature* (140: 3540), copyright (1937). In a letter to the editor of *Nature* (and his close friend), Richard Gregory, dated 23 September 1937, Wells wrote, 'Thank you for that leading article in *Nature*. I'm vain but not so vain as to be blind to the dominant share you have had in giving me a show in this B. A. affair' (Smith 1998, IV: 169).

2   'The Informative Content of Education' was delivered to the British Association meeting at Nottingham on 2 September 1937 and published in *World Brain* (1938, 65-90).

must rest. By a careful selection of topics it is possible in the period up to the dawn of adolescence to impart clear conceptions of material science, making for mechanical understanding and competence, and a vision of the history of life upon the earth and of human history and human conditions, hygienic, physiological, geographical and political, sufficient for adequate citizenship without any killing of the spirit of inquiry.

A much more realistic and serviceable knowledge than is generally attained, of economic life and of the legal conventions of property and of the process of finance which dominate our everyday lives, is possible before the school-leaving age, but it is possible only through the stringent elimination of any irrelevant matter and of any matter which distorts the general picture. The major fault of the knowledge system we build up to-day in the general mind is its lack of proportion. The historical intelligence, the political mind of the contemporary European citizen is a sort of hunchback[3] mind, in which the hole-and-corner facts of the national history and the petty details of the Jewish tribal records loom, preposterously exaggerated. The necessity of a drastic modernisation of the historical outlook has been shirked too long – with disastrous results to the world. History, the backbone of our fact system, needs to be straightened and that hunch removed.

Under modern conditions schooling is only foundation work. There is now no end to education throughout life. The primary fact system passes insensibly into a vast variety of technical learning and adult culture and so upward at its highest levels to the knowledge evoked by original inquiry and creative work. The proportion of those who contribute by observation and criticism to the common stock of knowledge and to its sifting and organisation is likely to increase very considerably in the future. Mass observation[4] as it is being developed by Harrisson and his group may have many important effects upon the public mentality.

---

3   A hunched or protuberant back.

4   A British social research organisation founded in 1937 and operating into the mid-1950s (and revived in 1981) which aimed to record everyday life in Britain through a panel of around 500 untrained volunteer observers who either maintained diaries or replied to open-ended questionnaires. It also paid investigators to record peoples conversation and behaviour at work, on the street and at various public occasions.

3.12: Social Relations of Science (1938)

Editorial: 'Social Relations of Science' (23 April 1938).[1]

'Science and its applications are not only transforming the physical and mental environment of men, but are adding greatly to the complexities of the social, economic and political relations among them'. This passage from a resolution of the Council of the American Association for the Advancement of Science, published in *Nature* on January 22,[2] is representative of the widespread growth of interest, in recent times, in the social relations of science. The American Association has resolved to take as one of its objectives an examination of the profound effects of science upon society. This resolve seems to have been partly inspired by the movement, started several years ago, to make the British Association the platform in Great Britain for the discussion of social problems which science had helped to create and might help to solve.

Alongside these national movements, international action on the same subject has been taken by the International Council of Scientific Unions[3] (I. C. S. U.). This important body, partly at the instance of the Academy of Sciences of Amsterdam,[4] set up in 1937 a Committee on Science and its Social Relations[5] (C. S. S. R.), as reported in *Nature* of April 24 and May 22, 1937 (139, 689, 869).[6] This Committee is charged to survey the influence of science on the world picture as well as on the material side of human life and society; it is to review science and its applications as a whole, and to promote the study of their social influence. Its initial plan is to prepare a report, with bibliographical material, to be presented at the next meeting of the I. C. S. U. in 1940, and thereafter, it is hoped, to be printed for wide circulation.

The collection of data on which the Committee on Science and its Social Relations will base this report is to be obtained from three sources: from national correspondents appointed by national academies or research councils, who will provide information on the national aspects of the social relations of sci-

---

1   Reprinted by permission from Macmillan Publishers Ltd: *Nature* (141: 3573), copyright (1938).

2   In the anonymous piece, 'News and Views' (1938).

3   An organisation for the promotion of international scientific activity, founded in 1931 and known as the International Council for Science since 1998.

4   Founded in 1851 in Amsterdam as an organisation dedicated to the advancement of science in the Netherlands, it was renamed the Royal Netherlands Academy of Arts and Sciences in 1938.

5   A body established by the International Council of Scientific Unions in 1937 to assess the influence of science on the material life and society.

6   In two anonymous articles, 'Social Responsibilities of Science' (1937) and 'International Council of Scientific Unions' (1937), respectively.

ence; from correspondents appointed by international bodies dealing with the several branches of science, who will report from the point of view of their particular sciences; and from individual correspondents having special interest in, or knowledge of, these matters. The appointed correspondents will in many cases find it desirable to enlist the aid of national or international groups of interested men of science, because the field of inquiry, especially for the national correspondents, is too wide to be covered by the knowledge of any single person. It is hoped that by this wide co-operation a report of great interest will be produced, though the difficulties to be faced in compiling it are obviously considerable.

To guide their correspondents in the collection and supply of information, the C. S. S. R. has drawn up a series of fairly detailed questionnaires, one for national correspondents, and others for the several branches of science on which the international scientific unions will report. It is hoped that the consideration and answering of these inquiries will play a useful part in stimulating and clarifying thought in scientific circles all over the world, on the social relations of science; and that the C. S. S. R. will receive from its many correspondents the support without which its efforts cannot but fall short of the great needs and opportunities before it.

The connection of the C. S. S. R. with such important and established bodies as the International Council of Scientific Unions, the various international scientific unions themselves, and, still more, with the (in most cases) much older national academies, gives it a representative position which could scarcely otherwise be obtained. These connections in turn impose a duty on the Committee to make its work as scientific in spirit as possible, and in no way to compromise or misrepresent its parent bodies by partisan views or statements. In particular, the C. S. S. R. is not to be, or to be regarded as, a propagandist body; its functions are to survey, to study, to report.

It is excellent that the national academies and international scientific unions should take part in setting up and helping the work of such a body as the C. S. S. R., but the preparation of a condensed report of world-wide scope, to appear two years hence, and perhaps triennially[7] thereafter, is far from sufficient to meet the need within each of the great nations, whose civilisation is now largely based on science, for thought, discussion and publication on the social relations of science. Nor does it seem that in Great Britain the provision for such discussion, at the annual meeting of the British Association, is adequate. Further, national scientific academies, such as the Royal Society, probably do well to limit their discussions and publications to the natural sciences, without extending their functions into that great bordering region which the C. S. S. R. is

---

7   Every three years.

charged to survey. Science itself has its controversies, sometimes keen despite the objectivity of the scientific method and spirit; in that border region beyond, though the like objectivity may be striven after, union of opinion and agreement in discussion will certainly be more difficult to attain. It would seem best for both sides, therefore, that the arena for the discussion of the social relations of science should be separate from those in which the natural sciences are considered, though many representatives of each should be interested in both.

To be explicit, it has been suggested that in Great Britain (and the same applies to the other great nations) there should be a Society for the Study of the Social Relations of Science[8] (S. R. S.), with a large individual membership, which should not be confined to men of science, though they should play the principal part in it. The Society should have its council, its regular meetings, its publications, and perhaps its committees for the study of selected questions. It should receive, read, discuss, and, after consideration by suitable referees, publish papers submitted to it; it might arrange symposia (by the spoken and written word) on special subjects within its range. Its field of work would inevitably trench on[9] questions that have a political importance, but its attitude towards papers submitted to it should be scientific and objective, and it should not in general express corporate opinions, but leave readers to accept or reject the statements in its publications, according to their view of the credit of the authors.

This research method and policy of publication have proved their success in serving science in general, as in the case of the Royal Society, and the many branches of science now organised in separate societies, too numerous to mention; there seems good prospect that a like success would attend the same method and policy applied to this new field. The S. R. S. would be a society for the advancement of knowledge, not a propagandist body for the advancement of science in the public councils and esteem (like the former British Science Guild) or for the advancement of professional scientific interests (like the Association of Scientific Workers). Despite the existence of such useful bodies as Political and Economic Planning[10] and the Engineers' Study Group,[11] which are doing valuable work on the social relations of science, it does not seem that they perform the functions that are suggested for the S. R. S. Questions of overlapping and other difficulties may present themselves, but public scientific opinion on these

---

8   This editorial and the debate it aroused resulted in the establishment of the Division for the Social and International Relations of Science within the British Association at the Association's meeting in August 1938.

9   Encroach.

10   Founded in 1931, a British political think-tank that merged into the Policy Studies Institute in 1978.

11   An organisation of the late-1930s and 1940s which reported on the impact of science (including social science) on society.

matters now seems to have reached a stage where the formation of such a society is appropriate.

With the object of obtaining representative opinions upon the subject of social repercussions of science, and the question of promoting their deliberate study by the formation of a new scientific society or otherwise, advance proofs of the above article were sent to a number of scientific workers and others, with a letter inviting the frank expression of their views. The replies received are published in succeeding pages of this Supplement, and are grouped under headings representing in a general way the fields of scientific work in which the correspondents are particularly interested. It will be observed that doubts are expressed as to the need of establishing a new scientific society, and suggestions are made that the desired objects might be obtained through co-operation with existing bodies. Notwithstanding this difference of opinion, it is evidently the decided view of a number of responsible scientific workers that steps should be taken to further the objective study of social relations of science in the hope that the knowledge obtained may make both science and society conscious of their common interests and responsibilities.[12]

Comment on the editorial: H. G. Wells, 'Representative Opinions: Sociology and Economics' (23 April 1938).[13]

The essential difficulty in working out any special social functions for scientific men lies in the fact that, so far as the great majority of sciences go, the individual worker has no special aptitude for social organisation. His time, his mental energy he owes to his special work. But this is less true of certain sciences than of others. It is less true, for example, of biology than of astronomy. It is less true of anthropology and psychology than of invertebrate anatomy. In the case of human ecology and social psychology, the man of science works in a field whose generalisations are almost immediately applicable to social organisation. Every

---

12 This editorial was followed by a large number of comments from scientists and others. Only Wells's comment, and that by F. G. Donnan (because of its 'Wellsian' reference), are reprinted below; for the rest of the debate see Bartlett 1938, Bernal 1938, Blackett 1938, Boswell 1938, Bragg 1938, Clark 1938, Crew 1938, Desch 1938, Egerton 1938, Farquharson 1938, Ferguson 1938, Fleure 1938, Florence 1938, Flugel 1938, Ginsberg 1938, Haldane 1938, Hall 1938, Hill 1938, Hopkins 1938, Huxley 1938, Kerr 1938, Laski 1938, Levy 1938, Lindemann 1938, Marquand 1938, Mitchell 1938, Myers 1938, Myres 1938, Needham 1938, Paget 1938, Philip 1938, Read 1938, Russell 1938, Ryle 1938, Salisbury 1938, Soddy 1938, Spearman 1938, Stopford 1938, Tizard 1938 and Wooster 1938.

13 Reprinted by permission from Macmillan Publishers Ltd: *Nature* (141: 3573), copyright (1938).

science insists upon integrity, explicitness and devotion to the extent of entire disinterestedness, and so the study and teaching of any science tends to brace the character and sweeten the social atmosphere. But it is through the pushing of the boundaries of science out into the field of rash generalisations and mischievous traditions known as human history, that the practical hope of mankind in science lies.

The S. R. S. claims the attention and frank criticism of every type of scientific mind, but if it is to operate efficiently it will have to create opportunities and support of an increasing number of social biologists and social psychologists. There is little advantage to be found in the distinguished experimentalist in physical science dissipating his time and genius in amateurish contributions to political and social theory. There is everything to be gained by an S. R. S. that will keep him in touch and co-operation with social scientific work and thought as intensive as his own.

Comment on the editorial: Frederick Donnan, 'Representative Opinions: Chemistry' (23 April 1938).[14]

As a foreign member of the Amsterdam Academy of Sciences, I am very glad to have had the opportunity of associating myself with the action taken by that body, an action which led to the recent setting up by the International Council of Scientific Unions of a 'Committee on Science and its Social Relations'. There can be no doubt that this Committee is destined to carry out most valuable work, and its formation on such a secure international basis may well mark the beginning of a new era in the history of mankind.

The proposal to found in Great Britain a Society for the Study of the Social Relations of Science is one which I wish to support most strongly. The existence of such a society in this country – and of similar societies in other countries – would be the surest guarantee for the success of the great work initiated by the formation of the international committee.

The impact of science on society – to employ a now famous expression – is of two kinds. In its less obvious and yet perhaps finally most important form, it alters the general 'climate' of thought and opinion. In the nineteenth century, when steam-driven machinery in factories, steam-boats and railway trains, and the application of electrical science in the telegraph,[15] telephone and electric

---

14 Reprinted by permission from Macmillan Publishers Ltd: *Nature* (141: 3573), copyright (1938).

15 A communication system consisting of a transmitter and a receiver joined by a wire along which an electric current passes, signals being related by making and breaking the circuit.

light were changing the social and economic relations of people, the work of Wallace, Darwin[16] and Huxley[17] caused a fundamental change of general outlook. So also in the present century, with its vast organisation of factory production and great power stations, its electric trains, motor-cars, aeroplanes, cinemas, radio, gramophones,[18] etc., the great discoveries in physics, chemistry and astronomy have produced a profound effect on the general climate of opinion; whilst it is probable that the biological sciences are destined in no very distant future to effect another and perhaps still more drastic development.

It is with no intention of underrating the enormous effects of applied science on the social and economic conditions of humanity that I mention these matters. I want simply to suggest that we must pay equal attention to the influence exerted on the actions of men by the general outlook which they derive from the current scientific philosophy presented to them. It is of very great importance that this 'ideology' should be the best available.

In spite of everything that has been written on the subject, it is perhaps not yet sufficiently realised that the inhabitants of this planet are witnessing at the present time a very peculiar epoch in its history – the epoch of the enormously rapid advance of science and its applications. Although speculative prophecy is usually of small value, I am inclined to hold the opinion that this epoch will be a relatively brief one, confined (bar 'accidents' of a terrestrial or extra-terrestrial character) to the next ten thousand, or possibly to the next two thousand, years. It is hard to say when the zenith of this peculiar period will be reached. Certainly nothing like it has ever been experienced before by the inhabitants of this earth. Will its effects be beneficial or catastrophic? That is the serious question to which civilised humanity is now slowly awakening. Modern science is the revelation to mankind of possibilities and potentialities undreamed of even by such giants as Galileo, Newton and Harvey – undreamed of, therefore, only a few hundred years ago. What will a Wellsian historian, writing, say, in the year 20,000, have to say of this epoch?

In the somewhat complacent mixture of romanticism and utilitarianism which characterised the nineteenth century, many men, intoxicated by the advances of that age, dreamed of a continuous upward progress of humanity. Wiser, or perhaps more disillusioned, than they, we of this century are by no means sure of such a continuous progress. Many see a possible, or even probable, danger of collapse. Such a crash of civilisation could never be due to the true advance of scientific knowledge, though it might be accelerated by the inhuman

---

16   I. e., Charles Darwin.

17   I. e., T. H. Huxley.

18   Instruments for reproducing recorded sound by the vibrations of a stylus travelling in an irregular spiral groove in a disc rotating on a turntable.

430

and anti-social use of this knowledge, and by a false ideology based on a perverted interpretation.

I think that one of the main objects of the new society will be the careful study of the reversible social-scientific reaction, science $\leftrightarrows$ human welfare;[19] how by the advance of science to increase human welfare, and how by the advance of human welfare to increase science. This is one of the great dynamic equilibria[20] of a beneficent and benevolent civilisation.

At the same time we must avoid the errors of an easy sentimentalism founded on august abstract nouns and grandiloquent phrases. Human society and its welfare are extremely difficult and complicated matters, the hard, concrete realities of which demand detailed and highly critical study. Although we may reject the application to human society of the holistic conceptions of the beehive and the territory,[21] or the idea of the flowering of a great aristocracy based on a partial de-humanisation[22] of the rest, it will be for the biological and psychological science of the future to say what are the possibilities and what may be the best available solution. Unlike traditional philosophy and traditional theology, science does not attempt to storm the citadel[23] of truth; it rests on patient experimental research, and offers no simple panacea and no facile Utopia. Great and immense, therefore, are the prospects and potentialities of the new society, for they will be based on the essential fluidity and adaptability of scientific thought, the steady progress of discovery, and the slow building of whatever conception of the *summum bonum*[24] mankind is capable of attaining. There may be room here for personal optimism or pessimism, but none for tears or an inaction born of despair.

Summary of Discussion: 'Summary' (23 April 1938).[25]

The comments in the foregoing letters may be conveniently summarised in three groups; *why* is it necessary to go deeper into the social relations of science, *what* are the activities envisaged, and *how* can they best be brought about.

---

19   The interaction of science on human welfare and human welfare on science.

20   States in which the influences of processes to which a thing is subject cancel one another and produce no overall change or variation.

21   More commonly, termitarium, a termite's nest.

22   The process of depriving one of human attributes.

23   Attack, metaphorically or actually, a physical or intellectual stronghold.

24   Latin, the highest good.

25   Reprinted by permission from Macmillan Publishers Ltd: *Nature* (141: 3573), copyright (1938).

The rapid and persistent growth of natural knowledge leads to effects which have to be corrected (Bragg, Fleure). There is need for intensification and direction in the study of the social relations of science (Boswell) and guidance in the organisation of society (Hall[26]). All is not well in the way science is applied to social life (Levy). The liberty of science is threatened (Hopkins). Social developments are ill-balanced (Bartlett, Philip) and may destroy civilisation (Bernal, Donnan, Kerr, Lindemann).

The social problems created by science can be solved by scientific method (Flugel) but educative action is needed both for scientific workers (Blackett) and for other citizens (Kerr). As the sciences become more specialised, the need for their synthesis increases (Desch, Salisbury, Spearman) and also that for a closer relationship between scientific and social workers (Laski, Marquand, C. S. Myers). It is the duty of scientific workers, as citizens, to study the social implications of science (Needham, Stopford) and to see that Government and legislature receive the best advice from those scientifically qualified (Egerton, Ryle).

The proposed organisation would provide a meeting place between men of science and others interested in statescraft[27] (Crew) and would prevent them from going about the business in the wrong way (Tizard). It should study the social background of science (Le Gros Clark), the historical relations between science and society (Blackett) and, in general, the reversible reaction science ⇌ society (Donnan). In particular, it would investigate the repercussions of science on social affairs and also likely future developments (Boswell, Russell[28]).

As specific problems, it might find out the number of scientific workers, how they are financed and how their work is co-ordinated (Bernal, Huxley,[29] Needham) and might draw up a code of ethics[30] for them (Hill[31]). The mechanism of production, the unsatisfactory method of dealing with new inventions, the imperfections of the financial system, the lack of statistics, problems of employment and ecological studies also deserve attention (Sargant Florence, Paget, Salisbury).

The organisation envisaged should eventually humanise scientific teaching (Read[32]), bring together results scattered in many journals (Boswell), act as

---

26   I. e., A. D. Hall.

27   The art of conducting state affairs; statesmanship.

28   I. e., John Russell.

29   I. e., Julian Huxley.

30   A set of guidelines for professional responsibility, intended to dispense with or help determine what professional behaviour is ethical.

31   I. e., A. V. Hill.

32   I. e., John Read.

co-ordinating body to other societies (C. S. Myers) and encourage them to study specific problems – for example, the anthropological and folklore[33] societies might inquire into the springs of human action (Fleure). It should obtain and distribute funds for research (Huxley, Hall, Wells) and might eventually act as information bureau and consultative body for administration and industry (Flugel, Huxley).

The need for preventing unnecessary duplication is stressed, particularly with reference to the activities of the British Association, the Royal Society and the Institute of Sociology[34] (Ferguson, Egerton, Desch). Sociologists would welcome co-operation (Farquharson) and the proposed organisation might grow into a section of the B. A. (Crew).

Other than scientific workers should be welcomed as members (Hopkins, Levy, Philip, Stopford). Sociology should be well represented (Ginsberg). Representatives of the chief societies interested in social questions should be included (C. S. Myers) but membership should be individual (Haldane[35]). Manual workers[36] should be allowed to join (Haldane) but economic quacks[37] should be excluded (Marquand).

Apart from one correspondent (J. L. Myres) the comments and criticisms are mostly constructive. The chief difficulties foreseen are in connection with retaining a cool, scientific attitude towards emotional and political subjects (Ferguson, Chalmers Mitchell, Stopford) and of obtaining a fair, unbiased board of referees for the publications (Blackett, Haldane, Levy). Here, perhaps, the First Interim Report on Schemes and Proposals for Economic and Social Reforms, published by the British Science Guild and the Engineers' Study Group (see *Nature*, May 25, 1935)[38] shows that at least one group of investigators found that the problem was not insoluble.

---

33 The traditional beliefs, customs, songs, tales, etc., preserved in oral tradition among a people.

34 An amateur organisation for the promotion of sociological research (1930-55).

35 I. e., J. B. S. Haldane.

36 Employees who perform their work with their hands, physical labourers, often distinguished from mental or brain workers.

37 Persons who profess a knowledge or skill which they do not have; charlatans.

38 The British Science Guild's *Engineers' Study Group on Economics* (1935) was noticed anonymously in *Nature* in 'Systems of Economic Reform' (1935).

3.13: Brenda Tripp, 'Science and the Citizen: The Public Understanding of Science' (3 April 1943).[1]

The Division for the Social and International Relations of Science of the British Association held a conference at the Royal Institution in London during March 20-21 to consider ways and means for increasing the public understanding and appreciation of science. For more than a hundred years the British Association through its annual conference has endeavoured to introduce science to the citizen, but the fact remains that to-day, in the midst of a scientific age, science and the citizen are still very insufficiently acquainted. As was so frequently stress during the course of the conference, we are living in an era in which the discoveries of science are becoming an essential constituent of our everyday life, and an understanding of the spirit and service of science is of the utmost importance for the people and its leaders if our civilisation is to survive.

[...]

Science and the Press

At the final session, the chair was taken by Sir Richard Gregory, who dealt with some prominent characteristics of the scientific movement following the publication of the works of Mill and Darwin.[2] These works had a great influence in releasing thought and inquiry from conventionalism and in revealing relationships between the nature of man and his environment. The foundation of *Nature* towards the latter part of the last century was a landmark in promoting this movement.

Mr Ritchie Calder, formerly science editor of the *Daily Herald*, was optimistic about the effect of the War[3] on the mental attitude of the average reader, the average journalist and the average scientific man. The newspapers have been purged, scientific men have been drawn from their isolated position into public life and the average reader, through national service,[4] has been given a new way of life and a new outlook. In a war of scientific weapons, they have become to a greater or lesser degree scientific. This new population will demand new treatment from the Press. He thinks that there will be a need for a British Institute of Scientific Information[5] linked with similar organisations throughout the world,

---

1   Reprinted by permission from Macmillan Publishers Ltd: *Nature* (151: 3831), copyright (1943).

2   I. e., Charles Darwin.

3   I. e., the Second World War.

4   Service in the armed forces under conscription for a specified period.

5   A non-profit organisation for the promotion of science proposed in 1943 by Calder but which apparently never came into existence.

which will maintain a regular supply of scientific information for dissemination in the various countries. A similar idea was put forward by Mr Henry Martin, of the Press Association.[6]

Mr J. G. Crowther put forward many suggestions for increasing the popular understanding of science, pointing out that there is no simple way of bringing this about. The improvement of science reporting in the Press depends on the simultaneous advance of several interests: the increasing interest and demand from the public; the effects of a higher standard of science teaching; the raising of the school-leaving age; the recognition by owners and editors of newspapers of the growing importance of science; recognition by the State and philanthropic bodies of the necessity for better public understanding of science; the efforts of scientific men themselves to make their activities better known and understood, and the promotion of scientific interest which arises from the increasing mechanisation of daily life. He advocates a full-time science editor for every newspaper, and a science news service providing reliable science news to all newspapers which subscribe to it.

The work which the Association of Scientific Workers is doing in publicising science was described by Dr D. S. Evans. The Association already has groups of people actively engaged in publicising science in a large number of its branches, and steps have been taken to train members in the technique of popular science writing. Their aims are to counteract the perverted ideas of science in the Press as instanced by astrology[7] pages and pseudo-scientific advertisements; to show the people what can be done by science during the period of reconstruction after the War and to protect the people from wrong systems of government offered in the light of arguments which appear to have a scientific background.

The Press was further criticised by Prof. J. B. S. Haldane, who said that more space is devoted to anti-science than to science. One of the first things to effect is a revision of the laws of libel so that some action could be taken against lies perpetrated in patent medicine[8] and other advertisements. He advocated a science news service; science features in every newspaper; a science reporter for every newspaper; and scientific and technical advisers attached to the staff of every newspaper to direct policy.

Mr Francis Williams considered how the Press, instead of giving occasional publicity to sensational science news, could become a vehicle for the consistent interpretation to the public of the social impact of scientific development

---

6   The national news agency of the United Kingdom, founded in 1868.

7   The supposed art of foretelling or counselling in human affairs by interpretation of the motions of celestial objects.

8   A proprietary medicine manufactured under patent and available without prescription.

upon the world. He considered the possibility of producing a paper independent of advertisement revenue.

It was at this final session on science and the Press that Mr H. G. Wells sounded the death knell[9] of newspapers as we know them to-day. The time has gone, he thinks, when we shall have to buy four daily newspapers in order to find out what is being concealed from us. He visualises a time not far off when we shall dial NEWS as we now dial TIM,[10] and receive the latest bulletin over the wires. There are promising signs that the public are demanding informative matter to read and will no longer tolerate newspapers which give no news and exist for the commodities advertised in them. Bound books will disappear. Ideas will be ventilated in paper-covered books and pamphlets, sold at a price within the reach of all, and these will do what the newspapers have failed to do. Finally, old, stale, out-of-date text-books must be burnt. The best-sellers of the future will be scientific books bringing to the citizen an awareness of the age in which he lives.

---

9   Figuratively, an event that heralds the end of something.

10   In Britain, the telephone dialling code formerly used to receive the correct time in words from 1936 to the early 1990s.

3.14: Fellowships of Imperial College, London (1943)

From 'Announcements' (10 July 1943).[1]

The governing body of the Imperial College of Science and Technology has elected to Imperial College fellowships the following old students of the college: Dr F. W. Lanchester, Dr J. G. Lawn, Dr F. C. Lea, Mr F. Twyman, and Mr H. G. Wells.

---

1   Reprinted by permission from Macmillan Publishers Ltd: *Nature* (152: 3845), copyright (1943).

3.15: Doctorates of the University of London (1943)

From 'Announcements' (6 November 1943).[1]

The following doctorates of the University of London have been conferred: *DSc*: Mr B. Katz, of University College; Mr H. G. Wells, an external student;[2] *DSc (Eng.)*: Mr G. Hughes, an external student; Prof. A. F. C. Pollard, University professor of (mechanical) instrument design, Imperial College of Science and Technology; *DSc (Econ.)*: Mr R. G. D. Allen, University reader in statistics, London School of Economics.

---

1   Reprinted by permission from Macmillan Publishers Ltd: *Nature* (152: 3862), copyright (1943).

2   A distance-learner taking a course of study through correspondence and only occasionally visiting the educational institution.

3.16: 'Thoughts on Reconstruction' (19 February 1944).[1]

The April, June and September 1943 issues of the *Krisson Bulletin*[2] contain a series of articles well designed to encourage the development of a more scientific outlook generally. The first, 'A Plea for Scepticism', should encourage a more critical attitude to some of the proposals for reconstruction and particularly to political theory. It includes a useful little bibliography. In the following issue are printed eleven paragraphs of 'The Universal Rights of Man' from a pamphlet by Mr H. G. Wells to be published later.[3] This is a development from the 'Declaration of the Rights of Man'.[4] This statement of the universal rights – the right to live, protection of minors, freedom to work, right to earn money, right to possess, freedom to go about, right to know, personal liberty, freedom from violence – which are in the nature of man and cannot be changed, but could be made the basis of a new and happier way of human life, is accompanied by an appeal not to take them for granted but to work for them and to guard them. The third article, 'Educated? It *is* my business', after quoting F. Sherwood Taylor's *The Century of Science*, pleads for an attempt to understand our environment and to take an intelligent place in human organisation.

---

1   Reprinted by permission from Macmillan Publishers Ltd: *Nature* (153: 3877), copyright (1944).

2   This publication has proved untraceable, and thus also the three articles mentioned below.

3   A reference to Wells's *The Rights of Man*, actually published in September 1943.

4   A reference to Wells's earlier version, *The Rights of Man*, published 1940.

3.17: The Death of H. G. Wells (1946)

i) From 'Announcements' (24 August 1946).[1]

We regret to announce the following deaths:

Nikolai Morozov, honorary member of the Academy of Sciences of the USSR, known for his general writings on scientific topics, on July 13, aged ninety-two.

Mr H. G. Wells, on August 13, aged seventy-nine.

ii) Richard Gregory, 'H. G. Wells: A Survey and Tribute' (21 September 1946).[2]

Creative ideas, and the influence of their expression, constitute a measure of material and intellectual advance displayed in the works of science and literature. Science is now commonly understood to be systematic and formulated natural philosophy; but with achievements in these fields of human understanding are also associated moral and social forces which, though not of a physical kind, are observable in their effects and admit of rational analysis and judgement.

This is the domain of what Wells defined as human ecology; and all his works – novels, fantastic and imaginative romances and books upon social, religious and political questions – are concerned, directly and indirectly, with individual and social factors involved in the biological whole. As a philosophy of matter, life and mind and their relationships to one another, he may be said to have expressed independently much the same evolutionary principles in diverse ways as those presented by General Smuts in his *Holism and Evolution*, published in 1926. Moral as well as material values enter into this new humanism, and the adaptation of them to worthy conditions of life must continually create new problems for civilised societies to face and to solve, the tendency always being towards integrations of increased complexity and therefore of increasing difficulty of adjustment.

This was consistently the attitude taken by Wells towards human thought and action. In a Friday Evening Discourse at the Royal Institution in 1902, on the 'Discovery of the Future', his thesis was 'that mankind was at the dawn of a great changeover from life regarded as a system of consequences to life regarded as a system of constructive effort.... We should be less and less bound by the engagements of the past and more and more ruled by a realisation of the creative

---

1   Reprinted by permission from Macmillan Publishers Ltd: *Nature* (158: 4008), copyright (1946).

2   Reprinted by permission from Macmillan Publishers Ltd: *Nature* (158: 4012), copyright (1946).

effects of our acts'. He did not say that the future could be foretold, but he held that its conditions could be foretold.

Thirty-four years later, in another Discourse at the Royal Institution, Wells again expressed what was always dominant in his mind – to relate effects to causes and arrive at generalisations and syntheses. His temperament and endeavour were those of a scientific enquirer into individual experiences and their collective relationships, with the same independence of customary authority as that of the Horatian[3] motto *Nullius in verba*[4] of the Royal Society, but with much greater perplexities to study than those of the concrete natural sciences. The subject of the Discourse at the Royal Institution was 'The Idea of a World Encyclopaedia',[5] and the object was the collation of all published knowledge in the world by, with and for the world.

The conspectus[6] of such a vast undertaking can be found in Wells's *Outline of History*, *The Science of Life*, with his eldest son, G. P. Wells, and Julian Huxley as joint authors, and *The Work, Wealth and Happiness of Mankind*, successively published from 1920 to 1932.[7] The *Outline* is a story of the earth as the abode of man from his earliest appearance on the planet to the Peace of Versailles; the *Life* deals with biology and social structures; and *Work* with ways in which humanity earns its living. As contributions to the history of man and his activities, these three works constitute a supreme achievement which could not have been conceived and constructed by any historian without his scientific credentials. He was as aware as anyone of certain weaknesses and deficiencies; but he welcomed suggestions to remedy them as well as to include new discoveries relating to human evolution and history, particularly in revised editions of the *Outline*.[8]

To have mastered such a vast body of human thought and action, and to have kept abreast, as Wells did, of current knowledge and opinion on many technical subjects, was an intellectual feat which no other modern man of letters could possibly have achieved. Referring to these historical surveys and attempts to bring economic, financial and social life into rational relationship, he said at the Royal Institution ten years ago that he had been engaged in the 'still more desperate struggle to estimate the possible consequences of this or that set of op-

---

3   Of the Roman poet Horace.

4   Latin, the motto of the Royal Society, meaning 'on the words of no one'.

5   Delivered on 20 November 1936.

6   A comprehensive mental survey.

7   The year of publication of the British first edition of *The Work, Wealth and Happiness of Mankind* (though it appeared the year before in the USA).

8   During Wells's lifetime the book was published in revised editions in 1923, 1925, 1930 and 1940 (the latter under the title *The Enlarged and Revised Outline of History*).

erating causes upon the future of mankind'. His imaginative romances, as well as his works on social, religious and political questions, reflect his reactions to historical or visionary influences upon modes of human existence. On the magic carpet[9] of his mind he could travel backward or forward in time and space and live in ideals so vividly that they became convincing realities in narrative.

The first scientific fantasy of this kind was *The Time Machine*, a rough draft of which appeared in the *Science Schools Journal*[10] when Wells was a young man of twenty-one years.[11] He had acquired a sound knowledge of the fundamental facts of astronomy and was able, therefore, to describe accurately the rapidly changing celestial scenes presented to the time traveller. The moon passed in an instant through all its phases, the sun became a band of fire and swayed up and down, from solstice[12] to solstice again in a minute or less, with spring and winter merging into one another in the picture. Wells knew, better than any other man of letters, what such natural events and processes had been and they were due to forces acting continually and uniformly. It was this scientific knowledge, combined with brilliant powers of expression, that made him unique in his own particular field.

After *The Time Machine* came *The War of the Worlds* as the second of a series of a dozen imaginative romances in which physical and biological factors were cleverly used. Lowell's work on the planet Mars, and his conclusions that the so-called canals had been artificially constructed by intelligent beings,[13] had been published three years earlier, so Wells had a good basis for his story. The Martians he conceived to invade the earth brought novel heat-rays[14] and a heavy gas with them as devastating means of conquest, but after a short time they themselves became masses of corruption due to insidious germs of disease which they had eliminated in their own planet and to which their bodies were, therefore, not immune. This end of the Martian invaders is a characteristic example of the application of scientific knowledge to forms and conditions of life woven into a story having also strong emotional appeal.

The First Men in the Moon, published in 1901, again revealed his genius for producing a story rich in human interest without disturbing the sensibilities

---

9   A mythical carpet able to transport a person on it to any desired place.

10   The student magazine of the Normal School of Science, South Kensington, founded by Wells in 1887 and later renamed the *Royal College of Science Magazine* (1891) and *Phoenix* (1904).

11   As 'The Chronic Argonauts' (1888).

12   Either of the two occasions in the year when the sun reaches its highest or lowest point in the sky.

13   Lowell expressed this theory in *Mars* (1895).

14   Laser beams.

of critical scientific minds. In this respect, Wells's novel was far in advance of Jules Verne's *Journey to the Moon*,[15] which had many scientific blunders and inconsistencies. Moreover, Verne's travellers did not reach the moon, whereas Wells's did land upon our satellite and found beings living inside it with thoughts and feelings which made contacts with human hearts.

So it was with the story *In the Days of the Comet*, published in 1906. Several years earlier a remarkable new star appeared, visible to the naked eye, and expanding at such a rate that it was thought by many people to be a minor planet approaching the earth.[16] Wells had a much better basis for his fancy when he made a comet cross the earth's orbit at a point near enough for us to pass through its tail, as actually happened in 1861. He let his imagination play with the idea that human nature might be changed by the introduction of a new spiritual element in the earth's atmosphere, represented by a peculiar greenish radiation from the comet's tail. After passing through the tail, the whole race was transfigured. Jealousy and hatred vanished, and with it war and poverty, in the vision of a world lifted out of acquisitive greed into a condition of celestial harmony. This poetic dream of what mankind might become by following paths of truth and righteousness and suppressing animal instincts is displayed in a number of Wells's works, often with hope but always conscious of the prevalence of evil tendencies in human nature.

In *The World Set Free* the transformation from old to new and better conditions of life and government was reached not through the swish of a comet's tail but as the result of a world war. The book was published early in 1914, but in substance and outlook it describes the Second World War even more closely than the First. The book was dedicated to Prof. Soddy's *Interpretation of Radium*, published in 1909; and the theme is that of the disintegration of the atom and the use of atomic bombs[17] and thousands of aeroplanes in modern warfare. As a story of the discovery and use of natural power to supplement man's animal strength, the first chapter of the book, entitled 'The Sun Snarers', states these developments with crystal clearness. It outlines the conquest of external power in the industrial applications of fire, steam, electricity, and new chemical elements, leading up to radium[18] and the release of the energy locked up in atoms, for use first with devastating effects in what was called 'The Last War'

---

15   Properly, *From the Earth to the Moon direct in 97 hours 20 minutes; and a trip round it* (1873).

16   This is probably a reference to the Great Comet of 1861 (C/1861 J1) which was visible to the naked eye from May to August; for two days, when the comet was at its closest, the earth was within its tail.

17   Nuclear weapons deriving their destructiveness from the splitting of an atom.

18   A radioactive metallic chemical element.

448

and then, in 1956, to liberate the race from obsessions and entanglements which impede moral and material growth.

'Already before the release of atomic energy the tensions between the old way of living and the new were intense' are words used in the last chapter to introduce the assembly summoned to place social organisation upon a new and nobler footing. This council was constituted in the spirit of the United Nations Organisation,[19] and it eventually led to the planning of a new common social order for the entire population of the earth. How close the realities will approach to Wells's ideals remains to be seen.

Other works in which the possible future of the human race was forecast are *When the Sleeper Wakes* (1899), *Anticipations* (1901), *Mankind in the Making* (1903), *The Food of the Gods* (1904), and *A Modern Utopia* (1905). Of *Anticipations* Sir Ray Lankester said, in a five-column review in *Nature* of March 13, 1902:

This is a profoundly interesting and suggestive book by a very remarkable man. Mr Wells was educated at the Royal College of Science; he has a thorough knowledge of, and considerable training in, the great branches of science – physics, chemistry, astronomy, geology and biology. This course of study operated, in the case of Mr Wells, upon a mind naturally gifted with an extraordinarily vivid imagination and the aptitude for true literary art.

This kind of encouragement from scientific friends was highly appreciated by Wells from the very beginning of his literary career to the end of his life. He was trained to become a science teacher, and during this formative period, as well as for several years later, his closest contacts were with workers in scientific fields. He knew that when he entered the world of letters, in which he afterwards attained international fame, he lost his place on the ladder on which he had been moving upward; but the fact that he continued to be regarded as a great scientific educator by leaders of his own generation, and an inspiration to the new, kept him continually in touch with advancing knowledge and contributed in no small measure to the remarkable responses represented in his works.

Anticipations projected the present into the future from the outlook tower[20] of modern science. It was an indictment of many existing customs and structures and a prophecy of what change might be expected in the near future. On the mechanical or inventive side, the predictions made in the book revealed an

---

19   An international organisation based in New York which aims to facilitate international cooperation in law, security, economic development, social progress and human rights, founded in 1945.

20   A tall building or structure from which to observe the approach of others.

insight which was truly marvellous. Motor-cars and motor-roads were largely to replace railway traffic. Land ironclads, armoured trains, armoured tortoises[21] or tanks and flying machines[22] with folded parachutes for escape were to be used in warfare. Forty years after this forecast all these machines were in action, but their development has not been accompanied by the changes of heart and social structure which Wells hoped for but had not the same scientific reasons to expect to be fulfilled.

In *A Modern Utopia* (1905), faith in the principles of a rational social biology is expressed in practical terms with hope as well as ingenuity. The system presented resembles that of the Platonic *Republic*, save that insistence is given to the preciousness of individual freedom and to toleration. Family allowances[23] were to be made to women, but criminals and certain other groups were not allowed to reproduce their kind, though they were free to follow their own proclivities in their own separate communities. The main idea was to keep learning and the applications of it progressive instead of fixed and pedantic, the sprit being, therefore, that of *The Discovery of the Future*. This kind of idealistic Utopia is found again in *Men Like Gods* (1923). It makes man the master of his own house and conceives the birth of a new race with noble qualities of mind and great physical strength, devoted to the understanding of Nature in all its aspects and its control for the progressive welfare of humanity.

Such projections as these into the future of man and society are not satires like Swift's *Gulliver's Travels* and Samuel Butler's *Erewhon*, or parodies of science found in novels of our own times. They rank with Plato's *Republic*, Thomas More's *Utopia* and William Morris's *News from Nowhere* in their social philosophy[24] and as vivid literature. The world of science has every reason to be proud that its spirit and service should have been translated so genuinely and loyally into 'Thoughts that breathe and words that burn'[25] with such unsurpassing power and influence as those possessed by Wells. He presented scientific workers to his readers as human beings and not as the travesties in which they figure in novels and romances written without his intimate knowledge of them and their impulses. That is why homage has always been gratefully paid to him in these columns and in other scientific periodicals.

'By science,' Wells once said, 'is meant a process of human intellectual energy which is exhaustively and reverently criticised, leading, it is hoped, to

---

21 Tanks.

22 Aeroplanes.

23 Child benefits paid by the state, legislated in Britain in 1945.

24 The philosophical study of questions about social behaviour.

25 A quotation from *Odes* (1757) by Thomas Gray.

action exhaustively criticised before it is exhaustively planned.'[26] In these words he expressed the whole of his faith, the whole of his belief in human life. How and why he acquired this faith and proclaimed it is comprehensively stated in the two volumes of his *Experiment in Autobiography* (1934), the sub-title of which reads 'Discoveries and Conclusions of a Very Ordinary Brain'. He looked at people and their actions against a background of knowledge never used before to paint pictures of aspects of individual and social life; and his insight as well as the breadth of his experiences made all the scenes and figures stand out with convincing reality, even when they were fanciful.

From first to last the characters in all Wells's works represent growing experiences and the responses of thought to them. Following scientific methods, he observed ways and means of life independently, described faithfully what he saw and deduced principles from this evidence. *Love and Mr Lewisham, Kipps, Mr Polly,* and *The Wheels of Chance* are stories in which he himself lived and struggled and thought. So it was with most of his other novels. When he left this field for that of scientific romances, literary critics deplored the change of front and his re-entry into a field into which he became the supreme interpreter.

Mention has already been made of the lines of these perspectives of space and time, and of some other adventures into the domain of human ecology. It is sufficient here to refer, in addition, to *The World of William Clissold*, three volumes (1926), *The Way the World is Going* (1928), *The Open Conspiracy* (1930), *After Democracy* (1932), *The Anatomy of Frustration* (1936), *Star Begotten* (1937), in which the idea is used that cosmic rays directed towards the earth might induce mutation of genes in human nuclei, *The Fate of Homo Sapiens* (1939), *The New World Order* (1940), *The Outlook for Homo Sapiens*, and *The Conquest of Time* and *Phoenix* (all in 1942), *'42 to '44*, which is a supplement to the *Autobiography*, and *Mind at the End of its Tether* (1945).

These, with other books already noted, comprise only a selected list of Wells's contributions to the study of social biology. They state the essential ideas of his life and draw the perspective of a world liberated from sectionalism,[27] with men and women of goodwill and wide outlook co-operating in the task of constructing and maintaining conditions and ways of life worthy of human powers and the availability of the natural resources of the universe.

In *Ann Veronica* (1909) – a novel which provoked a storm of indignation from a group of critics, because of its frank discussion of sex relationships – Wells makes one of the characters say: 'Find the thing you want to do intensely,

---

26 This quote comes from an impromptu address by Wells to the annual dinner of the British Science Guild on 23 May 1922 (see 3.4 for a report of this dinner).

27 Undue concern with local interests or petty distinctions at the expense of greater well-being.

make sure that's it, and do it with all your might. If you live, well and good: if you die, well and good. Your purpose is done.' Before he wrote these words, Wells had had several reminders that his physical system was weak in several parts and liable to breakdowns.[28] It was his indomitable spirit that urged him on to carry out his purpose for a much longer period than anyone who knew him when he began his literary career would have expected. This was maintained to the day of his death on August 13. A few weeks before his heart ceased to beat, he had planned to work hard at the scenario of a film to be *The Shape of Things to Come* brought up to date[29] with the new ideas and curiosities due to the popularisation of the principles of the nuclear disintegration of the atom and the manufacture of the atomic bomb.

To have had such an intention at seventy-nine years of age and after producing about a hundred notable volumes is an impressive example of the mental alertness and perseverance of purpose of Wells's life, the spirit of which remains in his works to enlighten the world for many generations. From his early days he was eager to learn and to master his circumstances. His father[30] was a small tradesman at Bromley, Kent, where Herbert George Wells (familiarly known as 'H. G.') was born on September 21, 1866. His mother[31] was a typical representative of the lower middle class of Victorian times, with fixed regard for the established order and its conventions. This led to Wells being sent to a local 'academy' as a child instead of going to a national school.[32]

With the same maternal desire that Wells should occupy a 'respectable' place in the social order, he was twice placed in drapery establishments, from both of which he came away with resentment at the life imposed upon him. Between these two experiences he was sent for a month's trial as an apprentice to a pharmaceutical chemist at Midhurst, Sussex; but this new start in life was abandoned for financial reasons. He began there, however, the study of Latin with lessons from the headmaster of the small grammar school,[33] at which he became a boarder[34] for a couple of months in the interim between the two drapery adventures. After breaking away from the second of these two trials, he wrote to

---

28 Following severe damage to a kidney during a football match in 1887, Wells suffered a number of breakdowns and was not physically strong until 1898, though he suffered from diabetes throughout his life.

29 This last film project was provisionally title 'The Way the World is Going'.

30 Joseph Wells.

31 Sarah Wells.

32 A school conducted and supported to a greater or less extent by the state.

33 Horace Byatt.

34 A pupil who boards at a school.

this headmaster, who, as the result, offered him a post as an usher[35] in the Preparatory Department of Midhurst Grammar School.[36]

It was at this place and under this influence that Wells made his first systematic acquaintance with modern science. There he attended evening classes under the Science and Art Department, and was so successful in gaining grant-earning certificates in a number of subjects that in 1884 he was accepted as a science teacher in training at the Normal School of Science, South Kensington, which later became the Royal College of Science.

After three years at the College, Wells left without being awarded the associateship, having failed in the examination in advanced geology. Even without this qualification he was able to obtain a post in a small private school in Wales,[37] where he had his left kidney crushed during a football game and was wrongly pronounced to be consumptive, but later to be diabetic, which proved to be true. In 1889 he became an assistant master in a private school at Kilburn, where Alfred Harmsworth (Lord Northcliffe) had been a pupil, and Wells taught mathematics and science to a class which included A. A. Milne, the novelist and playwright, son of the headmaster of the school.[38]

While at this Henley House School,[39] Wells passed the London Intermediate BSc examination with honours in zoology and was awarded the licentiateship of the College of Preceptors with the three prizes in theory and practice of education, mathematics and natural science. These successes led to the offer of a post on the staff of the University Tutorial College, where he went to teach biology and also geology to students at Red Lion Square working for the University of London examinations. While there he took his BSc degree in 1890 with first-class honours in zoology and was first in the second class in honours in geology. He also obtained the fellowship[40] diploma of the College of Preceptors with honours in two subjects and gained the Doreck Scholarship[41] for theory and practice of education, thus getting in front of university teachers in their own examination.

---

35   An assist to a schoolteacher.

36   Founded in 1672, a school which teaches 13 to 18 year olds.

37   Wells taught at Holt Academy, Wrexham, during 1887.

38   John Vine Milne.

39   Private secondary school in Kilburn, London, during the late-nineteenth century and until 1910.

40   A membership of a learned society or university.

41   A prize awarded for the student who came first in the theory and practice of education when studying for the Fellowship of the College of Preceptors. Established in 1877, it was named in honour of Beata Doreck and awarded to Wells in 1891.

His career as a professional teacher came to an end in 1893 with another breakdown of health. It was then that he began to earn his living by writing articles for the periodical press on common subjects in his own whimsical vein of reactions to them. His *Select Conversations with an Uncle* (1895) is a collection of such contributions from scores of other unsigned articles and tales. He also contributed a number of reviews to *Nature*, including one on Podmore's *Apparitions and Thought Transference*.[42] His first book was, however, Part I of a *Textbook of Biology* (1893), with an introduction by G. B. Howes, assistant professor of zoology at the Royal College of Science, followed two years later by Part II, and Gregory and Wells's *Honours Physiography*.[43] In the same year (1895) *The Time Machine* was published, and Wells found himself recognised, at twenty-nine years of age, as a bright star rising above the horizon of the world of letters to radiate a new penetrating light before men.

The honorary degree of DLit was conferred upon Wells by the University of London in 1936; and in 1943 he was awarded the DSc degree for a thesis on *The Quality of Illusion in the Continuity of the Individual Life in the Higher Metazoa, with Particular Reference to Homo sapiens*. He was president of the Educational Science Section of the British Association at the Nottingham meeting in 1937, when he gave an address on 'The Informative Content of Education', which led to the publication of two reports upon the subject by a research committee of the Association.[44] He was elected an honorary fellow[45] of the Imperial College of Science and Technology[46] in 1943, just fifty years after the publication of *The Time Machine*,[47] the first of the imposing series of works by which Wells became the greatest international scientific educator of his times.

iii) From 'Announcements' (19 October 1946).[48]

A meeting has been arranged by a committee representative of the Society of Authors, Playwrights and Composers,[49] the International PEN Club[50] (English

---

42   Wells's review was entitled 'Peculiarities of Psychical Research' (1894).

43   In fact both these books appeared in 1893.

44   These British Association reports have proved untraceable.

45   A distinction bestowed by a university on one of its retiring or former members.

46   British university, founded in 1907 as part of the University of London and gaining its independence from that university in 2007.

47   Forty-eight years after, in fact.

48   Reprinted by permission from Macmillan Publishers Ltd: *Nature* (158: 4016), copyright (1946).

49   Now simply the Society of Authors, an organisation which protects the rights and furthers the interests of authors, established in 1884.

50   An international union of writers, founded in 1921.

Centre), the National Book League,[51] and the British Association for the Advancement of Science, in memory of H. G. Wells. Lord Beveridge will preside, and tributes will be paid by Prof. G. D. H. Cole, Sir Richard Gregory, Mr David Low, Mr Desmond MacCarthy and Mr J. B. Priestley. The meeting, which is open to the public, will be held at the Royal Institution, Albemarle Street, London, W. 1, on October 30, 3.0 pm. Applications for tickets should be addressed to the Secretary, Wells Tribute Meeting, c/o The British Association, Burlington House, London, W. 1.

---

51 Founded in 1944 as an association of authors, publishers, booksellers, librarians and readers, known since 1986 as Booktrust.

Short Biographies

Edwin Abbott Abbott (1838-1926): headteacher of the City of London School (1865-89) and the author of mathematical and theological works.

Arthur Herbert Dyke Acland (1847-1926): British Liberal politician, MP for Rotherham (1885-99) and vice-president of the Council of Education (1892-94).

Richard Thomas Dyke Acland (1906-90): British Liberal (1935-42), Common Wealth (1942-45), Labour (1947-55) and Independent (1955) MP, co-founder of the Common Wealth Party (1941) and of the Campaign for Nuclear Disarmament (1958).

(Jean) Louis Rodolphe Agassiz (1807-73): Swiss-American professor of zoology and geology at Harvard University who first proposed the theory of ice ages.

George Edward Aldred (1816-68): a Jamaican-born British military surgeon.

Jean le Rond d'Alembert (1717-83): French Enlightenment mathematician, physicist and philosopher, permanent secretary of the *Académie française* (1772-83).

Alexander the Great (356 BC-323 BC): King of Macedon (336 BC-323 BC), an undefeated military leader who expanded Greek hegemony over most of the known world.

Albert Victor Alexander, 1st Earl Alexander of Hillsborough (1885-1965): British Labour MP (1922-31; 1935-50), First Lord of the Admiralty (1929-31; 1940-45; 1945-46), Minister of Defence (1946-50) and Chancellor of the Duchy of Cornwall (1950-51).

Dante Alighieri (1265-1321): Italian poet and greatest Italian wordsmith.

Roy George Douglas Allen (1906-83): British economist and mathematician, professor of statistics at the London School of Economics (1944-73).

George James Allman (1812-98): Irish naturalist, professor of botany at the University of Dublin (1844-56), and professor of natural history at the University of Edinburgh (1856-70).

(Ralph) Norman Angell (1872-1967): co-founder of the Union of Democratic Control (1914), Labour MP for Bradford North (1929-31) and active pacifist.

Antony the Great (c. 251-356): Egyptian Christian monk.

Edward Victor Appleton (1892-1965): professor of physics at King's College, London (1924-36), and of natural philosophy at the University of Cambridge (1936-39).

Thomas Aquinas (c. 1225-74): Roman Catholic saint, considered one of the greatest Catholic theologians and the model teacher for studying for the priesthood.

William Archer (1856-1924): British drama critic, principally for the *World* (1884-1905).

Archimedes of Syracuse (c. 287 BC-c. 212 BC): ancient Greek mathematician, physicist and engineer, generally considered one of the most important of the classical scientists.

Henry Edward Armstrong (1848-1937): professor of chemistry at the London Institution (1870-79), the City & Guilds Institute (1879-83) and the Central Technical Institution (1884-1914).

Thomas Arnold (1795-1842): British educationalist and historian, headteacher of Rugby School from 1828 to 1841.

Harold Avery (1869-1943): children's storywriter.

V. B.: this reviewer remains unidentified.

Arthur James Balfour, 1ˢᵗ Earl of Balfour (1848-1930): British Conservative politician, MP for Hertford (1874-85), Manchester East (1885-1906) and the City of London (1906-22), and prime minister (1902-05).

John Ball (d. 1381): English priest and prominent member of the Peasants' Revolt of 1381.

Ernest Barker (1874-1960): British political scientist, professor of political science at the University of Cambridge (1928-39).

Frederic Charles Bartlett (1886-1969): professor of experimental psychology at the University of Cambridge (1931-51).

Aubrey Vincent Beardsley (1872-98): British decadent illustrator and caricaturist.

Vladimir Mikhailovich Bechterev (1857-1927): Russian neurophysiologist and psychiatrist who founded the discipline of psycho-reflexology.

Henri Bégouën (1863-1956): French archaeologist and expert in prehistoric cave art.

(Joseph) Hilaire Pierre René Belloc (1870-1953): French-born British writer, Liberal politician and outspoken Catholic apologist.

Aristarkh Apollonovich Belopolsky (1854-1934): Russian astronomer and director of the Pulkovo Observatory (1916-18).

(Enoch) Arnold Bennett (1867-1931): British novelist and critic.

Arthur Christopher Benson (1862-1925): British essayist, poet and diarist, Housemaster at Eton College (1884-1915) and Master of Magdalene College, University of Cambridge (1915-25).

Jeremy Bentham (1748-1832): British utilitarian philosopher.

Henri-Louis Bergson (1859-1941): French philosopher, professor of modern philosophy at the *Académie des sciences morales et politiques* (1904-20).

John Desmond Bernal (1901-71): Irish-born British physicist and mathematician, professor of physics at Birkbeck College, London (1937-68), and an active member of the Communist Party.

Walter Besant (1836-1901): British novelist.

William Henry Besant (1828-1917): a distinguished mathematician at the University of Cambridge and the first recipient of a Doctorate of Science from that university.

William Henry Beveridge, 1st Baron Beveridge (1879-1963): British economist and social reformer, author of the 'Beveridge Report' which formed the basis of the British welfare state and director of the London School of Economics (1919-37).

Wilhelm Freiherr von Biela (1782-1856): German-born Austrian military officer and amateur astronomer who discovered the 3D / Biela Comet in 1826.

Rowland Henry Biffen (1874-1949): British botanist and geneticist and first professor of agricultural botany at the University of Cambridge (1908-31).

Patrick Maynard Stuart Blackett, Baron Blackett (1897-1974): British experimental physicist and professor of physics at the universities of London (1933-37) and Manchester (1937-53) and Imperial College, London (1953-63).

Louis Jean Joseph Charles Blanc (1811-82): French politician.

Louis Blériot (1872-1936): French aviation pioneer, the first person to fly across the English Channel (1909).

Jean de Bloch (1836-1901): Polish banker and railway financier who devoted his private life to the study of modern industrial warfare.

Ivan Parfenevitch Borodin (1847-1930): professor of botany at the Forestry Institute, St Petersburg.

Percy George Hamnall Boswell (1886-1960): British geologist, professor of geology at Imperial College, London (1930-39).

John Boyd Orr, 1st Baron Boyd-Orr (1880-1971): British teacher, doctor and politician, first Director-General of the United Nations Food and Agriculture Organisation (1945-48) and independent MP for the Combined Scottish Universities (1945-46).

John Theodore Cuthbert Moore-Brabazon, 1ˢᵗ Baron Brabazon of Tara (1884-1964): British aviation pioneer and politician, Conservative MP for Chatham (1918-29) and Wallasey (1931-42).

George Granville Bradley (1821-1903): Dean of Westminster (1881-1902).

William Henry Bragg (1862-1942): British physicist, graduate of the University of Cambridge, professor of mathematics at the University of Adelaide (1886-1908) and professor of physics at the University of Leeds (1909-15), University College, London (1915-23), and at the Royal Institution (1923-42).

Jean Louis Armand de Quatrefages de Bréau (1810-92): French naturalist, professor of natural history at the *Lycée Napoléon* (1850-55) and of anthropology and ethnography at the *Museum National d'Histoire Naturelle* (1855-92).

Henri Édouard Prosper Breuil (1877-1961): French archaeologist, anthropologist, ethnologist and geologist, an acknowledged expert on prehistoric cave paintings.

Percy Williams Bridgman (1882-1961): American physicist, professor of physics at Harvard University (1919-54).

Robert Stephen Briffault (1876-1948): French novelist, historian, social anthropologist and surgeon.

William Briggs (1862-1932): mathematician and law scholar, founder of the University Correspondence College in London and Cambridge (1887).

R. Brightman (d. 1968): A chemist and prolific reviewer for *Nature* from c. 1932 to 1967, but otherwise untraceable.

William Jennings Bryan (1860-1925): American lawyer, statesman and Democratic politician who crusaded against Darwinism and for the prohibition of alcohol.

Arthur Bryant (1899-1985): prolific British popular historian.

James Bryce, 1ˢᵗ Viscount Bryce (1838-1922): British jurist, historian and Liberal politician (1880-1907).

Robert Williams Buchanan (1841-1901): British poet, novelist and dramatist.

Gautama Buddha (c. 563 BC-c. 483 BC): spiritual teacher of ancient India and historical founder of Buddhism.

Georges-Louis Leclerc, Comte de Buffon (1707-88): French naturalist, mathematician, biologist and cosmologist whose pioneering evolutionary research influenced Jean-Baptiste Lamarck and Charles Darwin.

William Burke (1792-1829): Irish-born British serial killer.

William Gordon Burn-Murdoch (1862-1939): British artist and Arctic explorer, famous for his sketches of the Arctic.

Robert Burns (1759-96): British poet and lyricist, considered the national poet of Scotland.

Robert Burton (1577-1640): English scholar and vicar of St Thomas's Church, Oxford.

Dr Busby: This person has remained untraceable.

Samuel Butler (1835-1902): British Anglican clergyman and novelist.

Horace Byatt (1843-1907): British schoolteacher, headteacher of Burslem Endowed School (1876-80) and Midhurst Grammar School (1880-1903).

Alessandro di Cagliostro (1743-95): Italian forger and assumed mystic who claimed to have studied alchemy, the Kabbalah and magic, and who was imprisoned by the Catholic Church for being a Freemason.

Norman Robert Campbell (1880-1949): British physicist and philosopher of science.

Caractacus (1st century): a British chieftain who lead resistance to the Roman conquest.

Thomas Carlyle (1795-1881): British essayist, satirist and historian who was a severe critic of progress.

Andrew Carnegie (1835-1919): Scottish-born American steel magnate.

William Benjamin Carpenter (1813-85): British physiologist and naturalist, professor of physiology at the Royal Institution (1845-56) and registrar of the University of London (1856-79).

Alexander Morris Carr-Saunders (1886-1966): British sociologist, professor of social science at the University of Liverpool (1923-37) and director of the London School of Economics (1937-55).

Howard Carter (1874-1939): British archaeologist and Egyptologist, discoverer of the tomb of Tutankhamen (1922).

Edward Provan Cathcart (1877-1954): British physiologist, professor of physiology in the London Hospital (1913-19) and of physiological chemistry (1919-28) and physiology (1928-47) at the University of Glasgow.

(Arthur) Neville Chamberlain (1869-1940): British Conservative politician, MP for Birmingham Ladywood (1918-29) and Birmingham Edgbaston (1929-40), and prime minister (1937-40).

George Chapman (c. 1559-1634): English playwright.

Charles II (1630-85): Stuart King of England (1660-85).

Charles V (1500-58): Flemish-born Holy Roman Emperor (1530-56).

William Pitt, 1st Earl of Chatham (1708-78): known as 'the Elder', British statesman, Whig MP for Seaford (1747-54), Aldborough (1754-56), Okehampton (1756-57) and Bath (1757-66), and Prime Minister (1766-68).

Frederick Alexander Lindemann, 1st Viscount Cherwell (1886-1957): British physician and scientific advisor to the British government, professor of experimental philosophy at the University of Oxford (1919-56).

Winston Leonard Spencer Churchill (1874-1965): British Conservative (1900-04; 1924-64) and Liberal (1904-22) politician, MP for Oldham (1900-06), Manchester North West (1906-08), Dundee (1908-22), Epping (1924-45) and Woodford (1945-64), and prime minister (1940-45; 1951-55).

Charles Herbert Clark (1854-1924): American teacher, principal of Windsor High School, Waban, Massachusetts.

Wilfred Edward Le Gros Clark (1895-1971): British anatomist and surgeon, professor of anatomy at St Bartholemew's Hospital Medical College (1927-29), St Thomas's Hospital Medical School (1929-34) and the University of Oxford (1934-62).

William Kingdom Clifford (1845-79): British mathematician and author of philosophical works, professor of mathematics at University College, London (1871-79).

John Douglas Cockcroft (1897-1967): British physicist responsible, with Ernest Walton, for 'splitting the atom' (1932).

George Douglas Howard Cole (1889-1959): British political theorist, economist and historian, active in the Fabian Society and professor of social and political theory at the University of Oxford (1944-57).

(Isidore Marie) Auguste François Xavier Comte (1798-1857): French founder of positivism and the first modern sociologist.

Confucius (551 BC-479 BC): Chinese social philosopher.

Edwin Grant Conklin (1863-1952): American biologist, professor of biology at Princeton University (1908-33) and a leading defender of the effects of advanced technology on society.

Joseph Conrad (1857-1924): Polish-born British novelist.

Frank Challice Constable (1846-1937): British barrister and author of popular works on science and spiritualism.

James Fenimore Cooper (1789-1851): a popular American writer and novelist.

Edmund Vincent Cowdry (1888-1975): Canadian-born American anatomist, zoologist and cytologist, professor of anatomy at Peking Union Medical College (1917-21) and at the University of Washington, St Louis (1928-60).

William Cramp (1876-1939): British electrical engineer, professor of electrical engineering at the University of Birmingham (-1939).

Mina 'Margery' Crandon (1888-1941): Canadian-born American spiritualist.

Walter Crane (1845-1915): British artist and member of the Arts and Crafts Movement.

Francis Albert Eley Crew (1886-1973): British geneticist, professor of animal genetics (1928-44) and of public health and social medicine (1944-55) at the University of Edinburgh.

Wilfred Frank Crick (b. 1900): British economist with the Midland Bank (1928-62).

William Crookes (1832-1919), British chemist and physicist, president of the Royal Society (1913-15).

James Gerald Crowther (1899-1983): pioneering popular science journalist and author, science correspondent for the *Manchester Guardian* (1928-46) and Director of the Science Department of the British Council (1939-46).

William Bunting Crump (b. 1868): British school teacher and Yorkshire local historian.

Joseph Thomas Cunningham (1859-1935): British zoologist and biologist.

Pierre Curie (1859-1906): French physicist and pioneer in crystallography, magnetism and radioactivity, professor of sciences at the *Sorbonne*, Paris (1900-06).

Georges Léopold Chrétien Frédéric Dagobert Cuvier (1769-1832): French naturalist and zoologist appointed professor of natural history at the College de France in 1799.

John Dalton (1766-1844): British chemist, meteorologist and physicist, a pioneer of atomic theory.

John Ford Darling (1864-1938): British banker, and monetary reformer, director of the Midland Bank.

Raymond Dart (1893-1988): Australian anatomist.

Charles Robert Darwin (1809-82): British naturalist who developed the theory of evolution by natural selection in *The Origin of Species* (1859).

George Howard Darwin (1845-1912): British astronomer and mathematician.

Charles Benedict Davenport (1866-1944): American biologist and eugenicist, director of Cold Spring Harbor Laboratory (1910-34) and founder of the Eugenics Record Office (1910).

Arthur Morley Davies (1869-1959): British palaeontologist and reader of palaeontology at Imperial College, London.

George Edward Day (1815-72): professor of anatomy and medicine at the University of St Andrews (1849-63).

John Dee (1527-1609): English mathematician and astrologer who was a prominent spiritualist investigator.

Yves Delage (1854-1920): French marine zoologist, director of the *Station biologique de Roscoff* (1901-20).

Democritus (c. 460 BC-c. 370 BC): ancient Greek philosopher who first conceived of atoms as base units of all matter.

Réne Descartes (1596-1650): French philosopher, mathematician and scientist, considered the founder of modern philosophy.

Cecil Henry Desch (1874-1958): professor of metallurgy at the Royal Technical College, Glasgow (1918-20), and the University of Sheffield (1920-31).

Charles John Huffam Dickens (1812-70): British novelist.

Goldsworthy Lowes Dickinson (1862-1932): British historian and political activist.

Denis Diderot (1713-84): French Enlightenment philosopher and editor-in-chief of the *Encyclopédie* (1751-66).

Herbert Dingle (1890-1978): British astronomer and professor of natural philosophy at Imperial College, London (1938-46) and of history and philosophy of science at University College, London (1946-55).

Bramah Joseph Diplock (d. 1918): a quarry merchant and inventor of the pedrail.

Edward Travers Dixon (1862-1935): British mathematician.

Horatio Bryan Donkin (1845-1927): British medical doctor and Medical Adviser to the Prison Commission.

Frederick George Donnan (1870-1956): Ceylonese-born British chemist, professor of chemistry at University College, London (1913-37).

Beata Doreck (1833-75): German educationist.

Arthur Ignatius Conan Doyle (1859-1930): British crime and science fiction author and spiritualist.

Karl von Drais (1785-1851): German engineer and inventor.

Jack Cecil Drummond (1891-1952): British biochemist, professor of biochemistry at University College, London (1922-45), and of physiology at the Royal Institution (1942-44).

John Duncan (1866-1945): British symbolist painter, illustrator and muralist active in the Celtic Revivalist movement.

Wyndham Rowland Dunstan (1861-1949): British chemist, director of the Imperial Institute (1903-24).

Thomas Dwight (1843-1911): American anatomist, professor of anatomy at Harvard Medical School (1883-1911).

Alfred George Earl (1859-1937): British schoolteacher at Tonbridge School (1884-1918).

Arthur Stanley Eddington (1882-1944): British astrophysicist, professor of astronomy and experimental philosophy at the University of Cambridge (1913-44).

Percy Granville Edge (1881-1976): British teacher and statistician for the League of Nations, recording national vital statistics and assisting with census-taking.

Francis Ysidro Edgeworth (1845-1926): Irish economist and mathematician, professor of political economics (1888-90) and of economic science (1890-91) at King's College, London, and of political economy at the University of Oxford (1891-1922).

Thomas Alva Edison (1847-1931): American inventor and businessman, holding over 1000 patents in his lifetime, including the phonograph and the light bulb, and inventing the industrial research laboratory.

Edward IV (1442-83): English king of the House of York (1461-70; 1471-83).

Edward VIII (1894-1972): British king of the House of Windsor (1936) who abdicated, becoming the Duke of Windsor (1937-72).

Alfred Charles Glyn Egerton (1886-1959): British chemist, professor of chemical technology at Imperial College, London (1936-52).

Albert Einstein (1879-1955): German-born physicist, professor of physics at Charles University, Prague (1911-12), ETH Zurich (1912-14) and the University of Berlin (1914-32).

Robert Eisler (1882-1949): Austrian art historian, Biblical scholar and monetary reformer, assistant-director of the League of Nations Universities Interrelations Office (1925-31).

Euclid (c. 300 BC): ancient Greek mathematician known as the 'father of geometry'.

David Stanley Evans (1916-2004): British astronomer, professor of astronomy at the Macdonald Observatory, Texas (1968-77), and at the University of Texas (1977-86).

Alexander Farquharson (1882-1954): British sociologist and school teacher.

Frederic William Farrar (1831-1903): Master of Marlborough College (1871-76) and Dean of Canterbury Cathedral (1895-1903).

Louis Anderson Fenn (b. 1889): a British activist in the National Council Against Conscription during the Great War, writer of politics, popular science and economics books, supporter of the Popular Front in the 1930s, member of the Socialist League National Council (1935-36), and unsuccessful Labour parliamentary candidate for Birmingham Handsworth (1929; 1931).

Allan Hitchen Ferguson (1880-1951): British physicist and historian of science.

Herbert Albert Laurens Fisher (1865-1940): British historian, educator and politician, Liberal MP for Sheffield Hallam (1916-18) and the Combined English Universities (1918-26) and President of the Board of Education (1916-22).

James Maxwell McConnell Fisher (1912-70): British broadcaster, naturalist and ornithologist who made over 1000 radio and television programmes on natural history subjects.

Osmond Fisher (1817-1914): British Anglican clergyman and geologist, rector of Harlton Church (1867-1906).

James Elroy Flecker (1884-1915): British poet, novelist and playwright.

Walter Morley Fletcher (1873-1933): British physiologist, secretary of the Medical Research Council (1914-33).

Herbert John Fleure (1877-1969): British zoologist and geographer, professor of anthropology and geography at the University of Wales, Aberystwyth (1917-30), and of geography at Victoria University of Manchester (1930-44).

Philip Sargant Florence (1890-1982): professor of commerce at the University of Birmingham (1929-55).

John Carl Flugel (1884-1955): British psychoanalyst, assistant professor of psychology at University College, London (1929-44).

Henry Ford (1863-1947): founder of the Ford Motor Company (1903) and the initiator of the modern assembly line as used in mass production.

Michael Foster (1836-1907): British physiologist, professor of practical physiology at University College, London (1869-70), of physiology at the University of Cambridge (1883-1903) and Unionist MP for the University of London (1900-06).

(Edward) Francis Williams, Baron Francis-Williams of Abinger (1903-70): British publisher and journalist, editor of the *Daily Herald* (1936-40) and media adviser to the British government (1941-47).

Francisco Franco (1892-1975): Spanish general, leader of the victorious Nationalist forces during the Spanish Civil War (1936-39) and Spanish dictator (1939-75).

James George Frazer (1854-1941): British social anthropologist, influential in the development of the modern study of mythology and comparative religion.

Sigmund Freud (1856-1939): Austrian neurologist and psychologist who founded the psychoanalytical school of psychology.

Friedrich Wilhelm August Froebel (1782-1852): German educational pioneer, founder of the kindergarten.

Hans Friedrich Gadow (1855-1928): German ornithologist, curator of the Strickland Collection at the University of Cambridge (1884-1928).

Galen (129-c. 216): ancient Greek physician whose theories dominated Western medical science for over a millennium.

Galileo Galilei (1564-1642): Italian polymath, considered 'father of observational astronomy' and 'father of modern physics'.

Francis Galton (1822-1911): British polymath and founder of the pseudo-science of eugenics.

Mahatma Gandhi (1869-1948): Indian nationalist leader, and advocate of nonviolent protest.

Alejandro Lerroux Garcia (1864-1949): Spanish Radical Republican politician, and prime minister (1933; 1934-35).

James Clark Maxwell Garnett (1880-1958): British mathematician, principal of the Manchester School of Technology (1912-20) and secretary of the League of Nations Union (1920-38).

Charles André Joseph Marie de Gaulle (1890-1970): French military leader and president of France (1944-46; 1959-69).

Patrick Geddes (1854-1932): British biologist and botanist, professor of botany at the University College, Dundee (1888-1919) and of sociology at the University of Bombay (1919-24).

George III (1738-1820): British Hanoverian king (1760-1820).

Morris Ginsberg (1889-1970): British sociologist, professor of sociology at the London School of Economics (1929-54).

John Hall Gladstone (1827-1902): British chemist, professor of chemistry at the Royal Institution (1874-77).

William Ewart Gladstone (1809-98): British Liberal politician and prime minister (1868-74, 1880-85, 1886 and 1892-94).

Karl Immanuel Eberhard von Goebel (1855-1932): German botanist, professor of botany at the University of Marburg (1887-91) and the University of Munich (1891-1931).

Israel Gollancz (1863-1930): British medieval and Shakespearean scholar, professor of English language and literature at King's College, London (1903-30).

John Goodsir (1814-67): British anatomist, professor of anatomy at the University of Edinburgh (1846-67).

Hugh Gordon (b. 1863): British science teacher and inspector of elementary schools.

George Cornelius Gorham (1787-1857): Anglican clergyman.

Robert Bontine Cunninghame Graham (1852-1936): British politician.

Thomas Gray (1716-71): British poet.

Alfred George Greenhill (1847-1927): British mathematician, professor of applied mathematics at the Royal Indian Engineering College (1873) and of mathematics at the Artillery College, Woolwich (1876-1908).

Richard Arman Gregory (1864-1952): British science journalist, editor of *Nature* (1919-38).

Jacob Ludwig Carl Grimm (1785-1863): German linguist and collector of fairy tales.

Wilhelm Carl Grimm (1786-1859): German linguist and collector of fairy tales.

George Grossmith (1847-1912): British comedian, writer, actor and singer.

Edmund Gurney (1847-88): British psychologist and paranormal investigator.

Frederick Guthrie (1833-86): British chemist and physicist, professor of chemistry at the Royal College of Mauritius (1860-66) and of physics at the Normal School of Science, South Kensington (1881-86).

Malcolm Guthrie: British late-nineteenth century experimenter in thought transference.

T. LL. H.: an unidentified reviewer for *Nature*.

Ernst Heinrich Philipp August Haeckel (1834-1919): German naturalist and biologist, professor of comparative anatomy at the University of Jena (1862-1909).

John Burdon Sanderson Haldane (1892-1964): British geneticist and evolutionary biologist, professor of physiology at the Royal Institution (1930-32) and of genetics (1933-37) and biometry (1937-57) at University College, London.

John Scott Haldane (1860-1936): British physiologist, honorary professor of mining at the University of Birmingham (1921-36).

Alfred Daniel Hall (1864-1942): British agriculturist, director of the Rothamsted Experimental Station (1902-12) and the John Innes Horticultural Institution (1927-39).

Asaph Hall (1829-1907): American astronomer.

Charles Augustin Hanson (1840-1922): British Conservative politician, MP for Bodmin (1916-22) and Lord Mayor of London (1917-18).

Augustus George Vernon Harcourt (1834-1919): British chemist, reader in chemistry at the University of Oxford (1859-1902) and president of the Chemical Society (1895-97).

John Charlton Hardwick (b. 1885): chaplain of Ripon Hall, Oxford.

Frederic Harrison (1831-1923): British jurist, historian and leading positivist, professor of jurisprudence and international law at the Council of Legal Education (1877-89).

Tom Harrisson (1911-76): Argentinean-born British polymath, co-founder of Mass-Observation (1937) and curator of the Sarawak Museum (1947-66).

William Harvey (1578-1657): English medical doctor, the first person to correctly describe the circulatory system of the human body.

T. H. Hawkins: British educationist, education officer of the Educational Advance Board of the British Social Hygiene Council (-1941).

Dr Hayward: This person has remained untraceable.

Frederick Webb Headley (1856-1919): British ornithologist.

Gerald Heard (1889-1971): British science populariser and anthropologist, professor of historical anthropology at Duke University (1937-41).

Grace Heath (d. 1895): British school teacher at the North London Collegiate School for Girls (1888-94), founder of the school's Science Club (1890).

W. M. Heller: British teacher at Berners Street Board School, Hackney, London, catering for very poor students.

Olaus Magnus Friedrich Erdmann Henrici (1840-1918): Danish-born British mathematician, professor of mathematics at Bedford College for Women (1869-70) and University College, London (1870-80), of applied mathematics and mechanics at the latter (1880-84) and of mechanics and mathematics at the Central Technical College, London (1884-1911).

Henry VIII (1491-1547): Tudor king of England (1509-47).

Hero (10-70): ancient Greek engineer.

Robert Herrick (1591-1674): English clergyman and poet.

Frederick William Herschel (1738-1822): German-born British astronomer.

Archibald Vivian Hill (1886-1977): British biologist and politician, professor of physiology at the University of Manchester (1918-23) and University College, London (1923-51), professor of the Royal Society (1926-51) and an independent conservative MP for the University of Cambridge (1940-45).

Matthew Davenport Hill (b. 1872): science teacher and a master at Eton College (1896-1926).

Hippocrates (460 BC-370 BC): ancient Greek physician, considered the 'father of medicine'.

Hirst, Francis Wrigley (1873-1953): British journalist, editor of the *Economist* (1907-16) and *Common Sense* (1916-21).

Adolf Hitler (1889-1945): Austrian-born German politician, leader of the National Socialist German Workers Party (1920-45) and dictator of Germany (1933-45).

Ernest William Hobson (1856-1933): British mathematician, professor of mathematics at the University of Cambridge (1910-31).

Lancelot Thomas Hogben (1895-1975): British experimental zoologist and medical statistician, professor of zoology at the University of Cape Town (1927-30), of social biology at the London School of Economics (1930-37), of natural history at the University of Aberdeen (1937-41) and of zoology (1941-47) and medical statistics (1947-61) at the University of Birmingham.

Edwin Holmes (1842-1919): British astronomer, discoverer of 17P / Holmes Comet in 1892.

Homer (c. 8th century BC): ancient Greek poet.

Frederick Gowland Hopkins (1861-1947): British biochemist, professor of biochemistry at the University of Cambridge (1914-43).

Horace (65 BC-8 BC): ancient Roman poet.

Thomas Jeeves, 1ˢᵗ Baron Horder (1871-1955): British medical doctor and frequent medical advisor to the British government.

James Francis Horrabin (1884-1962): popular educator, political cartographer, pioneering television presenter and Labour MP for Peterborough (1929-31).

George Bond Howes (1853-1905): British zoologist, professor of zoology at the Royal College of Science, South Kensington (1895-1905).

G. Hughes: an unidentified recipient of an honorary doctorate of science in engineering from the University of London (1943).

Julian Sorell Huxley (1887-1975): British zoologist, professor of zoology at King's College, London (1925-27), and director-general of UNESCO (1946-48).

Thomas Henry Huxley (1825-95): British biologist, professor of natural history at the Royal School of Mines (1854-95), professor of physiology at the Royal Institution (1855-58, 1865-67) and professor of anatomy and physiology at the Royal College of Surgeons (1863-69).

William Ralph Inge (1860-1954): British Anglican prelate, professor of divinity at the University of Cambridge (1907-11) and Dean of St Paul's Cathedral (1911-34).

Osbert Peake, 1ˢᵗ Viscount Ingleby (1897-1966): British Conservative politician, MP for Leeds North (1929-55) and Leeds North East (1955-56).

Bruce Ingram (1877-1963): British journalist, editor of the *Illustrated London News* (1900-63).

Henry James (1843-1916): American novelist.

Karl Guthe Jansky (1905-50): American physicist, researcher with Bell Telephone Laboratories and a founding figure of radio astronomy.

James Hopwood Jeans (1877-1946): British physicist, astronomer and mathematician, professor of applied mathematics at Princeton University (1904-10) and of astronomy at the Royal Institution (1935-46).

Jengis Khan (1162-1227): more commonly, Genghis Khan, Mongol ruler and founder of the Mongol Empire.

Henry Charles Fleeming Jenkin (1833-85): British electrician and cable engineer, professor of engineering at University College, London (1866-68) and the University of Edinburgh (1868-85).

Jesus Christ (6 BC-30 AD): Galilean Jewish preacher and healer whose teachings led to the foundation of Christianity.

Samuel Johnson (1709-84): British writer and critic.

Henry Hamilton Johnston (1858-1927): British explorer, botanist and colonial administrator.

Robert Armstrong Jones (1857-1943): British psychiatrist, professor of physic at Gresham College (1917-27).

John Wesley Judd (1840-1916): British geologist, professor of geology at the Royal School of Mines (1876-1905).

Julius Caesar (c. 100 BC-44 BC): ancient Roman soldier and statesman, founder of the Roman Empire.

Carl Gustav Jung (1875-1961): Swiss psychiatrist, professor of psychology at the University of Zurich (1933-41) and the University of Basle (1944-61).

Pyotr Kapitza (1894-1984): Russian physicist, founder and head of the Institute for Physical Problems in Moscow (1934-46, 1953-84).

Alexander Petrovich Karpinsky (1846-1936): Russian geologist, director of mining research at the Mining Institute, St Petersburg (1885-1916).

Bernard Katz (1911-2003): German-born British biophysicist, professor of biophysics at University College, London (1952-78).

William Henry Kauntze (1887-1947): British specialist in tropical diseases.

John Keats (1795-1821): British poet.

Frederick William Keeble (1870-1952): British botanist, professor of botany at the University of Oxford (1920-27) and of physiology at the Royal Institution (1938-41).

Arthur Keith (1866-1955): British anatomist and anthropologist, editor of the *Journal of Anatomy* (1915-36).

Edward Kelly (1555-97): English spirit medium.

John Graham Kerr (1869-1957): British embryologist and politician, professor of zoology at the University of Glasgow (1902-35) and independent MP for the Scottish universities (1935-50).

John Maynard Keynes, 1ˢᵗ Baron Keynes (1883-1946): British economist who advised the British and American governments at various times throughout his career.

Hermann Alexander Keyserling (1880-1946): Russian-born German philosopher, founder of the *Gesellschaft für Freie Philosophie* (1920).

William Lyon Mackenzie King (1874-1950): Canadian Liberal MP (1909-11, 1919-48) and prime minister (1921-26, 1926-30, 1935-48).

Charles Kingsley (1819-75): British Anglican clergyman, novelist and historian, professor of modern history at the University of Cambridge (1860-69).

(Joseph) Rudyard Kipling (1865-1936): Indian-born British novelist, poet and children's story writer.

John Knox (1514-72): Scottish religious leader, instrumental in reforming the Scottish church along Calvinist lines.

Anatolii Fedorovich Koni (1844-1927): Russian jurist.

Alexander Korda (1893-1956): Hungarian-born British film producer.

Ernst Ludwig Krause (1839-1903): German biologist.

Walter G. Krivitsky (1899-1941): real name, Samuel Ginsberg, Soviet spy who defected to France in 1937 and is generally believed to have been assassinated by Soviet agents in the USA.

Tibulle François Ladevèze (1828-1901): French magistrate in Mas d'Azil and amateur archaeologist.

Jean-Baptiste Pierre Antoine de Monet, Chevalier de Lamarck (1744-1829): French naturalist, professor of botany at the *Jardin des Plantes* (1788-93) and of zoology at the *Muséum national d'histoire naturelle* (1793-1829), and advocate of the inheritance of acquired characteristics.

Frederick William Lanchester (1868-1946): British automotive engineer, co-founder of the Lanchester Engine Company (1900).

Edwin Ray Lankester (1847-1929): British zoologist, professor of zoology at University College, London (1874-90), of comparative anatomy at the University of Oxford (1891-98) and director of the Natural History Museum (1898-1907).

Lao Tse (4th century BC): ancient Chinese Taoist philosopher.

Harold Joseph Laski (1893-1950): British political theorist and economist, professor of political science at the London School of Economics (1926-50).

Vasily Vasilevich Latishev (1855-1921): Russian philologist and historian, a member of the St Petersburg Academy of Sciences (1893-1921).

C. Hugo Laubach: This person has remained untraceable.

James Gunson Lawn (1868-1952): British-born South African mining engineer, professor of mining at the School of Mines, Kimberley (1896-99), and the School of Mines and Technology, Johannesburg (1909-10).

William Lawrence (1783-1867): British surgeon, professor of anatomy and surgery at the Royal College of Surgeons of England (1815-19).

Frederick Charles Lea (1871-1952): British engineer, professor of civil engineering at the University of Birmingham (1913-24) and of mechanical engineering at the University of Sheffield (1924-36).

Gottfried Wilhelm Leibniz (1646-1716): German mathematician and philosopher.

Pierre-Edouard Lemontey (1762-1826): French politician, lawyer and social critic.

Vladimir Illych Lenin (1870-1924): Russian revolutionary, leader of the Bolsheviks and first leader of Soviet Russia (1917-24).

Hyman Levy (1889-1975): British mathematician, professor of mathematics at Imperial College, London (1923-54).

Sinclair Lewis (1885-1951): American novelist.

Thomas Linacre (c. 1460-1524): English humanist and physician.

Abraham Lincoln (1809-65): American Republican president (1861-65) who led the Unionists to victory in the American Civil War.

Carolus Linnaeus (1707-78): Swedish botanist.

Richard Winn Livingstone (1880-1960): British classical scholar and educational reformer.

David Lloyd George, 1st Earl Lloyd-George of Dwyfor (1863-1945): British Liberal MP (1890-1945) and prime minister (1916-22).

Oliver Joseph Lodge (1851-1940): British physicist and spiritualist, professor of physics and mathematics at University College Liverpool (1881-1900).

Jack London (1876-1916): American journalist, novelist and adventurer.

Henry Wadsworth Longfellow (1807-82): American poet.

Hendrik Willem van Loon (1882-1944): Dutch-born American historian and journalist, professor of history at Cornell University (1915-17).

David Alexander Cecil Low (1891-1963): New Zealand political cartoonist.

Percival Lowell (1855-1916): American amateur Orientalist and astronomer, founder of the Lowell Observatory in Flagstaff, Arizona.

Lucretius (c. 99 BC-c. 55 BC): ancient Roman poet and philosopher.

Savile Lumley (1876-1950): British poster designer and illustrator of children's annuals.

Anatoly Vasilievich Lunacharsky (1875-1933): Russian art critic and journalist, Soviet People's Commissar for Enlightenment (1917-29).

Martin Luther (1483-1546): German Protestant clergyman and leader of the Reformation.

Charles Lyell (1797-1875): British lawyer and geologist, professor of geology at King's College, London (1831-33).

Desmond MacCarthy (1878-1952): British literary critic and journalist.

James Ramsay MacDonald (1866-1937): British Labour (National Labour from 1931) MP (1906-18; 1922-37) and prime minister (1924, 1929-35).

Ernst Mach (1838-1916): Austrian physicist and philosopher, professor of experimental physics at Charles-Ferdinand University, Prague (1867-1901).

Niccolò di Bernardo dei Machiavelli (1469-1527): Italian political philosopher.

Charles Hodge Mackie (1862-1920): British artist associated with the Scottish 'Staithes Group'.

James Macalister Mackintosh (1891-1966): British medical doctor, professor of public health at the University of Glasgow (1941-44) and the University of London (1944-56).

Herbert McLeod (1841-1923): British chemist and bibliographer, professor or experimental science and of chemistry at the Royal Indian Engineering College, Coopers Hill, Egham (1871-1901).

(Frederick) Louis MacNiece (1907-63): Irish-born British poet and playwright.

Philip Magnus (1842-1933): British educationalist, Jewish religious minister and Liberal Unionist (1906-12) and Conservative (1912-22) MP for the University of London.

(Robert) Thomas Malthus (1766-1834): British demographer and political economist, professor of political economy at the East India Company College, Hertford (1805-34).

Guglielmo Marconi (1874-1937): Italian inventor of radiotelegraphy, founder of the Wireless Telegraph & Signal Company (1897) and member of the Fascist Grand Council (1930-37).

Hilary Adair Marquand (1901-72): British economist and politician, professor of industrial relations at University College, Cardiff (1930-45), and Labour MP for Cardiff East (1945-50) and Middlesborough East (1950-61), holding the posts of Paymaster-General (1947-48), Minister of Pensions (1948-51) and Minister of Health (1951).

Henry Newell Martin (1848-93): Irish-born British physiologist, professor of physiology at Johns Hopkins University, Baltimore (1876-93).

Francis Sidney Marvin (1863-1943): teacher, schools inspector and historian, professor of modern history at the Egyptian University, Cairo (1929-30).

Karl Heinrich Marx (1818-83): German philosopher, economist and revolutionary.

John Edward Masefield (1878-1967): British poet, novelist and children's author, Poet Laureate (1930-67).

William Mather (1838-1920): British industrialist and politician, chairman of Mathers and Platt Iron Manufacturers and Liberal MP for Salford (1885-86), Gorton (1889-98) and Rossendale (1900-04).

John Frederick Denison Maurice (1805-72): British theologian and socialist, professor of English history and literature (1840-53) and of divinity (1846-53) at King's College, London, of moral philosophy at the University of Cambridge (1866-72) and originator of the Christian socialist movement (c. 1830s).

Louis Ferdinand Alfred Maury (1817-92): French archaeologist, professor of moral history at the *Collège de France* (1862-92).

James Clerk Maxwell (1831-79): British mathematician and theoretical physicist, professor of natural philosophy at Marischal College, Aberdeen (1856-60), professor of physics and astronomy at King's College, London (1860-68), and professor of physics at the University of Cambridge (1871-79).

Raphael Meldola (1849-1915): British chemist, professor of organic chemistry at the University of London (1912-15).

Gregor Johann Mendel (1822-84): German clergyman and biologist.

William Cameron Menzies (1896-1957): American film director.

Charles Arthur Mercier (1852-1919): British psychologist and medical doctor.

John Stuart Mill (1806-73): British philosopher, political economist and politician, independent MP for the City of London and Westminster (1865-68).

Alan Alexander Milne (1882-1956): British playwright, children's author and poet, creator of Winnie-the-Pooh.

John Vine Milne (1845-1932): British teacher, headteacher of Henley House School, Kilburn, London (1878-94).

John Milton (1608-74): English poet, polemicist and civil servant.

Hermann Minkowski (1864-1909): Russian-born German mathematician and physicist, professor of mathematics at the universities of Bonn (1887-94), Königsberg (1894-96), Zurich (1896-1902) and Göttingen (1902-09).

Peter Chalmers Mitchell (1864-1945): British zoologist, secretary of the Zoological Society of London (1903-35).

St George Jackson Mivart (1827-1900): British biologist, professor of biology at the Roman Catholic University College, London (1874-77).

John Walter Edward Douglas Scott Montagu, 2nd Baron Montagu of Beaulieu (1866-1929): British politician, Conservative MP for the New Forest (1892-1905).

Thomas More (1478-1535): English statesman and writer.

Thomas Hunt Morgan (1866-1945): American geneticist and embryologist, professor of biology at Bryn Mawr College (1895-1904), of experimental zoology at Columbia University (1904-27) and of biology at California Institute of Technology (1928-42).

Nikolai Aleaxandrovich Morozov (1854-1946): Russian poet, scientist and revolutionary.

William Morris (1834-96): British artist, writer, publisher and socialist, a principle leader of the arts and crafts movement (c. 1880-c. 1910) and founder of the Socialist League (1885).

Moses (c. 1393 BC-c. 1273 BC): Hebrew religious leader, supposed author of the Jewish Torah.

John Fletcher Moulton, Baron Moulton (1844-1921): British mathematician, politician, barrister and judge, Liberal MP for Battersea (1885-86), South Hackney (1894-95) and Launceston (1898-1906).

Muhammad (c. 570-632): Arab soldier and prophet, founder of Islam.

Matthew Moncreiff Pattison Muir (1848-1931): British chemist.

Walther Müller (1905-79): German physicist, professor of physics at the University of Tübingen (1936-40).

James Watson Munro (1888-1968): British zoologist, professor of entomology (1926-34) and of zoology and applied entomology at Imperial College, London (1934-53).

(George) Gilbert Aimé Murray (1866-1957): Australian-born British classical scholar, professor of Greek at the University of Glasgow (1889-99) and the University of Oxford (1908-44).

J. Wickham Murray: A secretary of the Association of Teachers in Technical Institutions, he has remained otherwise untraceable.

Benito Amilcare Andrea Mussolini (1883-1945): Italian Fascist politician, dictator of Italy (1922-43).

Charles Samuel Myers (1873-1946): British psychologist, founder of the National Institute of Industrial Psychology (1921).

Frederic William Henry Myers (1843-1901): British poet and essayist.

John Linton Myres (1869-1954): British archaeologist, professor of Greek at the University of Liverpool (1907-10) and professor of ancient history at the University of Oxford (1910-39).

D. N.: an unidentified reviewer for *Nature*.

J. N.: an unidentified reviewer for *Nature*.

Napoleon I (1769-1821): French military leader and emperor (1804-14, 1815).

Joseph Terence Montgomery Needham (1900-95): British biochemist and scholar of the history of Chinese science.

John Henry Newman (1801-90): British Roman Catholic convert and cardinal (1879-90).

Isaac Newton (1643-1727): English scientific polymath, enunciator of the theory of gravity and MP for the University of Cambridge (1689; 1701-92).

Friedrich Nietszsche (1844-1900): German philosopher.

Alfred Charles William Harmsworth, 1ˢᵗ Viscount Northcliffe (1865-1922): Irish-born British journalist and newspaper magnate, founder of the *Daily Mail* (1896) and the *Daily Mirror* (1903) and owner of *The Times* and the *Observer*.

Alan Ian Percy, 8ᵗʰ Duke of Northumberland (1880-1930): British soldier and chancellor of the University of Durham (1929-30).

George Henry Falkiner Nuttall (1862-1937): American-born British bacteriologist, professor of biology at the University of Cambridge (1906-31).

William Gammie Ogg (1891-1979): British agricultural scientist and expert in soil reclamation.

Sergey Fyodorovich Oldenburg (1863-1934): Russian Orientalist, secretary of the Russian Academy of Sciences (1904-29).

Henry Fairfield Osborn (1857-1935): American geologist, palaeontologist and eugenicist, professor of comparative anatomy at Princeton University (1883-90), and of biology (1891-96) and zoology (1896-1909) at Columbia University.

Elise Charlotte Otté (1818-1903): American linguist, historian and noted translator.

Orville Ward Owen (1854-1924): American physician.

Walter Hines Page (1855-1918): American journalist.

Richard Arthur Surtees Paget (1869-1955): British barrister and philologist.

William Paley (1743-1805): British Anglican theologian.

Bernard Pares (1867-1949): British historian and educationalist, professor of Russian languages, literature and history at King's College, London (1919-39).

William Newton Parker (1861-1923): British biologist, professor of zoology at University College, Cardiff (1883-1922).

Sidney James Webb, 1ˢᵗ Baron Passfield (1859-1947): British socialist and economist, cofounder of the Fabian Society (1884), Labour MP for Seaham (1922-29), President of the Board of Trade (1924) and Secretary of State for Dominion Affairs (1929-30) and the Colonies (1929-31).

Louis Pasteur (1822-95): French chemist, early advocate of the germ theory of disease, professor of physics at Dijon Lycée (1848) and of chemistry at the University of Strasbourg (1848-54) and the Sorbonne (1867-95).

Paul of Tarsus (10-67): Christian saint and major theologian, author of a number of epistles in the New Testament Bible.

Robert William Paul (1869-1943): British film pioneer and producer.

Ivan Petrovich Pavlov (1849-1936): Russian physiologist, psychologist and physician, professor of pharmacology (1890-95) and of physiology (1895-1936) at the Institute of Experimental Medicine, St Petersburg.

Maria Pavlovna (1890-1958): a member of the Russian royal family forced to flee Russia during the 1917 Bolshevik Revolution.

Karl Pearson (1857-1936): British mathematician, socialist and eugenicist, professor of applied mathematics and mechanics at King's College, London (1884-1911), and of eugenics at the University of London (1911-33).

Samuel Pepys (1633-1703): English diarist, naval administrator and politician, MP for Harwich (1685-89).

Charles Perrault (1628-1703): French fairy tale collector.

John Perry (1850-1920): Irish-born British engineer, professor of engineering and mathematics at Finsbury Technical College (1881-96) and of mathematics and mechanics at the Central Institution, London (1896-1914).

(Jacques) Boucher de Crèvecoeur de Perthes (1788-1868): French geologist and customs officer, director of the douane at Abbeville (1825-68).

Peter the Hermit (c. 1050-1115): French priest and religious leader, popular leader during the First Crusade (1096-99).

James Charles Philip (1873-1941): British chemist, professor of physical chemistry at Imperial College, London (1913-38).

Henry Phillpotts (1778-1869): Anglican clergyman, Bishop of Exeter (1831-69).

Édouard Piette (1827-1906): French archaeologist.

Leonora Piper (1857-1950): American trance medium considered one of the most significant psychics in the history of paranormal research.

Plato (c. 428 BC-c. 348 BC): ancient Greek philosopher whose work has contributed to the philosophical foundations of Western culture.

Dr Platt: This person has remained untraceable.

Pierre Guillaume Frédéric Le Play (1806-82): French engineer, sociologist and economist, professor of metallurgy at the *École des Mines*, Paris (1840-56).

Frank Podmore (1856-1910): author, founder member of the Fabian Society and psychical researcher.

Edgar Allan Poe (1809-49): American poet, short story writer and man of letters.

Alan Faraday Campbell Pollard (1877-1948): British physicist, professor of instrument design at Imperial College, London.

Albert Frederick Pollard (1869-1948): British historian, professor of constitutional history at University College, London (1903-31), and editor of *History* (1916-22).

William Jackson Pope (1870-1939): British chemist, professor of chemistry at the University of Cambridge (1908-39).

Frederick York Powell (1850-1904): British historian, professor of modern history at the University of Oxford (1894-1904).

John Henry Poynting (1852-1914): British physicist, professor of physics at Mason Science College (University of Birmingham from 1900) (1880-1914).

John Boynton Priestley (1894-1984): British writer and broadcaster.

Joseph Proudman (1888-1975): British mathematician, professor of applied mathematics (1919-33) and of oceanography (1933-54) at the University of Liverpool.

Reginald Crundall Punnett (1875-1967): British geneticist, cofounder of the *Journal of Genetics* (1910) and professor of biology (1910-12) and of genetics (1912-40) at the University of Cambridge.

Edward Bouverie Pusey (1800-82): British Anglican clergyman, leader of the Oxford Movement and professor of Hebrew at the University of Oxford (1828-82).

Pythagoras of Samos (c. 580 BC-490 BC): ancient Greek philosopher, mathematician and religious leader, best known for his Pythagorean theorem.

Vasily Vasilievich Radlov (1837-1918): German-born Russian ethnographer, founder and director of the Peter the Great Museum of Anthropology and Ethnography (1894-1918).

Walter Raleigh (1552-1618): English explorer and writer, founder of the first English colonies in the Americas during the voyages of discovery.

William Ramsay (1852-1916): British chemist, professor of chemistry at University College, Bristol (1879-87), and University College, London (1887-1916).

Herbert Edward Read (1893-1968): British poet and literature and art critic.

John Read (1884-1963): British chemist, professor of chemistry at the University of Sydney (1916-23) and the University of St Andrews (1923-63).

(William) Winwood Reade (1838-75): British historian, explorer and philosopher.

Pierre-Auguste Renoir (1841-1919): French artist, leading member of the Impressionist school of painters.

Richard II (1367-1400): Plantagenet King of England (1377-99).

Charles Robert Richet (1850-1935): French physiologist, professor of physiology at the Collège de France (1887-1935).

Peter Ritchie Calder, Baron Ritchie-Calder (1906-82): British author, journalist and academic, a leading pacifist and internationalist activist.

William Halse Rivers Rivers (1864-1922): British anthropologist and psychiatrist, a pioneer in the treatment of 'shell shock' (combat stress reaction).

Maximilien François Marie Isidore de Robespierre (1758-94): French revolutionary leader.

George John Romanes (1848-94): Canadian-born British naturalist and psychologist.

Franklin Delano Roosevelt (1882-1945): Democratic president of the United States (1933-45).

Theodore Roosevelt, Jr (1858-1919): Republican president of the United States (1901-09).

Henry Enfield Roscoe (1833-1915): British chemist and politician, MP for Manchester South (1885-95) and professor of chemistry at Owen's College, Manchester (1857-87).

Archibald Philip Primrose, 5th Earl of Rosebery (1847-1929): British Liberal politician and prime minister (1894-95).

Edward John Routh (1831-1907): Canadian-born British mathematician and tutor at the University of Cambridge (1855-88).

John Ruskin (1819-1900): highly influential British art critic and social critic.

Bertrand Arthur William Russell, 3rd Earl Russell (1872-1970): British philosopher, mathematician, social critic and pacifist.

(Edward) John Russell (1872-1965): British agriculturist, director of the Rothamsted Experimental Station (1912-43).

William James Russell (1830-1909): British chemist and educationalist, professor of chemistry at Bedford College (1860-70).

Sydney Russell-Wells (1868-1924): British medical doctor, senior physician at the Seamen's Hospital, Greenwich, and physician at the National Hospital for Diseases of the Heart, London, vice-chancellor (1919-22) of and Conservative MP (1922-24) for the University of London.

Ernest Rutherford, 1st Baron Rutherford of Nelson (1871-1937): New Zealand nuclear physicist, professor of physics at McGill University, Montreal (1898-1907), and the University of Manchester (1907-17).

John Alfred Ryle (1889-1950): British medical doctor, professor of medicine at the University of Cambridge (1935-43) and of social medicine at the University of Oxford (1943-50).

F. C. S. S.: an unidentified reviewer for *Nature*.

T. B. S.: an unidentified correspondent to *Nature*.

Francis Bacon, 1st Viscount St Alban (1561-1626): English philosopher, essayist and statesman, the populariser of inductive methodology for scientific enquiry.

Edward James Salisbury (1886-1978): British botanist, director of the Royal Botanic Gardens, Kew (1943-56).

Frederick William Sanderson (1857-1922): British educationalist, headteacher of Oundle School (1892-1922).

John Sankey, 1st Viscount Sankey (1866-1948): British judge and politician, Lord Chancellor (1929-35).

Sargon of Akkad (c. 24th-23rd centuries BC): Akkadian king (c. 2334 BC-2279 BC) conqueror of Sumer.

(Franz) Arthur Friedrich Schuster (1851-1934): German-born British physicist, professor of applied mathematics (1881-88) and of physics (1888-1907) at Owen's College, Manchester.

Leonard F. Schuster: This person has remained untraceable.

John Thomas Scopes (1900-70): American school teacher.

Harry Govier Seeley (1839-1909): British palaeontologist, professor of geology and geography at King's College, London (1876-1909) and of geology and geography at Queen's College, London (1876-1909).

Ramón José Sender (Garcés) (1901-82): Spanish-born American novelist and Republican volunteer during the Spanish Civil War (1936-39).

Albert Charles Seward (1863-1941): British botanist and geologist, professor of botany at the University of Cambridge (1909-36).

William Shakespeare (1564-1616): English playwright and poet, generally considered the greatest writer in the English language.

George Bernard Shaw (1856-1950): Irish dramatist, novelist and essayist, and founding member of the Fabian Society (1884).

Mary Shelley (1797-1851): British novelist.

William Ashwell Shenstone (1850-1908): British chemist and teacher at Clifton College, Bristol.

Charles Scott Sherrington (1852-1957): British physiologist and neuroscientist, professor of physiology at the University of Liverpool (1895-1913) and the University of Oxford (1913-35).

Matthew Phipps Shiel (1865-1947): British fantasy and science fiction novelist, author of *The Purple Cloud* (1901).

Arthur Everett Shipley (1861-1927): British zoologist, Master of Christ's College, Cambridge (1910-27), and vice-chancellor of the University of Cambridge (1917-19).

Lewis Erle Shore (1863-1944): British physiologist and neurologist, lecturer at the University of Cambridge (1896-1930).

Henry Sidgwick (1838-1900): British philosopher and co-founder of the Society for Psychical Research, professor of philosophy at the University of Cambridge (1883-1900).

George Smith (1840-76): British Assyriologist and archaeologist, the foremost translator of cuneiform writing.

Arthur Smithells (1860-1939): British chemist, professor of chemistry at the University of Leeds (1885-1923) and director of the Salters' Institute of Industrial Chemistry (1923-37).

Jan Christiaan Smuts (1870-1950): South African statesman, soldier and philosopher, prime minister of South Africa (1919-24; 1939-48).

Charles Percy Snow, Baron Snow of the City of Leicester (1905-80): British novelist and government scientific advisor.

Socrates (c. 470 BC-399 BC): ancient Greek philosopher, generally credited with laying the foundations of western philosopher and being considered its most influential practitioner.

Frederick Soddy (1877-1956): British radiochemist, professor of chemistry at the University of Aberdeen (1914-19) and the University of Oxford (1919-37).

Charles Edward Spearman (1863-1945): British psychologist, professor of mind and logic (1911-28) and of psychology (1928-31) at University College, London.

Catherine Helen Spence (1825-1910): Australian political activist.

Herbert Spencer (1820-1903): British philosopher and political theorist.

Joseph Stalin (1878-1953): Georgian-born Russian revolutionary and dictator of the Soviet Union (1928-53).

Mr Stallard: This person has remained untraceable.

Josiah Charles Stamp, 1ˢᵗ Baron Stamp (1880-1941): British banker, industrialist and civil servant, a director of the Bank of England (1928-41).

(William) Olaf Stapledon (1886-1950): British philosopher and science fiction writer.

John Kemp Starley (1854-1901): British engineer and inventor of the modern bicycle.

Riccardo Stephens: British minor poet and novelist.

George Stephenson (1781-1848): British mechanical engineer, known as the father of railways.

Robert Louis Balfour Stevenson (1850-94): British novelist, poet and travel writer.

John Sebastian Bach Stopford, 1ˢᵗ Baron Stopford of Fallowfield (1888-1961): British anatomist, professor of anatomy (1919-56) at and vice-chancellor of the University of Manchester (1934-56).

James Stormonth (1824-82): British Episcopalian minister and lexicographer, compiler of *A Dictionary of the English Language* (1884).

Jonathan Swift (1667-1745): Irish cleric, satirist and essayist.

George Clarke, 1ˢᵗ Baron Sydenham of Combe (1848-1933): British engineer and colonial administrator, governor of Victoria, Australia (1901-03), and of Bombay (1907-13).

Nikolai Stepanovich Tagantzev (1843-1923): Russian lawyer and criminologist, professor of law at St Petersburg University and the Institute of Legal Studies (1867-1882) and chair of the Russian Association of Crimonologists (1915-17).

Richard Henry Tawney (1880-1962): British historian and economist, professor of economic history at the London School of Economics (1931-49).

Frank Sherwood Taylor (1897-1956): British chemist and historian of science, director of the Science Museum, London (1950-56).

Frederick Temple (1821-1902): British Anglican minister, Bishop of Exeter (1869-85) and of London (1885-96) and Archbishop of Canterbury (1896-1902).

Samuel John Gurney Hoare, 1st Viscount Templewood (1880-1959): British Conservative MP for Chelsea (1910-44), foreign secretary (1935) and home secretary (1937-39).

Alfred Tennyson, 1st Baron Tennyson (1809-92): British poet, Poet Laureate (1850-92).

Terence (c. 185 BC-c. 159 BC): Roman dramatist.

William Makepeace Thackeray (1811-63): British novelist.

William Turner Thiselton-Dyer (1843-1928): British botanist, professor of natural history at the Royal Agricultural College, Cirencester (1868-70), and of botany at the Royal College of Science, Dublin (1870-72) and the Royal Horticultural Society, London (1872-75), and director of the Royal Botanic Gardens, Kew (1885-1905).

John Arthur Thomson (1861-1933): British naturalist, professor of natural history at the University of Aberdeen (1899-1930).

Robert Henry Thouless (1894-1984): British psychologist and advocate of the scientific study of psychic phenomena.

Edward Thring (1821-87): British educationalist, headteacher of Uppingham School (1853-87).

Henry Thomas Tizard (1885-1959): British chemist and inventor, rector of Imperial College, London (1929-42).

Brenda M. H. Tripp: This person has remained untraceable.

William Ashbee Tritton (1875-1946): British machine engineer, and generally considered the co-inventor of the first practical tank (1916).

Frances Trollope (1780-1863): British novelist and travel writer.

Leon Trotsky (1879-1940): Russian revolutionary, founder of the Soviet Red Army (1918) and founder of the Fourth Socialist International (1938).

Wilfred Trotter (1872-1939): pioneering British neurosurgeon, professor of surgery at University College Hospital, London (1935-39).

Francis Adrian Joseph Turville-Petre (1901-41): British archaeologist.

Tutankhamen (1342 BC-1324 BC): ancient Egyptian pharaoh (1333 BC-1324 BC).

Frank Twyman (1876-1959): a British pioneer of applying science to industry, director of Hilger and Watts (1946-52).

Edward Burnett Tylor (1832-1917): British anthropologist, professor of anthropology at the University of Oxford (1896-1912).

John Tyndall (1820-93): Irish natural philosopher, professor of natural philosophy at the Royal Institution (1853-87).

James Ussher (1581-1656): Irish Anglican clergyman and scholar, Archbishop of Armagh and Primate of All Ireland (1625-56).

Robert Gilbert Vansittart, 1st Baron Vansittart (1881-1957): British diplomat, head of the British diplomatic service during the Second World War.

Herbert Alfred Vaughan (1832-1903): Roman Catholic prelate, Bishop of Salford (1872-92), Archbishop of Westminster (1892-1903) and cardinal (1893-1903).

Jules Gabriel Verne (1828-1905): French author, pioneer of science fiction.

Louis Marius Vialleton (1859-1929): French medical researcher, professor of anatomy, pathogy and histology (1889-95) and of histology (1895-1929) at the University of Montpellier.

Victoria (1819-1901): British Hanoverian queen (1837-1901).

Virgil (70 BC-19 BC): Classical Roman poet.

Andrei Januarievich Vishinsky (1883-1954): Russian jurist and diplomat, Soviet foreign minister (1949-53) and leading prosecutor during the Stalinist show trials.

Voltaire (1694-1778): Pen-name of François-Marie Arouet, French Enlightenment philosopher.

Johann Heinrich Voss (1751-1826): German poet.

Frederick William Walker (1829-1910): British educator, head teacher of Manchester Grammar School (1861-77) and St Paul's School, London (1877-1905).

Alfred Russel Wallace (1823-1913): British naturalist and biologist, pioneering researcher on evolution by natural selection.

Ernest Thomas Sinton Walton (1903-1995): Irish physicist, professor of natural and experimental philosophy at Trinity College, Dublin (1946-1974).

Mary Augusta Ward (1851-1920): Mrs Humphry Ward, British popular novelist.

James Watt (1736-1819): British engineer, inventor of the first practical steam engine.

(Martha) Beatrice Potter Webb (1858-1943): British political and sociological writer, and Fabian Society activist.

(Friedrich Leopold) August Weismann (1834-1914): German biologist, responsible for discrediting the theory of evolution by acquired characteristics in favour of the transmission of characteristics through germ plasm, professor of zoology at the Albert Ludwig University, Freiburg in Breisgau (1865-1912).

Amy Catherine Wells (1872-1927): British short story writer, the second wife of H. G. Wells (1895-1928).

Frank Richard Wells (1903-82): British documentary and educational film producer and writer.

George Philip Wells (1901-85): British zoologist, professor of zoology at the University of London (1954-68).

Herbert George Wells (1866-1946): British novelist, essayist, journalist, biographer and historian, student of biology at the Normal School of Science (1884-87) and external student at the University of London (1889-90), author of many popular science essays and reviews who used science as a foundation for much of his literature.

Joseph Wells (1828-1910): British gardener, shopkeeper and professional cricketer, father of H. G. Wells.

Sarah Wells (1822-1905): British domestic servant and shopkeeper, mother of H. G. Wells.

Geoffrey West (b. 1900): the pseudonym of Geoffrey Harry Wells, British biographer and bibliographer.

John Wheatley (1869-1930): Irish-born British Labour politician, MP for Glasgow Shettleston (1922-30), Minister of Health (1924).

William Cecil Dampier Whetham (1867-1952): British agriculturist, secretary of the Agricultural Research Council (1931-35).

(Alexander) Frederick Whyte (1883-1970): British politician, Liberal MP for Perth (1910-18) and president of the Indian National Assembly (1920-25).

Samuel Wilberforce (1805-73): Anglican clergyman, Bishop of Oxford (1845-69) and of Winchester (1869-73).

Wendell Lewis Wilkie (1892-1944): American Republican presidential candidate (1940).

William I (c. 1028-87): known as 'the Conqueror', the first Norman King of England (1066-87).

William Emrys Williams (1896-1977): British educationalist and publisher, director of the Army Bureau of Current Affairs (1941-45) and editor-in-chief of Penguin Books (1935-65).

(Thomas) Woodrow Wilson (1856-1924): American politician and academic, Democratic president (1913-21) and professor of jurisprudence and political economy at Princeton University (1890-1910).

Walter Gordon Wilson (1874-1957): British soldier and engineer, considered a co-inventor of the tank (1915).

Leslie John Witts (1898-1982): British physician, professor of medicine at St Bartholomew's Hospital, London (1935-37), and of clinical medicine at the University of Oxford (1938-65).

Thomas Barlow Wood (1869-1929): British agriculturist, professor of agriculture at the University of Cambridge (1907-29).

Arthur Smith Woodward (1864-1944): British palaeontologist, keeper of geology at the Natural History Museum, South Kensington, London (1901-24).

Charles Hagberg Wright (1862-1940): British bibliophile, librarian of the London Library (1893-1940).

Edward Livingston Youmans (1821-87): American popular science writer, founder of *Popular Science* (1872).

Zeno of Citium (333 BC-264 BC): ancient Greek philosopher, founder of the Stoic school of philosophy.

Zenobia (c. 240-c. 274): queen of the Palmyrene Empire and conqueror of Egypt (269).

Bibliography

Adami, J. G. (1925) comment, *Nature*, 116: 2907 (18 July), 103.

(1943) 'Announcements', *Nature*, 152: 3845 (10 July), 46.

(1943) 'Announcements', *Nature*, 152: 3862 (6 November), 534.

(1946) 'Announcements', *Nature*, 158: 4008 (24 August), 264.

(1946) 'Announcements', *Nature*, 158: 4016 (19 October), 548.

Archer, W. (1895) 'In Memoriam R. L. S.', *New Review*, January.

Armstrong, H. E. (1894) 'Scientific Method in Board Schools', *Nature*, 50: 1304 (25 October), 631-34.

Armstrong, H. E. (1925) letter to the editor, *Nature*, 116: 2909 (1 August), 172.

Armstrong, H. E. (1926) 'Education, Science and Mr H. G. Wells', *Nature*, 118: 2977 (20 November), 723-28.

Avery, H. (1899) *Dormitory Flag* (London: Nelson).

B., V. (1924) 'The Visioning of Science', *Nature*, 113: 2842 (19 April), 559-61.

Bacon, F. (1605) *Of the Proficience and Aduancement of Learning, divine and humane* (London: Tomes).

Bacon, F. (1623) *De Augmentis Scientiarum* (London: Haviland).

Bacon, F. (1626) *Nova Atlantis* (London: Haviland).

Ballard, F. (1925) comment, Supplement to *Nature*, 116: 2906 (11 July), 77-78.

Barker, E. (1925) comment, Supplement to *Nature*, 116: 2906 (11 July), 79.

Barnes, E. W. (1925) comment, Supplement to *Nature*, 116: 2906 (11 July), 74.

Bartlett, F. C. (1938) 'Representative Opinions: Psychology', Supplement to *Nature*, 141: 3573 (23 April), 729.

Bateson, W. (1925) comment, Supplement to *Nature*, 116: 2906 (11 July), 78.

Bather, F. A. (1925) comment, Supplement to *Nature*, 116: 2906 (11 July), 77.

Belloc, H. (1926) *A Companion to Mr Wells's Outline of History* (London: Sheed and Ward).

Belloc, H. (1926) *Mr Belloc still Objects to Mr Wells's Outline of History* (London: Sheed and Ward).

Belloc, H. (1927) 'Is Darwinism Dead?', *Nature*, 119: 2990 (19 February), 277.

Belloc, H. (1939) 'The Tiger', in *Cautionary Verses: The Collected Humorous Poems of H. Belloc* (London: Duckworth), 58.

Bernal, J. D. (1938) 'Representative Opinions: Physics', Supplement to *Nature*, 141: 3573 (23 April), 736.

Berry, S. M. (1925) comment, Supplement to *Nature*, 116: 2906 (11 July), 83.

Besant, W. (1882) *All Sorts and Conditions of Men*, 3 vols. (London: Chatto and Windus).

(1931) 'Biology and Human Life', *Nature*, 127: 3204 (28 March), 477-79.

(1929) 'Biology for All', *Nature*, 123: 3099 (23 March), 442-43.

Blackett, P. M. S. (1938) 'Representative Opinions: Physics', Supplement to *Nature*, 141: 3573 (23 April), 736-37.

Blanc, L. (1845) *L'Organisation du travail* (Paris: Cauville).

de Bloch, J. (1901) 'The Wars of the Future', *Contemporary Review*, 80 (September), 305-32.

Boswell, P. G. H. (1938) 'Representative Opinions: Agriculture and Geology', Supplement to *Nature*, 141: 3573 (23 April), 735.

Bragg, W. (1938) 'Representative Opinions', Supplement to *Nature*, 141: 3573 (23 April), 725.

Breuil, H. (1926) 'Scientific Neglect of the Mas d'Azil', *Nature*, 118: 2964 (21 August), 265.

Briffault, R. (1919) *Making of Humanity* (London: Allen and Unwin).

Brightman, R. (1933) 'The Cost of a New World Order', *Nature*, 131: 3302 (11 February), 183-84.

Brightman, R. (1944) 'The Supremacy of Reason', *Nature*, 154: 3900 (29 July), 129-30.

(1937) 'British-American Understanding', *Nature*, 139: 3522 (1 May), 747-48.

(1917) 'The British Science Guild', *Nature*, 99: 2479 (3 May), 186-87.

(1922) 'British Science Guild', *Nature*, 109: 2744 (3 June), 728.

British Science Guild (1935) *Engineers Study Group on Economics: First Interim Report on Schemes and Proposals for Economic and Social Reforms* (London: British Science Guild).

Brown, W. A. (1925) comment, Supplement to *Nature*, 116: 2906 (11 July), 70-71.

Bryce, Lord (1917) 'The Worth of Ancient Literature to the Modern World', *Fortnightly Review*, 107 (April), 52-69.

Buchanan, R. (1891) *The Coming Terror and Other Essays and Letters* (London: Heinemann).

Burton, R. (1621) *Anatomy of Melancholy* (Oxford: Lichfield & Short / Cripps).

Butler, S. (1872) *Erewhon, or over the range* (London: Trübner).

Campbell, N. R. (1925) 'Science and Intellectual Freedom', *Nature*, 116: 2910 (8 August), 208.

Campbell, R. J. (1925) comment, *Nature*, 116: 2907 (18 July), 104.

Campbell-Kelly, Martin (2006) 'From World Brain to the World Wide Web', *The British Society for the History of Mathematics / Gresham College Annual Lecture*, Gresham College, 9 November, http://www.gresham.ac.uk/event.asp?PageId=39&EventId=486.

Carlyle, T. (1840) *On Heroes and Hero-Worship and the Heroic in History* (London: Chapman and Hall).

[Carlyle, T.] (1849) 'Occasional Discourse on the Negro Question', *Fraser's Magazine*, 40 (December), 670-79.

Carr-Saunders, A. M. (1922) *Population Problem: A Study in Human Evolution* (Oxford: Clarendon).

C[arr]-S[aunders], A. M. (1928) 'The Way the World might go', *Nature*, 122: 3062 (7 July), 3-5.

Cattell, J. M. (1925) 'Science and Intellectual Freedom', *Nature*, 116: 2914 (5 September), 358.

(1925) 'The Centenary of Huxley', *Nature*, 65: 2897 (9 May), 697-752.

Château Margaux (2008) 'As the vintages go by', http://www.chateau-margaux.com/en/Millesime.aspx, accessed 10 February.

(1940) 'Civilisation and the Rights of Man', *Nature*, 145: 3668 (17 February), 237-39.

Clark, C. H. (1894) *Practical Methods in Microscopy* (Boston: Heath).

Clark, W. E. L. G. (1938) 'Representative Opinions: Biology', Supplement to *Nature*, 141: 3573 (23 April), 731.

Clodd, E. (1925) comment, Supplement to *Nature*, 116: 2906 (11 July), 82.

Committee of Investigation Appointed by the National Government at Burgos (1937) *The Second and Third Reports on the Communist Atrocities Committed in Southern Spain from July to October, 1936, by the Communist Forces of the Madrid Government* (London: Eyre and Spottiswoode).

Conrad, J. (1983) *The Collected Letters of Joseph Conrad: Volume 3, 1903-1907*, ed. F. R. Karl and L. Davies (Cambridge: Cambridge University Press).

Constable, F. C. (1902) 'A Lunar Romance', *Nature*, 65: 1684 (6 February), 318.

Cowdry, E. V., ed. (1930) *Human Biology and Racial Welfare* (London: Lewis).

Crew, F. A. E. (1938) 'Representative Opinions: Biology', Supplement to *Nature*, 141: 3573 (23 April), 732-33.

Crowther, J. G. (1940) review of *Babes in the Darkling Wood*, *Nature*, 146: 3713 (28 December), 822.

Crump, W. B. (1894) 'Science Teaching in Schools', *Nature*, 51: 1307 (15 November), 56.

(1922) 'Current Topics and Events', *Nature*, 109: 2745 (10 June), 755.

(1925) 'Current Topics and Events', *Nature*, 115: 2897 (9 May), 682-86.

Danahay, M. A., ed. (2003), *The War of the Worlds*, by H. G. Wells (Peterborough, Ont.: Broadview).

[D'Arcy], C. F., [Archbishop of] Armagh (1925) 'Science and Intellectual Freedom', *Nature*, 116: 2909 (1 August), 172.

Darwin, C. (1859) *On the Origin of Species by Means of Natural Selection* (London: Murray).

Darwin, C. (1871) *Descent of Man, and selection in relation to sex* (London: Murray).

Darwin, C. (1872) *The Origin of Species by Means of Natural Selection*, 6th edn. (London: Murray).

Day, A. F. (1925) comment, Supplement to *Nature*, 116: 2906 (11 July), 82-83.

Desch, C. H. (1938) 'Representative Opinions: Chemistry', Supplement to *Nature*, 141: 3573 (23 April), 741-42.

Dickens, C. (1842) *American Notes for General Circulation* (London: Chapman and Hall).

Diderot, D., and J. le Rond d'Alembert, eds. (1751-80) *Encyclopédie, ou dictionnaire raisonné des sciences, des arts et des métiers* (Paris: Briasson, Le Breton).

Dingle, H. (1942) 'The Triumph of Time', *Nature*, 150: 3807 (17 October), 444-46.

Dixey, F. A. (1925) comment, Supplement to *Nature*, 116: 2906 (11 July), 80.

Dixon, E. T. (1894) 'Peculiarities of Psychical Research', *Nature*, 51: 1313 (27 December), 200.

Dixon, E. T. (1895) 'Peculiarities of Psychical Research', *Nature*, 51: 1314 (3 January), 223-24.

(1926) 'Dr E. A. Abbott: Scholar, Critic, and Teacher', *Times* (13 October), 19.

(1919) 'The Dominion of Man', *Nature*, 104: 2615 (11 December), 371-72.

Donnan, F. G. (1938) 'Representative Opinions: Chemistry', Supplement to *Nature*, 141: 3573 (23 April), 740-41.

Earl, A. (1894) *Practical Lessons in Physical Measurement* (London: Macmillan).

Egerton, A. C. G. (1938) 'Representative Opinions: Chemistry', Supplement to *Nature*, 141: 3573 (23 April), 739-40.

(1925) 'Evolution and Intellectual Freedom', Supplement to *Nature*, 116: 2906 (11 July), 69-70.

(1925) 'Evolution and Intellectual Freedom', *Nature*, 116: 2907 (18 July), 102-03.

Ewart, J. C. (1925) comment, Supplement to *Nature*, 116: 2906 (11 July), 81.

Fallaize, E. N. (1925) comment, Supplement to *Nature*, 116: 2906 (11 July), 81.

Farquharson, A. (1938) 'Representative Opinions: Sociology and Economics', Supplement to *Nature*, 141: 3573 (23 April), 728.

F[enn], L. A. (1932) 'The Politics of Science', *Nature*, 129: 3255 (19 March), 415-17.

Ferguson, A. (1938) 'Knowledge and World Progress', *Nature*, 141: 3573 (23 April), 707-08.

Ferguson, A. (1938) 'Representative Opinions: Physics', Supplement to *Nature*, 141: 3573 (23 April), 738.

Fisher, O. (1902) 'King Og's Bed', *Nature*, 65: 1687 (27 February), 392.

Flecker, J. E. (1913) *The Golden Journey to Samarkand* (London: Goschen).

Fleure, H. J. (1938) 'Representative Opinions: Sociology and Economics', Supplement to *Nature*, 141: 3573 (23 April), 726.

Florence, P. S. (1938), 'Representative Opinions: Sociology and Economics', Supplement to *Nature*, 141: 3573 (23 April), 726-27.

Flugel, J. C. (1938) 'Representative Opinions: Psychology', Supplement to *Nature*, 141: 3573 (23 April), 728-29.

Foster, M., and L. E. Shore (1894) *Physiology for Beginners* (London: Macmillan).

Friend, H. (1925) comment, Supplement to *Nature*, 116: 2906 (11 July), 76-77.

Galton, F. (1889) *Natural Inheritance* (London: Macmillan).

Gardiner, J. S. (1925) comment, Supplement to *Nature*, 116: 2906 (11 July), 81-82.

Garfield, E. (1983) '"World Brain" or "Memex"? Mechanical and Intellectual Requitements for Universal Bibliographic Control', in *Essays of an Information Scientist*, vol. 6 (Philadelphia: ISI), 540-47.

G[arnett], J. C. M. (1921) 'Education and World Citizenship', *Nature*, 107: 2701 (4 August), 707-08.

Geddes, P., et. al. (1895) *The Evergreen. A Northern Seasonal* (London: Fisher Unwin).

Ginsberg, M. (1938) 'Representative Opinions: Sociology and Economics', Supplement to *Nature*, 141: 3573 (23 April), 727-28.

Goebel, K. (1882) *Grundzüge der systematik und speciellen pflanzenmorphologie* (Leipzig: Engelmann).

Gordon, H. (1893) *Elementary Course of Practical Science, Part I* (London: Macmillan).

Gray, T. (1757) *Odes* (London: Dodsley).

Gregory, J. W. (1925) comment, *Nature*, 116: 2907 (18 July), 104.

G[regory], R. A. (1898) 'Science in Fiction', *Nature*, 57: 1476 (10 February), 339-40.

Gregory, R. A. (1913) 'National Aspects of Education', *Nature*, 91: 2268 (17 April), 174.

Gregory, R. A. (1916) *Discovery, or, the Spirit and Service of Science* (London: Macmillan).

Gregory, R. A. (1916) letter to H. G. Wells, 2 October, University of Illinois Archives, Urbana-Champaign.

Gregory, R. A. (1946) 'H. G. Wells: A Survey and Tribute', *Nature*, 158: 4012 (21 September), 399-402.

Gregory, R. A., and H. G. Wells (1893) *Honours Physiography* (London: Hughes).

Greenhill, A. G. (1894) 'Historical Exposition of Mechanics', *Nature*, 51: 1307 (15 November), 49-52.

Gurney, E., F. W. H. Myers and F. Podmore (1886) *Phantasms of the Living*, vol. 1 (London: Trübner).

494

H., T. LL. (1934) 'Mr H. G. Wells Reveals Himself', *Nature*, 134: 3389 (13 October), 553-54.

Haeckel, E. (1868) *Natürliche Schöpfungsgeschichte* (Berlin: Reimer).

H[aldane], J. B. S. (1937) 'Messianic Radiation', *Nature*, 140: 3535 (31 July), 171.

Haldane, J. B. S. (1938) 'Representative Opinions: Biology', Supplement to *Nature*, 141: 3573 (23 April), 730-31.

H[aldane], J. S. (1923) 'Biology in Utopia', *Nature*, 111: 2792 (5 May), 591-94.

H[aldane], J. S. (1923) letter to the editor, *Nature*, 111: 2798 (16 June), 809.

Hall, A. D. (1936) 'A Social Analysis', *Nature*, 138: 3497 (7 November), 779-80.

Hall, [A.] D. (1938) 'Representative Opinions: Agriculture and Geology', Supplement to *Nature*, 141: 3573 (23 April), 734.

Hammond, J. R. (2004) *H. G. Wells's The Time Machine: A Reference Guide* (Westport, CT: Praeger).

H[ardwick], J. C. (1939) 'The Future of Mankind', *Nature*, 144: 3644 (2 September), 397-98.

Hardwick, J. C. (1942) 'Man's Present and Future', *Nature*, 149: 3777 (21 March), 316-17.

Harmer, S. (1925) comment, Supplement to *Nature*, 116: 2906 (11 July), 78-79.

Hawkins, T. H. (1944) 'Science and Broadcasting', *Nature*, 154: 3897 (8 July), 39-40.

Haynes, R. D. (1980) *H. G. Wells: Discoverer of the Future. The Influence of Science on His Thought* (New York and London: New York University Press).

H[eadley], F. W. (1904) 'The Future of the Human Race', *Nature*, 71: 1835 (29 December), 193-94.

H[eadley], F. W. (1905) 'Fact in Sociology', *Nature*, 71: 1842 (16 February), 366.

Heard, G. (1934) *These Hurrying Years: An Historical Outline* (London: Chatto and Windus).

Heath, G. (1894) letter to the editor, *Nature*, 51: 1307 (15 November), 56-57.

Henrici, O. (1894) 'Science Teaching in Schools', *Nature*, 51: 1309 (29 November), 106.

Henson, H. H. (1925) comment, *Nature*, 116: 2907 (18 July), 103-04.

Hickson, S. J. (1925) comment, Supplement to *Nature*, 116: 2906 (11 July), 81.

Hill, A. V. (1938) 'Representative Opinions: Biology', Supplement to *Nature*, 141: 3573 (23 April), 729-30.

Hill, A. V. (1941) 'Science, National and International, and the Basis of Co-operation', *Nature*, 147: 3722 (1 March), 250-52.

Hill, M. D. (1917) 'Classical Education and Modern Needs', *Nature*, 99: 2481 (17 May), 225.

Hogben, L. (1930) 'Social Biology', *Nature*, 126: 3183 (1 November), 705-06.

H[ogben], L. (1933) 'Mr Wells Comes Back', *Nature*, 132: 3338 (21 October), 620-22.

Hopkins, F. G. (1938) 'Representative Opinions', Supplement to *Nature*, 141: 3573 (23 April), 725.

Horder, Lord (1943) 'World Reorganisation', *Nature*, 151: 3831 (3 April), 374-75.

Huxley, J. S. (1938) 'Representative Opinions: Biology', Supplement to *Nature*, 141: 3573 (23 April), 733.

Huxley, J. S. (1939) 'The Uniqueness of Man', *Yale Review*, 28 (March), 474-500.

Huxley, J. S. (1941) *The Uniqueness of Man* (London: Chatto and Windus).

Huxley, J. S., H. G. Wells, J. B. S. Haldane, W. G. Ogg, J. C. Drummond, W. F. Crick, J. W. Munro, J. Fisher, W. H. Kauntze, L. J. Witts, P. G. Edge, J. M. Mackintosh and E. V. Appleton (1944) *Reshaping Man's Heritage: Biology in the Service of Man* (London: Allen and Unwin).

Huxley, T. H. (1893) 'Autobiography', in *The Collected Essays of Thomas Henry Huxley, Volume 1: Method and Results* (New York: Appleton), 1-17.

Huxley, T. H. (1893) 'The Darwin Memorial', in *The Collected Essays of Thomas Henry Huxley, Volume 2: Darwiniana* (New York: Appleton), 248-52.

Huxley, T. H. (1893) *Evolution and Ethics* (London: Macmillan).

Huxley, T. H. (1893) 'Mr Darwin's Critics', in *The Collected Essays of Thomas Henry Huxley, Volume 2: Darwiniana* (New York: Appleton), 120-86.

(1937) 'The Informative Content of Education', Supplement to *Nature*, 140: 3540 (4 September), 415-16.

Inge, W. R. (1919) *Outspoken Essay* (London: Longman).

Inge, W. R. (1940) 'Victorian Socialism', *Nature*, 145: 3663 (13 January), 45-46.

Inge, W. R. (1940) letter to the editor, *Nature*, 145: 3665 (27 January), 152.

(1937) 'International Council of Scientific Unions', *Nature*, 139: 3521 (22 May), 869-70.

James, H. (1907) *The American Scene* (London: Chapman and Hall).

Jones, R. A. (1941) 'The Man of Science as Aristocrat', *Nature*, 147: 3735 (31 May), 677.

Keats, J. (1816) 'On First Looking into Chapman's Homer', *Examiner*, 1 December.

Keith, A. (1925) comment, Supplement to *Nature*, 116: 2906 (11 July), 75.

Keith, A. (1927) 'Is Darwinism Dead?', *Nature*, 119: 2985 (15 January), 75-77.

Keith, A. (1927) letter to the editor, *Nature*, 119: 2990 (19 February), 277.

Kerr, J. G. (1925) comment, Supplement to *Nature*, 116: 2906 (11 July), 80.

Kerr, J. G. (1938) 'Representative Opinions: Biology', Supplement to *Nature*, 141: 3573 (23 April), 731-32.

Keynes, J. M. (1919) *The Economic Consequences of the Peace* (London: Macmillan).

Keyserling, H. (1934) *Révolution Mondiale et la Responsabilite de l'Esprit* (Paris: Stock).

Kingsley, C. (1880) *The Works of Charles Kingsley, Volume XIX: Scientific Lectures and Essays* (London: Macmillan).

Kingsley, C. (1901-03) *The Life and Works of Charles Kingsley*, 19 vols. (London: Macmillan).

Kipling, R. (1902) 'The Islanders', *Times* (4 January), 9.

Krause, E. (1880) *Werden und Vergehen: Eine Entwickelungsgeschichte des Naturganzen*, 2 vols. (Berlin: Borntraeger).

Krivitsky, W. G. (1939) *I Was Stalin's Agent* (London: Hamilton).

Lankester, E. R. (1880) *Degeneration: A Chapter in Darwinism* (London: Macmillan).

Lankester, E. R. (1902) 'The Present Judged by the Future', Supplement to *Nature*, 65: 1689 (13 March), iii-v.

Lankester, E. R. (1910) *Science from an Easy Chair* (London: Methuen).

Lankester, E. R. (1925) comment, Supplement to *Nature*, 116: 2906 (11 July), 71-72.

Laski, H. J. (1938) 'Representative Opinions: Sociology and Economics', Supplement to *Nature*, 141: 3573 (23 April), 727.

Lawrence, W. (1822) *Lectures on Physiology, Zoology, and the Natural History of Man* (London: Callow).

Lemontey, P.-E. (1801) 'Influence morale de la division du travail', in *Raison, Folie, Chacun son Mot: petit cours de morale mis à la portée des vieux enfants* (Paris: Imprimerie de Guilleminet).

Levy, H. (1927) 'Science in Literature', *Nature*, 120: 3023 (8 October), 503-04.

Levy, H. (1931) 'Science in Literature', *Nature*, 127: 3206 (11 April), 549-50.

Levy, H. (1934) 'The Autobiography of H. G. Wells', Supplement to *Nature*, 134: 3397 (8 December), 882-84.

Levy, H. (1934) letter to the editor, *Nature*, 134: 3399 (22 December), 972.

Levy, H. (1938) 'Representative Opinions: Physics', Supplement to *Nature*, 141: 3573 (23 April), 737-38.

Lewis, S. (1925) *Arrowsmith* (New York: Grosset & Dunlap).

Lidgett, J. S. (1925) Supplement to *Nature*, 116: 2906 (11 July), 82.

Lindemann, F. A. (1938) 'Representative Opinions: Physics', Supplement to *Nature*, 141: 3573 (23 April), 737.

Linnaeus, C. (1735) *Systema Naturae* (Netherlands: Lugduni Batavorum).

(1917) 'Literature and Science in Education', *Nature*, 98: 2466 (1 February), 432-33.

Livingstone, R. W. (1916) *A Defence of Classical Education* (London: Macmillan).

Livingstone, R. W. (1917) 'Classical Education and Modern Needs', *Nature*, 99: 2480 (10 May), 205.

(1937) 'The Living World', *Nature*, 140: 3542 (18 September), 484-85.

Lodge, O. J. (1895) 'Peculiarities of Psychical Research', *Nature*, 51: 1315 (10 January), 247.

Lodge, O. J. (1925) comment, Supplement to *Nature*, 116: 2906 (11 July), 83.

London, J. (1903) *The People of the Abyss* (New York: Macmillan).

Longfellow, H. W. (1838) 'A Psalm of Life', *Knickerbocker Magazine*, October.

van Loon, H. (1921) *The Story of Mankind* (New York: Boni & Liveright).

van Loon, H. (1922) *The Story of Mankind* (London: Harrap).

Lowell, P. (1895) *Mars* (Boston: Houghton, Mifflin).

Luckhurst, R. (2002) *The Invention of Telepathy* (Oxford: Oxford University Press).

Lucretius (1963) *De Rerum Natura* (Oxford: Clarendon).

(1902) 'A Lunar Romance', *Nature*, 65: 1680 (9 January), 218-19.

MacBride, E. W. (1925) comment, Supplement to *Nature*, 116: 2906 (11 July), 72-73.

Machiavelli, N. (1532) *Il Principe* (Rome: Blado).

McIntosh, W. C. (1925) comment, Supplement to *Nature*, 116: 2906 (11 July), 76.

MacKenzie, N., and J. MacKenzie (1987) *The Life of H. G. Wells: The Time Traveller*, rev. edn (London: Hogarth).

Magnus, P. (1893) 'Elementary Practical Science', *Nature*, 49: 1258 (7 December), 121-22.

Malthus, T. (1798) *Essay on Population* (London: Johnson).

Marett, R. R. (1925) comment, *Nature*, 116: 2907 (18 July), 105.

Marquand, H. A. (1938) 'Representative Opinions: Sociology and Economics', Supplement to *Nature*, 141: 3573 (23 April), 727.

Marvin, F. S. (1922) 'Unified Human History', *Nature*, 110: 2774 (30 December), 867-68.

Marx, K. (1867) *Das Kapital: Kritik der politischen Oekonomie*, vol. 1 (Hamburg: Meissner).

Marx, K. (1898) *Eighteenth Brumaire of Louis Napoleon*, trans. D. De Leon (New York: International Publishing).

Marx, K. (1981) *A Contribution to the Critique of Political Economy*, ed. M. Dobb (London: Lawrence & Wishart).

Masefield, J. (1909) *Multitude and Solitude* (London: Richards).

Maurice, F. D. (1853) *Theological Essays* (Cambridge: Macmillan).

Maxwell, J. C. (2004) 'To the Additional Examiner for 1875', in *Poems* (Paris: PoemHunter.com), 62-63.

Mercier, C. (1905) 'Discussion', in 'Eugenics: Its Definition, Scope and Aims', by F. Galton, in *Sociological Papers* (London: Macmillan), 55.

Milton, J. (1644) *Areopagitica* (London).

(1936) 'Mr H. G. Wells's Film *Things to Come*', *Nature*, 137: 3461 (29 February), 352.

Mitchell, P. C. (1894) *Outlines of Biology* (London: Methuen).

Mitchell, P. C. (1938) 'Representative Opinions: Biology', Supplement to *Nature*, 141: 3573 (23 April), 731.

Mivart, S. G. J. (1871) *On the Genesis of Species* (London: Macmillan).

Montagu of Beaulieu, E. Barker, E. P. Cathcart, A. S. Eddington, I. Gollancz, R. A. Gregory, P. C. Mitchell, B. Pares, A. Schuster, C. S. Sherrington, A. E. Shipley, H. G. Wells, A. S. Woodward and C. H. Wright (1921) 'The British Committee for Aiding Men of Letters and Science in Russia', *Nature*, 106: 2671 (6 January), 598-99.

de Monzie, A., and L. Febvre, eds. (1937-66), *Encyclopédie française*, 20 vols. (Paris: Société de gestion de l'Encyclopédie française / Larousse).

Moore-Brabazon, J. T. C. (1941) 'The Man of Science as Aristocrat', *Nature*, 147: 3731 (3 May), 544-45.

More, T. (1551) *Utopia*, trans. R. Robynson (London: Vele).

Morgan, C. L. (1925) comment, *Nature*, 116: 2907 (18 July), 103.

Morris, W. (1890) *News from Nowhere* (Boston: Roberts).

Murray, J. O. F. (1925) comment, *Nature*, 116: 2907 (18 July), 104-05.

Myers, C. S. (1938) 'Representative Opinions: Psychology', Supplement to *Nature*, 141: 3573 (23 April), 729.

Myres, J. L. (1938) 'Representative Opinions: Sociology and Economics', Supplement to *Nature*, 141: 3573 (23 April), 725-26.

N., J., and D. N. (1934) 'A Crystallographic *Arrowsmith*', Supplement to *Nature*, 134: 3397 (8 December), 890.

Needham, J. (1938) 'Representative Opinions: Biology', Supplement to *Nature*, 141: 3573 (23 April), 734.

(1930) 'News and Views', *Nature*, 126: 3183 (1 November), 694-95.

(1931) 'News and Views', *Nature*, 127: 3196 (31 January), 172-77.

(1938) 'News and Views', *Nature*, 141: 3560 (22 January), 150-56.

(1894) 'Notes', *Nature*, 51: 1312 (20 December), 182.

(1901) 'Notes', *Nature*, 63: 1640 (4 April), 546.

(1901) 'Notes', *Nature*, 64: 1662 (5 September), 454.

(1920) 'Notes', *Nature*, 106: 2663 (11 November), 352.

Nuttall, G. H. F. (1925) comment, Supplement to *Nature*, 116: 2906 (11 July), 83.

(1895) 'Our Book Shelf', *Nature*, 52: 1342 (18 July), 268.

(1906) 'Our Book Shelf', *Nature*, 75: 1936 (6 December), 124-25.

(1913) 'Our Bookshelf', *Nature*, 91: 2282 (24 July), 529.

(1925) 'Our Bookshelf', *Nature*, 116: 2923 (7 November), 671-72.

(1926) 'Our Bookshelf', *Nature*, 118: 2981 (18 December), 872.

Paget, R. A. S. (1938) 'Representative Opinions: Physics', Supplement to *Nature*, 141: 3573 (23 April), 738-39.

Paget, R. A. S. (1941), letter to the editor, *Nature*, 147: 3731 (3 May), 545.

P[arker], W. N. (1893) 'Vertebrate Biology', *Nature*, 47: 1226 (27 April), 605.

P[arker], W. N. (1893) 'Our Book Shelf', *Nature*, 49: 1259 (14 December), 148.

Parrinder, P., ed. (1972) *H. G. Wells: The Critical Heritage* (London: Routledge & Kegan Paul).

Parrinder, P. (1989) 'Introduction', in *The Discovery of the Future with The Common-Sense of World Peace and The Human Adventure*, by H. G. Wells, ed. P. Parrinder (London: PNL), 7-17.

Partington, J. S. (2003) *Building Cosmopolis: The Political Thought of H. G. Wells* (Aldershot: Ashgate).

Partington, J. S. (2005) 'Revising *Anticipations*: Wells on Race and Class, 1901 to 1905', *Undying Fire*, 4: 31-44.

Partington, J. S. (2007) 'H. G. Wells, "The Discovery of the Future" and the Cancelled Royal Institution Lecture', *H. G. Wells Newsletter*, 5. 14 (Summer), [13-16].

Paul, R. W. (1941) letter to the editor, *Nature*, 147: 3733 (17 May), 610.

Pearson, K. (1894) 'Peculiarities of Psychical Research', *Nature*, 51: 1311 (13 December), 153.

Pearson, K. (1894) letter to the editor, *Nature*, 51: 1313 (27 December), 200.

Pearson, K. (1895) 'Peculiarities of Psychical Research', *Nature*, 51: 1316 (17 January), 273-74.

Pearson, K. (1896) 'Reproductive Selection', *Natural History*, 8 (May), 321.

Pearson, K. (1923) 'Biology of Man', *Nature*, 111: 2798 (16 June), 809.

Perrault, C. (1697) *Contes de ma Mère l'Oye* (Paris: Barbin).

Perry, J. (1900) 'Railways and Moving Platforms', *Nature*, 62: 1609 (30 August), 412.

Perry, J. (1907) 'Social Problems in America', *Nature*, 75: 1942 (17 January), 265-66.

Philip, J. C. (1938) 'Representative Opinions: Chemistry', Supplement to *Nature*, 141: 3573 (23 April), 741.

Philmus, R. M., and D. Y. Hughes, eds. (1975) *H. G. Wells: Early Writings in Science and Science Fiction* (Berkeley, Los Angeles and London: University of California Press).

Plato (1904) *Republic of Plato*, trans. J. L. Davies and D. J. Vaughan (London: Macmillan).

Podmore, F. (1894) *Apparitions and Thought Transference* (London: Scott).

Poe, E. A. (1893) *The Murders in the Rue Morgue and Other Tales of Mystery* (London: Low).

Poynting, J. H. (1900) 'Recent Studies in Gravitation', *Nature*, 62: 1608 (23 August), 403-08.

P[roudman], J. (1916) 'Forecast by Mr Wells', *Nature*, 97: 2441 (10 August), 478.

Punnett, R. C. (1905) *Mendelism* (Cambridge: Macmillan & Bowes).

Punnett, R. C. (1925) comment, Supplement to *Nature*, 116: 2906 (11 July), 80.

De Quatrefages, A. (1857) *Rambles of a Naturalist*, trans. E. C. Otté (London: Longman, Brown, Green, Longmans & Roberts).

Read, J. (1938) 'Representative Opinions: Chemistry', Supplement to *Nature*, 141: 3573 (23 April), 741.

Reade, W. W. (1872) *The Martyrdom of Man* (London: Kegan Paul, Trench, Trübner).

Reed, J. R. (1982) *The Natural History of H. G. Wells* (Athens: Ohio University Press).

Reviewer, The (1902) letter to the editor, *Nature*, 65: 1684 (6 February), 318.

(1938) Review of *The Camford Visitation*, *Nature*, 141: 3563 (12 February), 267.

(1936) Review of *Man who could work Miracles*, *Nature*, 137: 3475 (6 June), 929.

(1935) Review of *The New America: the New World*, *Nature*, 136: 3427 (14 September), 414.

(1936) Review of *Things to Come*, *Nature*, 137: 3454 (11 January), 50.

Ruddick, N., ed. (2001) *The Time Machine: An Invention*, by H. G. Wells (Peterborough, Ont.: Broadview).

Ruskin, J. (1843-60) *Modern Painters*, 5 vols. (London: Smith, Elder).

Russell, B. (1916) *Principles of Social Reconstruction* (London: Allen and Unwin).

Russell, J. (1938) 'Representative Opinions: Agriculture and Geology', Supplement to *Nature*, 141: 3573 (23 April), 734-35.

Ryle, J. A. (1938) 'Representative Opinions: Biology', Supplement to *Nature*, 141: 3573 (23 April), 732.

S., F. C. S. (1905) 'Sociological Speculations', *Nature*, 72: 1867 (10 August), 337-38.

S., T. B. (1902) 'King Og's Bed', *Nature*, 65: 1686 (20 February), 366.

Salisbury, E. J. (1938) 'Representative Opinions: Biology', Supplement to *Nature*, 141: 3573 (23 April), 733.

Scheick, W. J., ed. (1995) *The Critical Response to H. G. Wells* (Westport, CT: Greenwood).

Schuster, L. F. (1921) 'Literature for Men of Letters and Science in Russia', *Nature*, 106: 2675 (3 February), 728.

(1895) 'Science in the Magazines', *Nature*, 51: 1315 (10 January), 259.

(1896) 'Science in the Magazines', *Nature*, 54: 1407 (15 October), 589.

Scott, D. H. (1925) comment, Supplement to *Nature*, 116: 2906 (11 July), 77.

Sender, R. J. (1936) *Seven Red Sundays*, trans. Peter Chalmers Mitchell (London: Faber & Faber).

Seward, A. C., ed. (1917) *Science and the Nation* (Cambridge: Cambridge University Press).

Shakespeare, W. (2005) *Twelfth Night* (Cambridge: Cambridge University Press).

[Shelley, M.] (1818) *Frankenstein; or, The Modern Prometheus*, 3 vols. (London: Lackington, Hughes, Harding, Havor & Jones).

Shenk, D. (1999) *The End of Patience: Cautionary Notes on the Information Revolution* (Bloomington: Indiana University Press).

Shiel, M. P. (1901) *The Purple Cloud* (London: Chatto & Windus).

Shipley, A. (1925) comment, Supplement to *Nature*, 116: 2906 (11 July), 73-74.

Smith, D. C. (1986) *H. G. Wells: Desperately Mortal. A Biography* (New Haven and London: Yale University Press).

Smith, D. C. (1998) ed., *The Correspondence of H. G. Wells*, by H. G. Wells, 4 vols. (London: London: Pickering & Chatto).

Smith, G. E. (1925) comment, Supplement to *Nature*, 116: 2906 (11 July), 75-76.

Smithells, A. (1925) comment, Supplement to *Nature*, 116: 2906 (11 July), 82.

Smuts, J. C. (1926) *Holism and Evolution* London: Macmillan).

Smuts, J. C. (1942) *The Basis of Trusteeship in South African Native Policy*, 'New Africa Pamphlet', 2 (Johannesburg: South African Institute of Race Relations).

Snow, C. P. (1934) *The Search* (London: Gollancz).

Snow, C. P. (1956) 'The Two Cultures', *New Statesman*, 53 (6 October), 413-14.

(1932) 'Social Economics', *Nature*, 129: 3259 (16 April), 558-60.

(1938) 'Social Relations of Science', Supplement to *Nature*, 141: 3573 (23 April), 723-24.

(1937) 'Social Responsibilities of Science', *Nature*, 139: 3521 (24 April), 689-91.

Soddy, F. (1909) *Interpretation of Radium* (London: Murray).

Soddy, F. (1938) 'Social Relations of Science', *Nature*, 141: 3574 (30 April), 784-85.

Sollas, W. J. (1925) comment, Supplement to *Nature*, 116: 2906 (11 July), 74-75.

Spearman, C. (1938) 'Representative Opinions: Psychology', Supplement to *Nature*, 141: 3573 (23 April), 728.

Spence, C. H. (2006) *An Autobiography* (Charleston, SC: BiblioBazaar).

Spencer, H. (1861) *Education: Intellectual, Moral and Physical* (London: Williams and Norgate).

Spencer, H. (1892) *Education: Intellectual, Moral and Physical* (London: Williams and Norgate).

Stapledon, O. (1930) *Last and First Men: A Story of the Near and Far Future* (London: Methuen).

Stapledon, O. (1935) *Odd John: A Story between Jest and Ernest* (London: Methuen).

Stapledon, O. (1937) *Star Maker* (London: Methuen).

Stevenson, R. L. (1896) 'If This Were Faith', in *Songs of Travel and other verses*, ed. S. Colvin (London: Chatto & Windus).

Stopford, J. S. B. (1938) 'Representative Opinions: Biology', Supplement to *Nature*, 141: 3573 (23 April), 730.

Stormonth, J. (1884) *A Dictionary of the English Language* (Edinburgh: Blackwood).

Stover, L. (1987) *The Prophetic Soul: A Reading of H. G. Wells's Things to Come Together with His Film Treatment, Whither Mankind? And the Postproduction Script (Both Never Before Published)* (Jefferson, NC: McFarland).

Stover, L., ed. (1996) *The Time Machine: An Invention. A Critical Text of the 1895 London First Edition, with an Introduction and Appendices*, by H. G. Wells (Jeferson, NC: McFarland).

(1938) 'Summary', Supplement to Nature, 141: 3573 (23 April), 742.

Swift, J. (1704) *A Tale of a Tub* (London: Nutt).

Swift, J. (1726) *Gulliver's Travels* (London: Curll.).

(1935) 'Systems of Economic Reform', *Nature*, 135: 3421 (25 May), 884-85.

Tawney, R. H. (1921) *The Acquisitive Society* (London: Bell).

Taylor, F. S. (1941) *The Century of Science* (London: Heinemann).

[Tennyson, A.] (1850) *In Memoriam* (London: Moxon).

Terence (1959) *Phormio*, ed. R. H. Martin (London: Methuen).

Thackeray, W. (1849-50) *The History of Pendennis*, 3 vols. (London: Bradbury and Evans).

Thiselton-Dyer, W. T. (1907) 'Mulattos', *Nature*, 77: 1989 (12 December), 126-27.

Thompson, D. W. (1925) comment, Supplement to *Nature*, 116: 2906 (11 July), 79.

(1944) 'Thoughts on Reconstruction', *Nature*, 153: 3877 (19 February), 220.

Thouless, R. H. (19123) *An Introduction to the Psychology of Religion* (Cambridge: Cambridge University Press).

Tizard, H. (1938) 'Representative Opinions: Physics', Supplement to *Nature*, 141: 3573 (23 April), 735-36.

(1920) 'A "Tour de Force"', *Nature*, 106: 2657 (30 September), 137-40.

Tripp, B. M. H. (1943) 'Science and the Citizen: The Public Understanding of Science', *Nature*, 151: 3831 (3 April), 382-85.

Trotter, W. (1916) *Instincts of the Herd in Peace and War* (London: Fisher Unwin).

(1925) 'Truth and Doctrine in Science and Religion', Supplement to *Nature*, 116: 2906 (11 July), 83-84.

(1917) 'University and Educational Intelligence', *Nature*, 99: 2476 (12 April), 138.

(1922) 'University and Educational Intelligence', *Nature*, 110: 2752 (29 July), 166.

(1922) 'University and Educational Intelligence', *Nature*, 110: 2763 (14 October), 530.

(1923) 'University and Educational Intelligence', *Nature*, 112: 2821 (24 November), 777.

Verne, J. (1865) *De la terre à la lune* (Paris: Hetzel).

Verne, J. (1870) *Autour de la lune* (Paris: Hetzel).

Verne, J. (1873) *From the Earth to the Moon direct in 97 hours 20 minutes; and a trip round it*, trans. L. Mercier and E. C. King (London: Low).

Vialleton, L. (1911) *Éléments de morphologie des vertébrés* (Paris: Octave Doin).

Virgil (1980) *Virgil's Eclogues: The Latin Text with a Verse Translation and Brief Notes*, trans. G. Lee (Liverpool: Cairns).

[Voltaire] (1764) *Dictionnaire philosophique* (Geneva).

Voss, J. H. (1777) 'Gesundheit', *Musenalmanach*, 107.

Wagar, W. W. (1961) *H. G. Wells and the World State* (New Haven: Yale University Press).

(1925) 'War Against Evolution: The Rising Tide Against Teaching Certain Conclusions of Science in the Public Schools – Voters Being Urged to Assert That as Taxpayers Who Pay for Teaching They Shall Say What Shall Be Taught', *Boston Evening Transcript*, (23 May), Section 3: 16.

Ward, Mrs H. (1888) *Robert Elsmere*, 3 vols. (London: Smith and Elder).

Waterhouse, E. S. (1925) comment, Supplement to *Nature*, 116: 2906 (11 July), 79.

Wells, H. G. (1888) 'The Chronic Argonauts', *Science Schools Journal*, 2: 11 (April), 312-20.

Wells, H. G. (1888) 'The Chronic Argonauts', *Science Schools Journal*, 2: 12 (May), 336-41.

Wells, H. G. (1888), 'The Chronic Argonauts', *Science Schools Journal*, 2: 13 (June), 367-71.

Wells, H. G. (1893) *Text-book of Biology, Part I: Vertebrata* (London: Clive / University Correspondence College).

Wells, H. G. (1893) *Text-book of Biology, Part II: Invertebrates and Plants* (London: Clive / University Correspondence College).

Wells, H. G. (1894) *Text-book of Biology*, 2 vols., 2nd edn (London: Clive / University Correspondence College).

Wells, H. G. (1894) 'Popularising Science', *Nature*, 50: 1291 (26 July), 300-01.

Wells, H. G. (1894) 'Science, in School and After School', *Nature*, 50: 1300 (27 September), 525-26.

Wells, H. G. (1894) letter to the editor, *Nature*, 51: 1309 (29 November), 106.

Wells, H. G. (1894) 'Peculiarities of Psychical Research', *Nature*, 51: 1310 (6 December), 121-22.

Wells, H. G. (1894) 'The Sequence of Studies', *Nature*, 51: 1313 (27 December), 195-96.

Wells, H. G. (1895) *Select Conversations with an Uncle, Now Extinct, and Two Other Reminiscences* (London: Lane).

Wells, H. G. (1895) *The Time Machine: An Invention* (London: Heinemann).

Wells, H. G. (1895) 'The Time Machine', *New Review*, 12 (January), 98-112.

Wells, H. G. (1895) 'Science Teaching – An Ideal and Some Realities', *Educational Times*, 48 (1 January), 23-29.

Wells, H. G. (1895) letter to the editor, *Nature*, 51: 1316 (17 January), 274.

Wells, H. G. (1895) 'The Time Machine', *New Review*, 12 (February), 207-21.

Wells, H. G. (1895) 'The Time Machine', *New Review*, 12 (March), 329-43.

Wells, H. G. (1895) 'The Remarkable Case of Davidson's Eyes', *Pall Mall Budget*, 28 March.

Wells, H. G. (1895) 'The Time Machine', *New Review*, 12 (April), 453-72.

Wells, H. G. (1895) 'The Time Machine', *New Review*, 12 (May), 577-88.

Wells, H. G. (1895) 'Bio-optimism', *Nature*, 52: 1348 (29 August), 410-11.

Wells, H. G. (1896) *The Island of Doctor Moreau* (London: Heinemann).

Wells, H. G. (1896) 'The Plattner Story', *New Review*, April.

Wells, H. G. (1896) 'Human Evolution, an Artificial Process', *Fortnightly Review*, 60 (October), 590-95.

Wells, H. G. (1896) *The Wheels of Chance: A Holiday Adventure* (London: Dent).

Wells, H. G. (1897) 'The Acquired Factor', *Academy*, 51 (9 January), 37.

Wells, H. G. (1897) 'The Star', *Graphic*, December.

Wells, H. G. (1898) *The War of the Worlds* (London: Heinemann).

Wells, H. G. (1898) 'The Man Who Could Work Miracles', *Illustrated London News*, July.

Wells, H. G. (1898) 'Mr Ledbetter's Vacation', *Strand Magazine*, 16 (October), 452-62.

Wells, H. G. (1899) *When the Sleeper Wakes* (London: Harper).

Wells, H. G. (1899), 'A Story of the Days to Come', *Pall Mall Magazine*, June-October.

Wells, H. G. (1900) *Love and Mr Lewisham* (London and New York: Harper).

Wells, H. G. (1901) *The First Men in the Moon* (London: Newnes).

Wells, H. G. (1901) 'Anticipations', *Fortnightly Review*, 75 (April), 747-60.

Wells, H. G. (1901) 'Anticipations', *Fortnightly Review*, 75 (May), 925-37.

Wells, H. G. (1901), 'A Dream of Armageddon', *Black and White Budget*, May-June.

Wells, H. G. (1901) 'Anticipations', *Fortnightly Review*, 75 (June), 1004-21.

Wells, H. G. (1901) 'Anticipations', *Fortnightly Review*, 76 (July), 170-88.

Wells, H. G. (1901) 'Anticipations', *Fortnightly Review*, 76 (August), 355-70.

Wells, H. G. (1901) 'Anticipations', *Fortnightly Review*, 76 (September), 538-55.

Wells, H. G. (1901) 'Anticipations', *Fortnightly Review*, 76 (October), 725-38.

Wells, H. G. (1901) 'Anticipations', *Fortnightly Review*, 76 (November), 911-26.

Wells, H. G. (1901) 'Anticipations', *Fortnightly Review*, 76 (December), 1063-82.

Wells, H. G. (1902) *Anticipations of the Reaction of Mechanical and Scientific Progress upon Human Life and Thought* (London: Chapman and Hall).

Wells, H. G. (1902) *The Discovery of the Future: A Discourse Delivered to the Royal Institution on January 24th, 1902* (London: Fisher Unwin).

Wells, H. G. (1902) 'The Discovery of the Future', *Nature*, 65: 1684 (6 February), 326-31.

Wells, H. G. (1902) letter to the editor, *Nature*, 65: 1686 (20 February), 366.

Wells, H. G. (1903) *Mankind in the Making* (London: Chapman and Hall).

Wells, H. G. (1903) 'The Land Ironclads', *Strand Magazine*, vol. 26 (December), 751-64.

Wells, H. G. (1904) *Anticipations of the Reaction of Mechanical and Scientific Progress upon Human Life and Thought*, cheap edn. (London: Chapman and Hall).

Wells, H. G. (1904) *The Food of the Gods and How It Came to Earth* (London: Macmillan).

Wells, H. G. (1904) 'The Country of the Blind', *Strand Magazine*, April.

Wells, H. G. (1904) 'Scepticism of the Instrument', *Mind*, 13: 51 (July), 379-93.

Wells, H. G. (1905) *Kipps: The Story of s Simple Soul* (London: Macmillan).

Wells, H. G. (1905) *A Modern Utopia* (London: Chapman and Hall).

Wells, H. G. (1905) 'Fact in Sociology', *Nature*, 71: 1840 (2 February), 319.

Wells, H. G. (1905) 'The Empire of the Ants', *Strand Magazine*, December.

Wells, H. G. (1906) *The Future in America: A Search After Realities* (London: Chapman and Hall).

Wells, H. G. (1906) *In the Days of the Comet* (London: Macmillan).

Wells, H. G. (1907) *This Misery of Boots* (London: Fabian Society).

Wells, H. G. (1907) 'Mulattos', *Nature*, 77: 1990 (19 December), 149.

Wells, H. G. (1908) *First and Last Things: A Confession of Faith and Rule of Life* (London: Constable).

Wells, H. G. (1908) *New Worlds for Old* (London: Constable).

Wells, H. G. (1909) *Ann Veronica* (London: Fisher Unwin).

Wells, H. G. (1910) *The History of Mr Polly* (London: Nelson).

Wells, H. G. (1910) 'My First Aeroplane', *Strand Magazine*, January.

Wells, H. G. (1910) 'Endowment of Motherhood', *Daily Mail* (22 June).

Wells, H. G. (1911) *The New Machiavelli* (London: Lane).

Wells, H. G. (1912) *Marriage* (London: Macmillan).

Wells, H. G. (1913) *The Passionate Friends* (London: Macmillan).

Wells, H. G. (1913) 'War and Common Sense, I: The Common Sense of Conscription', *Daily Mail* (7 April).

Wells, H. G. (1913) 'War and Common Sense, II: Put Not Your Faith in Dread-noughts', *Daily Mail* (8 April).

Wells, H. G. (1913) 'War and Common Sense, III: The Balance of Present and Future', *Daily Mail* (9 April).

Wells, H. G. (1914) *The Wife of Sir Isaac Harman* (London: Macmillan).

Wells, H. G. (1914) *The World Set Free* (London: Macmillan).

Wells, H. G. (1915) *The Research Magnificent* (London: Macmillan).

Wells, H. G. (1916) *Mr Britling Sees it Through* (London: Cassell).

Wells, H. G. (1916) *What is Coming? A Forecast of Things after the War* (London: Cassell).

Wells, H. G. (1917) *God, the Invisible King* (London: Cassell).

Wells, H. G. (1917) 'The Case Against The Classical Languages', *Fortnightly Review*, 107 (April), 567-74.

Wells, H. G. (1917) 'Education and Research', *Nature*, 99: 2477 (19 April), 141-42.

Wells, H. G. (1917) letter to the editor, *Nature*, 99: 2480 (10 May), 205.

Wells, H. G. (1919) *The Outline of History: Being a Plain History of Life and Mankind*, part 1 (London: Newnes).

Wells, H. G. (1920) *The Outline of History: Being a Plain History of Life and Mankind*, rev. edn. (London: Cassell).

Wells, H. G. (1920) 'Russia: The Effect in Europe. Russia in Collapse.... Will Western Europe Crash? The Folly of Marxism. The Real Maxim Gorky', *Sunday Express* (7 November).

Wells, H. G. (1920-21) 'The Probable Future of Mankind', *Review of Reviews* (October-January).

Wells, H. G. (1921) *The Salvaging of Civilisation* (London: Cassell).

Wells, H. G. (1922) *A Short History of the World* (London: Cassell).

Wells, H. G. (1923) *Men Like Gods* (London: Cassell).

Wells, H. G. (1923) *The Outline of History: Being a Plain History of Life and Mankind*, definitive edn. (London: Cassell).

Wells, H. G. (1923) *Socialism and the Scientific Motive* (London: Co-operative Printing Society).

Wells, H. G. (1924) 'An Introduction to the 1914 Edition of *Anticipations*', in *The Works of H. G. Wells: Atlantic Edition, Volume IV: Anticipations and Other Papers* (London T. Fisher Unwin), 276-82.

Wells, H. G. (1924) *The Story of a Great Schoolmaster: Being a Plain Account of the Life and Ideas of Sanderson of Oundle* (London: Chatto and Windus).

Wells, H. G. (1925) *The Outline of History: Being a Plain History of Life and Mankind*, 4th edn., 2 vols. (London: Cassell).

Wells, H. G. (1925) 'Science and Intellectual Freedom', *Nature*, 116: 2908 (25 July), 134.

Wells, H. G. (1925) letter to the editor, *Nature*, 116: 2912 (22 August), 280.

Wells, H. G. (1925-26) *The Outline of History: Being a Plain History of Life and Mankind*, rev. edn., parts 1-24 (London: Cassell).

Wells, H. G. (1926) *Mr Belloc Objects to 'The Outline of History'* (London: Watts).

Wells, H. G. (1926) *The World of William Clissold: A Novel at a New Angle*, 3 vols. (London: Benn).

Wells, H. G. (1926) 'Scientific Neglect of the Mas d'Azil', *Nature*, 118: 2963 (14 August), 228.

Wells, H. G. (1927) *The Short Stories of H. G. Wells* (London: Benn).

Wells, H. G. (1928) *Mr Blettsworthy on Rampole Island* (London: Benn).

Wells, H. G. (1928) *The Open Conspiracy: Blue Prints for a World Revolution* (London: Gollancz).

Wells, H. G. (1928) *The Way the World is Going: Guesses and Forecasts of the Years Ahead* (London: Benn).

Wells, H. G. (1930) *The Autocracy of Mr Parham: His Remarkable Adventures in this Changing World* (London: Heinemann).

Wells, H. G. (1930) *The Open Conspiracy: Blue Prints for a World Revolution* (London: Hogarth).

Wells, H. G. (1930) *The Outline of History: Being a Plain History of Life and Mankind*, 5th edn. (London: Cassell).

Wells, H. G. (1931) *What are We to do with our Lives?* (London: Heinemann).

Wells, H. G. (1931) *The Work, Wealth and Happiness of Mankind*, 2 vols. (New York: Doubleday, Doran).

Wells, H. G. (1932) *After Democracy: Addresses and Papers on the Present World Situation* (London: Watts).

Wells, H. G. (1932) *The Work, Wealth and Happiness of Mankind* (London: Heinemann).

Wells, H. G. (1933) *The Shape of Things to Come: The Ultimate Revolution* (London: Hutchinson).

Wells, H. G. (1934) *Experiment in Autobiography: Discoveries and Conclusions of a Very Ordinary Brain (since 1866)*, vol. 1 (London: Gollancz / Cresset).

Wells, H. G. (1934) *Experiment in Autobiography: Discoveries and Conclusions of a Very Ordinary Brain (since 1866)*, vol. 2 (London: Gollancz / Cresset).

Wells, H. G. (1934) 'Power in Social Psychology', *Nature*, 134: 3399 (22 December), 972.

Wells, H. G. (1935) *The New America: The New World* (London: Cresset).

Wells, H. G. (1935) *Things to Come* (London: Cresset).

Wells, H. G. (1936) *Anatomy of Frustration: A Modern Synthesis* (London: Cresset).

Wells, H. G. (1936) *The Idea of a World Encyclopaedia* (London: Hogarth).

Wells, H. G. (1936) *Man Who Could Work Miracles* (London: Cresset).

Wells, H. G. (1936) 'The Idea of a World Encyclopaedia', Supplement to *Nature*, 138: 3500 (28 November), 917-24.

Wells, H. G. (1937), *The Camford Visitation* (London: Methuen).

Wells, H. G. (1937) *Star Begotten: A Biological Fantasia* (London: Chatto and Windus).

Wells, H. G. (1938) *World Brain* (London: Methuen).

Wells, H. G. (1938) 'Representative Opinions: Sociology and Economics', Supplement to *Nature*, 141: 3573 (23 April), 725.

Wells, H. G. (1939) *The Fate of Homo Sapiens: An Unemotional Statement of the Things that are Happening to him Now, and of the Immediate Possibilities Confronting Him* (London: Secker and Warburg).

Wells, H. G. (1940) *Babes in the Darkling Wood* (London: Secker and Warburg).

Wells, H. G. (1940) *The Enlarged and Revised Outline of History*, 6th edn, 3 vols. (New York: Triangle Books).

Wells, H. G. (1940) *The New World Order: Whether it is Attainable, How it can be Attained, and What Sort of World a World at Peace will have to be* (London: Secker and Warburg).

Wells, H. G. (1940) *The Rights of Man, or what are we fighting for?* (Harmondsworth: Penguin).

Wells, H. G. (1940) 'Victorian Socialism', *Nature*, 145: 3665 (27 January), 152.

Wells, H. G. (1941) 'Biology for the Million', *Nature*, 147: 3722 (1 March), 247-48.

Wells, H. G. (1941) 'The Man of Science as Aristocrat', *Nature*, 147: 3729 (19 April), 465-67.

Wells, H. G. (1941) 'The Man of Science as Aristocrat', *Nature*, 147: 3733 (17 May), 610.

Wells, H. G. (1942) *Conquest of Time* (London: Watts).

Wells, H. G. (1942) *The Outlook for Homo Sapiens: An Unemotional Statement of the Things that are Happening to him Now, and of the Immediate Possibilities Confronting Him* (London: Secker and Warburg).

Wells, H. G. (1942) *Phoenix: A Summary of the Inescapable Conditions of World Reorganisation* (London: Secker and Warburg).

Wells, H. G. (1942) *The Quality of Illusion in the Continuity of the Individual Life in the Higher Metazoa, with particular reference to Home sapiens* (London: Watts).

[Wells, H. G.] (1943) *The Rights of Man: An Essay in Collective Definition* (Brighton: Poynings).

Wells, H. G. (1944) *'42 to '44: A Contemporary Memoir upon Human Behaviour during the Crisis of the World Revolution* (London: Secker and Warburg).

Wells, H. G. (1944) *The Illusion of Personality* (London: Nature).

Wells, H. G. (1944) 'The Illusion of Personality', *Nature*, 153: 3883 (1 April), 395-97.

Wells, H. G. (1945) *Mind At the End of Its Tether* (London: Heinemann).

Wells, H. G., and A. M. Davies (1909) *Text-book of Zoology*, 5th edn., rev. J. T. Cunningham (London: Clive / University Tutorial).

Wells, H. G., and A. M. Davies (1913) *Text-book of Zoology*, 6th edn., rev. J. T. Cunningham (London: Clive / University Tutorial).

Wells, H. G., J. Huxley and G. P. Wells (1929) *The Science of Life*, part 1 (London: Amalgamated).

Wells, H. G., J. Huxley and G. P. Wells (1930) *The Science of Life: A Summary of Contemporary Knowledge about Life and Its Possibilities*, 3 vols. (London: Amalgamated).

Wells, H. G., J. Huxley and G. P. Wells (1931) *The Science of Life* (London: Cassell).

Wells, H. G., J. Huxley and G. P. Wells (1934-37) *The Science of Life Series*, 9 vols. (London: Cassell).

West, G. (1930) *H. G. Wells: A Sketch for a Portrait* (London: Howe).

Whetham, W. C. D., and C. I. Whetham (1912) *An Introduction to Eugenics* (Cambridge: Bowes & Bowes).

(1941) *Who's Who*, 93rd edn. (London: A. & C. Black, 1941).

Wilson, H., ed. (1960), *Arnold Bennett and H. G. Wells: A Record of a Personal and a Literary Friendship* (London: Hart-Davis).

Wooster, W. A. (1938) 'Social Relations of Science', *Nature*, 141: 3576 (14 May), 879.

Workman, H. B. (1925) comment, Supplement to *Nature*, 116: 2906 (11 July), 83.

Arbeiten zur Literarischen Phantastik
Eine Schriftenreihe der Universität Leipzig

Herausgegeben von Elmar Schenkel and Alexandra Lembert

Band 1   Fanfan Chen: Fantasticism. Poetics of Fantastic Literature. The Imaginary and Rhetoric. 2007.

Band 2   John S. Partington (ed.): H. G. Wells's *Fin-de-Siècle*. Twenty-first Century Reflections on the Early H. G. Wells. 2007.

Band 3   John S. Partington (ed.): H. G. Wells in *Nature*, 1893–1946. A Reception Reader. 2008.

www.peterlang.de

John S. Partington (ed.)

H. G. Wells's *Fin-de-Siècle*

Twenty-first Century Reflections on the Early H. G. Wells
Selections from *The Wellsian*

Frankfurt am Main, Berlin, Bern, Bruxelles, New York, Oxford, Wien, 2007.
VI, 150 pp.
Arbeiten zur Literarischen Phantastik.
Edited by Elmar Schenkel and Alexandra Lembert. Vol. 2
ISBN 978-3-631-57111-8 · pb. € 32.–*

The essays contained in this collection focus on the early H. G. Wells, the scientific romancer, the comic novelist and the young author discovering the literary élite. Written at the crossroads of a new century, the authors of these essays use their own *fin-de-siècle* experiences to look back one hundred years and critically assess the writings of an earlier *fin-de-siècle*. With seven chapters dealing with *The Time Machine*, *The Wheels of Chance*, *The Island of Doctor Moreau*, *The War of the Worlds*, *Tono-Bungay* and *The History of Mr Polly*, readers receive a detailed overview of Wells's literary output between 1895 and 1910. Two further chapters treat Wells's literary friendships, assessing his personal and professional relationships with the Victorian realist, George Gissing, and the pioneering modernist, Joseph Conrad, while the final chapter reveals Wells as a 'time traveller', employing poststructuralist techniques fifty years before that expression was coined.

Contents: Science fiction · Comic novels · H. G. Wells · Joseph Conrad · George Gissing · Poststructuralism · *The Time Machine* · *The Wheels of Chance* · *The Island of Doctor Moreau* · *The War of the Worlds* · *Tono-Bungay* · *The History of Mr Polly* · *The Wellsian* · H. G. Wells Society

Frankfurt am Main · Berlin · Bern · Bruxelles · New York · Oxford · Wien
Distribution: Verlag Peter Lang AG
Moosstr. 1, CH-2542 Pieterlen
Telefax 00 41 (0) 32 / 376 17 27

*The €-price includes German tax rate
Prices are subject to change without notice
Homepage http://www.peterlang.de

Peter Lang · Internationaler Verlag der Wissenschaften